CONTEMPORARY Black Biography

ISSN-1058-1316

CONTEMPORARY
Black
Biography

Profiles from the International Black Community

Volume 71

GALE
CENGAGE Learning

Detroit • New York • San Francisco • New Haven, Conn • Waterville, Maine • London

St. Philip's College Library

Contemporary Black Biography, Volume 71

Kepos Media, Inc.: Paula Kepos and Derek Jacques, editors

Project Editor: Margaret Mazurkiewicz

Image Research and Acquisitions: Leitha Etheridge-Sims

Editorial Support Services: Nataliya Mikheyeva

Rights and Permissions: Margaret Abendroth, Jennifer Altschul

Manufacturing: Dorothy Maki, Cynde Bishop

Composition and Prepress: Mary Beth Trimper, Gary Leach

Imaging: John Watkins

© 2009 Gale, Cengage Learning

ALL RIGHTS RESERVED. No part of this work covered by the copyright herein may be reproduced, transmitted, stored, or used in any form or by any means graphic, electronic, or mechanical, including but not limited to photocopying, recording, scanning, digitizing, taping, Web distribution, information networks, or information storage and retrieval systems, except as permitted under Section 107 or 108 of the 1976 United States Copyright Act, without the prior written permission of the publisher.

This publication is a creative work fully protected by all applicable copyright laws, as well as by misappropriation, trade secret, unfair competition, and other applicable laws. The authors and editors of this work have added value to the underlying factual material herein through one or more of the following: unique and original selection, coordination, expression, arrangement, and classification of the information.

For product information and technology assistance, contact us at
Gale Customer Support, 1-800-877-4253.
For permission to use material from this text or product,
submit all requests online at www.cengage.com/permissions.
Further permissions questions can be emailed to
permissionrequest@cengage.com

While every effort has been made to ensure the reliability of the information presented in this publication, Gale, a part of Cengage Learning, does not guarantee the accuracy of the data contained herein. Gale accepts no payment for listing; and inclusion in the publication of any organization, agency, institution, publication, service, or individual does not imply endorsement of the editors or publisher. Errors brought to the attention of the publisher and verified to the satisfaction of the publisher will be corrected in future editions.

EDITORIAL DATA PRIVACY POLICY. Does this publication contain information about you as an individual? If so, for more information about our editorial data privacy policies, please see our Privacy Statement at www.gale.cengage.com.

Gale
27500 Drake Rd.
Farmington Hills, MI, 48331-3535

ISBN-13: 978-1-4144-1928-2
ISBN-10: 1-4144-1928-7

ISSN 1058-1316

This title is also available as an e-book.
ISBN 13: 978-1-4144-5688-1
ISBN-10: 1-4144-5688-3
Contact your Gale sales representative for ordering information.

Printed in the United States of America
1 2 3 4 5 6 7 13 12 11 10 09

Advisory Board

Emily M. Belcher
General and Humanities Reference Librarian
Firestone Library, Princeton University

Dr. Alton Hornsby, Jr.
Professor of History
Morehouse College

Dr. Ronald Woods
Professor, African American Studies Program
Eastern Michigan University

Contents

Introduction ix

Cumulative Nationality Index 173

Cumulative Occupation Index 187

Cumulative Subject Index 209

Cumulative Name Index 261

Jabari Asim 1
  Respected journalist and children's author
Richard Lewis Baltimore III..........................4
  Distinguished former U.S. ambassador
Lloyd Augustus Barbee.................................7
  Champion of school desegregation
Bertie Bowman 10
  Long-serving Capitol Hill staff member
Wayne Brady 12
  Talented comic and television personality
Kobe Bryant 15
  Los Angeles Lakers superstar
Juanita Bynum 20
  Inspiring evangelist and women's advocate
James E. Clyburn 23
  Influential Democratic legislator
Marva Collins 26
  Renowned Chicago educator
Ravi Coltrane 30
  Gifted jazz musician
Carl Craig...33
  Innovative techno artist and music producer
Eric Deggans 37
  Forthright media critic
Shelton Fabre 40
  Louisiana Catholic bishop
James A. Forbes Jr......................................43
  Activist minister

Cito Gaston..47
  Championship-winning baseball manager
Lorna Goodison 49
  Jamaican poet and illustrator
W. C. Gorden..52
  College football coach inducted into the Hall of Fame
Augustus O. Grant......................................55
  Respected cardiologist
Anthony Griffin 58
  Skilled plastic surgeon
Johnny Griffin..61
  Powerhouse jazz saxophonist
Lisa Gay Hamilton 65
  Obie Award-winning actress
Zelma Henderson 68
  Last-surviving plaintiff in Brown v. Board of Education
Edie Huggins 70
  Beloved television personality
Maulana Karenga 73
  Influential scholar and creator of Kwanzaa
R. Kelly 77
  Popular and controversial R&B artist
Kwame Kilpatrick 81
  Former Detroit mayor
Oni Faida Lampley 86
  Award-winning playwright and actor
Butch Lewis 89
  Successful boxing promoter and entrepreneur
Romany Malco..92
  Talented comedy actor
Mario...95
  Rising R&B star
Bryan Monroe 98
  Prize-winning journalist and publishing executive
Robert Mugabe 101
  Zimbabwean dictator
Cynthia Nance 107
  Esteemed law school dean

Sonny Okosuns 110
    Nigerian social protest singer
Will Packer 112
    Atlanta-based film producer of Stomp the Yard
Marjorie B. Parham 115
    Legendary Cincinnati Herald publisher
Paul Pierce 117
    NBA All-Star and captain of the Boston Celtics
Adrian Piper 120
    Thought-provoking artist and philosopher
Byron Pitts 123
    Prominent news correspondent who overcame illiteracy
Richard E. Prince 126
    Veteran journalist covering media diversity
LaTanya Richardson 129
    Versatile character actress
Patrick Robinson 132
    Rising fashion designer
Abdi Roble 136
    Important photographer of Somali diaspora
Lisa Salters 139
    Personable television sportscaster

Ellen Johnson Sirleaf 142
    Beloved president of Liberia
Samuel Snow 145
    Vindicated soldier accused in World War II riot
Emmitt Thomas 147
    Hall of Fame pro football player and coach
Reed V. Tuckson 150
    Dedicated physician and health-care executive
Michael Jai White 153
    Film actor in Spawn and The Dark Knight
Isabel Wilkerson 156
    Pulitzer Prize-winning journalist
Thomas Alphonso Wilkins 158
    Committed symphony conductor and music mentor
Maggie Williams 161
    Former chief of staff to Hillary Clinton
Stevie Williams 165
    Skateboarding idol and entrepreneur
Dwight D. York 167
    Imprisoned founder of Nuwaubian religious cult
Zane 170
    Best-selling author of urban erotica

Introduction

Contemporary Black Biography provides informative biographical profiles of the important and influential persons of African heritage who form the international black community: men and women who have changed today's world and are shaping tomorrow's. *Contemporary Black Biography* covers persons of various nationalities in a wide variety of fields, including architecture, art, business, dance, education, fashion, film, industry, journalism, law, literature, medicine, music, politics and government, publishing, religion, science and technology, social issues, sports, television, theater, and others. In addition to in-depth coverage of names found in today's headlines, *Contemporary Black Biography* provides coverage of selected individuals from earlier in this century whose influence continues to impact on contemporary life. *Contemporary Black Biography* also provides coverage of important and influential persons who are not yet household names and are therefore likely to be ignored by other biographical reference series. Each volume also includes listee updates on names previously appearing in *CBB*.

Designed for Quick Research and Interesting Reading

- **Attractive page design** incorporates textual subheads, making it easy to find the information you're looking for.
- **Easy-to-locate data sections** provide quick access to vital personal statistics, career information, major awards, and mailing addresses, when available.
- **Informative biographical essays** trace the subject's personal and professional life with the kind of in-depth analysis you need.
- **To further enhance your appreciation** of the subject, most entries include photographic portraits.
- **Sources for additional information** direct the user to selected books, magazines, and newspapers where more information on the individuals can be obtained.

Helpful Indexes Make It Easy to Find the Information You Need

Contemporary Black Biography includes cumulative Nationality, Occupation, Subject, and Name indexes that make it easy to locate entries in a variety of useful ways.

Available in Electronic Formats

Diskette/Magnetic Tape. Contemporary Black Biography is available for licensing on magnetic tape or diskette in a fielded format. Either the complete database or a custom selection of entries may be ordered. The database is available for internal data processing and nonpublishing purposes only. For more information, call (800) 877-GALE.

On-line. Contemporary Black Biography is available on-line through Mead Data Central's NEXIS Service in the NEXIS, PEOPLE and SPORTS Libraries in the GALBIO file and Gale's Biography Resource Center.

Disclaimer

Contemporary Black Biography uses and lists websites as sources and these websites may become obsolete.

We Welcome Your Suggestions

The editors welcome your comments and suggestions for enhancing and improving *Contemporary Black Biography*. If you would like to suggest persons for inclusion in the series, please submit these names to the editors. Mail comments or suggestions to:

The Editor
Contemporary Black Biography
Gale, Cengage Learning
27500 Drake Rd.
Farmington Hills, MI 48331-3535
Phone: (800) 347-4253

Jabari Asim

1962—

Journalist, children's author

Jabari Asim is a nationally recognized journalist and author who fueled the debate over America's most notorious racial epithet in *The N Word: Who Can Say It, Who Shouldn't, and Why* (2007). In the book Asim traced the history of the term and presented the case for its permanent eradication from the vernacular. "In the African-American community, the elders have consistently said that young people would not use this word if they only knew the history," Asim explained to Jane Henderson in the *St. Louis Post-Dispatch*. "I set out to condense that history and compile it in one convenient volume. I want it to be a primer and source book."

Born in 1962 in St. Louis, Missouri, Asim was an avid reader as a child and edited his school newspaper at Southwest High School. He entered Northwestern University in Evanston, Illinois, in 1980, to major in journalism. The school's program was one of the best in the nation, but Asim was an indifferent student. "I read tons but studied little," he confessed in the *Washington Post* online when he was serving as book editor of the paper years later. "Some of my best memories involve skipping classes and haunting the used-book stores in Evanston, Chicago and the surrounding environs, unearthing treasured volumes that I still have. I wanted to read all the time, but didn't want to do the requisite course work—exams, quizzes and term papers based on all I digested."

Asim dropped out of college one semester before graduation, later describing himself at the time as "arrogant, defiant, and clueless," according to Emily Christensen on the Web site of the Poynter Institute. Returning to St. Louis, he worked in retail and began a writing career that eventually brought both acclaim as a local playwright and a full-time job with the *St. Louis Post-Dispatch*. His first national byline came in the March 1992 issue of *Essence,* which published his personal essay "Getting Out Alive" about the decline of the St. Louis neighborhood where he was raised and still lived. Married and the father of young children by then, Asim wrote of the pervasive fear he felt every summer when violence in his neighborhood escalated along with the temperatures. "Ironically, I've long advocated city living, have sung the praises of remaining in the community and being a role model," he reflected in the article. "Today my optimism seems misguided and naive. It would require a massive infusion of dedicated, skilled African Americans to return our numerous deteriorating neighborhoods to their former glory. Those of us in the trenches are in desperate need of reinforcements, and I don't see them arriving."

Asim's tenure at the *St. Louis Post-Dispatch* included a stint as the book editor and arts editor of the weekend entertainment section. By 1998 he had joined the *Washington Post Book World* and was a regular reviewer for the section while working on his own projects. His first published book was *The Road to Freedom,* a young-adult novel that was published in 2000. A year later he served as editor for *Not Guilty: Twelve Black Men Speak Out on Law, Justice and Life.* Other contributors included *Straight Outta*

At a Glance ...

Born on August 11, 1962, in St. Louis, MO; married Liana; children: five. *Education:* Attended Northwestern University, c. 1980–84.

Career: Journalist, playwright, and children's author, 1992—. *St. Louis Post-Dispatch,* copy editor of the daily editorial and commentary pages, book editor after 1993, and arts editor of the weekend section *Get Out!* after 1995; *Washington Post Book World,* began as senior editor, became deputy editor, 2005; *The Crisis,* editor in chief, 2007—.

Addresses: *Home*—Baltimore, MD. *Office*—c/o *The Crisis,* 4805 Mt. Hope Dr., Baltimore MD 21215.

Compton author Ricardo Cortez Cruz and novelist E. Lynn Harris. Critiquing the volume in *Black Issues Book Review,* Tracy Grant asserted that through the work "Asim provides an opening into the hearts of black men coping with serious issues. He shatters the myth of black men as monolithic in their thinking."

In 2005 Asim was promoted to deputy editor of the *Washington Post Book World.* A year later three books of his for young readers—*Whose Knees Are These?, Daddy Goes to Work,* and *Whose Toes Are Those?*—were published by Little, Brown. In early 2007 Houghton Mifflin issued Asim's wide-ranging examination of the most racially charged epithet in American colloquial speech, *The N Word: Who Can Say It, Who Shouldn't, and Why.* He recounted the history of the word, finding its earliest reference in North America in an account of the first slaves that arrived by ship in 1619. A significant portion of the book addresses the debate over the appropriation of the word as a term of affection, which black users assert robs the word of its negative connotations. Asim disagreed with this line of thinking. "I challenge the conventional notion that white people cannot say them and black people can," he told Henderson. "I actually reserve my harshest criticism for African Americans who use the word, particularly gangsta rappers. Also, I call them the 'henchmen' for 'white supremacists.'"

On the other hand, Asim objected to efforts to legally ban the term, as some communities have done, which he claimed is a misguided effort and violation of some forms of artistic expression. Elaborating further in an interview on the *Tavis Smiley Show,* he told Smiley "if we say, 'Don't use the word at all,' we missed the opportunity to do something constructive—which is what Lenny Bruce did when he used the word. He was a white man who used the word. He used it to expose white racism very effectively—perhaps more so than I could have."

Asim stepped down from his position at the *Washington Post Book World* later in 2007 to take a new job as editor-in-chief of *The Crisis,* the official publication of the National Association for the Advancement of Colored People (NAACP). The bimonthly magazine, founded by W. E. B. DuBois in 1910, is mailed free of charge to all NAACP members. In its early decades it served as an important platform for emerging African-American writers shut out from mainstream print media sources. Its literary influence waned later in the century, but *The Crisis* remained a significant voice in political and cultural affairs as the official publication of the largest civil rights organization for African Americans. "I hope to make *Crisis* a must-read, the leading journal of African-American ideas and culture," he told Margena A. Christian in *Jet,* and also conceded that the idea of taking over at a publication once helmed by "DuBois proved too irresistible to pass up."

Selected writings

Books

The Road to Freedom (young adult novel), Jamestown Publishers, 2000.
(Editor) *Not Guilty: Twelve Black Men Speak Out on Law, Justice and Life,* HarperCollins, 2001.
The N Word: Who Can Say It, Who Shouldn't, and Why, Houghton Mifflin, 2007.

Juvenile

Daddy Goes to Work, illustrated by Aaron Boyd, Little, Brown, 2006.
Whose Knees Are These?, illustrated by LeUyen Pham, Little, Brown, 2006.
Whose Toes Are Those?, illustrated by LeUyen Pham, Little, Brown, 2006.
Also author of the plays *Caribbean Beat,* produced by Muny Student Theatre Project; *Peace, Dog,* produced by The New Theatre, 1993; author of lyrics to the musical *Testify,* produced by Gettys Productions, 1995; *New Blood Symphony,* 1992, and *Didn't It Rain,* both staged by Pamoja Theatre Workshop.

Sources

Periodicals

Black Issues Book Review, January-February 2002, p. 65; March-April 2007, p. 28.
Ebony, July 2007, p. 94.
Essence, March 1992, p. 40.
Jet, August 20, 2007, p. 30.
New York Times, February 25, 2007, p. A23.
St. Louis Post-Dispatch, April 18, 2007, p. E1.

Online

Asim, Jabari, "Schools and Kids," WashingtonPost.com, May 10, 2000, http://www.washingtonpost.com/wp-srv/liveonline/00/schools/schools0510.htm (accessed November 12, 2008).

Christensen, Emily, "On Depth and Context," Poynter.org, http://legacy.poynter.org/nww/stlouis2002/asim_christensen.htm (accessed November 12, 2008).

Other

"Jabari Asim," *Tavis Smiley Show,* PBS.org, April 17, 2007, http://www.pbs.org/kcet/tavissmiley/archive 200704/20070418_asim.html (accessed November 12, 2008).

—Carol Brennan

Richard Lewis Baltimore III

1947—

Diplomat

Richard Lewis Baltimore III is a former U.S. foreign official who served as ambassador to Oman and in a number of senior posts within the U.S. State Department during a career that spanned more than three decades. Following his service in Oman, Baltimore served in Kabul, Afghanistan, in 2006, and aided in that country's restoration of democracy. In 2007 Baltimore joined one of the largest development projects in the Middle East, the fourteen-square-mile project on Oman's coast known as Al Madina A'Zarqa, or Blue City.

Born into a Distinguished Family

Baltimore was born in New York City on the last day of 1947. The Baltimores were among the numerous accomplished, well-educated African-American families who lived in Harlem during its zenith. A free black born in Washington, DC, in 1852, his great-grandfather, Jeremiah D. Baltimore, was a self-taught inventor. A steam engine he built out of common household items won him some local acclaim, and he applied for a patent on it. "Emboldened by these events, he attempted to visit President [Ulysses S.] Grant but was shooed away by a White House guard," Baltimore told an audience in Oman in 2003. "Fortuitously, the President somehow learned of the young man's presence that day, sought him out, congratulated him on what he had done and instructed that he would be admitted to study at the United States Navy Yard. Notwithstanding persistent incidents of discrimination, he succeeded and went on to further study at the Franklin Institute in Philadelphia, the second black ever to do so." Jeremiah Baltimore went on to a career that included working with the U.S. Office of Coast Survey and as the chief engineer at Freedman's Hospital in the District of Columbia.

Baltimore's grandfather was Richard Lewis Baltimore Sr., who graduated from Howard University's Law School in 1905 and became an assistant U.S. attorney for the Southern District of New York in the 1920s. During the early 1930s Baltimore Sr. was involved in a dispute that led to the creation of a separate Federal Bar Association of New York and New Jersey when the national leadership of that organization ordered the New York chapter to rescind the membership offer extended to Baltimore Sr. and three other African-American attorneys. Baltimore's grandfather was later appointed by Governor Thomas E. Dewey as a workers's compensation referee for New York State in 1944, becoming the first African American to hold that post.

Finally, Baltimore's father, the attorney Richard L. Baltimore Jr., was president of the Knickerbocker Young Republicans Club in 1946 when it became the first black Republican group to join the Association of New York State Young Republican Clubs. Baltimore's father made history as the first African-American judge to sit on the bench of a Westchester County town in 1970.

At a Glance . . .

Born December 31, 1947, in New York, NY; son of Richard Lewis Baltimore Jr. (an attorney and judge) and Lois Madison Baltimore; married, 1980 (divorced, 1990); married Eszter Ekue, 1993; children: Krisztina, Josephine, Natalie. *Education:* Attended MacMurray College, 1967; George Washington University, BA, 1969; Harvard Law School, JD, 1972.

Career: U.S. State Department, foreign service officer; U.S. Embassy in Lisbon, Portugal, political and economic officer, 1973–75; U.S. Embassy in Pretoria, South Africa, political officer, 1976–79; special assistant to Secretaries of State Cyrus Vance, Edmund Muskie, and Alexander Haig, 1979–81; U.S. Embassy in Cairo, Egypt, political officer, 1981–83; U.S. Embassy in Budapest, Hungary, political chief, 1984–87; U.S. State Department Bureau of Near Eastern and South Asian Affairs, Regional Affairs Office, deputy director, 1987–88, director, 1988–90; U.S. Embassy Budapest, Hungary, deputy chief of mission, 1990–94; senior political adviser to the assistant secretary for European and Canadian affairs, 1994–95; U.S. Embassy in San Jose, Costa Rica, deputy chief of mission, 1996–99; U.S. Consul General in Jeddah, Saudi Arabia, 1999–2002; United States ambassador to the Sultanate of Oman, 2002–06; U.S. Embassy in Kabul, Afghanistan, counselor for the Rule of Law program, 2006; Blue City (Oman) development project, consultant, 2007—.

Addresses: *Office*—c/o Al Sawadi Investment & Tourism Company, Beit Lima Bldg., Beit Al Faraj St., PO Box 3619, Ruwi 112, Oman.

By that time Baltimore was at Harvard Law School, where he earned a *juris doctor* in 1972. Prior to this, he studied international affairs at George Washington University in preparation for a career in foreign service. He joined the U.S. State Department and in 1973 was posted to the U.S. Embassy in Lisbon, Portugal, as a political and economic officer. It was a heady time on the Iberian peninsula, with both Portugal and Spain under dictatorships. In 1974, during Baltimore's time in Lisbon, the Portuguese government was overthrown in a coup by left-wing military officers in what was known as the Carnation Revolution.

Served in South Africa during Apartheid

In March of 1976 Baltimore was posted to the U.S. Embassy in Pretoria, South Africa—an appointment that merited a mention in the *New York Times* with the headline "2 Black U.S. Diplomats Posted to South Africa." At the time, South Africa was a white-minority state, where blacks were denied basic political rights, including citizenship. Baltimore and another black State Department officer were only the second and third African-American diplomats ever to serve in an embassy or consular position there, and the *New York Times* article made a subtle reference to their heroism in noting that "both officers requested the assignments."

Returning to Washington in 1979, Baltimore became special assistant to three Secretaries of State—Cyrus Vance, Edmund Muskie, and Alexander Haig—during the administrations of presidents Jimmy Carter and Ronald Reagan. His first experience in the Middle East came with a 1981 posting to the U.S. Embassy in Cairo, Egypt, as a political officer; later in the decade he served in the same capacity at the U.S. Embassy in Budapest, Hungary. Back in Washington in 1987, Baltimore was appointed deputy director in the Regional Affairs Office of the State Department's Bureau of Near Eastern and South Asian Affairs, and became its director a year later. He returned to Budapest in 1990 for a four-year term of service as deputy chief of mission at the embassy.

In 1994 Baltimore became senior policy adviser to Assistant Secretary of State for European and Canadian Affairs, Richard C. Holbrooke, a role that called for seeking and signing private-sector support for the newly created Federation of Bosnia and Herzegovina during a tumultuous period on the Balkan peninsula. A year later Baltimore entered the U.S. State Department's rigorous Senior Seminar program, which trains diplomats for work in international and national security affairs at the highest executive levels abroad. He was elected president of his 1995–96 class.

Posted to Oman

Following completion of the Senior Seminar executive leadership program, Baltimore was posted to the U.S. Embassy in San Jose, Costa Rica, as deputy chief of mission. In 1999 he was appointed U.S. consul general in Jeddah, Saudi Arabia. Three years later, President George W. Bush appointed him as the new U.S. ambassador to the Sultanate of Oman, which borders Saudi Arabia, Yemen, and the United Arab Emirates on the Arabian Peninsula. The country is run by a hereditary sultan, but during Baltimore's time there Oman instituted universal suffrage in its first steps toward a representative democracy. He lived in the capital city of Muscat with his wife, daughters, and father, who was by then retired.

Baltimore served as ambassador to Oman until 2006, when he relocated to the U.S. Embassy in Kabul, Afghanistan, to assist with its Rule of Law Program. In 2007 he joined the Al Madina A'Zarqa/Blue City project in Oman as an international consultant. Blue City is one of the Middle East's famed "mega-city" developments and is projected to house 200,000 residents upon its completion in 2020. The fourteen-square-mile coastal development project, with integrated sites for education, housing, business, shopping, tourism, and entertainment, is planned as a rival to that of neighboring Dubai and its ultra-luxurious coastal showcase.

Baltimore developed an affinity for the Arab world during his long career with the State Department, after visiting ninety countries around the world during his long years of service. As the senior U.S. official in Oman, Baltimore was feted even in the remotest villages, where residents "insist that I join them for coffee, tea, dates, and often a meal. They have no idea who I am other than a guest in their country," he told Laura Ewald in the George Washington University alumni magazine, GW. He conceded that Oman—which had undergone a rapid modernization in the past few decades but still had a tribal-based political structure—and the United States diverged in some matters of foreign policy regarding the Gulf States region, "but what we have in common outweighs the differences. This is a safe country that has a long history of people-to-people friendship with the United States."

Sources

Periodicals

New York Times, March 14, 1976, p. 8.

Online

"Ambassador Baltimore's Remarks to Inaugurate the Celebration of African American History Month," U.S. Embassy—Muscat, February 1, 2003, http://www.usa.gov.om/blackhistorymonth.htm (accessed October 24, 2008).

Ewald, Laura, "Shaping Modern Oman," *GW Magazine,* Fall 2005, http://www.gwu.edu/~magazine/archive/2005_fall/docs/alumni_newsmakers/dept_alumni_oman.html (accessed October 24, 2008).

—Carol Brennan

Lloyd Augustus Barbee

1925–2002

Lawyer, politician, educator, civil-rights activist

A prominent lawyer, state representative, and civil-rights activist, Lloyd Barbee was the driving force behind efforts to desegregate public schools in Milwaukee, Wisconsin, a city long known for its deep racial divisions. The cornerstone of those efforts, a federal lawsuit known as *Amos et al. v. Board of School Directors of the City of Milwaukee,* occupied Barbee for more than a decade. Though the plaintiffs, for whom he acted as lead counsel, eventually prevailed, Barbee came to view the victory as a partial one. Still, he noted in comments quoted by Maxine Aldridge White and Joseph A. Ranney in the April 2004 issue of *Wisconsin Lawyer,* "I am not discouraged. I have seen more difficult times. We are not as well off as we could be, but we are better off than we were."

The youngest of three sons born to Earnest A. and Adlena G. Barbee, Barbee was born August 17, 1925, in Memphis, Tennessee. His mother died shortly after his birth, and he was raised by his father, who worked as a painting contractor, and an extended family that included several teachers and businesspeople. After attending segregated public schools, Barbee served in the U.S. Navy for three years, from 1943 to 1946, before entering LeMoyne College, a predominately African-American institution in Memphis. He received a bachelor's degree in social sciences from LeMoyne in 1949, then moved north to attend law school at the University of Wisconsin in Madison. Frustrated with the racist attitudes he encountered among professors and fellow students, Barbee dropped out after his first year. After spending several months as a student organizer for a social-change organization called Americans for Democratic Action, he returned to the university, where he received a law degree in 1956. His first major position after passing the bar exam was with the Madison-based Industrial Commission of Wisconsin (ICW), where he served as a law examiner for five years, from 1957 to 1962. He then moved to Milwaukee and began his own law firm.

Even while struggling with the demands of law school and his early career, Barbee worked many hours as a volunteer in a variety of civil-rights causes. Central to his work in this area was the National Association for the Advancement of Colored People (NAACP), an organization Barbee had joined in Memphis at the age of twelve. He would fill a variety of positions for the organization over the course of his career, including the presidencies of the Madison branch, from 1955 to 1960, and the Wisconsin chapter, from 1961 to 1964. At the same time, Barbee worked as a civil-rights consultant for state and local government, serving, for example, as legal consultant for the Wisconsin Governor's Commission on Human Rights in 1959. He also helped to draft the city of Madison's Equal Opportunity Ordinance (passed in 1964), one of the first of its kind in the country. While he most often worked behind the scenes, Barbee did not hesitate to lead nonviolent protests in the streets when he felt it necessary. In 1961, for example, he led a thirteen-day sit-in at the State Capitol in Madison, a dramatic event that galvanized support for several antidiscrimination bills then pending.

As energetic as Barbee had been as a civil-rights advocate in Madison, he redoubled his efforts after

At a Glance...

Born on August 17, 1925, in Memphis, TN; died December 29, 2002; son of Earnest A. (a painting contractor) and Adlena G. Barbee; married Roudaba Bunting, 1954 (divorced 1960); children: three. *Military service:* U.S. Navy, 1943–46. *Education:* LeMoyne College, BA, social sciences, 1949; University of Wisconsin–Madison, LLB, 1956.

Career: Industrial Commission of Wisconsin, law examiner, 1957–62; Governor's Commission on Human Rights, Wisconsin, legal consultant, 1959; lawyer in private practice, 1962–2002; Wisconsin State Assembly, representative, 1965–77; University of Wisconsin–Milwaukee, lecturer, 1976–80, adjunct professor, 1980–88.

Memberships: American Bar Association; National Bar Association; Wisconsin Bar Association; Wisconsin Black Lawyers Association; National Association of Black Veterans; NAACP, president of Madison, WI, chapter, 1955–60, president of Wisconsin conference, 1961–64.

Awards: Milwaukee Man of the Year, Alpha Phi Alpha, 1965; Medgar Evers Award, NAACP (Milwaukee chapter), 1969; Faculty Award, University of Wisconsin–Milwaukee, 1985; Black Excellence Award, *The Milwaukee Times,* 1994; Eunice Z. Edgar Award for Lifetime Libertarian Achievement, ACLU (Wisconsin chapter), 1995; City of Milwaukee, Proclamation of September 6 as Lloyd A. Barbee Day, 1997, dedication of West Barbee Street, 1997.

moving to Milwaukee, a city with a much larger African-American population and a troubled history of racial relations. With the encouragement of other civil-rights leaders, he ran successfully for the State Assembly, serving six terms, from 1965 to 1977, as the representative for Milwaukee's largely African-American "Inner Core" neighborhood. Shortly after taking office Barbee demanded that the Milwaukee Public School (MPS) system develop a comprehensive plan for ending the segregation visible in its institutions. While he acknowledged that segregation was not the result of an explicit policy by MPS, he argued that many of its day-to-day decisions served to concentrate African Americans in schools with inferior facilities and equipment. Particularly disturbing to Barbee in this regard was MPS's tendency to place African-American teachers only in predominately African-American schools and to deny requests by individual African-American students to transfer out of those schools. In response, MPS claimed that the racial disparities in its institutions were due to settlement patterns over which it had no control. With the stage thus set for a confrontation, Barbee immediately formed a group called the Milwaukee United School Integration Committee (MUSIC) in 1965 to coordinate reform efforts. While MUSIC's marches and protests brought some minor concessions by MPS, Barbee was not satisfied, and in July of 1965 he filed suit in federal court, arguing that MPS was violating African-American students' rights to equal protection under the law.

Amos et al. v. Board of School Directors of the City of Milwaukee proved one of the most important desegregation cases filed in a northern city in the civil-rights era. Barbee served as lead counsel for the plaintiffs throughout the case, often working alone as he scrutinized hundreds of hours of testimony and thousands of documents. In 1976, eleven years after the suit was filed, Judge John Reynolds ruled against MPS. Barbee's work was far from over, however, as Judge Reynolds asked him to help draft a comprehensive solution. MPS, meanwhile, appealed the decision. While the federal appeals court asked Judge Reynolds to reconsider certain technical points, the basic reasoning behind his decision was affirmed, and *Amos* has since become an important part of the nation's case law on the issue of desegregation. Despite this victory, Barbee felt much more work needed to be done, noting, in particular, the mixed results of the remedial steps he helped design and implement. While several of these steps, including innovative resource-sharing agreements with white-majority suburban school districts, have helped alleviate some of the worst racial disparities in Milwaukee's schools, the quest for what Barbee often called "equal educational opportunity" continues.

Following the end of the *Amos* case, Barbee concentrated on his private law practice, though he remained active in civil-rights causes and taught for twelve years, from 1976 to 1988, as a lecturer and adjunct professor at the University of Wisconsin's Milwaukee campus. He died on December 29, 2002, at the age of seventy-seven.

Sources

Periodicals

Wisconsin Lawyer, April 2004.

Online

"At the Heart of Barbee's Many Causes Was Education," JS Online (*Milwaukee Journal Sentinel*), January 31, 2004, http://www.jsonline.com/story/index.aspx?id=204117 (accessed August 11, 2008).

"Lloyd A. Barbee Papers, 1933–1982," University of Wisconsin Digital Collections, http://digital.library.wisc.edu/1711.dl/wiarchives.uw-whs-mil00016 (accessed August 11, 2008).

Ranney, Joseph A., "Attorney Lloyd Barbee," Wisconsin Court System, http://www.wicourts.gov/about/organization/history/article47.htm (accessed August 11, 2008).

—R. Anthony Kugler

Bertie Bowman

1931—

Civil servant

Bertie Bowman is the longest-serving African-American staff member on Capitol Hill. After arriving in the nation's capital in 1944 as a thirteen-year-old runaway, Bowman worked his way up from a janitorial position to become hearing coordinator for the U.S. Senate's powerful Foreign Relations Committee. In 2008 his autobiography, *Step by Step: A Memoir of Hope, Friendship, Perseverance, and Living the American Dream,* was published, with a forward by former President Bill Clinton.

Herbert "Bertie" Bowman was born outside the small town of Summerton, South Carolina, in 1931. As he noted in his autobiography, his precise birth date is uncertain, as the local courthouse records, often unreliable in that era, do not agree with family tradition. On the basis of the latter, however, Bowman believes he was born April 12, 1931. He was the fifth child of tenant farmers Robert Bowman and Mary Ragin Bowman; the household eventually included fourteen children.

Like most African-American families in the rural South of the 1930s, the Bowmans were poor, at times desperately so. Bowman wrote movingly of this poverty, noting, for example, that "the wind would whistle through the wooden boards of the house" in the winter. While he found much to enjoy as a child, particularly the social gatherings held each week at the local church, the burden of farm chores and his father's strict discipline made him dream of escape. He seized an opportunity to do so in 1944, after hearing U.S. Senator Burnet Maybank speak at a local store. As Bowman recalled the incident decades later, the senator, then running for re-election, invited his listeners to visit him if they were ever in Washington, DC. The thirteen-year-old Bowman took Maybank at his word and immediately resolved to leave Summerton for the nation's capital. Several nights later, he crept out of the house, caught a bus to the nearby town of Sumter, and boarded a train to Washington. Though he was unused to trains and travel, particularly among whites, he was reassured by the presence of numerous African-American porters, several of whom gave him advice and assistance. The excitement Bowman felt upon reaching Washington's Union Station was still apparent more than sixty years later, when he exclaimed to talk-show host Tavis Smiley in a 2008 broadcast, "When I got to the Union Station, man, I thought that Union Station was Washington. All those lights. I'd never seen that many lights before."

With few resources, Bowman had to rely initially on his charm and his wits. While he knew an older cousin lived in the city, he had lost the man's address. Seeing Senator Maybank thus became an urgent necessity. Once again, he received considerable assistance from workers and passersby. After spending several nights on the benches of Union Station, Bowman succeeded in meeting the senator, who quickly arranged what became Bowman's first job in Washington: sweeping the steps of the U.S. Capitol building for two dollars a week. It was only later that Bowman learned that the job had been an unofficial one; Maybank paid the salary out of his own pocket. Recalling the senator's kindness,

> **At a Glance . . .**
>
> Born Herbert Bowman on April 12, 1931, in Summerton, SC; son of Robert Bowman (a farmer) and Mary Ragin Bowman; married. *Military service:* U.S. Army, late 1940s.
>
> **Career:** Performed a wide variety of janitorial and other tasks in the U.S. Capitol, 1944–65; U.S. Senate Foreign Relations Committee, clerk and assistant hearing coordinator, 1965–90, hearing coordinator, 2000—; president, Bertie's Limousine Service, 1990—.
>
> **Memberships:** Board member, U.S. Senate Federal Credit Union.
>
> **Addresses:** *Office*—c/o Foreign Relations, 6225 U.S. Senate, Washington, DC 20510-6225.

Bowman commented to Alison McSherry in *Roll Call,* "I guess we Southerners stick together."

Bowman's acquaintance with Maybank was the first instance of what would become an unusual characteristic of his career: namely, his friendship with white politicians who, at least in their public lives, opposed racial integration and other civil-rights goals. Bowman grew particularly close, for example, to fellow South Carolinian Strom Thurmond, who first came to national prominence in 1948 as the presidential candidate of the States' Rights Democratic Party, a staunchly segregationist organization. Thurmond would later serve in the U.S. Senate for decades. Bowman, for his part, has repeatedly drawn a distinction between Thurmond's personal qualities and the positions he had to take to get elected at a time when public support for civil rights was not yet widespread. Any criticism of his relationship with Thurmond, Bowman told McSherry, therefore went "in one ear and out the other."

While still a sweeper, Bowman quickly established himself as a helpful, courteous jack-of-all-trades in and around the Capitol building. The array of official and unofficial jobs he performed during this period is vast. In general terms, however, he moved from sweeping the steps to working in the building's coffee shop, and from the coffee shop to the janitorial office. He also spent a brief period in the U.S. Army after being drafted in the late 1940s. By the middle of the 1950s he was working in the Capitol's barbershop, where he met and befriended future U.S. President Lyndon Johnson. The focus of his Capitol career, however, began about 1965, when he became a clerk for the U.S. Senate's Foreign Relations Committee (FRC), arguably the most powerful committee in Congress. Bowman was thus at the center of the nation's foreign-policy debate during one of the most tumultuous periods in its history, as controversy grew over the war in Vietnam. He also worked throughout the Watergate scandal of the early 1970s, when the nation's attention was riveted on the Capitol for months. By 1990, when Bowman announced his retirement, he had risen to become assistant hearing coordinator for the FRC, with significant responsibility for handling the logistical arrangements for all of the dozens of meetings the committee holds each year.

Bowman's work in the Capitol did not end in 1990, however, for he continued to work as a consultant to the FRC for the rest of the decade. It was also in 1990 that he took over his recently deceased father-in-law's limousine business. These activities kept him occupied until 1999, when another southern senator, Jesse Helms of North Carolina, altered the course of Bowman's life once more. Helms, who had just become chair of the FRC, remembered Bowman and thought highly of his abilities. In the course of his preparations to take over the committee, therefore, Helms asked Bowman to come out of retirement and serve as his hearing coordinator. Bowman agreed and began work the following year. As of 2008 he was still working in the Capitol he had first entered as a teenage runaway some sixty-four years earlier.

Selected writings

Step by Step: A Memoir of Hope, Friendship, Perseverance, and Living the American Dream, Ballantine Books, 2008.

Sources

Periodicals

Roll Call, May 20, 2008.

Online

"Bertie Bowman," *Tavis Smiley,* June 3, 2008, http://www.pbs.org/kcet/tavissmiley/archive/200806/20080603_bowman.html (accessed October 29, 2008).

"Board of Directors," U.S. Senate Federal Credit Union, http://www.ussfcu.org/board.php (accessed October 29, 2008).

Inskeep, Steve, "From Sweeper to Capitol Hill Staffer, 'Step by Step,'" NPR (National Public Radio), May 13, 2008, http://www.npr.org/templates/story/story.php?storyId=90394739&ft=1&f=1012 (accessed October 29, 2008).

—R. Anthony Kugler

Wayne Brady

1972—

Actor, comedian, singer

Brady, Wayne, photograph. Jean-Paul Aussenard/WireImage.

Emmy-award winning actor Wayne Brady is a versatile comedian and singer who rose to fame for his improvisational comedic skills on the hit television series *Whose Line Is It Anyway?* Displaying charm, humor, and vocal ability, the multitalented Brady also hosted a variety show, a daytime talk show, and the musical game show *Don't Forget the Lyrics.*

Wayne Brady was born on June 2, 1972, in Orlando, Florida. With his father, an army serviceman, posted overseas and his seventeen-year-old mother unable to take care of him, Brady was raised by his grandmother, Valerie Petersen. A shy boy, Brady "stuttered, had acne, was stick thin, couldn't get a girlfriend, and got beat up 'for breakfast, lunch, tea, and dinner' because he was in gifted classes and ROTC," , according to Jane Ganahl in the *San Francisco Chronicle.*

Began Acting in High School

Brady discovered his gift for entertaining when he was sixteen years old. Thinking that there was really nothing else for him to do, Brady had intended on going into the military after he completed high school. However, a friend of his pulled out of the school play and asked Brady to take over the one-line part. "As soon as I stepped onstage," Brady told *Jet,* "my stutter went away, my self-confidence went up, and with that first bit of applause, [I was] hooked." He graduated from Dr. Phillips High School in 1990 and began to focus on a career in entertainment. Brady started taking dance, singing, and acting lessons. He got jobs at a variety of places, including Walt Disney World, Universal Studios, and Great America. One of the parts he played at Disney World was that of Tigger in the Winnie the Pooh parade. At this time Brady was also involved in community theater, appearing in such productions as *A Chorus Line* and *Jesus Christ Superstar.*

In 1991, while still in Florida, Brady met and befriended Jonathan Magnum. The duo soon formed an improv group called the Houseful of Honkeys and moved to Los Angeles. Brady took parts in dinner theater companies and on cruise ships to pay the rent, as well as a number of walk-on roles on such television shows as *Superboy, I'll Fly Away, In the Heat of the Night, Clarissa Explains It All,* and the *Home Court.*

> **At a Glance...**
>
> Born on June 2, 1972, in Orlando, FL; married Mandie Taketa, 1999 (divorced 2008); one child, Maile.
>
> **Career:** Actor, comedian, and singer, 1990—; television host, 2003—.
>
> **Awards:** Daytime Emmy Awards for outstanding talk show, 2003, and outstanding talk show host, for *The Wayne Brady Show,* 2003, 2004; Emmy Award for outstanding individual performance in a variety or music program for *Whose Line Is It Anyway?* 2003.
>
> **Addresses:** *Office*—c/o *Don't Forget the Lyrics,* Fox Broadcasting Company, PO Box 900, Beverly Hills, CA 90213.

In 1996, while doing a musical revue in Hawaii, Brady met Mandie Taketa, and the couple was married three years later. It was also in 1996 that Brady was chosen to take part in an improvisational group called Kwik Witz. Although the show was not entirely improvisational—there was a disclaimer at the end of each performance that stated that the actors knew their topics beforehand—it still put Brady into the spotlight. It was there that he was noticed by the producers of the British television show *Whose Line Is It Anyway?*

When the American version of *Whose Line Is It Anyway?* debuted in 1998, Brady appeared as a rotating replacement, but soon became one of the regular members of the cast. He gained attention for his musical improvisations and was nominated in 2001 for an Emmy Award for Outstanding Performance in a Variety or Music Program. Drew Carey, Brady's costar on *Whose Line Is It Anyway?* was quoted by Hal Boedeker in the *Orlando Sentinel* as saying of Brady, "He's great, he's really super talented, really charismatic, and he's a thrill to work with. When he's onstage, he's something to see. I remember the first time I worked with him, I couldn't believe the stuff he was doing. It was like watching magic tricks."

Gained Fame on Whose Line?

The show brought Brady widespread fame, and he received much of the credit for the show's success. However, there was one thing that bothered Brady: Often people did not believe that the scenes staged on the show really were improvised. "That kind of ticks me off when people ask that," Brady told Diane Eicher in the *Denver Post.* Yet Brady realized it was also a compliment to the quick wit and talent of the actors. Viewers could not believe anyone could think up such humorous skits on the spot.

Of course, Brady had performed to sold out audiences at improvisational shows across the country for years, which was, according to Ganahl, "Pretty good for a [man] who bucks the notion that to sell out big venues, you've got to have R- or X-rated material." Not only did Brady achieve stardom for improvisational acting, but he did so on the strength of family-oriented material.

In 2001 Brady was given his own show, aptly named the *Wayne Brady Show,* which he hosted and starred in, along with Brooke Dillman, Jonathan Mangum, J. P. Manoux, and Missi Pyle. Brady described the show in *People*: "The template is Flip Wilson and Carol Burnett scrunched together, then laid on top of a human Muppet show. It's family TV." The show raised ABC's summer ratings in its Wednesday time slot by four million viewers. A *New York Post* reporter wrote, "I haven't laughed at a sketch show this much since my all-time favorite sketch show *In Living Color,* bit the dust, lo these many years ago…. Wayne Brady and co. are as funny a show as the old *Carol Burnett Show* ensemble company and the Wayans brothers combined."

Hosted Daytime Talk Show

Based on its success as a summer replacement program, the *Wayne Brady Show* was continued for six more episodes, but when its ratings dropped, ABC decided to change the format. The revamped *Wayne Brady Show* debuted in 2002 as a daytime talk show and was a critical success, with Brady awarded Daytime Emmy awards in 2003 and in 2004. Ratings sagged by its second season, however, and the show was cancelled in 2004. By this time Brady was seemingly omnipresent on television, serving as host of *Dick Clark's New Year's Rockin' Eve* and the Miss America Pageant. In 2004 Brady made his Broadway debut, joining the cast of *Chicago* for a limited run.

Brady returned to the small screen in 2006 as host of a new Fox musical series, *Celebrity Duets.* That show was short-lived, but the following year he landed a similar role as host of a new show called *Don't Forget the Lyrics,* a karaoke-influenced show in which contestants sing along with a band and are fed a portion of the lyrics, but must finish the words on their own from memory.

After releasing several singles over the years, he recorded his first album, *A Long Time Coming,* which was released in September of 2008. Meanwhile, Brady continued to tour comedy clubs and did several performances per week of the live show *Wayne Brady and Friends* at the Venetian resort in Las Vegas.

Selected works

Television

Superboy, 1990.
I'll Fly Away, 1993.
In the Heat of the Night, 1993.
On Promised Land, 1994.
Vinyl Justice, 1998.
Whose Line is It Anyway?, 1998–2003.
Hollywood Squares, 1999–2003.
Wayne Brady Show (variety), 2001.
Wayne Brady Show (daytime talk), 2002–04.
Celebrity Duets, 2006.
Everybody Hates Chris, 2006, 2008.
Don't Forget the Lyrics, 2007—.

Film

(Animated) *Clifford's Really Big Movie,* 2004.
Roll Bounce, 2005.
Stuart Little 3: Call of the Wild, 2005.
Crossover, 2006.
The List, 2006.

Albums

A Long Time Coming, Peak Records, 2008.

Sources

Periodicals

Advertising Age, March 1, 1999, p. 8.
Atlanta Journal-Constitution, August 8, 2001, p. C10.
Denver Post, March 1, 2001, p. F5.
Entertainment Weekly, August 10, 2001, p. 57.
Interview, September, 2001, p. 132.
Jet, August 27, 2001, p. 62; September 24, 2001; February 10, 2003, p. 56; June 9, 2003, p. 34; May 5, 2008, p. 33.
Kansas City Star, September 27, 2007.
Knight-Ridder/Tribune News Service, August 7, 2001, p. K2667.
Los Angeles Times, May 7, 1999, p.6; April 27, 2000, p. F7; August 8, 2001, p. F4; August 15, 2001, p. F11.
Mediaweek, August 27, 2001, p. 8.
Milwaukee Journal Sentinel, May 14, 2001, p. 6.
New York Post, August 8, 2001, p. 70.
Orlando Sentinel, July 26, 2001.
People, June, 2000, p. 70; September 3, 2001, p. 95; February 24, 2003, p. 71.
The Record (Bergen County, NJ), May 9, 2008, p. G38.
San Francisco Chronicle, May 2, 2001, p. B1.
Seattle Times, September 1, 2006, p. E2.
Washington Post, September 4, 2001, p. C1.

Online

"Biography," Wayne Brady, http://www.waynebrady.com/_bin/biography.cfm (accessed November 12, 2008).

—Catherine Victoria Donaldson
and Bob Jacobson

Kobe Bryant

1978—

Basketball player

Bryant, Kobe, photograph. Lisa Blumenfeld/Getty Images.

Kobe Bryant is a basketball superstar who has played for the Los Angeles Lakers since 1996, when at the age of eighteen he became the youngest player in the history of the National Basketball Association (NBA). Bypassing college, Bryant moved straight from high school to the NBA, a feat accomplished by only twenty-seven other players since the league was founded in 1946. During his professional career Bryant has won nearly every honor associated with the sport of basketball, including being consistently named an all-star, being chosen the league's most valuable player, and helping the Lakers to win three NBA championships.

Lived in Italy during Childhood

The youngest of three children born to Joe and Pam Bryant, Kobe Bryant was born in Philadelphia in 1978. The Lakers press guide said his parents named him after a type of steak they saw on a restaurant menu shortly before he was born. Bryant's father was in the midst of a sixteen-year professional basketball career that took the family from Philadelphia, to San Diego, Houston, and then to Italy. When not traveling with his team, Joe played sports with his children, teaching them his moves. Kobe proved to be a particularly apt student, and he adored his father. Said Bryant in the *New York Times,* "Other kids don't have a father. I don't have anything in common with them. My father's my best friend. Those kids say I lead a Beaver Cleaver life. I don't care." Kobe was five years old when his father left the NBA and moved the family to Pistoia, Italy. There the elder Bryant competed eight more years in the Italian Professional Basketball League. Since no one in the Bryant family could speak Italian at first, the bonds between them grew even closer as they struggled with learning another language. "We didn't have anybody to depend on but our family. We had to stick together," Bryant remembered in the Riverside, California, *Press-Enterprise.* Bryant got along well with his sisters Sharia and Shaya, and—when time allowed—he played hoops with his father. He also played soccer, a favorite sport in Italy.

When Joe Bryant's professional career ended in 1991, the family returned to the United States and settled in a comfortable home on the Main Line, the most prestigious of Philadelphia's suburban areas. Thirteen-

At a Glance . . .

Born August 23, 1978, in Philadelphia, PA; son of Joe (a professional basketball player and coach) and Pam Bryant; married Vanessa Laine, 2001; children: Natalia Diamante, Gianna Maria-Onore. *Education:* Graduate of Lower Merion High School, Ardmore, PA.

Career: Professional basketball player, Los Angeles Lakers, 1996—.

Awards: National High School Player of the Year, *USA Today*, 1996; Naismith Player of the Year, 1996; Gatorade Circle of Champions High School Player of the Year, 1996; McDonald's All-American, 1996; NBA Rookie All-Star, 1997; NBA All-Star, 1998, 2000–08; NBA All-Star game Most Valuable Player, 2002, 2007; All-NBA First Team, 2002–08; All-NBA Defensive First Team, 2002–08; NBA scoring champion, 2006, 2007; NBA Most Valuable Player, 2008; Gold Medal with U.S. Olympic men's basketball team, 2008.

Addresses: *Home*—Pacific Palisades, CA. *Office*—Los Angeles Lakers, Staples Center, 1111 S. Figueroa St., Los Angeles, CA 90015.

year-old Kobe surprised his fellow students at Lower Merion High School in Ardmore; they marveled at the young black man who could speak Italian fluently but who was relatively unaware of the hip urban attitudes popular among teens. In a *Los Angeles Times* profile, Bryant recalled that time: "It was kind of strange because, being away, I didn't know a lot of the slang that kids used. Kids would come up to me and say whatever, and I'd just nod."

Basketball helped bridge the gap between Bryant and his classmates at Lower Merion High. Tall and skilled, Bryant quickly became a starter for the varsity team and just as quickly began to make a name for himself in greater Philadelphia. His high school coach, Gregg Downer, encouraged him to aim for a professional career. "When I first met [Bryant], at age thirteen, and I saw him play, after five minutes I said, 'This kid is going to be a pro,'" Downer told the *Los Angeles Times.* "Never was there one moment I doubted that. That it would happen so quickly, I may have doubted that. But I knew if he progressed so quickly and continued to make good decisions, he would someday get there."

Bryant concluded his high school career as the all-time leading scorer in the history of Southeastern Pennsylvania basketball. His 2,883 points far surpassed the 2,359 points of Hall-of-Famer Wilt Chamberlain. As a junior, he was named Pennsylvania's high school player of the year. In Bryant's senior year he led the Lower Merion Aces to a season record of 31–3 and the Class-AAAA state championship. He averaged 30.8 points, 12 rebounds, 6.5 assists, 4 steals, and 3.8 blocked shots per game. Accolades poured in from both local and national sources. *USA Today* named him National High School Player of the Year, and he also won the Naismith Player of the Year citation. Downer told the *Los Angeles Times*, "I know the high school market very well and I've watched it for close to twenty years, and to think there could be another player come into my hands and be this good, that's an abstract concept. [Kobe's] blessed with a lot of natural ability and great genes, but the work ethic is his and it's very strong. Kobe has the skills and the maturity and everything you could want."

Bypassed College for the Pros

Not surprisingly, Bryant was offered scholarships to almost every major college and university in the country. Not only was he a brilliant basketball player, he was also a good student, scoring an above-average 1,100 on his Scholastic Aptitude Test. Bryant and his parents remained coy about his future, however. They realized that they faced a momentous decision: whether to bypass college completely and go straight into the NBA draft. Bryant, meanwhile, catapulted to national prominence when the media learned that he would be escorting the pop star Brandy to his high school prom in downtown Philadelphia.

Just before prom time, Bryant called a news conference to declare his decision to make himself available for the 1996 NBA draft in June. Philadelphia sports fans who had expected Bryant to enroll at one of the local colleges greeted the announcement with jeers. The criticism escalated when Joe Bryant quit his job as an assistant coach at La Salle University to manage his son's career. Answering all his detractors in the *New York Times,* Joe Bryant stated, "Would Kobe be more accepted going to the NBA if he'd been a dummy? Do you have to be poor, with five kids, living on welfare?" He concluded, "Kobe should have had the key to the city. Instead they tried to crucify him. No one saw how special he is."

No one, that is, except the Charlotte Hornets, who chose Bryant as the thirteenth pick in the first round of the 1996 NBA draft. No one but Adidas, who swooped in to sign the young star to a product endorsement contract. No one but Brandy, who praised her prom date as a terrific guy and invited him to guest-star on her television show, *Moesha.* And no one but the Los

Angeles Lakers, who traded veteran center Vlade Divac to obtain the untested rookie. A month shy of his eighteenth birthday, Bryant signed a three-year, $3.5 million contract with the Lakers and moved into a mansion in Pacific Palisades, California. If anyone could be said to be "on top of the world," it was Bryant.

Saw Limited Action as a Rookie

Poised for greatness, Bryant took the Southern California Summer Pro League by storm. He appeared in four games—drawing huge, overflow crowds—and netted twenty-seven points in one game and thirty-six in another. Then, just before training camp was due to start in September, he broke his wrist playing pickup ball and could not practice for five weeks. This setback effectively undercut his first chance to learn the NBA style of play. To make matters worse, he took a body shot from an opponent in Philadelphia during an exhibition game in October of 1996 and missed not only the rest of the preseason but also the season opener in November.

The injuries gave Bryant a huge disadvantage during the regular season. Lakers coach Del Harris explained in the *Press-Enterprise* that "You've got to figure that not only did [Bryant] skip college, he also skipped training camp. Given that, the fact that he was able to compete at this level by January [1997] is incredible—especially with a team that's been in first or second place all year, rather than a team that might say, 'Well, we're not going anywhere anyway, so let's play the young guys.'"

Harris saw Bryant as a novice who needed more training in the pro game and restricted his playing time accordingly. Bryant averaged 15.5 minutes of playing time, 7.6 points, 1.3 assists, and 1.9 rebounds per game in 71 regular season appearances. Naturally the former high school star felt frustrated by the limited play. "One of the hardest things this year was not knowing whether you're going to play or how many minutes you're going to play," Bryant acknowledged in an Associated Press report. "But at the same time that kind of helps you, because you just have to be ready every night."

Bryant's chance to shine as a rookie came during the All-Star break, when he scored thirty-one points in the Rookie All-Star Game and aced the slam-dunk title with a dramatic shot that began between his legs. That moment of fame was some compensation for his slow start as a professional, and it served to reinforce his coaches' conviction that he would make an impact within a year or two.

Adjusted to NBA Lifestyle

Debate, meanwhile, still raged over whether Bryant had taken a wrong turn when he decided to skip college. As Theresa Smith observed in the *Orange County Register,* "It's still too early.... If he hadn't turned pro, he'd be learning strategy and refining skills in frequent practice sessions, and starring for a Top 25 team two days a week. Instead, his practice time is limited by a rigorous game and travel schedule and his game time is limited by Harris, who has the incongruous task of developing young talent and winning at the same time." The *New York Times* quoted Harris as expressing similar frustrations: "I don't want to be remembered ... [as] the guy who wouldn't let Kobe Bryant play." He also observed, "I have to do it. I can't give him special treatment just because he's eighteen. He elected to come into a man's world and he'll have to play by a man's rules."

That "man's world" presented many challenges for a person of Bryant's age. Not yet old enough to order an alcoholic beverage legally and enormously wary of the multitude of other temptations beckoning NBA players, he generally kept to himself both at home and on the road. His parents often traveled with him, and they lived in his Pacific Palisades home.

In addition to his multimillion-dollar contract, Bryant had product endorsement deals for such companies as Adidas, Nintendo, Spalding, and Sprite. "I like getting out there for promotional appearances and having a good time and meeting people," he said in the *Los Angeles Times.* "I like to see the end product, and I take pride in it." At the same time, he added, "I understand basketball is what got me here and on top of that, I love to do it so much that it will always be my focal point."

Evolved into an Pro Star

By age twenty-one, Bryant was well on his way to becoming an elite player in the NBA. Rather than squander his money on the high life, Bryant became the co-owner of an Italian basketball team, Olimpia Milano. He also released a hip-hop album, *K.O.B.E.* Larry Brown, then coach of the Philadelphia 76ers, told *Sports Illustrated,* "Kobe's a model of what a young player should aspire to be. Year by year he has learned and made his game more solid, and now he's not just a highlight-film guy but an accomplished NBA player."

Along with the NBA's Most Valuable Player, Shaquille O'Neal, in 2000 Bryant helped the Lakers win their first championship in twelve years. The media frequently mentioned tension between O'Neal and Bryant. According to *Los Angeles Magazine,* "Shaq had never become an adult, while Kobe had never been a child."

The Lakers repeated as champions in 2001 and 2002. In 2003 Bryant was accused of sexual assault in Eagle County, Colorado. Prosecutors dropped the charge in

September of 2004, saying the accuser, a nineteen-year-old hotel employee, could not move forward with the case. She did, however, file a civil suit against Bryant. They settled the suit early in 2005, under terms that remained concealed. Bryant often took shuttle flights between the trial in Colorado and Lakers games. He still made the All-NBA first team. The Lakers reached the NBA Finals in 2004, losing four games to one to the Detroit Pistons. After the season, the team settled the simmering feud between Bryant and O'Neal by trading O'Neal to the Miami Heat and signing Bryant to a seven-year, $136 million contract extension. Coach Phil Jackson left the Lakers after the season, and during the 2004 offseason he wrote a book in which he said Bryant's trial and attitude in general wore down the team.

Bryant was again an All-Star in 2005, but the Lakers missed the playoffs for only the second time in twenty-nine years. After the season, team owner Jerry Buss rehired Jackson as head coach, and he and Bryant both publicly said they were at peace.

Early in 2006 Bryant scored 81 points in a game against the Toronto Raptors, the second-highest total ever scored in an NBA game. He was again named as a Western Conference starter for the NBA All-Star game, and ended the 2005–06 season as the NBA scoring champion, with an average 35.4 points per game. In July of 2006 he underwent arthroscopic surgery on his right knee, missing the Lakers' preseason exhibition games and the first two regular season games. With his knee progressing slowly, Bryant was back in the lineup by early November.

Bryant changed his jersey number from 8 to 24 for the 2006–07 season. He also won his second All-Star game MVP award, scoring 31 points as the West defeated the East, 153–132. After the season, during which the Lakers lost in the first round of the playoffs, Bryant alternately asked for a trade, then recanted. In one day, Bryant first told ESPN Radio: "I would like to be traded. And as tough as it is to say that, as tough as it is to come to that conclusion, there's no other alternative." However, later the same day he said on another broadcast: "I don't want to go anyplace else. I don't want to. I want to be a Laker. I want to be here for the rest of my career."

Competed in the 2008 Olympics

Bryant, who played on a five-stop tour of Asia before the start of the 2007–08 season, returned to the Lakers. Midway through the season, he was named a starter for the Western Conference All-Star team. He was to compete in his tenth All-Star game. Bryant went on to complete perhaps his finest NBA season yet, leading the Lakers to the NBA Finals, where they were defeated by the Boston Celtics. In May of 2008 he was named the league's Most Valuable Player for the season. He was also named to the NBA All-Defensive Team for the third consecutive year, and sixth time overall. The following month, Bryant was named to the U.S. men's basketball team that would compete in the 2008 Olympics in Beijing, China. The squad, dubbed the "Redeem Team" in reference to the U.S. men's futility in several previous international tournaments, included most of the NBA's biggest stars, including LaBron James, Dwyane Wade, Kevin Garnett, and just about every other perennial all-star.

In Beijing, Bryant was the most luminous of the American basketball stars. Chinese fans worshipped him as they did no other player, other than perhaps their compatriot Yao Ming. Off the court, Bryant was at his best, behaving as a gentleman in the press and drawing the praise of NBA officials for his conduct. On the court, Bryant adapted to the needs of the team, taking on the role of defensive stopper, assigned to guard the top scorer on each opposing team. The strategy worked remarkably well. With so many other capable scorers on the U.S. team, Bryant was able to focus on shutting down the opposing offense. Of course, Bryant did not entirely leave his offensive skills at the hotel. In the gold medal final against defending basketball world champions Spain, Bryant scored twenty points and took control of the game in the decisive fourth quarter.

Throughout his career Bryant has been saddled with inevitable comparisons to the great Michael Jordan. Regardless of whether those comparisons have been fair, they are now largely irrelevant. Bryant is without question one of the small handful of greatest players of his era, and perhaps even of all time.

Sources

Periodicals

Associated Press, November 10, 1996; April 29, 1997.
Esquire, June 5, 2008.
Fort Worth Star-Telegram, August 21, 2008.
Jet, April 24, 2000; July 10, 2000.
Los Angeles Magazine, June 2001, p. 58.
Los Angeles Times, October 15, 1996, p. C1; August 25, 2008.
New York Times Magazine, January 19, 1997, p. 23; January 1999, p. 66.
Orange County Register, January 5, 1997, p. C10.
Philadelphia Inquirer, November 3, 1996, pp. C1, C6; August 14, 2008.
Press-Enterprise (Riverside, CA), October 29, 1996, p. C1; February 8, 1997, p. C1.
San Diego Union Tribune, October 22, 1996, p. D2.
Sports Illustrated, April 24, 2000 p. 38; June 25, 2001, p. 42.
USA Today, August 21, 2008, p. 1A.

Online

"Bryant Asks for Trade, then Backtracks Slightly," ESPN, May 31, 2007, http://sports.espn.go.com/nba/news/story?id=2886927 (accessed November 13, 2008).

Jackson, Phil, "Balancing Act," SI.com, October 12, 2004, http://sportsillustrated.cnn.com/2004/basketball/nba/10/12/jackson/ (accessed November 14, 2008).

"Kobe Bryant Wins Most Valuable Player Award," NBA.com, http://www.nba.com/news/kobe_mvp_080506.html (accessed November 13, 2008).

Other

CBC News, November 3, 2006.

—Mark Kram, Christine Miner Minderovic, and Bob Jacobson

Juanita Bynum

1959—

Minister, author, gospel singer

Juanita Bynum is a minister, self-proclaimed prophetess, and author, who gained prominence by counseling women to find closure for previous relationships, adopt a chaste lifestyle, and be the kind of people they hoped to attract. Using her own mistakes as a basis for her sermons, Bynum dedicated herself to spreading a message of healing, while also preaching celibacy for singles. She became a leading televangelist by using her own colorful story in her efforts to save souls. Since the public demise in 2007 of her marriage to Bishop Thomas Weeks III, precipitated by domestic abuse charges against Weeks, Bynum has also emerged as a leading advocate for survivors of domestic abuse.

Growing up in Chicago with her parents, Katherine and Thomas, and siblings Janice, Kathy, Regina, and Thomas, Bynum embraced the church as a central part of her life. The family belonged to St. Luke Church of God in Christ, where her father was an elder. According to *Ministries Today,* Bynum was an outgoing child. Her charisma became apparent when she landed a starring role in her middle school's production of *My Fair Lady.* Her performance grabbed the attention of television agents, who wanted to cast her in programs similar to *Julia,* starring Diahann Carroll. Bynum's mother, however, declined the offers. "I used to make her stop playing outside and come in the house and just sit still," she told *Ministries Today.* "I wanted my daughter to listen to the voice of God."

Bynum, Juanita, photograph. Brandi Pettijohn/FilmMagic.

Began Preaching during Teen Years

Bynum attended Saints Academy of the Church of God in Christ high school in Lexington, Mississippi, and graduated second in her class. Soon after her graduation, Bynum, still a teenager, began preaching at churches and revivals. Eventually, she traveled to Port Huron, Michigan, to minister for pastor William T. Nichols and his wife, and ended up on an unanticipated journey that changed the course of her life.

At the age of twenty-one Bynum married, despite the warnings of her loved ones. "Everybody told me he wasn't right, but I was screamin', 'I'm in love. I can change him,'" she told *Essence.* As Bynum later found out, she could not change her husband, and she had married him for all the wrong reasons.

At a Glance...

Born Juanita Bynum on January 16, 1959, in Chicago IL; divorced from first husband, 1985; married Thomas Weeks III (a minister), 2002 (divorced 2008). *Religion:* Christian. *Education:* Graduated from Saints Academy of the Church of God in Christ in Lexington, Mississippi.

Career: Author of books and video presentations, 1997—; public speaker 1997—, including appearances at conferences "Woman, Thou Art Loosed!" 1998, and Women's Weapons of Power, 2001; minister, Morning Glory Ministries, c. 1999–2002; Global Destiny Church, 2002–08, Juanita Bynum Ministries, 2008—; founded the record label Flow, 2006; marriage counselor on television series *Divorce Court*, 2008—; actor in film and television, including *Lincoln Heights,* 2008, and *Mama, I Want to Sing!,* 2009.

Addresses: *Office*—PO Box 939, Waycross, GA 31501.

A virgin until her marriage, Bynum admitted in *Essence,* "I married for sex—and what the man looked like." Her husband left her in 1983 and divorced her in 1985. The pain of the failed relationship landed her in an institution, battling anorexia nervosa and questioning her life's turn of events. She began to question her faith, and sought refuge and healing through a series of empty affairs. As her emotional state deteriorated, so did her financial situation, and she went on welfare.

Worked as Hairdresser, Flight Attendant

In 1990 Bynum returned to Chicago, became a hairdresser, and managed to support herself without public assistance. She then moved to New York and found work as a flight attendant for Pan American Airways (Pan Am), a job she held until the company went out of business in 1991. Bynum told *Essence* that friends believed the fate of Pan Am was God's way of telling her that she was supposed to be a preacher. "I knew God was saying that this was my destiny, but I didn't want to hear it."

In New York, Bynum joined a new church and began ministering again. In 1996 she met a man who would prove to be a key figure in her transformation into a renowned preacher. Though he knew nothing of her story, Pentecostal evangelist Bishop T. D. Jakes invited her to a singles' conference he had organized in Dallas, Texas.

The conference turned out to be a steppingstone for Bynum's explosive rise to national prominence. Two years after attending the singles' conference, Bynum's role changed from attendee to keynote speaker. In 1998 she delivered a message titled "No More Sheets" to 17,000 people, mostly women, and brought the crowd to its feet.

Developed Successful Ministry to Singles

"No More Sheets" was a testimony of Bynum's transformation from promiscuity to righteous self-respect. She reached out to the crowd with brutal honesty, honing in on the concept that "single" is not synonymous with unmarried; instead "single" refers to those who are free from the remnants of past relationships. "In order for God to bring somebody else in your life, there's got to be room for that person in your life. You're not single yet," she told the crowd. "You're still attached."

Wrapped in sheets, Bynum explained that each sheet represented a past relationship and only God could peel those layers away in order to make people truly single—ready to receive their ordained mates. She shared a story of poverty that placed her in roach-infested projects, using McDonald's napkins as toilet paper. Bynum told the crowd that by allowing her to struggle, God was reconditioning her to release her dependence on men and embrace her dependence on Him. It was a sacrifice that she made in order to be blessed.

Bynum told *Essence* that when she was on stage, her message had a life of its own. "It wasn't me—it was God." The video of the presentation—of which more than a million copies were sold—captured thousands of entranced listeners chanting, "No More Sheets! No More Sheets!" Practically overnight, Bynum was much sought after as a speaker at inspirational gatherings all over the country.

Ended High-Profile Marriage after Abuse

With her popularity came the conception of Morning Glory Ministries, a venue that allowed people to find out exactly where Bynum would be delivering messages and to obtain information about her various activities. Videotapes like the now-famous, "No More Sheets" and others with such similarly provocative titles as "I'm Too Fat for the Yoke" and "The Limp of the Lord," as well as books and other materials, were available for purchase through the ministry. There was also the *Morning Glory* television show, which according to *Ministries Today* was airing in fifteen television markets across the country in 1999.

Bynum remained humble by remembering rougher times in the past. "If I close my eyes right now, I can see myself in the snow, wearing a black $2 coat and tennis shoes with no socks, waiting to get my $76 in food stamps," she was quoted as saying. "I can see myself in the hospital after my nervous breakdown, crying and throwing myself against the walls of the padded cell they put me in. When I remember the process it took to get myself from there to where I am today—and then I see a sister with no hope—I'm driven to get to that sister. I believe that the pain in each of our pasts gives us an opportunity to help others. If I honestly tell somebody what has happened to me, then maybe that person will be transformed."

Over the course of her travels Bynum made the acquaintance of Bishop Thomas Weeks III, the well-known founder of the Global Destiny Church in Washington, DC, and after a romance that reached storybook proportions in evangelical circles, the pair married in 2002. Together, they were a formidable Christian marketing force, selling thousands of books and CDs at packed conferences and online, though each retained their individual ministerial identity. In 2006 Bynum launched the record label Flow, on which she released her own gospel albums and a small number of recordings made by others.

In 2007 Bynum's high-profile marriage collapsed. In August of 2007, Weeks battered Bynum in the parking lot of an Atlanta hotel. Bynum sustained injuries serious enough to require a trip to the hospital. She filed for divorce in September, and in March of 2008 Weeks pleaded guilty to assault charges. He was sentenced to 200 hours of non-church-related community service. The sequence of events gave Bynum a new public role as an advocate for survivors of domestic violence. She appeared on *Divorce Court* to talk about the experience, and counseled women to help them overcome the scars of domestic violence.

Selected works

Books

Don't Get off the Train: En Route to Your Divine Destiny, Pneuma Life, 1997.
The Planted Seed, Pneuma Life, 1997.
The Juanita Bynum Topical Bible: King James Version, Pneuma Life, 1998.
No More Sheets: Devotional, Pneuma Life, 1998.
No More Sheets: The Truth about Sex, Pneuma Life, 1998.
Matters of the Heart, Charisma House, 2002.
Matters of the Heart Devotions for Women, Charisma House, 2003.
My Spiritual Inheritance, Charisma House, 2004.
(Juvenile; with Cathy Ann Johnson) *A Heart for Jesus,* Charisma Kids, 2004.
Matters of the Heart: Companion Study Guide, Charisma House, 2005.
My Spiritual Inheritance: Devotional, Charisma House, 2005.
My Spiritual Inheritance: Companion Study Guide, Charisma House, 2005.
The Threshing Floor, Charisma House, 2005.
Experiencing His Presence: The Threshing Floor Devotional, Charisma House, 2006.
Walking in Your Destiny, Charisma House, 2006.
Heart Matters, Charisma House, 2007.

Albums

Morning Glory, Vol. 1: Peace, Jet Star, 1999.
Morning Glory, Vol. 2: Be Still, Shekinah, 2000.
Christmas with Juanita Bynum, Flow, 2006.
Piece of My Passion, Flow, 2006.
Unplugged, Flow, 2007.
Pour My Love on You, Flow, 2008.

Sources

Periodicals

Atlanta Journal-Constitution, February 17, 2008, p. J1; June 21, 2008, p. J1.
Chicago Defender, August 20, 2008.
Essence, May 2001, p. 185; December 2007, p. 224; January 2008, p. 82.
Houston Chronicle, September 2, 2007, p. 17; September 23, 2007, p. 3.
Ministries Today, July/August 1999.

Online

"About Dr. Bynum," Juanita Bynum, http://www.juanitabynum.com/AboutUs.aspx (accessed November 14, 2008).

Other

Additional information was obtained from the video *No More Sheets,* T.D. Jakes Ministries, 1997.

—Shellie M. Saunders and Bob Jacobson

James E. Clyburn

1940—

Legislator

Clyburn, James E., photograph. Scott J. Ferrell/Congressional Quarterly/Getty Images.

Elected to the United States House of Representatives in 1992, James E. Clyburn was South Carolina's first black Representative in Congress since the Reconstruction era in the late nineteenth century. Graduating from college in the early 1960s, Clyburn became involved in the civil rights movement, later making a career for himself in the administration of government anti-poverty programs. He was elected by his African-American peers in Congress to head the Congressional Black Caucus beginning in 1999. He was one of the leaders who successfully delivered an unprecedented Southern black voter turnout in the 1998 national elections, making possible a series of unexpected victories for Democratic candidates in South Carolina and across the rest of the South. He broke new ground in 2006, when he was elected House Majority Whip, the highest Congressional post held by an African American at that time.

James E. Clyburn was born on July 21, 1940, in Sumter, South Carolina, in the lowlands east of Columbia, the state capital. His father was a minister. Clyburn attended South Carolina State College, one of the South's premier historically black educational institutions, earning a Bachelor of Science degree in 1962. Later, he worked in Congress to secure funds for the renovation of historically black colleges, which suffered financially as formerly segregated Southern state university systems opened to African-American students. After college Clyburn embarked on a career as a high school history teacher, but soon the political change that was sweeping the South began to have an impact on the direction of his life.

The so-called "Great Society" initiative of President Lyndon Johnson included several new programs designed to alleviate poverty in Southern black communities. For educated young Southerners like Clyburn, one effect was to open up new job opportunities in the administration of these government initiatives. Clyburn was named director of a program called the Neighborhood Youth Corps in 1966, and then became executive director of the South Carolina Commission for Farm Workers in 1968. He married Emily England, from the town of Moncks Corner, South Carolina, and the family grew to include three daughters.

At a Glance . . .

Born July 21, 1940, in Sumter, SC; son of a minister; married Emily England (a librarian), 1961; children: Mignon, Angela, and Jennifer. *Politics:* Democrat. *Education:* Graduated from South Carolina State College, 1962; attended University of South Carolina Law School, 1972–74.

Career: Social studies teacher, C. A. Brown High School, Charleston, SC, early 1960s. Director, Neighborhood Youth Corps, 1966–68; executive director, South Carolina Commission for Farm Workers, 1968–71; special assistant to South Carolina Governor for Human Resource Development, 1971–74; South Carolina Human Affairs Commissioner, 1974–92. U.S. Representative, South Carolina Sixth District, 1992—; elected chair, Congressional Black Caucus, 1998; vice chair, House Democratic Caucus, 2002–06; House Majority Whip, 2006—.

Memberships: NAACP, life member; Omega Psi Phi, Allen University Board of Governors.

Awards: Named one of *Ebony*'s Most Influential Black Americans, 2006; NAACP "Barrier Breaker" award, 2008; Lifetime Achievement Award, National Minority Quality Forum, 2008; Louis E. Martin Great American Award, Joint Center for Political and Economic Studies, 2008.

Addresses: *Office*—2135 Rayburn House Office Bldg., Washington, DC 20515.

Elected to Congress

Clyburn's career was advanced considerably in the 1970s when he entered the inner circle of South Carolina Governor John West. He became the governor's Special Assistant for Human Resources Development in 1971 and, with future political ambitions on his mind, enrolled in the University of South Carolina Law School from 1972 through 1974. That year Clyburn was named a South Carolina Human Affairs Commissioner, remaining in the post through 1992 and amassing a formidable network of political allies. While serving as Human Affairs Commissioner, Clyburn ran for the office of Secretary of State twice, losing by small margins both times but building name recognition and serving notice that he would be a force to be reckoned with in the future.

In 1992 Clyburn declared his candidacy for the U.S. Congress in South Carolina's black-majority Sixth District, an irregularly-shaped unit that includes parts of the cities of Charleston and Columbia, most of Orangeburg (home of Clyburn's alma mater, now renamed South Carolina State University), and parts of the state's tobacco-growing areas. He faced four opponents, all black, in the Democratic primary, the victor of which was virtually assured of election in November in this heavily Democratic district. Clyburn reaped the benefits of his years of statewide exposure, winning the primary with 56 percent of the vote. He won handily and was returned to Congress in each general election through 2008, winning in that year with more than two-thirds of the vote.

In Congress Clyburn established a liberal voting record, like most of his fellow African-American members, the vast majority of whom are Democrats. He worked to resist the attacks on affirmative action that surfaced in the Republican-dominated Congresses of the 1990s. Early on, Clyburn favored funding for enterprise zones, a program that offered tax breaks to corporations that located their operations in economically depressed areas. He broke with Democratic liberals, however, by supporting measures to require a balanced federal budget and by favoring term limits for those serving in office.

Became State and National Democratic Luminary

The 1998 Congressional elections, coming in the midst of the national trauma surrounding the impeachment of President Bill Clinton, were hotly contested everywhere, and nowhere more so than in South Carolina, where the veteran seventy-six-year-old Democratic Senator Ernest Hollings faced a stiff challenge from Representative Bob Inglis, a conservative Republican with whom Clyburn had clashed in the past. Clyburn emerged as one of the leaders in an unprecedented get-out-the-vote effort, crisscrossing the state in support of Hollings and Democratic gubernatorial candidate Jim Hodges.

Clyburn's efforts bore fruit. Although South Carolina has been considered one of the nation's most conservative and Republican states, both Hollings and Hodges emerged victorious, and Clyburn could rightly claim a large share of the credit for their victories. Quoted in the *New York Times,* Clyburn said Hodges was "a smart guy," who "knows where his margin of victory was." He continued, "I don't think there's going to be any problem getting our concerns addressed." At the same time, Clyburn was diplomatic. Declining to speak in terms of "demands," a word that had surfaced in connection with similar black-led victories across the South, Clyburn offered this advice in the same interview: "Let's not be too pointed in our language. We can do this without using those inflammatory terms."

Clyburn was elected without opposition to the post of chair of the Congressional Black Caucus after the 1998 elections in which he played such a crucial role. "He's a conciliator," said Representative Sheila Jackson Lee (D-TX) in an interview with the Associated Press. "He will bring the caucus together and at the same time work well with all Democrats." Clyburn promised to work toward the appointment of more black federal judges, particularly in the South; to address environmental concerns in minority residential areas; to maintain affirmative action programs; and to promote the sampling technique, thought by some to enumerate minorities more accurately, in the national census set for the year 2000.

Clyburn continued to rise in the ranks in Congress. In 2002 he was elected vice chair of the House Democratic Caucus, defeating two other contenders. He became the first African-American House Majority Whip in 2006, the third highest rank in that chamber, and was widely recognized as one of the real powers behind the scenes in the House. Back home in South Carolina, Clyburn was larger than life. His name was placed on everything from a golf center to a bus station to a pedestrian overpass. In 2007 Clyburn became the first African American to address a joint session of the South Carolina General Assembly. He used that opportunity to comment on the state's troublesome race relations history. As reported by Kevin Chappell in *Jet,* Clyburn said, "There is so much we can accomplish in South Carolina by joining our efforts and striving to achieve a larger vision for the people of our state."

In 2008 Clyburn received the Louis E. Martin Great American Award from the Joint Center for Political and Economic Studies for his "lifelong dedication to racial justice, his efforts to bridge racial and ethnic divides and his steady commitment to improving social and economic conditions for people of color." That description effectively sums up the career of one of the pre-eminent African-American politicians of this era.

Sources

Books

Barone, Michael, and Richard E. Cohen, *The Almanac of American Politics,* 2008 ed., National Journal Group, 2007.

Periodicals

Houston Chronicle, June 8, 2008, p. 28.
Jet, December 7, 1998, p. 4; April 23, 2007, p. 11; April 28, 2008, p. 31.
New Orleans Times-Picayune, November 18, 1998, p. A12.
New York Times, April 25, 2008, p. A24.
The Oregonian (Portland, OR), November 6, 1998, p. A16.
Spartanburg Herald-Journal, June 2, 1993.
Sun News (Myrtle Beach, SC), June 16, 2008.
U.S. News and World Report, March 5, 2007, p. 42.
Washington Post, May 12, 1998, p. A17.

Online

"James E. Clyburn Biography," *United States Congressman James E. Clyburn,* http://clyburn.house.gov/clyburn-biography.cfm (accessed November 15, 2008).

—James M. Manheim and Bob Jacobson

Marva Collins

1936—

Educator

Teachers need nothing more than "books, a blackboard, and a pair of legs that will last the day," Marva Collins told Dan Hurley in *50 Plus* magazine. These three things were essentially all that Collins had when she opened the Westside Preparatory School in Chicago, Illinois, in 1975 with the $5,000 she had contributed to her pension fund. Disillusioned after teaching in the public school system for sixteen years, Collins decided to open a school that would welcome students who had been rejected by other schools and labeled disruptive and "unteachable." She had seen too many children pass through an ineffective school system in which they were given impersonal teachers who did not challenge their students to excel.

A firm believer in the value of a teacher's time spent with a student, Collins rejected the notion that the way to solve the problems faced by U.S. schools was to spend more money. Collins also shunned the audiovisual aids so common in other classrooms because she believed that they created an unnecessary distance between teacher and student. By offering individual attention tempered with strict discipline and a focus on reading skills, Collins was able to raise the test scores of many students, who in turn went on to college and excelled. "It takes an investment of time to help your children mature and develop successfully," declared Collins in *Ebony*. Collins's methods spread to other schools, some of which took on her name, and she has gone on to disseminate her unique ideas about education all over the world through lectures, workshops, books and a variety of other materials available through her consulting company, Marva Collins Seminars, Inc.

Developed Confidence, Responsibility in Childhood

Marva Collins was born Marva Deloise Nettles on August 31, 1936, in Monroeville, Alabama. Collins has described her childhood as "wonderful" and filled with material comforts that included riding in luxury cars and having her own horse. Her father, Alex Nettles, was a successful merchant, cattle buyer, and undertaker. He lavished attention and praise on Marva and her younger sister, Cynthia. By challenging Marva to use her mind, he instilled in her a strong sense of pride and self-esteem.

"[My father] never presumed that any task was too challenging for me to try nor any concept too difficult for me to grasp," noted Collins in *Ebony*. "He gave me assignments that helped build my confidence and gave me a sense of responsibility." At a young age Collins managed the store's inventory, kept track of invoices, and deposited the store's money in the bank. From these early experiences, she developed the philosophy she would use later in life to teach children, one that entailed providing encouragement and positive reinforcement.

Collins attended Clark College in Atlanta, Georgia. After graduating in 1957 with a bachelor's degree in

At a Glance . . .

Born Marva Deloise Nettles, August 31, 1936, in Monroeville, AL; daughter of Alex L. (in business) and Bessie Maye (Knight) Nettles; married Clarence Collins (a draftsman), September 2, 1960; children: Eric Tremayne, Patrick, Cynthia. *Religion:* Baptist. *Education:* Clark College, BA, 1957; graduate studies at Chicago Teachers College and Columbia University, 1965–67.

Career: Public school teacher in Monroeville, AL, 1957–59, and in Chicago, IL, 1960–75; Mount Sinai Hospital, Chicago, IL, medical secretary, 1959–61; Westside Preparatory School, Chicago, founder and director, 1975–90; founder and president, Marva Collins Seminars, Inc., 1976—. Lecturer and workshop leader, mid-1980s—. Appeared on television programs, including *60 Minutes, Good Morning America,* and the *Phil Donahue Show.*

Memberships: President's Commission on White House Fellowships; National Advisory Board on Private Education.

Awards: Fred Hampton Image Award, Fred Hampton Foundation, and Watson Washburne Award, Reading Reform Foundation, both 1979; West Garfield Image Award, educator of the year awards from Phi Delta Kappa and Chicago Urban League, United Negro College Fund award, Sears Week of the Child Award, and Sojourner Truth Award, all 1980; Jefferson Award, American Institute for Public Service, 1981; Legendary Woman of the World, City of Birmingham, AL, 1982; National Humanities Medal, National Endowment for the Humanities, 2004. Received numerous honorary degrees from such institutions as Howard University, Dartmouth University, and Washington University.

Addresses: *Office*—Marva Collins Seminars, Inc., PO Box 6598, Hilton Head Island, SC 29938.

---

secretarial sciences, she returned to Alabama to teach typing, shorthand, bookkeeping, and business law at Monroe County Training School. Having never intended to be a teacher, she left the profession in 1959 to take a position as a medical secretary at Mount Sinai Hospital in Chicago. While in the city she met Clarence Collins, a draftsman, whom she married on September 2, 1960.

Established Westside Preparatory School

In 1961 Collins returned to teaching as a full-time substitute in Chicago's inner-city schools because she missed helping youngsters discover the joy of learning. Working against a tide of indifferent teachers who, in Collins's words, were creating "more welfare recipients" soon left her weary and angry. With her pension money and the support of her husband, Collins opened the Westside Preparatory School in the basement of Daniel Hale Williams University.

Collins made a point of not accepting federal funds because she did not want to abide by all the regulations that came with such backing. Craving more independence than she had in the university setting, Collins soon moved the school into the second floor of her home, which she and her husband renovated to accommodate approximately twenty children ranging from four to fourteen years old. Located in one of Chicago's poorest neighborhoods, the school was eventually moved to its own building near Collins's home. Shortly after this move, enrollment increased to more than two hundred students.

Collins started attracting media attention in 1977 after an article on her and the Westside Preparatory School appeared in the *Chicago Sun-Times.* Several national publications printed her story, and she was featured in an interview with Morley Safer on the popular television program *60 Minutes.* In 1981 CBS presented a Hallmark Hall of Fame special entitled *The Marva Collins Story,* starring Cicely Tyson.

Turned Down Government Posts

Late in 1980 Collins was considered for the post of secretary of education by President Ronald Reagan. Preferring to continue teaching and running her school, Collins announced that she would not accept the position if it were offered to her. She believed that she could make a bigger difference by working with the children in Chicago than she could by immersing herself in the bureaucratic grind of Washington. The Chicago school board and the Los Angeles County school system also offered her positions. Again, she declined.

Collins's method of teaching, spelled out in her 1982 book *Marva Collins' Way,* provides students with a nurturing atmosphere in which they learn the basics—reading, math, and language skills. Gym class and recess are considered superfluous. When writing about Collins and her school, many journalists comment on the familiar sight of young children reading such classics as Aesop's Fables and works by William Shakespeare and Geoffrey Chaucer. Each day students wrote papers and memorized a quotation of their choice. In addition, they were expected to read a new book every two weeks and to report on it.

Collins guided all of this activity with a strong dose of love and personal concern for each student. Any child who had to be disciplined was made to understand that it is the behavior, not the child himself, that was being criticized. In an interview in *Instructor* magazine, Collins pointed out that "teacher attitude is very important," and that she believed "children should be given a lot of my time."

Answered Criticism with Classroom Success

In 1982, however, just as she was receiving mountains of positive publicity, Collins was also assailed by criticism from several fronts. Charges against her ranged from accepting federal funds—she had always adamantly claimed that she would not—to reports that she had exaggerated her students' test scores. An independent investigation revealed that Collins received $69,000 through the Comprehensive Employment and Training Act (CETA). Collins refuted these charges early in 1982 as a guest on the *Phil Donahue Show*, during which she claimed that the CETA money had come to her through a social service agency and that she had no idea the money had originated in Washington, DC

A majority of the parents of Westside's students rallied behind her, declaring that they were pleased with the work Collins was doing with their children. Support also came from Morley Safer, who had stayed in contact with Collins after her appearance on *60 Minutes*. In the March 8, 1982, issue of *Newsweek*, Safer was quoted as saying: "I'm convinced that Marva Collins is one hell of a teacher."

Kevin Ross, a former Creighton University basketball star, represents one of Collins's success stories. Ross enrolled in Westside Preparatory School in the fall of 1982 because he had not acquired basic education skills after four years of college. Working with Collins, Ross was able to double his reading and math scores and triple his language score within one school year.

Collins chose Ross to deliver the commencement address at Westside's eighth-grade graduation. He was quoted in *Newsweek* as telling the graduating class to "learn, learn, and learn some more" so that the debate on the potential of inner-city school children would become "as obsolete as covered wagons on the expressway." Others also supported Collins's work. She received donations from many individuals, most notably the rock star Prince, who became cofounder and honorary chairman of Collins's National Teacher Training Institute, created so Collins could retrain teachers using her methodology, which she began doing through seminars in the mid-1980s.

Shortly before her fiftieth birthday, Collins was interviewed by *50 Plus* magazine and was asked if she felt, after all the media hype, that she had passed her peak. She responded: "All of that means nothing, except what I get for the children. Those were fleeting moments.... Being a celebrity isn't important. It's what the children learn that's important."

Closed School, Focused on Teacher Training

In 1990 one of the educators who had attended a Collins seminar founded a school in Cincinnati, Ohio, based on Collins's methods. About that time, Collins handed the day-to-day leadership of the Chicago school over to her daughter, Cynthia Collins—one of the school's first graduates—who became headmistress of Westside Preparatory. This allowed Collins to concentrate on spreading her message to teachers and school administrators across the globe, and eventually a large percentage of her work was being done abroad. The television program *60 Minutes* visited Westside again in 1996, documenting the accomplishments of a girl who had been labeled as borderline retarded before arriving at the school; the girl went on to graduate from college *summa cum laude*. A third Marva Collins school was launched in Milwaukee, Wisconsin, in 1997, and another was operating in Florida by this time. In 2004 Collins was honored by the National Endowment for the Humanities with a National Humanities Medal for her lifetime of achievements.

After a few years, however, Collins began questioning the use of her name on schools that were not under her supervision and control. In 2004 she demanded that the Milwaukee outpost, the Marva Collins Preparatory School of Wisconsin, stop using her name. The school remained in operation as of 2008, but under the name Milwaukee College Preparatory School. The following year she announced that she had no relationship with the Cincinnati school that bore her name, and wanted them to cease using her name. As of 2008 the Cincinnati school was fighting to retain the name, and the matter was being contested in court. Meanwhile, Collins had moved her base of operations to Hilton Head Island, South Carolina, from where she maintained a busy schedule of speaking engagements, workshops, and other consulting activities. At the end of the 2007–08 school year, Collins stunned parents by announcing the closing of the Westside Preparatory School in Chicago (which was now actually located on the South Side), citing financial issues as the reason. While parents mourned the demise of their beloved school, Collins's legacy remained alive and well through the work of hundreds of educators and students whose lives she had touched.

Selected writings

Books

(With Civia Tamarkin) *Marva Collins' Way,* J.P. Tarcher, 1982.
Ordinary Children, Extraordinary Teachers, Hampton Roads, 1992.

Sources

Periodicals

American Spectator, April 1983.
Black Enterprise, June 1982.
California Review, April 1983.
Chicago Tribune Book World, October 31, 1982.
Christian Science Monitor, November 20, 1981; September 9, 1982.
Ebony, February 1985; August 1986; May 1990; December 1996, p. 122.
Essence, October 1981; November 1985.
50 Plus, June 1986.
Good Housekeeping, September 1978.
Harper's Bazaar, December 1981.
Instructor, January 1982.
Jet, November 6, 1980; October 4, 1982; February 7, 1983; July 29, 1985; August 10, 1987; August 1, 1988; June 23, 2008, p. 14.
Life, spring 1990.
Los Angeles Times Book Review, December 12, 1982.
Milwaukee Journal Sentinel, December 3, 2004.
Newsweek, March 8, 1982; June 27, 1983.
New York Times, December 19, 1980; December 21, 1980; March 7, 1982; November 4, 1990.
People, December 11, 1978; February 21, 1983.
Saturday Review, April 14, 1979.
Time, December 26, 1977.
TV Guide, November 28, 1981.
Variety, June 18, 1986.
Wall Street Journal, March 15, 1981.
Washington Monthly, February 1980.
Washington Post Book World, November 14, 1982.

Online

"Eight Who Make a Difference: The National Endowment for the Humanities Medalists 2004," National Endowment for the Humanities, January/February 2005, http://www.neh.gov/news/humanities/2005-01/medals.html (accessed November 15, 2008).
"Illinois Hall of Fame: Marva Collins," Illinois State Society, December 23, 2006, http://illinoisstatesoceity.typepad.com/my_weblog/2006/12/illinois_hall_o_18.html (accessed November 15, 2008).
"Marva N. Collins Biography," Marva Collins Seminars, Inc., 2008, http://www.marvacollins.com/biography.html (accessed November 15, 2008).

Other

"Marva Collins School to Close," ABC7 Chicago, June 5, 2008, http://abclocal.go.com/wls/story?id=6188122&section=news/local (accessed November 15, 2008).
"Wisdom Watch: Famed Educator Marva Collins," *Tell Me More,* National Public Radio, September 5, 2007, http://www.npr.org/templates/story/story.php?storyId=14178874 (accessed November 15, 2008).

—Debra G. Darnell and Bob Jacobson

Ravi Coltrane

1965—

Jazz saxophonist, composer, music producer

Coltrane, Ravi, photograph. Laura Cavanaugh/UPI/Landov.

Ravi Coltrane knows that comparisons to his legendary father are inevitable. Ravi is, of course, the son of John Coltrane, the saxophonist and composer whose music helped shape modern jazz and inspired generations of musicians. Though he could easily have been forgiven for choosing a different profession, Ravi Coltrane has jumped right into the fray, picking up the tenor and soprano saxophone—exactly the same instrument his father played—and making a career as a jazz musician. Though he recognizes the profound influence of his father's work on his own style of jazz, he also seeks to transcend it, and to create music that is uniquely his own.

By all accounts, Coltrane has succeeded. Critics praised his 2005 release *In Flux,* his fourth recording as bandleader, pointing to its creativity and maturity as evidence that he had, at age forty, come into his own as a musician. Reviewer Mark Turner of the All about Jazz Web site observed of the album, "With wisdom and respect he has admirably upheld his revered namesake yet also developed a distinct voice if one listens closely."

Born to a Music Legend

Ravi Coltrane was born on August 6, 1965, in Long Island, New York, the second of three sons of John and Alice Coltrane. He was named for the Indian sitar player Ravi Shankar, a friend of his father. Both John and Alice Coltrane had deep attachments to India: John had become interested in the rhythms and sounds of Indian music in the early 1960s, forming a mutual admiration society with Shankar, and Alice was a lifelong student of Indian spiritualism. Both, too, were noted musicians—John as a saxophonist and bandleader, at the peak of fame by the time of Ravi's birth, and Alice as a classically trained pianist who often sat in with her husband.

John Coltrane died of liver cancer when Ravi was just two years old. After his death, Alice Coltrane moved the family to California, where they lived in a suburb of Los Angeles. Though Alice never pushed her children to follow in their parents' footsteps, the Coltrane household was filled with music of all kinds. Ravi Coltrane recalled in the biography on his Web site, "My mother was playing piano and organ in the house,

At a Glance . . .

Born on August 6, 1965, in Long Island, NY; son of John (a jazz saxophonist) and Alice (a pianist) Coltrane; married Kathleen Hennessy, 1999; children: William. *Education:* California Institute of the Arts, BFA, 1990.

Career: Side musician on thirty recordings, 1991–97; band leader, 1997—; RKM Music, co-owner, 2002—.

Addresses: *Web*—http://www.ravicoltrane.com. *Agent*—AMS Artists, 1153 River Rd., Teaneck, NJ 07666-1915.

---

every day. She took us to her performances and to recording sessions. She played my father's LPs and recordings of classical music. Early on, I listened to a lot of R and B, soul music, popular music of the day—James Brown, Stevie Wonder, Sly Stone, Motown music, Earth Wind and Fire. Later … I listened to more symphonic music—Stravinsky, Dvorak."

Coltrane began playing the clarinet in junior high school, but his interest in music was casual. Though he appreciated jazz, he knew little about his father's music. It was not until his late teens that his attitude began to change. In 1982 his older brother, John Jr., was killed in a car accident. The incident shook the family and prompted Ravi Coltrane to reconsider his direction in life. He began listening seriously to jazz—not just his father's recordings, but also other jazz musicians, such as Sonny Rollins and Charlie Parker. In 1998 he told Ben Ratliff in the *New York Times* that jazz "became something I couldn't live without."

In 1986 Coltrane was accepted into the music school at the California Institute of the Arts (CalArts)—more on the strength of his name than on his experience as a musician—and decided to study the tenor and soprano saxophone. Even then, he still was not sure that he wanted to make a career of music. "I enrolled to see if music was something I wanted to do or even could do," Coltrane remembered in an interview with R. J. DeLuke for All about Jazz in 2003. "It was a total experiment.… I didn't stand up and say, 'today I will be a musician.'"

Forged His Own Musical Path

Coltrane started playing gigs around Los Angeles while he was still in school, and within a year of completing his degree at CalArts, he moved to New York City. There, he apprenticed for two years under bandleader Elvin Jones, the influential drummer who had played with the John Coltrane Quartet in the 1960s, and later under fellow saxophonist Steve Coleman, who acted as a mentor to Coltrane as he developed his own style. During the 1990s Coltrane played as a sideman on more than thirty recordings, accompanying such musicians as Jack DeJohnette, Rashied Ali, Geri Allen, Kenny Barron, Wallace and Antoine Roney, Graham Hayes, Gerry Gibbs, Joe Lovano, Joanne Brackeen, and Cindy Blackman.

In 1998 Coltrane made his debut as bandleader, recording the album *Moving Pictures* with pianist Andy Milne, bassist Darryl Hall, and drummer Steve Hass. The inaugural work was well received by critics. In the *New York Times* that year, Ratliff noted, "'Moving Pictures' is a rare jazz record. It isn't dazzling. Ravi Coltrane's music works on you more slowly. He has a warm, streamlined tone, and he's partial to small, sharp motifs and pockets of silence rather than the endless stuffing of notes through complicated harmonic grids." Coltrane followed up with *From the Round Box* in 2000 and *Mad 6* in 2003. Turner for All about Jazz noted Coltrane's progression as an artist on these albums: "Each recording has shown different facets of the saxophonist in terms of performance, adaptation, and creativity, as he charts his own path as a musician."

The genre of Coltrane's music is best categorized as "American post-bop." This term describes a style of small-combination jazz that emerged in the mid-1960s, pioneered by John Coltrane, Miles Davis, Bill Evans, and Charles Mingus. The form incorporates elements of modal and free jazz, avant-garde music, and hard bop (a style of bebop influenced by gospel and rhythm and blues music).

In 2005 Coltrane released his fourth album, *In Flux,* featuring pianist Luis Perdomo, bassist Drew Gress, and drummer E. J. Strickland, his working band since 2003. Again, critics applauded. Turner in All about Jazz called the album Coltrane's "most striking and mature work to date." In the *New York Times* Ratliff reported in February 2005, "Mr. Coltrane avoids tired song structures and doesn't want to bore you. He's fascinated on one hand by miniatures and on the other by the idea of longer songs that sound like collective improvisation from start to finish. It's a record that you can point to and say: This is what jazz sounds like now in New York."

Preserved the Family Legacy

In addition to his recordings, in 2002 Coltrane launched a music label, RKM Music. He formed the company in the hope of giving artists more freedom to experiment without, as he told interviewer DeLuke, "the corporate filters applied to recording projects." For RKM, Coltrane has produced such musicians as trumpeter Ralph Alessi, saxophonist Michael McGinnis, guitarist David Gilmour (formerly of Pink Floyd), and fellow bandmate Perdomo.

As the family archivist and keeper of the John Coltrane legacy, Ravi Coltrane oversees a large collection of previously unreleased recordings kept by his mother, who died in 2007. In 1998 he shepherded the production of a new album, *One Down, One Up: Live at the Half Note,* featuring a pair of live performances by the John Coltrane Quartet in 1965. In 2002 he produced *Legacy,* a four-disc retrospective of his father's career for Verve Records, as well as the reissue of John Coltrane's *A Love Supreme* in a deluxe edition.

Ravi Coltrane has never sought to emulate his famous father; rather, he has paid tribute to John Coltrane's legacy by becoming his own musician, and by defying comparison to his father. In his biography on his Web site, Coltrane reflected, "I want to be involved with music that is truly honest—that's not trying to follow trends or fit into someone's idea about what jazz 'is.' For Bird, Miles, Monk, Coltrane, and Wayne Shorter, I hold the highest level of appreciation because their love and knowledge of tradition was never greater than their need to follow their own path—the need to be themselves—this is my goal—my aspiration—to acknowledge with love my influences while attempting to move forward—to be open and receptive to shifts in the musical terrain—to make music that is relevant to my present day experience."

Selected recordings

Moving Pictures, RCA Victor, 1998.
From the Round Box, RCA Victor, 2000.
Mad 6, 88/Columbia, 2003.
In Flux, Savoy Jazz, 2005.

Sources

Periodicals

New York Times, June 14, 1998; February 20, 2005; October 11, 2005.

Online

DeLuke, R. J., "Ravi Coltrane: His Own Man, His Own Thing," All about Jazz, October 8, 2003, http://www.allaboutjazz.com/php/article.php?id=391 (accessed August 14, 2008).

Ravi Coltrane official Web site, http://www.ravicoltrane.com (accessed August 14, 2008).

Turner, Mark F., "Ravi Coltrane: In Flux," All about Jazz, http://www.allaboutjazz.com/php/article_print.php?id=16765 (accessed August 14, 2008).

—Deborah A. Ring

Carl Craig

1969—

Music producer, recording artist

Craig, Carl, photograph. Chris Gordon/WireImage.

Music producer and DJ Carl Craig is one of the most important artists in the development of the electronic music genre. Based in Detroit, Michigan, Craig has gained international recognition for breaking new ground in techno music by incorporating jazz, soul, hip-hop, and avant-garde influences. Throughout his career he has issued music under various aliases that correspond with his musical moods, including futuristic house beats under the name Paperclip People, harder edge techno as 69, and experimental jazz works with the Innerzone Orchestra. According to the *Washington Post,* "Craig's musical expression has always gone beyond the artistic purity associated with techno." Craig summarized his unique approach in *Billboard,* saying, "I've always had a concept of dodging boundaries."

Experimented with Electronica

Born in 1969, Craig listened to a variety of music while attending Detroit's famed Cooley High, including Prince, the German avant-garde duo Kraftwerk, Parliament, Led Zeppelin, the Smiths, and the Motown legend Stevie Wonder. Craig played guitar and was exposed to the dance-music scene by a cousin who was doing lighting for parties in the Detroit area. He first became interested in electronic music while listening to Detroit techno pioneer Derrick May's radio show on radio station WJLB. Craig experimented with recording on dual-deck cassette players until he convinced his parents to buy a synthesizer and sequencer. He began studying electronic music, including the work of artists such as Morton Subotnick, Wendy Carlos, and Pauline Oliveros.

In an electronics course, Craig passed along a tape of his homemade productions to a friend of May's. May was interested in Craig's work and invited him to re-record the track "Neurotic Behavior." Craig did not own a drum machine, so the track's original mix was completely beatless, but inspired nonetheless. As Detroit techno music developed a strong following in England and other countries, May invited Craig to join his Rhythim Is Rhythim DJ group on its 1989 European tour. Craig subsequently lent his hand to May's classic "Strings of Life" and the Rhythim Is Rhythim single "The Beginning." While on the tour, he also recorded several of his own tracks at Belgium's R&S

At a Glance...

Born on May 22, 1969, in Detroit, MI; married Hannah Sawtell; children: one. *Education:* Attended Cooley High School, Detroit, MI.

Career: Music producer and DJ, 1989—; joined Derrick May's Rhythim Is Rhythim DJ group, 1989; co-founded RetroActive label, 1990 (label dissolved); founded Planet E Communications record label, 1991; signed with Blanco Y Negro; organized and served as creative director of Detroit Electronic Music Festival and Ford Focus/Detroit Electronic Music Festival, 2000–01; participated in The Detroit Experiment, a collaboration with jazz artists, 2003; launched Demon Days series of club nights in North American cities.

Awards: Best Label Award for Planet E and Best Remix Award for "The Climax (Basic Channel Remake)," Musik und Maschine Awards, 2001; honored by the City of Detroit for contributions to music and the Detroit community, 2001; Grammy Award nomination for Best Remix for remix of Junior Boys' "Like a Child," 2008.

Addresses: *Office*—Planet E Communications, PO Box 27218, Detroit, MI 48207.

Studios, some of which were released on the *Crackdown* EP that Craig recorded as Psyche on May's Transmat record label.

Craig and partner Damon Booker founded RetroActive Records in 1990. Between shifts at a copy shop, Craig recorded tracks in his parents' basement, and from 1990 to 1991 he released six slick singles on RetroActive under his own name and the monikers BFC and Paperclip People. A falling out with Booker led to RetroActive's demise, but Craig wasted no time establishing his own label, Planet E Communications. Under the Planet E banner, he recorded a deliberately lo-fi and funky EP called *4 Jazz Funk Classics*, which he released under the name 69. Craig's work during the rest of 1991 bounced from hip-hop to techno. His 1992 single, "Bug in the Bass Bin," which he recorded as Innerzone Orchestra, was considered an early influence on the British drum 'n' bass and jungle genres. DJs and producers played the 33-rpm single at 45-rpms to create a ready-made, high-speed beat. His Paperclip People release "Throw" showcased Craig's disco and funk influences.

Gained Fame Producing Remixes

"In the past, remixing was simply layering some percussion over a track and maybe adding a few samples," Craig said in an interview in *Billboard*. "Now, it seems as though the art of remixing has morphed into an almost completely new method of songwriting." Craig made his mark as a remixer in 1994 with the music of Tori Amos in a ten-minute rendition of her song "God," and with songs by Maurizio, La Funk Mob, and others. The Amos remix led to Craig's first contract with a major label, and he signed with the Blanco y Negro European imprint of Warner Bros. Records. *Landcruising*, Craig's first full-length release, exposed his broad range and vision to a market far wider than he had known before.

As Craig gained recognition more for his broad vision, his work and identity began to drift from his Detroit-techno roots. He became increasingly uncomfortable branding his music as Detroit techno, opting instead to call it "urban" or "soul," if it need be labeled at all, he told the *Washington Post*. Craig released one of his most important full-length collections, *More Songs about Food and Revolutionary Art*, on Planet E in 1996.

In 1999 Craig released Innerzone Orchestra's *Programmed*, and played a number of very well-received dates with what *Billboard* called the "free jazz meets techno" group. Craig remixed live instrumentation by former Sun Ra drummer Francisco Mora, jazz keyboardist Craig Taborn, and bassist Paul Randolph, and added vocals and digital enhancement. The result, according to Amanda Nowinski in *Billboard*, was "21st-century jazz whose roots are grounded in the past but technologically enhanced." The release, she continued, "signifies the aesthetic maturity of an artist whose training began in the early days of techno." Citing what experimental artists like Sun Ra, Miles Davis, and John Coltrane did with jazz, Craig told *Billboard*, "You need to know the history in order to learn and develop the future."

Craig showcased an extensive collection of his remixes from the previous eight years in *Designer Music: The Remixes* (2000). Craig reworked the music of such artists as R&B's Incognito, Belgian Euro-disco act Telex, Ron Trent, and Italian synth-pop/disco artist Alexander Robotnik "with the discipline of a gene splicer," according to reviewer Pat Blashill in *Rolling Stone*. The standout piece was "Buena Vida," Craig's rewiring of Detroit techno pioneer Kevin Saunderson's 1988 anthem, "Good Life."

Directed Detroit Electronic Music Festival

In 2000 Craig conceived and served as creative director for the first Detroit Electronic Music Festival (DEMF). He used his influence in the music industry to book leading performers in the genre and expected a turnout of about 200,000 to 300,000 fans over the course of three days. His estimate was wrong—more than a million people flooded downtown Detroit over Memorial Day weekend, setting a record as the largest electronic music event in history. Though national and international acts performed, Craig's emphasis was on Detroit talent. The festival "instantly catapulted Motown's techno artists from almost total anonymity in their own hometown to front-page news in the local papers," according to writer Mike Rubin in *Rolling Stone.* "It was definitely a feeling of vindication for all the Detroit-based artists that have been in the business for the past ten or fifteen years," Craig told *Billboard.*

The second annual festival in 2001 was even bigger than the first. The world-class artist roster, which included Kid Koala, Mix Master Mike, and De La Soul, still emphasized Detroit talent, with performances by Stacey Pullen, Kenny Larkin, Juan Atkins, and Kevin Saunderson, among many others. In all, eighty artists played on four stages. The crowd grew and downtown hotels were packed full of foreign tourists. Ford Motor Company and Miller Genuine Draft beer, sensing the festival's promotional value, sponsored the event, and it was renamed the Ford Focus/Detroit Electronic Music Festival, much to the chagrin of those fans who lamented the festival's commercialization.

In an abrupt turn, however, festival organizer Carol Marvin fired Craig days before the festival for "very murky reasons," according to Rubin in *Rolling Stone.* A subsequent outcry and e-mail campaign flooded Marvin's inbox and those of executives at Ford and J. Walter Thompson, Ford's advertising company. Ford responded by claiming it was not "the corporate monster you worry about," according to the *Wall Street Journal.* Craig struck back by suing Marvin for breach of contract.

Honored by City of Detroit

Despite the controversy, Craig was vindicated to some degree when on the final day of the festival he was honored by Detroit Mayor Dennis W. Archer. Just as the second DEMF was coming to a close, Craig accepted a special commendation from the City of Detroit recognizing his founding role in the festival and in helping raise Detroit's music industry profile. "Craig has endeared himself to an international audience of electronic music lovers with his artistic vision, intellectual curiosity, and his willingness to identify with and promote the work of other artists," the mayor's proclamation read. "He has ... enhanced the image of the city of Detroit"

In 2003 Craig collaborated with several of Detroit's best jazz musicians, including trumpeter Marcus Belgrave and percussionist Francisco Mora, on a project called the Detroit Experiment, which led to the release of a recording of the same name. In 2005 Craig was back in the techno limelight with the release of *Fabric 25,* his contribution to the acclaimed series of recordings curated by the London nightclub Fabric. That year, he also launched a series of club nights called Demon Days, which took place at popular nightclubs in major cities across North America. Demon Days were still taking place as of the fall of 2008. Meanwhile, Craig's prowess as a remixer was recognized by the mainstream music industry with a Grammy nomination for his reworking of the single "Like a Child" by the Junior Boys.

Awards, however, were not a priority for Craig. As he told *Code* magazine, "It's about making your mark and leaving something behind for the generations to come, so they can expand on the concepts and ideas and take them to the next level." He believed that contemporary music, "especially black music, is just so stagnant. It's so focused on materialism ... Chasing money, being greedy ... there's just no future in it.... Someone has to stick his neck out and take that chance. The way I see it, if that person isn't me, then who's it gonna be?"

Selected discography

(As Psyche) *Crackdown* (vinyl EP), Zomba Music/Transmat, 1990.
(As 69) *4 Jazz Funk Classics* (vinyl EP), Planet E, 1991.
Intergalactic Beats, Planet E, 1992.
(As Innerzone Orchestra) *Bug in the Bass Bin* (vinyl EP), Planet E, 1992.
Landcruising, Blanco Y Negro, 1995.
Stevie Knows, Planet E, 1995.
DJ Kicks, !K7, 1996.
More Songs about Food and Revolutionary Art, SSR, 1996.
(As Paperclip People) *The Floor* (vinyl EP), Planet E, 1996.
Acid Tunes, Nova Tekk, 1997.
House Party 013: A Planet E Mix, Next Era, 1999.
(As Innerzone Orchestra) *Programmed,* Planet E, 1999.
Designer Music: The Remixes, Vol. 1, Planet E, 2000.
The Detroit Experiment, Planet E, 2002.
The Album Formerly Known As..., Planet E, 2005.
Fabric 25, Fabric, 2005.
Sessions, Planet E, 2008.

Sources

Periodicals

Billboard, July 17, 1999, p. 29; August 5, 2000, p. 34.

Code, October 2000, p. 28.

Fader, January 19, 2007.

Remix, March 1, 2008.

Rolling Stone, September 28, 2000, p. 60; July 5, 2001, p. 40.

SF Weekly, February 7, 2007.

Wall Street Journal, May 25, 2001, p. B2.

Washington Post, August, 30, 2000, p. C5.

Wire: Adventures in Modern Music, May 2008.

Online

Nasrallah, Dimitri, "Carl Craig: Intergalactic Beats," *Exclaim,* March 2008, http://www.exclaim.ca/articles/multiarticlesub.aspx?csid2=9&fid1=29999&csid1=119 (accessed November 20, 2008).

Patel, Joseph, "A History of Carl Craig," Planet E Demon Days, December 2007, http://www.demon-days.com/CarlCraig.html (accessed November 20, 2008).

—Brenna Sanchez and Bob Jacobson

Eric Deggans

1965—

Television and media critic

Deggans, Eric, photograph. Kevin Winter/Getty Images.

Professional athletes know that if the opposing team's fans are booing, the athletes are doing something right. The same is true for today's media pundits: If one is not getting called nasty names, one is not pushing the envelope far enough. So when Fox News host Bill O'Reilly started hurling invectives at Eric Deggans, media critic for the Florida-based *St. Petersburg Times,* he knew that he had arrived. Since starting at the *Times* in 1995—becoming the paper's first-ever media critic—Deggans has provided timely and thoughtful, and sometimes controversial, reporting on trends in the national media, with a particular focus on the way in which minorities are portrayed. In his columns and blogs, he presses readers to reconsider racial stereotypes and to observe how they play out in the popular media.

Deggans was born in Washington, DC, in 1965, but grew up in the industrial city of Gary, Indiana. He attended Indiana University at Bloomington, where he earned a bachelor's degree in political science and journalism. He began his professional career as a reporter in Pittsburgh, Pennsylvania, contributing to the *Pittsburgh Press* from 1990 to 1992 and to the *Pittsburgh Post-Gazette* from 1990 to 1993. During that time he helped to create a minority affairs reporting position at the *Post-Gazette,* and worked with the Pennsylvania State Troopers Academy to develop a training program on racial sensitivity for new recruits. In 1993 Deggans moved to the *Asbury Park Press* newspaper in New Jersey, writing as a music critic. Notably, he covered the Woodstock '94 music festival and wrote an important feature on the antiracist skinhead movement.

In 1995 Deggans was hired by the *St. Petersburg Times,* where he started out as a pop music critic, covering events such as the MTV Music Video Awards in New York City. Within a few years he expanded his role to cover media and television, writing reviews and news stories as well as longer features on trends in the local and national media. He joined the *Times*'s editorial board in 2004, then returned to writing criticism, first as a media critic in 2005 and then as a television critic in 2006.

Deggans entered the blogosphere in 2006, writing the *Feed,* a blog on television, media, and pop culture published by the *St. Petersburg Times,* and occasion-

At a Glance...

Born in November of 1965 in Washington, DC; married Barbara; children: four, including Marcus, Zoe, and Jessica. *Education:* Indiana University at Bloomington, BA, political science and journalism, 1990.

Career: *Pittsburgh Press,* reporter, 1990–92; *Pittsburgh Post-Gazette,* reporter, 1990–93; *Asbury Park Press,* music critic, 1993–95; *St. Petersburg Times,* music critic, television and media critic, and editorial writer/columnist, 1995—; has worked as a lecturer and educator.

Memberships: Tampa Bay Area Chapter of the National Association of Black Journalists, president; National Association of Black Journalists, Media Monitoring Committee, chair; Television Critics Association.

Awards: Award of Excellence, Mid-Florida Chapter, Society of Professional Journalists, 1999, 2000, 2001, and 2003; Best Newspaper Columnist, *Weekly Planet* magazine, 2000; First Place, Criticism, Florida Society of Newspaper Editors, 2003; Let's Do It Better! Award for Excellence in Race and Ethnicity Coverage, Columbia University Graduate School of Journalism, 2005; Chuck Stone Award, National Association of Black Journalists, 2005; First Place, Minority News, Florida Press Club, 2007.

Addresses: *Office*—c/o St. Petersburg Times, 490 First Ave. S., St. Petersburg, FL 33701-4223. *Web*—http://ericdeggans.com/index.htm.

---

ally for the Huffington Post, a liberal news Web site. Though his criticism encompasses all aspects of the popular media, Deggans focuses on media portrayals—particularly stereotypes—of minorities.

For example, in a 2004 column in the *St. Petersburg Times,* "Jayson Blair and the Fear Factor," Deggans considered the aftershocks of the scandal surrounding Jayson Blair, the discredited *New York Times* reporter accused of plagiarism and fabrication. Describing what Deggans saw as an impossible double standard for journalists of color, he wrote, "Minority journalists, already worried about being taken seriously in their newsrooms, now see a new hurdle to overcome. Taught that we have to be twice as good to get half as far, we now worry there's no room for error." He went on to say, "It's an unfortunate truth: If a black journalist turns out to be a mediocre hire or worse, the finger-pointing begins in a way white journalists rarely face." If Blair had been a middle-aged white reporter rather than a young black one, Deggans wondered, would he have received the same treatment?

Over the course of several years, Deggans became known for arousing the ire of conservative Fox News host Bill O'Reilly, who famously called Deggans a "race baiter" in 2008. Indeed, Deggans had been an outspoken opponent of O'Reilly since at least 2002, when he called the Fox host a "gasbag" in a column about O'Reilly's use of racially charged language when talking about rap music. Deggans continued his jabs in 2005, criticizing the stereotypes employed by O'Reilly and other conservative pundits to characterize the mainly black victims of Hurricane Katrina. O'Reilly fired back two days later on the Fox News Web site, calling Deggans a "dishonest, racially motivated correspondent writing for perhaps the worst newspaper in the country."

In September of 2007 Deggans again took aim at O'Reilly, commenting on the latter's infamous trip to a Harlem restaurant and the surprise he expressed on his show at having been treated so well. Blogging for the Huffington Post, Deggans wrote, "In O'Reilly's world, black people were either vocal protesters like [Al] Sharpton and Jesse Jackson, or straight-up thugs like N.W.A. After his trip to Sylvia's, O'Reilly seems amazed to meet black folks who don't fit his disconnected stereotype of what we are."

The war of words between Deggans and O'Reilly came to a head in April of 2008, after Deggans mentioned a reference to lynching that O'Reilly had made on his radio program. In his "Talking Points" column for April 8, 2008, O'Reilly wrote, "One of the biggest race baiters in the country writes for the *St. Petersburg Times* newspaper. Eric Deggans also serves as the chairman of the Black Journalist Media Monitoring Committee. Deggans takes delight in branding people racist. Senator Joseph McCarthy would love this guy." At the time, Deggans served as chair of the Media Monitoring Committee of the National Association of Black Journalists, which "monitor[s] the national media for discrimination and other injustices to people in the African diaspora in their coverage and employment practices," according to the association's Web site. Taking O'Reilly's comments as a sign of his success as a critic, Deggans blogged on the Huffington Post, boasting it was "My Proudest Moment as a Pundit."

In addition to his writing, Deggans has spoken as a guest lecturer at Indiana University, the University of South Florida, and St. Petersburg College, and he has taught as an adjunct faculty member at Eckerd College in St. Petersburg and the University of South Florida. In 2003–04 he was an ethics fellow at the Poynter Institute for Media Studies in St. Petersburg, and in

2005 he lectured at Columbia University's prestigious School of Journalism as the winner of its Let's Do It Better! Award for coverage of race and ethnicity.

Deggans has received numerous awards for his criticism. The Mid-Florida Chapter of the Society of Professional Journalists granted him its Award of Excellence four times, in 1999, 2000, 2001, and 2003. The Atlanta chapter of that organization named him a finalist in the criticism category for its Green Eyeshades Award in 1999 and awarded him a second-place prize in 2003. The Florida Society of Newspaper Editors named Deggans the top critic in 2003, and he earned a second-place award in criticism writing from the Florida Press Club as well that year. In 2005 he received the Chuck Stone Salute to Excellence Award from the National Association of Black Journalists for his column "Jayson Blair and the Fear Factor." The Florida Press Club once again recognized him in 2007 with another second-place award in criticism writing, as well as with a first-place award in the minority news category.

Selected writings

Periodicals

"Wallowing in Corruption," *St. Petersburg Times,* March 28, 2002, p. 1D.

"Jayson Blair and the Fear Factor," *St. Petersburg Times,* March 21, 2004, p. 1P.

"Add to Katrina's Toll Race-Tinged Rhetoric," *St. Petersburg Times,* September 14, 2005, p. 6A.

"A Year Later, Imus' Racist Remarks Scandal Yields Surprising Conclusions," *St. Petersburg Times,* April 4, 2008.

Online

"Judging Bill O'Reilly: Why His Comments about Lunch in Harlem Matter," Huffington Post, September 26, 2007, http://www.huffingtonpost.com/eric-deggans/judging-bill-oreilly-wh_b_65914.html (accessed October 24, 2008).

"My Proudest Moment as a Pundit: Bill O'Reilly Calls Me a Race Baiter," Huffington Post, April 8, 2008, http://www.huffingtonpost.com/eric-deggans/my-proudest-moment-as-a-p_b_95610.html (accessed August 27, 2008).

Sources

Online

"Eric Deggans," Huffington Post, http://www.huffingtonpost.com/eric-deggans (accessed August 27, 2008).

"Eric Deggans, TV & Media Critic," *St. Petersburg Times* online, http://www2.sptimes.com/pdfs/profiles06/deggans_eric.pdf (accessed October 24, 2008).

O'Reilly, Bill, "Celebrating America's Tragedy," Fox News, September 16, 2005, http://www.foxnews.com/story/0,2933,169563,00.html (accessed August 27, 2008).

O'Reilly, Bill, "White Backlash against Reverend Wright and Racist Accusations," Fox News, April 8, 2008, http://www.foxnews.com/story/0,2933,347969,00.html (accessed August 27, 2008).

—Deborah A. Ring

Shelton Fabre

1963—

Catholic bishop

In late 2006 Pope Benedict XVI surprised and gladdened the Catholic community of Baton Rouge, Louisiana, by elevating one of their own, Father Shelton Fabre, to the position of auxiliary bishop of New Orleans. Fabre, a lifelong Louisiana resident who had distinguished himself as a thoughtful and devoted leader in the Catholic Church, became just the tenth active African-American bishop in the nation and the youngest in the country. Ministering to the people of New Orleans, a community still wracked by the destruction of Hurricane Katrina in 2005, Fabre reached out to his new parishioners, promising to aid them in rebuilding their lives. The bishop's motto made his commitment clear: "Comfort My People."

Fabre, Shelton, photograph. Michael DeMocker/Newhouse News Service/Landov.

Shelton Joseph Fabre was born on October 25, 1963, in New Roads, Louisiana, the fifth of six children of Luke and Theresa Fabre. He attended Catholic elementary and secondary schools in New Roads, being graduated as valedictorian from Catholic High School of Pointe Coupee in 1981. Fabre enrolled in St. Joseph Seminary College in St. Benedict, Louisiana, earning a bachelor's degree in history in 1985. He continued his education at the American College of the Immaculate Conception of the Catholic University of Louvain in Belgium, completing bachelor's and master's degrees in religious studies.

Fabre was ordained as a priest on August 5, 1989, by Bishop Stanley J. Ott at St. Joseph Cathedral in the Diocese of Baton Rouge. Fabre began his career in the church as an associate pastor at St. Alphonsus Liguori Parish in Greenwell Springs, Louisiana, and then at St. George Parish in Baton Rouge. During 1994 he spent a brief period as a chaplain at the Louisiana State Penitentiary at Angola. In the mid-1990s he served as an associate pastor at St. Isidore the Farmer Parish in Baker, Louisiana, and then at St. Joseph Cathedral in Baton Rouge. From 1996 to 2004 he served as pastor of the parishes of St. Joseph in Grosse Tete, Louisiana, and Immaculate Heart of Mary in Maringouin, Louisiana, and from 2004 to 2007 as pastor of Sacred Heart of Jesus Parish and chaplain to St. Joseph's Academy, both in Baton Rouge.

During his eighteen years in Baton Rouge, Fabre served the church in many important administrative capacities as well. He was director of the Office of Black Catholics and acted as a liaison to black Catholics

At a Glance . . .

Born Shelton Joseph Fabre on October 25, 1963, in New Roads, LA; son of Luke (a bricklayer) and Theresa Vallet Fabre. *Religion:* Catholic. *Education:* St. Joseph Seminary College, BA, history, 1985; American College of the Immaculate Conception, Catholic University of Louvain, BA, religious studies, 1987, MA, religious studies, 1989.

Career: St. Alphonsus Liguori Church, associate pastor, 1989–92; St. George Church, associate pastor, 1992–94; Louisiana State Penitentiary, chaplain, 1994; St. Isidore the Farmer Church, associate pastor, 1994–95; St. Joseph Cathedral, associate pastor, 1995–96; St. Joseph Church, and Immaculate Heart of Mary Church, pastor, 1996–2004; Sacred Heart of Jesus Parish, pastor, and chaplain to St. Joseph's Academy, 2004–07; Archdiocese of New Orleans, auxiliary bishop, and pastor of Our Lady of the Rosary Church, 2007—.

Memberships: Greater Baton Rouge Food Bank, board member; Diocese of Baton Rouge, director of Office of Black Catholics, advisory board member of Catholic Community Services, member-at-large of Presbyteral Council, College of Consulters, clergy representative of Diocesan School Board, member-at-large of Clergy Personnel Board, dean of Northwest Deanery, and chair of Pastoral Planning Committee.

Addresses: *Office*—c/o Archdiocese of New Orleans, 7887 Walmsley Ave., New Orleans, LA 70125-3431.

in the diocese from 1990 to 2005. He also chaired the Pastoral Planning Committee of the Diocese of Baton Rouge, acted as dean of the Northwest Deanery of the diocese, served on the Diocesan School Board, and was a member of the College of Consulters and Presbyteral Council.

On December 13, 2006, the Vatican announced that Pope Benedict XVI had appointed Father Fabre auxiliary bishop in the archdiocese of New Orleans, the second-oldest see (bishop's seat) in the United States. Speaking of the appointment, in a statement issued by the Diocese of Baton Rouge, Bishop Robert W. Muench of Baton Rouge described Fabre as a "devoted, gifted, exemplary and highly respected priest, who comes from a faith-filled family." He went on, "He exhibits strong intellect, genuine piety and true fidelity to Christ and the Church. He is especially noted for his humble demeanor, perceptive judgment, zealous ministry and articulate preaching." Bishop Muench also noted that in appointing Fabre to the bishopric, the pope had "recognized the vibrancy of the Catholic faith in the African-American community."

Fabre was consecrated as bishop on February 28, 2007, in a ceremony held at the Cathedral-Basilica of St. Louis, King of France, in New Orleans. More than four hundred clergy attended the mass, in addition to Fabre's parents and family. As reported in the *New Orleans Clarion Herald,* during the ordination New Orleans archbishop Alfred C. Hughes, who presided—aided by Bishop John H. Ricard of Florida, Fabre's cousin, and Bishop Muench—called on Fabre to "comfort a people devastated by tragedy." Alluding to Fabre's father, who had worked as a bricklayer, Hughes said, "You are now to build up God's church, not with lifeless bricks, but the living stones of God's people." Going further, Hughes asked Fabre to help New Orleans unite in the face of its difficulties: "Help us to become one people across racial, ethnic and economic lines."

It is customary for each Catholic bishop to adopt an episcopal motto that becomes part of his coat of arms. This motto serves as a public statement of the bishop's priorities, describing what he intends to achieve in his position and how he will work with his parishioners. Bishop Fabre selected the motto "Comfort My People," taken from Isaiah 40:1, as a signal of his commitment to the people of New Orleans, many of whom still struggled to recover from Hurricane Katrina. In an address delivered upon his appointment, Fabre reflected on the challenges facing the city: "I know that life in this great city has changed for so many because of Hurricane Katrina. Your resiliency in faith in response to this tragedy has been witnessed by many.... As so many here in New Orleans seek to rebuild their lives and to renew their hope, it is my fervent desire and prayer that to the best of my ability I will be able in some way to bring assistance, comfort and the assurance of God's love and presence to all who are suffering."

At the time of his ordination, Fabre, then forty-three years old, was the youngest Catholic bishop in the United States. (He no longer holds this distinction, however: On June 2, 2008, Father Oscar Cantú was ordained as bishop in San Antonio, Texas, at age forty-one.) Fabre was also one of only ten active African-American bishops out of the 275 nationwide and the first African American to be appointed bishop by Pope Benedict XVI. During his ordination Fabre, the third African-American auxiliary bishop to serve the New Orleans archdiocese, received the pastoral staff that had belonged to Archbishop Joseph Rummel, who in 1962 set a civil rights precedent by excommunicating three parishioners who opposed his plan to integrate the city's Catholic schools.

In his new position as auxiliary bishop, Fabre took on the duties of vicar general, aiding Bishop Hughes in the administration of the archdiocese, including the ordination of priests and deacons. He also took on the job of pastor at Our Lady of the Rosary Church in New Orleans.

Sources

Periodicals

Black Catholic News, December 13, 2006.
New Orleans Clarion Herald, March 10, 2007.

Online

"Bishop Shelton Fabre Ordained," Roman Catholic Diocese of Baton Rouge, http://www.diobr.org/news/070301a.htm (accessed August 22, 2008).

"Curriculum Vitae Most Reverend Shelton Joseph Fabre," National Black Catholic Congress, http://www.nbccongress.org/aboutus/congress-directory/african-american-catholic-bishop-shelton-fabre.asp (accessed August 22, 2008).

"New Bishop for New Orleans a 'Devoted, Gifted, Exemplary' Priest," Catholic News Agency, December 13, 2006, http://www.catholicnewsagency.com/new.php?n=8272 (accessed August 22, 2008).

"Statement of Bishop-Elect Shelton Fabre on Appointment as Auxiliary Bishop of the Archdiocese of New Orleans," Roman Catholic Diocese of Baton Rouge, December 13, 2006, http://www.diobr.org/news/061213d.htm (accessed August 22, 2008).

"Statement of Bishop Muench, Bishop of Baton Rouge, on the Appointment of Father Shelton Fabre as an Auxiliary Bishop of New Orleans," Roman Catholic Diocese of Baton Rouge, December 13, 2006, http://www.diobr.org/news/061213b.htm (accessed August 22, 2008).

—Deborah A. Ring

James A. Forbes Jr.

1935—

Interfaith pastor

Forbes, James A., Jr., photograph. AP Images.

As senior minister of the historic Riverside Church in New York City for nearly two decades, the Reverend James A. Forbes Jr. could not shy away from controversy—it is simply part of the job description. Throughout the church's progressive history, its leaders have used the pulpit as a national platform for advocating social justice and civil rights. Forbes continued that tradition during his tenure, speaking out as a vocal critic of President George W. Bush and as a proponent of gay marriage. Nevertheless, Forbes's greatest challenge would prove to be dissent within his own congregation over his financial leadership of the church's sizable endowment and his Pentecostal-influenced style of preaching—divisions that finally caused him to step down in 2007 from one of the most prestigious positions in the contemporary religious and political arena.

Valued Church and Community

James Alexander Forbes Jr. was born on September 6, 1935, in Burgaw, North Carolina, one of eight children. His parents, James A. Forbes Sr. and Mabel Clemons Forbes, were both deeply religious, and they raised their children in the traditions of the black Pentecostal church. The elder Forbes supported his large family by working as a candy salesman while serving as pastor of the Providence United Holy Church in Raleigh, North Carolina, where they lived together in a three-bedroom apartment on Bloodworth Street. Mabel Forbes worked as a domestic for a white family on the opposite side of town. As a child, the junior Forbes attended Sunday school and sang in the choir at his father's church.

Forbes's family life centered around the church, and he and his brothers and sisters were brought up to value community and, most important, service to the community. In an interview with Bill Moyers for PBS, Forbes recalled, "Church was the center of your social life. Church was the place where you developed your talent. This was the life. And every major holiday, there was a church festival, a convention, somewhere or another, designed to keep you out of mischief. But also, to keep you in a context where the values of the church, and your associates, were all of a common

At a Glance...

Born on September 6, 1935, in Burgaw, NC; son of James A. Forbes Sr. (a minister and candy salesman) and Mabel Clemons Forbes; married Bettye Franks Forbes; children: James A. Forbes III. *Religion:* Pentecostal Baptist. *Education:* Howard University, BS, chemistry, 1957; Union Theological Seminary, MDiv, 1962; Colgate-Rochester Divinity School, DMin, 1975.

Career: Holy Trinity Church, pastor, 1960–65; St. Paul's Holy Church, pastor, 1960–69; St. John's United Holy Church of America, pastor, 1965–73; Virginia Union University, campus minister, 1968–70; Union Theological Seminary, Brown and Sockman Associate Professor of Preaching, 1976–85, Joe R. Engle Professor of Preaching, 1985–89; Riverside Church, senior minister, 1989–2007, senior minister emeritus, 2007—; Healing of the Nations Foundation, founder, 2007.

Memberships: Congress of National Black Churches; Martin Luther King Fellows, past president; Partnership of Faith; board of directors, Bertram M. Beck Institute on Religion and Poverty at Fordham University, Harlem Congregations for Community Improvement, Interfaith Alliance, Mailman School of Public Health at Columbia University, Manhattanville College, United Way, and Values Institute of America.

Awards: Earle B. Pleasant Clergy of the Year Award, Religion in American Life, 2000; Unitas Distinguished Alumni Award, Union Theological Seminary, 2001; Distinguished Service Medal, Teachers College of Columbia University, 2003; Cronkite Faith and Freedom Award Partnership of Faith, 2004; numerous honorary doctorates from colleges and universities, including Colgate University, DePauw University, Fairleigh Dickinson University, Lehigh University, Princeton University, and Trinity College.

Addresses: *Office*—c/o Riverside Church, 490 Riverside Dr., New York, NY 10027-5788.

In 1953 Forbes left his community in Raleigh to study at Howard University in Washington, DC. Initially, he intended to become a doctor, believing that a career in medicine would allow him to combine his love of science with his love of people. By his junior year of college, however, Forbes was beginning to doubt his choice, feeling that he was being called in a more spiritual direction. As he questioned his life's purpose, Forbes told Moyers that he remembered thinking, "I think God wants me to be a healer but a healer of a different sort. Healing body, mind and spirit. Healing individuals and maybe healing in the culture as well." From that moment, Forbes knew that he would dedicate himself to the church.

Began a Life of Faith

Forbes finished his bachelor's degree in chemistry in 1957, then returned to North Carolina to contemplate his path. He wished to attend the Divinity School at Duke University in Durham, but was turned down because of his race. Instead, he enrolled at the Union Theological Seminary in New York City—across the street from Riverside Church—where he earned a master of divinity degree.

After finishing his degree, Forbes returned, once again, to North Carolina. As the civil rights struggle reached its peak in the racially segregated South, Forbes's brother, David, organized sit-ins at Woolworth's lunch counters, where blacks were traditionally denied service. James Forbes participated in those protests. Recalling to Moyers the first time he was able to order a meal at the counter, Forbes said, "When I came into the store and sat down, there was a white woman who had just received her meal. As immediately upon my sitting down, she got up and ran out of the store." He went home and composed the following poem, which appeared in the *New York Times* on October 12, 2004:

> Why did she move when I sat down?
>
> Surely she could not tell so soon that my Saturday bath had worn away,
>
> Or that savage passion had pushed me for a rape.
>
> Perhaps it was the cash she carried in her purse.
>
> She could not risk a theft so early in the month.
>
> And who knows that on tomorrow t'would fall her lot
>
> To drink her coffee from a cup my darkened hands had clutched?
>
> So horrible was that moment, I too should have run away,
>
> For prejudice has the odor of a dying beast.
>
> Whether racist or rapist, both fall into the savage class.

mind about what righteousness looks like, and what holiness looks like."

And the greatest theft of all is to rob one's right to be.

Forbes began his career in the church as pastor at Holy Trinity Church in Wilmington, North Carolina. He went on to minister at St. Paul's Holy Church in Roxboro, North Carolina, and at St. John's United Holy Church of America in Richmond, Virginia, while completing a doctor of ministry degree at Colgate-Rochester Divinity School. In 1976 he returned to New York to take a position at his alma mater, Union Theological Seminary, where he taught homiletics (the art of preaching) for thirteen years.

Took the National Pulpit

By 1989 Forbes had developed a reputation as an inspiring preacher and a sought-after lecturer. That year, he was selected from more than two hundred applicants to become senior minister of the well-known Riverside Church in New York, replacing the outgoing William Sloane Coffin. Only the fifth senior minister in the church's nearly sixty-year history, Forbes was also its first African-American leader.

The Riverside Church, located at the intersection of Morningstar Heights and Harlem on the Upper West Side of Manhattan, was established in 1930 with the support of John D. Rockefeller Jr. Today, it is an interdenominational, interracial, and international church affiliated with both the American Baptist Churches and the United Church of Christ. Long known for its commitment to progressive causes, Riverside was described by the New York Times in 2008 as "a stronghold of activism and political debate," with its pulpit considered one of the most "influential on the nation's religious and political landscapes."

As senior minister of Riverside Church, Forbes became one of the leading voices in American religion, known as a "preacher's preacher" for his charismatic style. In 1993 Ebony magazine named him one of the nation's greatest black preachers, and in 1996 Newsweek recognized him as one of the twelve most effective preachers in the English-speaking world.

Like his predecessors, Forbes did not shy away from the political fray. He welcomed gays and lesbians into the church and spoke out in support of gay marriage, setting himself apart from most other black clergy. During the 2004 presidential election, he openly criticized the policies of the Bush administration and promoted the candidacy of John Kerry, delivering an important address at the Democratic National Convention that year.

Brought Down by Internal Conflict

Despite his record of activism, Forbes's tenure as senior minister was marked by internal conflict almost from the beginning. In 1992 the congregation divided over Forbes's leadership and manner of preaching. Some parishioners objected to his lengthy and interactive sermons, a hallmark of the oral tradition of the black Pentecostal church in which Forbes was raised. Others cited declining attendance and donations, noting that many white members had left the congregation, turned off by what they perceived as Forbes's fundamentalism. Still others were dismayed when Forbes attempted to fire the church's number-two man, the Reverend David Dyson, without consulting the church council. The situation became so heated that a professional mediator was called in to help resolve the disputes.

In 2002, once again, a group of parishioners questioned Forbes's leadership, this time charging mismanagement of church funds. Critics, led by longtime parishioner and former budget committee chair George Bynoe, claimed that Forbes had taken money from the church's endowment to finance operations and that his administration "[did] not follow, deliberately and with malicious intent, proper church governance," the New York Times reported. After a court-appointed receiver examined the church's accounts and found no evidence of wrongdoing, the case was dismissed. Nonetheless, several vocal opponents within the congregation continued to challenge Forbes.

Divisions within the church, it seemed, could not be healed. In September of 2006 Forbes announced that he would step down the next year as senior minister—after eighteen years of service—citing a desire to start a new ministry "aimed at maximizing the witness for spiritual revitalization," he was quoted as saying in the New York Times. Forbes retired from Riverside on June 1, 2007, though he retained the title of senior minister emeritus. Later that year he established the Healing of the Nations Foundation, which is dedicated to the "spiritual revitalization and healing of our country," according to the organization's Web site, and hosted the program The Time Is Now on Air America Radio.

Sources

Periodicals

New York Times, February 6, 1989; May 18, 1992; July 21, 2002; October 12, 2004; September 18, 2006; August 4, 2008.

Online

Healing of the Nations Foundation, http://www.healingofthenations.com (accessed August 25, 2008)

James A. Forbes Jr., interview by Bill Moyers, NOW with Bill Moyers, PBS, December 26, 2003, http://www.pbs.org/now/transcript/transcript248_full.html (accessed August 25, 2008).

"Senior Minister Emeritus," Riverside Church, http://www.theriversidechurchny.org/about/?minister-emeritus (accessed August 25, 2008).

—Deborah A. Ring

Cito Gaston

1944—

Baseball player, manager

Cito Gaston has spent more than forty years in professional baseball as a player, coach, and manager. Best known for leading the Toronto Blue Jays to back-to-back World Series triumphs in 1992 and 1993, he is widely respected for his quiet, unassuming demeanor and studious approach to the game. Only the fourth African-American manager in major-league history, he was the first to win a world title.

The son of a truck driver, Clarence Edwin Gaston was born March 17, 1944, in San Antonio, Texas. The nickname "Cito" was not acquired until his teens. Gaston attended local schools in San Antonio and Corpus Christi, Texas, receiving his high-school diploma in the latter city in 1962. After graduation, he played semi-professional baseball in local leagues for roughly two years. About 1964, however, a scout for the Milwaukee (now Atlanta) Braves spotted him at a game and immediately signed him. After several years of playing outfield for Braves-affiliated teams in the minor leagues, he made his major league debut on September 14, 1967, close to the end of the season. He played eight more games for the Braves that year, then missed the following season (1968), when he was chosen by a new team, the San Diego Padres, in an expansion draft. The Padres' preparations for entering the league were not complete until the start of the 1969 season, when Gaston returned to the field. In six seasons with the Padres (1969–74), he compiled an impressive record. His best year was in 1970, when he hit .310, had twenty-nine home runs, and made the National League All-Star team. After the 1974 season he was traded back to the Braves, for whom he played another four seasons (1975–78). In September of 1978 the Braves traded him to the Pittsburgh Pirates. After playing only two games as a Pirate, Gaston's playing career in the major leagues came to an end.

Gaston, Cito, photograph. J. Meric/Getty Images.

With the exception of the 1970 season, Gaston's statistics were merely respectable, not outstanding. What most impressed his fellow players and coaches was not his performance on the field, but the quiet dedication with which he studied the finer points of technique, particularly with regard to batting. This studious approach would serve him well after the end of his playing career, when his reputation for understanding the mechanics and psychology of batting landed him a job in 1981 as a minor-league batting instructor

At a Glance...

Born March 17, 1944, in San Antonio, TX; married Denise (divorced); married Linda; four children.

Career: Atlanta Braves, outfielder, 1967, 1975–78; San Diego Padres, outfielder, 1969–74; Pittsburgh Pirates, outfielder, 1978; Atlanta Braves, minor-league batting coach, 1981; Toronto Blue Jays, batting coach, 1982–89, 2000–01, manager, 1989–97 and 2008—, guest coach, 2005–07, goodwill ambassador and assistant to team president, 2007–08.

Awards: Member of National League All-Star Team, 1970; Toronto Blue Jays, "Level of Excellence," 1999; Canadian Baseball Hall of Fame, 2002. Received honorary doctorate from University of Toronto, 1994.

Addresses: *Office*—c/o Toronto Blue Jays Baseball Club, 1 Blue Jays Way, Ste. 3200, Rogers Centre, Toronto, ON M5V 1J1, Canada.

---

for the Braves, one of his old teams. The following year he returned to the major leagues as the batting coach for the Toronto Blue Jays, a position he held for the next seven years. By his own account, Gaston would have been happy to remain a coach for the rest of his career. In May of 1989, however, the struggling Blue Jays fired manager Jimy Williams and asked Gaston to take his place on an interim basis. Though Gaston declined the position at first, he relented after several players asked him to reconsider. A quiet, private man, he had to adjust quickly to the intense media scrutiny under which managers must work. "The worst part" of his new job, Gaston told George Vescey in the *New York Times* in September of 1989, "is the questions from the press. When the games start, I relax."

The Blue Jays thrived under Gaston's direction, and the 1989 season that had started so poorly under Williams ended with a division title. They won three more (1991–93) over the course of the next four seasons. In 1992 the team went on to win the American League and World Series titles, the first Canadian team ever to do so. They then repeated that feat in 1993. By all accounts, much of the credit for the team's remarkable success belonged to Gaston, whose calm demeanor reduced players' anxiety and strengthened their confidence. Joe Carter, whose ninth-inning home run clinched the 1993 series, told Walter Leavy in *Ebony*, "Cito knows how to work with each individual, treating everyone like a human being.... When you have a manager like that, it makes you want to play for the guy. We'd go to war for him. What Cito has done for the Blue Jays can't be taken lightly."

The success of 1992–93 was followed by a series of disappointing seasons, with the Blue Jays finishing no better than third in their division between 1994 and 1997. Gaston, hitherto a favorite of the Toronto press, began facing harsh criticism. His defenders pointed out that the expectations created in the wake of the 1993 season were unrealistic, as only a handful of teams in the history of the game had ever won three World Series titles in a row. Many observers, and Gaston himself, detected a note of racism in some of the most strident criticism. The most notorious incident in this regard involved a cartoon that appeared in 1997 in the *Toronto Star*, one of the city's leading papers. In the words of Peter Schmuck in the *Sporting News*, the cartoon "showed Gaston sleeping in the dugout with a 'Do Not Disturb' sign around his neck, and what looked like a liquor bottle in the batting rack." Though many players and fans rallied to Gaston's defense, criticism mounted as the team continued to struggle, and he was fired in the final week of the 1997 season.

Gaston spent the next few years traveling and exploring his options. Though he interviewed several times for managing positions, he did not return to baseball until 2000, when he once again became the Blue Jays' batting coach. He left that position at the end of the 2001 season, only to return to the team in 2005 for temporary assignments as a "guest coach." In 2007 he became a good-will ambassador for the team and an assistant to its president, Paul Godfrey. He was serving in those capacities on June 20, 2008, when Godfrey asked him to take over managing duties from John Gibbons. This time, Gaston accepted the job without hesitation. "I didn't have to think too long about it because of where it was going to be," Gaston told Allan Ryan in the *Toronto Star*. "It's Toronto, the city I love."

Sources

Periodicals

Ebony, May 1993; May 1994.
Jet, October 29, 2007.
New York Times, June 6, 1989; September 24, 1989; October 26, 1992.
Sporting News, November 1, 1993; July 7, 1997.
Toronto Star, June 22, 2008.

—R. Anthony Kugler

Lorna Goodison

1947—

Poet, short-story writer, illustrator

Lorna Goodison never intended to become a poet. As a young woman in her native Jamaica, Goodison kept her writing a secret, publishing poems anonymously in the local newspaper because she was unsure of her talent. Before long, however, as her creative voice demanded to be heard, it became clear that Goodison was meant to be a poet. Today, she is considered one of the foremost Caribbean authors writing in English, standing alongside Nobel Prize winner Derek Wolcott and poet Edward Kamau Brathwaite. Through her sympathetic yet realistic portrayals of the downtrodden, and particularly the struggles of women, she offers powerful testimony to the strength and resilience of the Jamaican spirit.

Resisted Becoming a Poet

Lorna Gaye Goodison was born on August 1, 1947, in Kingston, Jamaica, the eighth of nine children of Vivian Marcus and Doris Louise Goodison. Her parents grew up in the rural Jamaican countryside, but financial hardship forced them to move into the city, where the family lived on a noisy street in a lower-middle-class neighborhood. As a girl, Goodison would travel fourteen hours to visit her extended family in the village of Harvey River, named for her maternal great-grandfather, Englishman William Harvey. The lush landscape of the Jamaican countryside "was to shape my imagination for the rest of my life," she wrote in her memoir *From Harvey River: A Memoir of My Mother and Her People* (2007).

The Goodison household never wanted for literature; as a girl, Lorna had access to a large library of books and magazines brought in by her mother and sister, both voracious readers. Goodison attended St. Hugh's High School, a well-known Anglican academy in Kingston, where she began writing poems and stories. Her parents and teachers, however, believed that her writing paled in comparison to that of a studious older sister, and so she hid her creative work, publishing her first poems anonymously in the *Jamaica Gleaner* newspaper.

After graduation from high school, Goodison worked for a year in the bookmobile of the Jamaican Library Service, a job that again took her into rural Jamaica. In 1967 she enrolled in the Jamaica School of Art, where she pursued her twin passions, writing and painting, and then went on to New York City to study at the school of the Art Students League. Returning to Jamaica the following year, Goodison held a series of jobs, working in advertising and teaching creative writing and art to high school and college students.

Gave In to Her Poetic Voice

Though Goodison believed that she was first and foremost a painter, by the time she was in her twenties the urge to write poetry was becoming more insistent. In an interview with the *Guardian,* quoted in the introduction to her 1986 collection of poetry, *I Am Becoming My Mother,* she said, "I'm a poet, but I didn't choose poetry—it chose me ... it's a dominating, intrusive tyrant. It's something I have to do—a wicked

At a Glance...

Born Lorna Gaye Goodison on August 1, 1947, in Kingston, Jamaica; daughter of Vivian Marcus and Doris Louise (Harvey) Goodison; married Don Topping (a Jamaican radio personality), 1972 (divorced, 1978); children: Miles Goodison Fearon. *Education:* Jamaica School of Art, 1967–68; Art Students League, New York City, 1968–69.

Career: Jamaican Library Service, bookmobile assistant, 1960s; teacher of creative writing and art, 1960s; Radcliffe College, visiting fellow, 1991; University of Toronto, visiting fellow, 1991; University of Michigan, visiting professor, 1992–93, 1995, associate professor, 2008—.

Memberships: Board for Review of Jamaican Copyright Laws; Grace Foundation for Gifted Children; Jamaican National Commission, United Nations Educational, Scientific and Cultural Organization.

Awards: Commonwealth Writers' Prize, Americas region, Commonwealth Foundation, 1987; Commonwealth Universities Fellowship, 1990–91; Musgrave Gold Medal, Institute of Jamaica, 1999; British Columbia Award for Canadian Non-Fiction, 2008.

Addresses: *Office*—c/o University of Michigan, Department of English, 435 S. State St., 3187 Angell Hall, Ann Arbor, MI 48109-1003.

---

force." Finally succumbing to her poetic voice, Goodison began to publish poems under her own name in the *Jamaica Journal* and gave readings to audiences across the island. The experience of sharing her work gave Goodison a sense of confidence, and she began to devote herself seriously to the craft of poetry. "I honestly feel I was given this work to do. It took me a long while to accept it because I used to fight it," Goodison told the *Jamaica Observer.*

Goodison published her first volume of poetry, *Tamarind Season*, in 1980. The collection's title is a reference to a Jamaican phrase describing the period before the harvest when food is scarce and times are hard; this motif of struggle and hardship is one that Goodison would return to again and again in her work. She followed up with *I Am Becoming My Mother*. The volume was her first work to be widely recognized both on the island and internationally, earning Goodison the Commonwealth Writers' Prize the following year.

Goodison's subsequent volumes of poetry include *Heartease* (1988), *To Us, All Flowers Are Roses* (1995), *Turn Thanks* (1999), *Guinea Woman* (2000), *Travelling Mercies* (2001), *Controlling the Silver* (2005), and *Goldengrove* (2006). In addition, she has penned two collections of short stories: *Baby Mother and the King of Swords* (1990) and *Fool-Fool Rose Is Leaving Labour-in-Vain Savannah* (2005).

Wrote of Jamaican People and Culture

Goodison's poetry and prose pay tribute to the scenery, people, and language of Jamaica. In an interview with the *Jamaica Observer*, Goodison noted, "I am definitely a poet of place. Even when I am not writing about Jamaica, it is always on my heart." Like many West Indian writers of her generation, she blends many different dialects in her verse, sometimes writing in "proper" English, sometimes in Jamaican English, and sometimes in Jamaican Creole or "dread talk," a patois spoken by Rastafarians. She may use all of these languages in the same poem, and even in the same line. At the same time, allusions to poets such as Samuel Butler Yeats and William Wordsworth are evidence of her grounding in the canon of English literature.

Many of Goodison's poems focus on women and their struggles. Whereas some poems pay homage to great women—such as novelist Jean Rhys in "Lullaby for Jean Rhys," activist Winnie Mandela in "Bedspread," and civil rights pioneer Rosa Parks in "For Rosa Parks"—many more focus on ordinary women and their daily lives.

In one of her most famous poems, "For My Mother (May I Inherit Half Her Strength)," published in both *Tamarind Season* and *I Am Becoming My Mother*, she pays tribute to her mother's memory and all that she endured:

> She could work miracles, she would make a garment from a square of cloth in a span that defied time. Or feed twenty people on a stew made from fallen-from-the-head cabbage leaves and a carrot and a cho-cho and a palmful of meat.

> And she rose early and sent us clean into the world and she went to bed in the dark, for my father came in always last.

In "Guinea Woman," from the collection of the same name, she writes of her maternal ancestor,

> Great grandmother was a guinea woman wide eyes turning the corners of her face could see

behind her her cheeks dusted with a fine rash of jet-bead warts that itched when the rain set up.

In her highly acclaimed memoir, *From Harvey River*, Goodison continues this "fleshing out of her mother," in the words of critic Edward Baugh, offering a sensitive portrait of the Harvey family in the early 1900s and, along with it, a glimpse into the culture and history of Jamaica. Writing for the *Toronto Star*, Donna Bailey Nurse praised the book: "The work is a feat of history, imagination and artistic achievement. Rather than forcing a narrative from the rich but limited details of her forebears' lives, Goodison simply presents those details and allows them to speak for themselves. The result is a sumptuous montage of landscapes, portraits and anecdotes—sepia-toned period pieces—that impress vividly upon the mind." *Washington Post* reviewer Carolyn See noted, "This is Goodison's tribute to her mother, but more than that, it is a window that opens onto a society that most of us will never know." *From Harvey River* earned Goodison the British Columbia Award for Canadian Non-Fiction in 2008.

Since the 1990s Goodison has divided her time between Jamaica and North America. She began teaching creative writing as a visiting fellow at Radcliffe College and the University of Toronto in 1991, and as a visiting professor at the University of Michigan in 1992. As of 2008 she served as a full-time faculty member in the English Department at the University of Michigan and maintained a home in Toronto. In addition to her writing and teaching, Goodison remained an accomplished painter, illustrating most of her book covers and exhibiting her artwork throughout Jamaica and North America.

Selected writings

Poetry

Tamarind Season, Institute of Jamaica Press, 1980.
I Am Becoming My Mother, New Beacon, 1986.
Heartease, New Beacon, 1988.
To Us, All Flowers Are Roses, University of Illinois Press, 1995.
Turn Thanks, University of Illinois Press, 1999.
Guinea Woman, Carcanet, 2000.
Travelling Mercies, McClelland & Stewart, 2001.
Controlling the Silver, University of Illinois Press, 2005.
Goldengrove, Carcanet, 2006.

Stories

Baby Mother and the King of Swords, Longman, 1990.
Fool-Fool Rose Is Leaving Labour-in-Vain Savannah, Ian Randle, 2005.

Nonfiction

"How I Became a Writer," in *Caribbean Women Writers: Essays from the First International Conference,* edited by Selwyn R. Cudjoe, University of Massachusetts Press, 1990, pp. 290–294.
(With E. Kamau Brathwaite and Mervyn Morris) *Three Caribbean Poets on Their Work,* edited by Victor L. Chang, Institute of Caribbean Studies, 1993.
From Harvey River: A Memoir of My Mother and Her People, McClelland & Stewart, 2007.

Sources

Periodicals

Halcyon: The Newsletter of the Friends of the Thomas Fisher Rare Book Library, November 1998.
Jamaica Observer, August 13, 2007.
New York Times, March 30, 2008.
Toronto Star, February 25, 2007.
Washington Post, March 21, 2008.

Online

"Artist Biography: Lorna Goodison," Voices from the Gaps: Women Artists and Writers of Color, an International Website, 2005, http://voices.cla.umn.edu/vg/Bios/entries/goodison_lorna.html (accessed August 12, 2008).

—Deborah A. Ring

W. C. Gorden

1930—

Football coach

W. C. Gorden is a legend among alumni and supporters of Jackson State University in Mississippi as the most successful coach in the history of the school's renowned football program. Gorden led the Tigers for sixteen seasons and compiled a record of 119 wins, 47 losses, and 5 ties. His tenure included a stunning twenty-eight-game winning streak during the late 1980s. Credited with making Jackson State's football program a powerhouse in the Southwestern Athletic Conference (SWAC) during that era, he was inducted into the College Football Hall of Fame in 2008. When the honor was announced, Michael Rubenstein, executive director of the Mississippi Sports Hall of Fame, hailed the retired coach in the Jackson *Clarion-Ledger* as "representative of everything that's good about college football."

Born in 1930 in Nashville, Gorden graduated from the city's all-black Pearl High School and went on to Tennessee State University, a historically black college in Nashville. He was a wide receiver for its football team and was also an outstanding baseball player who captained the team. After graduating in 1952 with a degree in health and physical education, he went on to earn a master's degree from the school as well. In 1956 he took a job at Eva Gordon High School in Magnolia, Mississippi, as the school's athletic director and head football, baseball, basketball, and track coach. A decade later, he worked at Temple High School in Vicksburg as its head football coach and athletic director before he was hired at what was then called Jackson State College in 1967.

Gorden initially held two jobs at Jackson State—head baseball coach and defensive coordinator for the football team—before being promoted to head football coach in 1977. One of the several historically black schools in the SWAC in Division I-AA of the National Collegiate Athletic Association (NCAA), Jackson State was already producing future National Football League pros by the time Gorden arrived on campus. "Football is a large part of the soul of this predominantly black state school," noted Leigh Montville in *Sports Illustrated.* Montville cited a long list of former Tigers who went on to NFL careers, including Lem Barney and Walter Payton, and wrote that scouts for professional teams arrived "every year to weigh and measure and take two and three and four players to the big cities and the big noise." A *New York Times* article by Ray Glier on the history of black college football programs reiterated Jackson State's legendary status. "In a 1980 study by *The Chronicle of Higher Education,* Jackson State had 21 players in the NFL, more than Alabama, more than Michigan, more than Florida and more than Texas," wrote Glier. "Only six universities that season had more players in pro football than the Tigers."

Gorden is credited with much of that legacy. Under his watch the Tigers—often referred to as the Blue Bengals by supporters—won eight Southwestern Athletic Conference championships; between 1985 and 1989, they racked up twenty-eight consecutive victories in league play. One of the best years under Gorden's direction was the 1985 season, which ended with an 8–3 record; Gorden also coached the SWAC All-Star team that year to a 16–14 win in the Freedom Bowl over the Mideast-

At a Glance . . .

Born June 30, 1930, in Nashville, TN; married Vivian Howard; children: Craig, Robin. *Education:* Earned undergraduate degree in health and physical education from Tennessee State University, 1952; later earned master's degree from Tennessee State University.

Career: Eva Gordon High School, athletic director and head football, baseball, basketball, and track coach, 1956–66; Temple High School, head football coach and athletic director, 1966–67; Jackson State University, head baseball coach, 1967–72, defensive coordinator for football team, 1967–77, head football coach, 1977–91, athletic director, 1991–94.

Memberships: Make-A-Wish Foundation (board member), Pearl River Valley Water Supply District (board member).

Awards: Coach of the Year, Southwestern Athletic Conference (six times); Coach of the Year, National Sports Foundation, 1985; inducted into the Mississippi Sports Hall of Fame & Museum, 1997; inducted into the College Football Hall of Fame, 2008.

Addresses: *Home*—Jackson, MS. *Office*—c/o College Football Hall of Fame, 111 South St. Joseph St., South Bend, IN 46601.

---

ern Athletic Conference All-Star team and was named Coach of the Year by the National Sports Foundation.

Amid all of these triumphs were also a string of tragedies: in 1970, when Gorden was still an assistant coach, the campus was the scene of a notorious incident in which Mississippi Highway Patrol officers fired into a women's dormitory during a campus disturbance, killing two and wounding seven. In 1988, at the height of the team's success, defensive back Antonio Rogers died in an automobile accident. Sixteen months later, running back Earl Eatman met the same fate.

The most wrenching loss for Gorden and the school, however, came on Easter weekend in 1990, when three of his players—Casey Conner, Charles Ford, and Michael Kimble—were killed in a car crash. In *Sports Illustrated* Montville reported on the impact of the deaths, and described the subdued mood on campus and in the locker room. "I got the call at 3:35 on Monday morning," Gorden told Montville. "Casey's sister was on the phone. I hate a phone call after 12 o'clock. It never is good. I have two grown children of my own, and I'm responsible for 95 football players.... I hadn't said anything before this vacation, but I made it a point to talk to the team before spring break in March about being careful," he continued. "I talked about the things that had happened the past two years. I told a story about myself when I was in college. I was going to summer school. We had a break for the Fourth of July. I came back to class and the desk next to me was empty. I said, 'Hey, where's So-and-So?' I was told, 'Oh, he was in a crash. He died.' Just like that. I told the kids to watch themselves."

Gorden coached until 1992, then served as Jackson State's athletic director for two years before retiring. In 1997 he was honored by the Mississippi Legislature with a proclamation that cited him as "the winningest football coach in the history of Jackson State University," but also commended him "for his hard-nosed academic oversight policy, under which he led his players to a higher graduation rate than any public school in his conference, and also graduated his players at a higher rate than the rest of the student body during his coaching tenure."

In May of 2008 the National Football Foundation announced that Gorden would be inducted into the College Football Hall of Fame at a July ceremony. Former Minnesota Viking wide receiver and sports broadcaster Ahmad Rashad spoke at the ceremony about Gorden's impressive leadership of the Tigers for sixteen seasons. "Those guys were always ready for the NFL when they left," Rashad said. "They had speed. Discipline. They were a step ahead of us when they got to the league."

By then the halcyon days of black college football had become a mere footnote in the history of American sports. "Integration hurt us, so did the big television contracts, and the improvements to stadiums at the bigger schools," Gorden told Glier in 2003. "We fell behind." He was immensely honored by the recognition from the College Football Hall of Fame, as he told Kareem Copeland in the *Clarion-Ledger.* "It means so much because there are a lot of people that are not aware of the history, the successes and the athletes that matriculated at Jackson State University. In a sense, they played in anonymity. By honoring me, it brings recognition to (them)."

Sources

Periodicals

Clarion-Ledger (Jackson, MS), September 24, 2007; May 8, 2008; July 21, 2008.
New York Times, September 4, 2003, p. D2.
Sports Illustrated, April 30, 1990, p. 42.

Online

"House Concurrent Resolution 152," Mississippi Legislature, 1997, http://billstatus.ls.state.ms.us/documents/1997/HC/HC0152SG.htm (accessed October 25, 2008).

Recek, Travis, "Hall of Fame Awaits W. C. Gorden," Fox40News.com, July 17, 2008, http://www.fox40now.com/sports/college/25525114.html (accessed October 25, 2008).

—Carol Brennan

Augustus O. Grant

1946(?)—

Cardiologist

Each year, more than 960,000 people die in the United States as a result of heart disease—including heart attack, stroke, and other cardiac disorders. As one of the top cardiologists in the country, Dr. Augustus O. Grant has dedicated his career to treating and preventing this killer. For nearly thirty years he has been a part of two of the leading health institutions in the United States, serving as a physician and faculty member at Duke University Medical Center—ranked among the ten best heart centers nationwide—and as a president of the American Heart Association, one of the largest voluntary health organizations in the United States. In his work, Grant has vigorously promoted heart health and underscored the important partnership between physicians and patients in fighting heart disease.

Augustus Oliver Grant was born in 1946 in Jamaica. He attended the distinguished St. Jago High School in Spanish Town, earning the Jamaica Scholarship in 1963. He left Jamaica to attend the University of Edinburgh in Scotland, where he earned undergraduate and medical degrees, and then went on to the University of California at San Francisco to study pharmacology, completing a doctorate in 1975.

Grant trained as a medical resident at the University of Manitoba in Canada from 1975 to 1977. He began his association with Duke University in 1977 as a fellow in cardiology, joining the faculty at Duke's School of Medicine in 1980. In 1986–87 he traveled to Germany as an Alexander von Humboldt research fellow at the University of Saarland.

From 1992 to 1994 Grant served as president of the Association of Black Cardiologists, an organization that is dedicated to eliminating disparities related to cardiovascular disease among people of color. Under his leadership the association created the Annual Cardiology Fellows program, which provides scholarships to medical students and sponsorship for fellows and residents to attend medical conferences and workshops.

In his research and clinical practice, Grant has focused on the understanding and treatment of patients with cardiac arrhythmias—that is, patients with heartbeats that are too slow, too fast, or irregular. Although arrhythmia is a common cardiac condition, its mechanisms are still not well understood by physicians, and it is a frequent cause of death. Grant's work aims to identify new ways to diagnose, treat, and prevent arrhythmias.

In 2003 Grant was elected president of the American Heart Association (AHA), the nation's largest organization dedicated to fighting heart disease, stroke, and other cardiovascular disorders. He was the first Duke cardiologist to be named to the post. By this time, Grant already had a long history of service to the AHA, beginning nearly three decades earlier in 1974, when he first received a grant to support his graduate research at the University of California. Since then he has served as an active member of the AHA, reviewing grant applications and organizing scientific meetings.

As president of the AHA, Grant acted as the public face of the 22.5-million-member organization and as a

At a Glance . . .

Born Augustus Oliver Grant in 1946(?) in Jamaica. *Education:* University of Edinburgh, MB, ChB, 1971; University of California at San Francisco, PhD, pharmacology, 1975.

Career: University of Manitoba, medical resident, 1975-77; Duke University Medical Center and School of Medicine, fellow in cardiology, 1977-80, professor of medicine, 1980—, vice dean for faculty enrichment, 2007—.

Memberships: American College of Cardiology; American Heart Association, past president; American Society of Clinical Investigation; Association of Black Cardiologists, past president; Biophysical Society; Heart Rhythm Society; National Advisory Council for Biomedical Imaging; Sarnoff Cardiovascular Research Foundation.

Awards: Gold Heart Award for volunteer service, American Heart Association, 2008; Distinguished Faculty Award, Duke Medical Alumni Association, 2008.

Addresses: *Office*—Duke University Medical Center, Box 3504 DUMC, Durham, NC 27710.

---

national advocate for heart health. At the beginning of his presidency Grant announced that one of the AHA's major goals would be to reduce the incidence of heart attack and stroke by 25 percent by 2010 through clinical research, physician training, and especially more proactive patient education. "We have developed many expensive technologies for treating heart disease, and while these have saved many lives, patients have an important role to play by leading healthier lives," Grant said in a July of 2002 interview with *Inside,* a newsletter published by the Duke University Medical Center. "The AHA can play a crucial role in educating patients about the control they have in preventing heart disease and stroke."

At the same time that Grant was asking individuals to take more responsibility for their own health, in January of 2004 the AHA put pressure on the U.S. Congress to do more at the legislative level to support Americans' cardiovascular health. "Many Americans promised themselves they would improve their health in the New Year—eat better and get more exercise," Grant wrote in a letter to members of Congress outlining the AHA's priorities, as reported on the Science Blog Web site that month. The letter went on to say: "Now it is Congress's turn to make the same pledge to all Americans. Heart disease, stroke, and other cardiovascular diseases claim far too many lives—nearly 1 million per year—and almost a quarter of all Americans are afflicted with at least one type of cardiovascular disease." Grant also asked Congress to support the fight against cardiovascular disease by passing stroke treatment and prevention legislation, enhancing funding for the Centers for Disease Control and Prevention, reauthorizing a child nutrition program, supporting regulation of tobacco products, and providing more money for 911 emergency systems.

Grant's term as AHA president ended in 2004. He continued to serve as a professor of medicine at Duke University Medical Center and as codirector of the hospital's Heart Station, where patients receive noninvasive cardiac care. In 2007 he took on the position of vice dean of faculty enrichment in the School of Medicine. According to *U.S. News & World Report,* Duke ranked among the top ten hospitals in the nation for cardiac care and heart surgery in 2008.

In addition to his clinical practice and teaching duties, Grant remained active in the medical community. He was a fellow of the American College of Cardiology and the American Heart Association and a member of the Association of Black Cardiologists, the Biophysical Society, the Heart Rhythm Society, and the American Society of Clinical Investigation. He has sat on the editorial boards of *Circulation, Circulation Research,* and the *Journal of Molecular and Cellular Cardiology,* and he served as deputy editor of the *Journal of Cardiovascular Electrophysiology* and consulting editor to the *American Journal of Physiology.* He continued to act as a benefactor to St. Jago High School in his native Jamaica through the Grant Foundation.

In 2008 Grant received the Gold Heart Award from the American Heart Association, the organization's highest honor recognizing distinguished service in advancing the goals of the AHA, and the Distinguished Faculty Award from the Duke Medical Alumni Association.

Sources

Periodicals

Inside, July 1, 2002; September 16, 2002.

Online

"Best Hospitals: Heart & Heart Surgery," *U.S. News & World Report,* 2008, http://www.usnews.com/directories/hospitals/index_html/specialty+ihqcard (accessed August 26, 2008).

Biography of Augustus O. Grant, Duke University School of Medicine, http://medschool.duke.edu/modules/som_administration/index.php?id=27 (accessed August 26, 2008).

Other

"American Heart Association Challenges Congress to Commit to Americans' Health," news release, January 20, 2004, Science Blog, http://www.scienceblog.com/community/older/archives/K/0/pub0605 .html (accessed August 26, 2008).

—Deborah A. Ring

Anthony Griffin

1960—

Plastic surgeon

Griffin, Anthony, photograph. Frazer Harrison/Getty Images.

Only a few decades ago, plastic surgery was considered by many people to be the exclusive domain of white doctors serving white patients. Few African Americans underwent plastic surgery—either for cosmetic or for reconstructive purposes—not only because of concerns about scarring, a common problem for patients with darker skin, but also because many believed that such procedures would wipe away their ethnic features, making them look "too white." And until recently, only a handful of African-American doctors practiced plastic surgery in the United States. When Dr. Anthony Griffin, the Beverly Hills plastic surgeon featured on ABC TV's *Extreme Makeover* series, first told friends and family that he wanted to pursue the specialty, "Everyone was laughing at me saying, 'Black folks don't get plastic surgery,'" he related to *Jet* magazine in 2004.

These trends, however, have begun to change. As a result of new surgical techniques that minimize scarring—pioneered by doctors such as Griffin—and fueled by the popularity of reality television shows focused on plastic surgery, cosmetic procedures are no longer considered taboo among African Americans. According to the American Society of Plastic Surgeons, between 2000 and 2007 cosmetic plastic surgery procedures increased 129 percent among African Americans. Today, the most commonly requested procedures among African Americans are nose reshaping, liposuction, and breast reduction.

Griffin is one of a small but growing number of black plastic surgeons—about one hundred nationwide. He is considered one of the nation's top authorities on plastic surgery for African Americans and other ethnic skin types. In his practice he has sought to demonstrate that blacks need not emulate traditional ideals of beauty. "Minorities no longer feel like they have to look like Barbie dolls, and that's the way it should be," Griffin wrote in an *Ebony* magazine column in 2008. "One's natural ethnic features ... are now something to be proud of." In 2002 Griffin took his practice to the national stage, appearing on the hit ABC reality series *Extreme Makeover*. He has used his celebrity status to bring attention to what he considers his most important work: Operation Smile, a medical mission that provides free surgical care to children with deformities in developing countries. It is this social

At a Glance . . .

Born Anthony Charles Griffin on March 1, 1960, in Kenosha, WI; married Belle. *Education:* Brown University, BA, biology; Washington University School of Medicine, MD and MA/MS, pharmacology, 1987.

Career: Washington University, surgical intern at Barnes Hospital, 1987–89, surgical resident, 1988–90; University of Chicago Pritzker Medical School, resident in general surgery, 1990–91; University of Southern California, resident in plastic and reconstructive surgery, 1991–94; Cedars-Sinai Medical Center, surgical staff, 1995; University of California, Los Angeles–Charles Drew University, surgical staff, 1998; Beverly Hills Cosmetic Surgery Institute and Beverly Hills Robertson Surgery Center, medical director, 1998—.

Memberships: American College of Surgeons; American Medical Association; American Society of Plastic Surgeons; American Society for Aesthetic Plastic Surgery; National Medical Association; California Medical Association; California Society of Plastic Surgeons; Beverly Hills Chamber of Commerce; Los Angeles County Medical Association; Los Angeles Society of Plastic Surgeons; Charles Drew Medical Society; Rhinoplasty Society.

Awards: Outstanding Achievement Award, National Association for the Advancement of Colored People; Golden Cannula Award, Lipoplasty Society, 1993.

Addresses: *Office*—Beverly Hills Cosmetic Surgery Institute, 8641 Wilshire Blvd., Ste. 305, Beverly Hills, CA 90211-2921. *Web*—http://www.griffinmd.com.

---

mission that Griffin sees as ultimately defining his life's work.

Anthony Charles Griffin was born on March 1, 1960, in Kenosha, Wisconsin. Growing up with a brother who had asthma, Griffin and his family were in and out of emergency rooms frequently, and the experience instilled in him a desire to pursue medicine as a career. But Griffin was also a creative child—he loved art class and often sketched comic book characters in his notebooks.

When, as a teenager, Griffin came across an *Ebony* magazine article profiling several black plastic surgeons, he knew immediately that was the career for him. Plastic surgery would allow him to combine his passions for art and medicine. "You have to have an eye for proportion and be able to see what you are going to do before doing it. Essentially, you are an artist. The ... human body is probably the most difficult medium to sculpt," he explained in 2006 to interviewer Deardra Shuler of the Web site Black World Today.

Griffin attended Brown University, completing a bachelor's degree in biology, and then went on to the School of Medicine at Washington University in St. Louis, Missouri. There, he earned both a doctorate in medicine and a master's degree in pharmacology. He trained as a general surgeon at the University of Chicago, then moved to California to complete a two-year residency in plastic surgery at the University of Southern California, specializing in burn reconstruction, plastic and reconstructive surgery, and hand surgery. After stints on the surgical staff at Cedars-Sinai Medical Center and on the faculty of University of California, Los Angeles–Charles Drew University, Griffin opened his own practice, becoming medical director of the Beverly Hills Cosmetic Surgery Institute in 1998.

In his private practice Griffin has developed three signature procedures. The most popular, the Brazilian Butt Lift, relocates fat from the patient's abdomen to create a more rounded, voluptuous posterior such as that of celebrities Jennifer Lopez and Beyoncé. The Six-Pack Tummy Tuck creates a slimmer, flatter abdomen, and the No-Tell Nose Job is purported to reshape the nose while leaving no scarring. Griffin specializes in scar-free surgery for scar-prone ethnic skin types (African American, Hispanic, and Asian), using techniques that do not require external incisions or that work with the natural folds and creases of the skin.

Griffin approaches his patients in much the same way that a psychologist does: He wants to understand what is driving them to seek cosmetic surgery. In an interview with the Web site LoveToKnow, he described his view: "My philosophy is that I think there are two different types of plastic surgery. One is vanity plastic surgery. That is the plastic surgery that most people think of.... Then, I think there is self-esteem surgery. People are born with certain distractions or have distractions that take away from their confidence and their ability to engage in life." It is the latter type of surgery that Griffin focuses on—surgery that, he believes, has a purpose beyond the patient's external appearance.

In 2002 Griffin was approached by ABC network executives to take part in a new reality television series called *Extreme Makeover*. Producers had learned of his work from Dr. William Dorfman, Griffin's dentist, who had already committed to being featured on the program. During the show, which ran until 2007, ordinary men and women received extensive makeovers that included plastic surgery, dental work, exercise programs, hair and makeup, and wardrobe.

Though Griffin was initially reluctant to put himself in the spotlight, he proved to be one of the show's most popular doctors, as audiences were attracted by his skill, compassion, and sensitivity. Griffin's role on *Extreme Makeover* has made him a celebrity in his own right, leading to appearances on CNN, the Discovery Health Channel, and the Learning Channel, as well as features in *Time, Essence,* and *National Geographic* magazines.

On top of an already demanding private practice, since 1995 Griffin has donated his time to the volunteer organization Operation Smile, a medical mission that provides free reconstructive surgery to children suffering from cleft lips and palates in developing countries. He has worked as part of a team of forty to sixty doctors, nurses, and therapists, performing as many as two hundred operations in a week. Operation Smile has taken him across the globe to Peru, China, the Middle East, the Philippines, and other locations. It was during a mission to Kenya that Griffin met his wife, Belle, who was then working as a volunteer nurse.

For Griffin, Operation Smile is by far his most gratifying work as a surgeon. "It's just absolutely changed my whole life and perspective," he told the *Los Angeles CityBeat* newspaper in 2006.

Selected writings

"What You Should Know before Getting That Nip & Tuck: Choosing the Right Surgeon Is the First Step," *Ebony,* April 2008.

Sources

Periodicals

Black Enterprise, November 2000.
Ebony, August 2004.
Jet, April 12, 2004.
Los Angeles CityBeat, February 2, 2006.

Online

Anthony Griffin, interview with LoveToKnow Skincare, http://skincare.lovetoknow.com/Interview_with_Dr._Anthony_Griffin,_%22Extreme_Makeover%22_Surgeon (accessed August 19, 2008).

Anthony Griffin official Web site, http://www.griffinmd.com (accessed August 19, 2008).

"Beverly Hills Plastic Surgery and the Path of an Unlikely Artist," beverlyhillspeople.com, http://www.beverlyhillspeople.com/pages/Dr-Griffin.html (accessed August 19, 2008).

"Cosmetic Plastic Surgery Procedures for Ethnic Patients Up 13 Percent in 2007," American Society of Plastic Surgeons, March 25, 2008, http://www.plasticsurgery.org/media/press_releases/Cosmetic-Plastic-Surgery-Procedures-for-Ethnic-Patients-Up-13-Percent-in-2007.cfm (accessed August 19, 2008).

Shuler, Deardra, "Dr. Anthony Griffin: The Expert on Ethnic Skin," Black World Today, September 13, 2006, http://www.tbwt.org/index.php?option=content&task=view&id=805&Itemid=2 (accessed August 19, 2008).

—Deborah A. Ring

Johnny Griffin

1928–2008

Jazz saxophonist, bandleader

Griffin, Johnny, photograph. Greetsia Tent/WireImage.

Johnny Griffin, the great jazz tenor saxophonist, was nicknamed "The Little Giant" for his diminutive stature, but he towered over his contemporaries as a musical force. He mastered complex harmonies and rapid-fire tempos, even those of the most demanding bandleaders, in a way that less-accomplished musicians could only envy. For his incredible speed and technical prowess, he earned the distinction "world's fastest saxophonist," but he could also play a ballad just as skillfully as his peers. Over a career that spanned more than six decades, Griffin accompanied many of the jazz greats of the swing and bop eras—most notably John Coltrane and Thelonious Monk, but also Lionel Hampton, Joe Morris, Arnett Cobb, Art Blakey, and many others. Griffin was tireless to the end, honking out blues rhythms quite literally until the day he died.

Born a Musician

John Arnold Griffin III was born on April 24, 1928, on the South Side of Chicago. Music was a fixture in the Griffin household: His father had been a cornet player, though he gave up the instrument before Johnny was born, and his mother played the piano and sang in the church choir. Griffin, who clearly had a talent for music from the start, began playing the piano at age six, studying for four years, and then tried his hand at the Hawaiian steel guitar. But then, at age twelve, he heard Gene Ammons play the saxophone with King Kolax's big band at the Parkway Ballroom in Chicago, and he knew that was the instrument for him.

Griffin attended DuSable High School in Chicago, where he studied music under the famous Captain Walter Dyett, who had trained such jazz greats as Nat King Cole and Dinah Washington, as well as saxophonists Ammons and Von Freeman. Though Griffin was eager to learn the alto saxophone, Dyett insisted that Griffin cut his teeth on other instruments first, and so he learned the clarinet, oboe, and English horn before finally taking up the sax in earnest. Griffin began playing with schoolmates in a group called the Baby Band and occasionally with blues guitarist T-Bone Walker.

Coming of age during the 1940s, Griffin was inspired by Charlie "Bird" Parker and Dizzy Gillespie, who were leading the way in popularizing the up-tempo bebop

At a Glance...

Born John Arnold Griffin III on April 24, 1928, in Chicago, IL; died on July 25, 2008, in Availles-Limouzine, France; married Miriam; children: Jo-Onna, Ingrid, John, Cynthia. *Military service:* U.S. Army, 1951–53.

Career: Played tenor saxophone with Lionel Hampton, 1945–57, Joe Morris, 1947–50, Art Blakey's Jazz Messengers, 1957, Thelonious Monk, 1958, Eddie "Lockjaw" Davis, 1960–62, and Kenny Clarke and Francy Boland, 1967–69; led groups including the Johnny Griffin Sextet, 1958, and the Big Soul Band, 1960; collaborated with other artists including Philly Joe Jones, Percy Heath, Jo Jones, Gene Ramey, Arnett Cobb, Bud Powell, Babs Gonzales, Kenny Drew, Art Taylor, and Martial Solal.

style of jazz. Griffin saw both musicians play in 1945 with Billy Eckstine's band. He also admired the sounds of saxophonists Johnny Hodges and Ben Webster, reflecting in the book *Talking Jazz,* "These cats were really my masters; to me, the greatest sounds ever."

Became a Professional Sax Man

Griffin began his profession just days after his high school graduation in 1945, traveling to Toledo, Ohio, to join up with well-known bandleader Hampton. At the last minute, Griffin was asked to switch from alto to tenor saxophone—forcing him to dash back to Chicago, where he had left his tenor sax, before going out on tour—but it was a change he was happy to make, as he preferred the latter instrument.

When trumpeter Joe Morris split from Hampton in 1947 to form his own rhythm and blues band, Griffin followed. He toured with Morris for the next three years, and played often with noted musicians Philly Joe Jones, Percy Heath, Jo Jones, Gene Ramey, and Cobb.

In 1951 Griffin was drafted into the U.S. Army in the same company as seven other black men from the South Side of Chicago. When they learned that they were destined for Fort Chaffee, in Arkansas, the men refused, knowing what kind of treatment they could expect in the racially charged South. Instead, the group was sent to Hawaii. There, Griffin learned of an opening for an oboist in the army band, and he so impressed a drunken colonel whom he performed for that he was reassigned. The rest of his battalion was sent to Korea, where most died. Griffin later credited the oboe for having saved his life.

Collaborated with Jazz Greats

After his discharge from the army in 1953, Griffin spent several years at home in Chicago before heading back to New York to join drummer Art Blakey's Jazz Messengers as tenor saxophonist in 1957. The group's 1958 recording featuring the legendary Monk on piano marked a turning point in Griffin's career, as it brought him international recognition and initiated a brief but important collaboration between Griffin and Monk. A few months later Griffin left Blakey to join Monk's quartet, replacing Coltrane on the tenor saxophone.

Monk, a pioneer of bebop jazz, was a notoriously difficult bandleader, particularly when playing his own compositions. His improvisational style and complex harmonies made it hard for lesser musicians to keep up. In *Talking Jazz,* Griffin described the experience of playing live with Monk: "I found it difficult at times, I mean, DIFFICULT. I enjoying playing with him, enjoying playing music, but when I'm playing my solos ... the way his comping [accompaniment] is so strong ... it's almost like you're in a padded cell. I mean, trying to express yourself, because his music, with him comping, is so overwhelming, like it's almost like you're trying to break out of a room made of marshmallows." Nonetheless, Griffin identified Monk as one of his most rewarding partnerships: "The way he composed, the logic of his compositions, immensely influenced me," Griffin said, as quoted in his obituary in the *Independent.*

At the same time he was working with Monk, Griffin was emerging as a bandleader in his own right. In 1957 he recorded the now-classic album *A Blowin' Session* with fellow saxophonists Coltrane and Hank Mobley. In a twist of fate Coltrane had not originally been slated to play on the album—he happened to bump into Griffin and Mobley while they were walking to the recording studio, and they asked him to come along and play with them. In 1958 Griffin fronted the Johnny Griffin Sextet, recording an album of the same name, and in 1960 he led the fourteen-piece Big Soul Band, allowing him to explore the possibilities of a much larger ensemble than he was used to.

From 1960 to 1962 Griffin teamed up with fellow saxophonist Eddie "Lockjaw" Davis to form a popular two-tenor quintet. In their recordings and performances Griffin and Davis would challenge each other to improvisational duels, to the delight of audiences. The group was informally known as the "Tough Tenors," a term that would be applied to an entire group of saxophonists—including Ammons, Illinois Jacquet, and Houston Person, in addition to Griffin and Davis—who played an aggressive, fast-paced style of hard bop that incorporated elements of gospel and blues.

Griffin in particular was known for his lightning-fast, energetic, tireless playing, earning him the epithet "world's fastest saxophonist." In a 1958 review in

Down Beat magazine, music critic Ralph J. Gleason remarked, "Unquestionably Johnny Griffin can play the tenor saxophone faster, literally, than anyone else alive.... And in the course of playing with this incredible speed, he also manages to blow longer without refueling than you would ordinarily consider possible. With this equipment he is able to play almost all there could possibly be played in any given chorus."

Left America for Europe

As jazz declined in popularity—and commercial success—in the United States during the early 1960s, many jazz musicians moved to Europe, where they felt the environment was more receptive. Griffin, staying true to his bebop roots, held a special disdain for the free or avant-garde jazz that was then all the rage in America. "A lot of those cats can't play. And others can play, but can't swing. How can jazz all of a sudden go completely crazy and have no form," he said, according to his obituary in the *Independent*. In 1963, facing tax problems and marital difficulties with his first wife, he relocated to Paris, where he played at the Blue Note with other American expatriates such as Bud Powell, Kenny Clarke, Kenny Drew, and Art Taylor. From 1967 to 1969 he was a soloist with the multinational big band led by Clarke and Belgian Francy Boland.

Griffin maintained his exile until 1978, when he made a triumphant return to the United States to tour with Dexter Gordon and to record the album *Return of the Griffin*. Though he continued to make his home in Europe—moving to the Netherlands in 1973, then to the Côte d'Azur in 1980, and finally settling in the rural village of Availles-Limouzine in midwestern France—he made a trip home to Chicago each year during the week of his birthday (April 28) to appear at the Jazz Showcase, usually ending with a week at the Village Vanguard jazz club in New York.

Griffin kept up a vigorous pace of recording and touring well into his sixties and seventies. In 1990 he recorded the album *The Cat*, followed by *Chicago, New York, Paris* in 1994. The high point of the later years of his career was a collaboration with Algerian pianist Martial Solal on the album *In and Out* in 2000. Moderating the furious tempo of his earlier music, Griffin's later recordings display a greater attention to ballads and long solos.

Throughout six decades, Griffin never lost his enthusiasm for the music. "I got so excited when I played and I still do," he said, according to his obituary in the *Independent*. "I want to eat up the music like a child eating candy." Just days before his death, Griffin played a concert in Hyères, France, and was slated to sit in with American organist Rhoda Smith for a show in Saint-Georges-sur-Cher on the evening of his death, July 25, 2008. Griffin died at his home in Availles-Limouzine at the age of eighty.

Selected recordings

Chicago Calling, Blue Note, 1956.
Introducing Johnny Griffin, Blue Note, 1956.
A Blowin' Session, Blue Note, 1957.
The Congregation, Blue Note, 1957.
Art Blakey's Jazz Messengers with Thelonious Monk, Atlantic, 1958.
Johnny Griffin Sextet, Riverside, 1958.
Thelonious in Action, Fantasy, 1958.
Way Out!, Riverside, 1958.
The Little Giant, Riverside, 1959.
Griff and Lock, Jazzland, 1960.
Tough Tenors, 1960.
Wade in the Water, Riverside, 1960.
The Kerry Dancers and Other Swinging Folk, Riverside, 1961.
Lookin' at Monk, Jazzland, 1961,
White Gardenia, Riverside, 1961.
The Man I Love, Polydor, 1967.
You Leave Me Breathless, Black Lion, 1967.
Blues for Harvey, SteepleChase, 1973.
Live in Tokyo, Philips, 1976.
Bush Dance, Galaxy, 1978.
Return of the Griffin, Galaxy, 1978.
Paris Reunion Band, Sonet, 1985.
Take My Hand, Who's Who in Jazz, 1988.
The Cat, Antilles, 1990.
Dance of Passion, Antilles, 1992.
Chicago, New York, Paris, Verve, 1994.
In and Out, Dreyfus, 2000.
Woe Is Me, A Jazz Hour With, 2000.
Johnny Griffin & Steve Grossman Quintet, Dreyfus, 2001.
Close Your Eyes, Minor Music, 2003.
Johnny Griffin and the Great Danes, Stunt, 2003.
Live/Autumn Leaves, Universal International, 2003.
Pisces, Ojc, 2004.
Johnny Griffin & Lockjaw Davis in Copenhagen, Storyville, 2007.

Sources

Books

Hennessey, Mike, *The Little Giant: The Story of Johnny Griffin,* Northway, 2008.
Sidran, Ben, *Talking Jazz: An Oral History,* revised edition, Da Capo Press, 1994, pp. 195–208.

Periodicals

Guardian (London), July 26, 2008.
Independent (London), July 28, 2008.
New York Times, July 26, 2008.

Online

Jarenwattananon, Patrick, "Fleet Jazz Saxophonist Johnny Griffin Dies," National Public Radio Music, July 25, 2008, http://www.npr.org/templates/

story/story.php?storyId=92943737 (accessed August 20, 2008).

"Johnny Griffin: Biography," allmusic, http://www.allmusic.com/cg/amg.dll?p=amg&sql=11:jifwxqt5ldse~T1 (accessed October 28, 2008).

—Deborah A. Ring

Lisa Gay Hamilton

1964—

Actor

Hamilton, Lisa Gay, photograph. Jean-Paul Aussenard/WireImage.

Lisa Gay Hamilton is a classically trained actress whose work encompasses film, television, and theater. She made her movie debut in the 1985 cult favorite *Krush Groove,* appeared in a number of New York Shakespeare Festival productions during the 1990s, and won an Obie Award for her performance in Athol Fugard's *Valley Song.* To television viewers Hamilton is best known for her portrayal of Rebecca Washington on the Emmy-winning legal drama *The Practice.*

Hamilton was born in 1964 in Los Angeles but grew up in the Long Island, New York, community of Stony Brook. Her mother, Tina, was a social service executive, while her father, Ira, was an engineer who later moved to Florida after the marriage ended when Hamilton was in her early teens. The Hamiltons were the only African-American family in their neighborhood. "I had rocks thrown at me when I was riding my bicycle," she told journalist Alvin Klein in the *New York Times,* and she was called racial epithets at school. Hamilton recounted one particularly upsetting episode when she was cast in a school production of the musical *West Side Story.* She played the female lead, Maria, but the boy who won the male leading role was forced to drop out when his father objected to the interracial casting.

Graduated from NYU, Julliard

Hamilton earned a degree in theater from New York University in 1985. Soon afterward she made her screen debut as Aisha in the urban-music movie *Krush Groove,* a depiction of New York City's early hip-hop scene presenting a fictionalized account of Russell Simmons's pioneering Def Jam Recordings label. Hamilton harbored more serious ambitions, however, and applied to the Yale School of Drama. The graduate program offered immense opportunity for any actor who hoped for a career on the stage, and especially for African-American performers. At the time, the school's artistic director was the esteemed black actor and director Lloyd Richards, and August Wilson held regular readings of his acclaimed Pittsburgh Cycle plays with the company. "I knew, especially as a woman of color, I really, really wanted to go to Yale," she told Jesse McKinley in the *New York Times.* However, according to Hamilton, she failed the tryout. "My audition was a dog. And I was just crushed because all

> **At a Glance . . .**
>
> Born March 25, 1964, in Los Angeles, CA; daughter of Ira (an engineer) and Tina (a social worker) Hamilton. *Education:* New York University, BA, theater, 1985; Juilliard School, MA, 1988.
>
> **Career:** Film, stage, and television actor. Made directorial debut with the documentary film *Beah: A Black Woman Speaks*, 2003.
>
> **Awards:** Obie Award for performance, *Village Voice*, 1996, for *Valley Song*.
>
> **Addresses:** *Agent*—Paradigm Agency, 10100 Santa Monica Blvd. Ste. 2500, Los Angeles, CA 90067.

I ever wanted was to be in the ring," she said, referring to the cycle of plays by Wilson.

Hamilton instead entered the Juilliard School in Manhattan, another well-regarded training ground for Broadway hopefuls. However, pursuing a master's degree did not immediately afford the types of opportunities she desired. In Juilliard productions she was consistently cast in supporting roles that were usually "black, old women," she told John Rockwell in the *New York Times*. "I never kissed at school—never had a love scene, ever." Her next screen role came in *Reversal of Fortune* (1990) a Barbet Schroeder film about the legal case involving Claus von Bulow, who had been convicted twice of the attempted murder of his heiress wife. That same year, Hamilton achieved her goal of appearing in a work by Wilson when she won a role in the original Broadway production of *The Piano Lesson*, which went on to win a Pulitzer Prize.

During the early 1990s Hamilton was cast in a number of New York Shakespeare Festival productions, which are held in an outdoor setting on the Delacorte Stage in Central Park during the summer and in the Public Theater of New York during colder months. When Hamilton was asked to read for the role of a prostitute in *Henry IV, Part II*, she bristled at what she considered typecasting and asked the director to let her read for a much larger role, that of Lady Percy. Hamilton wound up auditioning for Joseph Papp, founder of the Shakespeare Festival, and won the part. "They may not have thought of me in the first place," she told Klein in the *New York Times*. "But then I felt if actors of color can challenge the system and get directors and producers to see new possibilities—well, they did."

Won Obie Award

Hamilton went on to appear in Athol Fugard's acclaimed *Valley Song*, set in contemporary South Africa following the end of apartheid. The drama opened in December of 1995 at the Manhattan Theater and earned her an Obie Award—the honors bestowed by the *Village Voice* on the best off-Broadway actors and productions of the season. In *Valley Song* she played a young woman named Veronica, who aspires to become a singer in Johannesburg now that freedom has come to black South Africans. "It is a performance of both subtlety and panache, and a lesson in the art of transformation," asserted reviewer Peter Marks in the *New York Times*.

Hamilton appeared in the highly regarded Quentin Tarantino film *Jackie Brown* in 1997, the same year she made her debut in the ABC television drama *The Practice*. Her character, Rebecca Washington, was a receptionist and paralegal at a Boston law firm, but secretly attends law school and passes the bar over the course of the next few seasons and becomes an attorney. It was not the first television role for Hamilton, but it was her most visible to date. "I got it purely by auditioning," she told David Sheward in *Back Stage*. "Like most actors, I made the annual pilgrimage" to Los Angeles in the winter and early spring months for what is known as pilot season.

Hamilton's years on *The Practice* restricted her ability to audition for New York stage plays because of the show's shooting schedule on the West Coast. She did, however, appear in the movie *Beloved* in 1998, the screen adaptation of Toni Morrison's Pulitzer Prize-winning novel. She played the younger version of Sethe, the character who was played in older age by Oprah Winfrey. Living in Southern California for part of the year did allow Hamilton to take on more film roles, and she appeared in the Clint Eastwood drama *True Crime* (1999) and in *The Sum of All Fears* (2002), an espionage thriller that starred Ben Affleck and Morgan Freeman. After seven seasons on *The Practice*, Hamilton was released from her contract along with half of the cast, including Camryn Manheim, Lara Flynn Boyle, and Dylan McDermott, after the show's producer, David E. Kelley, was forced to make budget cutbacks.

Directed Documentary Film

Hamilton made her own foray into filmmaking with her documentary *Beah: A Black Woman Speaks* (2003). Its star was Beah Richards, best known for portraying the mother of Sidney Poitier's character in the 1967 comedy *Guess Who's Coming to Dinner*. Richards was a veteran actress who was nominated for an Academy Award for that role, but also had a long career on Broadway that included performing in the original production of *A Raisin in the Sun*. Hamilton compiled more than seventy hours of interviews with Richards to make the documentary, but sadly her subject never saw the finished product before she died in 2000. As Hamilton told a writer in the *Houston Chronicle*, Richards "set a standard a lot of black actresses have been trying to achieve in their own work. She had her own approach to acting, and she also respected me and encouraged me to continue on my own path to find out who I am."

Hamilton later performed in *Nine Lives* (2005)—a work by filmmaker Rodrigo García, son of the novelist Gabriel García Márquez—and *Honeydripper* (2007), which takes its story from the mythical birth of rock and roll at a blues club in the Mississippi Delta in 1950. She played Delilah, the wife of Tyrone "Pinetop" Purvis (Danny Glover), who owns the club of the film's title. In 2008 she appeared in *The Soloist*, a film about the real-life musical prodigy Nathaniel Ayers (Jamie Foxx), who was living on the streets of Los Angeles as a homeless schizophrenic. The mother of a young son, Hamilton has said in interviews that she envisions a future for herself as a drama teacher—perhaps even at her alma mater, Juilliard. "So few actors of color are classically trained," she noted in the interview with Klein in the *New York Times*. "Families don't encourage them. Schools don't do enough to recruit them."

Selected works

Plays

The Piano Lesson, Walter Kerr Theater, 1990.
Henry IV, Part I, New York Shakespeare Festival, 1991.
Henry IV, Part II, New York Shakespeare Festival, 1991.
Measure for Measure, New York Shakespeare Festival, 1993.
Two Gentlemen of Verona, New York Shakespeare Festival, 1994.
Valley Song, Manhattan Theater Club, 1995.
Gem of the Ocean, Walter Kerr Theater, 2004.

Television

The Practice, 1997–2003.

Films

Krush Groove, 1985.
Reversal of Fortune, 1990.
Naked in New York, 1993.
Twelve Monkeys, 1995.
Jackie Brown, 1997.
Beloved, 1998.
True Crime, 1999.
The Sum of All Fears, 2002.
The Truth about Charlie, 2002.
(As director) *Beah: A Black Woman Speaks*, 2003.
Nine Lives, 2005.
Honeydripper, 2007.
Deception, 2008.
The Soloist, 2008.

Sources

Periodicals

Back Stage, September 5, 1997, p. 5.
Houston Chronicle, September 16, 2000, p. 5.
New York Times, July 25, 1993; January 12, 1996; January 26, 2003, p. 9; December 19, 2004, p. AR6.

—Carol Brennan

Zelma Henderson

1920–2008

Civil rights activist

At the time of her death in 2008, Zelma Henderson was the last surviving plaintiff in *Brown v. Board of Education of Topeka,* the historic 1954 U.S. Supreme Court decision that outlawed segregated schools in the United States. As a young girl in rural Kansas during the 1920s, Henderson attended an integrated elementary school, and she became a plaintiff in the landmark class-action lawsuit because she wanted her own children to have the same opportunity. "None of us knew that this case would be so important and come to the magnitude it has," she said in 1994, according to an obituary in the *New York Times.* "What little bit I did, I feel I helped the whole nation."

Henderson was born Zelma Hurst on February 29, 1920, in Colby, Kansas, the seat of Thomas County in the western part of the state. Her parents were farmers who eventually moved to nearby Oakley, which had a few more black households than Colby. Oakley was later the inspiration for the fictional town of Jericho in the CBS television drama of the same name that depicts the citizens of a remote town adjusting to life in the aftermath of nuclear attacks on the United States.

In the era before the *Brown v. Board of Education* ruling, states and communities were free to establish their own laws and rules governing public education for African-American students. During Henderson's girlhood, Kansas law stipulated that communities with a population of 15,000 or more had to have separate elementary schools for black children; middle schools and high schools were integrated. Both Colby and Oakley, where Henderson grew up, had populations far less than 15,000, and therefore she went all the way through school in the same classes as the white children in her neighborhood.

Henderson moved to Topeka, the Kansas state capital, in 1940, and entered the Kansas Vocational School, a blacks-only institution. She trained as a cosmetologist but also became a skilled typist, and though she searched for an office job she was unable to land one because of her race. In 1943 she married Andrew Henderson, and began a family that soon included two children, Donald and Vicki. She ran an at-home business as a hairdresser in their house on N.E. Jefferson Street in North Topeka. It was only when Donald, her older child, was almost of school age that she realized that because of the state law her children would be riding a bus to an all-black school, not attending the one that was closest to their home. "I was quite surprised," she told Erin Adamson in the *Topeka Capital Journal,* "because in small cities, they integrated them and we got along fine together. And I could not see why they couldn't get along here, too."

Henderson was a member of the Topeka chapter of the National Association for the Advancement of Colored People (NAACP), and in 1950 learned that the civil rights organization was planning to file a suit against the Topeka school board over segregation. In an interview in the 2004 book *The Unfinished Agenda of Brown v. Board of Education,* she recalled that "one of the attorneys asked me if I would be a plaintiff. I was glad to be involved because I didn't think it was right." Instructed to take her children to the nearby

At a Glance . . .

Born Zelma Cleota Hurst on February 29, 1920, in Colby, KS; died of pancreatic cancer on May 20, 2008, in Topeka, KS; married Andrew Henderson, 1943; children: Donald, Vicki (died 1984). *Religion:* African Methodist Episcopal. *Education:* Trained as a cosmetologist at the Kansas Vocational School, early 1940s.

Career: Worked as a hairdresser.

---

whites-only elementary school, Quincy Elementary, and enroll them there, she did so, and school officials denied the request.

From there Henderson signed on to the class-action suit filed on behalf of twenty African-American youngsters in Topeka by their parents. A Topeka rail yard worker and part-time minister, Oliver L. Brown, was one of the thirteen plaintiffs, along with Henderson, and it is his name that became part of the historic court case, which was filed in U.S. District Court in 1951. Henderson testified at that trial at the Topeka courthouse in June of 1951, recalling in the interview with Adamson that "it was kind of frightening and yet, when you're determined, you get a little more strength. They had to calm me down a time or two, but I made it through." The three-judge panel, however, rejected the plaintiffs' plea by citing the legal precedence set in the 1896 U.S. Supreme Court decision in *Plessy v. Ferguson,* which ruled that "separate but equal" schools and other public facilities did not violate the Equal Protection Clause of the U.S. Constitution.

The NAACP legal team appealed the judges' decision to the U.S. Supreme Court. It agreed to hear the *Brown* arguments in combination with several similar pending cases from other states. On May 17, 1954, the nine U.S. Supreme Court justices ruled unanimously in favor of Henderson's two children and dozens more whose parents had filed suit on their behalf. "We conclude that in the field of public education the doctrine of 'separate but equal' has no place," Chief Justice Earl Warren wrote in his decision. "Separate educational facilities are inherently unequal."

With that ruling, the era of segregated public schools in America officially ended, though many states in the South posed legal challenges for years to come. The *Brown v. Board of Education* decision opened the door to further legal challenges elsewhere in the United States—and especially in the South—and is often cited as the day the civil rights movement began, along with Rosa Parks's act of resistance on a segregated bus in Montgomery, Alabama, the following year.

By then, Henderson had returned to a quiet life with her family and community. She continued to work as a hairdresser, was active in her African Methodist Episcopal (AME) church as a deaconess, and was involved in the establishment of a Brown v. Board National Historic Site in a Topeka schoolhouse. Her husband died in 1971, and thirteen years later her daughter Vicki passed away. The sole element that separated Henderson from her neighbors and fellow churchgoers was the fact that she was regularly interviewed by journalists from across the United States when milestone anniversaries for *Brown v. Board of Education* occurred. In 2004, on the fiftieth anniversary, she was eighty-four years old and one of three surviving plaintiffs of the original thirteen Topeka parents. Within four years of that milestone, she was the last surviving plaintiff and was ill with pancreatic cancer. She died in Topeka on May 20, 2008, at the age of eighty-eight. Speaking at Henderson's funeral, Kansas governor Kathleen Sebelius said, "Let's promise to never forget the lessons of Zelma Henderson—that ordinary people, with moral courage and stamina can indeed change the world."

Sources

Books

Black Issues in Higher Education, James Anderson, and Dara N. Byrne, *The Unfinished Agenda of Brown v. Board of Education,* Diverse: Issues In Higher Education, 2004, pp. 141–42.

Periodicals

New York Times, May 12, 2004, p. B8; May 22, 2008, p. C12.
Topeka Capital Journal, May 11, 2003, p. B1; May 9, 2004, p. A12; May 28, 2008, p. 1.

Online

"U.S. Supreme Court: Brown v. Board of Education, 347 U.S. 483 (1954)," Findlaw.com, http://caselaw.lp.findlaw.com/scripts/getcase.pl?court=US&vol=347&invol=483 (accessed October 26, 2008).

—Carol Brennan

Edie Huggins

1935–2008

Television news personality

Edie Huggins was not just another talking head on the evening news. To scores of Philadelphians who grew up watching her on local television, she was very much a part of the community. Over the course of a broadcasting career that spanned more than four decades, Huggins endeared herself to viewers with her thoughtful reporting, zest for life, and genuine interest in the people she interviewed. As the first African-American woman to appear on television news in Philadelphia, she broke gender and color barriers, paving the way for future generations of journalists. Huggins's death in 2008 prompted an outpouring of emotion as colleagues and viewers honored the incredible accomplishments of the woman whom many fondly referred to as "Miss Edie."

Huggins was born Edith Lou Thompson on August 14, 1935, in St. Joseph, Missouri, approximately thirty miles north of Kansas City. A popular girl known to friends as "Eddie Lou," she was introduced to broadcasting at age fourteen when she won a contest that gave her the chance to appear on KRES, a local radio station. Station executives were so impressed with Eddie Lou that they gave her a weekly Saturday evening show for teenagers, making her the city's first African-American disc jockey. At Bartlett High School she developed a talent for music, learning the cornet and marching with the band, as well as playing piano at church. Classmate Theresa Rowlett remembered that Eddie Lou always had a way with people. "She could mingle with anybody," she told the *St. Joseph News-Press* in 2008.

When she was denied entrance to the University of Missouri because of her race, she instead attended the University of Nebraska on a music scholarship. There, she was the first African American to be crowned Miss Cornhusker, in 1954. She dropped out of school to marry U.S. Air Force officer Hastings Huggins, with whom she had a son and a daughter. When Hastings Huggins left the military and took a job with IBM, the family moved to New York City.

Eddie Lou Huggins, as she was still known, went back to school at the State University of New York in Plattsburgh, graduating cum laude with a bachelor's degree in science in 1963. She took a job as a registered nurse, working at both Bellevue and Flower-Fifth Avenue hospitals. While working nights as a nurse, she embarked on a more glamorous career during the day as an actress, playing Nurse Spencer on the NBC soap opera *The Doctors,* also serving as an informal consultant to the show. She also made appearances on the CBS soaps *The Edge of Night* and *Love of Life,* and in the film *A Man Called Adam* (1966) starring Sammy Davis Jr.

In 1966 Huggins was spotted by Bruce Bryant, general manager at WCAU television in Philadelphia, who was looking for a features reporter for the station's evening news. He asked Huggins to audition. Bryant offered her the job, on one condition—that she change her name. Eddie Lou Huggins became Edie Huggins, and soon she and her children (she was now divorced) moved to Philadelphia.

At a Glance . . .

Born Edith Lou Thompson on August 14, 1935, in St. Joseph, MO; died on July 29, 2008, in Philadelphia, PA; daughter of Edward W. Thompson (a pharmacist); married Hastings Huggins, late 1950s (divorced, 1960s); married Ray Bryant (a jazz pianist), 1975 (divorced, 1982); children: Hastings Edward, Laurie Linn. *Religion:* Baptist. *Education:* State University of New York at Plattsburgh, BA, science, 1963.

Career: Bellevue and Flower-Fifth Avenue hospitals, registered nurse, 1963–66; television actress, late 1960s; WCAU-TV (now NBC 10), news reporter, anchor, and program host, 1966–2008.

Memberships: National Association of Black Journalists.

Awards: Communicator of the Year, Philadelphia Chapter, American Women in Radio and Television, 1993; Philadelphia Broadcast Pioneers Hall of Fame, 2002; Outstanding African-American Philadelphians of the 20th Century, Urban League of Philadelphia, 2002; Hall of Fame Award, American Federation of Television and Radio Artists, 2006; Board of Governors' Award, Mid-Atlantic Chapter, National Academy of Television Arts and Sciences, 2008; Lifetime Achievement Award, Philadelphia Association of Black Journalists, 2008.

Huggins started out as a feature reporter on the Big News Team with John Facenda. As the first African-American woman on Philadelphia television news, she was both exhilarated and terrified. Recalling her first days on air in Philadelphia, she told WCAU/NBC 10, "I was a trailblazer, and I guess that's where ... the fear came in because I was getting mail, fan mail. Some of it good, some of it not so good, you know like, why do they have to go to New York to find someone, why do they have to get a colored woman—we were 'colored' then."

Before long, Huggins was getting more air time. In the early 1970s she appeared with Herb Clarke on *What's Happening,* a midday news program, and from 1974 to 1976 she hosted *Morningside,* a daily one-hour program featuring segments on health, finance, and entertainment, with interviews with newsmakers. Huggins became a mainstay at the station, anchoring the news, conducting interviews with local personalities and politicians, reporting new stories, and conducting investigative reports. Though she was a respected and skilled journalist, it was her charm and compassion that endeared her to colleagues and viewers, and even to those she interviewed. Pennsylvania governor Ed Rendell, for instance, recalled to WCAU/NBC 10, "If Edie wanted an interview it was simply impossible to say no to her. Her charm, grace and overall likeability were her greatest assets, but they didn't stop her from asking tough questions about some of the challenges that faced our city and region."

Huggins was a passionate advocate of community service and devoted time to many organizations in Philadelphia. One of her most popular segments was "Huggins' Heroes," a weekly profile of ordinary people doing extraordinary deeds. Huggins said in an interview with WCAU/NBC 10, "I love people. I love learning about people ... their troubles and their aches and pains." She went on, "I just want to be remembered as someone who cares ... about others."

Huggins acted as a mentor to many young journalists during her more than forty years at WCAU, having forged a path for others to follow. "In her uniquely dignified way, Edie helped open the doors and blazed the trail that made it possible for so many of us to be here," said WCAU/NBC 10 vice president Chris Blackman. Former Congressman Bill Gray, Edie's former pastor, reflected, "She was a beautiful person in every sense of the word and a role model.... She was really committed to giving back." A longtime member of Bright Hope Baptist Church in Philadelphia, Huggins established a scholarship for women to pursue nursing, which continues as her legacy.

Huggins was a founding member of the National Association of Black Journalists, which honored her in 2005. She received many awards for her journalism and for her community service. In 2002 she was inducted into the Broadcast Pioneers of Philadelphia's Hall of Fame, and she was named by the Urban League of Philadelphia as one of the Outstanding African-American Philadelphians of the 20th Century. She received the Hall of Fame Award from the American Federation of Television and Radio Artists in 2006, and in 2008 she earned the Board of Governors' Award of the Mid-Atlantic Chapter of the National Academy of Television Arts and Sciences, as well as the Lifetime Achievement Award of the Philadelphia Association of Black Journalists. The Philadelphia City Council declared March 30 "Edie Huggins Day" in 2006, in honor of her forty years of dedication.

Huggins died on July 29, 2008, following a long battle with cancer. Shortly before her death Huggins, as quoted by Michael Klein in the *Philadelphia Inquirer,* summed up her life and career positively, reflecting: "I've had a wonderful, wonderful life and the people that I've met, I don't think I'd trade it for anything. I can't think of anything, truly, that I would rather do or rather spend the past 42-plus years than what I've done."

Sources

Periodicals

Philadelphia Daily News, July 30, 2008.
Philadelphia Inquirer, July 29, 2008; August 7, 2008.
St. Joseph News-Press, August 6, 2008.

Online

"Edie Huggins," Broadcast Pioneers of Philadelphia, http://www.broadcastpioneers.com/ediehuggins.html (accessed August 27, 2008).

"Huggins Says She Wants to Be Remembered as Someone Who Cares," WCAU/NBC 10, July 29, 2008, http://www.nbc10.com/news/17031520/detail.html (accessed August 27, 2008).

"NBC 10's Edie Huggins Dies at 72," WCAU/NBC 10, July 29, 2008, http://www.nbc10.com/news/17026230/detail.html?dl=mainclick (accessed August 27, 2008).

—Deborah A. Ring

Maulana Karenga

1941—

Professor, social activist

Maulana Karenga is a scholar of African and African-American studies who is best known for creating the celebration of Kwanzaa in the mid-1960s. Karenga downplayed his personal role in launching the seven-day December festival that celebrates African history, community, and culture, but in 1998 he gave a lengthy interview to Henry Louis Gates of Harvard University, considered America's foremost scholar of African-American studies, for the PBS series *Frontline*. "I tell my classes each year that you're the only person I know who invented a holiday," Gates told Karenga. "And in our time, it's a very rare thing to do."

Adopted Swahili Name

Karenga was born Ronald McKinley Everett in Parsonsburg, Maryland, in 1941, and was one of fourteen children. His father was a Baptist minister, but the family's income also came from the chicken farm on which Karenga was raised. In 1958 Karenga moved to Southern California to enroll in a special program at Los Angeles City College for those who had not yet earned their high school diplomas. He went on to earn a bachelor's degree from the school while becoming the first African-American ever to be elected president of its student body. From there, Karenga entered the University of California's Los Angeles campus and graduated with a master's degree in political science and African studies. He also taught Swahili in night-school classes and adopted a new name in the pan-African tongue: "Maulana" meant "master teacher," and "Karenga" connoted "nationalist."

Karenga was working toward a doctorate in linguistics with a specialty in African languages when riots broke out in Watts, a predominantly black neighborhood in Los Angeles in August of 1965. His activism had already brought him into contact with Malcolm X, who had been gunned down at a Harlem event just six months earlier, and he was inspired by his meeting with the black Muslim leader to launch a similar initiative on the West Coast to help healed the frayed community. In the weeks after the riots in Watts, he created US, sometimes referred to as Organization US. Karenga's group took its name from the idea of "us" versus "them." Its members adopted African-style dress, wore shaved heads instead of Afros, and renamed themselves with Swahili-inspired monikers. "We name ourselves," Karenga explained to Thomas A. Johnson in the *New York Times*. "Only slaves and dogs are named by their masters." In that same 1966 article he spoke of the need to defend African-American communities like Watts, noting that earlier initiatives like "love, prayer, and picketing have not worked."

In Johnson's *New York Times* article, Karenga asserted that "we are making our own customs" and had formulated a set of beliefs that are "more functional than spiritual in working for the day-to-day good of black people." He devised a set of tenets around the concept of *Nguzo Saba,* or the Seven Principles of Blackness. These were *Umoja,* or unity; *Kujichagulia,* or self-determination; *Ujima,* or collective work and responsibility; *Ujamaa,* or cooperative economics; *Nia,* or purpose; *Kuumba,* or creativity; and *Imani,* or faith. With these principles in mind, Karenga and his

> ### At a Glance...
>
> Born Ronald McKinley Everett, on July 14, 1941, in Parsonsburg, MD; son of a Baptist minister; married Tiamoya, 1967; children: two sons, one daughter. *Education:* University of California—Los Angeles, BA, cum laude, political science, 1963, MA, 1964; U.S. International University, PhD, 1976; University of Southern California, PhD, 1994.
>
> **Career:** Formed the black nationalist organization US, 1965; Ujima Housing Projects/ Mafundi Institute, Los Angeles, CA, co-planner; California State University at Long Beach, professor of black studies, c. 1991, and chair of President's Task Force on Multicultural Education and Campus Diversity; also director, African-American Cultural Center, Los Angeles; member of executive council of the Million Man March/Day of Absence.
>
> **Awards:** President's Award, African Heritage Studies Association, 1999; C.L.R. James Award, National Council for Black Studies, 2002; Paul Robeson-Zora Neale Hurston Award, National Council for Black Studies, 2003; Peace Education Award, California State University-Sacramento Center for African Peace and Conflict Resolution, 2004; Nguzo Saba Philosophical Award, Molefi Kete Asante and Haki Madhubuti, 2005. Honorary doctorate, University of Durban, Westville, South Africa, 1998.
>
> **Addresses:** *Office*—California State University—Long Beach, Department of Africana Studies, 1250 Bellflower Blvd., Long Beach, CA 90840.

fellow US members began establishing independent schools for youth, and encouraged the formation of black student unions on college campuses.

Established Kwanzaa Festival

Based on those ideas of Nguzo Saba, the first Kwanzaa celebration took place in Los Angeles in December of 1966 with Karenga's US friends and family members. The term "Kwanzaa" was taken from a Swahili term, *matunda yakwanza*, meaning "first fruit." Swahili is spoken widely throughout East Africa and is a blend of the sub-Saharan Bantu tongue and Arabic, and is reflective of the multicultural character of this part of the continent. Swahili was of particular interest to scholars of black nationalism because its widespread use did not reflect the hegemony of one particular African tribe or nation over another; even prior to European encroachment many parts of Africa had been scarred by internecine wars.

Matunda yakwanza, sometimes spelled *matunda ya kwanza*, may also mean "first harvest," and as a celebration of the earth's bounty and gratitude to nature for its benevolence Kwanzaa is not unlike celebrations found in nearly every other world culture. After refining its rituals, Karenga promulgated the seven-day ceremony, and it began to catch on with other African Americans. The *mkeka*, or straw mat, serves as the centerpiece of several symbolic items, and itself represents the foundation. Central is the *kinara*, or candleholder, which holds seven candles. The kinara is a symbol of the ancestral stalk from which all blacks—and humans—originated. The colors of the candles—three red, three green, and one black—were borrowed from the teachings of early twentieth-century black nationalist visionary Marcus Garvey, as Karenga explained in an interview with Aldore Collier in *Ebony*. "Black is for Black people, first. Red is for struggle, and green is for the future and the promise that comes from struggle." The future is represented by the *muhindi*, or ears of corn laid on the mat by the children of the household. On December 31, the sixth day, a feast is called for, and Imani, the next day, is one for "reassessment and recommitment," Karenga told Veronica Chambers in *Essence*. "We meditate on the meaning and mission of our lives and recommit ourselves to our people, our struggle, our culture, and to ever-higher levels of human life." Gifts were given as part of the celebration, but were meant to reflect African heritage and given to children to signify the work achieved in the past year in reaching their own goals.

Kwanzaa quickly took hold throughout African-American communities and mainstream publications including the *New York Times* began reporting on Kwanzaa festivities as early as 1971. In the first mention of Kwanzaa in that newspaper, a reporter witnessed schoolchildren in Harlem being instructed in the seven Nguzo Saba principles by a sixteen-year-old activist and ordained Pentecostal minister named Alfred Sharpton, who told reporter Charlayne Hunter that "as black people, we need to stress the educational, cultural and communal aspects of the holiday," which was often referred to as the "Black Christmas" in its early years. "Doing things this way," Sharpton continued, "gives us the feeling of unity that we need."

The *New York Times* article mentioned that the teenaged Sharpton was the founder of the National Youth Movement, an outgrowth of the Southern Christian Leadership Conference founded by Martin Luther King Jr. Sharpton's organization was founded to combat the growing scourge of illegal drugs in African-American communities, and was one of scores of similar groups active in urban communities at the time. The most famous among them was the Black Panther

Party, which had early ties to Karenga's US organization in Los Angeles. The US group actually pre-dated the founding of the Black Panthers in Oakland, California, in 1966, but the Bay-area black-power advocates would go on to achieve a much higher profile in the mainstream media. Both were founded on many of the same principles, and as Karenga recalled in the interview with Gates on *Frontline,* the Panthers "borrowed a lot of techniques from our community alert patrol of following the police around, taking their names, giving legal defense and counsel to people who were harassed by the police, and actually checking the police."

Targeted by Federal Agents

Karenga was one of the most active academics among the leadership of the black consciousness movement during the late 1960s. He began working with Adam Clayton Powell, Jr., who represented Harlem in Congress, to organize the first National Conference on Black Power in 1966 in Washington, DC. Two more conferences followed, in Newark in 1967 and Philadelphia in 1968. Yet both Karenga's group and the Black Panthers were targeted by a special counterintelligence division within the Federal Bureau of Investigation (FBI). Documents released later revealed that the FBI actively attempted to destabilize both groups by instigating a gangland-style animosity.

In one notorious incident, Karenga was arrested on charges that he had subjected two female members of his group to torture after accusing them of trying to poison his food. One of the victims cut a deal with prosecutors to testify against him in exchange for the release of a pending charge against her for auto theft; the other woman had reportedly fled the country by the time the case went to trial in 1971. Karenga denied all charges, but was sentenced to one to ten years in prison on the torture charges. He entered California's San Luis Obispo Prison in September of 1971. He was released in 1975 thanks to the efforts of sympathetic state and local lawmakers. Later journalists who tried to track down the two women, whose names appeared in court testimony, were never able to locate either of them.

Karenga spent his time behind bars productively, working in the prison library and leading discussion groups. He also worked toward completing a doctorate in social ethics, and was granted a PhD from the University of Southern California in 1994. For much of his career he has taught at California State University at Long Beach, where he chairs the school's Department of Black Studies. In 1995 he was a member of the executive council for the Million Man March/Day of Absence and authored the event's mission statement.

In the decades since its inception, the Kwanzaa cultural festival has become a worldwide phenomenon. Some twenty million people celebrate it, and Karenga has since expanded the principles of Nguzo Saba to embrace a community of humankind, not just those of African descent. "I have been blessed to see my work flourish," he reflected in *Ebony.* "Many people in history—Marcus Garvey, Ida B. Wells, Martin Luther King Jr., Malcolm X—never lived to see their work flourish. I have seen people around the world embrace my philosophy and principles, involving themselves in a cultural institution that my organization and I created."

Selected writings

Books

Kwanzaa: Origin, Concepts, Practice, Kawaida Publications, 1977.

The African American Holiday of Kwanzaa: A Celebration of Family, Community & Culture, University of Sankore Press, 1988.

The Book of Coming Forth by Day: The Ethics of the Declarations of Innocence, University of Sankore Press, 1990.

(Editor) *Reconstructing Kemetic Culture: Papers, Perspectives, Projects,* University of Sankore Press, 1990.

Introduction to Black Studies, University of Sankore Press, 1993.

(Editor, with Haki R. Madhubuti) *Million Man March/Day of Absence: A Commemorative Anthology,* Third World Press/University of Sankore Press 1996.

Kwanzaa: A Celebration of Family, Community, and Culture, University of Sankore Press, 1998.

Maat, the Moral Ideal in Ancient Egypt: A Study in Classical African Ethics, Routledge, 2004.

(Editor, with Molefi Kete Asante) *Handbook of Black Studies,* Sage Publications, 2006.

Kawaida and Questions of Life and Struggle: African American, Pan-African, and Global Issues, University of Sankore Press, 2007.

The Message and Meaning of Kwanzaa: Bringing Good into the World: The Founder's Annual Statements 1994–2006, University of Sankore Press, 2007.

Sources

Periodicals

Black Collegian, February 1997, p. 160.

Ebony, January 1998, p. 116; December 2004, p. 38; December 2007, p. 146.

Essence, December 1992, p. 96.

Journal of Black Studies, November 1997, p. 157.

New York Times, May 27, 1966, p. 30; September 2, 1968, p. 13; January 24, 1969, p. 44; October 8, 1970, p. 35; December 24, 1971, p. 28; January 5, 1976, p. 22.

Online

Gates, Henry Louis, "Interview: Maulana Karenga," *Frontline*, PBS.org, http://www.pbs.org/wgbh/pages/frontline/shows/race/interviews/karenga.html (accessed October 26, 2008).

—Carol Brennan

R. Kelly

1967—

Singer, songwriter, music producer

Kelly, R., photograph. Lawrence Lucier/FilmMagic.

R. Kelly is a music producer and recording artist who dominated the rhythm and blues (R&B) charts during the early and mid-1990s with a series of impeccably arranged recordings that were frankly sexual in nature. He was besieged by serious image and legal troubles, however, when a videotape was sent anonymously to the *Chicago Sun-Times* that allegedly showed Kelly having sex with a thirteen-year-old girl. The newspaper went public with the story, and in June of 2002 Kelly was indicted on charges including child pornography. Six years after the initial charges were brought, a jury in Chicago found Kelly not guilty on all charges. Nevertheless, he faced numerous accusations and lawsuits from other young women claiming they either were unknowingly taped during intimate moments with Kelly or were underage at the time they were with him. No other criminal charges held up, however, and Kelly continued pursuing his music career throughout.

Received Classical Vocal Training

Born Robert Sylvester Kelly in Chicago in 1967, R. Kelly was raised by his mother, Joann, a single parent struggling to make a living on the city's South Side. His singing career began in a storefront church choir when he was a boy. He stayed clear of the city's growing gang scene, and along with his four siblings gained admission to the Kenwood Academy, a top-quality high school operated by the Chicago Public Schools in the Hyde Park neighborhood, which is in the shadow of the prestigious University of Chicago. The same school also produced the disco superstar Chaka Khan and rapper Da Brat. At Kenwood, Kelly received a thorough grounding in classical vocal technique from teacher Lena McLin. "She was my second mother," Kelly told *Ebony*. McLin recalled in *Vibe* magazine the broad musical studies that helped Kelly accomplish so much so quickly when he reached adulthood: "Music history, theory, piano, choir, opera workshop, jazz workshop—Robert took it all." He also accompanied her to a music educators' conference in Austria.

Kelly never finished high school and, according to the *Chicago Sun-Times,* he admitted years later that he could not read very well. After leaving high school, Kelly quickly directed his ambitions toward a musical career. A single afternoon spent playing and singing

At a Glance . . .

Born Robert Sylvester Kelly on January 8, 1967, in Chicago, IL; son of Joann (a schoolteacher); married Aaliyah (a singer), 1994 (annulled); married Andrea Lee (a dancer), 1996; children: Joanne, Jaya, and one son.

Career: MGM (R&B group), founder, late 1980s; recording and performing artist, 1989—; music producer, 1990—; Atlantic City Seagulls, player, 1997.

Awards: Grammy Awards, Best Male R&B Vocal Performance, Best Song Written for a Motion Picture or for Television, and Best R&B Song, all for "I Believe I Can Fly," 1997; Soul Train Music Awards, Sammy Davis Jr., Entertainer of the Year Award, 1999; Billboard Music Awards, R&B/Hip-Hop Artist of the Year, 1999; American Music Awards, Male Soul/R&B Artist, 2000; Vibe Awards, R&B Vanguard Award, 2003; Billboard Music Awards, R&B Producer of the Year and R&B Songwriter of the Year, 2004.

Addresses: *Office*—Barry Hankerson, Midwest Management, 15250 Ventura Blvd., Sherman Oaks, CA 91403.

---

under Chicago's elevated railroad tracks netted him $400 and gave the young singer an indication of his ability to move a crowd. He formed an R&B group called MGM, which took home the $100,000 grand prize on a television talent search program. Kelly was discovered by Wayne Williams, an executive at Jive Records, singing at a backyard barbecue. He was placed in an all-male group, Public Announcement, and signed to the record company.

Kelly's first release with the group, the 1992 album *Born into the 90s*, was certified platinum for sales of over a million copies, but Kelly left the group to pursue a solo career. One year later, the multiplatinum smash *12 Play* put the artist in *Billboard*'s top ten for three months, and several of its singles topped the R&B charts. "Bump n' Grind" remained at number one on the Hot R&B chart for longer than any other R&B single of the previous thirty years. The music on *12 Play* fixed Kelly's style in the public mind. He became known for self-composed and self-produced recordings such as "Sex Me," uninhibited, explicitly erotic odes with intense rhythm tracks and a distinctive tension-filled vocal style. On stage, recalled a writer for *Ebony*, Kelly was "the 'Prince of Pillowtalk,' who dropped his pants during his concerts to the delight of thousands of screaming women."

Had Controversial Relationships and Marital Troubles

No matter how explicit Kelly's lyrics became, music critics and fans always considered his arrangements and compositions varied and full of interesting musical detail—possibly as a result of his classical training. Kelly produced his own recordings, and other artists sought him out as a producer and songwriter, intrigued by the palette of sounds he seemed to have at his command. Kelly worked with Whitney Houston, Quincy Jones, Toni Braxton, Gladys Knight, and, most famously, Michael Jackson, as composer of the number-one hit "You Are Not Alone," which was released on Jackson's *HIStory: Past, Present, and Future, Book I* album in 1995.

Another creative collaboration made headlines in the nation's music press when rumors began spreading that Kelly had married the fifteen-year-old vocalist Aaliyah while producing her debut album, *Age Ain't Nothing but a Number*. Even though Kelly maintained the relationship was nothing more than platonic, reports of the relationship circulated widely. In reality, the twenty-seven-year-old Kelly had married Aaliyah in a hotel-room ceremony in Chicago on August 31, 1994. To get a marriage license, Aaliyah had claimed to be eighteen. When her family learned of the marriage, they intervened, and an annulment was granted in Detroit in October of 1994.

In 1996 Kelly married Andrea Lee, one of the dancers in his live shows. The couple had three children together, but most sources claim the marriage was rocky from the start. According to the *Chicago Sun-Times*, Lee's family distrusted and felt alienated by him, saying they were not allowed to visit or speak to Lee on the telephone. For her part, Lee admitted Kelly had some control issues, and in 2005 a judge granted her request for an emergency protection order after she claimed Kelly physically abused her when she told him she wanted a divorce. A few weeks later Lee dropped the protection order, saying she and Kelly were trying to reconcile, albeit living separately. In *Essence* in 2007, she again said they were in the process of divorcing.

Produced Own Recordings; Moved toward Gospel

Meanwhile, Kelly's music began to move in a new stylistic direction. Like many other African-American musicians, Kelly had made no secret of the fact that he drew heavily on the gospel music that he had sung as a youth. He stated in *Ebony*, "Take away the sexy bump and grind, and you can easily put in gospel lyrics."

Following his mother's death from cancer in 1993, Kelly began making music that connected with gospel more directly. His third album, *R. Kelly*, included several gospel tunes, and he broke through to a wider pop audience than he had ever previously reached with his huge 1996 hit "I Believe I Can Fly," from the soundtrack of the film *Space Jam*. Although not strictly a religious song, "I Believe I Can Fly" bowed toward gospel in its quotation of the turn-of-the-century revival hymn "Leaning on the Everlasting Arms" and in the swelling choral lines that generated its climax. The song deftly fused gospel with inspirational language, and soon became a fixture of high-school choir presentations all over the country. Kelly won three Grammy Awards for the single in 1997.

Making a guest appearance at a 1997 concert by the gospel phenomenon Kirk Franklin, according to a report in *Ebony*, Kelly proclaimed: "I used to be flying in sin—now I'm flying in Jesus." He told Franklin, "You know I'm sick and tired of being sick and tired, and I really want to get some things in my life right with the Lord," and it became clear that Kelly was considering performing gospel music himself. If he made the switch, he would follow in the footsteps of some illustrious predecessors—Al Green and Little Richard being the best known. The influential R&B critic Nelson George, quoted in *Ebony*, pointed out that Kelly had several options open: "He could do gospel and R&B, or he could simply write love songs with less explicit language.... It will all depend on whether he plans to sing true gospel, R&B, or that funny thing in the middle."

Not long after making his religious announcement, Kelly fulfilled another one of his dreams: playing professional basketball. Though it was not with the world-renowned National Basketball Association, he played a full eight-week season in the summer of 1997 for the Atlantic City Seagulls of the United States Basketball League. Soon, Kelly returned to his musical career, releasing his fourth album, *R.*, in 1998. The album featured several spiritual songs, including a duet with the Canadian singer Celine Dion. Kelly blended his former song styles with his religious leanings in his next album *TP-2.Com*, released in 2000, which featured both spiritual and more explicitly sexual songs.

Charged with Improprieties

Kelly's public image was marred by several allegations of sexual relations with minors, along with numerous incidents of erratic and violent behavior. He settled with four women who filed suits against him in 1996, 2001, and 2002, but he was charged with twenty-one counts of possessing child pornography in 2002. Kelly was charged with, among other things, enticing an underage girl into performing illicit acts and directing and producing a videotape of the acts. The tape was sent anonymously to the *Chicago Sun-Times* on the day Kelly performed at the Winter Olympics wrapped in an American flag. Kelly was released on $750,000 bond. In 2003 Kelly was arrested in Florida on twelve counts of possessing child pornography. He was released on a $12,000 bond. The case was dropped, though, when a judge ruled that police did not have enough evidence to search Kelly's property.

The Chicago case dragged on for six years before finally going to trial in May of 2008, with fourteen felony counts against him—seven had been dropped since the initial charges were brought. Legal analysts were stumped as to why the process had taken so long. The judge ruled that the jurors would watch the entire video in question, which authorities said showed a grown man performing sexual acts with a girl as young as thirteen. In the end the jury of nine men and three women took less than a day to find Kelly not guilty.

Despite his troubles with the law, Kelly's music continued to resonate with fans. His albums *TP-2.Com* and *Chocolate Factory*, released in 2003, both reached the top of the *Billboard* chart. In 2001 Kelly won several top R&B music awards, including the Source R&B Artist of the Year and the Billboard Top R&B Artist of the Year, and in 2003 he won the Black Entertainment Award for Best Male R&B Artist and several awards at the Billboard Music Awards. In 2006 and 2008 Kelly was nominated for Grammy Awards for Best Long Form Music Video for his "urban opera" *Trapped in the Closet*, a series of "chapters" with a continuing storyline that were released from 2004 to 2007.

Selected discography

(With Public Announcement) *Born into the 90s*, Jive, 1992.
12 Play, Jive, 1993.
R. Kelly, Jive, 1995.
(With other artists) *Space Jam* (soundtrack; contains "I Believe I Can Fly"), Jive/Atlantic/Warner Bros., 1996.
R., Jive, 1998.
TP-2.Com, Jive, 2000.
(With Jay-Z) *The Best of Both Worlds*, Universal, 2002.
Chocolate Factory, Jive, 2003.
Unfinished Business, Jive, 2004.
Happy People/U Saved Me, Jive/Zomba, 2004.
TP.3 Reloaded, Jive, 2005.
Double Up, Jive/Zomba, 2007.
12 Play: 4th Quarter, Jive, 2008.

Sources

Periodicals

Atlanta Journal-Constitution, August 15, 2003.
Chicago Sun-Times, May 8, 2008.

Chicago Tribune, January 26, 1998; June 13, 2008.
Ebony, July 1996, p. 127; June 1997, p. 104.
Essence, February 1996, p. 58; May 3, 2007.
Jet, August 26, 1996, p. 34; March 24, 1997, p. 54; June 8, 1998, p. 54; May 27, 2002, p. 56.
Newsweek, April 14, 2003, p. 54.
People, May 30, 1994, p. 95.
Vibe, August 1997, p. 48.

Online

R. Kelly Official Web site, http://www.r-kelly.com (accessed November 3, 2008).

Vineyard, Jennifer, "R. Kelly's Wife Says He Isn't in Alleged Sex Tape—Though She Hasn't Seen It," MTV News, http://www.mtv.com/news/articles/1558650/20070503/kelly_r.jhtml (accessed November 3, 2008).

—James M. Manheim, Sara Pendergast, and Nancy Dziedzic

Kwame Kilpatrick

1970—

Former mayor

Kwame Kilpatrick was the youngest mayor to lead the city of Detroit, Michigan, and the city's first mayor to resign the office after being charged with a felony. What began as an administration full of promise for both Kilpatrick and the beleaguered city in 2002 ended in scandal, ignominy, and near financial disaster after several years of rumors and reports that tied the mayor to everything from lying under oath to the murder of an exotic dancer. When Kilpatrick pleaded guilty to two felony counts in a plea agreement in September of 2008, he addressed the people of Detroit: "For those who have supported me through the years ... I thank you with all my heart.... I know supporting me has not always been easy, but you have to know that it has not been boring, either."

Raised in a Politically Active Family

Kwame Malik Kilpatrick was born in Detroit and raised on the city's west side. Kilpatrick knew by the fifth grade that he wanted to be the mayor. At the time, his mother, Carolyn Cheeks Kilpatrick, was serving in the Michigan State House of Representatives, a position she held from 1979 to 1996, when she was elected to the U.S. House of Representatives. With his father working as an aide to the county's highest executive, Kilpatrick had politics in his blood.

Kilpatrick attended the arts-focused magnet school Lewis Cass Technical High School. He left Detroit to attend college at Florida A&M University (FAMU), where he graduated with honors. Kilpatrick was certified as a teacher while at FAMU and received his bachelor of science degree in political science in 1992.

After teaching at Rickards High School in Tallahassee, Florida, Kilpatrick accepted a teaching position at Marcus Garvey Academy and returned to Detroit. At the school Kilpatrick took on the role of basketball coach and the more important role of mentor. He remained at the academy for four years, but when the opportunity to enter politics arose, Kilpatrick was ready. He earned a law degree in 1999 at Michigan State University's Detroit College of Law.

Elected to State House of Representatives

Congresswoman Kilpatrick decided to make her transition from state representative to U.S. representative in 1995. She won the congressional election, leaving the state seat available. Kilpatrick won the seat vacated by his mother in 1996, when he was just twenty-six years old. By that time, he also had married Carlita Poles, whom he met while at FAMU, and the couple had twin sons, Jalil and Jelani.

As a state representative Kilpatrick split his time between the state capital in Lansing and his home on the west side of Detroit. By 1998 he helped develop the $675 million Clean Michigan Initiative. Kilpatrick was able to designate 60 percent of the funds to Detroit, which was both Michigan's largest city and the one

At a Glance . . .

Born Kwame Malik Kilpatrick on June 6, 1970, in Detroit, MI; son of Bernard Kilpatrick and Carolyn Cheeks Kilpatrick (U.S. representative); married Carlita Poles, 1995; children: Jalil, Jelani, Jonas. *Education:* Florida A&M University, BS, political science, 1992; Detroit College of Law at Michigan State University, JD, 1999.

Career: Rickards High School, Tallahassee, FL, teacher; Marcus Garvey Academy, Detroit, teacher and basketball coach, 1992–96; Michigan House of Representatives, state representative, 1996–2002; mayor, 2002–08.

Memberships: Alpha Phi Alpha Fraternity; Mount Pavan Lodge Number 2; National Association for the Advancement of Colored People.

Addresses: *Home*—Detroit, MI.

---

most in need. He also helped secure millions of dollars to fight lead poisoning in the city. At the time, more child-related lead poisoning cases were reported in Detroit then throughout the rest of the state combined. Other priorities for Kilpatrick included expanded health care for the poor and elderly, school safety, and environmental clean-up of the city.

He was still doing great things for the city and proving himself to fellow representatives when the opportunity arose to run for state house minority leader in 2000. Though many thought he was too young, he won the position in January of 2001. Kilpatrick was not only the first African American to be chosen as minority leader but also the youngest person to ever hold that position, at the age of thirty. Kilpatrick stepped into the national spotlight at the Democratic National Conventions in 2000 and 2004, when he was given speaking spots at both. He was named by the Democratic Leadership Council as an up-and-coming young Democrat to watch.

Ran a Successful Bid for Mayor

Kilpatrick was just settling into the role of minority leader when in April of 2001 Dennis Archer, the mayor of Detroit, announced that he would not run for reelection. With this news, Kilpatrick saw the opportunity to take on the job he had dreamed of since 1980. Once again the main obstacle Kilpatrick faced on the campaign trail was his age; people thought he was too young. He would be the youngest person ever to be elected to the position of mayor in Detroit's history. "At 31 ... Kilpatrick may seem to some to be too young to lead a city renowned for its decades of decay," reported David Schepp of the BBC News. "His presence, however, is commanding, and his call for government reform much welcomed."

Kilpatrick joined the race, trailing a group of twenty-one candidates. By the primary election on September 11, 2001, however, Kilpatrick walked away with 50.2 percent of the votes, compared with 34.4 percent for his closest competitor, the Detroit city councilman Gill Hill. Kilpatrick won the election for the office on November 6, 2001, and was sworn in January 4, 2002, as mayor of Detroit. In his inaugural speech he outlined a three-point initiative for the term: to improve the police department; to begin Mayor's Time, a program for the city's youth; and to head a citywide cleanup effort. An important part of Kilpatrick's approach was to let the people of Detroit know how sincere he was about creating a better city. "My entire family dwells within the walls of the city of Detroit," he said in the *Detroit News*. "This position is personal to me. It's much more than just politics."

Kilpatrick, who had inherited a troubled city with declining industry, an underfunded and underperforming school system, persistent poverty and unemployment, and a disastrous national image, brought a sense of hope to Detroit, and during his tenure he achieved several remarkable feats that appeared to put the city on the road to national prominence, most notably hosting Major League Baseball's All-Star Game at Comerica Park in 2005 and the National Football League's Super Bowl XL at Ford Field in 2006. Both events were hailed in the national press as outstanding. Businesses and suburban residents—who had largely fled the city following the racial-based civil unrest of the late 1960s—flocked to downtown Detroit, and, for the first time in decades, new residential housing boomed in the city.

Earned Unsavory Reputation

At the same time, however, Kilpatrick's lifestyle in the mayor's residence, the Manoogian Mansion, was growing more lavish and less scrupulous, earning him a reputation as the "hip-hop mayor"—a moniker many of the city's black residents, who still largely supported the mayor, found insulting. Rumors circulated of wild parties featuring strippers, one of whom ended up killed in a drive-by shooting shortly after her alleged appearance at a Kilpatrick-hosted gathering that was said to have included a confrontation with Carlita Kilpatrick. Further outrage erupted when it was discovered that Kilpatrick had used city funds to lease a Lincoln Navigator for his wife's personal use and spent city money for travel and entertainment. Many observers were shocked when Kilpatrick won his bid for reelection in 2005.

Things began to unravel for Kilpatrick when two Detroit police officers—Deputy Chief Gary Brown and Harold Nelthrope, who had been assigned to the mayor's security detail—brought a suit against the city and the mayor's office alleging the state's Whistleblower Protection Act had been violated when they were fired for taking part in an internal investigation into claims of misconduct in the mayor's security detail. One allegation in particular would eventually derail the mayor's career altogether: that Kilpatrick had used his city-issued security unit to cover up extramarital affairs, including one with Christine Beatty, his chief of staff. Both Kilpatrick and Beatty denied under oath that they had ever been involved romantically, and Kilpatrick maintained that Brown had not been fired but "unassigned." The lynchpin of the officers' accusations was a notorious party in the fall of 2002, at which exotic dancer Tamara Greene had performed and allegedly been assaulted by the mayor's wife, who returned home unexpectedly during the party. Michigan attorney general Mike Cox and the Michigan State Police investigated the allegations but never found any concrete evidence that the party had even happened. Cox called the party an urban legend, and the investigation was dropped. Brown, Nelthrope, and others in the city's department of internal affairs continued to look into the case.

In the meantime, on April 30, 2003, Tamara Greene was shot to death outside the strip club where she worked. A Detroit police lieutenant named Alvin Bowman, who was investigating the case, claimed in an affidavit that Greene had been shot with a police-issued weapon and that his evidence indicated that a police officer had done the shooting. According to Bowman, Greene had long been involved in prostitution, drugs, and money laundering and was demanding money from the mayor's office to keep quiet about the 2002 party. Bowman maintained she was murdered in retaliation by someone trying to cover up corruption in the Kilpatrick administration. The official investigation, however, failed to support Bowman's claims. According to the police report, Greene could have been killed by any number of men, including two with whom she had gotten into a scuffle at a motel party two weeks before her death. Bowman claimed he was prevented from investigating any further by Police Chief Jerry Oliver and his successor, Ella Bully-Cummings, and that the department even went so far as to alter police records. Lawyers representing the city and the mayor called Bowman's charges ridiculous. In 2008 a former city employee named Joyce Carolyn Rogers came forward in a signed affidavit claiming she had seen a police report in late 2002 that described an altercation between Greene and Carlita Kilpatrick at the Manoogian Mansion on the night that the party supposedly took place. Rogers has not, however, proven to be a credible witness, and Greene's murder remained unsolved.

On September 11, 2007, the jury in the trial at Wayne County Circuit Court found in favor of Brown and Nelthrope, awarding them a combined $6.5 million. Outraged, Kilpatrick planned to appeal, but a deal was struck a few weeks later after the mayor learned that evidence may have surfaced proving that Kilpatrick and Beatty had perjured themselves when they denied having an affair. Kilpatrick agreed to an $8.4 million settlement, to be paid to Brown, Nelthrope, and Walter Harris, a plaintiff in another lawsuit against the city. The Detroit City Council approved the settlement agreement despite the anger of many Detroit residents, who believed they were being made to pay for the mayor's indiscretions. Still, Detroit residents thought the worst was behind them and the mayor could move beyond the scandals toward the more important business of running the city.

Caught in Text-Messaging Scandal

In January of 2008 the *Detroit Free Press* obtained and published sexually charged excerpts from some of the fourteen thousand text messages sent between Kilpatrick and Beatty. The messages proved the two had lied under oath about the nature of their relationship and also that Brown was in fact fired. Beatty resigned days later. A contrite Kilpatrick appeared on Detroit television with his wife, explaining they had been through difficult times and all had been forgiven. Kilpatrick's pastor even went public, assuring the city that he was counseling the mayor. Kilpatrick further outraged many citizens on March 11, however, when in his annual state-of-the-city address he likened media coverage of the case to a lynch mob and used the N-word. On March 18, the city council passed a nonbinding resolution asking Kilpatrick to resign, with one council member dissenting. Business leaders, city council members, and others also called for the mayor to step down, but he refused, saying the situation was a private matter.

Wayne County prosecutor Kym Worthy disagreed, finding the evidence of perjury and other misconduct to be a very public matter. She launched an investigation and, on March 24, 2008, announced she was filing twelve felony counts—including perjury, obstruction of justice, misconduct, and conspiracy—against Kilpatrick and Beatty. At a news conference, Worthy disputed city attorneys' charges that the case was guided by prurience. "Let me be very, very clear," Worthy said. "This was not an investigation focused on lying about sex. Gary Brown, Harold Nelthrope, and Walter Harris, their lives were forever changed. They were ruined financially and their reputations were completely destroyed because they chose to be dutiful police officers. The public trust was violated. This investigation is whether public dollars were used unlawfully and much, much more." Among the things revealed in the text messages was the city's awarding $45 million in contracts to Bobby Ferguson, a local businessman and friend of Kilpatrick and Beatty, after passing him information on other contractors' bids and plans. Due to the amount of suspected nepotism in city hiring during his tenure, Kilpatrick's administration earned the label "the friends and family plan."

Once the charges were announced on March 24, Beatty turned herself in to the Wayne County Sheriff's Department, and Kilpatrick followed later in the day. Both were fingerprinted, and the mug shots taken showed up on the evening news. *Detroit Free Press* editorial page editor Ron Dzwonkowski was quoted by the Associated Press as saying of Kilpatrick after the booking, "At this point, he's more trouble than he's worth. It seems pretty clear it's going to be months getting this resolved. He's the city's public image. At best, he's a distraction, and at worst, he's a bad guy in a position with a lot of power." Furthermore, the *Detroit Free Press* called for the mayor to resign before things got even worse.

Jailed for Violating Bond

As the case dragged on through the summer and Detroit residents steadily lost patience with the mayor's defiant attitude about his legal troubles, Kilpatrick found himself in another sticky situation. In August of 2008 he was found to have violated his bond agreement by leaving the country without permission. Kilpatrick maintained he had no choice but to attend meetings in Windsor, Ontario—just across the Detroit River—to work on a deal to sell Detroit's half of the underwater tunnel connecting the two countries. In court Kilpatrick apologized for his mistake and asked Judge Ronald Giles for lenience. Giles rejected the plea, revoked Kilpatrick's bond, and sent him to the Wayne County Jail for a night.

When he was released the next day, Kilpatrick found himself in trouble yet again, this time due to a July incident in which the mayor had allegedly shoved and injured a Wayne County sheriff's deputy and another officer trying to serve a subpoena to Kilpatrick's friend Bobby Ferguson. The mayor was charged with assaulting an officer and booked on August 9. At his arraignment he pleaded not guilty, and his attorneys maintained the exchange between Kilpatrick and the officers had been friendly. Judge Thomas Jackson of the U.S. Circuit Court ordered Kilpatrick to wear an ankle monitor and remain in the Detroit metropolitan area. After posting a $25,000 bond, Kilpatrick returned to work at city hall later in the day. He did, however, eventually agree not to petition the court to attend the Democratic National Convention in Denver later in the month, even though he was a Democratic Party superdelegate.

At the urging of the Detroit City Council, Michigan governor Jennifer Granholm agreed to schedule a hearing to explore the possibility of removing Kilpatrick from office. From a legal standpoint, Granholm was the only person with authority to force Kilpatrick's resignation, but she had until then been reluctant to interfere in the legal process. Not surprisingly, the lead-up to the hearing did not go smoothly, with Kilpatrick's attorneys attempting to block Granholm from proceeding. When the hearing finally began on September 3, Kilpatrick was not present. Public scrutiny, however, was intense, with Detroit residents divided between those who continued to support the mayor and those who demanded punishment. Anti-Kilpatrick protesters marched outside the building, and longtime Detroit news broadcasters weighed in with televised editorials. One thing everyone agreed on was the need for closure to the case so that the city could move forward.

Resigned in Disgrace

The next day closure came: Kilpatrick turned himself in and admitted to two counts of obstruction of justice in exchange for the prosecutor's office dropping the remaining six charges, including the perjury counts. According to the terms of the plea agreement, Kilpatrick would resign from office, give up his law license and state pension, serve four months in the Wayne County Jail, spend five years on probation, and pay $1 million in restitution to the city. He also pleaded no contest to one of the assault charges pending against him. Prosecutor Worthy had hoped the mayor would spend six months in jail, but in general she was pleased with the results, commenting, "You have to have some consequences for your actions. You don't just lose your job."

Kilpatrick officially left office and moved out of the Manoogian Mansion on September 18, 2008. Beatty, who had been expected to accept a plea deal of her own, instead chose to take her chances with a jury. Her trial was set to begin in January of 2009; if convicted, she faced nineteen to thirty months in jail. Police Chief Bully-Cummings resigned shortly after Kilpatrick did. On September 19, City Council president Ken Cockrel Jr. was sworn in as interim mayor. Cockrel's first official acts were appointing a deputy mayor and a police chief. When he resigned in court, Kilpatrick delivered a defiant twenty-minute speech in which he questioned Governor Granholm's motives for pursuing the removal hearing and declared, "I want to tell you, Detroit, that you done set me up for a comeback."

Sources

Periodicals

Associated Press, March 24, 2008; September 5, 2008.
Campaigns & Elections, October 2001.
Chicago Tribune, September 5, 2008.
Crain's Detroit Business, November 20, 2000; January 21, 2001; January 7, 2002; March 18, 2002.
Detroit Free Press, March 24, 2008; July 13, 2008; September 4, 2008.

Detroit News, January 5, 2002; March 10, 2002; March 14, 2008; September 4, 2008.
Jet, November 26, 2001.
Los Angeles Times, August 8, 2008; August 9, 2008.

Online

"Bio: Mayor Kwame Kilpatrick," Alliance of National Heritage Areas, http://www.nationalheritageareas.com/ihdc.php?recordID=5&code=93 (accessed November 4, 2008).

"Detroit Cops Win $6.5 Million Suit against Mayor," CBS News, http://www.cbsnews.com/stories/2007/09/11/national/main3251871.shtml (accessed November 4, 2008).

"No Deal: Christine Beatty Headed to Trial," WXYZ.com, http://www.wxyz.com/content/news/detroitmayorinvestigation/story.aspx?content_id=e72fc3a6-66f6-4806-970d-a43ac0af62ab (accessed November 4, 2008).

Schepp, David, "Detroit's Renaissance on Hold," BBC News, http://news.bbc.co.uk/2/low/business/1746121.stm (accessed November 4, 2008)

Stevens, Andrew, "Kwame Kilpatrick, Mayor of Detroit," City Mayors, http://www.citymayors.com/mayors/detroit_mayor.html (accessed November 4, 2008).

—Leslie Rochelle and Nancy Dziedzic

though
Oni Faida Lampley

1959–2008

Playwright, actor, essayist

Oni Faida Lampley was an admired actor and writer whose award-winning plays explored issues of race, identity construction, and terminal illness. Her personal experience with disease—Lampley suffered from and eventually died of breast cancer—strongly informed her later plays and essays, in which she openly shared her struggles, fears, and eventual acceptance of herself and her body. She died in April of 2008.

Not much is known about Lampley's early life. She was born Vera Lampley in Oklahoma City, Oklahoma, in 1959. She attended a predominantly white, Catholic girls' school, and this experience went on to influence her work and lay the foundations of one of her most acclaimed autobiographical plays, *The Dark Kalamazoo* (1999). In *The Dark Kalamazoo* Lampley depicted her mother as a strong black woman, with a cigarette in one hand and a Scotch glass in the other, sending letters to her daughter full of what a reviewer in the *Daily Variety* called "hard-won wisdom, motherly warmth and bitter defensiveness."

Studied Abroad

Lampley graduated from high school and went on to attend Oberlin College in Oberlin, Ohio, and majored in creative writing. During her second year of college, she sought out opportunities to study abroad, especially the possibility to travel to Africa. Oberlin had no programs that interested Lampley, so she traveled abroad through Kalamazoo College in Kalamazoo, Michigan.

In 1979 Lampley departed on a study abroad trip to Ghana in West Africa. Expecting a warm welcome in "the Motherland," Lampley was shocked when she arrived and was met with prejudice. Being the only African-American student in the program of twenty people, she was given the hurtful nickname "Dark Kalamazoo" by the Africans she met—which would become the title of her autobiographical play about the experience. In the United States she actively tried to escape the view society had of her as an outsider, but she realized that in Africa she was equally outside the status quo.

A civil war in Ghana forced a change in plans, and Lampley traveled to Freetown, Sierra Leone. Her experiences in Africa affected her perception of herself as an African American and later influenced her work as a playwright. In an interview with writer Zinta Aistars about her play *The Dark Kalamazoo,* Lampley stated, "Study abroad was a huge milestone for me. It was the biggest step away from my customary life that I have ever made, a step away to see how others saw me—from a distance—and step out of my own self-absorption."

After her travels to West Africa, Lampley returned to Oberlin and received a Bachelor of Arts degree in 1981. She then attended the Lila Acheson Wallace American Playwrights program at the Juilliard School in New York City. There, Lampley studied the craft of playwriting, but she also had the opportunity to take classes on poetry and theater history. Her work at Juilliard and the pieces that came out of her personal

> **At a Glance . . .**
>
> Born Vera Lampley on April 15, 1959, in Oklahoma City, OK; died on April 28, 2008, in New York City, NY; married Tommy Abney; two children: Olu and Ade. *Education:* Oberlin College, BA, 1981; New York University, graduate degree in acting; Juilliard School, attended playwriting program; National Theater in London, playwriting residency, 2007.
>
> **Career:** Actor, 1980s–2008; playwright, 1991–2008; essayist, 1993–2008.
>
> **Memberships:** Drama Department, New York Theatre Workshop.
>
> **Awards:** Helen Hayes Award for Outstanding New Play, 1991; Lincoln Center Lecomte du Noüy Award.

experience garnered a Lincoln Center Lecomte du Noüy Award.

Her first play, *Mixed Babies,* won a 1991 Helen Hayes Award for Outstanding New Play. Her next play, *The Dark Kalamazoo,* received a nomination for a Barrymore Award for Outstanding Leading Actress. Lampley was nominated for another Helen Hayes Award for *The Dark Kalamazoo* in 1999.

Fought Cancer by Embracing Theater

In 1996 Lampley was diagnosed with breast cancer. Initially stunned by the diagnosis and her body's response to aggressive treatment, Lampley was overcome by shame, feeling that she was somehow to blame for having cancer. In a 2006 essay in *Self* magazine, Lampley wrote of the exhaustion caused by chemotherapy and radiation: "Perhaps the hardest part of this enforced stillness was my fear that those who loved me would be disappointed if I ceased to be the do-it-all survivor. And then I felt ashamed, once again: There was a 'right' way of having cancer, and I was doing it wrong." Nonetheless, Lampley continued working throughout her long battle with the disease, even after it had metastasized to her brain. She became active in breast cancer charities as well. In 2001 she wrote and performed the play *Shame the Devil* at a Carnegie Hall benefit, Artists for a Cure. She revived the piece for a 2003 performance in New York for the second installment of the series "My Soul to Keep," a cancer awareness show.

Out of her long struggle came her play *Tough Titty* in 2003. In a press release from the BRIC Studio in New York, Lampley explained the work as "part of digging out of the hole of seven years of breast cancer survivorship." She continued, "As an artist, my way of digesting life's events is to write. I've known for years, as events unfolded after diagnosis, that there is a useful story in this event." In the play, a thirty-seven-year-old mother of an infant receives a diagnosis of breast cancer and goes through the same waves of guilt, shame, and terror that plagued Lampley. The play also examines the effects of terminal illness on marriage and family. Before her death, Lampley learned that her play was set to be performed at San Francisco's Magic Theater in 2009.

Besides her work on the stage, Lampley was also an accomplished film and television actor. She made appearances on the television shows *Law & Order, Third Watch, Oz, NYPD Blue,* and *Homicide: Life on the Streets.* She performed roles in such films as *Money Train* with Woody Harrelson and Wesley Snipes, *Jungle 2 Jungle* with Tim Allen, *Bullet* with Tupac Shakur, Mickey Rourke, and Adrien Brody, and the Oscar-nominated John Sayles film *Lone Star.* Additionally, she performed in contemporary and classical material in regional theater and off-Broadway. Lampley appeared on Broadway in productions of *The Ride down Mt. Morgan* and *Two Trains Running.* In 1999 she was featured in the Peter Sellers operatic staging of Stravinsky's *Biblical Pieces* in Amsterdam, Netherlands.

Lampley was a founding member of the Drama Department, a New York theater project, and was a Usual Suspect at the New York Theatre Workshop. In 1993 she began to write essays and columns for various women's magazines. She was also a participant in the 1998 Sundance Screenwriters Lab to develop *The Dark Kalamazoo* into a film. Before her death she completed a screenplay based on a work by Robert Coles about African-American migrant farm workers in the 1960s.

Selected works

Film

The Keeper, 1995.
Money Train, 1995.
Lone Star, 1996.
Jungle 2 Jungle, 1997.
The Misadventures of Margaret, 1998.
Advice from a Caterpillar, 1999.
The Bumblebee Flies Anyway, 1999.
Dragonfly, 2002.
Brother to Brother, 2004.

Plays

Mixed Babies, 1991.
The Dark Kalamazoo, 1999.
Shame the Devil, 2001.
Tough Titty, 2003.

Television

Homicide: Life on the Streets, NBC, 1993.
NYPD Blue, ABC, 1993.
One Life to Live, NBC, 1994, 1997.
... First Do No Harm (movie), 1997.
Oz, HBO, 1999–2000.
Third Watch, NBC, 2000–01.
Law & Order, NBC, 1993, 1996, 2002, 2003.
The Jury, 2004.

Theatrical performances

Two Trains Running, Broadway Production, 1990s.
Mule Bone, Ethel Barrymore Theater, 1991.
Biblical Pieces, Amsterdam, Netherlands, 1999.
The Ride down Mt. Morgan, Ambassador Theater, 2000.
The Bluest Eye, Hartford Stage, 2008.

Other

"No More Shame," *Self,* October 2006.
Grand Theft Auto IV (voice), 2008.

Sources

Periodicals

Daily Variety, September 26, 2002, p. 31.
Entertainment Weekly, June, 28, 2002, p. 100.
Playbill, May 2, 2008.

Online

"Oni Faida Lampley," New Dramatists, http://newdramatists.org/oni_faida_lampley.htm (accessed November 4, 2008).
"Oni Faida Lampley, Actor," Drama Department, http://www.dramadept.org/who/bios/lampley-oni-faida.html (accessed November 4, 2008).
Oni Faida Lampley Memorial Web site, http://www.theonifund.com (accessed November 4, 2008).
Tough Titty, BRIC Studio, http://www.briconline.org/bricstudio/FY04_popups/oni.asp (November 4, 2008).

—Adam R. Hazlett and Nancy Dziedzic

Butch Lewis

1946—

Boxing promoter, entertainment executive

Lewis, Butch, photograph. Ray Tamarra/Getty Images.

Butch Lewis first came to prominence as a promoter for some of the biggest boxing matches of the 1970s and 1980s, including the famous 1978 fight in which Leon Spinks, then a relative unknown, upset reigning heavyweight champion Muhammad Ali. During the 1990s Lewis expanded from boxing into movies and television, building partnerships with such entertainment magnates as Robert L. Johnson, the founder and chairman of Black Entertainment Television. Lewis also devoted much of his time to Voicez Music Group, an independent record label he founded in 2005.

Scant information is available about Lewis's early life. Born Ronald Lewis on June 26, 1946, in New Jersey, he was raised by his mother and grandmother. According to a biographical statement posted on the Voicez Music Group Web site, the family's circumstances were "humble." After attending local schools, Lewis got a job as a car salesman, a profession in which his considerable personal charm proved an asset. "I'm in the people business," Lewis told Robert Mladinich on the *Sweet Science,* boxing Web site. "Selling cars is a people business. Boxing is a people business."

The switch from automobiles to prizefights seems to have been a gradual one. Like most boxing promoters, Lewis started on a small scale, organizing local and regional matches for a share of the ticket receipts. The late 1960s and early 1970s were a period of expanding opportunities in boxing, however, as public interest in the sport grew with the rise of talented and charismatic young fighters like Muhammad Ali. To capitalize on this interest, the television networks increased their boxing broadcasts, a development that vastly increased a promoter's potential profits. Lewis thrived in this tumultuous, fiercely competitive atmosphere. Perhaps his greatest single coup came in the aftermath of the 1976 Summer Olympics, when his new company, Butch Lewis Productions, signed promotional agreements with brothers Michael and Leon Spinks, both of whom had won gold medals for the United States. In February of 1978 he arranged a televised fight in Las Vegas, Nevada, between Leon Spinks and Ali, the heavyweight champion and one of the most recognized celebrities in the world. Ali, expecting an easy fight, failed to train sufficiently, and Spinks, in only his eighth professional bout, won a unanimous decision that

> **At a Glance . . .**
>
> **B**orn Ronald Lewis in New Jersey on June 26, 1946; children: four.
>
> **Career:** Founder, chairman, and CEO, Butch Lewis Productions, 1978—, Butch Lewis Entertainment, 1991—, Voicez Music Group, 2005—.
>
> **Awards:** Butch Lewis Day proclamation, State of Delaware, 1996; Candle Award in Business and Entertainment, 2006, and Doctor of Humane Letters, 2007, Morehouse College.
>
> **Addresses:** *Office*—c/o Voicez Music Group, 250 West 57th St., Ste. 311, New York, NY 10019.

shocked the world of sport. Lewis built on this initial success by staging a rematch several months later in New Orleans, Louisiana. This time, Ali was much better prepared, beating Spinks before the largest stadium crowd in boxing history. Lewis's share of the profits from these two events is difficult to determine, but it undoubtedly amounted to millions of dollars. The former car salesman was suddenly a celebrity in his own right.

Lewis continued to promote boxers and boxing matches throughout the 1980s and 1990s. His career in this period was not without occasional setbacks. He had, for example, several bitter public disputes with boxers under his management, usually over money. The worst of these quarrels involved Bernard Hopkins, a prominent middleweight, whose unproven accusations of dishonesty reportedly moved Lewis to tears. In general, however, Lewis maintained his ascent, scoring another triumph in September of 1985, when he arranged a match between Michael Spinks, Leon's brother, and heavyweight champion Larry Holmes. Spinks won in a unanimous decision, thus breaking Holmes's streak of forty-eight consecutive wins. Lewis also oversaw a 1988 match with Mike Tyson that would prove Spinks's last professional fight. Though Tyson knocked Spinks out in the first round, the match was a financial windfall for both fighters and for Lewis, who shared what was then the largest guaranteed purse in boxing history.

Though Lewis has never abandoned the boxing ring, he has increasingly focused on opportunities outside professional sports, notably in entertainment. In 1991 he formed an offshoot of Butch Lewis Productions called Butch Lewis Entertainment. The first production of this new enterprise was an immensely popular pay-per-view concert featuring soul star James Brown.

Lewis then moved into feature films and television, often serving as a coproducer in partnership with BET, a cable network founded by his friend Robert L. Johnson. Lewis helped produce several prominent works, notably *Out of Sync* (1995), a crime drama starring rapper LL Cool J; the highly-regarded historical drama *Once upon a Time...When We Were Colored* (1995), starring Al Freeman, Jr., and Phylicia Rashad; and *Linc's,* a popular series that aired from 1998 to 2000 on the Showtime cable network.

In 2005 Lewis expanded his business interests once again, moving forcefully into the music business. The independent record label he established in February of that year, Voicez Music Group, is a partnership with Island Def Jam Music Group, one of the most powerful organizations in the music industry, with particular strength in rap, pop, hip-hop, and R&B. Voicez has signed a number of performers in these genres, including Kinfolk, a rap duo from South Carolina, and hip-hopper Troy Ave. Lewis's daughter Sita is the company's senior vice president of operations, and his son Brandon is the senior vice president of artists and repertoire (A&R). Lewis himself serves as Voicez' chairman and chief executive officer.

Outside work, Lewis devotes considerable time to philanthropic causes. He focused much of his early philanthropy on the antiapartheid struggle in South Africa, a country he first visited in 1991 at the invitation of revered antiapartheid activist Nelson Mandela. Lewis returned there five years later, again at the invitation of Mandela, who had been elected president in the interim. Following Mandela's triumph, Lewis seems to have shifted the bulk of his charitable giving to the United States. In 2001, for example, J. Zamgba Browne reported in the *New York Amsterdam News* that Lewis's charitable organization, the Butch Lewis Foundation, had joined a number of other groups in donating holiday toys to seven hundred underprivileged children in Harlem. In addition, according to the Voicez Web site, he has frequently paid the tuition of deserving students who would otherwise be unable to afford college. In recognition of these activities, Lewis has received a number of awards. In 1996, for example, an official "Butch Lewis Day" was declared throughout Delaware, his current home, by then-Governor Thomas R. Carper. Lewis also received a Candle Award in Business and Entertainment in 2006 from Morehouse College, a historically black, all-male institution in Atlanta, Georgia; the same school presented him with an honorary doctorate the following year.

Sources

Periodicals

Jet, August 5, 1996.
New York Amsterdam News, December 26, 2001.

Online

"About Us," Voicez Music Group, http://voicezmusicgroup.com/ (accessed October 30, 2008).

"Biography: Butch Lewis," *Charlie Rose,* http://www.charlierose.com/guests/butch-lewis (accessed October 30, 2008).

Mladinich, Robert, "TSS Where Are They Now: Butch Lewis," Sweet Science, October 27, 2007, http://www.thesweetscience.com/boxing-article/5462/tss-where-are-they-now-butch-lewis/ (accessed October 30, 2008).

—R. Anthony Kugler

Romany Malco

1968—

Actor

Romany Malco is a successful actor best known for his roles in the comedy film *The 40-Year-Old Virgin* and the cable-television drama *Weeds*. He began his entertainment career as a rapper and music producer, but turned to acting during the mid-1990s. Within a decade he had achieved stardom through supporting roles in a series of projects featuring such notable comedians as Will Ferrell, Tina Fey, and Mike Meyers, among others.

Began Career as a Rapper

Malco, Romany, photograph. Dimitrios Kambouris/WireImage.

Malco was born in 1968 in Brooklyn, New York, and grew up in a West Indian family whose roots were in Trinidad. A natural-born performer, he was an early rap artist as a seven-year-old who billed himself as Kid Nice. In his teens he formed a rap act called R.M.G., and after a stint in the military relocated to Los Angeles with the group. With a name change to College Boyz, they were signed to Virgin Records and had success with a 1992 LP titled *Radio Fusion*. Its first single, "Victim of the Ghetto," climbed to No. 1 on the *Billboard* rap singles chart. Malco wrote a number of songs for the group's second release, *Nuttin' Less Nuttin' Mo'*, which was issued on Capitol in 1994. For a time the group toured with Mark Wahlberg (then known as Marky Mark), who also later turned to acting.

Malco moved on to music producing, working with such artists as Paula Abdul and CeCe Peniston, for whom he produced the 1996 LP *I'm Movin' On*. He began producing music for movie soundtracks, and in 1997 worked with actor-comedian John Leguizamo on the movie *The Pest*. Leguizamo urged him to try his luck in front of the camera, and Malco heeded the advice. His first roles came in episodes of *Touched by an Angel* and *For Your Love* in 1998, and he went on to gain experience in films over the next few years.

In 2001 Malco costarred in *The Château,* a comedy that paired him with Paul Rudd as his brother in an adoptive family. The duo inherit a piece of luxury property in France and travel there to investigate its potential. Malco played Rex, an Internet entrepreneur with a profitable sex advertising business, while Rudd was cast as the less ambitious Graham. They soon learn the estate in question is saddled with debt. In the *San Francisco Chronicle* film critic Mick LaSalle noted that "Malco comically and adeptly shows us who Rex

At a Glance . . .

Born Romany Romanic Malco Jr., on November 18, 1968, in Brooklyn, NY. *Military service:* Served in the U.S. armed forces.

Career: Recording artist, College Boyz, 1992–94; actor in films and television, 1999—.

Addresses: *Agent*—c/o Mosaic Media Group, 9200 W. Sunset Blvd., 10th Fl., Los Angeles, CA 90069.

thinks he is (a hotshot entrepreneur) and who he really is (someone only slightly smarter than his helpless brother)."

Cast in High-Profile Television Roles

Malco also appeared in the VH1 movie *Too Legit: The MC Hammer Story* (2001) as the adult MC Hammer. Reviewing the telefilm for the *Houston Chronicle*, Mike McDaniel asserted that "Malco is a knockout dancer who lip-synchs Hammer's master recordings well. He has a ton of stage presence and sometimes even resembles Hammer." Yet McDaniel faulted a formulaic script in what he termed "a perfunctory message movie," noting that "I never fully bought into the performance. Then again, Malco can't perform what's not on the page."

Malco gained commercial success in 2005, when *Weeds* premiered on Showtime. The acclaimed series starred Mary Louise Parker as suburban mom and new widow Nancy Botwin. In order to maintain her comfortable suburban lifestyle, Botwin turns to drug dealing. Her first supplier is a no-nonsense older black woman named Heylia (Tonye Patano) whose grandson Conrad Shepard (Malco) develops a business relationship with Parker's character that *evolves* into something deeper. "You got a black man selling drugs," Malco said of Conrad in an interview with Gary Strauss in *USA Today*. "But he's cerebral and subtle, not the reactionary guy you're accustomed to seeing." Though the illicit drug trade was the centerpiece of *Weeds*, it was a complicated family drama, too. "The thing that appealed to me is how vulnerable everyone is," Malco told Strauss in *USA Today*. "The protective veneer is stripped away."

The story arc on *Weeds* took Malco through the first three seasons, with less frequent appearances in Season 4, which began airing on Showtime in June of 2008. By then Malco was enjoying a string of comedic film successes that began with a few scene-stealing moments in the Judd Apatow comedy *The 40-Year-Old Virgin*. Debuting in theaters in August of 2005 just a few days after the premiere of *Weeds*, *The 40-Year-Old Virgin* starred Steve Carell in the title role as Andy Stitzer, a middle-aged man who lacks experience with the opposite sex. Malco was cast as Jay, Andy's coworker at an electronics retailer who tries to help him finally succeed with women.

Performed in Hit Comedy Films

In 2007 Malco had a minor role in *Blades of Glory*, the Will Ferrell ice-skating comedy, and a year later acted in *Baby Mama*, which starred Tina Fey and Amy Poehler. Fey was cast as Kate Holbrook, a career woman in her late thirties who hires a surrogate (Poehler) to fulfill her goal of becoming a mother. According to Katey Rich in *Film Journal International*, "the script takes [the two lead characters] through a series of misunderstandings and lies that most rational adults are capable of avoiding. But the characters are compelling, and are backed up by an embarrassment of riches in the supporting roles, with Romany Malco as an enthusiastic doorman and especially Steve Martin as Kate's loony New Age boss."

Malco also appeared in the Mike Myers comedy *The Love Guru* (2008). He played Darren Roanoke, a National Hockey League star whose game suffers when his girlfriend leaves him for another player (Justin Timberlake). Myers played Guru Pitka, the self-help expert whose services are enlisted to bring Roanoke's focus back to the ice. Malco had never skated in his life, but began training arduously in preparation for the role. "I really wanted to be good, because I didn't want to be in a sports movie and come off looking like I don't care about the sport," he told Arash Markazi in an interview on SI.com. "I wanted to put as much energy as I could into learning how to skate and play hockey. I like it when you're able to cut seamlessly and the audience knows, 'Hey, that guy is really skating.'"

Though *The Love Guru* was generally panned by critics, it did serve to introduce Malco to his fiancé, Taryn Dakha, who was the skating double for Jessica Alba's character in the movie. Malco and Dakha became engaged in late 2007. "Having a significant other," Malco enthused to Sarah Z. Wexler in *Marie Claire* "and potentially having your own family is much more exciting than 'What's the next movie I'm gonna do?'"

Selected works

Films

Corrupt, 1999.
The Wrecking Crew, 1999.
The Prime Gig, 2000.
True Vinyl, 2000.
The Château, 2001.

Ticker, 2001.
The Tuxedo, 2002.
White Boy, 2002.
Churchill: The Hollywood Years, 2004.
Death and Texas, 2004.
The 40-Year-Old Virgin, 2005.
Fast Track, 2006.
Blades of Glory, 2007.
Baby Mama, 2008.
The Love Guru, 2008.
Saint John of Las Vegas, 2009.

Television

Level 9, UPN, 2000–01.
Too Legit: The MC Hammer Story (movie), VH1, 2001.
Weeds, Showtime, 2005—.

Albums (with College Boyz)

Radio Fusion, Virgin Records, 1992.
Nuttin' Less Nuttin' Mo', Capitol, 1994.

Sources

Periodicals

Film Journal International, June 2008, p. 40.
Houston Chronicle, December 19, 2001, p. 12.
Marie Claire, June 2008, p. 70.
People, November 20, 2006, p. 140.
San Francisco Chronicle, September 6, 2002, p. D5.
USA Today, August 9, 2007, p. 1D.

Online

"Biography," Romany Malco Web Site, http://www.romanymalco.com/ (accessed October 27, 2008).
Markazi, Arash, "Q&A: Romany Malco," SI.com, June 9, 2008, http://sportsillustrated.cnn.com/2008/writers/arash_markazi/06/09/malco.qa/ (accessed October 27, 2008).

—Carol Brennan

Mario

1986—

Rhythm and blues singer

Mario, photograph. AP Images.

By the tender age of twenty-one, Mario Barrett, known to fans simply as Mario, had achieved more than most aspiring entertainers could dream of. Since making his debut at age fifteen, he has recorded three hit albums—with another on the way—appeared in three Hollywood films, and played live to throngs of adoring fans. Appearing on the wildly popular ABC TV series *Dancing with the Stars* in 2008, Mario showcased another of his talents—he can move as well as he can sing—and opened himself up to a whole new audience. Where will Mario take his career next? He has set his sights on nothing short of the top: "I want to be an icon," he told Naomi West in the *Telegraph*. "I want young artists to look up to me and say, 'Wow, I wanna be like that.'"

Launched to Teen Stardom

Mario Dewar Barrett was born on August 27, 1986, in Baltimore, Maryland, one of three sons of mother Shawn Hardaway. He began singing at age four, urged on by his mother. Mario recalled in an interview with *Ebony* magazine that his biggest influence was "my mother standing by me and encouraging me to sing…. She kept good music around me, which helped me to see other options. Sam Cooke is an artist I've grown to love; also Earth, Wind & Fire. And my mother played the piano. It was her way of keeping me away from the negative influences in our environment." Despite the early encouragement that Mario received from his mother, their relationship was difficult. Mario grew up not knowing his father, and his mother struggled with a substance abuse problem. He was raised mostly by his grandmother, who died when Mario was twelve years old.

Throughout his childhood Mario competed in talent competitions, dreaming of becoming a star. That dream started to become a reality when he was eleven years old. After performing a Boyz II Men song at a local talent show, Mario signed with his first manager, Troy Patterson—who also became something of a surrogate parent to him when Mario's mother was in the throes of addiction. Three years later Mario came to the attention of legendary music executive Clive Davis—the former president of Arista Records and, more importantly, the man who had discovered such

At a Glance...

Born Mario Dewar Barrett on August 27, 1986, in Baltimore, MD; son of Shawn Hardaway.

Career: Recording artist with J Records, 2000—.

Awards: Billboard Award for R&B/hip-hop single, 2005, for "Let Me Love You."

Addresses: *Office*—c/o J Records, 745 5th Ave., New York, NY 10151. *Web*—http://www.mario2u.com.

performers as Bruce Springsteen, Billy Joel, Whitney Houston, and legions of other recording artists during the course of his career. After meeting with Mario and hearing him sing, Davis was impressed with the young man's talent and immediately signed him to his J Records label.

Mario released his first single, "Just a Friend 2002," a remix of the 1989 hit by Biz Markie (who also acted as a producer on Mario's version), in May of 2002. The song outperformed the original single on the Billboard Hot 100, peaking at number four. Mario's self-titled debut album appeared that July, featuring the singles "Braid My Hair," "Put Me On," and "C'Mon." The record debuted at number nine on the Billboard Top 10 and went gold within months of its release, selling more than seven hundred thousand copies by 2008. At only fifteen years old, Mario and his image were carefully molded to appeal to teenage girls, and many of the album's songs describe innocent pleasures. Natalie Nichols in the *Los Angeles Times* described *Mario* as "recalling the more innocent days of Michael Jackson, or maybe Prince at his most sweet-talking."

Polished His Image

After taking a couple of years off to finish high school, Mario returned with his sophomore offering, *Turning Point,* in December of 2004. This album, launched just a few months after Mario turned eighteen, was still targeted to female listeners, but it displayed a greater sense of maturity—attributable partly to the more sensual material, partly to the singer's deeper and more masculine voice, and partly to a more polished, adult image designed to draw in a wider audience beyond teenyboppers. Mario had traded his youthful braids and sneakers for a more refined look, sporting a crisp, tailored suit and neatly manicured facial hair.

The smooth, soulful single "Let Me Love You" was a runaway success, holding on to the number-one spot on the Billboard Hot 100 for nine weeks and hitting number two on the U.K. Singles Chart. Notably, the single broke the record set by Usher—with whom Mario is often compared—gaining 191 million radio listeners following its release. Whereas his first album had made Mario a pop idol, *Turning Point* brought him the critical acclaim he desired. He earned two Grammy Award nominations, for male rhythm and blues (R&B) vocal performance and contemporary R&B album, and won the Billboard Award for top R&B/hip-hop single for "Let Me Love You."

Mario released his third recording, the much-anticipated *Go!*, in December of 2007, dedicating the album to his mother. The record features collaborations with a number of noted R&B and hip-hop producers—including Jermaine Dupri, Ne-Yo, Scott Storch, Jimmy Jam and Terry Lewis, Timbaland, The Neptunes, Akon, Polow da Don, and Stargate—and produced the hit singles "How Do I Breathe," "Crying Out for Me," and "Music for Love."

While recording *Go!*, Mario agreed to allow MTV to film a documentary about his troubled relationship with his mother and her continuing struggle with heroin addiction. *I Won't Love You to Death: The Story of Mario and His Mom,* which aired in October of 2007, chronicled their everyday lives and emotional pains as Mario attempted to get his mother into rehab. "I found myself really feeling [that] if she didn't get her life together that I didn't want to be a part of her life," Mario said in an interview with *Jet* magazine in 2008. "It was affecting me every day to the point where I couldn't create." Since completing a stint in a drug rehab facility in 2007, Hardaway has remained sober.

Became a Triple Threat

In addition to his music career, Mario has branched out into acting as well. In 2006 he appeared in the dance-themed movie *Step Up,* and in 2007 he starred alongside Oscar-winning actress Hilary Swank in the film *Freedom Writers*. His next film role was a small part in *Destination Fame*.

Seeking to develop his talents and widen his fan base even further, in 2008 Mario appeared on the sixth season of the hit ABC series *Dancing with the Stars,* on which celebrities are paired with professional dancers and square off in weekly competitions judged by viewers at home. Teaming up with Karina Smirnoff, Mario waltzed, tangoed, and quickstepped for eight weeks, but was eliminated from the show on May 6. Media critics were quick to point out that the show offered Mario an opportunity to reach more audiences. Talent executive Biff Warren told the *Baltimore Sun,* "This will benefit him and open more doors for him when it comes to television and film. Even in his own music career, it will make him more recognizable in different radio formats, because the show is so popular across the board."

In late 2008 Mario planned to release his fourth album, pleased with the success he has achieved in such a short time. In his biography on his Web site, he reflected, "I feel like this is what I'm supposed to be doing. I'm supposed to be at this place in every aspect of my life, from personal to business. This is where I am, this is where I chose to be."

Selected works

Recordings

Mario, J Records, 2002.
Turning Point, J Records, 2004.
Go!, J Records, 2007.

Films

Step Up, 2006.
Freedom Writers, 2007.
Destination Fame, 2008.

Television

I Won't Love You to Death: The Story of Mario and His Mom, 2007.
Dancing with the Stars, 2008.

Sources

Periodicals

Baltimore Sun, May 8, 2008.
Ebony, May 2005.
Jet, May 5, 2008.
Los Angeles Times, July 21, 2002.
Telegraph, March 31, 2005.

Online

Mario official Web site, http://www.mario2u.com (accessed August 21, 2008).

—Deborah A. Ring

Bryan Monroe

1965—

Journalist, publishing executive

Monroe, Bryan, photograph. AP Images.

Bryan Monroe is a Pulitzer Prize–winning journalist and publishing executive who gained recognition for overseeing a team of journalists working to keep a Biloxi, Mississippi, newspaper publishing after Hurricane Katrina in 2005. He began his career as a photography intern for a local newspaper and worked his way up to become an executive in the Knight Ridder news organization and president of the National Association of Black Journalists. In 2006 Monroe joined the venerable Johnson Publishing Company as vice president and editorial director of *Ebony* and *Jet* magazines.

Monroe was born in Munich, Germany, in 1965, but by the time he reached his early teens his family had settled in the community of Lakewood, Washington, in Pierce County. He earned a bachelor's degree in communications from the University of Washington in 1987, and spent a few months at the *Seattle Times* as a photography intern. Over the next few years he worked as a photographer for the United Press International news service and the *Roanoke Times,* and then as director of photography and design for the *Sun News* in Myrtle Beach, South Carolina. The *Sun News* belonged to the Knight Ridder newspaper group, and in the early 1990s Monroe was promoted to assistant director of Knight Ridder's 25/43 Project, which was aimed at attracting new readers to its publications. He spent most of the 1990s with one of Knight Ridder's flagship properties, the *San Jose Mercury News,* as a reporter, assistant city editor, design director, and assistant managing editor. In 2002 he was made assistant vice president for news within Knight Ridder's corporate offices.

Urged Newspapers to Embrace Diversity

In 2003 Monroe was named a Nieman Fellow, an honor given to journalists at mid-career that comes with a stint at the Nieman Foundation for Journalism at Harvard University. Monroe chose to examine diversity in the newsroom as his field of inquiry, and discussed the topic in an article in *Nieman Reports,* the Foundation's scholarly journal. His essay touched on the controversy over Jayson Blair, a *New York Times* reporter who was fired after it was discovered that he had plagiarized or fabricated many of the articles that ran under his byline. Blair was once a promising writer

At a Glance...

Born Bryan K. Monroe on August 22, 1965, in Munich, Germany; son of James W. and Charlyne W. Monroe; married Tahirah Monroe (a teacher); children: Seanna, Jackson. *Education:* University of Washington, BA, 1987.

Career: *Seattle Times,* photography intern, 1987; World News and United Press International, photographer; *Roanoke Times,* photographer; Myrtle Beach *Sun News,* director of photography and design; *San Jose Mercury News,* began as reporter, 1991, became assistant city editor, design director, and assistant managing editor by 2006; Knight Ridder News, assistant director for the 25/43 Project, and assistant vice president for news, 2002–06; Johnson Publishing Company, vice president and editorial director for *Ebony* and *Jet* magazines, 2006—.

Memberships: Bay Area Black Journalists Association, Unity: Journalists of Color, National Association of Black Journalists (vice president for print, 2001–05, president, 2005–07).

Awards: Nieman Fellow, Harvard University, 2003; Pulitzer Prize Gold Medal for Public Service, 2006.

Addresses: *Office*—Johnson Publishing Company, Inc., 820 S. Michigan Ave., Chicago, IL 60605.

at the paper, and some accused his superiors of overlooking warning signs that others had raised about the accuracy of his work. Monroe's article noted that some had dubbed Blair "the poster child for what's wrong with newsroom diversity, claiming that it has taken over the newsroom and lowered standards." Yet Monroe disagreed, quoting from an industry survey that found "the overwhelming majority of American newspapers—some 97 percent of those that responded—are miles away from having staffing that reflects the racial richness of their local communities."

After the Nieman fellowship ended, Monroe returned to the Knight Ridder corporate office in San Jose and to his post as assistant vice president. In August of 2005 he was elected president of the National Association of Black Journalists (NABJ) after having served four years as vice president for print in the 3,300-member organization. Just a few weeks later he led a team of Knight Ridder journalists striving to keep the Biloxi *Sun Herald* publishing daily in the aftermath of Hurricane Katrina. The paper's regular staff numbered about fifty, "but they can't find half of them; don't know if they are in shelters, left the city or are dead," he wrote in a dispatch that appeared on the NABJ Web site. In Biloxi, under circumstances of extreme privation, Monroe helped the *Sun Herald* team gather news and then file their stories with another Knight Ridder paper, the *Columbus (Georgia) Ledger-Enquirer,* which then printed the Biloxi newspapers. "And the next morning, someone puts the papers on the truck and trucks them in five hours here," Monroe wrote. Monroe often took part in the distribution efforts, as well, handing out papers to locals on the streets of a devastated Biloxi. "It's amazing how grateful people are just to have a newspaper," he wrote. "It brought tears to my eyes."

In 2006 Monroe shared the Pulitzer Prize Gold Medal for Public Service with his colleagues at the *Sun Herald* for their efforts in Biloxi. A few months later Knight Ridder was sold to the McClatchy Company, and days after that announcement Monroe took a new job with the Johnson Publishing Company in Chicago as vice president and editorial director of *Ebony* and *Jet* magazines.

Used Position to Fight Racism

In his new position Monroe wrote feature articles and editorials for Johnson's flagship publications. In February of 2007 his essay "Enough! Why Blacks—and Whites—Should Never Use the 'N-word' Again" was published in *Ebony.* Noting the racial epithet had inarguable negative impact when it was used by whites, he called on African Americans to stop using it to connote "affection or an insider status." Monroe noted, "We use it on the basketball courts and in our hip-hop music. We ignore its acidic purpose and transpose its meaning. We want it to imply nothin' but love. But in that act, we forget its origins, its roots, its deadly history." His editorial announced that "from here on, after you read the powerful discussion of that term in these subsequent pages of *Ebony,* you will likely never see that word used in this magazine—or our sister magazine, *Jet*—again. On the very rare occasion that its use is central to the telling of an important story, I, as the editor, will need to sign off on it personally." His crusade to symbolically bury the term gained steam later that year when the NAACP officially "buried" the word at its national convention.

Monroe stepped into the middle of a controversy involving radio talk show host Don Imus in the spring of 2007 after Imus made racist remarks about the women's basketball team at Rutgers University. The NABJ issued a strongly worded statement calling for Imus to resign, and Monroe explained the organization's position in a debate with Imus on Al Sharpton's radio show. "Mr. Imus, I have a daughter," he said. "I think you have a daughter. What would you do if a sixty-seven-year-old man went in front of millions of people and called your daughter what you called these women? Mr. Imus, what do you think the consequences of those words should be? Should an apology be enough?" Three days later, CBS Radio announced they were canceling Imus's daily show, though it was later resurrected on another radio network.

Monroe is married to Tahirah Monroe, an elementary school teacher, with whom he has two children. His family served as the impetus for undergoing gastric-bypass surgery in the summer of 2006, which helped him drop from 441 pounds to 282 pounds a little over a year later. In 2004—a year before he turned forty—Monroe was diagnosed with Type 2 diabetes, and already knew he suffered from high blood pressure. In November of 2007 Ebony ran a feature story on the procedure and interviewed him along with Khaliah Ali, daughter of the boxing legend Muhammad Ali, and radio talk-show host Joe Madison, both of whom had also chosen to have the surgery to improve their health and life expectancy. In the interview Monroe cited his two children, Seanna and Jackson, as the most important factors in making his decision. "Along with my wife, Tahirah, they are my heart and joy, and I really wanted to be around to see them graduate from high school, go to college and bring me a few grandkids."

Sources

Periodicals

Ebony, February 2007, p. 198; November 2007, p. 180.
New York Times, April 9, 2007.
Nieman Reports, Winter 2002, p. 111; Fall 2003, p. 29.
Seattle Times, May 17, 2007.

Online

"New Dispatch from Hurricane Katrina," National Association of Black Journalists, November 7, 2007, http://www.nabj.org/pres_corner/v-print/story/22745p-32365c.php (accessed October 2, 2008).

—Carol Brennan

Robert Mugabe

1924—

President of Zimbabwe

Robert Mugabe, Zimbabwe's president, decided while in his twenties to help his black countrymen achieve independence from British colonial rule. He fulfilled his goal in 1980, after eleven years in prison and a bloody seven-year guerrilla war. Since 1987 Mugabe has presided over a land whose economy is in shambles, and Amnesty International named Mugabe one of the ten worst dictators in the world.

Learned about Racial Injustice

Robert Mugabe was born in 1924, four months after Southern Rhodesia became a British Crown colony. In a land ruled by a theoretically multiracial Legislative Assembly that was actually overwhelmingly white, life was not easy for the Shona people of Mugabe's native Kutama village. Their freedom was curtailed by laws, their job opportunities were regulated by industry's need for unskilled labor, and their education, in most cases, was limited to the grammar-school level.

Mugabe was one of the few who escaped this fate. His education was supervised by Father O'Hea, the director of the nearby Jesuit mission, who was an unshakably moral and defiantly liberal man. An unabashed iconoclast, O'Hea held the philosophy that all people are equal and should be treated that way and that students should be educated as far as their capabilities can take them. He imbued the intelligent young Mugabe with both of these maxims and encouraged him to pass them on to others by becoming a teacher.

In 1945 Mugabe left O'Hea's guidance behind for a wider Southern Rhodesia, where new settlers were pouring into the country at a rate of ten thousand each year. Prime Minister Godfrey Huggins, intent on providing security for them, was firmly in favor of racial separation, a method of administration that had been buttressed by the Land Apportionment Act. Implemented in 1930, the act decreed that much of the nation's unincorporated land should be divided evenly between blacks and whites despite a huge demographic imbalance of only 50,000 whites and 650,000 blacks. The growing population and the increasing industrialization of the country forced more and more blacks to move. By the time Mugabe returned home to start his teaching career in 1946, about three hundred thousand black families had been displaced from their homes and packed into already overcrowded areas. It was a situation destined to fester into open warfare.

Southern Rhodesia was still seething in 1949, when Mugabe won a scholarship to the University of Fort Hare in South Africa. Because South Africa was also part of the British Commonwealth, he found little change in the external society, though life was different inside the all-black university. For the first time since he had left the mission, he saw active protest against segregation and an eagerness to explore different political philosophies. One that he found attractive was Marxism.

Mugabe's interest in communism grew into admiration after 1957, when he was invited by Kwame Nkrumah to teach in Ghana. Recently independent and proudly Marxist, the Ghanaian government was intent on bringing universal education and opportunity to those

At a Glance...

Born Robert Gabriel Mugabe on February 21, 1924, in Kutama, Zimbabwe; son of Gabriel Mugabe and Bona Mugabe; married Sally Heyfron, February 21, 1961; two children; married Grace Marufa, August 16, 1996; three children. *Education:* University of Fort Hare, South Africa, BA, 1951; University of London, LLB.

Career: Taught at various mission schools in Zimbabwe, 1951–55; taught at Chalimbana Training College, Zambia, 1955–58, and St. Mary's Training College, Takoradi, Ghana, 1958–60; National Democratic Party, publicity secretary, 1960–61; Zimbabwe African People's Union, publicity secretary, 1961–62; Zimbabwe African National Union, founder and leader, 1963–76, president, 1976–80; arrested in 1963 and jailed 1964–74; Republic of Zimbabwe, prime minister, 1980–87, minister of defense, 1985; president, 1987—.

Awards: African Leadership Prize, 1988.

Addresses: *Office*—Office of the President, Private Bag 7700, Causeway, Harare, Zimbabwe.

---

formerly at the lowest levels of society. Mugabe noted that most Ghanaians gladly seized the chance to better themselves. Enjoying the cheerful public spirit, he plunged eagerly into teaching and working with the country's youth groups, and he took a deep interest in all aspects of Ghanaian politics.

Became Opposition Leader in Zimbabwe

In 1960 he visited his homeland to introduce his mother to his Ghanaian fiancée, Sally Heyfron. The country was no longer the Southern Rhodesia he remembered. The white population had grown to 223,000, a formidable number of whom supported the federation that had been established between Northern and Southern Rhodesia and Malawi. However, no such enthusiasm existed among the country's 450,000-strong black voting force. The federation's government refused to implement black majority rule, so politically aware blacks were adamantly opposed to it. Mugabe was astounded by their bold new vehemence and the protest groups they had formed to express it.

In July of 1960 black fury exploded into a protest later called the March of 7,000. People gathered at the town hall of Salisbury's Harare Township to protest the arrest of their leaders. Mugabe was persuaded to address the gathering. He told his seething audience about the egalitarian new Ghanaian society and its rise from colonialism, and found that he had generated public interest that outlasted the day of the protest. He ignored the threatening, almost unlimited police power of the Law and Order Act that was enacted after the march and began to give many speeches about Ghanaian pride in its Marxist independence. He also decided to stay and help achieve the same status for Southern Rhodesia.

Within weeks of the March of 7,000, he was elected publicity secretary of the National Democratic Party. Seeing his first task as introducing the uninitiated to the possibility of black independence, he organized a semimilitant youth league like those he had worked with in Ghana. Just as he had done in Accra, he attracted Rhodesian teenagers with political discussions and the cultural dancing and music that would give them pride in their heritage. His efforts soon paid off. Even though the party itself was banned by the government on December 9, 1961, it left behind enough supporters to regroup immediately into the Zimbabwe African People's Union (ZAPU). As Southern Rhodesia's first effective black political movement, it functioned for nine months before it was banned the following September.

The tumultuous events in Southern Rhodesia had not escaped the notice of the British Foreign Office, which in 1959 ordered a comprehensive enquiry under Lord Monckton. The following year the Monckton Commission disclosed its conclusion that there was too much black opposition to the federation for it to continue to exist in its present form. If the federation were to survive, Monckton concluded, a new constitution providing majority rule would have to be enacted. Britain agreed, relinquishing control of Southern Rhodesia's domestic affairs and drawing up a new constitution allowing majority rule.

The new constitution did not appease black Rhodesians, however. It lacked a definite target date for adopting majority rule and it proposed a two-tier electoral system whose upper level was accessible only to voters with a secondary education. Because this effectively excluded most of the black population, blacks received only half the voting power of the better-educated whites, who were also eligible to vote on the lower roll. As a result, the country's far-smaller white population could elect fifty of the Legislative Assembly's sixty-five members. The vociferous opposition of 450,000 blacks spurred ZAPU leader Joshua Nkomo to visit the United Nations (UN), which in turn called on Britain to suspend the new constitution and initiate discussions about true majority rule.

Nkomo's negotiations with the British stalled. Nkomo was perceived by many, including Mugabe, as accepting Britain's vague promises of eventual majority rule rather than insisting on a definite timetable. Along with other ZAPU supporters, Mugabe was so furious about these equivocations that he openly began to advocate a guerrilla war. In April of 1961, noted Mugabe's biographers David Smith and Colin Simpson, Mugabe even snapped at a policeman at Salisbury Airport who stopped a party supporter suspected of carrying a weapon: "We are taking over this country, and we will not put up with this nonsense."

Mugabe's defiant attitude made him the target of constant police surveillance, especially after he split from Nkomo's party in 1963. In August of that year he and several other ex-Nkomo supporters formed the Zimbabwe African National Union (ZANU) in Dar es Salaam, Tanzania. The Rhodesian police, aware of these activities, waited for their opportunity to arrest him. Their chance came in December, when Mugabe returned to his homeland. He was jailed for eleven years. In prison, Mugabe was not as isolated as the police hoped. Secret communications networks between him and his supporters brought him the news that the former Nyasaland was now Malawi, that the former Northern Rhodesia was now Zambia, and that the independence of both countries had caused the collapse of the federation. He also knew that an attack on a white Rhodesian farmstead in 1964 had signaled the start of guerrilla operations to liberate Southern Rhodesia.

Watched the Majority Rule Prevail

Mugabe had been in prison for about two years when former Royal Air Force Pilot Ian Smith became Rhodesia's prime minister. An experienced politician, Smith assured white Southern Rhodesians that majority rule would not come to pass during his tenure. He went to London for the constitutional talks, but his stance did not impress the new Labor government. Nevertheless, he stuck obstinately to his agenda, going so far as to issue a unilateral declaration of independence on November 11, 1965, though still professing allegiance to the British Crown. In response, the UN imposed sanctions that quickly damaged the Rhodesian economy. Chrome, copper, asbestos, tobacco, and sugar previously bound for export never left the country, and shipments of badly needed oil were kept out.

However, sanctions were just one of Smith's problems. Far worse was the 1975 independence of Mozambique, a staunch former ally in its days as a Portuguese colony. Mozambique was now a Marxist state, with long, sparsely patrolled borders that were ideal bases of operations for Mugabe's Zimbabwe African National Liberation Army (ZANLA) and the Chinese allies eager to help it with training and arms. Neighboring South Africa, Smith's last remaining ally, was now also teetering insecurely. Encouraged by South African leaders, Smith had Mugabe released from prison to attend a 1974 conference in Lusaka. Mugabe seized this opportunity and escaped across the border into Mozambique, stopping on the way to recruit young Rhodesians for guerrilla training.

By the end of the 1970s a savage and stealthy war and a devastated economy had convinced Smith that majority rule was inevitable. Unsuccessfully, he tried to reach a mutually suitable transition schedule with Mugabe, but there was no progress until 1979, when Britain convened a conference at Lancaster House in London. Topics discussed at the conference were the British-monitored transition to black majority rule, the assurance of white minority representation for a specific period after independence, and a new constitution. With all these matters settled, on December 16 the UN lifted the sanctions.

Became Prime Minister

On April 18, 1980, British rule ended in Southern Rhodesia and the nation was renamed the Republic of Zimbabwe. Elected over candidates from ten competing parties, including Nkomo, the ZANU took power, with Mugabe as prime minister. Despite his Marxist leanings, he tried his best not to frighten whites by immediately scrapping the capitalist economy. Instead, he tried to persuade them to stay and share their skills by announcing that the change to socialism would proceed in gradual phases. White Rhodesians were not convinced that they could find security in a country run by a recently murderous enemy, however, and in 1980 alone, over seventeen thousand of them fled from the country.

Mugabe ignored their departure and turned his attention to badly needed reforms. By New Year's Day 1981, the country boasted free primary school education for all students as well as guaranteed admission to secondary school for all who qualified. Free medical care was provided for those with low income levels, and a new housing law granted freehold ownership to home-renters of thirty years' standing. In other innovations, Mugabe had city boundaries reshaped to ensure multiracial political representation and replaced whites with educated blacks in key positions relating to educational institutions.

Nevertheless, problems remained. Fighting broke out in February of 1981 between Mugabe's forces and Nkomo's Zambia-based faction. Most troublesome was Nkomo himself, who was fired from the government in 1982 after his intention to launch an antigovernment coup was revealed. This action touched off a flurry of robberies and led to the murder of several tourists. It also brought retaliation from Mugabe's forces in the form of rapes and murders in Nkomo's stronghold area of Matabeleland.

An atmosphere of resentment smoldered on through the national elections of 1985, when Mugabe triumphed a second time over Nkomo. Friction between the ZANU and Nkomo's ZAPU supporters continued until November of 1987, when fifteen Matabeleland missionaries were murdered with axes by Mugabe supporters. This tragedy caused Nkomo and Mugabe to settle their differences.

Became Zimbabwe's President

On December 22, 1987, the ZANU and the ZAPU merged in a unity agreement designed to begin healing the country, which was now split along tribal lines. One week later Mugabe was installed as the country's new president, and Nkomo was named one of three supervising senior ministers. The friction eased, allowing President Mugabe to concentrate on bettering an economy starved for foreign currency as a result of prolonged drought, a worldwide recession, and the lingering effects of sanctions against the Smith government. Despite his efforts, imported spare parts for the mining and manufacturing industries became scarce, and levies on tobacco and alcohol had to be instituted to offset the soaring unemployment rate.

By 1989 the economy required major restructuring. The International Monetary Fund and the World Bank helped create a five-year adjustment program that restructured the government, relaxed price controls, and gave farmers the right to set their own prices. Still, shortages of staples such as brake fluid and cooking oil; the drought-induced rises in the cost of maize, wheat, and dairy products; and a new policy of charging for education and medical care overshadowed most of the adjustment programs' benefits and darkened the national mood. By 1994, however, the structural adjustment had produced some improvements, with slight growth beginning in agriculture, manufacturing, and mining. Mugabe's vision of security under majority rule in Zimbabwe had begun to move forward.

In 1996 Mugabe took the controversial stance of supporting the seizure of white-owned land without compensation to reverse the economic imbalances that disadvantaged the majority blacks. He also refused to revise the constitution that is tailored to a one-party state, or release his hold on the media.

In September of 1998 Mugabe's government held an international conference to raise money for land distribution, but potential donor countries refused to give Mugabe any money until he came up with a plan for reducing rural poverty. Since no plan was proposed, no money was received.

Then in April of 2000 Zimbabwe passed a constitutional amendment that held Britain, as a former colonial power, responsible for paying for land stolen from Africans during colonial rule. Mugabe threatened to seize land without compensation if Britain did not pay. Some critics, however, pointed out that when the British arrived in Africa at the end of the nineteenth century, they were only helping themselves to land that was not being used by anyone else.

In a presidential election in March of 2002, Mugabe officially won reelection by 430,000 votes. However, there were widespread allegations that Mugabe had stuffed the ballot box with enough votes to give him his margin of victory. The allegations had sufficient credibility to cause the United States, the European Union, and many other developed countries to impose sanctions on Zimbabwe, including an arms embargo. In 2003 a hearing was held by the High Court of Zimbabwe, though no decision was immediately made and Mugabe and his party retained power.

Was Unable to Help Zimbabwe's Economy

By October of 2002 Zimbabwe's commercial agriculture, which had formerly sustained the economy, had ground to a halt. With widespread hunger (half the population was said to be experiencing famine), food donations were pouring into the country. There were reports that Mugabe's government had been distributing donated food on the basis of the recipient's political affiliation. Other reports stated the government would only buy farmers' products if they supported Mugabe, which contributed to the food problem.

Food shortages, however, were only the tip of the iceberg for Mugabe. Since early 2000 the economy had experienced a steep decline. The gross domestic product had fallen 24 percent, inflation had reached 135 percent, the value of the country's currency had fallen 96 percent, and the arrears on the foreign debt of $3.4 billion had reached 30 percent. Earnings from tourism had fallen 80 percent, gold production was down by half, and 300,000 of the county's 1.3 million workers were unemployed. In addition to bad economic news, 35 percent of all adults had AIDS. Many people left the country, whose population declined by nearly 2.5 million between 1992 and 2002.

Though Zimbabwe's economic, social, and cultural situations were growing more desperate, Mugabe tightened his grip on the country. In September of 2003 a government commission essentially banned Zimbabwe's only independent daily newspaper from future publication. The paper regularly criticized Mugabe. Though Mugabe was in control, he did face some uncertainty before the 2005 parliamentary elections. Besides factional infighting in his political party and controversy over who would be Mugabe's successor when he decided to leave office, several important people in Mugabe's government, including the Zimbabwean ambassador to Mozambique, were charged with selling state secrets to foreign agents.

During his campaign, Mugabe said he believed the mining industry would take Zimbabwe out of its economic doldrums, and he looked forward to the opening of the country's first big diamond mine in 2005. The government also invested funds to encourage more platinum mining. Furthermore, Mugabe spoke out against the violence expected to accompany the elections. Despite being named one of the world's ten worst dictators by Amnesty International in 2004, Mugabe was expected to win the election and stay in power until at least 2008, when he said he would retire.

His retirement did not come soon enough, however, as Mugabe's party did indeed retain power in the 2005 parliamentary elections. By that time, the country had further descended into a shocking state of chaos and economic ruin. The collapse had begun in 2000, with the enactment of the threatened forcible appropriation of thousands of white-owned farms. The ensuing destruction of the agricultural base (output fell by 80 percent) resulted in an approximate decline of 50 percent in the gross national product, an annual inflation rate of 400%, and a dizzying drop in tourist revenues. The problems were further worsened by Operation Murambatsvina (variously translated as "Clean up Filth," "Drive out Trash," and "Restore Order"), which was started in May of 2005. Described by the government as a civic beautification program, the initiative displaced an estimated seven hundred thousand people and affected nearly two million more, thousands of whom were rendered homeless within months. Mugabe denied any such situation and refused UN assistance for its alleged victims. Nonetheless, by November of 2005 the average life expectancy had halved in a decade, four million people faced famine, and the unemployment rate hovered around 70%.

Attempts to deal with the economic collapse, including printing more and more money, led to runaway inflation. It rose from 1,000 percent in 2005 to an unimaginable 40 million percent in 2008. In 2007 Celia W. Dugger of the *New York Times* reported that "the government had to lop 10 zeros off the currency … to keep the nation's calculators from being overwhelmed." Zimbabweans faced monthly limits of how much money they were allowed to take out of the banks, amounting to only a dollar or two. The once-prosperous Zimbabwe had declined into a beleaguered country fit, perhaps, only for its president.

Corrupted the 2008 Elections

In March of 2007 Zimbabwean riot police broke up opposition rallies, and Movement for Democratic Change (MDC) leader Morgan Tsvangirai and several other opposition leaders were beaten and hospitalized. The United States announced that it would hold Mugabe personally responsible for the attacks. In August of 2007 Mugabe forbade all businesses in Zimbabwe to increase their prices or wages for the next six months. The move was an attempt to fight Zimbabwe's runaway inflation, but it had little or no effect on the country's economic problems. In December British prime minister Gordon Brown refused to attend a summit involving the European Union and African nations because of Mugabe's presence there. At the summit, representatives of other countries criticized Mugabe for his human-rights record.

Late in 2007 Mugabe's party and the opposition began holding talks in South Africa aimed at national reconciliation. However, in January of 2008 police used tear gas to break up an opposition rally. A few days later, the Mugabe regime announced that it would hold presidential and parliamentary elections on March 29 of that year, and Mugabe would run for reelection. Mugabe ran on the slogan "This is the final battle for total control." Opposition leaders insisted that changes to the constitution should precede new elections, and they threatened to boycott the vote unless changes were made to ensure the elections would be free and fair, including a relaxation of tough security laws used to suppress political rallies.

The March 29, 2008, elections pitted Mugabe against opposition leader Morgan Tsvangirai of the MDC. Electoral authorities took more than a month to release results. In the meantime, on April 6, Mugabe asked the Zimbabwe Electoral Commission to recheck the results of the presidential elections before publicly releasing the outcome. The MDC sued in Zimbabwe's High Court to block this order. The MDC believed Mugabe was trying to steal the election and argued that Mugabe could not legally ask for a recount until after the results were released. The MDC also demanded that the results of the election be published immediately.

When election results were finally released on May 2, they showed that Tsvangirai took 47.9% of the vote and that Mugabe only won 43.2%. This meant the two would have to compete in a run-off election, because to win in the first round the top vote-getter had to win more than half of the vote. The MDC alleged that Tsvangirai had indeed won more than 50% of the vote in the first round of the election and that Mugabe's government had manipulated the vote-counting process to prevent Tsvangirai from taking office.

On May 16, 2008, the Zimbabwe Electoral Commission announced that the run-off election between Mugabe and Tsvangirai would be held on June 27, 2008. Tsvangirai declared he would compete in the run-off election, despite his assertions that the vote-counting in the first round of the election had been rigged. However, in June of 2008 Mugabe said he would not allow Tsvangirai or the MDC to take power in Zimbabwe as long as he was alive. BBC News noted that Tsvangirai withdrew his candidacy just days before the election because, he said, "the outcome is determined by … Mugabe himself" and because as many as two hundred thousand MDC supporters had been forced from their homes, and others had been beaten and even killed. On June 29, the Zimbabwe Electoral Commission announced that Mugabe had won 85.5% of the vote in the June 27 election. Shortly after the announcement, Mugabe was sworn in for another term.

Several international organizations that monitored the election, including the Southern African Development Community and the Pan-African Parliament, condemned Mugabe's reelection. The monitors declared the voting had been so unfair that the results could not be trusted. Many African leaders insisted at that time that Mugabe enter into talks with opposition leaders to relinquish some of the total control of the Zimbabwean government that he had exercised for twenty-eight years.

Agreed to Potential Power-Broking Deal

In response to international criticism, negotiations between Mugabe and Tsvangirai and mediated by President Thabo Mbeki of South Africa began in July of 2008. In September Mugabe signed an agreement with Tsvangirai to share responsibilities for running Zimbabwe. It was unclear how the power-sharing agreement would work, although at that time Mugabe was introduced as president and Tsvangirai as prime minister of the country. Within days, however, the deal faltered as Mugabe insisted on retaining control of the police and security forces, as well as other crucial ministries—finance, foreign affairs, information, mines, land, agriculture, and justice.

In early October of 2008 Mugabe announced that the ZANU would retain control of crucial ministries, including those that control both the military and the police force, whereas control of the finance ministry was still unresolved. Opposition leaders declared they would not join a government formed under such circumstances.

In late October Botswana's president Seretse Khama put pressure on other African leaders to call for a new election in Zimbabwe if the power-sharing deal remained at an impasse. Mediators referred stalled negotiations to the Southern African Development Community. By November of 2008 the situation was not yet resolved. Human rights groups suggested that Mugabe and his supporters might be jeopardizing the talks, fearing that they would face human rights trials should they allow the opposition to take part in government.

Sources

Books

Legum, Colin, ed., *Africa Contemporary Record: Annual Survey and Documents, 1980–1981*, Africana, 1981, p. B922.

Nelson, Harold D., ed., *Zimbabwe: A Country Study*, American University, 1983.

Rasmussen, R. Kent, *Historical Dictionary of Rhodesia/Zimbabwe*, Scarecrow Press, 1979.

Smith, David, and Colin Simpson, *Mugabe*, Sphere, 1981.

Periodicals

Africa News Service, May 20, 2004; September 4, 2004; December 9, 2004; December 16, 2004; December 30, 2004; December 31, 2004.

Africa Report, May–June 1981, p. 62; January–February 1985, p. 61; March–April 1988, p. 66; July–August 1988, p. 41; May–June 1989, p. 41; January–February 1990, p. 36; November–December 1991, p. 56; July–August 1993, p. 64; July–August 1993, p. 66.

Asia Africa Intelligence Wire, October 29, 2002.

Associated Press, October 31, 2008.

BBC News, March 19, 2007; August 31, 2007; January 26, 2008; April 6, 2008; June 22, 2008; June 30, 2008; September 15, 2008; October 28, 2008; October 31, 2008.

Catholic Insight, September 2005.

Daily Telegraph, September 26, 2006.

Economist, February 15, 1992, p. 47; June 13, 1992, p. 46; November 27, 2004, p. 48.

Guardian, April 3, 2005, November 8, 2005.

International Herald Tribune, November 14, 2005.

New Republic, January 31, 1983, p. 18.

New Statesman, June 5, 1992, p. 26.

Newsweek, December 5, 2005.

New York Times, February 20, 1980, p. 7; April 18, 1980, p. 1; February 14, 1980, p. 4; July 7, 1985, p. 1, Sec. 4, p. 3; January 28, 1992, p. 17; August 22, 1993, p. 5; September 29, 2003; November 10, 2003; May 3, 2008; September 15, 2008; October 1, 2008; September 18, 2008; September 22, 2008; October 11, 2008; October 20, 2008; October 28, 2008.

Reuters, February 15, 2008; June 14, 2008.

Time, March 17, 1980, p. 43.

Times (London), May 17, 2008.

Online

"Timeline: Zimbabwe," BBC News, http://news.bbc.co.uk/2/hi/africa/country_profiles/1831470.stm (accessed November 6, 2008).

Winter, Joseph, "Robert Mugabe: The Survivor," BBC News, http://news.bbc.co.uk/2/hi/africa/3017678.stm (accessed November 6, 2008).

—Gillian Wolf and Melissa Doak

Cynthia Nance

1958—

Lawyer, educator, college dean

Cynthia Nance is a widely respected lawyer and legal scholar who became dean of the School of Law at the University of Arkansas (UA) in 2006. Nance was the first African-American woman to become dean of a school or college in the history of the university. She was also the first woman and the first African American to be named head of the law school.

Cynthia Eleanor Nance, often known as Cyndi, was born September 3, 1958, in Chicago, Illinois. The first member of her family to attend college, Nance worked in management for the Ace Hardware Corporation while majoring in economics at Chicago State University. She graduated in 1986, earning a bachelor's degree with high honors. Despite a longtime interest in law, Nance hesitated to attend law school because, as she told an unnamed interviewer in the *Iowa Advocate* in 2007, "the thought of going back to school and being broke wasn't appealing to me." The persuasive recruiting efforts of Dennis Shields, then the law-school admissions director for the University of Iowa, convinced her otherwise, however. Once in Iowa, she studied for two degrees simultaneously, earning both a master's degree in finance and a law degree in 1990. It was at this time that Nance began intensive work in what have since become her specialties of employment law and labor law. Following her admission to the Iowa bar, she taught at both the law school, where she served as a faculty fellow, and at the university's Labor Center, a division of its continuing education program. According to its Web site, the Labor Center "annually reaches over 3,000 Iowa union leaders with a wide range of non-credit educational programs in the areas of practical industrial relations, labor law, labor history, communication, leadership, and citizenship skills."

In 1994 Nance moved from Iowa to the University of Arkansas, where she accepted a position as an assistant professor in the School of Law. Among the courses she taught were classes in Labor Law, Workplace Legislation, Employment Law, Torts [wrongful acts or injuries], and Worker's Compensation. Her reputation grew steadily throughout this period, as she published papers in legal journals, spoke at international conferences, and served, often as chair, on a number of boards and councils for legal professionals, including the Employment Law and Labor & Employment Law sections of the American Association of Law Schools. Visible in all of these activities, according to acquaintances, was a profound concern for her students, her colleagues, and the university. In a letter posted on the University Provost's Web site on the occasion of Nance's promotion to dean in 2006, for example, former student Caroline L. Curry wrote of Nance, "I know of no one else who has loved our institution and served it so well."

In August of 2005, Richard B. Atkinson, longtime dean of the law school, died. While Professor Howard W. Brill served as an interim replacement, a nationwide search was launched for a permanent successor. In the end, however, it was Nance, an internal candidate, who won the job in the spring of 2006. According to a press release issued by the university on May 23, 2006, "Professor Nance was the unanimous choice of the Law School faculty, Chancellor [John] White and Pro-

At a Glance . . .

Born Cynthia Eleanor Nance on September 3, 1958, in Chicago, IL; daughter of Eual Dean and Fern Elizabeth Nance. *Religion:* Evangelical Lutheran. *Education:* Chicago State University, BS, economics, 1986; University of Iowa, MA, finance, 1990, JD, 1990.

Career: University of Iowa Labor Center, labor educator, c.1990–94; University of Iowa Law School, faculty fellow, c.1990–94; University of Arkansas School of Law, associate professor, 1994–2006, dean, 2006—.

Memberships: Alpha Kappa Alpha; American Association of Law Schools; American Bar Association; Arkansas Association of Women Lawyers; Arkansas Bar Association; Law School Admissions Council, board member; Lutheran Immigration and Refugee Service, board member; National Association for Law Placement Foundation for Law Career Research and Education, board member; National Bar Association; Phi Delta Phi; W. B. Putman American Inn of Court.

Awards: Faculty Distinguished Achievement Award for Public Service, University of Arkansas Alumni Association, 2004; Outstanding Lawyer-Citizen, Arkansas Bar Association, 2005; NIA Professional Achievement Award, Northwest Arkansas Minority Awards Committee, 2006; Arthur A. Fletcher Lifetime Achievement Award, American Association for Affirmative Action, 2007.

Addresses: *Office*—c/o University of Arkansas, School of Law, Fayetteville, AR 72701; *E-mail*—cnance@uark.edu.

---

vost Bob Smith." Her initial two-year appointment has since been extended.

In and interview in the journal *Diverse Issues in Higher Education* (*DIHE*), Nance outlined her philosophy as an administrator. Asked whether a dean "can really impact the direction of a law school," she answered in the affirmative, remarking, "I think the faculty wants leadership. They want someone to help them get the institution to a new level. And so I really do think that you can [have an impact], particularly if you are willing to say, 'I don't know everything, and I'm willing to listen to you, and let's do this together.'" Among other initiatives, Nance has worked to improve the ethnic, racial, and economic diversity of the student body, noting in a "Message from the Dean" on the school's Web site, "We have made significant progress in attracting one of the most diverse student bodies in American legal education, while significantly improving the academic profiles of our entering classes." While her presence as an African-American woman has undoubtedly helped attract minority students to the school, Nance has modestly downplayed her own trailblazing role, emphasizing instead her efforts to convince all students of the benefits diversity holds for them. As she pointed out in *DIHE*, "If you haven't interacted with people who are not like you, you are at a disadvantage when you get out into your professional life."

Nance has also brought to the law school a new emphasis on public service, an area she has stressed in her own life as well. Nance was a board member of the Lutheran Immigration and Refugee Service (LIRS), an organization that has facilitated the resettlement of nearly 350,000 refugees since 1939. As part of her work for LIRS, Nance once traveled to Mexico to investigate conditions in shelters for women and youth. Such activities have brought her a number of public-service awards, notably a Faculty Distinguished Achievement Award for Public Service from the University of Arkansas Alumni Association in 2004 and recognition as an "Outstanding Lawyer-Citizen" from the Arkansas Bar Association the following year.

Nance has also devoted much time to the Good Shepherd Lutheran Church of Fayetteville, Arkansas, teaching Sunday school and chairing several committees. In a 2008 article in the online edition of the *ABA Journal*, a publication of the American Bar Association, writer Debra Cassens Weiss noted that Nance sees her work as a lawyer and educator as an expression of her religious faith. "As lawyers, we're called to be a voice for those whose voices wouldn't be heard otherwise," Nance said in remarks quoted by Weiss that first appeared in *The Lutheran* magazine. "I hope that I've been able to blend my legal knowledge with what I believe I'm called to do as a person of faith."

Sources

Periodicals

All Things Academic (University of Arkansas), September 2006.
Diverse Issues in Higher Education, July 12, 2007.
Iowa Advocate, Winter 2007.
The Lutheran, May 2008.

Online

Curry, Caroline L., personal communication to University Provost Bob Smith [posted by permission], May

23, 2006, http://libinfo.uark.edu/ata/v7no3/Chronolog050106083106.pdf (accessed October 30, 2008).

"Cyndi Nance," University of Arkansas School of Law, http://law.uark.edu/cyndi_nance.php (accessed October 30, 2008).

"History," University of Iowa Labor Center, http://www.continuetolearn.uiowa.edu/laborctr/html/about.html (accessed October 30, 2008).

"Nance Named New Dean of UA School of Law," University of Arkansas Daily Headlines, May 23, 2006, http://dailyheadlines.uark.edu/8800.htm (accessed October 30, 2008).

Weiss, Debra Cassens, "Arkansas Law Dean Wants to be Known as Lawyer of Faith," *ABA Journal,* May 1, 2008, http://www.abajournal.com/news/arkansas_law_dean_wants_to_be_known_as_lawyer_of_faith (accessed October 30, 2008).

—R. Anthony Kugler

Sonny Okosuns

1947–2008

Musician, minister

Nigerian singer-songwriter Sonny Okosuns was a pioneer of African liberation music, the songs of social protest that gave voice to native political movements on the continent. His work influenced a generation of musicians, both in Africa and around the world. Douglas Martin described Okosuns's style in the *New York Times* as "a catchy, rock-inflected cocktail of funk, reggae, Afrobeat and more…. The result was a zestful, funky strand in what has come to be called world music." At the time of his death in 2008 Okosuns was working on material for what would have been his fortieth album.

Okosuns's family name was originally "Okosun"—he later added the "s" himself. He was born on the first day of 1947 in Benin City, Nigeria, into a family of Esan ethnicity. The Esan, sometimes referred to as "Ishan" in the West, were one of the larger groups in Edo State, in which Benin City served as the provincial capital. Okosuns childhood was a time of extreme poverty, he told the writer Ogbonna Amadi in an Africa News Service interview. "We ate rice four times a year. Whenever my father collected his salary and he is not owing anybody, we ate rice. At Christmas, we ate rice and the final rice we'd eat will be in the new year."

Okosuns's parents belonged to a Pentecostal Christian sect called the Eternal Sacred Order of the Cherubim and Seraphim Church, which had been founded during the 1920s by Moses Orimolade Tunolase, later called Baba Aladura. Okosuns's family later moved to Enugu, also known as Coal City because it was the center of Nigeria's coal-mining industry, and his formal schooling ended after just a few years. A fan of Western rock music, he taught himself to play the guitar and learned the songs of Elvis Presley and the Beatles. In 1965, at age eighteen, Okosuns joined the Eastern Nigerian Theatre, a drama troupe that was invited to perform at the Commonwealth Arts Festival in London in the summer of 1965. Back in Nigeria, he formed a cover band called the Postmen, and after 1969 performed regularly with Victor Uwaifo, a popular Nigerian singer-songwriter a few years his senior. Uwaifo was a pioneer in a style of music known by the interchangeable terms "highlife" or *joromi* and described in the *Guardian* by Graeme Ewens as a "hugely popular form of west African dance music characterised by blazing horns and complex, interweaving guitar melodies."

Okosuns's second band, founded in 1972, was originally called Paperback Ltd. but he soon changed the name to Ozziddi, which meant "message" in the Igbo language. Ozziddi's exuberant highlife sounds were bolstered by infusions of reggae, the West Indian music that was also a form of social protest. Okosuns sang in Esan, Igbo, Hausa, and Yoruba. He recorded most of his thirty-nine albums in Nigeria, which had a thriving musical scene during the 1960s before a devastating civil war and series of military coups. He attained immense fame, and "Ozzidism, as it came to be known, evolved into a personal pan-African philosophy of liberation," wrote Ewens. In 1981 he gave a concert in London—where his 1977 LP, *Ozziddi for Sale,* had been recorded the famed Abbey Road studios of the EMI label—and among the attendees was Sally Mugabe, wife of Zimbabwean leader Robert Mugabe.

At a Glance . . .

Born Francis Sonny Okosun, on January 1, 1947, in Benin City, Nigeria; died on May 24, 2008, in Washington, DC; married several times; children: Sydney, Michael, Ebony, Adesuwa, and others. *Religion:* Evangelical Christian.

Career: Actor and performer with the Eastern Nigerian Theatre after 1965; formed first band, the Postmen, 1966; after 1969 performed with Victor Uwaifo; formed the band Paperback Ltd., 1972, and later renamed it Ozziddi; recorded gospel albums in the 1990s under the name "Evangelist Sunny Okosuns"; founded the House of Prayer Ministries, 1998.

As a result, Okosuns was invited to perform at Zimbabwe's first anniversary independence celebrations in Harare, the capital of what had until recently been the white-controlled enclave called Rhodesia.

Liberation music—and Okosuns's—was already focused on South Africa, the remaining holdout of white power on the African continent. His 1977 song "Fire in Soweto" was a blistering attack on apartheid, South Africa's system of segregation, and though it was banned by the government there it nevertheless became a massive underground hit in black townships. Another track from that same year, "Papa's Land," also reflected the dire situation for blacks in South Africa. Other songs he recorded paid homage to Nelson Mandela, the jailed South African leader of African National Congress.

Holy Wars, released in 1978, featured protest songs from Okosuns that reflected the wider struggle for independence across all of southern Africa, including Mozambique. In 1985 he took part in a benefit record along with several well-known musical stars in the West—among them Run-D.M.C., Bob Dylan, Bruce Springsteen, and Miles Davis—under the collective name Artists United Against Apartheid. The song, "Sun City," referred to an infamous luxury resort that catered to white South Africans but was located in a nominally independent black homeland.

With the end of apartheid in the early 1990s, liberation music's popularity died out, and Okosuns's record sales—which rarely reflected his success anyway, because pirated music was so rampant across Africa at the time—began to flag. He turned to Christianity in 1993, billing himself anew as "Evangelist Sunny Okosuns," and began releasing gospel albums. *Songs of Praise,* from 1994, reportedly sold 500,000 copies in Nigeria and other countries. In 1998 he founded his own church, the House of Prayer Ministries, out of his home in Lagos, Nigeria's largest city. He had several wives and many more children, and some of the young people who came to stay at his home legally took his surname. One of his legitimate daughters graduated from Pace University in the New York City area in May of 2008, and Okosuns traveled there for the commencement ceremony. Already ill from colon cancer, his health took a turn for the worse, and he died on May 24, 2008, at Howard University Hospital in Washington, DC. He was eulogized in both the Western media and back in Nigeria. Nseobong Okon-Ekong of the Africa News Service wrote of the worldwide appeal of Okosuns and his music, noting that "to his people in Edo State, he was a worthy son who unashamedly borrowed from the common local culture, propagating their folk tales and proverbs to a wider audience. To Nigerians, he tried to cut the image of an all-Nigerian personality who cared for the greater good."

Selected works

Albums

Ozidizm, Capitol/EMI Nigeria, 1976.
Living Music, Capitol/EMI Nigeria, 1977.
Ozziddi for Sale, Capitol/EMI Nigeria, 1977.
Papa's Land, EMI Nigeria, 1977.
Holy Wars, EMI Nigeria, 1978.
Sonny Okosun in 1980, EMI Nigeria, 1980.
Live in Varadero, EMI Nigeria, 1982.
Mother and Child, Oti, 1982.
Which Way Nigeria?, EMI Nigeria, 1984.
Revolution II, EMI Nigeria, 1985.
Africa Now or Never, EMI Nigeria, 1986.
Togetherness, Celluloid, 1990.
African Soldiers, Profile Records, 1991.
Songs of Praise, Ivory Music, 1994.
The Ultimate Collection, AVC Music, 1996.
Celebrate! & Worship in Caribbean Rhythms, God's Glory Records, 2000.
Be Glorified, God's Glory Records, 2001.
The Glory of God, Ivory Music, 2002.

Sources

Periodicals

Africa News Service, May 26, 2008; June 2, 2008; June 9, 2008.
Guardian (London), August 4, 2008. p. 30.
New York Times, August 28, 1985; June 25, 2008, p. A21.

—Carol Brennan

Will Packer

1974(?)—

Film producer, screenwriter

Packer, Will, photograph. Maury Phillips/WireImage.

Atlanta-based film producer Will Packer scored a surprise hit with the 2007 step-dance drama *Stomp the Yard.* Its box-office success prompted the industry trade journal *Daily Variety* to place Packer on their "Ten Producers to Watch" list. Packer asserted that his company, Rainforest Films, was merely putting out the kind of movies that the market demanded. "You've got this whole upwardly mobile, affluent African-American portrayals on-screen. It's higher concept with intelligent story lines," he told Bob Longino in the *Atlanta Journal-Constitution.* "People are embracing it."

Packer graduated from St. Petersburg High School in Florida in 1991 and went on to study engineering at Florida A&M University, a historically black school in Tallahassee. He pledged the same Alpha Phi Alpha fraternity to which his father, William Sr., had belonged, and later noted that it had enriched his college experience. "They had a great community service program, they gave out a lot of scholarships, they had the best parties," he said in an interview with Dalia Wheatt in the *St. Petersburg Times.* In 1994 Packer and his fraternity brother Rob Hardy set up Rainforest Films, a film production company. Their first project was *Chocolate City,* a story about a young man at Florida A&M, which Hardy directed and Packer produced.

Signed with Sony Pictures

After graduating in 1996, Packer and Hardy moved to Atlanta and opened Rainforest offices there. Their next project was *Trois,* a racy tale about a romantic triangle from a screenplay they wrote themselves. Shot on a budget of just $250,000, *Trois* (2000) benefited from Packer and Hardy's innovative idea to work outside the standard film distribution channels—they personally visited theater owners in predominantly African-American communities and convinced them to take a chance on showing it. In the end, *Trois* earned $1 million in box-office receipts, and netted Rainforest a financing and distribution deal with the Screen Gems unite of Sony Pictures.

Packer served as producer for two sequels to *Trois*: *Pandora's Box* in 2002 and *Trois 3: The Escort. Motives* (2004) was another erotic thriller that starred

At a Glance . . .

Born c. 1974, in St. Petersburg, FL; son of William Sr. and Birice (a community-service volunteer) Packer; married Nina; children: two daughters. *Education:* Florida A&M University, BS, electrical engineering, 1996.

Career: Film producer. Projects include: *Chocolate City,* 1994; *Trois,* 2000; *Pandora's Box,* 2002; *Motives,* 2004; *Trois 3: The Escort,* 2004; *The Gospel,* 2005; *Puff, Puff, Pass,* 2006; *Stomp the Yard,* 2007; *This Christmas,* 2007; *Obsessed,* 2009; *Bone Deep,* 2009.

Addresses: *Home*—Conyers, GA. *Office*—Rainforest Films, 2141 Powers Ferry Rd., Ste. 300, Marietta, GA 30067.

Shemar Moore and Vivica A. Fox. The first film to be released with the help of Screen Gems was *The Gospel* (2005), which starred Boris Kodjoe and Idris Elba. Kodjoe played a major-label R&B star, David, who returns to the Atlanta area and reconnects with Frank (Elba), who has taken over the pastorship of the church where both sang as young choir members. "This is a project we wanted to do for a long time but we got pigeonholed in the erotic thriller genre," Packer told Steve Persall in the *St. Petersburg Times.* "But that's okay because that gave us a chance to learn and understand our core demo(graphics), and to understand grass roots marketing." With music for the film written by gospel great Kirk Franklin, *The Gospel* was shot on a budget of $3 million and earned $8 million at the box office in the first week alone. Packer's mother, active in her St. Petersburg–area church, was thrilled to finally be able to show her friends and fellow churchgoers what her son was doing with his life. "This was an answer to my prayer, that he'd do something in praise and honor of the Lord," Birice Packer told Persall. "When I cry, it's tears of joy because he did what his mother asked him to do."

Packer's next project, a drug-themed comedy called *Puff, Puff, Pass* (2006), served as actor Mekhi Phifer's directorial debut. Rainforest next collaborated with Screen Gems on *Stomp the Yard,* a college musical set in Atlanta. Released in January of 2007—traditionally the dead-zone period for movie premieres—the movie earned $25 million at the box office in its opening weekend. Packer and Hardy had originally wanted to make a movie similar to *Chocolate City,* but used step-dancing as a hook to lure financing. "Stepping was the perfect vehicle because it is so visually attractive," Packer told Wheatt. "I felt like we would get them in the door with something that was really, really cool like stepping, but then once there, we were able to slide in some nuggets about black college life and about fraternities and sororities and about the importance of higher education."

Succeeded with Stomp the Yard

Stomp the Yard stars Columbus Short as DJ, a Los Angeles–area step dancer whose crew becomes embroiled in a rivalry that turns violent and leaves DJ's younger brother dead. Sent to live with his uncle in Atlanta, DJ enrolls in a historically black college, where he finds that the step-dancing scene is dominated by the school's intensely competitive black fraternities. He joins the underdog group, and "from there," wrote Justin Chang in *Daily Variety,* "the story's trajectory could hardly be more predictable—DJ must get schooled, get hazed and, of course, get the girl and the trophy, while dealing with his repressed grief and learning the meaning of teamwork." Despite the lack of critical plaudits, *Stomp the Yard* nevertheless proved such a financial windfall that it brought Packer serious recognition in Hollywood, and later that year he was named one of "Ten Producers to Watch" by *Daily Variety.*

Packer's next project for Rainforest was a family-oriented holiday drama, *This Christmas,* released near the end of 2007. Filmed in Los Angeles, the movie starred some well-known actors, including the aforementioned Elba and Phifer along with Delroy Lindo, Loretta Devine, and Regina King. "It was great because everybody came to work with such a drive, focus and energy that was contagious," Packer told Sarah Hoye in the *Tampa Tribune* about working with such screen veterans. "It was really like a family, and like a family, there is crying and drama, but if you believe in family and have faith in faith, it's all good at the end of the day." The story centers on the grown children who return to the home of Ma'Dere (Devine)—who attempts to hide the fact that she and Joe (Lindo) are living together—and the dilemma over whether or not to sell the family's dry-cleaning business. All of the children, it turns out, have their own secrets. Critics gave *This Christmas* a warmer reception than Packer's previous efforts, with Lael Loewenstein in *Variety* calling it "a rare holiday treat, a package that's both thoughtfully selected and sure to please its intended recipients."

Packer's subsequent projects include *Obsessed,* featuring Beyoncé Knowles as the victim of a stalker, and the basketball drama *Phenom.* Rainforest was also working on an all-black remake of the popular 1984 movie *The Big Chill* and a biopic about Kemba Smith, a young woman who spent six years in prison on federal drug charges. All of the productions kept him often away from his home in Conyers, Georgia, which he shares with wife, Nina, and their two daughters. Making time for everything he wanted to do was a problem,

Packer conceded to Longino. "I always know I could be doing a better job with the balance. It tilts both ways. I get all the big-picture stuff—the PTAs, the programs the girls are in. I don't miss any of that. It's the little stuff. Like, 'She scraped her knee.'"

Selected writings

Screenplays

Trois, 2000.
Pandora's Box, 2002.

Sources

Periodicals

Atlanta Journal-Constitution, November 18, 2007, p. K12.
Daily Variety, January 8, 2007, p.11.
Film Journal International, March 2007, p. 41; December 2007, p. 68.
St. Petersburg Times (St. Petersburg, FL), October 14, 2005, p. E1; January 12, 2007, p. E1.
Tampa Tribune, November 23, 2007, p. 17.
Variety, October 10, 2005, p. 76; October 29, 2007, p. 51.

—Carol Brennan

Marjorie B. Parham

1918—

Publisher, editor

Marjorie B. Parham is a newspaper publisher who spent more than three decades at the helm of the *Cincinnati Herald,* a newspaper that served the city's African-American community. Parham took over as publisher and editor in 1963 after the unexpected death of her husband, the newspaper's founder, Gerald Porter. Though she had negligible experience in journalism, Parham worked overtime to ensure the *Herald* stayed on firm financial footing. "I did everything—edited, wrote, took pictures, did the payroll, balanced the books, sold ads, swept the floor," she told Jim Knippenberg in the *Cincinnati Enquirer* in 2005. "I worked weekends, holidays, late night. I didn't know what a 40-hour week was."

Born in 1918 in Clermont County, Ohio, Parham graduated from Batavia High School and went on to Wilberforce University, a historically black college in Ohio. She later took classes at the University of Cincinnati, but as she explained to Knippenberg, "when a black girl graduated high school in 1935, she had to be a teacher, a nurse or a social worker. I didn't want any part of that. I wanted a business career. That's why I never graduated from college. I was getting pushed away from what I wanted to do."

Parham's marriage to William Spillers produced a son, but she was single again by 1946 and took a job as a clerk with the U.S. Veterans Administration in Cincinnati. In 1954 she wed Gerald Porter, who a year later founded the *Cincinnati Herald,* a weekly newspaper aimed at an African-American readership in the city. The *Herald* was not the first black-owned newspaper in Cincinnati, but took the place of the *Union,* which had shut down in the early 1950s. In 1961 Porter launched a sister publication, the *Dayton Tribune.*

Parham retired from the Veterans Administration in 1961 to take over the *Dayton Tribune,* which her son had been running until he was drafted by the U.S. military. Her husband died in an automobile accident two years later. "He was taken to a hospital on (Cincinnati's) east side, and they refused to treat him," Parham recalled in the *Cincinnati Enquirer.* "The nurse's exact words were, 'We don't accommodate Negro bed patients.' Do you believe that? She wasn't even subtle about it." Despite her loss, Parham did not want to see her late husband's efforts die with him, and she decided to take over the business. Her son received an early release from military service and returned home to help her run the papers. A family friend, Hartwell Parham, provided business and editorial advice, and he later became Parham's third husband.

Parham eventually shut down the Dayton paper, but as publisher of the *Herald* she continually sought new sources of revenue. She traveled to New York City and called at the offices of major advertising agencies in order to secure lucrative national ads, and also reached out to local businesses and readers by making the *Herald*'s classified advertising section a convenient place for buyers and sellers. On the editorial side, she strove to make the paper a must-read. "We had a slogan at the *Herald,* 'Know the truth,'" she told a gathering of the Cincinnati Chamber of Commerce in 2007. "We tried to get to the bottom of things and report them as they really were."

At a Glance . . .

Born in Clermont County, OH, in 1918; married William Spillers (marriage ended 1946); married Gerald Porter (a newspaper publisher; died 1963), 1954; married Hartwell Parham (died 1981); children: William M. Spillers Jr. *Education:* Attended Wilberforce University and the University of Cincinnati.

Career: Clerk with the U.S. Veterans Administration, 1946–61; *Dayton Tribune*, publisher, 1961–63; *Cincinnati Herald*, president and publisher, 1963–96, became publisher emerita, 1996. Trustee, University of Cincinnati, after 1982; National Afro-American Museum and Cultural Center, board chair.

Memberships: National Newspaper Publishers Association (former treasurer; trustee); Greater Cincinnati Urban League.

Awards: Community Service Media Award, National Conference of Christians and Jews, 1977; Trailblazer Award, National Association of Black Journalists, 1993; inducted into the Ohio Women's Hall of Fame, 1994; named Great Living Cincinnatian, Cincinnati Chamber of Commerce, 2007.

Addresses: *Office*—c/o Cincinnati Herald, 354 Hearne Ave., Cincinnati, OH 45229.

Parham became a respected figure in the greater Cincinnati community through both her newspaper work and her involvement in numerous civic organizations. In 1982 she became the second African American ever to serve as a trustee of the University of Cincinnati, and also chaired the board of the National Afro-American Museum and Cultural Center in Wilberforce, Ohio. She was also active in the Urban League, the American Red Cross, and scouting groups. Hartwell Parham died in 1981.

In 1993 Parham retired from day-to-day operations, with her son taking over her duties as publisher and president. In 1996 they sold the *Herald* to Sesh Communications, a local company that published a Cincinnati guide and magazine. Parham still retained the title "publisher emerita" on the masthead of the *Herald*, and occasionally made collection calls to advertisers late on their invoices on behalf of the trio of young African-American professionals now running the paper.

In 2007 Parham was honored as a "Great Living Cincinnatian" by the Cincinnati Regional Chamber of Commerce. She spoke at the award ceremony, reflecting back on her unexpected, thirty-three-year career as a newspaper publisher. "One reason why a black paper has been so vital is that, without it, the only kind of news we could get in the newspaper was bad news," she told the gathering. "The satisfaction you get is the ability to present what the major media does not present to the public. I had the privilege of showcasing the good things."

Sources

Periodicals

Cincinnati Enquirer, March 15, 2005, p. E1.
Cincinnati Post, June 24, 1999, p. 16A.
Kentucky Post (Covington, KY), December 16, 2006, p. A2; February 23, 2007, p. A3.

Online

"Cincinnati Herald," Cincinnati Historical Society Library, http://library.cincymuseum.org/aag/history/herald.html (accessed October 11, 2008).
"Great Living Cincinnatians," Cincinnati Chamber of Commerce, http://www.cincinnatichamber.com/cham_a.aspx?menu_id=144&id=2100 (accessed October 11, 2008).

—Carol Brennan

Paul Pierce

1977—

Professional basketball player

Paul Pierce is a professional basketball player best known for leading his team, the Boston Celtics, to victory in the 2008 National Basketball Association (NBA) championship series. He has also garnered attention for his charitable work with underprivileged children and for his remarkable recovery following a near-fatal stabbing in September of 2000.

Born on October 13, 1977, in Oakland, California, Paul Anthony Pierce moved with his mother, Lorraine Hosey, and two half brothers to Inglewood, a predominately African-American neighborhood in Los Angeles, California, about 1989. When his brothers, both older, left home, Pierce found companionship on the basketball courts of Inglewood's Rogers Park Community Center. An important early mentor was Scott Collins, a police officer and assistant basketball coach at Inglewood High School, who allowed Pierce and several of his friends to practice on the school's court every morning before classes began. Pierce would later credit these early-morning sessions with developing his character, particularly his work ethic. A standout star on the school's basketball team in his junior and senior years, he won an athletic scholarship to the University of Kansas (UK), which he entered in the fall of 1995.

Pierce, Paul, photograph. Gabriel Bouys/AFP/Getty Images.

Pierce's impact on the UK basketball team was immediate. In his first year (1995–96), he started in thirty-three out of thirty-four games, averaging nearly twelve points each time. Cowinner of Freshman of the Year honors from the Big Eight Conference, Pierce's performance only improved over the course of the next two seasons. In his junior year (1997–98), for example, he averaged more than twenty points per game and was named a first-team All American by the Associated Press. These achievements brought him to the attention of NBA scouts, and the Boston Celtics selected him as their first-round choice, and the tenth pick overall, in the 1998 NBA draft. After the draft Pierce decided to skip his senior year at Kansas; as of 2008 his undergraduate degree in crime and delinquency studies remained unfinished.

When he joined the team, the Boston Celtics were a struggling franchise with a rich history. Though the Celtics remained the most successful team in the league's history, with sixteen titles to their credit, their last championship season had been in 1985–86, a

At a Glance . . .

Born Paul Anthony Pierce on October 13, 1977, in Oakland, CA; son of Lorraine Hosey. *Education:* Majored in crime and delinquency studies at the University of Kansas, 1995–98.

Career: Boston Celtics, guard/forward, 1998—, cocaptain, 2000–03, captain, 2003—.

Awards: Freshman of the Year (cowinner), Big Eight Conference, 1995–96; First-Team All American, Associated Press, 1997–98; Rookie of the Month, 1999 and Player of the Month, 2001, both from the National Basketball Association; Home Team Community Service Award, 2002; named to Eastern Conference All-Star Team, 2002–06 and 2008; named Player of the Game (twice) and Most Valuable Player, NBA Championship Series, 2008, all National Basketball Association.

Addresses: *Office*—c/o Boston Celtics, 226 Causeway St., 4th Fl., Boston, MA 02114.

---

dozen years earlier. Though Pierce quickly established himself as a key contributor, averaging more than sixteen points and six rebounds per game in his rookie year (1998–99), the team continued to struggle, winning only nineteen of fifty games during that strike-shortened season. Though the team's record, and Pierce's personal statistics, improved over the next three seasons, an unsettling incident occurred in the fall of 2000, when he was the victim of a brutal stabbing in a Boston nightclub. In the early-morning hours of September 25, three men attacked Pierce from behind, striking him on the face with a broken bottle and stabbing him eleven times with a knife. While most of the wounds were superficial, one penetrated six inches into his chest and within a quarter inch of his heart. Pierce was lucky to receive medical attention within minutes. Even so, the speed of his recovery was extraordinary. After surgery to repair a partially collapsed lung, Pierce was out of the hospital and practicing with his teammates within three weeks.

The circumstances surrounding Pierce's assault remain unclear. In an article that appeared in *The Sporting News* in December of 2000, Michael Silverman wrote that the incident was "believed to be related to an incident from the night before, reportedly when Pierce said or did something to a mutual female acquaintance that sparked some jealous feeling." Pierce himself soon put the attack behind him, telling Silverman, "I don't think about the negative things that happened to me because basketball is my life right now."

After another disappointing season (36 wins, 46 losses) for the Celtics in 2000–01, the following year proved a turning point for the team, which reached the playoffs for the first time since 1995, and for Pierce himself, who was named to the Eastern Conference Team for the NBA All-Star Game. That honor would be repeated five times in the next six years (2003, 2004, 2005, 2006, and 2008). He was also selected to play for the United States in the 2002 World Championships in Indianapolis, Indiana.

A cocaptain of the Celtics since 2000, Pierce became sole captain in 2003. Under his leadership, the team returned several times to the playoffs. In 2006–07, however, the Celtics stumbled badly, finishing the season with one of the worst records (24 wins, 58 losses) in franchise history. Pierce's frustration was apparent. "I'm the classic case of a great player on a bad team, and it stinks," he remarked in comments quoted a year later by Billy Witz in the *New York Times*. Boston's fortunes improved immediately, however, following General Manager Danny Ainge's astute off-season acquisition of two veteran players, Ray Allen (formerly of the Seattle SuperSonics) and Kevin Garnett (formerly of the Minnesota Timberwolves), whose playing styles meshed well with Pierce's. "They like each other," Celtics head coach Doc Rivers told David DuPree in*USA Today* in November of 2007. "They've all decided that they don't need anything individually and it is all about what's best for the team." In a surprisingly fast turnaround, the team finished the 2007–08 season with the best record in the league (66 wins, 16 losses) and went on to win the championship title in a six-game series with the Los Angeles Lakers. Pierce was named Player of the Game in the first and fourth games and Most Valuable Player in the series as a whole.

As of 2008 Pierce had revealed few of his plans for retirement. He has said several times that he finds satisfaction in working with underprivileged children, an activity he pursues through a charitable organization, The Truth Fund, he founded in May of 2002. According to its Web site, "The mission of The Truth Fund is to provide educational and life-enriching opportunities for underprivileged youth by offering resources and programs that foster safe and stable environments." As a result of The Truth Fund's work in Inglewood and Boston, Pierce received the NBA's Home Team Community Service Award in 2002.

Sources

Periodicals

New York Times, June 1, 2008; June 10, 2008.
Sporting News, December 4, 2000.
Time, February 25, 2008.
USA Today, November 13, 2007.

Online

"Celtics History: Season Recaps—2000s," National Basketball Association, http://www.nba.com/celtics/history/Recap_2000s.html (accessed October 31, 2008).

"Paul Pierce Bio Page," National Basketball Association, http://www.nba.com/playerfile/paul_pierce/bio.html (accessed October 31, 2008).

"The Truth Fund," Paul Pierce Official Fan Club, http://www.paulpierce.net/go.cfm?do=Page.View&pid=17 (accessed October 31, 2008).

—R. Anthony Kugler

Adrian Piper

1948—

Artist, philosopher

Adrian Piper is an artist and academic who has been in the vanguard of several significant movements in contemporary art since beginning her career in the late 1960s. Piper's works range from photographs that document her performance-art pieces to video installations that guide viewers into examining their own prejudices and preconceptions about women, African Americans, and human kinship. "I want my work to help people stop being racist whether they ask for it or not," she said in the *Winston-Salem Journal*. "Just as movies and encounter groups can change people, so, maybe, can my art."

Born in 1948 in New York City, Piper grew up in Harlem and attended a progressive, integrated private school. By the time she earned an associate degree from the School of Visual Arts in 1969 she had become associated with a circle of artists, musicians, and writers in downtown Manhattan's vibrant art scene whose daring exploits helped define the American cultural landscape for decades to come. One of her first jobs as was an assistant to conceptual artist Sol LeWitt, and while working toward her bachelor's degree at the City College of the City University of New York she began to hone her skills as a performance artist. This involved carefully staged and documented events, such as striding down New York City streets wearing a shirt covered in wet paint with a sign bearing the caution, "Wet Paint," or riding the subway while wearing clothes that she had soaked in a horrific mixture of raw egg, cod-liver oil, and vinegar. There was also the *Mythic Being,* an angry, swaggering black male—actually Piper wearing an Afro wig and mustache—that stalked the urban landscape. "In an era when some politicians and much of the popular press seemed to be stoking racial fear," noted Holland Cotter in the *New York Times,* "she was turning fear into farce—but serious, and disturbing, farce, intended to punch a hole in pervasive fictions while acknowledging their power."

Explored Racial Issues through Art

Piper earned a bachelor's degree in philosophy in 1974 and entered graduate school at Harvard University to pursue a master's in the subject. She completed her graduate degree in 1977 and studied at the University of Heidelberg, then returned to Harvard to begin doctoral studies. She was granted a doctorate in 1981. Her most notable performance project during this period was *Funk Lessons,* staged at the Walker Art Center in Minneapolis, the San Francisco Art Institute, and the California Institute of Art, among other places, over several months in 1983 and 1984. Tom Patterson, writing in the the *Winston-Salem Journal,* explained the piece as "a series of scholarly, participatory demonstrations in which she attempted to teach largely white audiences how to dance to funk music. These grew out of her observation that many whites seemed uncomfortable with the music's basis in black working-class culture, its references to sexual activity and its related body movements."

Piper was a light-skinned African-American female, and occasionally found herself in uncomfortable situa-

At a Glance...

Born Adrian Margaret Smith Piper on September 20, 1948, in New York, NY. *Education:* School of Visual Arts, AA, 1969; City College of the City University of New York, BA (summa cum laude), 1974; Harvard University, MA, 1977, PhD, 1981; also attended the University of Heidelberg, 1977–78.

Career: Assistant to artist Sol LeWitt, late 1960s; performance artist, 1968–88; video artist, 1988—; University of Michigan, assistant professor of philosophy, 1979–82, 1984–86; Stanford University, Mellon Research Fellow, 1982–84; Georgetown University, associate professor of philosophy, 1986–88; University of California—San Diego, associate professor of philosophy, 1988–90; Wellesley College, professor of philosophy, 1990–2008; Royal Danish Academy of Art, visiting guest professor, 2005–07; Adrian Piper Research Archive, director.

Memberships: American Association of University Professors, American Philosophical Association, American Society for Political and Legal Philosophy, Society for Philosophy and Public Affairs, North American Kant Society.

Awards: Fellowships from the National Endowment for the Humanities (1979, 1998), the National Endowment for the Arts (1979, 1982), the Guggenheim Foundation (1989), and the J. Paul Getty Foundation 1998–99. Skowhegan Medal for Sculptural Installation, Skowhegan School of Painting and Sculpture, 1995.

Addresses: *Home*—Berlin, Germany. *Office*—Adrian Piper Research Archive, Postfach 54 02 04, D-10042 Berlin, Germany. *Gallery*—Elizabeth Dee Gallery, 545 West 20th St., New York, NY 10011.

---

tions inside the New York art scene, which she turned into another performance piece in the late 1980s. This project was titled *My Calling (Card) #1: A Reactive Guerilla Performance for Dinners and Cocktail Parties* (1986–90). Its singular element was the printed card that Piper sometimes handed out, which read: "Dear Friend: I am black. I am sure you did not realize this when you made/laughed at/agreed with that racist remark. In the past I have attempted to alert white people to my racial identity in advance. Unfortunately, this invariably causes them to react to me as pushy, manipulative or socially inappropriate. I regret any discomfort my presence is causing you, just as I am sure you regret the discomfort your racism is causing me."

Many of Piper's pieces have been documented on video, dating all the way back to her *Mythic Being* project in 1973. Later in her career, she began to examine the "one-drop" theory of race, a discredited idea that a person with one drop of blood from an African ancestor was in fact classifiable as a black person. Piper's 1988 work *Cornered* addressed this idea. "Facing us through the camera, speaking with the soothing composure of a social worker or grief counselor, she said that, according to statistics, if we were white Americans, chances were very high that we carried at least some black blood," wrote Cotter in the *New York Times*. "That was the legacy of slavery. She knew we would be upset. She was sorry. But [it] was the truth."

Taught Philosophy at Leading Universities

Piper further explored the conundrum of race in America in her 1991 essay, "Passing for White, Passing for Black." In the first paragraph, she recounted her first social encounter at Harvard when she entered the graduate program in philosophy. "The most famous and highly respected member of the faculty observed me for awhile from a distance and then came forward," she wrote. "Without introduction preamble he said to me with a triumphant smirk, 'Miss Piper, you're about as black as I am.'" She recounted that she was at a loss for the proper response, feeling that the remark was so distasteful on so many levels. In the same essay she also related a pervasive sense of alienation from both the white and black worlds that had followed her throughout much of her life. "My family was one of the very last middle-class, light-skinned black families left in our Harlem neighborhood after most had fled to the suburbs," she wrote. "Visibly black working-class kids my age yanked my braids and called me 'pale-face.' Many of them thought I was white, and treated me accordingly."

Over the years Piper has held a number of teaching appointments at such schools as Stanford, Georgetown, and the University of Michigan. In 1990 she joined the faculty of Wellesley College in Massachusetts. With this post, Piper became the first tenured African-American female professor of philosophy in the United States, and for a time was one of just three black professors of philosophy in the nation. Her field of specialty is the work of eighteenth-century German theorist Immanuel Kant, but she has also taught courses that delve into the teachings of the *Bhagavad Gita* and other tenets of Eastern philosophy. After a two-year stint at the Royal Danish Academy of Art as visiting guest professor, however, Piper's position was terminated by Wellesley in 2008 when she refused to return to the United States because her name surfaced on the U.S. Transportation Security Administration's Suspicious Traveler Watch List.

Fluent in German, Piper lives in Berlin where she serves as director of the Adrian Piper Research Archive. On her official Web site is a "Dear Editor" letter in which she enjoins those who write about her not to describe her as "an African American artist. Please don't call me an African American philosopher.... Please don't call me an artist and philosopher who happens to be black and a woman...Please don't call me a philosopher and artist who happens to be African American and female." After dozens more variations on these descriptive terms, she concludes, "I write to inform you that I have earned the right to be called an artist. I have earned the right to be called a philosopher. I have earned the right to be called an artist and philosopher. I have earned the right to be called a philosopher and artist."

Selected works

Writings

Talking to Myself: The Ongoing Autobiography of an Art Object (in English and Italian), Marilena Bonomo, 1975.
Colored People, Bookworks, 1991.
Decide Who You Are, Paula Cooper Gallery, 1992.
Out of Order, Out of Sight, Volume I: *Selected Writings in Meta-Art, 1968–1992,* Volume II: *Selected Writings in Art Criticism,* 1967–1992, MIT Press, 1996.

Solo exhibitions

One Man (sic), One Work, New York Cultural Center, New York City, 1971.
Adrian Piper, Gallery One, Montclair State College, Montclair, NJ, 1976.
Adrian Piper at Matrix 56, Wadsworth Atheneum, Hartford, CT, 1980.
Adrian Piper: Reflections 1967–1987, Alternative Museum, New York (retrospective), 1987.
Out of the Corner, Whitney Museum of American Art, Film and Video Gallery, New York, 1990.
Space, Time and Reference 1967–1970, John Weber Gallery, New York, 1992.
Decide Who You Are, Grey Art Gallery, New York, 1992.
Installations by Adrian Piper, New Langton Arts, San Francisco, 1993.
Cornered/Decide Who You Are, SUNY Buffalo, New York, 1994.
Ashes to Ashes, John Weber Gallery, New York, 1995.
Who Are You? Selected Works by Adrian Piper, Davis Museum and Cultural Center, Wellesley College, Wellesley, MA, 1997.
Adrian Piper: A Retrospective 1965–2000, Fine Arts Gallery, University of Maryland Baltimore County, Baltimore, 1998.
MEDI(t)Ations: Adrian Piper's Videos, Installations, Performances and Soundworks, 1968–1992, Los Angeles Museum of Contemporary Art, 1998.
The Mythic Being, 1972–1975, Thomas Erben Gallery, New York, 1999.
The Color Wheel Series: First Adhyasa. Annomayakosha, Paula Cooper Gallery, New York, 2000.
Adrian Piper: seit 1965, Generali Foundation, Vienna, 2002.
Adrian Piper Videos, ARTSADMIN, London, 2004.
Adrian Piper, Index, Swedish Contemporary Art Foundation, Stockholm, 2005.
Adrian Piper: The Mythic Being, Smart Museum of Art, Chicago, 2006.

Sources

Periodicals

Art Journal, Winter 2001, p. 63.
Nation, February 3, 1997, p. 25.
New York Times, March 30, 2008, p. 1.
Winston-Salem Journal (Winston-Salem, NC), October 7, 2001, p. E1.

Online

"Curriculum Vitae," adrianpiper.com, http:// http://www.adrianpiper.com/docs/CV_rev_12_07_o.pdf (October 27, 2008).
"Dear Editor," Adrian Piper Research Archive, http://www.adrianpiper.com/dear_editor.shtml (accessed October 27, 2008).
Piper, Adrian, "Passing for White, Passing for Black," *Frontline,* PBS.org, http://www.pbs.org/wgbh/pages/frontline/shows/secret/readings/piper.html (accessed October 27, 2008).

—Carol Brennan

Byron Pitts

1960—

Journalist

Pitts, Byron, photograph. CBS/Landov.

Byron Pitts is an award-winning journalist who overcame illiteracy and a debilitating stutter to travel the globe as a CBS news correspondent. His journalism credits include stints in Afghanistan and Iraq as an embedded reporter, achievements made more impressive by the fact that Pitts was functionally illiterate at the age of twelve. In an interview with Howard Kurtz in the *Washington Post,* he recalled how he felt when school officials told his mother. "It was humiliating. It was awful," Pitts said, noting that it was the first time he ever saw his mother cry. "You sort of live your life in disguise…. When you live in the 'hood, you have to wear a mask."

Pitts was born in 1960 and grew up on the east side of Baltimore in a single-parent household. His mother, Clarise, worked in a factory that produced raincoats. In his early elementary school years, Pitts was a quiet child who had a stutter and consistently stayed out of trouble—unlike some of his more unruly classmates. At home, he asked his older siblings to help him memorize passages that he needed to know for reading aloud in class, and would volunteer to read at the right time. On multiple-choice tests, he would make patterns coloring in the dots and score a few correct ones by chance.

"The trajectory of my life was prison or an early grave," he asserted in a speech to a Florida literacy group quoted in the *Palm Beach Post.*

When Pitts's inability to read was discovered, some education professionals informed his mother that he was probably a borderline mental-retardation case and suggested institutionalizing him. Instead, his mother found an experimental literacy program and enrolled him, and within a year he was able to read aloud a letter from his tutor to his mother that he had brought home. "It still gives me goosebumps," he told the Palm Beach audience about that moment.

Despite the progress, Pitts still had many more obstacles to face. When he entered high school, he was reading at the fifth-grade level, and at Archbishop Curley High School—a private Roman Catholic school—he had to take remedial courses. He went on to Ohio Wesleyan University in Delaware, Ohio, and chose journalism and speech communication as his major, to the surprise of many. Again, he struggled to complete his schoolwork, and wound up on academic probation. When he failed an introductory English course for the second time, the professor told him,

At a Glance . . .

Born on October 21, 1960, in Baltimore, MD; son of Clarise (a factory worker); married Lyne Pitts (a news producer and network vice president); five children. *Education:* Ohio Wesleyan University, BA, 1982.

Career: WNCT-TV, Greenville, NC, reporter and weekend sports anchor, 1983–84; WAVY-TV, Virginia, military reporter, 1984–86; WESH-TV, Orlando, FL, reporter, 1986–88; WFLA-TV, Tampa, FL, reporter and substitute anchor, 1988–89; WCBV-TV, Boston, MA, special assignment reporter, 1989–94; WSB-TV, Atlanta, GA, general assignment reporter, 1994–96; CBS News, Newspath correspondent, 1997–98; CBS News correspondent from Miami, 1998–99, from Atlanta, 1999–2001, and from New York, 2001–; became national correspondent, 2006.

Memberships: National Association of Black Journalists.

Awards: Journalist of the Year, National Association of Black Journalists, 2002.

Addresses: *Home*—Upper Montclair, NJ. *Office*—CBS News, 524 W. 57th St., New York, NY 10019.

"your presence at Ohio Wesleyan University is a waste of my time and the government's money. I think you should leave," Pitts recalled in a speech at Cazenovia College in 2008. Defeated, he picked up the necessary forms and was filling them out in tears when a woman approached and asked him if he was all right. He recounted to her what had happened, and she instructed him to hold off on filing the forms and to come to her office tomorrow. The woman turned out to be a professor in the English department, and gave Pitts extra assistance to help him pass his courses. His dormitory roommate, meanwhile, helped Pitts overcome his stutter by working with him on a word-a-day plan, in which Pitts chose a word out of the dictionary to learn and repeat until he spoke it clearly.

Pitts graduated from Ohio Wesleyan in 1982 and was hired by a Greenville, North Carolina, television station as a reporter and weekend sports anchor. In 1984 he moved on to WAVY-TV, the NBC affiliate in the Norfolk, Virginia, area, where he reported on military news. He spent two years there before working in two separate Florida markets. In 1989 he was hired by WCBV-TV in Boston, Massachusetts, as a special assignment reporter. Five years later he relocated to Atlanta to work at WSB-TV. His coverage of the 1996 Summer Olympics in the city—along with a pair of bomb explosions in Olympic Park that left one dead and 111 wounded—caught the attention of executives at CBS News, who hired him as a correspondent for Newspath, the twenty-four-hour news service for CBS affiliate stations. In May of 1998 Pitts became a regular correspondent for CBS News, reporting first from Miami, then Atlanta, and finally in 2001 from the network headquarters in New York City.

During his first year in New York, Pitts was in the office early on the morning of September 11, when initial reports came in about a plane striking one of the World Trade Center towers. "I thought, gee how awful, a novice pilot accidentally flew into the World Trade Center," he recalled in the Cazenovia College speech. He rushed downtown to cover the breaking news, and later that morning, after the second tower had also been hit and was in flames, "I was standing with two New York City cops when we looked up and saw what we thought was a giant piece of paper floating to the ground," he told the Cazenovia audience. "We thought it was a message from someone stranded above us.... Perhaps it was a giant sheet saying, 'Send help.' But soon we realized that the floating piece of paper was a person falling to their death."

When the first tower began to crumble, Pitts ran into a nearby school to escape the debris. He remained shaken by the experience even as the first anniversary of the disaster loomed, telling Michele Greppi in *Electronic Media* that it was still difficult to think about the traumas he witnessed. "Who am I to feel sorry for myself because I happened to be there? I got to go home to my family," he said. "I got to write about it with some personal distance." It had been an eventful year for Pitts: in addition to the 9/11 attack he also covered the execution of Oklahoma City bomber Timothy McVeigh and the U.S. invasion of Afghanistan for CBS. In recognition of his work the National Association of Black Journalists named him Journalist of the Year in 2002. He subsequently covered such events as the fall of Baghdad in the Iraq War in 2003, the 2004 Asian tsunami, and Hurricane Katrina in 2005. He became a national correspondent for CBS News in 2006.

Pitts is the father of five and is married to Lyne Pitts, an executive producer and vice president at NBC News. In 2002 his eldest son graduated from Ohio Wesleyan University, also with a journalism degree, and is a reporter with WRAL-TV in Raleigh, North Carolina. Pitts continues to devote himself to eradicating literacy, working with organizations such as the National Center for Family Literacy. "I want to be a witness for people that if I can do okay in my life then anyone can," he told a Pittsburgh audience in 2006, according to a report by television station KDKA. "I'm not ashamed of where I come from, I'm not ashamed of the struggles I had."

Sources

Periodicals

Boys' Life, March 2008, p. 28.
Columbus Dispatch, May 12, 2006.
Electronic Media, September 16, 2002, p. 3.
Palm Beach Post, March 29, 2008, p. C6.
Washington Post, May 7, 2007, p. C1.

Online

Pitts, Byron, "Keynote Address," Cazenovia College, 2008, http://www.cazenovia.edu/Default.aspx?tabid=1168 (accessed August 11, 2008).
"Pitts Overcame Obstacles, Willed Way to Success," KDKA.com, October 18, 2006, http://kdka.com/local/Byron.Pitts.CBS.2.385480.html?detectflash=false (accessed August 18, 2008).

—Carol Brennan

Richard E. Prince

1947—

Journalist

Richard Everett Prince is a veteran journalist widely respected for his work as a reporter, editor, and columnist. Since 2002 he has devoted much of his time to an influential online column, *Richard Prince's Journal-isms,* focused on issues of diversity in the media. Jeanne Fox-Alston in *Fusion* magazine cited *Journal-isms* as a prime example of what she called Prince's "dogged, leave-no-stone-unturned" style.

Richard Everett Prince, the son of Jonathan Joseph and Audrey Elaine Prince, was born July 26, 1947, in New York City. While a student at New York University, he began working as a newspaper reporter, first for the *Newark Star-Ledger* in nearby New Jersey (1967–68) and then, starting in 1968, for the *Washington Post,* one of the most influential papers in the country. Among the stories he helped cover for the *Post* was a 1977 hostage drama involving twelve Muslim extremists who seized three prominent buildings in Washington, paralyzing the nation's capital for several days. More typical were his stories on the impact of street crime on daily life in Washington's neighborhoods. On February 25, 1977, for example, he wrote poignantly of the botched robbery of a small store in an impoverished area. Several weeks later (April 5, 1977), he described the determination of a small business owner to reopen his clothing store after a devastating act of arson. Prince also wrote frequently about education and local government.

In 1972 Prince joined six other African-American reporters in filing a landmark complaint against the *Post* with the U.S. Equal Employment Opportunity Commission (EEOC). The group, which came to be known as the Metro Seven, charged the *Post* with denying its African-American employees equal opportunity, particularly with regard to job assignments and promotions. While the EEOC's staff found reasonable cause to believe that discrimination existed, its commissioners declined to pursue the matter. Despite this ambiguous and, to the Metro Seven, disappointing conclusion, the case sparked a number of similar complaints against newspapers around the country. Many of these later complaints proved more successful.

After almost a decade at the *Post,* Prince left in 1977 to pursue a career as a freelance journalist and photographer. Two years later, however, he accepted a position as assistant metro editor at a newspaper in upstate New York, the Rochester *Democrat and Chronicle,* owned by the Gannett Company. He remained there for the next fifteen years, receiving a number of promotions. The first of these occurred in 1981, when he became assistant news editor, a post he held until 1985, when he became an editorial writer and columnist. Many of his columns between 1988 and 1994 were syndicated by the Gannett News Service, a division of the Gannett Company, for publication in other newspapers across the country. Prince thus began to reach a nationwide audience during the late 1980s. In one of his most memorable columns from this period (December 13, 1988), Prince described being pulled over by Seattle police officers at two A.M. and searched without a warrant. The harrowing experience, Prince wrote, was "reaffirmation that being black in America

At a Glance . . .

Born Richard Everett Prince on July 26, 1947, in New York, NY; son of Jonathan Joseph and Audrey Elaine (White) Prince. *Military service:* U.S. Air Force Reserve, sergeant, 1968–73. *Education:* New York University, BS, 1969.

Career: *Newark Star-Ledger,* reporter, 1967–68; *Washington Post,* reporter, 1968–77; freelance writer, 1977–79; *Democrat and Chronicle* (Rochester, NY), assistant metro editor, 1979–81, assistant news editor, 1981–85, editorial writer and columnist, 1985–94, op-ed editor, 1993–94; Gannett News Service, syndicated columnist, 1988–94; Communities In Schools, publications editor, 1994–98; National Association of Black Journalists, interim director of communications, 1998–99; *Washington Post,* foreign-desk copy editor (part-time), 1999–; *Black College Wire,* editor, 2002–07; founder and writer of *Richard Prince's Journal-isms* (online column), 2002—.

Memberships: National Association of Black Journalists; National Conference of Editorial Writers; The Trotter Group.

Awards: Column Contest, second prize, National Society of Newspaper Columnists, 1989; Writing Competition, third prize for commentary, National Association of Black Journalists, 1987, 1998, 1989; President's Award, National Association of Black Journalists, 2003; Let's Do It Better Award, Columbia University Graduate School of Journalism, 2007.

Addresses: *Office*—c/o Maynard Institute for Journalism Education, 1211 Preservation Pkwy., Oakland, CA 94612; *E-mail*—rprince@maynardije.org.

is a full-time job, no matter what one's perceived station."

In 1993 Prince was appointed the editor of the opinions-and-editorials, or "op-ed," page of the *Democrat and Chronicle.* He served in this capacity until the following year, when he left Rochester to become the publications editor of Communities In Schools (CIS), arguably the nation's leading dropout-prevention program. According to its Web site, Virginia-based CIS "helps students stay in school and make right choices by connecting schools with needed community resources." As part of that effort, Prince oversaw the development of publications aimed at a variety of audiences, including educators, volunteers, policymakers, and the public. In 1998 Prince left CIS to become interim director of communications at the National Association of Black Journalists (NABJ) from 1998 to 1999. Prince was a natural choice for the position, as he had been heavily involved in NABJ's publications program for several years, serving as coeditor of the monthly *NABJ Journal* from 1989 to 1993 and as associate editor from 1994 to 1997.

Once the NABJ had found and hired a permanent communications director, Prince stepped down to pursue a variety of projects. He returned, for example, to the *Washington Post,* where he served as a part-time copy editor on the foreign desk beginning in 1999. Increasingly, however, he focused on Internet projects, including the *Black College Wire* (*BCW*), an online news source designed, according to its Web site, "to promote the journalistic work of students at predominantly black colleges and universities." Prince served as the editor of *BCW* from 2002, when it began, to 2007.

Prince's most prominent project, however, was the online column entitled *Richard Prince's Journal-isms.* As Prince told Fox-Alston in *Fusion,* the column began in the *NABJ Journal* about 1991 and ran there for the next seven years. Then, in 2002, Prince restarted *Journal-isms* in an online-only format on the Web site of the Robert C. Maynard Institute for Journalism Education. Named for a pioneering African-American newspaper editor and publisher, the Maynard Institute promotes diversity in journalism through training programs and outreach activities. *Journal-isms* is closely aligned with that broader mission; as Prince told Fox-Alston, the column's goal is "to report on news involving diversity issues in the news media, and journalists of color."

While Prince has long been known for the care with which he prepares his columns, his diligence, according to industry insiders, is particularly visible in *Journal-isms.* According to Alexander LeMaine in the student newspaper published by the American Society of Newspaper Editors (ASNE), for example, "Prince spends hours each day reporting and scouring the Web to compile material." This distinctive combination of traditional reporting and intensive online research offers, in LeMaine's words, "angles that may not have received much attention elsewhere." Among the topics covered in *Journal-isms* in the summer of 2008 were the lack of diversity in the upper management of television news networks; the 2007 murder in Oakland, California, of Chauncey Bailey, an African-American reporter, and the ongoing efforts of Bailey's colleagues to keep attention focused on the case; and the views of presidential candidates Barack Obama and John McCain on affirmative action.

According to Mallary Jean Tenore on the journalism Web site Poynter Online, *Journal-isms* was receiving an average of 60,000 unique visitors per month as of July, 2008. "I enjoy doing it even though it is a lot of work," Prince told LeMaine. "It's just not the journalists of color that need to know these things."

Selected writings

(Contributor) Wickham, DeWayne, ed., *Thinking Black: Some of the Nation's Best Black Columnists Speak Their Mind,* Crown Press, 1996.

(Contributor) The Trotter Group (DeWayne Wickham, ed.), *Black Voices in Commentary,* August Press, 2006.

Sources

Periodicals

ASNE Reporter, April 14, 2005.
Washington Post, March 11, 1977; April 5, 1977.

Online

"About Us," Black College Wire, http://www.blackcollegewire.org/index.php?option=com_content&task=view&id=1086&Itemid=39 (accessed October 31, 2008).

Fox-Alston, Jeanne, "Five Minutes with Richard Prince," Newspaper Association of America, http://www.naa.org/Resources/Publications/Fusion Magazine/FUSION-Magazine-2005-Summer/Diversity-Fusion-Five-Minutes-with-Richard-Prince/Diversity-Fusion-Five-Minutes-with-Richard-Prince.aspx (accessed October 31, 2008).

"How CIS works," Communities In Schools, http://www.cisnet.org/about/how.asp (accessed October 31, 2008).

Prince, Richard E., "Richard Prince: 'Vintage' Columns," The Trotter Group, http://www.trottergroup.org/prince_cols.htm (accessed October 31, 2008). Includes "The Supreme Court Wasn't Open at 2 a.m.," reprinted from the *Seattle Times,* December 13, 1988.

Tenore, Mallory Jean, "'Journal-isms' That Engage and Inform Diverse Audiences," Poynter Online, July 11, 2008, http://www.poynter.org/column.asp?id=58&aid=146549 (accessed October 31, 2008).

Other

Additional information for this profile was obtained through personal correspondence with Richard E. Prince, 2008.

—R. Anthony Kugler

LaTanya Richardson

1949—

Actor, director

LaTanya Richardson has had a long and distinguished career as an actress and director on film, television, and stage. While her marriage to Samuel L. Jackson, one of Hollywood's most prominent leading men, has occasionally overshadowed the public's awareness of her accomplishments, she has established a reputation among industry insiders as a character actress of rare intensity.

Richardson was born October 21, 1949, in Atlanta, Georgia, where she attended public schools before entering Spelman College, a predominately African-American institution in that city. A theater major, she was heavily involved in student productions. Because Spelman admitted women only, and many of the plays staged there were joint productions with Morehouse College, a neighboring men's school, also predominately African-American. It was at a rehearsal for one of these joint productions, Bertolt Brecht's *The Three-Penny Opera,* that Richardson met Morehouse student Samuel L. Jackson. The two began dating shortly thereafter, and were married in 1980. Their daughter, Zoe, was born in 1982.

Richardson, LaTanya, photograph. Stephen Lovekin/Getty Images.

After receiving a bachelor's degree from Spelman in 1974, Richardson left Atlanta for New York City, where she completed a graduate program in drama at New York University and auditioned for roles. Richardson thrived in the intensely competitive atmosphere of New York theater. Her first important break was in 1977, when she landed a major role in the New York Shakespeare Festival's world-premiere production of Aishah Rahman's *Unfinished Women Cry in No Man's Land While a Bird Dies in a Gilded Cage.* Richardson played Wilma, one of five pregnant teenagers, the "unfinished women" of the title, who must decide over the course of a single day whether to keep their children or put them up for adoption. Only weeks later, Richardson won a substantial role in a traveling production (1977–78) of Ntozake Shange's *For Colored Girls Who Have Considered Suicide When the Rainbow Is Enuf.* Richardson's performance as the Lady in Red was well received by critics in cities across the country, and she was asked to reprise the role for a production mounted by the Alliance Theatre Company of Atlanta several months later (1979–80). The actress then returned to New York, where in 1980 and 1981

> **At a Glance . . .**
>
> Born October 21, 1949, in Atlanta, GA; married Samuel L. Jackson (an actor), 1980; children: Zoe. *Education:* Spelman College, BA, theater, 1974; New York University, MA, drama.
>
> **Career:** Actor in theater, film and television, 1970s—. Directed several plays at the New Federal Theatre, 1985–86. Directed *Hairstory* (short film), 2000.
>
> **Awards:** Frederick D. Patterson Award (cowinner with Samuel L. Jackson), United Negro College Fund, 2005.
>
> **Addresses:** *Manager*—Peg Donegan, Framework Entertainment, 9057 Nemo St., Ste. C, West Hollywood, CA 90069.

she played the role of Carrie in the New Federal Theatre's production of African-American playwright Hughes Allison's 1937 play *The Trial of Dr. Beck*.

During the early 1980s Richardson withdrew from acting for several years to care for her young daughter. The decision to postpone her career was not an easy one. "I cried like a banshee," she recalled to Joy Bennett Kinnon of *Ebony* in 2006. "I still believe in family," Richardson continued, "so I had to deal with my feelings. I wasn't going to be good with just nannies raising Zoe." She returned to theater with renewed determination in 1985, when she both starred in and directed a New Federal Theatre production of Laurie Carlos's *Nonsectarian Conversations with the Dead*, which ran until the following year. She then directed another New Federal Theatre production, Bill Harris's *Stories about the Old Days* (1986), before taking the stage again herself with starring roles in Wesley Brown's *Boogie Woogie and Booker T*, in which she played the anti-lynching activist Ida B. Wells (New Federal Theatre, 1987); the Negro Ensemble Company's 1987–88 production of Ed Smith's *From the Mississippi Delta*; the Apple Corps Theatre's production of Cassandra Medley's *Ma Rose* (1988); Richard Wesley's *The Talented Tenth*, at the Manhattan Theatre Club's Stage II (1989); and Constance Congdon's *Casanova*, at the Public Theatre (1991).

Despite her growing success on stage, the late 1980s and early 1990s were a difficult period for Richardson, largely because of her husband's well-publicized struggles with drug and alcohol addiction. In an interview with Diane Weathers in*Essence* in 1999, Richardson described her determination to keep her marriage intact as Jackson descended further into addiction. "I stayed with him because I had to," she told Weathers. "I made a promise to God that I would be there, [and that] I wasn't going to let him die." At her insistence, and with the help of friends and family, Jackson entered a rehabilitation program, which he completed successfully in time to star in Spike Lee's 1991 film *Jungle Fever*. As Jackson's movie career resumed, Richardson began to appear in films herself, with roles in no less than three major Hollywood productions in 1991 alone (*The Super*, *Hangin' with the Homeboys*, and *Fried Green Tomatoes*). This frenetic pace continued for the rest of the decade. Among her best-known roles from this period are Nurse Ruth in the drama *Lorenzo's Oil* (1992); Lorraine in the biographical drama *Malcolm X* (1992); Harriet in the romantic comedy *Sleepless in Seattle* (1993); Caroline Jones in the drama *Losing Isaiah* (1995); and Deputy Marshal Cooper in the action film *U.S. Marshals* (1998).

In addition to her film and theater work, Richardson has made a number of memorable appearances on television, most notably as Judge Atallah Sims in the courtroom drama *100 Centre Street*, which ran on the A&E cable network from 2001 to 2002. Peter Marks described Richardson's careful preparations for the role in the *New York Times*, noting that she visited the real-life courtrooms at 100 Centre Street in New York and asked a retired judge for guidance on handling a courtroom. Following the end of *100 Centre Street*, Richardson concentrated increasingly on a return to the theater, her favorite venue. As she told Bennett in *Ebony*, the theater "allows me to work on my own terms, and I'm definitely an 'on my own terms' type of person." While she has continued to make occasional appearances on film and television, including the 2003 action movie *Kill Bill* and the 2006 drama *Freedomland*, she has said repeatedly that Hollywood no longer holds much attraction for her. A clear sign of her return to her roots in theater came in the summer of 2005, when she starred in Carson McCullers's *The Member of the Wedding* at a small but highly-regarded theater in Connecticut, the Westport Country Playhouse. She has also expressed a strong desire to do more work as a producer and director. To that end, she has reportedly acquired the rights to a number of books and screenplays, including the novel *Babylon Sisters* by fellow Spelman alumna Pearl Cleage.

Selected works

Films

Fried Green Tomatoes, 1991.
Hangin' with the Homeboys, 1991.
The Super, 1991.
Juice, 1992.
Lorenzo's Oil, 1992.
Malcolm X, 1992.
Sleepless in Seattle, 1993.
The Last Laugh, 1994.
When a Man Loves a Woman, 1994.

Losing Isaiah, 1995.
Lone Star, 1996.
Julian Po, 1997.
Loved, 1997.
U.S. Marshals, 1998.
(Director) *Hairstory* (short), 2000.
The Fighting Temptations, 2003.
Kill Bill, 2003.
Freedomland, 2006.
All about Us, 2007.
Blackout, 2007.

Television

One Life to Live, 1992.
Introducing Dorothy Dandridge, 1999.
100 Centre Street, 2001–02.

Theater

Unfinished Women Cry in No Man's Land While a Bird Dies in a Gilded Cage, New York Shakespeare Festival, 1977.
For Colored Girls Who Have Considered Suicide When the Rainbow Is Enuf, traveling production, 1977–78, Alliance Theatre Company, 1979–80.
The Trial of Dr. Beck, New Federal Theatre, 1980–81.
(And director) *Nonsectarian Conversations with the Dead,* New Federal Theatre, 1985–86.
(Director) *Stories about the Old Days,* New Federal Theatre, 1986.
Boogie Woogie and Booker T, New Federal Theatre, 1987.
From the Mississippi Delta, Negro Ensemble Company, 1987–88.
Ma Rose, Apple Corps Theatre, 1988.
The Talented Tenth, Manhattan Theatre Club, 1989.
Casanova, Public Theatre, 1991.
The Member of the Wedding, Westport Country Playhouse, 2005.

Sources

Periodicals

Ebony, March 2006.
Essence, December 1999; May 2002.
Melus, Autumn 1989–Autumn 1990.
New York Times, May 11, 2001.

—R. Anthony Kugler

Patrick Robinson

1966—

Fashion designer

Robinson, Patrick, photograph. Jamie McCarthy/WireImage.

Designer Patrick Robinson was heralded by fashion industry insiders as a star in the making after designing for some of the premier names in American and European sportswear, as well as launching a collection under his own name. "Watch this guy," declared Jennifer Jackson and Andrea Linett in *Harper's Bazaar* in 1998. "He has the potential for first-name designer status." A brief stint with the fashion house Perry Ellis International ended badly in 2004, and another with Paco Rabanne failed to reinvigorate the brand, but Robinson continued to have a loyal following of customers who appreciated the approach he took in his own collection. By May of 2007 the American public was familiar enough with his name and reputation that the discount retailer Target—long known for being both affordable and fashion-forward—featured Robinson in its GO International line, which is meant to appeal to a hip, young audience. From there Robinson was drafted as head designer to resuscitate the ailing Gap clothing chain. His ascent at Gap was greeted with a mix of enthusiasm and skepticism.

Interested in Fashion during Teen Years

Robinson was born in Memphis, Tennessee, in 1966, but he grew up southeast of Los Angeles, California, in the affluent area of Orange County. His father was a doctor, and Robinson, one in a family of five children, went to high school in Fullerton and worked at the Nordstrom department store at the Cerritos mall as a teen. He told Rose-Marie Turk in the *Los Angeles Times* that he grew up in a fashion-conscious family. His parents, he said, "subscribed to every magazine in the world and we had a big library." Besides working at the mall, Robinson also loved to surf, and he began his own line of surf wear. He decided to pursue a career as a fashion designer in earnest when he saw a film that featured homegrown American talent such as Calvin Klein and Jeffrey Banks.

Robinson was accepted into the renowned Parsons School of Design in New York City, and he also spent time at the American College in Paris. While there, he worked as first assistant for an up-and-coming young

At a Glance . . .

Born on September 8, 1966, in Memphis, TN; married Virginia Smith (in public relations and marketing); children: Wyeth. *Education:* Received degree from Parsons School of Design; also attended the American College in Paris.

Career: Worked at Nordstrom department store, Cerritos, CA, mid-1980s; affiliated with designer Patrick Kelly, Paris, and with design houses Albert Nippon and Herman Geist, 1980s; Le Collezioni White Label by Giorgio Armani, Turin, Italy, design director, 1990–94; Anne Klein Collection, New York City, designer, 1994–96; launched own collection, 1997–2003; Perry Ellis International, creative director, 2003–04; Paco Rabanne, Paris, artistic director, 2005–07; featured designer for Target Corporation's GO International line, May 2007; Gap Inc., San Francisco, CA, executive vice president for design, 2007—.

Addresses: *Office*—Gap Inc. Headquarters, Two Folsom St., San Francisco, CA 94105.

African-American designer named Patrick Kelly. After finishing school, Robinson worked for the design houses Albert Nippon and Herman Geist, and was hired by noted Italian designer Giorgio Armani for his bridge line, Le Collezioni. He got the job only when he agreed to start the next day and had to fly to Italy on extremely short notice. He completed an entire season's worth of clothes just ten days after arriving. "I've done a lot at a young age, but I pushed myself hard, and I gave up a lot of my personal life for my work," Robinson admitted to Julia Chance in *Essence.*

Robinson recognized that being associated with the Armani name was an invaluable experience. "In the '90s, Robinson was responsible for many of the Giorgio Armani power suits that female big shots have relied upon when dealmaking and strong-arming," wrote Robin Givhan in the *Washington Post.* In late 1994 he was wooed away from Le Collezioni by the Japanese owners of the Anne Klein Collection. The New York–based design house was one of the top purveyors of classic executive gear for American women, but had fallen on hard times during the 1990s. Its image had suffered as its look grew to be considered a bit too staid. The company had hired Hollywood designer Richard Tyler to revitalize it, but the move backfired and the collection was critiqued as too young and too sexy for the true Anne Klein loyalist. Tyler was unceremoniously fired from the collection in late 1994 after sales plummeted, and Robinson, still a relative unknown in the industry, was brought on board.

Became Head Designer for Fashion Collection

When he arrived back in New York to take over, Robinson found himself the head designer of a major collection at the age of only twenty-eight—yet among his predecessors at Anne Klein there had been equal novices: Donna Karan was just twenty-six when she took the same job in 1973. "This is the only company in America where you can become head designer and really be the designer," Robinson told Chance. The first few weeks were rough, however. He was introduced to baffled staff in the company showroom in a private meeting, and as he recalled in an interview with Kim France in *Harper's Bazaar,* he faced "a bunch of frowning little monsters." One witness to the meeting, Virginia Smith, then head of public relations for the company, told France that the young designer "looked slightly mortified to be in front of this group of people, and I thought, I feel kind of sorry for him."

Just before the debut of his first collection for Anne Klein, Robinson termed himself "28 going on 50" in an interview with Turk. However, he loved being back on familiar territory after years abroad. "This is the best country on Earth," he told Turk. "Everything works, I'm the only person, I think, walking around New York grinning." Yet some suspected that Anne Klein, after its Tyler debacle, was a sinking ship. Robinson recalled about this time "that it was almost more important for me to focus on bettering the name," as he told *Harper's Bazaar,* and because of this, he and Smith spent a great deal of time strategizing. A romance eventually blossomed, which they kept secret for as long as they could.

Meanwhile, Robinson dedicated himself to making the Anne Klein Collection a success. With his first collection of clothes, he visited several cities and held seminars with store executives and sales personnel that showed what Turk termed a return to the true Anne Klein look: "safe, sexy, understated, finely tailored day and evening wear in luxurious fabrics." Reviews were mixed: "There are some who think that Patrick Robinson is in way over his head," sniped *Women's Wear Daily* in a late 1995 issue that previewed the spring 1996 designer lines. Robinson's third collection for Anne Klein was not even shipped to stores when Japanese executives decided to close the Anne Klein Collection (its lower-priced line, Anne Klein II, was still commercially successful).

Launched His Own Line of Clothing

Fortunately for Robinson, his paramour was still gainfully employed—Smith had been offered a job at Calvin Klein shortly before the dark day of the announcement.

Out of a job, Robinson traveled through Asia for several weeks as a tonic. When he returned, he set up a design house in his New York City loft, hired a staff, and began courting backers. A line of clothing finally bearing his own name was launched for the fall/winter season of 1997 after Robinson signed a deal with the Italian manufacturer Coba. He was rather fortunate in light of the terms of the agreement: Coba, based near Urbino, did not invest in his company and receive a controlling interest, but rather gave him a break on the costs of manufacturing the clothes in return for a promise that the designer would stay with the firm when his business grew successful. "We think Patrick is a very talented designer, even if he didn't have a brilliant experience at Anne Klein," Domenico Toselli, Coba's sole director, told Samantha Conti in *Women's Wear Daily.* "He's young and good, and we want to give him a hand," Toselli continued.

Robinson's first trunk show sold $65,000 the first day at Saks Jandel in Washington, DC. He presented Asian-influenced sportswear carrying price tags ranging from $125 to $1,000. Givhan praised the debut collection and noted the line was lacking the standard "high-concept theme" that most designers attempt. She wrote, "He simply has created beautiful garments in brushed alpaca, nubuck, python and pony…. The clothes have shelf life and relevance."

The Asian mood of his first collection fit in perfectly with a late-1990s vibe. His catalysts, Robinson told Givhan, would always be global. Theorizing about his "signature look," he said it would always reflect "something about adventure, something with lots of cultures mixed in." He explained to Givhan that "I'm looking not only to America for inspiration, but the world…. I'm a black man and I love being that. I love being different than other people. That's part of it, too." Early in 1998 Robinson was able to move out of his Soho loft into a separate workspace on Wooster Street. There he continued creating lines under his own name, which were sold at such high-end retailers as Barney's, Bergdorf Goodman, and Neiman Marcus.

Experienced Mixed Success in Fashion World

In 2003 Robinson was offered the position of creative director of Perry Ellis International, which he readily accepted. "I am truly enthusiastic about this exciting opportunity. The Perry Ellis name has always epitomized for me what American sportswear is," Robinson announced. However, the union was to be short lived. Reaction to Robinson's first two seasons of designs for Perry Ellis was generally good, and retail outlets where the collection was sold were pleased with sales. In July of 2004 *New York Times* fashion reporter Ruth La Ferla quoted Ed Burstell, vice president and general manager of the upscale New York–based department store Henri Bendel, as saying of Robinson's designs, "They were exactly what was needed to blow the dust off the brand." However, La Ferla suggested that Burstell's opinion was not widely shared by those in the fashion community, and in December of 2004 she reported that Robinson had left the company after "six months of fraught negotiations over creative control of the brand." More to the point, according to La Ferla, Robinson's designs simply did not appeal to the mass-market audience Perry Ellis wanted to target. "A former Perry Ellis executive, who still works in the industry and insisted on not being named, termed Mr. Robinson's stint at the company an outright disaster, charging that he had catered exclusively to an elite circle of buyers and editors."

In the meantime, Robinson had married Virginia Smith, who had taken a position as market editor at *Vogue* and had given birth to the couple's son, Wyeth, in 2003. When Robinson took his next job, as artistic director of the fashion house Paco Rabanne, it meant a move to Paris and regular commutes to New York City to see his family. By most accounts, Robinson's tenure at Paco Rabanne was successful. He was praised for designing collections that were luxurious and wearable but with a nod to the fashion house's edgy, innovative past use of elements such as chain mail and plastic. Nonetheless, his line was shut down after just three seasons. After that Robinson designed a limited-edition line for the popular discount retailer Target, which was especially well received by the store's younger shoppers. Still, Robinson could not resist the next challenge, when he was courted by the Gap to help revive its brand, which had been steadily losing its youth market since the 1990s to stores such as Abercrombie and Fitch and H&M.

Gap Inc.'s decision to bring on Robinson was not without controversy, but observers agreed that something had to be done. The company's sales had dipped dramatically. According to *MarketWatch,* the Gap's 2007 holiday sales fell 8 percent, with net sales falling 4 percent. There was even speculation that the company might be ripe for a takeover. In August of 2008 Eric Wilson wrote in the *New York Times,* "On the one hand, the company has continued to report weak sales, including an 11 percent drop last month in stores open at least a year, and on Tuesday, Brand Keys, a research consultancy, announced that Gap ranked last in customer loyalty. On the other, some retail analysts long critical of Gap's merchandising efforts and management choices have joined the chorus that is singing Mr. Robinson's praises." Whether or not Robinson's presence would make a difference to the company's financials—or its fashions—remained to be seen as of the fall of 2008.

Sources

Periodicals

Essence, September 1995, p. 22.
Harper's Bazaar, March 1998; June 1998.

Los Angeles Times, June 29, 1995, p. E1.
MarketWatch, January 4, 2007.
New York Times, July 13, 2004; December 12, 2004; August 20, 2008; August 21, 2008.
Washington Post, August 21, 1997, p. F3.
Women's Wear Daily, December 21, 1994, p. 8; March 1, 1995, p, 8; August 8, 1995, p. G8; November 2, 1995, p. 6; January 7, 1997, p. 2; January 28, 1997, p. 6.

Online

"Gap Inc. Names Patrick Robinson Head of Design of Gap Adult, Gapbody," Gap Inc., http://www.gapinc.com/public/Media/Press_Releases/med_pr_PatrickRobinson052307.shtml (accessed November 4, 2008).

—Carol Brennan and Nancy Dziedzic

Abdi Roble

1964—

Documentary photographer

Born and raised in Somalia, Abdi Roble is an important contributor to contemporary documentary photography. Through his work he is recording the Somali Diaspora—the emigration of his people from their native land to escape poverty and civil conflict. In particular, Roble has documented the immigration of fellow Somalis to his adopted country, the United States, and their attempts to maintain their cultural identity in a new land. In 2007 he began compiling a similar record on Somalis relocating to Europe.

Using black-and-white photographic film and natural light, Roble captures images of recent immigrants who are still engaging in their native cultural practices but are beginning to adapt to their new lives. Roble began his work in 2003 in an effort to document this ongoing event, to help draw worldwide attention to the plight of the Somali people and others who are forced to leave their homelands, and to provide the Somali people with an archival record of this life-changing experience. In doing so, Roble is not only documenting history, but he is also making history: Never before has the diaspora of a people been documented as Roble is doing.

Immigrated to the United States

Abdi Roble was born in Somalia in February of 1964. During his childhood Roble traveled the countryside with his father, a veterinarian who provided free care for the farm animals of the poor. As Roble grew, his interest became focused on playing soccer. His ability to play the sport with great skill soon brought him international acclaim. Nonetheless, Roble left Somalia and his status as a soccer star due to the poor political and economic conditions in the country, which had been stricken by decades of civil war and regional conflicts. He first moved to Jidda, Saudi Arabia, and then in 1989 to Washington, DC. In 1990 Roble settled in Columbus, Ohio, after fellow Somali immigrants described the city as less expensive and less crowded than the nation's capital. Columbus is where Roble developed an interest in photography.

When he first arrived in the United States, Roble bussed tables in restaurants and worked in hotels to make a living. However, browsing through a flea market in Columbus one day in 1992, Roble saw a camera among the wares, and it piqued his interest. He bought the camera and taught himself the craft.

Within a few years, Roble was a freelance photographer for Columbus-area newspapers. In addition, *Leica View,* a publication of camera manufacturer Leica, published some of Roble's photographs. While gaining a foothold in the photography profession, Roble augmented his income by working at the Midwest Photo Exchange, a Columbus photography store. During the late 1990s Roble formed two photography groups: the Focus Group in 1998, an association of students and professionals, and the African American Photographers of North America in 1999, a group that works with young people to interest and involve them in photography and the arts.

Roble traveled extensively, viewing the world through the lens of his camera. His personal photographic

At a Glance...

Born on February 2, 1964, in Mogadishu, Somalia; son of a veterinarian and a housewife; dual citizenship, Somalia and the United States; single; no children. *Religion:* Muslim. *Education:* Ohio State University, attended for two years during the 1990s.

Career: Professional soccer player for the Mogadishu team, 1980-85; freelance photographer, 1995-98; Midwest Photo Exchange, camera salesman, 1997-2007; documentary photographer 1999—.

Awards: Individual Artist Award, Ohio Arts Council, 2004; Individual Artist Award, Greater Columbus Arts Council, 2006; Arts Freedom Award, South Side Settlement House and Huntington Bank, 2006.

Addresses: *Email*—abdi@somaliproject.org.

---

journeys included trips to Argentina, Brazil, Cuba, Ecuador, France, Germany, Italy, Japan, Switzerland, and Uruguay. He used photographs from his trips to develop exhibitions supported by Leica and Midwest Photo, including One Month in Europe with Leica in 2000, Leica Portrait of Cuba in 2002, and Japan: A Leica Perspective in 2004.

Formed the Somali Documentary Project

In 2003 Roble created the Somali Documentary Project along with writer Doug Rutledge, editor Stanley Kayn, and project manager Tariq Tarey. Thus began the heart of Roble's career—documenting the dispersal of the Somali people from an economically depraved and war-torn land to places of hope and prosperity. Roble was motivated by his interest in social justice and love for the people of his native country. In May of 2005 the first collection of Roble's documentary photos, Scenes from the Somali Diaspora, comprised a lobby exhibition outside the Ohio Arts Council's Riffe Gallery in Columbus. In 2006 Roble's work was exhibited at Intermedia Arts in Minneapolis, Minnesota, with the title Against Forgetting: Beyond Genocide and Civil War, along with works by Paul Corbit Brown and Mike Rosen. Together these photographers captured images of people struggling to survive against extreme adversity.

In the fall of 2007 the Columbus Museum of Art presented Stories of the Somali Diaspora: Photographs by Abdi Roble—the first major solo exhibition of his work on the Somali Documentary Project. Of his work, Roble told the Associated Press in November of 2007: "My role was a photographer, and all I have is a roll of film and a camera. That was my philanthropy. The idea was to archive and educate the hosting community and bring international attention to the plight of Somalia." The Roble exhibition traveled to the Bates College Museum of Art in Lewiston, Maine; the Weisman Art Museum in Minneapolis, Minnesota; and the Plains Art Museum in Fargo, North Dakota. In addition to these exhibitions, the Somali Documentary Project compiled *The Somali Diaspora: A Journey Away* (2008), a book that presents photos by Roble and narrative by Doug Rutledge.

Roble's work on the Somali Documentary Project began with recording the Somali immigration to the United States, focusing on families that settled in Ohio, Minnesota, California, and Maine. In the summer of 2007 he began photographing Somali refugees from the Dadaad refugee camp in Kenya who settled in new homes in Germany, Greece, and Malta. In this phase of his work, Roble planned to compare the U.S. and European immigration experiences.

Roble and the Somali Documentary Project have brought together a group of Somalis and Americans from the Columbus, Ohio, area, to form the Friends of the Dadaad. In 2007 the group raised $25,000 for schools at the refugee camp. The United Nations High Commission for Refugees is helping determine how best the money can be used in the schools. Thus Roble and the Somali Documentary Project are doing more than their groundbreaking work in recording the Somali diaspora; they are aiding Somali refugees during their transition to a new life.

Selected works

Books

(With Doug Rutledge) *The Somali Diaspora: A Journey Away,* University of Minnesota Press, 2008.

Exhibits

One Month in Europe with Leica, MPX Gallery (Columbus, OH), 2000.
Leica Portrait of Cuba, MPX Gallery, 2002.
Japan: A Leica Perspective, MPX Gallery, 2004.
Scenes from the Somali Diaspora, Verne Riffe Center for Government and the Arts (Columbus, OH), University of Minnesota Institute for Advanced Study (Minneapolis), Sibyl Center (Stanley, ND), and CHARISM Neighborhood Resource Centers (Fargo, ND), 2005-06.
(With Paul Corbit Brown and Mike Rosen) Against Forgetting: Beyond Genocide and Civil War, Intermedia Arts (Minneapolis), 2006.
Stories of the Somali Diaspora: Photographs by Abdi Roble, Columbus Museum of Art (OH), September 2007 to November 2007; Bates College Museum of Art (Lewiston, ME), January 2009 to May 2009;

Weisman Art Museum (Minneapolis, MN), June 2009 to September 2009; Plains Art Museum (Fargo ND), October 2009 to January 2010.

Sources

Periodicals

Associated Press, November 21, 2007.
Columbus Dispatch, April 25, 2000, p. F8; June 16, 2005; May 6, 2006, p. B3; October 8, 2006, p. D2; November 1, 2007.
PR Newswire, December 1, 2006.
Washington Post, November 22, 2007.

Online

"Abdi Roble," Intermedia Arts, 2007, http://www.intermediaarts.org/pages/programs/against_forgetting/af_2006/af_roble.htm (accessed September 3, 2008).
"Bios: Abdi Roble," The Somali Documentary Project, http://www.somaliproject.org/index.elements/bios_abdi.html (accessed September 3, 2008).
"Columbus Museum of Art Presents *Stories from the Somali Diaspora: Photographs by Abdi Roble,*" Columbus Museum of Art, July 17, 2007, http://www.columbusmuseum.org/about/news.php?id=8 (accessed September 3, 2008).

Other

Additional information for this profile was obtained through an interview with Abdi Roble on September 18, 2008.

—Sandra Alters

Lisa Salters

1966(?)—

Journalist

Lisa Salters is a television sportscaster who covers a range of topics as a general assignment reporter for the cable-television channel ESPN. She began her career in broadcast journalism as a network news correspondent, which made her an ideal choice for a position on *E:60,* an investigative-journalism program that debuted on ESPN in the fall of 2007. Salters also reports from the sideline during broadcasts of college football and professional basketball games, and she conducts hours of pregame research in order to prepare to interview players. "I find that the more personable you are with them, the more they open up to you," she told Melody K. Hoffman in *Jet* about interviewing athletes. "You try to find out who they are as human beings."

Salters was raised in King of Prussia, Pennsylvania, near Philadelphia, and graduated from Upper Merion Area High School. At Pennsylvania State University, she studied broadcast journalism and briefly played college basketball despite her relatively diminutive stature at five feet, two inches. She earned a spot on Penn State's Lady Lions after appearing at an open tryout, and played during the 1986–87 season as a guard. Twenty years later, she still held the distinction of being the shortest player in the history of Penn State basketball. "People ask me if I get nervous before going on the air," she said in an interview with Matt Herb on the Penn State athletics Web site FightOnState.com. "I tell them there's nothing that frightens me more than having to run. As long as no one is saying, 'Ladies, line up,' I'm happy. To me, that was hard work. Basketball was hard work. What I do now, watching people work out and not having to do it with them, is perfect."

Salters, Lisa, photograph. Monika Graff/UPI/Landov.

After graduating in 1988, Salters was hired by WBAL-TV in Baltimore as a general assignment reporter. She covered local news before moving on to international stories, traveling as far as Rwanda and Somalia to report on human-rights stories there. In February of 1995, Salters joined NewsOne, the affiliate news service for the ABC network, as a West Coast correspondent. Two years later she moved to ABC News as Los Angeles bureau correspondent. In both roles she reported on major stories of the day, including the O. J. Simpson trial in California, the crash of TWA Flight 800 in the Atlantic Ocean in July of 1996, the murder of Matthew Shepard in Wyoming, and the 1998 Winter Olympics in Nagano, Japan.

At a Glance . . .

Born Alisia Salters, c. 1966, daughter of Glen and Helen Salters. *Education:* Pennsylvania State University, BA, communications, 1988.

Career: WBAL-TV, Baltimore, MD, general assignment reporter, 1988–95; NewsOne (ABC affiliate news service), West Coast correspondent, 1995–97; ABC News, Los Angeles bureau correspondent, 1997–2000; ESPN/ESPN on ABC, general assignment reporter, 2000—, and correspondent on the newsmagazine program *E:60* after 2007.

Memberships: Association for Women in Sports Media, National Association of Black Journalists.

Awards: Alumni Fellow Award, Penn State Alumni Association, 2007.

Addresses: *Office*—ESPN, ESPN Plaza, Bristol, CT 06010.

Salters surprised many of her colleagues when she left ABC News for ESPN in March of 2000. "When you're at a network, there's kind of an elitist attitude," she told Herb. "They think, 'We're it, this is network TV, the top of the heap.'" Both ESPN and ABC, however, share a corporate parent—the Walt Disney Company and the Hearst Corporation, which have joint ownership—and Salters's move to general assignment reporter at the all-sports channel seemed to coincide with its push to bring a more news-oriented slant to its programming lineup.

At ESPN Salters became a regular contributor to *Outside the Lines*, a newsmagazine program. One of her more sensational assignments for it was the 2000–01 murder-conspiracy trial of Rae Carruth, a Carolina Panthers player who was sent to prison for his role in the death of his pregnant girlfriend. In early 2003, just before the start of the Iraq War, Salters and an ESPN camera crew traveled to the Persian Gulf nation of Qatar for a special *Outside the Lines* assignment. Her interview subjects included U.S. military personnel who had some professional, collegiate, or Olympic athletic experience. She and the crew also spent time on board a pair of U.S. Navy carriers in the Persian Gulf. Many of the servicemen and servicewomen they encountered would ask about their home teams or other sports news. She told Chuck Finder in the *Pittsburgh Post-Gazette*, "What I found is just how pervasive sports is in our society. To hear how their team is doing, they were thrilled. It was something to take their mind off what they were doing during war."

Salters covered both the 2004 Summer Olympics in Athens, Greece, and the 2006 Winter Olympics in Turin, Italy, and also served as the primary sideline reporter for ABC's coverage of National Basketball Association (NBA) games and for the Saturday night college football games broadcast as ESPN's *College Football Saturday Primetime*. In both roles her task was to interview players, coaching personnel, and sometimes even the celebrities who have courtside seats for their favorite NBA teams. As she explained to Hoffman in *Jet*, "the announcers really have to be looking right at the game the entire time. We are looking at people's reactions; we are looking at the bench to see somebody getting chewed out by the coach. We literally are the eyes and the ears for the viewer." She also admitted to being occasionally surprised, as she told Mary Schmitt Boyer in the Cleveland *Plain Dealer*, such as the time when she asked Ed Snider, owner of the NBA's Philadelphia 76ers, if its star player Allen Iverson had asked to be traded. Snider, she said, "let it all hang out.... I thought to myself, 'Wow.' I really had to regroup, because I'd been prepared for him not to answer."

In October of 2007 ESPN premiered *E:60*, a new program that showcased investigative journalism by Salters, Jeremy Schaap, Rachel Nichols, Tom Farrey, and Michael Smith. Salters's debut story involved the legacy of Jason Ray, who wore the horned-sheep mascot costume for the University of North Carolina Tar Heels teams. Ray was struck by a car on a highway during the National Collegiate Athletic Association's men's basketball tournament in March of 2007, and his organs were donated to four people. Critiquing *E:60* in the *New York Times*, Richard Sandomir called her segment "the gem, a moving and original report" in which "Salters extended the story to the people who received Ray's heart, lungs, liver and pancreas. This example of intelligent journalism ended with a meeting between Ray's parents and some of those who received their son's organs."

Sources

Periodicals

Jet, May 26, 2008, p. 53.
New York Times, October 18, 2007, p. D5.
Plain Dealer (Cleveland, OH), January 29, 2007, p. C4.

Online

Finder, Chuck, "The Big Picture: Ex-Penn Stater Gets War Story for ESPN," PittsburghPost-Gazette.com, April 3, 2003, http://www.post-gazette.com/sports/columnists/20030403thebig6.asp (accessed August 12, 2008).

Herb, Matt, "PSU Grad Shines at ESPN," FightOn-State.com, March 20, 2005, http://pennstate.scout.com/2/361617.html (accessed August 12, 2008).

—Carol Brennan

Ellen Johnson Sirleaf

1938—

President of liberia

Sirleaf, Ellen Johnson, photograph. Joe Corrigan/Getty Images.

Ellen Johnson Sirleaf is the president of Liberia, a small West African nation founded by freed American slaves in the nineteenth century. An economist by training, Sirleaf took office in 2006 as the first democratically elected female president in postcolonial Africa. Though she enjoyed considerable good will at home and abroad, Sirleaf faced an array of immense problems, the legacy of a devastating civil war (1989–2003) that left 250,000 people—nearly a tenth of the population—dead and the country's roads and power plants in shambles. Sirleaf made considerable progress in office, notably in persuading Liberia's creditors to forgive some of its crushing foreign debt. However, more than 80 percent of the adult population remained unemployed and large areas of the country were still without electric power more than two years into her administration.

The daughter of a lawyer and a teacher, Sirleaf was born Ellen Johnson on October 29, 1938, in the Liberian capital of Monrovia. About 1955, when she was still a teenager, she married James Sirleaf; their union produced four sons but ended in divorce. Amid her family obligations, Sirleaf doggedly pursued her education at Monrovia's College of West Africa, where she began her study of economics. Following her divorce in 1960 or 1961, she moved to the United States, where she enrolled at Madison Business College, a small school in Madison, Wisconsin, and supported herself as a waitress and store clerk. After receiving a bachelor's degree in business administration from Madison in 1964, she moved west to enroll at the University of Colorado, where she earned a bachelor's degree in economics in 1970. She then moved on to Harvard University, which granted her a master's degree in public administration in 1971.

Driven Twice into Exile

As she was completing her education in the United States, Sirleaf made regular trips back to Liberia, where in 1965 she began working for the government as a financial specialist. By 1979 she had risen to become Minister of Finance in the administration of William Tolbert. When Tolbert was deposed and executed in 1980 in a coup led by army sergeant Samuel K. Doe, Sirleaf lost her position. Though Doe subsequently appointed her president of the Liberian Bank for

At a Glance . . .

Born Ellen Johnson on October 29, 1938, in Monrovia, Liberia; married James Sirleaf, c.1955 (divorced); children: four sons. *Education:* Studied accounting and economics at the College of West Africa, late 1950s; Madison Business College, BBA, accounting, 1964; University of Colorado, BA, economics, 1970; Harvard University, MPA, 1971.

Career: Government of Liberia, financial specialist, 1965-79, Minister of Finance, 1979-80; Liberian Bank for Development and Investment, president, c.1980-81; Citicorp, vice president of regional office for Africa, 1980s; World Bank, senior loan officer, 1980s; elected to Liberian legislature (did not take office), 1985; Equator Bank, vice president, late 1980s-early 1990s; United Nations Development Programme, assistant administrator and director of regional bureau for Africa, 1992-97; candidate for president of Liberia, 1996; Governance Reform Commission (Liberia), chair, 2003-05; President of Liberia, 2006—.

Memberships: International Institute for Women in Political Leadership, founding member; Open Society Initiative for West Africa, founding chair; Women Waging Peace Network.

Awards: Freedom of Speech Award, Franklin & Eleanor Roosevelt Institute, 1988; IRI Freedom Award, International Republican Institute, 2006; David Rockefeller Bridging Leadership Award, University for a Night, 2006; Common Ground Award, Search for Common Ground, 2006; Africa Prize for Leadership for the Sustainable End of Hunger, The Hunger Project, 2006; Freedom Award, National Civil Rights Museum, 2007; Presidential Medal of Freedom, United States Government, 2007.

Addresses: *Office*—c/o Embassy of Liberia, 5201 16th St. NW, Washington, DC 20011.

Development and Investment, she served only briefly in that position, resigning when the extent of Doe's human-rights abuses became clear. With her life in danger from Doe's security forces, she fled into exile in Kenya, where she worked for several years as vice president of the regional office of Citicorp and as a senior loan officer for the World Bank.

In 1985, several months after Doe announced that he would allow free elections, Sirleaf returned to Liberia to run for a seat in the nation's Senate. While she won the election, she refused to take office when Doe claimed, contrary to the findings of election observers, that he had defeated the presidential candidate from Sirleaf's party (the Liberian Action Party). As popular opposition to Doe increased following the controversial election, he began arresting dozens of his political opponents, including Sirleaf, who was detained at the end of 1985. Subjected to harrowing psychological abuse and sentenced to ten years in prison for allegedly plotting against the government, Sirleaf was incarcerated for seven months. Her release in 1986 came only after vociferous international protest, particularly from the United States, where she moved immediately to escape further harassment. There she became a vice president at Washington's Equator Bank, an institution with a strong focus on Africa. In 1992 she left that position to become assistant administrator and director of the African bureau of the United Nations Development Programme.

In Liberia, meanwhile, Doe's abuse of power had worsened simmering ethnic and economic tensions, sparking a full-fledged civil war. Fighting first broke out in 1989, when two rebel coalitions, one led by Charles Taylor and the other by Prince Johnson, vied to unseat Doe, who was captured and executed by Johnson's forces the following year. It was Taylor, however, who soon gained the upper hand, amid human rights abuses on all sides. Taylor's growing reputation for brutality was particularly painful for Sirleaf because she had supported him briefly before the war in her eagerness to see the country free of Doe. When, in 1996, international peacekeepers succeeded in quelling the violence sufficiently to allow elections, Sirleaf returned to Liberia, despite considerable personal risk, in order to run for president against Taylor. She finished second in a field of fourteen, with 10 percent of the vote to Taylor's 75 percent. Despite his victory, Taylor continued to harass his opponents, and Sirleaf was forced for the second time into exile.

Sirleaf spent much of her time in exile trying to increase international awareness of the chaos and violence that was consuming her country. Taylor, meanwhile, was increasingly entangled in another, equally brutal civil war, this one in neighboring Sierra Leone. In 2002, as Taylor's position at home and abroad grew more precarious, Sirleaf bravely returned to Liberia to lead the Unity Party. Taylor banned all political parties in response, an act that prompted Sirleaf to remark, according to an Associated Press report in the *Washington Post,* "I did not realize that I was that powerful." The following year, intense international pressure finally forced Taylor to step down and go into exile himself. Taking his place was a new organization, the National Transitional Government of Liberia. Sirleaf was immediately selected chair of the Governance Reform Commission (GRC), one of the new administration's most important posts. Working with the GRC from 2003 to 2005, Sirleaf was responsible for designing and implementing a thorough reorganization of the country's governing structures, which had been weakened by years of corruption and mismanagement.

By 2005 Liberia was stable enough to hold elections again. Sirleaf was a frontrunner from the beginning of the campaign, with only one serious challenger, a former soccer star named George Weah. While Weah proved popular among young men, his relative lack of education and experience damaged his standing among women and older voters. In a run-off election on November 8, 2005, Sirleaf, with nearly 60 percent of the vote, defeated Weah handily. Though some of Weah's supporters challenged the fairness of the election, there was little evidence of fraud, and the results were certified by both the national election commission and international observation teams. Sirleaf thus became the first democratically elected female president in modern African history.

Enjoyed International Support

When she took office in January of 2006, Sirleaf enjoyed an immense outpouring of support from the international community and from her fellow Liberians, many of whom referred to her affectionately as "Ma" or, in a tribute to her determination, "The Iron Lady." For many of her supporters, Sirleaf personified the nation's ability to recover from the long nightmare of civil war. In a broader sense, however, she also represented new hope for Africa, particularly for African women, who have long borne the brunt of the violence, instability, and poverty that plague the continent. One indication of the hope her election inspired was the large number of prizes and honors she received in 2006 and 2007, among them a Presidential Medal of Freedom, the highest civilian honor bestowed by the United States. Perhaps Sirleaf's greatest single challenge as she began her term was to transform those hopeful expectations into immediate improvements in the country's abysmal standard of living. With the end of the war, hundreds of thousands of demobilized soldiers, many of them still armed, were suddenly on the streets without work. Crime was increasing rapidly, and the unemployment rate stood at more than 80 percent. Useable roads, electricity, sanitation, and running water, meanwhile, had been essentially unavailable for decades, even in the capital. The vast majority of the population depended on foreign charities for health care, and Liberians' life expectancy remained among the lowest in the world.

Sirleaf concentrated on the problems she believed were both pressing and relatively easy to solve. The first of these, and the one with which she had the most early success, concerned the country's massive foreign debt. Under Doe and Taylor, Liberia borrowed billions of dollars. As the interest alone on that debt threatened to cripple any budget Sirleaf and her administration devised, the president used her contacts in the international business world and her considerable personal charm to negotiate favorable settlements with a number of creditors, notably the U.S. government, which forgave $358 million in Liberian debt in February of 2007. This relief allowed Sirleaf's government to begin raising the salaries of policemen and other civil servants, a fundamental step in the struggle against corruption. (Many Liberian civil servants said they had been forced to take bribes because they were unable to feed their families on their official salary.) Sirleaf, for her part, vowed to root out corruption and to prosecute the worst offenders. While the management of government funds and contracts improved quickly, thanks in part to help from an international partnership known as the Governance and Economic Management Assistance Programme (GEMAP), small-scale corruption remained rampant.

Early results from the president's other initiatives were similarly mixed. While significant portions of Monrovia regained electrical service under her administration, most of the rest of the country was still without power in 2008. Without reliable electricity, economic development in the country was difficult to sustain. As Sirleaf told Julianne Malveaux in *Essence* in 2006, "Liberia is not a poor country. We have mineral and forest resources, fisheries and agriculture. We just need sound economic policies and a stable environment." While Sirleaf made significant progress toward those goals during her first two years in office, much more remained to be done.

Sources

Periodicals

The Economist, December 16, 2006.
Essence, March 2006.
New York Times, February 22, 2008.
Washington Post, April 30, 2002.

Online

"Biographical Brief of Ellen Johnson Sirleaf," Government of the Republic of Liberia: Executive Mansion, http://www.emansion.gov.lr/content.php?sub=President's%20Biography&related=The%20President (accessed October 31, 2008).

Toweh, Alphonso, "Liberia Leader Sets Up Anti-Corruption Commission," Reuters, August 22, 2008, http://africa.reuters.com/country/LR/news/usnLM96200.html (accessed October 31, 2008).

—R. Anthony Kugler

Samuel Snow

1923–2008

Custodian

Samuel Snow was a twenty-one-year-old U.S. Army private when he was wrongfully convicted by court-martial for a 1944 riot at a military base near Puget Sound, Washington. It was one of the largest court-martial cases of the World War II era, but those prosecuted believed they had been betrayed by the military service they had sworn to protect and serve. Several decades later the truth about the Fort Lawton riots emerged, but justice came too late for nearly all of them. In 2007 Snow was one of only two survivors among the twenty-eight soldiers who received apologies from the Army admitting that it had erred in prosecuting the case. "It means a lot to me that it's going to come out in the paper," Snow told William Yardley in the *New York Times*. "Now people are going to see that I wasn't a villain."

Snow was born in 1923 in Fort White, Florida, a small community near the Ichetucknee River. His father was a farm laborer, and his mother took in laundry to help support their six children, of whom Snow was the youngest. He attended segregated schools in the area, and spent a year living with his mother and an aunt in Leesburg to attend the Lake County Training School. At the height of World War II, Snow joined the U.S. Army. He hoped to become a mechanic once his service ended and he could access the benefits of the G.I. Bill, which provided college or trade school tuition. After completing basic training in Louisiana in July of 1944, he was granted two weeks' leave before he was to be shipped out to New Guinea with the 650th Port Company, an all-black unit. In August he reported to Fort Lawton, on Puget Sound in Washington State, to await a carrier that would take him to the Pacific theater of war.

Accused in Fort Lawton Riot

Fort Lawton was a common point of departure for combat troops, but several hundred prisoners of war (POWs) were also held there. The largest contingent were Italian men, but because Italy had surrendered to Allied forces a year earlier, they were not considered very much of a threat and were allowed to leave the base. Such casual treatment angered many, including white soldiers who had fought against the Italians as enemy combatants, and black soldiers who were still relegated to segregated units and in some cases enjoyed fewer freedoms than the POWs. A day after Snow arrived, a fight broke out between the Italian POWs and African-American soldiers. It quickly reached the proportions of an all-out riot, and an Italian prisoner of war named Guglielmo Olivotto was found hanged to death. Snow recalled hearing the whistle that summoned soldiers to stand at attention in front of their barracks, and headed outside. Once there, he was knocked unconscious. When he was revived in the hospital, he learned he was about to be placed in the stockade, or military prison, for his involvement in the melee.

Snow was one of forty-three black soldiers brought up on charges relating to Olivotto's death and the riot, and one of twenty-eight prosecuted. Only two lawyers were assigned to represent all of the defendants, and they had less than two weeks to prepare for the trial.

At a Glance . . .

Born on September 23, 1923, in Fort White, FL; died July 26, 2008, in Seattle, WA; son of Kid (a laborer) and Ruley (a laundress) Snow; married Margaret, 1947; children: Maurice (died, 2007), Kay (died, 1968); Ray. *Military service:* U.S. Army, 1944. *Religion:* African Methodist Episcopal.

Career: Morrison Methodist Church, Leesburg, FL, custodian for two decades.

Twenty-six of the men were convicted of rioting and two on manslaughter charges. Snow was among the first group, and spent more than a year in a military jail. After his release on March 2, 1946, he returned to Leesburg, Florida, where his father helped him burn his dishonorable discharge papers. "I didn't want anyone to see them," he told John Barry in the *St. Petersburg Times.* "No one wants to be a failure." Believing he was wrongly charged and convicted, Snow twice tried to have his military record corrected. In 1949 the Army Board for Correction of Military Records rejected his case, but in 1975 a second petition resulted in a change in his discharge status from dishonorable to general under honorable conditions.

Snow never told anyone what had happened to him during the war. For members of the so-called Greatest Generation, wartime service was almost universal among men of his age, and a dishonorable discharge was a black mark on one's record no matter what the extenuating circumstances. Not even his wife, Margaret, whom he married in 1947, nor his three children knew about the Fort Lawton riot. For the next several decades Snow worked as a custodian at a church or in other odd jobs, in part because an employment application to a company or government organization would have included a space in which he was expected to reveal his military record.

Cleared of Wrongful Conviction

In 1987 the story of the Fort Lawton riot piqued the interest of a Seattle television reporter named Jack Hamann. Knowing it was rare for blacks to lynch someone, as the army prosecutors had claimed, Hamann researched the incident. He discovered an unpublished report on the riot written by brigadier general Elliott Cooke, who "concluded that the case was a sham," wrote Barry in the *St. Petersburg Times.* "It lacked any physical evidence. The crime scene—an obstacle course where the Italian soldier had been found hanging from a cable—had been trampled over. Even the barracks where the fighting occurred had been repainted. The whole case was based on the testimony of two POWs and four black soldiers, whom Cooke believed had scores to settle." Hamann wrote a book about the case, *On American Soil: How Justice Became a Casualty of World War II,* that was published in 2005 and aided in reviving interest in what was the largest Army court-martial during World War II. The book linked the actual hanging of Olivotto to a white military police (MP) officer, and also noted that none of the Fort Lawton MPs acted quickly enough to stop the riot, and had perhaps even taunted the black GIs into attacking the Italians.

In 2007 the Board for Correction of Military Records finally admitted the prosecution of the African-American men had been a deeply flawed one. With that, Snow was now eligible for back pay for the year he spent in military prison, and later that year received a check for $725. There was no adjustment for inflation or interest, and Snow did not cash the check. A U.S. senator from Florida, Bill Nelson, took up the case of Snow and the other wrongfully convicted men, and calculated that his amount should rightfully be about $80,000. There was only one other surviving member of the twenty-seven others, but the families of the deceased were still eligible to receive the benefits.

Snow told the press he was more interested in a formal apology from the Army than any cash windfall, and that came in the summer of 2008, when Army officials scheduled an event at Fort Lawton for July 26. Now eighty-four years old and in failing health, Snow nevertheless traveled to Seattle for the ceremony. After a celebratory dinner in Seattle with Hamann and others on July 25, Snow began to experience issues with the pacemaker that regulated his heart, and he was taken to the hospital. His son Ray attended the ceremony the next day, and returned to his father's bedside with the honorable discharge papers. Just hours later, Snow died. "My father never held any animosity," Ray Snow said at the ceremony, according to Barry in the *St. Petersburg Times.* "He said, 'Son, God has been good to me. If I hold this in my heart, then I can't walk in forgiveness.'"

Sources

Books

Hamann, Jack, *On Native Soil: How Justice Became a Casualty of World War II,* Algonquin Books of Chapel Hill, 2005.

Periodicals

New York Times, October 27, 2007, p. A1; December 1, 2007, p. A10; July 30, 2008, p. A10.
Orlando Sentinel, July 27, 2008.
St. Petersburg Times (St. Petersburg, FL), November 9, 2007, p. E1; July 29, 2008, p. A1.

—Carol Brennan

Emmitt Thomas

1943—

Professional football player, coach

Thomas, Emmitt, photograph. Getty Images.

Emmitt Thomas capped his forty-two years in the National Football League with an induction into the Pro Football Hall of Fame in Canton, Ohio, in August of 2008. Thomas played thirteen seasons with the Kansas City Chiefs before starting the second phase of his career as an assistant coach for a succession of teams, including the Atlanta Falcons. "My personal road to Canton is very simple," Thomas said in his Hall of Fame acceptance speech, according to ESPN.com. "I love playing football. I never wanted to cheat the fans, my organization, my teammates or my coaches by not giving my best at all times."

Thomas was born on June 3, 1943, in Angleton, Texas, the seat of Brazoria County. His mother, Carrie, died when he was eight, and he had little contact with his father. His grandparents, Lewis and Virginia Fyles, raised Thomas and his three siblings. "Growing up, I was resentful and angry at other families around us because they seemed fully intact," he recalled in his Hall of Fame speech. "I'd often lay awake at night wondering why our family had to be different."

At Marshall High School, Thomas played just one season of football before entering Bishop College, a historically black college founded in Marshall, Texas, in 1881, that relocated to Dallas in 1961. His baseball coach suggested he try out for the football team, and he emerged as a skilled wide receiver and occasional quarterback. He was eligible for the 1966 National Football League (NFL) draft, but the roster was especially heavy with defensive players that year, and he stood little chance against players from the top-tier schools. The Kansas City Chiefs, however, had been looking for new talent among athletes from historically black colleges like Bishop, and gave Thomas a tryout. Initially, the rookie played wide receiver, but then "they called me in one day, and I thought I was getting cut," he recounted in an interview with Kent Youngblood in the Minneapolis *Star Tribune*. Instead the Chiefs' coach, Hank Stram, told Thomas he was being moved to defensive back under assistant coach Tom Bettis. "I was raw. I mean, I could run and jump and catch. But Tom taught me everything else."

Thomas wound up in the Chiefs' cornerback position, where his main role was to intercept forward passes. When he first donned his No. 18 Chiefs' jersey, the franchise was part of the now-defunct American Foot-

At a Glance...

Born Emmitt Earl Thomas on June 3, 1943, in Angleton, TX; son of Lewis Fyles Jr. and Carrie Thomas; married Gloria Diane Campbell (divorced); married Jacqui; children: (with Campbell) Derek, Dedra.

Career: Kansas City Chiefs, cornerback, 1966–78; Central Missouri State University, member of coaching staff, 1979–80; St. Louis Cardinals, receivers coach, 1981–85; Washington Redskins, receivers coach, 1986–87, secondary coach, 1987–94; Philadelphia Eagles, defensive coordinator, 1995–98; Green Bay Packers, defensive coordinator, 1999; Minnesota Vikings, defensive coordinator, 2000–01; Atlanta Falcons, senior defensive assistant/secondary coach, 2002—, interim head coach, December 2007–January 2008.

Awards: Inducted into the Pro Football Hall of Fame, 2008.

Addresses: *Home*—Suwanee, GA. *Office*—Atlanta Falcons, 4400 Falcon Pkwy., Flowery Branch, GA 30542.

---

ball League (AFL), and in 1969 Thomas led the AFL with nine interceptions. A year later the Chiefs became part of the NFL, and Thomas had twelve interceptions during the 1974 season, which again made him the League leader. One of his most famous interceptions came during Super Bowl IV in 1970, when the Chiefs beat the heavily favored Minnesota Vikings by a score of 23–7.

Thomas was a five-time Pro Bowl selection, and when he retired in 1978 he ended his career with fifty-eight interceptions, a Chiefs record that still held thirty years later. His first coaching job was at Central Missouri State University in Warrensburg. In 1981 he was hired by the St. Louis Cardinals as a receivers coach, and spent four seasons with the team. He joined the coaching staff of the Washington Redskins in 1986 in the same position, and was made secondary coach a year later. In all, Thomas spent eight seasons with the Redskins before moving to Philadelphia to take a job as the Eagles' defensive coordinator. He worked under head coach Ray Rhodes and moved with Rhodes when he became head coach of the Green Bay Packers in 1999. At the time—with Thomas as defense coach and Sherman Lewis serving as offensive coordinator—it marked the first time that an NFL team had a trio of African Americans in its top three coaching slots.

Thomas served as defensive coordinator for the Minnesota Vikings before joining the staff of the Atlanta Falcons in 2002 as the senior defensive assistant coach and secondary coach. The team went through a succession of head coaches over the next five years: first Dan Reeves, then Jim Mora, and finally in December of 2007 Bobby Petrino abruptly resigned to take a coaching job with the University of Arkansas Razorbacks in the midst of a dismal season for the Falcons in which they had won just three out of thirteen games. Thomas was named interim head coach for the Falcons on December 12, 2007, and given the task of shepherding the team through the rest of the season. "This organization has been good to me," Thomas told D. Orlando Ledbetter in the *Atlanta Journal-Constitution* when the announcement was made. "I am hoping that I'm able to step up for them and get this thing done for them for the next three games." The Falcons ended their 2007 season with a 44–41 win over the Seattle Seahawks at Atlanta's home field, the Georgia Dome.

In January of 2008 Thomas handed over coaching duties to new hire Mike Smith. A few weeks later, the Pro Football Hall of Fame announced that Thomas was to become one of its Class of 2008 inductees. Prior to the ceremony in August, Thomas requested his name be listed in the official records as Emmitt Earl Fyles Thomas, with the "Fyles" added in honor of his late grandfather Lewis, who "is still my hero," Thomas told family, friends, and colleagues who had gathered for the ceremony. "I remember those long hot summer nights sitting on the porch listening to baseball games and prize fights and other sporting events. It was during these times that he taught me life's greatest lesson. He taught me about honor, commitment, love, religion, hard work and respect."

Thomas became one of 247 members of the Pro Football Hall of Fame though his twenty-year eligibility window had closed long ago. He was chosen by the Hall of Fame seniors committee, which can make exceptions to that rule, and at the August ceremony was introduced by his son Derek, who serves as the basketball coach for the Western Illinois University Fighting Leathernecks. The younger Thomas recalled wondering why his father—whose fifty-eight career interceptions remain among the top ten in NFL history—had not yet been inducted into the Hall of Fame. "He'd always said good things come to people who wait," Derek Thomas told Rick Gosselin in the *Dallas Morning News*. "He'd tell me, 'If it happens, it happens. But if it doesn't, I know what I did. You know what I did. I'm at peace with that.'"

Sources

Periodicals

Atlanta Journal-Constitution, December 13, 2007, p. B1; August 2, 2008, p. B1.

Dallas Morning News, February 1, 2008; February 2, 2008.

Star-Ledger (Newark, NJ), December 30, 1996, p. 41.

Star Tribune (Minneapolis, MN), July 23, 2000, p. 1C.

Online

Porter, Todd, "Bet on the Tears: Six New Immortals Bare Their Hearts," CantonRepository.com, August 3, 2008, http://www.cantonrep.com/hof/article.php?ID=424082 (accessed October 27, 2008).

"Thomas: 'I Am Truly Humbled,'" ESPN.com, http://proxy.espn.go.com/nfl/halloffame08/news/story?id=3516486 (accessed October 27, 2008).

—Carol Brennan

Reed V. Tuckson

1951(?)—

Physician, health care executive

Reed V. Tuckson is a physician and advocate for healthcare reform in the United States. He served as public health commissioner in Washington, DC, as president of a Charles R. Drew medical school, in executive appointments within the American Medical Association and the March of Dimes, and in a high-ranking position with a managed-health care organization. The role of organized medicine, Tuckson told Deborah L. Shelton in *American Medical News,* is to serve as "an unequivocal advocate, a conscience for the nation, that says to the American people that the first order of business of a civilized and democratic society has to be whether or not the people of that society have the opportunity to live to their fullest capacity and to the greatest extent possible. Health is the most important determinant of the quality of life for any society."

A native of Washington, DC, Tuckson was born into an accomplished family during the early 1950s. His father was Dr. Coleman Tuckson, a dentist who was a key figure in the founding of Howard University's school of dentistry and helped launch the school's oral radiology department in the early 1960s. Tuckson's mother,

Tuckson, Reed V., photograph. Roger L. Wollenberg/UPI/Landov.

Evelyn, was a visiting nurse during the golden age of the U.S. public health mission in the mid-twentieth century. One of her duties was to visit new mothers and their infants to ensure both were doing well, a service that was part of a generously funded campaign that had been launched earlier in the century to reduce infant mortality rates in the United States.

Tuckson earned an undergraduate degree from Howard University in 1973 and went on to graduate from Georgetown University's School of Medicine in 1978. His residency was spent at the Hospital of the University of Pennsylvania, where he trained as a specialist in internal medicine. Part of this time he spent as an admitting doctor at the Veterans Affairs hospital in Philadelphia, where on a single day he signed in five new patients with end-stage heart disease. "I realized that so many causes of heart disease are preventable; it really bothered me," he told Rebecca Voelker in *American Medical News.* "I could have done an intellectually satisfying work-up and presented an advanced course of therapeutics. But what became most important was how to redesign our health system to prevent these diseases from occurring."

At a Glance...

Born c. 1951, in Washington, DC; son of Coleman (a dentist) and Evelyn (a nurse) Tuckson; married Margie Malone; four children. *Education:* Howard University, BS, 1973; Georgetown University School of Medicine, MD, 1978; studied heath care administration and policy at the Wharton School of Business, 1981–83.

Career: Hospital of the University of Pennsylvania, intern and resident, c. 1978–81; Elmira Jeffries Nursing Home, Philadelphia, founding medical director, 1981–85; Mental Retardation and Developmental Disabilities Administration, Washington, DC, administrator, 1983–85; deputy commissioner of public health, District of Columbia, 1985–86, and commissioner of public health, 1986–90; March of Dimes Birth Defects Foundation, senior vice president for programs, 1990–91; Charles R. Drew University of Medicine and Science, president, 1991–97; American Medical Association, group vice president for professional standards, 1997–2000; United Health Group, senior vice president of consumer health and medical-care advancement, 2000–06, executive vice president and chief of medical affairs, 2006—.

Memberships: American Medical Association.

Addresses: *Office*—United Health Group, PO Box 1459, Minneapolis, MN 55440-1459.

While still a resident physician, Tuckson launched a radio program aimed at African-American listeners and their health issues, and organized a support group for sickle-cell anemia sufferers. His interest in public health led to a Clinical Scholars fellowship from the Robert Wood Johnson Foundation, and with that stipend he studied health care administration and policy at the University of Pennsylvania's Wharton School of Business from 1981 to 1983. During some of this period he also worked as a medical director for a nursing home, and when he returned to Washington he took a job as administrator for the District of Columbia's Mental Retardation and Developmental Disabilities Administration. In 1985 Tuckson became the deputy commissioner of public health in the city, and a year later was promoted to commissioner of public health. He spent the next four years attempting to improve the quality of life for District of Columbia residents on a budget that consistently shrank every year because of cutbacks in federal spending.

In 1990 Tuckson resigned as public health commissioner to take a post with the March of Dimes Birth Defects Foundation as senior vice president for programs. A year later, he moved to Los Angeles when he was appointed the new president of the Charles R. Drew University of Medicine and Science, a private school known as a center for health-care professionals seeking to treat those in urban or medically underserved areas. As Tuckson explained to Voelker, "Drew University was created out of the ashes of the Watts riots of the 1960s by the community because they knew no access to health care. Our mission is to develop new knowledge to serve this community." Tuckson's increasing prominence brought him to the attention of President Bill Clinton, who placed First Lady Hillary Rodham Clinton at the head of a special White House task force on health-care reform in the early 1990s. Tuckson was one of four dozen medical professionals whom President Clinton invited to serve on the review panel in the spring of 1993 before the administration presented its recommendations to Congress.

Tuckson left Drew University in 1997 to take a post with the American Medical Association, the leading organization for physicians in the United States. He served as group vice president for professional standards until 2000, when he accepted an offer from the United Health Group in Minneapolis, Minnesota, as senior vice president of consumer health and medical-care advancement. The managed-care company was the second-largest health insurer in the nation, but its member-physicians—342,000 under contract at the time—were deeply dissatisfied with United Health's policies. There were lawsuits that claimed the physicians were deliberately underpaid for patient services submitted, and others that charged the company with arbitrarily denying claims. Tuckson was brought in to resolve these issues.

In December of 2006 Tuckson was made executive vice president and chief of medical affairs at United Health. Despite his role as an executive with a health-care group, he remains a staunch advocate for proposals to help uninsured Americans, including one put forth in 2007 that was endorsed by the American Medical Association. There were some flaws in the plan, Tuckson conceded to Robert Pear in the *New York Times,* but the point was to help the forty-seven million Americans without health insurance. "Day after day, there is debate and discussion." "Day after day, people die. We are sick and tired of the debate. We are focusing on what is achievable."

Though Tuckson is well known in medical circles, his name surfaced in a slew of mainstream media reports in July of 2008 when he was booked as a guest on *Fox*

News Sunday. Seated next to Rev. Jesse Jackson in a studio awaiting their interview segments, Tuckson posed a question to Jackson about Democratic presidential hopeful Barack Obama, and Jackson responded with disparaging remarks about the candidate, mistakenly thinking his microphone was turned off. The scurrilous comments later surfaced in the news media, and Jackson issued a public apology.

A father of four, Tuckson is married to Margie Malone, the sister of the late Vivian Malone Jones, who played a historic role in integrating the University of Alabama in 1963. He credited his family with instilling in him the belief that all people have a right to high-quality health care. "My mother is a very powerful symbol for me of what it means to be in this profession, what it means to be a health professional who cares for people," he told Shelton in the *American Medical News.* "I understand very deeply the commitment we must have to the health of the American people."

Sources

Periodicals

American Medical News, November 1, 1993, p. 18; October 27, 1997, p. 7.
Essence, November 1994, p. 162.
Modern Healthcare, September 25, 2000, p. 24; September 17, 2007, p. S15.
New York Times, January 19, 2007, p. A21.

Online

"Reed Tuckson, M.D., Named One of *Ebony*'s Most Influential Black Americans," Reuters.com, April 14, 2008, http://www.reuters.com/article/pressRelease/idUS199906+14-Apr-2008+BW20080414 (accessed October 12, 2008).

—Carol Brennan

Michael Jai White

1967—

Actor

White, Michael Jai, photograph. Brad Barket/Getty Images.

Actor and martial-arts expert Michael Jai White became the first black superhero in a major motion picture when he starred in 1997's cult hit *Spawn*. The movie—based on the popular comic-book series of the same name—starred White as a slain government agent who makes a deal with the devil in order to see his family once again. In an interview in *Jet*, White described the saga as "very Shakespearean," noting that his character's skin color was ultimately of little importance to the story. "People will be able to identify because it's a universal thing; it's not a distinction set for any race," he said. "A hero is defined by what he has to overcome."

White's own saga bears some traces of the heroic. Born in 1967 and raised by a single mother who was a teacher, he never knew his father and spent the first years of his life in a gritty part of Brooklyn known as East New York. The neighborhood's changing racial demographic brought some notorious disturbances between a Italian Americans and African Americans during White's childhood, including a night in June of 1973 when three African-American New York City police officers in plainclothes were attacked; that same night, an African-American woman's apartment was firebombed and groups of teens hurled rocks at one another.

White and his mother escaped the violence of East New York when she took a job in Bridgeport, Connecticut, about the time he started second grade. His new best friend was a neighbor who took karate classes. "I wasn't allowed to go because my mom thought it was too dangerous," White recalled in an interview with Shawn Perine in *Muscle & Fitness*. "So when they came back from class I'd have them teach me everything they learned." Renel White finally relented and agreed to let her son visit the karate dojo, where his friends told the sensei that he had already learned everything they had taught him. The master asked to see a demonstration and was impressed enough to let White enroll for free.

White had a black belt by the time he reached his teens and began weight training as well. Tensions at home increased, however, and he left home at age fourteen. He fell in with a bad crowd in Bridgeport, and became known as an enforcer for local thugs. At fifteen he was shot twice: one bullet in his arm, and the other in his hip. "It didn't seem like a big deal at the time," he told Perine. "A lot of people I knew had been shot." The

At a Glance...

Born on November 10, 1967, in Brooklyn, NY; son of Renel (a teacher); married Courtenay Chatman (a physician), August 2005; children: Jai, Devin. *Education:* Attended the University of Connecticut and Southern Connecticut State University; studied acting in New York City.

Career: Middle school teacher, c. 1989–92; actor.

Addresses: *Agent*—Writers & Artists Agency, 8383 Wilshire Blvd., Ste. 550, Beverly Hills, CA 90211.

---

incident served as a wake-up call, and White began devoting more time to his schoolwork and sports instead. Before he graduated from Bridgeport Central High School in 1982, he set a school record in the shot put (45 feet 9 inches) that still remained more than twenty-five years later.

In college White switched majors a few times, discarding political science and engineering at the University of Connecticut and Southern Connecticut State University. He eventually became a teacher of emotionally disturbed middle-school students in Bridgeport, but took acting classes and occasionally ventured back to New York City for auditions. After television commercial work and roles in the daytime dramas *Loving* and *All My Children*, White made his film debut in *The Toxic Avenger, Part II* in 1989. Three years later, he quit teaching altogether to pursue acting as a full-time career in Los Angeles.

White's early work included appearances on episodes of *Saved by the Bell, Martin, Living Single,* and *NYPD Blue*. His break came when his agent suggested he audition for the title role in a planned HBO biographical movie about world heavyweight boxing champion Mike Tyson, who was serving a three-year prison term at the time. "I thought I didn't look or sound anything like Mike, so I didn't even see any point in going," White said in *Muscle & Fitness*, but White beat out nearly a thousand other contenders for the title role in 1995's *Tyson* because of his impressive martial arts. Writing in the *New York Times*, Robert Lipsyte asserted that White's "eerie mimicry of Iron Mike's sweet retreats and dangerous rages offers some humanity to what is basically a fight film," while Ginia Bellafante in *Time* commended the "eerie emotional vacancy" White brought to the role. Bellafante further noted that White "is not given much dialogue, which serves to emphasize Tyson's position as little more than a pawn of handlers."

White's next starring role came in *Spawn* in 1997. The movie's plot was based on a popular comic-book series from Todd McFarlane, who had revived the *Super-Man* franchise in the 1980s, and the *Spawn* anti-hero was notable as one of the rare African-American crime fighters in the genre. Media reviews were mostly negative, faulting a reliance on dazzling special effects over character and storyline. Roger Ebert did note in the *Chicago Sun-Times*, however, that the lead actor "makes a powerful Spawn with a presence both menacing and touching."

White went on to appear in several major Hollywood productions, including the Jerry Springer comedy *Ringmaster* and an Alec Baldwin/Andre Braugher thriller *Thick as Thieves*, both from 1998. In 1999 he appeared with action star Jean-Claude Van Damme in *Universal Soldier: The Return*, and two years later he was cast alongside Steven Seagal in *Exit Wounds*. Other film appearances include *Getting Played* and the Tyler Perry comedy *Why Did I Get Married?* In 2008 White performed in one of the all-time top-grossing films, *The Dark Knight*, as Gambol, an underworld figure. Later that year the actor took on starring roles in *Black Dynamite*—a reworking of the 1970s-era blaxploitation-genre films—and *Blood and Bone*, in which he was cast as a man drawn into an underworld-controlled street-fighting ring.

White holds seven separate black belts in various martial arts, including kyokushin karate, tae kwon do, goju ryu, and tang soo do. His childhood friend from Bridgeport, the neighbor who introduced him to karate, grew up to become professional bodybuilder Troy Alves. Looking back on the path they had each traveled, White was levelheaded about his success in Hollywood. "I never forget that it's all just make-believe," he told Perine. "I enjoy what I do, but I don't pretend for a minute that acting is any more important than teaching or being a doctor. I'm just an adult who's getting paid to pretend."

Selected works

Films

The Toxic Avenger, Part II, 1989.
True Identity, 1991.
Full Contact, 1993.
Lion Strike, 1995.
City of Industry, 1997.
Spawn, 1997.
The Bus Stop, 1998.
Ringmaster, 1998.
Thick as Thieves, 1998.
Breakfast of Champions, 1999.
Universal Soldier: The Return, 1999.
Exit Wounds, 2001.
Honor among Thieves, 2002.
Pandora's Box, 2002.
Justice, 2003.
Getting Played, 2005.
Undisputed II: Last Man Standing, 2006.

Why Did I Get Married?, 2007.
Black Dynamite, 2008.
Blood and Bone, 2008.
The Dark Knight, 2008.
The Slammin' Salmon, 2008.

Sources

Periodicals

Chicago Sun-Times, August 1, 1997.
Jet, September 22, 1997, p. 35.
Muscle & Fitness, July 2006, p. 186.
New York Times, April 30, 1995.
Time, May 8, 1995, p. 98.

Online

"Boys' Track Records," Central High School (Bridgeport, CT), http://bridgeport.ct.schoolwebpages.com/education/components/scrapbook/default.php?sectiondetailid=5121 (accessed October 12, 2008).

—Carol Brennan

Isabel Wilkerson

1961—

Journalist, educator

One of the most prominent reporters in the country, Isabel Wilkerson first gained national attention in 1994, when she became the first African-American woman to win a Pulitzer Prize for journalism. During her career at the *New York Times,* she developed her own distinctive style of narrative reporting, one that requires an unusual degree of empathy and close attention to detail.

Isabel Wilkerson was born in Washington, DC, in 1961. Her parents, both natives of the South, had remained in Washington after meeting at Howard University, one of the city's leading institutions. Their migration northward would later inspire Wilkerson to begin work on a narrative history of the other African Americans, millions in number, who made similar migrations out of the South between 1900 and the end of the civil-rights era. Commenting on this Great Migration, Wilkerson noted in 2006 to Kim Urquhart in the *Emory Report,* "It was something in my history that I had taken for granted, but if my parents had not been participants in this movement, I wouldn't be here today."

Wilkerson's work in journalism began with her high-school newspaper, which she edited. After graduation, she entered Howard University, where she immediately began work as a reporter for *The Hilltop,* its highly regarded campus paper. She soon rose to become its editor-in-chief. By 1983, when she received her bachelor's degree, she had attracted the attention of newspaper editors across the country, thanks in part to her determined and successful pursuit of internships at the *Washington Post* and other influential papers. Also helpful in this regard was the Mark of Excellence Award she received from the Society of Professional Journalists for the best feature writing by a college student. After a year as a feature writer at the *Detroit Free Press* Wilkerson moved in 1984 to the *New York Times,* where she worked as a metropolitan reporter, covering court news and local politics, for two years. Then, in 1986 she was promoted to national correspondent, a post she held until 1991. Based in Detroit, Michigan, and Chicago, Illinois, Wilkerson covered a variety of Midwestern stories that she and her editors believed deserved a national audience. In 1986, for example, she wrote movingly of the controversy surrounding an Indiana judge's imposition of the death penalty on a sixteen-year-old girl convicted of a brutal murder; the sentence was later commuted to sixty years in prison. A year later, she portrayed the miraculous survival of a four-year-old girl after a fiery plane crash in Detroit.

Even at this relatively early stage of her career, Wilkerson's obvious empathy for the people she interviewed set her stories apart from those of her peers. Describing her approach in the *Emory Report,* Wilkerson told Urquhart, "In the end, nothing really matters until I can see from the perspective of the human heart." Noting the enthusiastic response of readers, the management of the *Times* offered Wilkerson the job of Chicago bureau chief in 1991. It was an almost unprecedented promotion for someone only about thirty years of age.

Wilkerson thrived as a bureau chief, in part because the position allowed her to spend weeks, even months,

At a Glance . . .

Born in 1961 in Washington, DC; married. *Education:* Howard University, BA, 1983.

Career: *Detroit Free Press,* feature writer, 1983–84; *New York Times,* metropolitan reporter, 1984–86, national correspondent, 1986–91, Chicago bureau chief, 1991–95, senior writer, 1995–; Princeton University, Ferris Professor of Journalism, 1996–97; Emory University, James M. Cox Professor of Journalism, 2006—.

Awards: Mark of Excellence Award for best feature writing by a college student, Society of Professional Journalists, early 1980s; George Polk Award for regional reporting, Long Island University, 1993; Pulitzer Prize for feature writing, 1994; Journalist of the Year, National Association of Black Journalists, 1994.

Addresses: *Office*—c/o Journalism Program, Mailstop 1535-001-1AB, Emory University, Atlanta, GA 30322; *E-mail*—iwilker@emory.edu.

---

covering a single story. This methodical approach paid dividends in 1993, when she received from Long Island University the annual George Polk Award for regional reporting. Nineteen ninety-three was also the year in which three of her best-known stories appeared. Two of these concerned the aftermath of a devastating flood in the small Missouri town of Hardin. The third was an in-depth study of a ten year-old boy's daily life in one of the poorest neighborhoods in Chicago. Wilkerson spent weeks with the boy, Nicholas, and his family. The profile that resulted, entitled "First Born, Fast Grown: The Manful Life of Nicholas, 10," is a wrenching portrayal of a boy forced by desperate circumstances to assume an adult's responsibilities. "He is all boy—squirming in line, sliding down banisters, shirt-tail out, shoes untied, dreaming of becoming a fireman so he can save people—but his walk," Wilkerson wrote of Nicholas, "is the stiff slog of a worried father behind on the rent."

Nicholas's story and the two Missouri pieces brought Wilkerson the 1994 Pulitzer Prize for feature writing. The award was a milestone in American journalism. Though African-American women had won Pulitzers in other fields, none had won for journalism. Wilkerson was also the first African American, male or female, to win for individual reporting. In the citation (quoted by an anonymous writer in the *New York Times* on April 13, 1994) that accompanied the award, the Pulitzer Committee praised "the high literary quality and originality" of Wilkerson's work.

The year after her Pulitzer, Wilkerson stepped down as Chicago bureau chief to become a senior writer for the *Times,* with the authority to pursue stories across the nation. In the late 1990s, however, she took a leave of absence to undertake a variety of outside projects, several of which involved teaching. In 1996–97, for example, she served as Ferris Professor of Journalism at Princeton University. She has also lectured at Harvard University, Northwestern University, and Emory University, where she was named the James M. Cox Professor of Journalism in 2006. Her courses at Emory have included one on the history and ethics of journalism. In addition to teaching, Wilkerson has continued to contribute occasional articles to the *Times* and other publications. Particularly notable in this regard was a 2005 follow-up piece in the *Times* on the mother of Nicholas, the Chicago boy she had profiled a dozen years earlier. Entitled "Angela Whitiker's Climb," the article was reprinted in *Class Matters* (Times Books, 2005), a collection of essays on the changing boundaries of social class in America.

In 2008 Wilkerson was concentrating on her history of the Great Migration, a book that has occupied her for many years. She first won support for the project during the late 1990s, receiving a publisher's advance in 1997 and a research fellowship from the Guggenheim Foundation the following year. Since that time, however, the work has grown to monumental proportions. In a sign of the painstaking approach that has long been her trademark, Wilkerson had personally conducted more than 1,500 interviews for the book, tentatively titled *North by South.*

Selected writings

(Contributor) *Class Matters,* Times Books, 2005.

Sources

Periodicals

Emory Report, September 25, 2006.
Quadrangle (Emory University), Spring 2008, pp. 4–5.
New York Times, November 2, 1986; August 19, 1987; April 4, 1993; April 13, 1994; June 12, 2005.

Online

Estrov, Anya, "Isabel Wilkerson," New York University Journalism Department, http://journalism.nyu.edu/pubzone/race_class/thiercernese/speaker5.htm (accessed November 6, 2008).
"Isabel Wilkerson, Journalism," Emory University Provost's Office, September 2007, http://www.emory.edu/PROVOST/greatscholars/IsabelWilkerson.htm (accessed November 6, 2008).

—R. Anthony Kugler

Thomas Alphonso Wilkins

1956—

Conductor

Wilkins, Thomas Alphonso, photograph. Mathew Imaging/WireImage.

Conductor Thomas Wilkins became music director of the Omaha Symphony in 2005, making him one of just a handful of African Americans conducting a major orchestra in the United States. Known for his commitment to music education and mentoring programs as well as a sharp wit, Wilkins is sometimes asked if he has ever broken his baton in the middle of a performance. He admitted to a writer in the *Tampa Tribune* that he once split one in half on his podium during "the last chord of the first movement of Beethoven's *Symphony No. 1*. It went straight up in the air. I and about 1,200 other people watched as it took about eight minutes to make it back to the ground."

Wilkins was born in 1956 in Norfolk, Virginia, where he was raised by a single mother in the Young Park public housing projects. He attended the nearby Young Park Elementary School, which served the predominantly black community, and settled upon his chosen career during a school field trip in the third grade. His class went to the Norfolk Arena Theater to see a special performance of the Norfolk Symphony Orchestra, and it was Wilkins's first encounter with any kind of live music. "When I saw the conductor as opposed to the other people in the orchestra, he seemed to be the person that was shaping and playing and being surrounded by all that sound," he recalled in an interview with Cathy Gant Hill in the *News & Record*. "And that was where I wanted to be...I went home and took my toy soldiers out and arranged them all in orchestra seating."

Wilkins began playing violin in the school orchestra in fourth grade. In high school he played cello in the orchestra and tuba in the marching band. Growing up during the late 1960s and early 1970s in a rapidly disintegrating urban environment, Wilkins stayed on a narrowly focused path. "I look at music as the thing that probably saved my life," he asserted in an interview on LAist.com. "In poverty in an inner-city neighborhood, you are not overrun with positive choices. Because I had chosen music a lot of my critical life questions were answered: who I would hang out with, whether or not I would go to college, what do I do with my spare time."

Wilkins earned a bachelor's degree in music education from Shenandoah Conservatory of Music in Winchester, Virginia, in 1978, and went on to the prestigious New England Conservatory of Music in Boston, which

At a Glance . . .

Born on September 10, 1956 in Norfolk, VA; son of Wallace Y. Wilkins Sr.; married Sheri-Lee (a physical therapist), June 14, 1985; children: Erica, Nicole. *Education:* Shenandoah Conservatory of Music, BME 1978; New England Conservatory of Music, MM 1982.

Career: Shenandoah Conservatory Symphony, assistant conductor, 1976–78; Busch Entertainment Corporation, music director, 1981–82; New England Conservatory Repertory Orchestra, assistant conductor, 1981–82; Northwest Indiana Youth Orchestra, assistant conductor, conductor, 1983; North Park College Orchestra, music director; University of Tennessee—Chattanooga, director orchestral studies, 1987–89; has also taught at North Park University and Virginia Commonwealth University; Richmond Symphony, associate conductor; Florida Orchestra, resident conductor, c. 1994–02; Detroit Symphony Orchestra, resident conductor, 2000—; Omaha Symphony, music director, 2005—; Hollywood Bowl Orchestra, principal guest conductor, 2008—.

Memberships: Raymond James Charitable Fund, board chair.

Awards: Classical Roots Musical Achievement Award, Detroit Symphony Orchestra, 2007.

Addresses: *Home*—Omaha, NE. *Office*—Omaha Symphony, 1605 Howard St., Omaha, NE 68102-2705.

granted him a master of music degree in orchestral conducting in 1982. By this point Wilkins had some teaching and conducting experience on his résumé, including a stint at the Busch Gardens theme park in Williamsburg, Virginia, where he conducted six performances every day, six days per week. That experience instilled in him a deep work ethic, he told LAist.com. "One of the things that was impressed upon us as young musicians in 'show business' is that when you get to the sixth show on the sixth day, it is still the first show for the people in the audience. They deserve the same enthusiasm, energy, and passion that you gave to the first show on the first day."

Wilkins taught at North Park College in the Chicago area and at the Chattanooga campus of the University of Tennessee in the 1980s. He began conducting in earnest with Virginia's Richmond Symphony orchestra in the early 1990s and by 1995 was serving as resident conductor of the Florida Orchestra in Tampa under Indonesian-born music director Jahja Ling. He held that post for nearly a decade, while also taking a resident conductor job with the Detroit Symphony Orchestra in 2000. For two years he divided his time between Tampa and Detroit, but left the Tampa Bay area in 2002 to devote his energies to the Detroit Symphony Orchestra. In 2005 he became music director of the Omaha Symphony, which was his first full-time assignment as principal conductor. The post gave him much greater authority in choosing the season's program, he explained to John Fleming in the *St. Petersburg Times*. "If I run across a young emerging artist or composer, I don't have to clear it with anyone now to get that person heard. That part of it is very exciting."

Wilkins commuted between Detroit and Omaha for a time, but moved his family to Nebraska in 2007 once his contract was renewed until 2012. He has twin daughters who were teenagers by that point, and not surprisingly were talented musicians in their own right. Recognizing the role his earliest mentors played in his own career, Wilkins has consistently returned the favor. He teaches at Shenandoah Conservatory's performing-arts camp every summer, and has been a vital part of the Detroit Symphony Orchestra's pioneering Classical Roots program, which nurtures the careers of up-and-coming African-American composers, some of them still in college.

Journalists sometimes ask Wilkins about the relevance of classical music in the twenty-first century, and he admits that outreach programs are vital. "If I didn't believe that, it would be time to do something else," he told Ashley Hassebroek in the *Omaha World-Herald*. "It's hard for me to be an orchestra evangelist and not believe there are potential flocks out there. We keep talking about the graying of symphony audiences. Guess what? People continue to gray. We're not just one thing—we're many different things. That's why we have to be more aware that we are a versatile instrument and we should pursue that versatility."

Wilkins is also a popular guest conductor elsewhere, and in 2008 became principal guest conductor of the Hollywood Bowl Orchestra in Los Angeles. In his spare time, he is an avid golfer and professes a love of such old television shows as *Star Trek, The Flintstones,* and *The Mary Tyler Moore Show.* His favorite pop music is the work of singer-songwriter James Taylor. Asked if he could provide any advice to youth who hoped for a career in the performing arts, he reiterated on LAist.com what he often told young people. "The first is to understand that their biggest competition is ignorance, not the person sitting next to them. That is something I actually borrowed from Wynton Marsalis many years ago. It stuck with me. The second piece of advice is to understand that if you wake up in the morning intent on doing battle with your biggest competitor, you always end up learning something by the end of the day."

Sources

Periodicals

Detroit Free Press, February 5, 2003.
News & Record (Piedmont Triad, NC), November 14, 2002, p. 6.
Omaha World-Herald, June 10, 2007.
St. Petersburg Times (St. Petersburg, FL), March 23, 2008, p. 2E.
Tampa Tribune, November 2, 1998, p. 1.

Online

"LAist Interview: Thomas Wilkins, Principal Guest Conductor of the Hollywood Bowl," LAist.com, June 18, 2008, http://laist.com/2008/06/18/laist_interview_thomas_wilkin_princ.php (accessed October 28, 2008).

—Carol Brennan

Maggie Williams

1954—

Government official

A public relations consultant and Democratic campaign strategist, Maggie Williams is a powerful and controversial figure in American politics. During the 1990s she served in the White House as chief of staff to First Lady Hillary Rodham Clinton and as an assistant to President Bill Clinton and was the first African-American woman appointed to these positions in a presidential administration. She later served as manager of Hillary Clinton's presidential campaign in 2008. Williams is known for her skills in negotiation and people management as well as her commitment to the causes in which she believes. "I just have this thing about injustice," Williams told Martha Sherrill in the *Washington Post*. "Everybody hates the big injustices—I know. But I hate even the little injustices, even the way a salesclerk treats somebody who is shabbily dressed and happens to go into a nice store."

Excelled in School

The daughter of a schoolteacher and a government worker, Williams credits her work ethic to her solid family ties and childhood experiences. She grew up in

Williams, Maggie, photograph. Luke Frazza/AFP/Getty Images.

Kansas City, Missouri, and was taught that a strong belief in God and pride in her African-American heritage would help her make a difference in the world. After graduating from an all-girls Catholic high school, she moved to Washington, DC, to attend Trinity College.

Her professors at Trinity considered her a remarkable student with a great understanding of the political process. While there, she began to develop her sense of political savvy. As one of only a handful of African-American students at a school that was situated in a city with a large minority population, Williams resented the fact that the school ignored the issues happening around it. In an effort to make her fellow classmates, professors, and the Trinity administration aware of the struggles that people of color were facing at the time, she and Peggy Lewis, who was the editor of the school newspaper, published an issue of the paper that was devoted entirely to African-American concerns.

When Williams and Lewis were called on by the administration to explain, they justified their actions by quoting from the school brochure, which insisted that the school was concerned about the problems of the

At a Glance . . .

Born Margaret Ann Williams on December 25, 1954, in Kansas City, MO; daughter of a schoolteacher and government worker; married William Barrett, 1997. *Politics:* Democrat. *Education:* Trinity College, BA, political science, 1977; University of Pennsylvania, Annenberg School for Communication, MA, 1992.

Career: Aide to Congressman Morris K. Udall of Arizona, 1977–78; Democratic National Committee (DNC), deputy press secretary, 1979–80, manager of convention press office, 1980; campaign press secretary for Congressman Robert G. Torricelli of New Jersey, 1982; Center on Budget and Policy Priorities, director of media relations; convention staff member managing backstage and podium activities for the DNC, 1984; Children's Defense Fund (CDF), communications director, 1984–89; Bill Clinton–Albert Gore Jr. presidential campaign, member, 1992; assistant to President Clinton and chief of staff to First Lady Hillary Rodham Clinton, 1993–97; independent communications consultant, Paris, France, 1997–2000; Fenton Communications, president, 2000–05; Delta Financial Corporation, director of the board of directors, 2000–07; Hillary Rodham Clinton presidential campaign, manager, 2008.

Memberships: Institute of Politics, John F. Kennedy School of Government, Harvard University, board member; City Year, member of board of trustees.

Addresses: *Office*—Griffin Williams Critical Point Management, 17 Watch Hill Rd. Westerly, RI 02891.

surrounding community. "We turned the brochure back on them," Lewis told Karen De Witt in the *New York Times*. "[Maggie] was very good at strategy from the beginning and always had a sense of self, a sense of culture and identity."

Worked for Children's Welfare

Williams gained first-hand experience with the political process soon after she graduated from Trinity in 1977 with a degree in political science. Her first job was as an aide to Congressman Morris K. Udall of Arizona. Even though she worked for him for only one year, she learned a lot about the system and how politics operates. Williams spent the next year in Paris, where she worked as an au pair.

She returned to Washington in 1979 and took a job as deputy press secretary for the Democratic National Committee (DNC). Her tenacity and dedication paid off as she worked her way into various positions throughout the Washington political scene. For the next several years, Williams functioned in a variety of capacities, acting as manager of the convention press office for the DNC, campaign press secretary for Congressman Robert G. Torricelli of New Jersey, and director of media relations for the Center on Budget and Policy Priorities.

In 1984 Williams took a job with the Children's Defense Fund (CDF), which is considered the most powerful child advocacy group in the country. One of her first tasks was to develop a public service campaign to address the problem of teen pregnancy. Marian Wright Edelman, the founder and director of the CDF, credited Williams with making the program a huge success. "She conceptualized how to mobilize people," Edelman told Patrice Gaines in *Emerge*, "and put teenage pregnancy on the national agenda and on the black and white agenda. She understood we needed to sell kids as effectively as Procter & Gamble sells its products."

Williams persuaded Fallon McElligott, an advertising agency in Minneapolis, Minnesota, to create a teen pregnancy prevention campaign; she made such a good impression on the agency that it offered her a job. Williams, however, was satisfied in knowing that the award-winning campaign would bring the problem of teen pregnancy to the attention of the American people. The CDF was also impressed with her work and promoted her to director of communications.

The conservative policies of the Republican administrations of Presidents Ronald Reagan and George H. W. Bush left Williams feeling frustrated and defeated. In 1990 she left the CDF to pursue a master's degree at the University of Pennsylvania's Annenberg School for Communication. Williams told Sherrill, "It didn't make sense to me anymore, that I had to beg people to treat children right or to persuade people in government that [pregnancy] prevention for children was important. I got tired and it seemed real obvious to me that nothing was going to change. It didn't look hopeful to me."

Recruited by Clinton, a Former Coworker

While working on her degree, Williams started receiving phone calls from a former CDF board member and friend, Hillary Rodham Clinton, who was looking for media advice. Clinton was so impressed with Williams that she asked her to join the Bill Clinton–Albert Gore Jr. presidential campaign. Williams declined the generous offer, preferring to finish her degree instead.

Having written a master's thesis on the relationship between black public officials and black reporters who work for mainstream news organizations, Williams graduated from the Annenberg School in the spring of 1992. While waiting to enter the school's doctoral program to study media, the phone calls from Clinton increased in regularity.

Williams had been following the campaign and was increasingly upset with the way the media was portraying Hillary Clinton, especially during the Republican National Convention. Finally, after polite persuasion from several friends, Williams joined the campaign in August of 1992 to serve as Hillary Clinton's media adviser. Almost immediately, Clinton's image in the minds of Americans began to improve. Williams's strategy was simple: Let Hillary be Hillary.

When Bill Clinton won the presidential election, Williams agreed to stay on as Hillary Clinton's transition director. When the Clintons moved into the White House, they—along with some friends and colleagues—were able to persuade Williams to take a job with the Clinton administration.

As a tribute to her talents, Williams was given the title of assistant to the president and chief of staff to the first lady. No previous White House official had ever held this dual role. Her duties required that she keep two offices, one in the Old Executive Office Building, where her staff worked, and another in the West Wing of the White House.

As the manager of Hillary Clinton's staff of thirteen, Williams had a host of responsibilities that included everything from speech writing to schedule organization to testifying before Congress on the first lady's behalf. Her loyalty to Hillary Clinton was unquestionable. According to *Time,* Williams considered herself a "counterpart" to the president's chief of staff, and while some argued that her responsibilities were indeed tremendous, others felt that she may have broken White House etiquette by making an assumption of "equal rank." Still, many in Washington believed that Williams's expertise as a media strategist greatly benefited Hillary Clinton. Paul Costello, a leading public relations executive and political consultant, commented to Vanessa Gallman in *Essence,* "Maggie has helped [Hillary Clinton] rise above all the questions about her role, and she has helped shape the image of Hillary as someone concerned with helping people."

Implicated in White House Scandal

Williams did, however, run into problems during what became known as the "Whitewater controversy," an inquiry into the legality of some of the Clintons' real estate dealings during the 1970s and 1980s. The investigation failed to produce evidence that the Clintons had broken any laws, but Williams was implicated in the affair when a Secret Service agent testified under oath that he had seen her leaving the home of White House counsel Vince Foster carrying documents after Foster's suicide. Williams, for her part, denied the charges and continued to support the Clintons. Additionally, Williams was part of a campaign finance scandal in which she allegedly accepted an illegal $50,000 contribution to the Democratic Party from a Taiwanese businessman named Johnny Chung, who was eventually convicted of numerous charges involving fraud and tax evasion. By the time Williams left her position at the White House, she had racked up more than $300,000 in legal fees to defend herself and was ready for a change.

In 1997 Williams married William Barrett, who had worked in the U.S. Department of State under the Clinton administration. The couple moved to Paris, where Williams worked as a communications consultant for three years. In 2000 she returned to Washington, DC, when she was named president of Fenton Communications, one of the largest public relations firms in the United States. With this position, Williams became the highest-ranking African-American woman at a top-fifty public relations agency. At the same time, Williams was recruited in April of 2000 to serve as director of the board at Delta Financial Corporation, a mortgage lending institution. According to Glenn Thrush in the *Chicago Tribune,* Williams believed the company's policy of focusing on mortgage lending to minorities would help lift many low-income families into the middle class. However, as the subprime mortgage crisis began unfolding in 2007, it became clear that such lending was often more predatory than helpful. Williams again became caught in controversy, but she remained in her position as director until the company filed for bankruptcy in December of 2007.

The following month Williams, who had been serving as an adviser, was tapped by Hillary Clinton to manage her presidential campaign. While Clinton's campaign for presidency ultimately was unsuccessful, Williams remained a loyal friend and adviser. She continued consulting through the firm Griffin Williams Critical Point Management and as a board member supported the Institute of Politics at Harvard University and the national service organization City Year.

Sources

Periodicals

Emerge, May 1993, p. 47.
Essence, October 1993, p. 61.
Jet, October 16, 2000.
Los Angeles Times, February 16, 2008.
New York Daily News, February 11, 2008.
New York Times, November 29, 1993, p. B-6.
Time, March 21, 1994, p. 28.
Washington Post, January 15, 1993, p. B1; February 11, 1993, p. D1.

Online

Thrush, Glenn, "Clinton Campaign Head Made $200,000 with Subprime Lender," Newsday.com, March 30, 2008, http://www.newsday.com/news/nationworld/nation/ny-ushill305631627mar30,0,857842.story (accessed November 5, 2008).

—Joe Kuskowski and Nancy Dziedzic

Stevie Williams

1979—

Skateboarder, business owner

Williams, Stevie, photograph. Frederick M. Brown/Getty Images.

Professional skateboarder Stevie Williams is a celebrity among skateboarding enthusiasts and one of a relatively small number of African-American daredevils to achieve fame in the sport. When he first began skateboarding during the early 1990s in his Philadelphia neighborhood, he was often the target of derision among his peers and faced disparaging comments from white teens when he moved beyond his immediate surroundings. He was undeterred, however. "Skating's big enough for people to be into whatever they're into," he told Charlotte Philby in the *Independent*. "There's something for each kid to relate to."

Williams was born on December 17, 1979, in Philadelphia, and grew up in a house on North 41st Street. He received his first skateboard at age eleven, and practiced his first ramp moves off the table in his living room when his mother was out of the house. Basketball was the dominant sport in his North Philadelphia neighborhood, and others ridiculed him for his interest in skateboarding. "People would say then that skateboarding was corny, why you acting like a white boy, stuff like that," he recalled in an interview with Jarrett Carter on BlackSportsNetwork.com. "I didn't let it affect me; it was just something I loved to do."

Williams began heading to downtown Philadelphia's Love Park, which is less a park than a sweeping concrete vista in Center City more formally known as JFK Plaza; it takes its name from an iconic Robert Indiana sculpture of the word "love" situated on the site. Love Park was a favorite haunt for Philly skateboarders because of its wide-open spaces, railings, and precipitous staircases, and had already gained some international repute among the skater community. Videographers regularly showed up to film the gravity-defying tricks of skaters who competed with one another for camera time. Once Williams and his friends began to show up at Love Park, other skaters "would tell the camera crews that we were dirty ghetto kids and that we didn't have any talent," Williams explained to Carter. "We were doing our thing, but people looked down on us because of what neighborhood we were from or because our gear wasn't the freshest."

Williams soon appropriated the term "Dirty Ghetto Kids" for his own use, later abbreviating it to DGK. It

At a Glance . . .

Born on December 17, 1979, in Philadelphia, PA; son of Steve Lassiter (a teacher and social worker); two children.

Career: Professional skateboarder with the Chocolate Skateboards Tour after 1999; signed sponsorship deal with DC Shoes, 2001; founded DGK, 2002; signed a sponsorship deal with Reebok, 2004; cofounder of L&K Limited skate shop, Oceanside, CA, 2006; launched DGK Skateboards, 2006, and a line of shoes and apparel sold under the name DGK RBK, 2008; appears in several video games under the Tony Hawk brand, including *American Wasteland, Project 8,* and *Proving Ground.*

Addresses: *Office*—c/o Reebok International Ltd., 1895 J.W. Foster Blvd., Canton, MA 02021; Educate to Skate Foundation, PO Box 6601, Philadelphia, PA 19149.

traveled with him when he left home at age fourteen, hitchhiking to San Francisco and living in such dire poverty for a few years that he was essentially a homeless teen at times. His break came in 1999, when he won a spot on the first Chocolate Skateboards tour, a recently launched company that featured several up-and-coming new skaters. The tour was a success and is considered a pivotal moment in skateboarding when the "street" style began to gain a wider audience. Until then, the sport had been dominated by "vert" skaters, whose moves relied on steep vertical ramps and had originated in the mid-1970s in California, when a statewide draught left many in-ground swimming pools empty. As Ben Detrick explained in the *New York Times* in 2007, "over the last two decades, the sport shifted away from ramp-based vert skating to street skating, a variation that made use of urban structures like stairways, curbs and railings. As the importance of access to ramps dwindled, skateboarding's fan base grew increasingly diverse."

Williams's teen years in California remained difficult ones, despite the fame he gained on the Chocolate tour and a sponsorship deal with DC Shoes. After moving south to Los Angeles, he told a writer on Vice.com, "I didn't really leave the house for a month cause I was just intimidated by the whole place." A friend from the Chocolate tour, Keenan Milton, showed up one day and urged him to come with him to a party in Malibu. Williams acquiesced, but left Milton there and felt uneasy on the way home, he told Vice.com. He learned the next morning that Milton had drowned in the pool after being struck in the head by another guest who had jumped from a balcony into the pool. "That was a dark time right there and it was on the 4th of July," Williams said. "Every year I get the same dark chill on Independence Day. After that I was back in the house for like two months."

In 2002 Williams launched his own company, called DGK, and two years later became the first skateboarder ever to sign a sponsorship contract with athletic-gear maker Reebok. In 2006 he opened the L&K Limited skate shop in Oceanside, California, with fellow-skater Nick Lockman. He has also appeared as himself in the top-selling line of video games from skateboarding professional Tony Hawk, including *American Wasteland* and *Project 8.* In 2008 Williams's DGK brand partnered with Reebok for a new line of Williams-designed shoes and apparel under the name "DGK RBK." Reebok is also the sponsor of the DGK professional team in which Williams competes alongside teammates Darren Harper, Evan Hernandez, Marcus McBride, and Lenny Rivas.

Williams and his father, Steve Lassiter, cofounded the Educate to Skate Foundation in 2004, which runs afterschool skateboarding programs for at-risk youth in Philadelphia. "Dropping out of school, running away from home, some of those decisions I made when I was 14 I look back on and wonder how I got to where I am now," he told Carter on BlackSportsNetwork.com. "If I can bring some different elements to the hood, then I can help build the block and uplift the community."

Sources

Periodicals

Independent (London, England), October 6, 2007, p. 11.
New York Times, November 11, 2007.

Periodicals

Carter, Jarrett, "Stevie Williams: Everlasting Grind," BlackSportsNetwork.com, http://www.blacksportsnetwork.com/articles/features/skate_122206.asp (accessed August 13, 2008).
"Stevie Williams Knows Fear," Vice.com, February 10, 2007, http://vice.typepad.com/vice_magazine/2007/10/stevie-williams.html#more (accessed October 23, 2008).

—Carol Brennan

Dwight D. York

1945—

Religious leader

Dwight D. York is the founder of a religious group known as the United Nuwaubian Nation of Moors. Characterized alternately as an African-American utopian community and as a black supremacist cult with unorthodox sexual practices, the Nuwaubians occupied a compound in rural Georgia until 2004, when York was convicted of multiple child molestation charges stemming from his activities with the group. His case was the largest child molestation prosecution of a single defendant in U.S. history. York was sentenced to 135 years in prison and is housed in the U.S. federal prison system's Supermax facility in Florence, Colorado, along with such high-profile offenders as Theodore Kaczynski, who was convicted of the infamous Unabomber attacks, and Zacarias Moussaoui, the only co-conspirator arrested in the 9/11 attacks on the World Trade Center and the Pentagon.

Founded Religious Group

York was born in 1945 and has been known by several different names, including Malachi Z. York, Amunnubi Rooakhptah, Imaam Isa Abdullah, and Chief Black Thunderbird Eagle. His birthplace was Boston, Massachusetts, not Omdurman, Sudan, as he has sometimes claimed. Over the years York concocted elaborate and sometimes contradictory genealogies linking him to various historical and religious figures. He asserted, for example, that his father was descended from the slave known only as York who accompanied Meriwether Lewis and William Clark on their historic 1804–06 overland expedition to the Pacific Ocean. In other instances he connected his ancestry to Yusuf Ben Ali, also known as Bilali Muhammad, a slave from Sapelo Island, Georgia, who wrote a significant manuscript on sharia, or Islamic law, in West African societies that was discovered after his death in 1857. Later, York borrowed a spelling variant of the Yamasee, a Native American tribe that led an aggressive war against European encroachment in South Carolina between 1715 and 1717. In a blending of the last two claims, he developed a theory that his followers were descended from what they called Native American Moors, or travelers from Africa who had crossed the Atlantic not on slave ships but rather in prehistoric times over a land bridge that later vanished.

York spent his teen years in Teaneck, New Jersey, and in 1964, at the age of nineteen, he received a sentence of probation for sexually assaulting a thirteen-year-old female. He was arrested several months later on a different assault charge, with weapons possession and resisting arrest added to his record, and spent three years in prison. Upon his release in 1967, he became active in the Black Panther movement. Following the lead of some of the group's key figures, he made a pilgrimage to Africa and began to explore Islam. In the early 1970s he founded the Ansaaru Allah Community, or "Allah's Helpers" in the Coney Island section of Brooklyn. For a time the group ran a bookstore and printing press on Flatbush Avenue, and later moved the operation to Bushwick Avenue in Brooklyn. York wrote scores of pamphlets and other materials detailing his emerging theology and black nationalist ideas. Somewhat incongruously, he also had a career in music,

At a Glance...

Born June 26, 1945, in Boston, MA; son of David Piper York and Mary C. (Williams) York.

Career: Singer and musician who recorded with the Delfonics and Evelyn "Champagne" King; lead vocalist for the groups Jackie and the Starlights, the Students, and Passion; also recorded under the name "Doctor York"; founded the Ansaaru Allah Community, c. 1970; later changed name of group to United Nuwaubian Nation of Moors.

Addresses: *Home*—Dwight D. York, Prisoner No. 17911-054, USP Florence ADMAX, U.S. Penitentiary, PO Box 8500, Florence, CO 81226.

---

appearing on recordings by such Philly soul acts as the Delfonics and working with disco singer Evelyn "Champagne" King. He fronted three different musical groups—Jackie and the Starlights, the Students, and Passion—and during the mid-1980s recorded under the name "Doctor York."

During the early 1990s York and his followers moved to a parcel of land in upstate New York near the town of Liberty. In 1993 they relocated to Eatonton, Georgia, the seat of Putnam County and located about an hour's drive from Atlanta. The new compound, called Tama-Re, was set on 476 acres. The move seems to have coincided with a name change from Ansaaru Allah to the United Nuwaubian Nation of Moors and a shedding of its Muslim overtones. His followers now called themselves Nuwaubians, and built at Tama-Re flimsy structures—some made from Styrofoam—modeled after the architecture of ancient Egypt, including sphinxes, obelisks, and pyramids. By this point York's theology began to take on more cosmic elements, including a claim that on May 5, 2003, a spaceship would arrive and transport him and his followers to a far-off galaxy.

Officials in Putnam County were alarmed by York, Tama-Re, and the 150 or so Nuwaubians. Routine traffic stops escalated into heated exchanges in which the Nuwaubians claimed they belonged to a separate nation and thus were not bound by county, state, or federal laws. Reports began to surface that the group was actually a cult, and health-care professionals alerted local officials to an unusually high number of Nuwaubian teenagers giving birth. York told a reporter for the *Atlanta Journal-Constitution* that the charges against him were part of a smear campaign. "I see the game. They don't want a positive black image here," he told Bill Osinski, who first profiled the group in the newspaper in 1998. "They're making me out to be a monster. I'm not a monster." That same year, Putnam County sheriffs padlocked a facility on Tama-Re that the Nuwaubians had been using as a nightclub. The building was only zoned for use as a storage facility, and a $45,000 fine was levied.

Charged with Racketeering, Molestation

York claimed that county officials were targeting him and his African-American community, and even won some public support from local politicians and civil rights activists. In the spring of 2000, a new twist in the story piqued national interest: the actor Wesley Snipes, who was preparing to acquire a parcel of land adjacent to York's compound, applied to Putnam County for its rezoning so that the land could be used for weapons storage. The actor and martial-arts aficionado hoped to launch a training school for bodyguards, which would have included a firing range, but officials were wary that Snipe's "Royal Guard of Amen-Ra" school and York's group were collaborating, and denied the rezoning request. There were fears that the Nuwaubians might one day mount a well-armed standoff with law-enforcement authorities like the one in Waco, Texas, in 1993 that ended disastrously with seventy-six deaths.

The child molestation case began not long afterward when authorities received anonymous letters with allegations of sexual abuse, but it took nearly two years before a victim was willing to come forward. In the spring of 2002 a Georgia grand jury indicted York on seventy-four counts of child molestation, and some two hundred Federal Bureau of Investigation (FBI) agents plus eighty Georgia sheriff's deputies raided Tama-Re and arrested York. The charges against him included federal racketeering, transporting minors across state lines for immoral purposes, and child molestation. At the trial, more bizarre details of life at Tama-Re emerged. Followers lived in trailers, while York lived in a modern house where daughters of compound members, some as young as twelve, were recruited to serve as his housekeeping staff; older women then asked them questions about their level of sexual experience and explained what York would expect of them. They were instructed to tell no one, not even their parents, and were told by him that this was a sure path to reach heaven. Thirteen witnesses testified against York, and those who came forward in his defense included the mother of one of the victims, who claimed her child had lied on the stand.

York was convicted in January of 2004 and sentenced to 135 years in prison. The verdict also granted authorities the right to seize his property, including Tama-Re and houses elsewhere in Georgia. He was incarcerated at the United States Penitentiary Administrative Maximum Facility in Florence, Colorado, known as a Supermax facility where inmates are kept in solitary confinement for twenty-three hours per day.

York's supporters claim he is a political prisoner of the U.S. government and continue to publicize their case on the Internet. One of their assertions is that an impostor was actually the York who was tried in U.S. District Court, and that York's son is actually guilty of the child-molestation charges. Another attempt involves a claim that in 1999 York was appointed consul general of Monrovia, the capital of Liberia, by that country's notorious warlord, Charles Taylor, and therefore has diplomatic immunity from prosecution in the United States.

Selected works

Albums

(As Doctor York) *New York,* Hot Melt Records, 1985.

Sources

Periodicals

Atlanta Journal-Constitution, September 20, 1998, p. C1; January 24, 2004, p. D1.
Fulton County Daily Report, July 27, 2007.
Macon Telegraph (Macon, GA), June 10, 2005; May 20, 2007.
New York Press, November 8, 2000.
Orange County Register (Santa Ana, CA), April 22, 2004.
Time, July 12, 1999, p. 32.
Washington Times, June 2, 2002, p. A5.

—Carol Brennan

Zane

1967(?)—

Novelist

Zane is a literary pseudonym used by the writer of bestselling erotic fiction whose works consistently dominate the *Essence* bestseller lists. With sales of six million books in less than a decade, Zane is the leading name in a fiction genre dubbed urban erotica. "Once I got into it, I knew it was my calling," Zane told Lynette R. Holloway in *Ebony*. Noting that she hopes her books and their assertive, confident heroines serve to empower her largely female readership, Zane said, "Men never hesitate to tell a woman what they want. Women need to learn to speak up and do the same."

Zane, photograph. Frederick M. Brown/Getty Images.

Zane was born Kristina LaFerne Roberts in Washington, DC, in about 1967. In interviews, she has revealed that her father is a professor of theology and religion with teaching stints at Oxford, Duke, Yale, and Howard universities, and her mother an elementary school teacher; both are supportive of her literary efforts, and Zane's sister works as an editor for Strebor Books, the publishing company Zane founded.

Zane has said that she never planned to become a writer. She earned a degree in chemical engineering from Howard University before embarking on a career in insurance sales. Her first child, a son, was born in the late 1980s, and a daughter arrived in the mid-1990s. A few years later, as a single parent living in North Carolina, she began writing after her children had gone to bed. She completed her first piece of erotic fiction in November of 1997, e-mailing it off to a few friends, who then forwarded it to others; soon, Zane's e-mail inbox was flooded with requests for more stories.

Zane launched her own Web site, www.eroticanoir.com, and soon it had 8,000 regular visitors. An e-zine, or Internet newsletter, of her stories followed that, and then an ad on her site for a printed collection of stories—which she photocopied and bound herself—netted a terrific response. Word of her self-publishing success reached publishing executives, and she fielded a few offers but declined because all had recommended that she tone down the more sexually explicit passages. In 1999 she created Strebor Books—her surname spelled backwards—and issued her first collection of short stories under the title *The Sex Chronicles: Shattering the Myth*. She wrote her first novel, *Addicted*, in less than three weeks, and it became an underground bestseller. The story of an art-gallery

At a Glance...

Born Kristina LaFerne Roberts c. 1967, in Washington, DC; daughter of a theology professor and a teacher; married Wayne (an environmental engineer), c. 2002; children: two sons, one daughter, one stepchild. *Education:* Earned degree in chemical engineering from Howard University, c. 1989.

Career: Worked as a sales executive in the insurance industry until 2001; Strebor Books, founder and publisher, 1999–2005; DePasse/Zane Entertainment, principal, 2005—.

Addresses: *Office*—c/o Author Mail, Atria Books/Simon & Schuster, 1230 Avenue of the Americas, New York, NY 10020.

owner whose solid marriage is threatened by her extramarital dalliances, *Addicted* sold 50,000 copies in its first six months, and was picked up for distribution first by book wholesalers and then by major chain bookstores, whose customers had been requesting it.

Zane quit her sales job in 2001 and signed a deal with Simon & Schuster for new trade paperback editions of *Addicted* and *The Sex Chronicles*. With the greater distribution came some of the first mainstream media reviews for her books. Writing in *Black Issues Book Review*, Kimberley White called *Addicted* "a novel with all the elements necessary for a best-seller.... Every character is motivated by their dark secrets." Subsequent works including *Shame on It All, The Heat Seekers,* and *Skyscraper* all sold equally well, and at one point in 2004 Zane had three books on the *Essence* bestseller list, which ranks the previous month's sales at bookstores catering to African-American readers. Her titles even began making appearances on the *New York Times* list, which gave her the distinction of being only the third African-American woman—after Toni Morrison and Terry McMillan—to have a title on the *Times*'s fiction rankings since 2000. Citing her success, Dwight Garner asserted in the *New York Times Book Review* that the works "are filled with smart, believable and self-deprecating young and middle-aged black characters.... They are also filled with sex scenes that will smoke your fingerprints off."

Though her stories were known for those racy scenes, Zane always tried to impart an underlying message or moral caution in her books. In some cases the characters' sexual addiction or behavior masks deeper issues that they come to realize as the plot draws to a conclusion, and usually decide to seek professional help. "When I sit down and write each book, I have something different in mind of what I'm trying to get across," she told Margena A. Christian in *Jet*. "I do it in a comedic and in a sexual way, but I always have a deeper purpose."

Despite the fact that so little was known about the pseudonymous author—some even speculated that "Zane" was a male writer—she gained a devoted fan base, and finally agreed to make public appearances for the first time in 2004 on the book tour for *Afterburn*. She did so in part because others were claiming to be her and holding book signings, she told *New York Times* writer Ginia Bellafante. "Once, I was online and noticed someone saying she was on her way to a reading of mine in Atlanta," she recalled. "I wasn't in Atlanta. I was in my house."

Zane's own publishing company, Strebor, was by then doing a brisk business publishing the works of other writers, and not just the erotic fiction submissions. Strebor issued titles from dozens of up-and-coming authors whose styles ranged from religious tales to crime stories. Zane also edited various anthologies for Strebor, including *Breaking the Cycle,* a collection of tales about women exiting abusive relationships. The stories in it—including her own—were every bit as graphic as the erotic fiction, she noted in *Jet*. "The stories are very harsh. I wanted them to be that way because I want people, when they put the book down, to say, 'Wow, I really need to get out.' And if they know someone in that situation, for them to say, 'I've really got to help them.'"

In 2005 Zane sold Strebor's back catalog to Simon & Schuster and Strebor became part of Atria, Simon & Schuster's African-American-focused imprint. This freed her to devote more time to her own fiction. A year later, she inked a deal with Lionsgate Films to bring *Addicted* to the big screen through a new company, De Passe/Zane Entertainment, that the writer formed with onetime Motown Records film and television executive Suzanne de Passe.

Since she began publishing her best-selling erotic fiction, Zane married her childhood sweetheart, who is an environmental engineer, and had a second son. She and her family live in suburban in Maryland. "My life is boring," she told Holloway. "I grocery shop, cook, clean the house, and attend soccer games and PTA meetings."

Selected works

Books

The Sex Chronicles: Shattering the Myth, Strebor Books International, 1999, reprinted as *Zane's Sex Chronicles,* Atria Books, 2008.
Addicted, Strebor Books International, 2001.
Shame on It All, Strebor Books International, 2001.
Gettin' Buck Wild: Sex Chronicles II, Atria Books, 2002.

The Heat Seekers, Atria Books, 2002.
Of Royal Blood, Silhouette, 2002.
Nervous, Atria Books, 2003.
The Sisters of APF: The Indoctrination..., Atria Books, 2003.
Skyscraper, Atria Books, 2003.
(Compiler) *Chocolate Flava: The Eroticanoir.com Anthology,* Atria Books, 2004.
Afterburn, Atria Books, 2005.
Dear G-Spot: Straight Talk about Sex and Love, Atria Books, 2005.
(Editor and contributor) *Breaking the Cycle,* (anthology), Strebor Books, 2005.
(Editor) *Caramel Flava: The Eroticanoir.com Anthology,* Atria Books, 2006.
Blackgentlemen.com, Atria Books, 2007.
(Editor) *Honey Flava,* Atria Books, 2008.

Sources

Periodicals

Black Issues Book Review, November-December 2001, p. 58; September-October 2005, p. 10.
Daily Variety, May 10, 2006, p. 1.
Ebony, March 2005, p. 100.
Entertainment Weekly, August 13, 2004, p. 94.
Jet, October 4, 2004, p. 56.
New York Times, August 22, 2004, p. ST1.
New York Times Book Review, January 30, 2005, p. 22.
Publishers Weekly, July 15, 2002, p. 20.
St. Petersburg Times (St. Petersburg, FL), October 26, 2006, p. 14K.

—Carol Brennan

Cumulative Nationality Index

*Volume numbers appear in **bold***

American
Aaliyah **30**
Aaron, Hank **5**
Abbott, Robert Sengstacke **27**
Abdul-Jabbar, Kareem **8**
Abdur-Rahim, Shareef **28**
Abele, Julian **55**
Abernathy, Ralph David **1**
Aberra, Amsale **67**
Abu-Jamal, Mumia **15**
Ace, Johnny **36**
Adams, Eula L. **39**
Adams, Floyd, Jr. **12**
Adams, Jenoyne **60**
Adams, Johnny **39**
Adams, Leslie **39**
Adams, Oleta **18**
Adams, Osceola Macarthy **31**
Adams, Sheila J. **25**
Adams, Yolanda **17, 67**
Adams-Campbell, Lucille L. **60**
Adams Earley, Charity **13, 34**
Adams-Ender, Clara **40**
Adderley, Julian "Cannonball" **30**
Adderley, Nat **29**
Adkins, Rod **41**
Adkins, Rutherford H. **21**
Adu, Freddy **67**
Agyeman, Jaramogi Abebe **10, 63**
Ailey, Alvin **8**
Akil, Mara Brock **60**
Akon **68**
Al-Amin, Jamil Abdullah **6**
Albright, Gerald **23**
Alcorn, George Edward, Jr. **59**
Alert, Kool DJ Red **33**
Alexander, Archie Alphonso **14**
Alexander, Clifford **26**
Alexander, Joyce London **18**
Alexander, Khandi **43**
Alexander, Margaret Walker **22**
Alexander, Sadie Tanner Mossell **22**
Alexander, Shaun **58**
Ali, Hana Yasmeen **52**
Ali, Laila **27, 63**
Ali, Muhammad **2, 16, 52**
Allain, Stephanie **49**
Allen, Byron **3, 24**
Allen, Claude **68**
Allen, Debbie **13, 42**
Allen, Ethel D. **13**
Allen, Marcus **20**
Allen, Robert L. **38**
Allen, Samuel W. **38**
Allen, Tina **22**
Allen-Buillard, Melba **55**
Alston, Charles **33**
Amaker, Norman **63**
Amaker, Tommy **62**
Amerie **52**
Ames, Wilmer **27**
Amos, Emma **63**
Amos, John **8, 62**
Amos, Wally **9**
Anderson, Anthony **51**
Anderson, Carl **48**
Anderson, Charles Edward **37**
Anderson, Eddie "Rochester" **30**
Anderson, Elmer **25**
Anderson, Jamal **22**
Anderson, Marian **2, 33**
Anderson, Michael P. **40**
Anderson, Mike **63**
Anderson, Norman B. **45**
Anderson, William G(ilchrist), D.O. **57**
Andrews, Benny **22, 59**
Andrews, Bert **13**
Andrews, Raymond **4**
Angelou, Maya **1, 15**
Ansa, Tina McElroy **14**
Anthony, Carmelo **46**
Anthony, Wendell **25**
Appiah, Kwame Anthony **67**
Archer, Dennis **7, 36**
Archie-Hudson, Marguerite **44**
Ardoin, Alphonse **65**
Arkadie, Kevin **17**
Armstrong, Louis **2**
Armstrong, Robb **15**
Armstrong, Vanessa Bell **24**
Arnez J **53**
Arnold, Tichina **63**
Arnwine, Barbara **28**
Arrington, Richard **24**
Arroyo, Martina **30**
Artest, Ron **52**
Asante, Molefi Kete **3**
Ashanti **37**
Ashe, Arthur **1, 18**
Ashford, Emmett **22**
Ashford, Evelyn **63**
Ashford, Nickolas **21**
Ashley-Ward, Amelia **23**
Asim, Jabari **71**
Atkins, Cholly **40**
Atkins, Erica **34**
Atkins, Juan **50**
Atkins, Russell **45**
Atkins, Tina **34**
Aubert, Alvin **41**
Auguste, Donna **29**
Austin, Gloria **63**
Austin, Jim **63**
Austin, Junius C. **44**
Austin, Lovie **40**
Austin, Patti **24**
Autrey, Wesley **68**
Avant, Clarence **19**
Avery, Byllye Y. **66**
Ayers, Roy **16**
Babatunde, Obba **35**
Bacon-Bercey, June **38**
Badu, Erykah **22**
Bahati, Wambui **60**
Bailey, Buster **38**
Bailey, Chauncey **68**
Bailey, Clyde **45**
Bailey, DeFord **33**
Bailey, Philip **63**
Bailey, Radcliffe **19**
Bailey, Xenobia **11**
Baines, Harold **32**
Baiocchi, Regina Harris **41**
Baisden, Michael **25, 66**
Baker, Anita **21, 48**
Baker, Augusta **38**
Baker, Dusty **8, 43**
Baker, Ella **5**
Baker, Gwendolyn Calvert **9**
Baker, Houston A., Jr. **6**
Baker, Josephine **3**
Baker, LaVern **26**
Baker, Maxine B. **28**
Baker, Thurbert **22**
Baker, Vernon Joseph **65**
Baldwin, James **1**
Ballance, Frank W. **41**
Ballard, Allen Butler, Jr. **40**
Ballard, Hank **41**
Baltimore, Richard Lewis, III **71**
Bambaataa, Afrika **34**
Bambara, Toni Cade **10**
Bandele, Asha **36**
Banks, Ernie **33**
Banks, Jeffrey **17**
Banks, Michelle **59**
Banks, Paula A. **68**
Banks, Tyra **11, 50**
Banks, William **11**
Banner, David **55**
Baquet, Dean **63**
Baraka, Amiri **1, 38**
Barbee, Lloyd Augustus **71**
Barber, Ronde **41**
Barber, Tiki **57**
Barboza, Anthony **10**
Barclay, Paris **37**
Barden, Don H. **9, 20**
Barker, Danny **32**
Barkley, Charles **5, 66**
Barlow, Roosevelt **49**
Barnes, Roosevelt "Booba" **33**
Barnes, Steven **54**
Barnett, Amy Du Bois **46**
Barnett, Etta Moten **56**
Barnett, Marguerite **46**
Barney, Lem **26**
Barnhill, David **30**
Barrax, Gerald William **45**
Barrett, Andrew C. **12**
Barrett, Jacquelyn **28**
Barrino, Fantasia **53**
Barry, Marion S(hepilov, Jr.) **7, 44**
Barthe, Richmond **15**
Basie, Count **23**
Basquiat, Jean-Michel **5**
Bass, Charlotta Spears **40**
Bass, Karen **70**
Bassett, Angela **6, 23, 62**
Bates, Daisy **13**
Bates, Karen Grigsby **40**
Bates, Peg Leg **14**
Bath, Patricia E. **37**
Batiste, Alvin **66**
Battle, Kathleen **70**
Baugh, David **23**
Baylor, Don **6**
Baylor, Helen **36**
Beach, Michael **26**
Beal, Bernard B. **46**
Beals, Jennifer **12**
Beals, Melba Patillo **15**
Bearden, Romare **2, 50**
Beasley, Jamar **29**
Beasley, Phoebe **34**
Beatty, Talley **35**
Bechet, Sidney **18**
Beckford, Tyson **11, 68**
Beckham, Barry **41**
Belafonte, Harry **4, 65**
Bell, Derrick **6**
Bell, James "Cool Papa" **36**
Bell, James A. **50**
Bell, James Madison **40**

Bell, Michael **40**
Bell, Robert Mack **22**
Bellamy, Bill **12**
Bellamy, Terry **58**
Belle, Albert **10**
Belle, Regina **1, 51**
Belton, Sharon Sayles **9, 16**
Benberry, Cuesta **65**
Benét, Eric **28**
Ben-Israel, Ben Ami **11**
Benjamin, Andre **45**
Benjamin, Regina **20**
Benjamin, Tritobia Hayes **53**
Bennett, George Harold "Hal" **45**
Bennett, Gwendolyn B. **59**
Bennett, Lerone, Jr. **5**
Benson, Angela **34**
Bentley, Lamont **53**
Berry, Halle **4, 19, 57**
Berry, Bertice **8, 55**
Berry, Chuck **29**
Berry, Fred "Rerun" **48**
Berry, Mary Frances **7**
Berry, Theodore **31**
Berrysmith, Don Reginald **49**
Bethune, Mary McLeod **4**
Betsch, MaVynee **28**
Bettis, Jerome **64**
Beverly, Frankie **25**
Beyoncé **39, 70**
Bibb, Eric **49**
Bibb, Henry and Mary **54**
Bickerstaff, Bernie **21**
Biggers, John **20, 33**
Biggers, Sanford **62**
Bing, Dave **3, 59**
Birch, Glynn R. **61**
Bishop, Sanford D., Jr. **24**
Black Thought **63**
Black, Albert **51**
Black, Barry C. **47**
Black, Keith Lanier **18**
Blackburn, Robert **28**
Blackmon, Brenda **58**
Blackshear, Leonard **52**
Blackwell, Kenneth, Sr. **61**
Blackwell, Robert D., Sr. **52**
Blackwell, Unita **17**
Blacque, Taurean **58**
Blair, Jayson **50**
Blair, Paul **36**
Blake, Asha **26**
Blake, Eubie **29**
Blake, James **43**
Blakey, Art **37**
Blanchard, Terence **43**
Bland, Bobby "Blue" **36**
Bland, Eleanor Taylor **39**
Blanks, Billy **22**
Blanks, Deborah K. **69**
Blanton, Dain **29**
Blassingame, John Wesley **40**
Blayton, Jesse B., Sr. **55**
Bleu, Corbin **65**
Blige, Mary J. **20, 34, 60**
Blockson, Charles L. **42**
Blow, Kurtis **31**
Bluford, Guy **2, 35**
Bluitt, Juliann S. **14**
Bobo, Lawrence **60**
Bogle, Donald **34**
Bogues, Tyrone "Muggsy" **56**
Bolden, Buddy **39**

Bolden, Charles F., Jr. **7**
Bolden, Frank E. **44**
Bolden, Tonya **32**
Bolin, Jane **22, 59**
Bolton, Terrell D. **25**
Bolton-Holifield, Ruthie **28**
Bond, Beverly **53**
Bond, Julian **2, 35**
Bonds, Barry **6, 34, 63**
Bonds, Bobby **43**
Bonds, Margaret **39**
Bonet, Lisa **58**
Bontemps, Arna **8**
Booker, Cory Anthony **68**
Booker, Simeon **23**
Borders, James **9**
Bosley, Freeman, Jr. **7**
Boston, Kelvin E. **25**
Boston, Lloyd **24**
Bow Wow **35**
Bowe, Riddick **6**
Bowman, Bertie **71**
Bowser, Yvette Lee **17**
Boyd, Edward **70**
Boyd, Gerald M. **32, 59**
Boyd, Gwendolyn **49**
Boyd, John W., Jr. **20**
Boyd, T. B., III **6**
Boykin, Keith **14**
Bradley, David Henry, Jr. **39**
Bradley, Ed **2, 59**
Bradley, J. Robert **65**
Bradley, Jennette B. **40**
Bradley, Thomas **2, 20**
Brady, Wayne **32, 71**
Brae, C. Michael **61**
Braithwaite, William Stanley **52**
Branch, William Blackwell **39**
Brand, Elton **31**
Brandon, Barbara **3**
Brandon, Terrell **16**
Brandy **14, 34**
Branham, George, III **50**
Brashear, Carl **29**
Brashear, Donald **39**
Braugher, Andre **13, 58**
Braun, Carol Moseley **4, 42**
Brawley, Benjamin **44**
Braxton, Toni **15, 61**
Brazile, Donna **25, 70**
Bridges, Sheila **36**
Bridges, Todd **37**
Bridgewater, Dee Dee **32**
Bridgforth, Glinda **36**
Brimmer, Andrew F. **2, 48**
Briscoe, Connie **15**
Briscoe, Marlin **37**
Britt, Donna **28**
Broadbent, Hydeia **36**
Brock, Lou **18**
Bronner, Nathaniel H., Sr. **32**
Brooke, Edward **8**
Brooks, Tyrone **59**
Brooks, Aaron **33**
Brooks, Avery **9**
Brooks, Derrick **43**
Brooks, Golden **62**
Brooks, Gwendolyn **1, 28**
Brooks, Hadda **40**
Brooks, Mehcad **62**
Brower, William **49**
Brown, Angela M. **54**
Brown, Bobby **58**

Brown, Byrd **49**
Brown, Cecil M. **46**
Brown, Charles **23**
Brown, Clarence Gatemouth **59**
Brown, Claude **38**
Brown, Cora **33**
Brown, Corrine **24**
Brown, Cupcake **63**
Brown, Donald **19**
Brown, Eddie C. **35**
Brown, Elaine **8**
Brown, Erroll M. **23**
Brown, Foxy **25**
Brown, George Leslie **62**
Brown, Homer S. **47**
Brown, James **15, 60**
Brown, James **22**
Brown, Janice Rogers **43**
Brown, Jesse **6, 41**
Brown, Jesse Leroy **31**
Brown, Jim **11**
Brown, Joe **29**
Brown, Joyce F. **25**
Brown, Lee Patrick **1, 24**
Brown, Les **5**
Brown, Lloyd Louis **42**
Brown, Marie Dutton **12**
Brown, Oscar, Jr. **53**
Brown, Patrick "Sleepy" **50**
Brown, Robert **65**
Brown, Ron **5**
Brown, Sterling Allen **10, 64**
Brown, Tony **3**
Brown, Uzee **42**
Brown, Vivian **27**
Brown, Warren **61**
Brown, Wesley **23**
Brown, Willa **40**
Brown, Willard **36**
Brown, Willie L., Jr. **7**
Brown, Zora Kramer **12**
Browne, Roscoe Lee **66**
Broyard, Anatole **68**
Broyard, Bliss **68**
Bruce, Blanche Kelso **33**
Bruce, Bruce **56**
Bruce, Isaac **26**
Brunson, Dorothy **1**
Bryan, Ashley F. **41**
Bryant, John **26**
Bryant, John R. **45**
Bryant, Kobe **15, 31, 71**
Bryant, Wayne R. **6**
Bryant, William Benson **61**
Buchanan, Ray **32**
Buckley, Gail Lumet **39**
Buckley, Victoria (Vikki) **24**
Bullard, Eugene **12**
Bullins, Ed **25**
Bullock, Steve **22**
Bully-Cummings, Ella **48**
Bumbry, Grace **5**
Bunche, Ralph J. **5**
Bunkley, Anita Richmond **39**
Burgess, John **46**
Burgess, Marjorie L. **55**
Burke, Selma **16**
Burke, Solomon **31**
Burke, Yvonne Braithwaite **42**
Burks, Mary Fair **40**
Burleigh, Henry Thacker **56**
Burnett, Charles **16, 68**
Burnim, Mickey L. **48**

Burns, Eddie **44**
Burns, Ursula **60**
Burnside, R.L. **56**
Burrell, Tom **21, 51**
Burris, Chuck **21**
Burris, Roland W. **25**
Burroughs, Margaret Taylor **9**
Burrows, Stephen **31**
Burrus, William Henry "Bill" **45**
Burt-Murray, Angela **59**
Burton, LeVar **8**
Busby, Jheryl **3**
Bush, Reggie **59**
Butler, George, Jr. **70**
Butler, Jerry **26**
Butler, Leroy, III **17**
Butler, Louis **70**
Butler, Octavia **8, 43, 58**
Butler, Paul D. **17**
Butts, Calvin O., III **9**
Bynoe, Peter C.B. **40**
Bynum, Juanita **31, 71**
Byrd, Donald **10**
Byrd, Eugene **64**
Byrd, Michelle **19**
Byrd, Robert **11**
Cadoria, Sherian Grace **14**
Caesar, Shirley **19**
Cage, Byron **53**
Cain, Herman **15**
Caldwell, Benjamin **46**
Caldwell, Earl **60**
Caldwell, Kirbyjon **55**
Callender, Clive O. **3**
Calloway, Cab **14**
Camp, Kimberly **19**
Campanella, Roy **25**
Campbell, Bebe Moore **6, 24, 59**
Campbell, Bill **9**
Campbell, Donald J. **66**
Campbell, E. Simms **13**
Campbell, Mary Schmidt **43**
Campbell-Martin, Tisha **8, 42**
Canada, Geoffrey **23**
Canady, Alexa **28**
Cannon, Katie **10**
Cannon, Nick **47**
Cannon, Reuben **50**
Carr, Johnnie **69**
Cardozo, Francis L. **33**
Carew, Rod **20**
Carey, Mariah **32, 53, 69**
Cargill, Victoria A. **43**
Carr, Kurt **56**
Carr, Leroy **49**
Carroll, Diahann **9**
Carroll, L. Natalie **44**
Carruthers, George R. **40**
Carson, André **69**
Carson, Benjamin **1, 35**
Carson, Julia **23, 69**
Carson, Lisa Nicole **21**
Carter, Anson **24**
Carter, Benny **46**
Carter, Betty **19**
Carter, Butch **27**
Carter, Cris **21**
Carter, Joe **30**
Carter, Joye Maureen **41**
Carter, Kenneth **53**
Carter, Mandy **11**
Carter, Nell **39**
Carter, Pamela Lynn **67**

Carter, Regina 23
Carter, Robert L. 51
Carter, Rubin 26
Carter, Stephen L. 4
Carter, Vince 26
Carter, Warrick L. 27
Cartey, Wilfred 1992 47
Cartiér, Xam Wilson 41
Carver, George Washington 4
Cary, Lorene 3
Cary, Mary Ann Shadd 30
Cash, Rosalind 28
Cash, Swin 59
Cashin, Sheryll 63
CasSelle, Malcolm 11
Catchings, Tamika 43
Catlett, Elizabeth 2
Cayton, Horace 26
Cedric the Entertainer 29, 60
Cee-Lo 70
Chadiha, Jeffri 57
Chamberlain, Wilt 18, 47
Chambers, Julius 3
Chaney, John 67
Chapman, Nathan A., Jr. 21
Chapman, Tracy 26
Chappell, Emma 18
Chappelle, Dave 50
Charles, Ray 16, 48
Charleston, Oscar 39
Chase, Debra Martin 49
Chase, Leah 57
Chase-Riboud, Barbara 20, 46
Chatard, Peter 44
Chavis, Benjamin 6
Cheadle, Don 19, 52
Checker, Chubby 28
Cheeks, Maurice 47
Chenault, John 40
Chenault, Kenneth I. 4, 36
Cherry, Deron 40
Chesnutt, Charles 29
Chestnut, Morris 31
Chideya, Farai 14, 61
Childress, Alice 15
Chinn, May Edward 26
Chisholm, Samuel 32
Chisholm, Shirley 2, 50
Christian, Barbara T. 44
Christian, Spencer 15
Christian-Green, Donna M. 17
Christie, Angella 36
Chuck D 9
Ciara 56
Ciara, Barbara 69
Claiborne, Loretta 34
Clark, Celeste 15
Clark, Joe 1
Clark, Kenneth B. 5, 52
Clark, Mattie Moss 61
Clark, Patrick 14
Clark, Septima 7
Clark-Cole, Dorinda 66
Clarke, Cheryl 32
Clarke, Hope 14
Clarke, John Henrik 20
Clarke, Kenny 27
Clark-Sheard, Karen 22
Clash, Kevin 14
Clay, Bryan Ezra 57
Clay, William Lacy 8
Clayton, Constance 1
Clayton, Eva M. 20

Clayton, Mayme Agnew 62
Clayton, Xernona 3, 45
Claytor, Helen 14, 52
Cleage, Pearl 17, 64
Cleaver, Eldridge 5
Cleaver, Emanuel 4, 45, 68
Cleaver, Kathleen 29
Clements, George 2
Clemmons, Reginal G. 41
Clemons, Clarence 41
Clemons, Michael "Pinball" 64
Clendenon, Donn 26, 56
Cleveland, James 19
Cliff, Michelle 42
Clifton, Lucille 14, 64
Clifton, Nathaniel "Sweetwater" 47
Clinton, George 9
Clyburn, James E. 21, 71
Coachman, Alice 18
Cobb, Jewel Plummer 42
Cobb, W. Montague 39
Cobb, William Jelani 59
Cobbs, Price M. 9
Cochran, Johnnie 11, 39, 52
Cohen, Anthony 15
Colbert, Virgis William 17
Cole, Johnnetta B. 5, 43
Cole, Keyshia 63
Cole, Lorraine 48
Cole, Nat King 17
Cole, Natalie 17, 60
Cole, Rebecca 38
Coleman, Bessie 9
Coleman, Donald 24, 62
Coleman, Gary 35
Coleman, Ken 57
Coleman, Leonard S., Jr. 12
Coleman, Mary 46
Coleman, Michael B. 28
Coleman, Ornette 39, 69
Coleman, Wanda 48
Coleman, William F., III 61
Colemon, Johnnie 11
Colescott, Robert 69
Collins, Albert 12
Collins, Barbara-Rose 7
Collins, Bootsy 31
Collins, Cardiss 10
Collins, Janet 33, 64
Collins, Lyn 53
Collins, Marva 3, 71
Collins, Patricia Hill 67
Collins, Paul 61
Colter, Cyrus J. 36
Coltrane, Alice 70
Coltrane, John 19
Coltrane, Ravi 71
Combs, Sean "Puffy" 17, 43
Comer, James P. 6
Common 31, 63
Cone, James H. 3
Coney, PonJola 48
Connerly, Ward 14
Conyers, John, Jr. 4
Conyers, Nathan G. 24, 45
Cook, (Will) Mercer 40
Cook, Charles "Doc" 44
Cook, Samuel DuBois 14
Cook, Suzan D. Johnson 22
Cook, Toni 23
Cook, Will Marion 40
Cooke, Marcia 60
Cooke, Marvel 31

Cooper Cafritz, Peggy 43
Cooper, Andrew W. 36
Cooper, Andy "Lefty" 63
Cooper, Anna Julia 20
Cooper, Barry 33
Cooper, Charles "Chuck" 47
Cooper, Cynthia 17
Cooper, Edward S. 6
Cooper, Evern 40
Cooper, J. California 12
Cooper, Margaret J. 46
Cooper, Michael 31
Copeland, Michael 47
Corbi, Lana 42
Corley, Tony 62
Cornelius, Don 4
Cornish, Sam 50
Cornwell, Edward E., III 70
Cortez, Jayne 43
Corthron, Kia 43
Cortor, Eldzier 42
Cosby, Bill 7, 26, 59
Cosby, Camille 14
Cose, Ellis 5, 50
Cotter, Joseph Seamon, Sr. 40
Cottrell, Comer 11
Cowans, Adger W. 20
Cowboy Troy 54
Cox, Ida 42
Cox, Joseph Mason Andrew 51
Cox, Renée 67
Cox, William E. 68
Craig, Carl 31, 71
Craig-Jones, Ellen Walker 44
Crawford, Randy 19
Cray, Robert 30
Creagh, Milton 27
Crennel, Romeo 54
Crew, Rudolph F. 16
Crew, Spencer R. 55
Crite, Alan Rohan 29
Crocker, Frankie 29
Crockett, George W., Jr. 10, 64
Croom, Sylvester 50
Cross, Dolores E. 23
Crothers, Scatman 19
Crouch, Andraé 27
Crouch, Stanley 11
Crowder, Henry 16
Cruse, Harold 54
Crutchfield, James N. 55
Cullen, Countee 8
Cullers, Vincent T. 49
Culpepper, Daunte 32
Cummings, Elijah E. 24
Cuney, William Waring 44
Cunningham, Evelyn 23
Cunningham, Randall 23
Currie, Betty 21
Curry, George E. 23
Curry, Mark 17
Curtis, Christopher Paul 26
Curtis-Hall, Vondie 17
Daemyon, Jerald 64
Daly, Marie Maynard 37
Dandridge, Dorothy 3
Dandridge, Ray 36
Dandridge, Raymond Garfield 45
D'Angelo 27
Daniels, Lee Louis 36
Daniels-Carter, Valerie 23
Danner, Margaret Esse 49
Dara, Olu 35

Darden, Calvin 38
Darden, Christopher 13
Dash, Damon 31
Dash, Julie 4
Dash, Leon 47
Datcher, Michael 60
David, Keith 27
Davidson, Jaye 5
Davidson, Tommy 21
Davis, Allison 12
Davis, Angela 5
Davis, Anthony 11
Davis, Arthur Paul 41
Davis, Artur 41
Davis, Belva 61
Davis, Benjamin O., Jr. 2, 43
Davis, Benjamin O., Sr. 4
Davis, Charles T. 48
Davis, Chuck 33
Davis, Danny K. 24
Davis, Ed 24
Davis, Eisa 68
Davis, Ernie 48
Davis, Errol B., Jr. 57
Davis, Frank Marshall 47
Davis, Gary 41
Davis, George 36
Davis, Guy 36
Davis, James E. 50
Davis, Mike 41
Davis, Miles 4
Davis, Nolan 45
Davis, Ossie 5, 50
Davis, Piper 19
Davis, Ruth 37
Davis, Shani 58
Davis, Terrell 20
Davis, Thulani 61
Davis, Tyrone 54
Davis, Viola 34
Dawes, Dominique 11
Dawkins, Wayne 20
Dawson, Matel "Mat," Jr. 39
Dawson, Michael C. 63
Dawson, William Levi 39
Day, Leon 39
Days, Drew S., III 10
de Passe, Suzanne 25
De Veaux, Alexis 44
De' Alexander, Quinton 57
Dean, Mark E. 35
DeBaptiste, George 32
DeCarava, Roy 42
Deconge-Watson, Lovenia 55
Dee, Merri 55
Dee, Ruby 8, 50, 68
Deezer D 53
DeFrantz, Anita 37
Deggans, Eric 71
Delaney, Beauford 19
Delaney, Joseph 30
Delany, Bessie 12
Delany, Martin R. 27
Delany, Sadie 12
Delany, Samuel R., Jr. 9
Delco, Wilhemina 33
DeLille, Henriette 30
Dellums, Ronald 2
DeLoach, Nora 30
Delsarte, Louis 34
Demby, William 51
Dennard, Brazeal 37
Dent, Thomas C. 50

DePriest, James 37
DeVard, Jerri 61
Devers, Gail 7
Devine, Loretta 24
Dickens, Helen Octavia 14, 64
Dickenson, Vic 38
Dickerson, Debra J. 60
Dickerson, Eric 27
Dickerson, Ernest R. 6, 17
Dickey, Eric Jerome 21, 56
Diddley, Bo 39
Diesel, Vin 29
Diggs, Charles C. 21
Diggs, Taye 25, 63
Diggs-Taylor, Anna 20
Dillard, Godfrey J. 45
Dinkins, David 4
Divine, Father 7
Dixon, Dean 68
Dixon, Ivan 69
Dixon, Julian C. 24
Dixon, Margaret 14
Dixon, Sharon Pratt 1
Dixon, Sheila 68
Dixon, Willie 4
DMX 28, 64
Dobbs, Mattiwilda 34
Doby, Lawrence Eugene, Sr. 16, 41
Dodson, Howard, Jr. 7, 52
Dodson, Owen Vincent 38
Doley, Harold, Jr. 26
Domino, Fats 20
Donald, Arnold Wayne 36
Donaldson, Jeff 46
Donegan, Dorothy 19
Dorrell, Karl 52
Dorsey, Lee 65
Dorsey, Thomas 15
Dortch, Thomas W., Jr. 45
Dougherty, Mary Pearl 47
Douglas, Aaron 7
Dourdan, Gary 37
Dove, Rita 6
Dove, Ulysses 5
Downing, Will 19
Draper, Sharon Mills 16, 43
Dre, Dr. 10, 14, 30
Drew, Alvin, Jr. 67
Drew, Charles Richard 7
Drexler, Clyde 4, 61
Driskell, David C. 7
Driver, David E. 11
Drummond, William J. 40
Du Bois, David Graham 45
DuBois, Shirley Graham 21
DuBois, W. E. B. 3
Ducksworth, Marilyn 12
Dudley, Edward R. 58
Due, Tananarive 30
Duggins, George 64
Duke, Bill 3
Duke, George 21
Dukes, Hazel Nell 56
Dumars, Joe 16, 65
Dumas, Henry 41
Dunbar, Paul Laurence 8
Dunbar-Nelson, Alice Ruth Moore 44
Duncan, Michael Clarke 26
Duncan, Tim 20
Dungey, Merrin 62
Dungy, Tony 17, 42, 59
Dunham, Katherine 4, 59

Dunlap, Ericka 55
Dunn, Jerry 27
Dunner, Leslie B. 45
Dunnigan, Alice Allison 41
Dunston, Georgia Mae 48
Duplechan, Larry 55
Dupri, Jermaine 13, 46
Dutton, Charles S. 4, 22
Dworkin, Aaron P. 52
Dwight, Edward 65
Dye, Jermaine 58
Dyson, Michael Eric 11, 40
Early, Gerald 15
Earthquake 55
Easley, Annie J. 61
Ebanks, Michelle 60
Eckstine, Billy 28
Edelin, Ramona Hoage 19
Edelman, Marian Wright 5, 42
Edley, Christopher 2, 48
Edley, Christopher F., Jr. 48
Edmonds, Kenneth "Babyface" 10, 31
Edmonds, Terry 17
Edmonds, Tracey 16, 64
Edmunds, Gladys 48
Edwards, Esther Gordy 43
Edwards, Harry 2
Edwards, Herman 51
Edwards, Melvin 22
Edwards, Teresa 14
Edwards, Willarda V. 59
El Wilson, Barbara 35
Elder, Larry 25
Elder, Lee 6
Elder, Lonne, III 38
Elders, Joycelyn 6
Eldridge, Roy 37
Elise, Kimberly 32
Ellerbe, Brian 22
Ellington, Duke 5
Ellington, E. David 11
Ellington, Mercedes 34
Elliott, Missy "Misdemeanor" 31
Elliott, Sean 26
Ellis, Clarence A. 38
Ellis, Jimmy 44
Ellison, Keith 59
Ellison, Ralph 7
Elmore, Ronn 21
Emanuel, James A. 46
Emeagwali, Dale 31
Ephriam, Mablean 29
Epperson, Sharon 54
Epps, Archie C., III 45
Epps, Mike 60
Epps, Omar 23, 59
Ericsson-Jackson, Aprille 28
Ervin, Anthony 66
Erving, Julius 18, 47
Escobar, Damien 56
Escobar, Tourie 56
Esposito, Giancarlo 9
Espy, Mike 6
Estes, Rufus 29
Estes, Simon 28
Estes, Sleepy John 33
Eubanks, Kevin 15
Eugene-Richard, Margie 63
Europe, James Reese 10
Evans, Darryl 22
Evans, Etu 55
Evans, Faith 22

Evans, Harry 25
Evans, Mari 26
Eve 29
Everett, Francine 23
Evers, Medgar 3
Evers, Myrlie 8
Fabio, Sarah Webster 48
Fabre, Shelton 71
Fair, Ronald L. 47
Faison, Donald 50
Faison, Frankie 55
Faison, George 16
Falana, Lola 42
Falconer, Etta Zuber 59
Fargas, Antonio 50
Farley, Christopher John 54
Farmer, Art 38
Farmer, Forest J. 1
Farmer, James 2, 64
Farmer-Paellmann, Deadria 43
Farr, Mel 24
Farrakhan, Louis 2, 15
Farris, Isaac Newton, Jr. 63
Fattah, Chaka 11, 70
Faulk, Marshall 35
Fauntroy, Walter E. 11
Fauset, Jessie 7
Favors, Steve 23
Fax, Elton 48
Feelings, Muriel 44
Feelings, Tom 11, 47
Felix, Allyson 48
Felix, Larry R. 64
Fenty, Adrian 60
Ferguson, Roger W. 25
Ferrell, Rachelle 29
Fetchit, Stepin 32
Fiasco, Lupe 64
Fielder, Cecil 2
Fielder, Prince Semien 68
Fields, C. Virginia 25
Fields, Cleo 13
Fields, Evelyn J. 27
Fields, Felicia P. 60
Fields, Julia 45
Fields, Kim 36
Files, Lolita 35
Fine, Sam 60
Finner-Williams, Paris Michele 62
Fishburne, Laurence 4, 22, 70
Fisher, Antwone 40
Fitzgerald, Ella 1, 18
Flack, Roberta 19
Flanagan, Tommy 69
Flavor Flav 67
Fleming, Raymond 48
Fletcher, Arthur A. 63
Fletcher, Bill, Jr. 41
Flowers, Sylester 50
Flowers, Vonetta 35
Floyd, Elson S. 41
Forbes, Calvin 46
Forbes, James A., Jr. 71
Ford, Cheryl 45
Ford, Clyde W. 40
Ford, Harold E(ugene) 42
Ford, Harold E(ugene), Jr. 16, 70
Ford, Jack 39
Ford, Johnny 70
Ford, Nick Aaron 44
Ford, Wallace 58
Forman, James 7, 51
Forrest, Leon 44

Forrest, Vernon 40
Forte, Linda Diane 54
Foster, Ezola 28
Foster, George "Pops" 40
Foster, Henry W., Jr. 26
Foster, Jylla Moore 45
Foster, Marie 48
Fowler, Reggie 51
Fox, Vivica A. 15, 53
Foxx, Jamie 15, 48
Francis, Norman (C.) 60
Franklin, Aretha 11, 44
Franklin, C. L. 68
Franklin, J. E. 44
Franklin, Kirk 15, 49
Franklin, Shirley 34
Frazer, Jendayi 68
Frazier, E. Franklin 10
Frazier, Joe 19
Frazier, Kevin 58
Frazier, Oscar 58
Frazier-Lyde, Jacqui 31
Freelon, Nnenna 32
Freeman, Aaron 52
Freeman, Al, Jr. 11
Freeman, Charles 19
Freeman, Harold P. 23
Freeman, Leonard 27
Freeman, Marianna 23
Freeman, Morgan 2, 20, 62
Freeman, Paul 39
Freeman, Yvette 27
French, Albert 18
Friday, Jeff 24
Fryer, Roland G. 56
Fudge, Ann (Marie) 11, 55
Fulani, Lenora 11
Fuller, A. Oveta 43
Fuller, Arthur 27
Fuller, Charles 8
Fuller, Howard L. 37
Fuller, Hoyt 44
Fuller, Meta Vaux Warrick 27
Fuller, S.B. 13
Fuller, Solomon Carter, Jr. 15
Fuller, Vivian 33
Funderburg, I. Owen 38
Fuqua, Antoine 35
Futch, Eddie 33
Gaines, Brenda 41
Gaines, Clarence E., Sr. 55
Gaines, Ernest J. 7
Gaines, Grady 38
Gaither, Alonzo Smith (Jake) 14
Gaither, Israel L. 65
Gantt, Harvey 1
Gardner, Chris 65
Gardner, Edward G. 45
Garnett, Kevin 14, 70
Garrett, Joyce Finley 59
Garrison, Zina 2
Gary, Willie E. 12
Gaskins, Eric 64
Gaston, Arthur George 3, 38, 59
Gaston, Cito 71
Gaston, Marilyn Hughes 60
Gates, Henry Louis, Jr. 3, 38, 67
Gates, Sylvester James, Jr. 15
Gaye, Marvin 2
Gaye, Nona 56
Gayle, Addison, Jr. 41
Gayle, Helene D. 3, 46
Gaynor, Gloria 36

Gentry, Alvin 23
George, Nelson 12
George, Zelma Watson 42
Gibson, Althea 8, 43
Gibson, Bob 33
Gibson, Donald Bernard 40
Gibson, Johnnie Mae 23
Gibson, Josh 22
Gibson, Kenneth Allen 6
Gibson, Ted 66
Gibson, Truman K., Jr. 60
Gibson, Tyrese 27, 62
Gibson, William F. 6
Giddings, Paula 11
Gidron, Richard D. 68
Gilbert, Christopher 50
Flanagan, Tommy 69
Gill, Johnny 51
Gilles, Ralph 61
Gillespie, Dizzy 1
Gilliam, Frank 23
Gilliam, Joe 31
Gilliam, Sam 16
Gilliard, Steve 69
Gilmore, Marshall 46
Ginuwine 35
Giovanni, Nikki 9, 39
Gist, Carole 1
Givens, Adele 62
Givens, Robin 4, 25, 58
Glover, Corey 34
Glover, Danny 1, 24
Glover, Nathaniel, Jr. 12
Glover, Savion 14
Goapele 55
Goines, Donald 19
Goings, Russell 59
Goldberg, Whoopi 4, 33, 69
Golden, Marita 19
Golden, Thelma 10, 55
Goldsberry, Ronald 18
Golson, Benny 37
Golston, Allan C. 55
Gomes, Peter J. 15
Gomez, Jewelle 30
Gomez-Preston, Cheryl 9
Goode, Mal 13
Goode, W. Wilson 4
Gooden, Dwight 20
Gooding, Cuba, Jr. 16, 62
Goodnight, Paul 32
Gorden, W. C. 71
Gordon, Bruce S. 41, 53
Gordon, Dexter 25
Gordon, Ed 10, 53
Gordone, Charles 15
Gordy, Berry, Jr. 1
Goss, Carol A. 55
Goss, Tom 23
Gossett, Louis, Jr. 7
Gotti, Irv 39
Gourdine, Meredith 33
Gourdine, Simon 11
Grace, George H. 48
Graham, Lawrence Otis 12
Graham, Lorenz 48
Graham, Stedman 13
Granderson, Curtis 66
Grant, Augustus O. 71
Grant, Bernie 57
Grant, Gwendolyn Goldsby 28
Granville, Evelyn Boyd 36
Gravely, Samuel L., Jr. 5, 49

Graves, Denyce Antoinette 19, 57
Graves, Earl G. 1, 35
Gray, Darius 69
Gray, F. Gary 14, 49
Gray, Farrah 59
Gray, Fred 37
Gray, Ida 41
Gray, Macy 29
Gray, William H., III 3
Gray, Willie 46
Gray, Yeshimbra "Shimmy" 55
Greaves, William 38
Greely, M. Gasby 27
Green, A. C. 32
Green, Al 13, 47
Green, Darrell 39
Green, Dennis 5, 45
Green, Grant 56
Green, Jonathan 54
Greene, Joe 10
Greene, Maurice 27
Greene, Petey 65
Greene, Richard Thaddeus, Sr. 67
Greenfield, Eloise 9
Greenhouse, Bunnatine "Bunny" 57
Greenlee, Sam 48
Greenwood, Monique 38
Gregory, Ann 63
Gregory, Dick 1, 54
Gregory, Frederick 8, 51
Gregory, Wilton 37
Grier, David Alan 28
Grier, Mike 43
Grier, Pam 9, 31
Grier, Roosevelt 13
Griffey, Ken, Jr. 12
Griffin, Anthony 71
Griffin, Bessie Blout 43
Griffin, Johnny 71
Griffin, LaShell 51
Griffith, Mark Winston 8
Griffith, Yolanda 25
Griffith-Joyner, Florence 28
Grimké, Archibald H. 9
Grooms, Henry R(andall) 50
Guillaume, Robert 3, 48
Guinier, Lani 7, 30
Gumbel, Bryant 14
Gumbel, Greg 8
Gunn, Moses 10
Guy, George "Buddy" 31
Guy, Jasmine 2
Guy, Rosa 5
Guy-Sheftall, Beverly 13
Guyton, Tyree 9
Gwynn, Tony 18
Haddon, Dietrick 55
Hageman, Hans 36
Hageman, Ivan 36
Hailey, JoJo 22
Hailey, K-Ci 22
Hale, Clara 16
Hale, Lorraine 8
Haley, Alex 4
Haley, George Williford Boyce 21
Hall, Aaron 57
Hall, Arsenio 58
Hall, Arthur 39
Hall, Elliott S. 24
Hall, Juanita 62
Hall, Kevan 61
Hall, Lloyd A. 8
Halliburton, Warren J. 49

Ham, Cynthia Parker 58
Hamblin, Ken 10
Hamer, Fannie Lou 6
Hamilton, Anthony 61
Hamilton, Samuel C. 47
Hamilton, Lisa Gay 71
Hamilton, Virginia 10
Hamlin, Larry Leon 49, 62
Hammer, M. C. 20
Hammond, Fred 23
Hammonds, Evelynn 69
Hammons, David 69
Hampton, Fred 18
Hampton, Henry 6
Hampton, Lionel 17, 41
Hancock, Herbie 20, 67
Handy, W. C. 8
Hannah, Marc 10
Hansberry, Lorraine 6
Hansberry, William Leo 11
Hardaway, Anfernee (Penny) 13
Hardaway, Tim 35
Hardin Armstrong, Lil 39
Harding, Vincent 67
Hardison, Bethann 12
Hardison, Kadeem 22
Hare, Nathan 44
Harkless, Necia Desiree 19
Harmon, Clarence 26
Harold, Erika 54
Harper, Ben 34, 62
Harper, Frances Ellen Watkins 11
Harper, Hill 32, 65
Harper, Michael S. 34
Harrell, Andre 9, 30
Harrington, Oliver W. 9
Harris, Alice 7
Harris, Barbara 12
Harris, Barry 68
Harris, Carla A. 67
Harris, Corey 39
Harris, E. Lynn 12, 33
Harris, Eddy L. 18
Harris, Jay T. 19
Harris, Kamala D. 64
Harris, Leslie 6
Harris, Marcelite Jordon 16
Harris, Mary Styles 31
Harris, Monica 18
Harris, Patricia Roberts 2
Harris, Richard E. 61
Harris, Robin 7
Harris, Sylvia 70
Harrison, Alvin 28
Harrison, Calvin 28
Harsh, Vivian Gordon 14
Hart, Alvin Youngblood 61
Harvard, Beverly 11
Harvey, Steve 18, 58
Harvey, William R. 42
Haskins, Clem 23
Haskins, James 36, 54
Hassell, Leroy Rountree, Sr. 41
Hastie, William H. 8
Hastings, Alcee L. 16
Hatcher, Richard G. 55
Hatchett, Glenda 32
Hathaway, Donny 18
Hathaway, Isaac Scott 33
Hathaway, Lalah 57
Hawkins, Augustus F. 68
Hawkins, Coleman 9
Hawkins, Erskine 14

Hawkins, La-Van 17, 54
Hawkins, Screamin' Jay 30
Hawkins, Steven 14
Hawkins, Tramaine 16
Hayden, Carla D. 47
Hayden, Palmer 13
Hayden, Robert 12
Hayes, Cecil N. 46
Hayes, Dennis 54
Hayes, Isaac 20, 58
Hayes, James C. 10
Hayes, Roland 4
Hayes, Teddy 40
Haynes, George Edmund 8
Haynes, Marques 22
Haynes, Trudy 44
Haysbert, Dennis 42
Haywood, Gar Anthony 43
Haywood, Jimmy 58
Haywood, Margaret A. 24
Hazel, Darryl B. 50
Healy, James Augustine 30
Heard, Gar 25
Heard, Nathan C. 45
Hearns, Thomas 29
Hedgeman, Anna Arnold 22
Height, Dorothy I. 2, 23
Hemphill, Essex 10
Hemphill, Jessie Mae 33, 59
Hemsley, Sherman 19
Henderson, Cornelius Langston 26
Henderson, David 53
Henderson, Fletcher 32
Henderson, Gordon 5
Henderson, Rickey 28
Henderson, Stephen E. 45
Henderson, Thelton E. 68
Henderson, Wade J. 14
Henderson, Zelma 71
Hendrix, Jimi 10
Hendryx, Nona 56
Hendy, Francis 47
Henries, A. Doris Banks 44
Henry, Aaron 19
Henry, Clarence "Frogman" 46
Henson, Darrin 33
Henson, Matthew 2
Henson, Taraji 58
Herbert, Bob 63
Hercules, Frank 44
Herenton, Willie W. 24
Herman, Alexis M. 15
Hernandez, Aileen Clarke 13
Hernton, Calvin C. 51
Hickman, Fred 11
Higginbotham, A. Leon, Jr. 13, 25
Higginbotham, Jay C. 37
Higginsen, Vy 65
Hightower, Dennis F. 13
Hill, Andrew 66
Hill, Anita 5, 65
Hill, Bonnie Guiton 20
Hill, Calvin 19
Hill, Donna 32
Hill, Dulé 29
Hill, Grant 13
Hill, Janet 19
Hill, Jesse, Jr. 13
Hill, Lauryn 20, 53
Hill, Leslie Pinckney 44
Hill, Oliver W. 24, 63
Hillard, Terry 25
Hillary, Barbara 65

Hilliard, Asa Grant, III 66
Hilliard, David 7
Hilliard, Earl F. 24
Hilliard, Wendy 53
Himes, Chester 8
Hinderas, Natalie 5
Hine, Darlene Clark 24
Hines, Earl "Fatha" 39
Hines, Garrett 35
Hines, Gregory 1, 42
Hinton, Milt 30
Hinton, William Augustus 8
Hoagland, Everett H. 45
Hobson, Julius W. 44
Hobson, Mellody 40
Hogan, Beverly Wade 50
Holder, Eric H., Jr. 9
Holder, Laurence 34
Holdsclaw, Chamique 24
Holiday, Billie 1
Holland, Endesha Ida Mae 3, 57
Holland, Kimberly N. 62
Holland, Robert, Jr. 11
Holland-Dozier-Holland 36
Holloway, Brenda 65
Hollowell, Donald L. 57
Holmes, Amy 69
Holmes, Clint 57
Holmes, Larry 20, 68
Holmes, Shannon 70
Holt, Lester 66
Holt, Nora 38
Holton, Hugh, Jr. 39
Holyfield, Evander 6
Honeywood, Varnette P. 54
Honoré, Russel L. 64
Hooker, John Lee 30
hooks, bell 5
Hooks, Benjamin L. 2
Hope, John 8
Hopkins, Bernard 35, 69
Horn, Shirley 32, 56
Horne, Frank 44
Horne, Lena 5
Horton, Andre 33
Horton, James Oliver 58
Horton, Suki 33
House, Son 8
Houston, Charles Hamilton 4
Houston, Cissy 20
Houston, Whitney 7, 28
Howard, Ayanna 65
Howard, Desmond 16, 58
Howard, Juwan 15
Howard, M. William, Jr. 26
Howard, Michelle 28
Howard, Ryan 65
Howard, Sherri 36
Howard, Terrence Dashon 59
Howlin' Wolf 9
Howroyd, Janice Bryant 42
Hoyte, Lenon 50
Hrabowski, Freeman A., III 22
Hubbard, Arnette Rhinehart 38
Hudlin, Reginald 9
Hudlin, Warrington 9
Hudson, Cheryl 15
Hudson, Jennifer 63
Hudson, Wade 15
Huggins, Edie 71
Huggins, Larry 21
Huggins, Nathan Irvin 52
Hughes, Albert 7

Hughes, Allen 7
Hughes, Cathy 27
Hughes, Ebony 57
Hughes, Langston 4
Hughley, D.L. 23
Hull, Akasha Gloria 45
Humphrey, Bobbi 20
Humphries, Frederick 20
Hunt, Richard 6
Hunter, Alberta 42
Hunter, Clementine 45
Hunter, Torii 43
Hunter-Gault, Charlayne 6, 31
Hurston, Zora Neale 3
Hurt, Byron 61
Hurtt, Harold 46
Hutch, Willie 62
Hutcherson, Hilda Yvonne 54
Hutchinson, Earl Ofari 24
Hutson, Jean Blackwell 16
Hyde, Cowan F. "Bubba" 47
Hyman, Earle 25
Hyman, Phyllis 19
Ice Cube 8, 30, 60
Iceberg Slim 11
Ice-T 6, 31
Ifill, Gwen 28
Imes, Elmer Samuel 39
India.Arie 34
Ingram, Rex 5
Innis, Roy 5
Irvin, Michael 64
Irvin, Monford Merrill 31
Irvin, Vernon 65
Irving, Larry, Jr. 12
Irvis, K. Leroy 67
Isley, Ronald 25, 56
Iverson, Allen 24, 46
Ja Rule 35
Jackson Lee, Sheila 20
Jackson, Alexine Clement 22
Jackson, Alphonso R. 48
Jackson, Earl 31
Jackson, Edison O. 67
Jackson, Fred James 25
Jackson, George 14
Jackson, George 19
Jackson, Hal 41
Jackson, Isaiah 3
Jackson, Jamea 64
Jackson, Janet 6, 30, 68
Jackson, Jesse 1, 27
Jackson, Jesse, Jr. 14, 45
Jackson, John 36
Jackson, Judith D. 57
Jackson, Mae 57
Jackson, Mahalia 5
Jackson, Mannie 14
Jackson, Maynard 2, 41
Jackson, Michael 19, 53
Jackson, Millie 25
Jackson, Milt 26
Jackson, Randy 40
Jackson, Reggie 15
Jackson, Samuel 8, 63
Jackson, Sheneska 18
Jackson, Shirley Ann 12
Jackson, Tom 70
Jackson, Vera 40
Jacob, John E. 2
Jacobs, Regina 38
Jacquet, Illinois 49

Jaheim 58
Jakes, Thomas "T.D." 17, 43
Jamal, Ahmad 69
Jamerson, James 59
James, Charles H., III 62
James, Daniel, Jr. 16
James, Donna A. 51
James, Etta 13, 52
James, Juanita 13
James, LeBron 46
James, Rick 19
James, Sharpe 23, 69
James, Skip 38
Jamison, Judith 7, 67
Jarreau, Al 21, 65
Jarret, Vernon D. 42
Jarvis, Charlene Drew 21
Jarvis, Erich 67
Jasper, Kenji 39
Jay-Z 27, 69
Jazzy Jeff 32
Jealous, Benjamin 70
Jefferson, William J. 25
Jeffries, Leonard 8
Jemison, Mae C. 1, 35
Jemison, Major L. 48
Jenifer, Franklyn G. 2
Jenkins, Beverly 14
Jenkins, Ella 15
Jennings, Lyfe 56, 69
Jerkins, Rodney 31
Jeter, Derek 27
Jimmy Jam 13
Joe, Yolanda 21
John, Daymond 23
Johns, Vernon 38
Johnson, Angela 52
Johnson, Avery 62
Johnson, Beverly 2
Johnson, Buddy 36
Johnson, Charles 1
Johnson, Charles S. 12
Johnson, Clifford "Connie" 52
Johnson, Earvin "Magic" 3, 39
Johnson, Eddie Bernice 8
Johnson, George E. 29
Johnson, Georgia Douglas 41
Johnson, Harry E. 57
Johnson, Harvey, Jr. 24
Johnson, J. J. 37
Johnson, Jack 8
Johnson, James Weldon 5
Johnson, Je'Caryous 63
Johnson, Jeh Vincent 44
Johnson, John H. 3, 54
Johnson, Johnnie 56
Johnson, Katherine (Coleman Goble) 61
Johnson, Kevin 70
Johnson, Larry 28
Johnson, Levi 48
Johnson, Lonnie 32
Johnson, Mamie "Peanut" 40
Johnson, Mat 31
Johnson, Michael 13
Johnson, Norma L. Holloway 17
Johnson, R. M. 36
Johnson, Rafer 33
Johnson, Robert 2
Johnson, Robert L. 3, 39
Johnson, Robert T. 17
Johnson, Rodney Van 28
Johnson, Sheila Crump 48

Johnson, Shoshana 47
Johnson, Virginia 9
Johnson, William Henry 3
Jolley, Willie 28
Jones, Absalom 52
Jones, Alex 64
Jones, Bill T. 1, 46
Jones, Bobby 20
Jones, Carl 7
Jones, Caroline 29
Jones, Clara Stanton 51
Jones, Cobi N'Gai 18
Jones, Donell 29
Jones, Doris W. 62
Jones, E. Edward, Sr. 45
Jones, Ed "Too Tall" 46
Jones, Edith Mae Irby 65
Jones, Edward P. 43, 67
Jones, Elaine R. 7, 45
Jones, Elvin 14, 68
Jones, Etta 35
Jones, Frederick McKinley 68
Jones, Gayl 37
Jones, Hank 57
Jones, Ingrid Saunders 18
Jones, James Earl 3, 49
Jones, Jonah 39
Jones, Lois Mailou 13
Jones, Lou 64
Jones, Marion 21, 66
Jones, Merlakia 34
Jones, Orlando 30
Jones, Quincy 8, 30
Jones, Randy 35
Jones, Sarah 39
Jones, Thad 68
Jones, Thomas W. 41
Jones, Van 70
Jones, Wayne 53
Jones, William A., Jr. 61
Joplin, Scott 6
Jordan, Barbara 4
Jordan, June 7, 35
Jordan, Michael 6, 21
Jordan, Montell 23
Jordan, Vernon E. 3, 35
Joseph, Kathie-Ann 56
Josey, E. J. 10
Joyner, Marjorie Stewart 26
Joyner, Matilda Sissieretta 15
Joyner, Tom 19
Joyner-Kersee, Jackie 5
Julian, Percy Lavon 6
July, William 27
Just, Ernest Everett 3
Justice, David 18
Kaigler, Denise 63
Kaiser, Cecil 42
Kani, Karl 10
Karenga, Maulana 10, 71
Karim, Benjamin 61
Kaufman, Monica 66
Kay, Ulysses 37
Kearney, Janis 54
Kearse, Amalya Lyle 12
Kee, John P. 43
Keflezighi, Meb 49
Keith, Damon J. 16
Keith, Floyd A. 61
Kelis 58
Kelley, Elijah 65
Kelley, Malcolm David 59
Kellogg, Clark 64

Kelly, Patrick 3
Kelly, R. 18, 44, 71
Kem 47
Kendrick, Erika 57
Kendricks, Eddie 22
Kennedy, Adrienne 11
Kennedy, Florynce 12, 33
Kennedy, Randall 40
Kennedy-Overton, Jayne Harris 46
Kenney, John A., Jr. 48
Kenoly, Ron 45
Kenyatta, Robin 54
Kerry, Leon G. 46
Keyes, Alan L. 11
Keys, Alicia 32, 68
Khan, Chaka 12, 50
Khanga, Yelena 6
Kidd, Mae Street 39
Killens, John O. 54
Killings, Debra 57
Killingsworth, Cleve, Jr. 54
Kilpatrick, Carolyn Cheeks 16
Kilpatrick, Kwame 34, 71
Kimbro, Dennis 10
Kimbro, Henry A. 25
Kincaid, Bernard 28
Kincaid, Jamaica 4
King, Alonzo 38
King, B. B. 7
King, Barbara 22
King, Bernice 4
King, Colbert I. 69
King, Coretta Scott 3, 57
King, Dexter 10
King, Don 14
King, Gayle 19
King, Martin Luther, III 20
King, Martin Luther, Jr. 1
King, Preston 28
King, Reatha Clark 65
King, Regina 22, 45
King, Robert Arthur 58
King, Woodie, Jr. 27
King, Yolanda 6
Kirby, George 14
Kirk, Ron 11
Kitt, Eartha 16
Kitt, Sandra 23
Kittles, Rick 51
Klugh, Earl 59
Knight, Etheridge 37
Knight, Gladys 16, 66
Knight, Suge 11, 30
Knowles, Tina 61
Knowling, Robert E., Jr. 38
Knox, Simmie 49
Knuckles, Frankie 42
Komunyakaa, Yusef 9
Kong, B. Waine 50
Kool Moe Dee 37
Kotto, Yaphet 7
Kountz, Samuel L. 10
Kravitz, Lenny 10, 34
KRS-One 34
Kunjufu, Jawanza 3, 50
La Salle, Eriq 12
LaBelle, Patti 13, 30
Lacy, Sam 30, 46
Ladd, Ernie 64
Ladner, Joyce A. 42
Lafontant, Jewel Stradford 3, 51
Lampkin, Daisy 19
Lampley, Oni Faida 43, 71

Lane, Charles 3
Lane, Vincent 5
Langhart Cohen, Janet 19, 60
Lanier, Bob 47
Lanier, Willie 33
Lankford, Ray 23
Larkin, Barry 24
Larrieux, Amel 63
Lars, Byron 32
Larsen, Nella 10
Laryea, Thomas Davies, III 67
Lashley, Bobby 63
Lassiter, Roy 24
Lathan, Sanaa 27
Latimer, Lewis H. 4
Lattimore, Kenny 35
Lavizzo-Mourey, Risa 48
Lawless, Theodore K. 8
Lawrence, Jacob 4, 28
Lawrence, Martin 6, 27
Lawrence, Robert H., Jr. 16
Lawrence-Lightfoot, Sara 10
Lawson, Jennifer 1, 50
Leary, Kathryn D. 10
Leavell, Dorothy R. 17
Lee, Annie Francis 22
Lee, Barbara 25
Lee, Canada 8
Lee, Debra L. 62
Lee, Joe A. 45
Lee, Joie 1
Lee, Spike 5, 19
Lee, Bertram M., Sr. 46
Lee-Smith, Hughie 5, 22
Leevy, Carrol M. 42
Leffall, Lasalle, Jr. 3, 64
Legend, John 67
Leggs, Kingsley 62
Leland, Mickey 2
Lemmons, Kasi 20
Lennox, Betty 31
LeNoire, Rosetta 37
Lenox, Adriane 59
Leon, Kenny 10
Leonard, Buck 67
Leonard, Sugar Ray 15
Lester, Bill 42
Lester, Julius 9
Lesure, James 64
LeTang, Henry 66
Letson, Al 39
Levert, Eddie 70
Levert, Gerald 22, 59
Lewellyn, J. Bruce 13
Lewis, Ananda 28
Lewis, Aylwin 51
Lewis, Butch 71
Lewis, Byron E. 13
Lewis, Carl 4
Lewis, David Levering 9
Lewis, Delano 7
Lewis, Edmonia 10
Lewis, Edward T. 21
Lewis, Emmanuel 36
Lewis, Henry 38
Lewis, John 2, 46
Lewis, Marvin 51
Lewis, Norman 39
Lewis, Oliver 56
Lewis, Ramsey 35, 70
Lewis, Ray 33
Lewis, Reginald F. 6
Lewis, Samella 25

Lewis, Shirley A. R. 14
Lewis, Terry 13
Lewis, Thomas 19
Lewis, William M., Jr. 40
Lewis-Thornton, Rae 32
Ligging, Alfred, III 43
Lil' Kim 28
Lil Wayne 66
Liles, Kevin 42
Lincoln, Abbey 3
Lincoln, C. Eric 38
Lindsey, Tommie 51
Lipscomb, Mance 49
LisaRaye 27
Lister, Marquita 65
Liston, Sonny 33
Little Milton 36, 54
Little Richard 15
Little Walter 36
Little, Benilde 21
Little, Robert L. 2
Littlepage, Craig 35
LL Cool J 16, 49
Lloyd, Earl 26
Lloyd, John Henry "Pop" 30
Lloyd, Reginald 64
Locke, Alain 10
Locke, Eddie 44
Lofton, James 42
Lofton, Kenny 12
Logan, Onnie Lee 14
Logan, Rayford W. 40
Lomax, Michael L. 58
Long, Eddie L. 29
Long, Loretta 58
Long, Nia 17
Long, Richard Alexander 65
Lopes, Lisa "Left Eye" 36
Lorde, Audre 6
Lott, Ronnie 9
Louis, Errol T. 8
Louis, Joe 5
Loury, Glenn 36
Love, Darlene 23
Love, Ed 58
Love, Laura 50
Love, Nat 9
Lover, Ed 10
Loving, Alvin, Jr., 35, 53
Loving, Mildred 69
Lowe, Herbert 57
Lowe, Sidney 64
Lowery, Joseph 2
Lowry, A. Leon 60
Lucas, John 7
Lucien, Jon 66
Luckett, Letoya 61
Lucy, William 50
Lucy Foster, Autherine 35
Ludacris 37, 60
Luke, Derek 61
Lumbly, Carl 47
Lyles, Lester Lawrence 31
Lymon, Frankie 22
Lynch, Shola 61
Lyons, Henry 12
Lyttle, Hulda Margaret 14
Mabley, Moms 15
Mabrey, Vicki 26
Mabry, Marcus 70
Mac, Bernie 29, 61
Madhubuti, Haki R. 7
Madison, Joseph E. 17

Madison, Paula 37
Madison, Romell 45
Mahal, Taj 39
Mahorn, Rick 60
Majette, Denise 41
Major, Clarence 9
Majors, Jeff 41
Malco, Romany 71
Mallett, Conrad, Jr. 16
Mallory, Mark 62
Malone Jones, Vivian 59
Malone, Annie 13
Malone, Karl 18, 51
Malone, Maurice 32
Malveaux, Floyd 54
Malveaux, Julianne 32, 70
Manigault, Earl "The Goat" 15
Manigault-Stallworth, Omarosa 69
Manley, Audrey Forbes 16
Marable, Manning 10
March, William Carrington 56
Mariner, Jonathan 41
Marino, Eugene Antonio 30
Mario 71
Marrow, Queen Esther 24
Marsalis, Branford 34
Marsalis, Delfeayo 41
Marsalis, Wynton 16
Marsh, Henry, III 32
Marshall, Bella 22
Marshall, Kerry James 59
Marshall, Paule 7
Marshall, Thurgood 1, 44
Martin, Darnell 43
Martin, Helen 31
Martin, Jesse L. 31
Martin, Louis E. 16
Martin, Roberta 58
Martin, Roland S. 49
Martin, Ruby Grant 49
Martin, Sara 38
Mase 24
Mason, Felicia 31
Mason, Ronald 27
Massaquoi, Hans J. 30
Massenburg, Kedar 23
Massey, Brandon 40
Massey, Walter E. 5, 45
Massie, Samuel Proctor, Jr. 29
Master P 21
Mathis, Greg 26
Mathis, Johnny 20
Matthews Shatteen, Westina 51
Matthews, Mark 59
Maxey, Randall 46
Maxis, Theresa 62
Maxwell 20
May, Derrick 41
Mayfield, Curtis 2, 43
Mayhew, Richard 39
Maynard, Robert C. 7
Maynor, Dorothy 19
Mayo, Whitman 32
Mays, Benjamin E. 7
Mays, Leslie A. 41
Mays, William G. 34
Mays, Willie 3
Mayweather, Floyd, Jr. 57
MC Lyte 34
McAnulty, William E., Jr. 66
McBride, Bryant 18
McBride, James C. 35
McCabe, Jewell Jackson 10

McCall, H. Carl 27
McCall, Nathan 8
McCann, Renetta 44
McCarthy, Sandy 64
McCarty, Osceola 16
McClendon, Lisa 61
McClurkin, Donnie 25
McCoo, Marilyn 53
McCoy, Elijah 8
McCrary Anthony, Crystal 70
McCray, Nikki 18
McCullough, Geraldine 58
McDaniel, Hattie 5
McDonald, Audra 20, 62
McDonald, Erroll 1
McDonald, Gabrielle Kirk 20
McDougall, Gay J. 11, 43
McDuffie, Dwayne 62
McEwen, Mark 5
McFadden, Bernice L. 39
McFarlan, Tyron 60
McFarland, Roland 49
McFerrin, Bobby 68
McGee, Charles 10
McGee, James Madison 46
McGlowan, Angela 64
McGriff, Fred 24
McGruder, Aaron 28, 56
McGruder, Robert 22, 35
McGuire, Raymond J. 57
McKay, Claude 6
McKay, Nellie Yvonne 17, 57
Mckee, Lonette 12
McKenzie, Vashti M. 29
McKinney, Cynthia Ann 11, 52
McKinney, Nina Mae 40
McKinney-Whetstone, Diane 27
McKinnon, Isaiah 9
McKissick, Floyd B. 3
McKnight, Brian 18, 34
McLeod, Gus 27
McMillan, Rosaylnn A. 36
McMillan, Terry 4, 17, 53
McMurray, Georgia L. 36
McNabb, Donovan 29
McNair, Ronald 3, 58
McNair, Steve 22, 47
McNeil, Lori 1
McPhail, Sharon 2
McPherson, David 32
McPherson, James Alan 70
McQueen, Butterfly 6, 54
McWhorter, John 35
Meadows, Tim 30
Meek, Carrie 6, 36
Meek, Kendrick 41
Meeks, Gregory 25
Mell, Patricia 49
Memphis Minnie 33
Mengestu, Dinaw 66
Mercado-Valdes, Frank 43
Meredith, James H. 11
Merkerson, S. Epatha 47
Metcalfe, Ralph 26
Mfume, Kweisi 6, 41
Micheaux, Oscar 7
Michele, Michael 31
Mickelbury, Penny 28
Miles, Buddy 69
Millender-McDonald, Juanita 21, 61
Miller, Bebe 3
Miller, Cheryl 10
Miller, Dorie 29

Miller, Reggie 33
Miller, Warren F., Jr. 53
Miller-Travis, Vernice 64
Millines Dziko, Trish 28
Mills, Florence 22
Mills, Joseph C. 51
Mills, Sam 33
Mills, Stephanie 36
Mills, Steve 47
Milner, Ron 39
Milton, DeLisha 31
Mingo, Frank 32
Mingus, Charles 15
Minor, DeWayne 32
Mitchell, Arthur 2, 47
Mitchell, Brian Stokes 21
Mitchell, Corinne 8
Mitchell, Elvis 67
Mitchell, Kel 66
Mitchell, Leona 42
Mitchell, Loften 31
Mitchell, Nicole 66
Mitchell, Parren J. 42, 66
Mitchell, Russ 21
Mitchell, Stephanie 36
Mo', Keb' 36
Mohammed, Nazr 64
Mohammed, W. Deen 27
Monica 21
Mo'Nique 35
Monk, Art 38
Monk, Thelonious 1
Monroe, Bryan 71
Monroe, Mary 35
Montgomery, Tim 41
Moon, Warren 8, 66
Mooney, Paul 37
Moore, Barbara C. 49
Moore, Chante 26
Moore, Dorothy Rudd 46
Moore, Gwendolynne S. 55
Moore, Harry T. 29
Moore, Jessica Care 30
Moore, Johnny B. 38
Moore, Melba 21
Moore, Minyon 45
Moore, Shemar 21
Moore, Undine Smith 28
Moorer, Michael 19
Moose, Charles 40
Morgan, Garrett 1
Morgan, Gertrude 63
Morgan, Irene 65
Morgan, Joe Leonard 9
Morgan, Rose 11
Morgan, Tracy 61
Morial, Ernest "Dutch" 26
Morial, Marc H. 20, 51
Morris, Garrett 31
Morris, Greg 28
Morrison, Sam 50
Morrison, Toni 2, 15
Morton, Azie Taylor 48
Morton, Jelly Roll 29
Morton, Joe 18
Mos Def 30
Moses, Edwin 8
Moses, Gilbert 12
Moses, Robert Parris 11
Mosley, Shane 32
Mosley, Walter 5, 25, 68
Moss, Carlton 17
Moss, J. 64

Moss, Preacher 63
Moss, Randy 23
Mossell, Gertrude Bustill 40
Moten, Etta 18
Motley, Archibald, Jr. 30
Motley, Constance Baker 10, 55
Motley, Marion 26
Mourning, Alonzo 17, 44
Moutoussamy-Ashe, Jeanne 7
Mowry, Jess 7
Moyo, Karega Kofi 36
Moyo, Yvette Jackson 36
Muhammad, Ava 31
Muhammad, Elijah 4
Muhammad, Khallid Abdul 10, 31
Mullen, Harryette 34
Mullen, Nicole C. 45
Murphy, Eddie 4, 20, 61
Murphy, John H. 42
Murphy, Laura M. 43
Murray, Albert L. 33
Murray, Cecil 12, 47
Murray, Eddie 12
Murray, Lenda 10
Murray, Pauli 38
Murray, Tai 47
Murrell, Sylvia Marilyn 49
Muse, Clarence Edouard 21
Musiq 37
Mya 35
Myers, Walter Dean 8, 70
Myles, Kim 69
Nabrit, Samuel Milton 47
Nagin, C. Ray 42, 57
Nance, Cynthia 71
Nanula, Richard D. 20
Napoleon, Benny N. 23
Nas 33
Nash, Joe 55
Nash, Johnny 40
Nash, Niecy 66
Naylor, Gloria 10, 42
Ndegéocello, Me'Shell 15
Ne-Yo 65
Neal, Elise 29
Neal, Larry 38
Neal, Raful 44
Nelly 32
Nelson Meigs, Andrea 48
Nelson, Jill 6, 54
Neville, Aaron 21
Neville, Arthel 53
Newcombe, Don 24
Newkirk, Pamela 69
Newman, Lester C. 51
Newsome, Ozzie 26
Newton, Huey 2
Nicholas, Fayard 20, 57
Nicholas, Harold 20
Nichols, Nichelle 11
Nissel, Angela 42
Nix, Robert N. C., Jr. 51
N'Namdi, George R. 17
Noble, Ronald 46
Norman, Christina 47
Norman, Jessye 5
Norman, Maidie 20
Norman, Pat 10
Norton, Eleanor Holmes 7
Notorious B.I.G. 20
Nottage, Lynn 66
Nugent, Richard Bruce 39
Nunn, Annetta 43

Nutter, Michael 69
Obama, Barack 49
Obama, Michelle 61
Odetta 37
Oglesby, Zena 12
Ogletree, Charles, Jr. 12, 47
Ojikutu, Bayo 66
Ojikutu, Bisola 65
Ol' Dirty Bastard 52
Olden, Georg(e) 44
O'Leary, Hazel 6
Oliver, Jerry 37
Oliver, Joe "King" 42
Oliver, John J., Jr. 48
Oliver, Kimberly 60
Oliver, Pam 54
O'Neal, Ron 46
O'Neal, Shaquille 8, 30
O'Neal, Stanley 38, 67
O'Neil, Buck 19, 59
Onyewu, Oguchi 60
Orlandersmith, Dael 42
Orman, Roscoe 55
Osborne, Jeffrey 26
Osborne, Na'taki 54
Otis, Clarence, Jr. 55
Otis, Clyde 67
Owens, Helen 48
Owens, Jack 38
Owens, Jesse 2
Owens, Major 6
Owens, Terrell 53
P.M. Dawn 54
Pace, Betty 59
Pace, Orlando 21
Packer, Daniel 56
Packer, Will 71
Packer, Z. Z. 64
Page, Alan 7
Page, Clarence 4
Paige, Rod 29
Paige, Satchel 7
Painter, Nell Irvin 24
Palmer, Keke 68
Palmer, Rissi 65
Palmer, Violet 59
Parham, Marjorie B. 71
Parish, Robert 43
Parker, Charlie 20
Parker, Jim 64
Parker, Kellis E. 30
Parker, Nicole Ari 52
Parker, Pat 19
Parker, Star 70
Parks, Bernard C. 17
Parks, Gordon 1, 35, 58
Parks, Rosa 1, 35, 56
Parks, Suzan-Lori 34
Parr, Russ 51
Parsons, James 14
Parsons, Richard Dean 11, 33
Paterson, Basil A. 69
Paterson, David A. 59
Patrick, Deval 12, 61
Patterson, Floyd 19, 58
Patterson, Frederick Douglass 12
Patterson, Gilbert Earl 41
Patterson, Louise 25
Patterson, Mary Jane 54
Patton, Antwan 45
Patton, Paula 62
Payne, Allen 13
Payne, Donald M. 2, 57

Payne, Ethel L. 28
Payne, Freda 58
Payne, Ulice 42
Payne, William D. 60
Payton, Benjamin F. 23
Payton, John 48
Payton, Walter 11, 25
Peck, Carolyn 23
Peete, Calvin 11
Peete, Holly Robinson 20
Peete, Rodney 60
Pena, Paul 58
Pendergrass, Teddy 22
Peoples, Dottie 22
Perez, Anna 1
Perkins, Edward 5
Perkins, James, Jr. 55
Perkins, Marion 38
Perkins, Pinetop 70
Perkins, Tony 24
Perren, Freddie 60
Perrineau, Harold, Jr. 51
Perrot, Kim 23
Perry, Laval 64
Perry, Lowell 30
Perry, Tyler 40, 54
Perry, Warren 56
Person, Waverly 9, 51
Peters, Margaret and Matilda 43
Petersen, Frank E. 31
Peterson, James 38
Peterson, Marvin "Hannibal" 27
Petry, Ann 19
Phifer, Mekhi 25
Phillips, Charles E., Jr. 57
Phillips, Helen L. 63
Phillips, Teresa L. 42
Phipps, Wintley 59
Pickens, James, Jr. 59
Pickett, Bill 11
Pickett, Cecil 39
Pierce, Paul 71
Pierre, Percy Anthony 46
Pincham, R. Eugene, Sr. 69
Pinchback, P. B. S. 9
Pinckney, Bill 42
Pinckney, Sandra 56
Pindell, Howardena 55
Pinderhughes, John 47
Pinkett Smith, Jada 10, 41
Pinkett, Randal 61
Pinkney, Jerry 15
Pinkston, W. Randall 24
Pinn, Vivian Winona 49
Piper, Adrian 71
Pippen, Scottie 15
Pippin, Horace 9
Pitts, Byron 71
Pitts, Leonard, Jr. 54
Player, Willa B. 43
Pleasant, Mary Ellen 9
Plessy, Homer Adolph 31
Poitier, Sidney 11, 36
Poitier, Sydney Tamiia 65
Pollard, Fritz 53
Porter, James A. 11
Potter, Myrtle 40
Pough, Terrell 58
Poussaint, Alvin F. 5, 67
Powell, Adam Clayton, Jr. 3
Powell, Bud 24
Powell, Colin 1, 28
Powell, Debra A. 23

Powell, Kevin 31
Powell, Maxine 8
Powell, Michael 32
Powell, Mike 7
Powell, Renee 34
Pratt, Awadagin 31
Pratt, Geronimo 18
Pratt, Kyla 57
Premice, Josephine 41
Pressley, Condace L. 41
Preston, Billy 39, 59
Price, Florence 37
Price, Frederick K.C. 21
Price, Glenda 22
Price, Hugh B. 9, 54
Price, Kelly 23
Price, Leontyne 1
Price, Richard 51
Pride, Charley 26
Primus, Pearl 6
Prince 18, 65
Prince, Richard E. 71
Prince, Ron 64
Prince, Tayshaun 68
Prince-Bythewood, Gina 31
Pritchard, Robert Starling 21
Procope, Ernesta 23
Procope, John Levy 56
Prophet, Nancy Elizabeth 42
Prothrow-Stith, Deborah 10
Pryor, Rain 65
Pryor, Richard 3, 24, 56
Puckett, Kirby 4, 58
Purnell, Silas 59
Puryear, Martin 42
Quarles, Benjamin Arthur 18
Quarles, Norma 25
Quarterman, Lloyd Albert 4
Queen Latifah 1, 16, 58
Quigless, Helen G. 49
Quince, Peggy A. 69
Quivers, Robin 61
Rabb, Maurice F., Jr. 58
Rahman, Aishah 37
Raines, Franklin Delano 14
Rainey, Ma 33
Ralph, Sheryl Lee 18
Ramsey, Charles H. 21, 69
Rand, A. Barry 6
Randall, Alice 38
Randall, Dudley 8, 55
Randle, Theresa 16
Randolph, A. Philip 3
Randolph, Linda A. 52
Randolph, Willie 53
Rangel, Charles 3, 52
Raoul, Kwame 55
Rashad, Ahmad 18
Rashad, Phylicia 21
Raspberry, William 2
Raven 44
Rawls, Lou 17, 57
Ray, Charlotte E. 60
Ray, Gene Anthony 47
Razaf, Andy 19
Reagon, Bernice Johnson 7
Reason, J. Paul 19
Record, Eugene 60
Reddick, Lance 52
Reddick, Lawrence Dunbar 20
Redding, J. Saunders 26
Redding, Louis L. 26
Redding, Otis 16

Redman, Joshua 30
Redmond, Eugene 23
Reed, A. C. 36
Reed, Ishmael 8
Reed, Jimmy 38
Reems, Ernestine Cleveland 27
Reese, Della 6, 20
Reese, Milous J., Jr. 51
Reese, Pokey 28
Reese, Tracy 54
Reeves, Dianne 32
Reeves, Gregory 49
Reeves, Rachel J. 23
Reeves, Triette Lipsey 27
Reid, Antonio "L.A." 28
Reid, Irvin D. 20
Reid, Senghor 55
Reid, Tim 56
Reid, Vernon 34
Reynolds, Star Jones 10, 27, 61
Rhames, Ving 14, 50
Rhimes, Shonda Lynn 67
Rhoden, Dwight 40
Rhoden, William C. 67
Rhodes, Ray 14
Rhone, Sylvia 2
Rhymes, Busta 31
Ribbs, Willy T. 2
Ribeau, Sidney 70
Ribeiro, Alfonso 17
Rice, Condoleezza 3, 28
Rice, Constance LaMay 60
Rice, Jerry 5, 55
Rice, Linda Johnson 9, 41
Rice, Louise Allen 54
Rice, Norm 8
Richards, Beah 30
Richards, Hilda 49
Richards, Sanya 66
Richardson, Desmond 39
Richardson, Donna 39
Richardson, LaTanya 71
Richardson, Nolan 9
Richardson, Rupert 67
Richardson, Salli 68
Richie, Leroy C. 18
Richie, Lionel 27, 65
Richmond, Mitch 19
Rideau, Iris 46
Ridley, John 69
Riggs, Marlon 5, 44
Riley, Helen Caldwell Day 13
Riley, Rochelle 50
Ringgold, Faith 4
Riperton, Minnie 32
Rivers, Glenn "Doc" 25
Roach, Max 21, 63
Roberts, Darryl 70
Roberts, Deborah 35
Roberts, Marcus 19
Roberts, Mike 57
Roberts, Robin 16, 54
Roberts, Roy S. 14
Robertson, Oscar 26
Robeson, Eslanda Goode 13
Robeson, Paul 2
Robinson, Aminah 50
Robinson, Bill "Bojangles" 11
Robinson, Bishop L. 66
Robinson, Cleo Parker 38
Robinson, David 24
Robinson, Eddie G. 10
Robinson, Fatima 34

Robinson, Fenton 38
Robinson, Frank 9
Robinson, Jackie 6
Robinson, LaVaughn 69
Robinson, Malcolm S. 44
Robinson, Matt 69
Robinson, Max 3
Robinson, Patrick 19, 71
Robinson, Rachel 16
Robinson, Randall 7, 46
Robinson, Reginald R. 53
Robinson, Sharon 22
Robinson, Shaun 36
Robinson, Smokey 3, 49
Robinson, Spottswood W., III 22
Robinson, Sugar Ray 18
Robinson, Will 51, 69
Roble, Abdi 71
Roche, Joyce M. 17
Rochon, Lela 16
Rock, Chris 3, 22, 66
Rock, The 29, 66
Rodgers, Johnathan 6, 51
Rodgers, Rod 36
Rodman, Dennis 12, 44
Rodriguez, Jimmy 47
Rodriguez, Cheryl 64
Rogers, Jimmy 38
Rogers, Joe 27
Rogers, Joel Augustus 30
Rogers, John W., Jr. 5, 52
Roker, Al 12, 49
Roker, Roxie 68
Rolle, Esther 13, 21
Rollins, Charlemae Hill 27
Rollins, Howard E., Jr. 16
Rollins, Jimmy 70
Rollins, Sonny 37
Rose, Anika Noni 70
Ross, Charles 27
Ross, Diana 8, 27
Ross, Don 27
Ross, Isaiah "Doc" 40
Ross, Tracee Ellis 35
Ross-Lee, Barbara 67
Roundtree, Richard 27
Rowan, Carl T. 1, 30
Rowell, Victoria 13, 68
Roxanne Shante 33
Roy, Kenny 51
Rubin, Chanda 37
Rucker, Darius 34
Rudolph, Maya 46
Rudolph, Wilma 4
Ruley, Ellis 38
Rupaul 17
Rush, Bobby 26
Rush, Otis 38
Rushen, Patrice 12
Rushing, Jimmy 37
Russell, Bill 8
Russell, Brenda 52
Russell, Herman Jerome 17
Russell, Nipsey 66
Russell-McCloud, Patricia A. 17
Rustin, Bayard 4
Saar, Alison 16
St. Jacques, Raymond 8
Saint James, Synthia 12
St. John, Kristoff 25
St. Julien, Marlon 29
St. Patrick, Mathew 48
Sallee, Charles 38

Salters, Lisa **71**
Samara, Noah **15**
Sample, Joe **51**
Sampson, Charles **13**
Sanchez, Sonia **17, 51**
Sanders, Barry **1, 53**
Sanders, Deion **4, 31**
Sanders, Joseph R., Jr. **11**
Sanders, Malika **48**
Sanders, Pharoah **64**
Sanford, Isabel **53**
Sapp, Warren **38**
Sapphire **14**
Satcher, David **7, 57**
Savage, Augusta **12**
Sayers, Gale **28**
Sayles Belton, Sharon **9, 16**
Scantlebury-White, Velma **64**
Schmoke, Kurt **1, 48**
Schuyler, George Samuel **40**
Schuyler, Philippa **50**
Scott, C(ornelius) A(dolphus) **29**
Scott, David **41**
Scott, George **55**
Scott, Harold Russell, Jr. **61**
Scott, Hazel **66**
Scott, Jill **29**
Scott, John T. **65**
Scott, "Little" Jimmy **48**
Scott, Milton **51**
Scott, Robert C. **23**
Scott, Stuart **34**
Scott, Wendell Oliver, Sr. **19**
Scurry, Briana **27**
Seals, Son **56**
Sears, Stephanie **53**
Sebree, Charles **40**
Seele, Pernessa **46**
Sengstacke, John **18**
Serrano, Andres **3**
Shabazz, Attallah **6**
Shabazz, Betty **7, 26**
Shabazz, Ilyasah **36**
Shakur, Afeni **67**
Shakur, Assata **6**
Shakur, Tupac **14**
Shange, Ntozake **8**
Sharper, Darren **32**
Sharpton, Al **21**
Shavers, Cheryl **31**
Shaw, Bernard **2, 28**
Shaw, William J. **30**
Sheard, Kierra "Kiki **61**
Sheffield, Gary **16**
Shell, Art **1, 66**
Shepherd, Sherri **55**
Sherrod, Clayton **17**
Shinhoster, Earl **32**
Shipp, E. R. **15**
Shippen, John **43**
Shirley, George **33**
Short, Bobby **52**
Showers, Reggie **30**
Shropshire, Thomas B. **49**
Shuttlesworth, Fred **47**
Sifford, Charlie **4, 49**
Sigur, Wanda **44**
Silas, Paul **24**
Silver, Horace **26**
Simmons, Bob **29**
Simmons, Gary **58**
Simmons, Henry **55**
Simmons, Kimora Lee **51**
Simmons, Russell **1, 30**
Simmons, Ruth J. **13, 38**
Simone, Nina **15, 41**
Simpson, Carole **6, 30**
Simpson, Lorna **4, 36**
Simpson, O. J. **15**
Simpson, Valerie **21**
Simpson-Hoffman, N'kenge **52**
Sims, Howard "Sandman" **48**
Sims, Lowery Stokes **27**
Sims, Naomi **29**
Sinbad **1, 16**
Singletary, Mike **4**
Singleton, John **2, 30**
Sinkford, Jeanne C. **13**
Sisqo **30**
Sissle, Noble **29**
Sister Souljah **11**
Sizemore, Barbara A. **26**
Skinner, Kiron K. **65**
Sklarek, Norma Merrick **25**
Slater, Rodney E. **15**
Slaughter, John Brooks **53**
Sledge, Percy **39**
Sleet, Moneta, Jr. **5**
Slocumb, Jonathan **52**
Slyde, Jimmy **70**
Smaltz, Audrey **12**
Smiley, Rickey **59**
Smiley, Tavis **20, 68**
Smith, Anna Deavere **6, 44**
Smith, B(arbara) **11**
Smith, Barbara **28**
Smith, Bessie **3**
Smith, Bruce W. **53**
Smith, Cladys "Jabbo" **32**
Smith, Clarence O. **21**
Smith, Damu **54**
Smith, Danyel **40**
Smith, Dr. Lonnie **49**
Smith, Emmitt **7**
Smith, Greg **28**
Smith, Hilton **29**
Smith, Ian **62**
Smith, Jane E. **24**
Smith, Jessie Carney **35**
Smith, John L. **22**
Smith, Joshua **10**
Smith, Kemba **70**
Smith, Lonnie Liston **49**
Smith, Lovie **66**
Smith, Mamie **32**
Smith, Marie F. **70**
Smith, Marvin **46**
Smith, Mary Carter **26**
Smith, Morgan **46**
Smith, Nate **49**
Smith, Roger Guenveur **12**
Smith, Stephen A. **69**
Smith, Stuff **37**
Smith, Trixie **34**
Smith, Tubby **18**
Smith, Vincent D. **48**
Smith, Will **8, 18, 53**
Smith, Willi **8**
Smith, Zadie **51**
Smythe Haith, Mabel **61**
Sneed, Paula A. **18**
Snipes, Wesley **3, 24, 67**
Snoop Dogg **35**
Snow, Samuel **71**
Snowden, Frank M., Jr. **67**
Solomon, Jimmie Lee **38**
Sommore **61**
Southern, Eileen **56**
Southgate, Martha **58**
Sowell, Thomas **2**
Sparks, Jordin **66**
Spaulding, Charles Clinton **9**
Spears, Warren **52**
Spencer, Anne **27**
Spikes, Dolores **18**
Spiller, Bill **64**
Sprewell, Latrell **23**
Spriggs, William **67**
Stackhouse, Jerry **30**
Staley, Dawn **57**
Stallings, George A., Jr. **6**
Stampley, Micah **54**
Stanford, John **20**
Stanford, Olivia Lee Dilworth **49**
Stanton, Robert **20**
Staples, "Pops" **32**
Staples, Brent **8**
Staples, Mavis **50**
Stargell, Willie **29**
Staton, Candi **27**
Staton, Dakota **62**
Staupers, Mabel K. **7**
Stearnes, Norman "Turkey" **31**
Steave-Dickerson, Kia **57**
Steele, Claude Mason **13**
Steele, Lawrence **28**
Steele, Michael **38**
Steele, Shelby **13**
Steinberg, Martha Jean "The Queen" **28**
Stephens, Charlotte Andrews **14**
Stew **69**
Steward, David L. **36**
Steward, Emanuel **18**
Stewart, Alison **13**
Stewart, Ella **39**
Stewart, James "Bubba," Jr. **60**
Stewart, Kordell **21**
Stewart, Maria W. Miller **19**
Stewart, Paul Wilbur **12**
Still, William Grant **37**
Stingley, Darryl **69**
Stinson, Denise L. **59**
Stokes, Carl B. **10**
Stokes, Louis **3**
Stone, Angie **31**
Stone, Chuck **9**
Stone, Toni **15**
Stoney, Michael **50**
Stoudemire, Amaré **59**
Stout, Juanita Kidd **24**
Stout, Renee **63**
Stoute, Steve **38**
Strahan, Michael **35**
Strawberry, Darryl **22**
Strayhorn, Billy **31**
Street, John F. **24**
Streeter, Sarah **45**
Stringer, C. Vivian **13, 66**
Stringer, Korey **35**
Stringer, Vickie **58**
Studdard, Ruben **46**
Sudarkasa, Niara **4**
Sudduth, Jimmy Lee **65**
Sullivan, Leon H. **3, 30**
Sullivan, Louis **7**
Sullivan, Maxine **37**
Summer, Donna **25**
Sun Ra **60**
Sundiata, Sekou **66**
Sutton, Percy E. **42**
Swann, Lynn **28**
Sweat, Keith **19**
Sweet, Ossian **68**
Swoopes, Sheryl **12, 56**
Swygert, H. Patrick **22**
Sykes, Roosevelt **20**
Sykes, Wanda **48**
Syler, Rene **53**
Tademy, Lalita **36**
Tait, Michael **57**
Talbert, David **34**
Talley, André Leon **56**
Tamar-kali **63**
Tamia **24, 55**
Tampa Red **63**
Tancil, Gladys Quander **59**
Tanksley, Ann **37**
Tanner, Henry Ossawa **1**
Tate, Eleanora E. **20, 55**
Tate, Larenz **15**
Tatum, Art **28**
Tatum, Beverly Daniel **42**
Taulbert, Clifton Lemoure **19**
Taylor, Billy **23**
Taylor, Cecil **70**
Taylor, Charles **20**
Taylor, Ephren W., II **61**
Taylor, Helen (Lavon Hollingshed) **30**
Taylor, Jason **70**
Taylor, Jermain **60**
Taylor, Koko **40**
Taylor, Kristin Clark **8**
Taylor, Lawrence **25**
Taylor, Marshall Walter "Major" **62**
Taylor, Meshach **4**
Taylor, Mildred D. **26**
Taylor, Natalie **47**
Taylor, Regina **9, 46**
Taylor, Ron **35**
Taylor, Susan C. **62**
Taylor, Susan L. **10**
Taylor, Susie King **13**
Terrell, Dorothy A. **24**
Terrell, Mary Church **9**
Terrell, Tammi **32**
Terry, Clark **39**
Tharpe, Rosetta **65**
Thigpen, Lynne **17, 41**
Thomas, Alma **14**
Thomas, Arthur Ray **52**
Thomas, Clarence **2, 39, 65**
Thomas, Claudia Lynn **64**
Thomas, Debi **26**
Thomas, Derrick **25**
Thomas, Emmitt **71**
Thomas, Frank **12, 51**
Thomas, Franklin A. **5, 49**
Thomas, Irma **29**
Thomas, Isiah **7, 26, 65**
Thomas, Michael **69**
Thomas, Mickalene **61**
Thomas, Rozonda "Chilli" **34**
Thomas, Rufus **20**
Thomas, Sean Patrick **35**
Thomas, Trisha R. **65**
Thomas, Vivien **9**
Thomas-Graham, Pamela **29**
Thompson, Bennie G. **26**
Thompson, Cynthia Bramlett **50**
Thompson, Don **56**

Thompson, John W. 26
Thompson, Kenan 52
Thompson, Larry D. 39
Thompson, Tazewell 13
Thompson, Tina 25
Thompson, William C. 35
Thoms, Tracie 61
Thornton, Big Mama 33
Thornton, Yvonne S. 69
Thrash, Dox 35
Thrower, Willie 35
Thurman, Howard 3
Thurman, Wallace 16
Thurston, Stephen J. 49
Till, Emmett 7
Tillard, Conrad 47
Tillis, Frederick 40
Tillman, George, Jr. 20
Timbaland 32
Tinsley, Boyd 50
Tirico, Mike 68
Tisdale, Wayman 50
Todman, Terence A. 55
Tolliver, Mose 60
Tolliver, William 9
Tolson, Melvin 37
Tolton, Augustine 62
Tomlinson, LaDainian 65
Tonex 54
Tooks, Lance 62
Toomer, Jean 6
Toote, Gloria E.A. 64
Torres, Gina 52
Torry, Guy 31
Touré, Askia (Muhammad Abu Bakr el) 47
Touré, Faya Ora Rose 56
Toussaint, Allen 60
Towns, Edolphus 19
Townsend, Robert 4, 23
Tresvant, Ralph 57
Tribble, Israel, Jr. 8
Trotter, Donne E. 28
Trotter, Lloyd G. 56
Trotter, Monroe 9
Trueheart, William E. 49
Tubbs Jones, Stephanie 24
Tubman, Harriet 9
Tucker, C. Delores 12, 56
Tucker, Chris 13, 23, 62
Tucker, Cynthia 15, 61
Tucker, Rosina 14
Tuckson, Reed V. 71
Tunie, Tamara 63
Tunnell, Emlen 54
Turnbull, Charles Wesley 62
Turnbull, Walter 13, 60
Turner, Henry McNeal 5
Turner, Ike 68
Turner, Tina 6, 27
Tyler, Aisha N. 36
Tyree, Omar Rashad 21
Tyson, Andre 40
Tyson, Asha 39
Tyson, Cicely 7, 51
Tyson, Mike 28, 44
Tyson, Neil deGrasse 15, 65
Uggams, Leslie 23
Underwood, Blair 7, 27
Union, Gabrielle 31
Unseld, Wes 23
Upshaw, Gene 18, 47
Usher 23, 56

Usry, James L. 23
Ussery, Terdema, II 29
Utendahl, John 23
Valentino, Bobby 62
Van Lierop, Robert 53
Van Peebles, Mario 2, 51
Van Peebles, Melvin 7
Vance, Courtney B. 15, 60
VanDerZee, James 6
Vandross, Luther 13, 48, 59
Vanzant, Iyanla 17, 47
Vaughan, Sarah 13
Vaughn, Countess 53
Vaughn, Gladys Gary 47
Vaughn, Mo 16
Vaughn, Viola 70
Vaughns, Cleopatra 46
Vega, Marta Moreno 61
Velez-Rodriguez, Argelia 56
Verdelle, A. J. 26
Vereen, Ben 4
Verrett, Shirley 66
Vick, Michael 39, 65
Vincent, Marjorie Judith 2
Von Lipsey, Roderick K. 11
Waddles, Charleszetta "Mother" 10, 49
Wade, Dwyane 61
Wade-Gayles, Gloria Jean 41
Wagner, Annice 22
Wainwright, Joscelyn 46
Walker, A'lelia 14
Walker, Albertina 10, 58
Walker, Alice 1, 43
Walker, Bernita Ruth 53
Walker, Cedric "Ricky" 19
Walker, Cora T. 68
Walker, Dianne 57
Walker, George 37
Walker, Herschel 1, 69
Walker, Hezekiah 34
Walker, John T. 50
Walker, Madame C. J. 7
Walker, Maggie Lena 17
Walker, Margaret 29
Walker, Rebecca 50
Walker, T. J. 7
Wallace, Ben 54
Wallace, Joaquin 49
Wallace, Michele Faith 13
Wallace, Perry E. 47
Wallace, Phyllis A. 9
Wallace, Rasheed 56
Wallace, Sippie 1
Waller, Fats 29
Ward, Andre 62
Ward, Benjamin 68
Ward, Douglas Turner 42
Ward, Lloyd 21, 46
Ware, Andre 37
Ware, Carl H. 30
Warfield, Marsha 2
Warner, Malcolm-Jamal 22, 36
Warren, Michael 27
Warwick, Dionne 18
Washington, Alonzo 29
Washington, Booker T. 4
Washington, Denzel 1, 16
Washington, Dinah 22
Washington, Fredi 10
Washington, Gene 63
Washington, Grover, Jr. 17, 44
Washington, Harold 6

Washington, Harriet A. 69
Washington, Isaiah 62
Washington, James, Jr. 38
Washington, James Melvin 50
Washington, Kenny 50
Washington, Kerry 46
Washington, Laura S. 18
Washington, MaliVai 8
Washington, Mary T. 57
Washington, Patrice Clarke 12
Washington, Regynald G. 44
Washington, Val 12
Washington, Walter 45
Wasow, Omar 15
Waters, Benny 26
Waters, Ethel 7
Waters, Maxine 3, 67
Waters, Muddy 34
Watkins, Donald 35
Watkins, Levi, Jr. 9
Watkins, Perry 12
Watkins, Shirley R. 17
Watkins, Tionne "T-Boz" 34
Watkins, Walter C. 24
Watley, Jody 54
Watson, Bob 25
Watson, Carlos 50
Watson, Diane 41
Watson, Johnny "Guitar" 18
Watt, Melvin 26
Wattleton, Faye 9
Watts, J. C., Jr. 14, 38
Watts, Reggie 52
Watts, Rolonda 9
Wayans, Damon 8, 41
Wayans, Keenen Ivory 18
Wayans, Marlon 29
Wayans, Shawn 29
Weathers, Carl 10
Weaver, Afaa Michael 37
Weaver, Robert C. 8, 46
Webb, Veronica 10
Webb, Wellington 3
Webber, Chris 15, 30, 59
Webster, Katie 29
Wedgeworth, Robert W. 42
Weeks, Thomas, III 70
Weems, Carrie Mae 63
Weems, Renita J. 44
Wein, Joyce 62
Welburn, Edward T. 50
Welch, Elisabeth 52
Wells, Henrietta Bell 69
Wells, James Lesesne 10
Wells, Mary 28
Wells-Barnett, Ida B. 8
Welsing, Frances Cress 5
Wesley, Dorothy Porter 19
Wesley, Valerie Wilson 18
West, Cornel 5, 33
West, Dorothy 12, 54
West, Kanye 52
West, Togo D., Jr. 16
Westbrook, Kelvin 50
Westbrook, Peter 20
Westbrooks, Bobby 51
Whack, Rita Coburn 36
Whalum, Kirk 37, 64
Wharton, Clifton R., Jr. 7
Wharton, Clifton Reginald, Sr. 36
Wheat, Alan 14
Whitaker, Forest 2, 49, 67
Whitaker, Mark 21, 47

Whitaker, Pernell 10
White, Barry 13, 41
White, Bill 1, 48
White, Charles 39
White, Dondi 34
White, Jesse 22
White, John H. 27
White, Josh, Jr. 52
White, Linda M. 45
White, Lois Jean 20
White, Maurice 29
White, Michael Jai 71
White, Michael R. 5
White, Reggie 6, 50
White, Walter F. 4
White, Willye 67
White-Hammond, Gloria 61
Whitfield, Fred 23
Whitfield, Lynn 18
Whitfield, Mal 60
Whitfield, Van 34
Wideman, John Edgar 5
Wilbekin, Emil 63
Wilbon, Michael 68
Wilder, L. Douglas 3, 48
Wiley, Kehinde 62
Wiley, Ralph 8
Wilkens, J. Ernest, Jr. 43
Wilkens, Lenny 11
Wilkerson, Isabel 71
Wilkins, Ray 47
Wilkins, Roger 2
Wilkins, Roy 4
Wilkins, Thomas Alphonso 71
will.i.am 64
Williams, Anthony 21
Williams, Armstrong 29
Williams, Bert 18
Williams, Billy Dee 8
Williams, Clarence 33
Williams, Clarence 70
Williams, Clarence, III 26
Williams, Daniel Hale 2
Williams, David Rudyard 50
Williams, Deniece 36
Williams, Doug 22
Williams, Dudley 60
Williams, Eddie N. 44
Williams, Evelyn 10
Williams, Fannie Barrier 27
Williams, Frederick (B.) 63
Williams, George Washington 18
Williams, Gregory 11
Williams, Hosea Lorenzo 15, 31
Williams, Joe 5, 25
Williams, John A. 27
Williams, Ken 68
Williams, Lauryn 58
Williams, Maggie 7, 71
Williams, Malinda 57
Williams, Marco 53
Williams, Mary Lou 15
Williams, Montel 4, 57
Williams, Natalie 31
Williams, O. S. 13
Williams, Patricia 11, 54
Williams, Paul R. 9
Williams, Pharrell 47
Williams, Preston Warren, II 64
Williams, Robert F. 11
Williams, Ronald A. 57
Williams, Russell, II 70
Williams, Samm-Art 21

Williams, Saul 31
Williams, Serena 20, 41
Williams, Sherley Anne 25
Williams, Stanley "Tookie" 29, 57
Williams, Stevie 71
Williams, Terrie M. 35
Williams, Tony 67
Williams, Vanessa A. 32, 66
Williams, Vanessa L. 4, 17
Williams, Venus 17, 34, 62
Williams, Walter E. 4
Williams, Wendy 62
Williams, William T. 11
Williams, Willie L. 4
Williamson, Fred 67
Williamson, Mykelti 22
Willie, Louis, Jr. 68
Willingham, Tyrone 43
Willis, Bill 68
Willis, Dontrelle 55
Wilson, August 7, 33, 55
Wilson, Cassandra 16
Wilson, Chandra 57
Wilson, Charlie 31
Wilson, Debra 38
Wilson, Dorien 55
Wilson, Ellis 39
Wilson, Flip 21
Wilson, Gerald 49
Wilson, Jackie 60
Wilson, Jimmy 45
Wilson, Mary 28
Wilson, Nancy 10
Wilson, Natalie 38
Wilson, Phill 9
Wilson, Sunnie 7, 55
Wilson, William Julius 20
Winans, Angie 36
Winans, BeBe 14
Winans, CeCe 14, 43
Winans, Debbie 36
Winans, Marvin L. 17
Winans, Ronald 54
Winans, Vickie 24
Winfield, Dave 5
Winfield, Paul 2, 45
Winfrey, Oprah 2, 15, 61
Winkfield, Jimmy 42
Wisdom, Kimberlydawn 57
Withers, Bill 61
Withers, Ernest C. 68
Withers-Mendes, Elisabeth 64
Witherspoon, John 38
Witt, Edwin T. 26
Wolfe, George C. 6, 43
Womack, Bobby 60
Wonder, Stevie 11, 53
Woodard, Alfre 9
Woodruff, Hale 9
Woodruff, John 68
Woods, Georgie 57
Woods, Granville T. 5
Woods, Jacqueline 52
Woods, Mattiebelle 63
Woods, Scott 55
Woods, Sylvia 34
Woods, Teri 69
Woods, Tiger 14, 31
Woodson, Carter G. 2
Woodson, Robert L. 10
Woodward, Lynette 67
Worrill, Conrad 12
Worthy, James 49

Wright, Antoinette 60
Wright, Bruce McMarion 3, 52
Wright, Charles H. 35
Wright, Deborah C. 25
Wright, Jeffrey 54
Wright, Jeremiah A., Jr. 45, 69
Wright, Lewin 43
Wright, Louis Tompkins 4
Wright, Nathan, Jr. 56
Wright, Rayfield 70
Wright, Richard 5
Wyatt, Addie L. 56
Wynn, Albert R. 25
X, Malcolm 1
X, Marvin 45
Xuma, Madie Hall 59
Yancy, Dorothy Cowser 42
Yarbrough, Camille 40
Yarbrough, Cedric 51
Yette, Samuel F. 63
Yoba, Malik 11
York, Dwight D. 71
York, Vincent 40
Young Jeezy 63
Young, Andrew 3, 48
Young, Coleman 1, 20
Young, Donald, Jr. 57
Young, Jean Childs 14
Young, Jimmy 54
Young, Lester 37
Young, Roger Arliner 29
Young, Whitney M., Jr. 4
Youngblood, Johnny Ray 8
Youngblood, Shay 32
Zane 71
Zollar, Alfred 40
Zollar, Jawole Willa Jo 28
Zook, Kristal Brent 62

Angolan
Bonga, Kuenda 13
dos Santos, José Eduardo 43
Neto, António Agostinho 43
Roberto, Holden 65
Savimbi, Jonas 2, 34

Antiguan
Spencer, Winston Baldwin 68
Williams, Denise 40

Aruban
Williams, David Rudyard 50

Australian
Freeman, Cathy 29
Mundine, Anthony 56
Rose, Lionel 56

Austrian
Kodjoe, Boris 34

Bahamian
Christie, Perry Gladstone 53
Ingraham, Hubert A. 19
Spence, Joseph 49

Barbadian
Arthur, Owen 33
Brathwaite, Kamau 36
Clarke, Austin C. 32
Foster, Cecil 32
Grandmaster Flash 33, 60
Kamau, Kwadwo Agymah 28
Lamming, George 35

Rihanna 65

Batswana
Masire, Quett 5

Belizean
Barrow, Dean 69
Jones, Marion 21, 66

Beninese
Gantin, Bernardin 70
Hounsou, Djimon 19, 45
Joachim, Paulin 34
Kerekou, Ahmed (Mathieu) 1
Kidjo, Anjelique 50
Mogae, Festus Gontebanye 19
Soglo, Nicéphore 15

Bermudian
Cameron, Earl 44
Gordon, Pamela 17
Smith, Jennifer 21

Brazilian
da Silva, Benedita 5
dos Santos, Manuel Francisco 65
Gil, Gilberto 53
Nascimento, Milton 2, 64
Pelé 7
Pitta, Celso 17
Ronaldinho 69

British
Abbott, Diane 9
Adjaye, David 38
Akinnuoye-Agbaje, Adewale 56
Akomfrah, John 37
Amos, Valerie 41
Anderson, Ho Che 54
Anthony, Trey 63
Appiah, Kwame Anthony 67
Armatrading, Joan 32
Barnes, John 53
Bassey, Shirley 25
Berry, James 41
Blackwood, Maureen 37
Boateng, Ozwald 35
Boateng, Paul Yaw 56
Breeze, Jean "Binta" 37
Campbell, Naomi 1, 31
Carby, Hazel 27
Christie, Linford 8
Crooks, Garth 53
D'Aguiar, Fred 50
David, Craig 31, 53
Davidson, Jaye 5
Edwards, Trevor 54
Ejiofor, Chiwetel 67
Elba, Idris 49
Emmanuel, Alphonsia 38
Garrett, Sean 57
Gladwell, Malcolm 62
Hamilton, Lewis 66
Harewood, David 52
Harris, Naomie 55
Henriques, Julian 37
Henry, Lenny 9, 52
Holmes, Kelly 47
Ibrahim, Mo 67
Jamelia 51
Jean-Baptiste, Marianne 17, 46
Jordan, Ronny 26
Julien, Isaac 3
Kay, Jackie 37
King, Oona 27

Lester, Adrian 46
Lewis, Denise 33
Lewis, Lennox 27
Lindo, Delroy 18, 45
Markham, E.A. 37
McKinney Hammond, Michelle 51
Morris, William "Bill" 51
Newton, Thandie 26
Okonedo, Sophie 67
Pitt, David Thomas 10
Regis, Cyrille 51
Scantlebury, Janna 47
Seacole, Mary 54
Seal 14
Siji 56
Smith, Anjela Lauren 44
Smith, Richard 51
Taylor, John (David Beckett) 16
Thomason, Marsha 47
Walker, Eamonn 37

Burkinabé
Somé, Malidoma Patrice 10

Burundian
Ndadaye, Melchior 7
Ntaryamira, Cyprien 8

Cameroonian
Bebey, Francis 45
Beti, Mongo 36
Biya, Paul 28
Kotto, Yaphet 7
Milla, Roger 2
Oyono, Ferdinand 38

Canadian
Auguste, Arnold A. 47
Augustine, Jean 53
Bell, Ralph S. 5
Boyd, Suzanne 52
Brand, Dionne 32
Brathwaite, Fred 35
Brown, Rosemary 62
Brown, Sean 52
Carnegie, Herbert 25
Chanté, Keshia 50
Chong, Rae Dawn 62
Clarke, Austin 64
Clarke, George 32
Cools, Anne 64
Cooper, Afua 53
Cox, Deborah 28
Curling, Alvin 34
Dixon, George 52
Doig, Jason 45
Elliot, Lorris 37
Foster, Cecil 32
Fox, Rick 27
Fuhr, Grant 1, 49
Grand-Pierre, Jean-Luc 46
Hammond, Lenn 34
Harris, Claire 34
Iginla, Jarome 35
Isaac, Julius 34
Jean, Michaëlle; 70
Jenkins, Fergie 46
Johnson, Ben 1
Laraque, Georges 48
Mayers, Jamal 39
McKegney, Tony 3
Mollel, Tololwa 38
Neale, Haydain 52
O'Ree, Willie 5

Peterson, Oscar 52
Philip, Marlene Nourbese 32
Reuben, Gloria 15
Richards, Lloyd 2
Rodrigues, Percy 68
Sadlier, Rosemary 62
Salvador, Bryce 51
Scarlett, Millicent 49
Senior, Olive 37
Sparks, Corinne Etta 53
Vanity 67
Verna, Gelsy 70
Weekes, Kevin 67
Williams, Denise 40

Cape Verdean
Evora, Cesaria 12
Pereira, Aristides 30

Caymanian
Ebanks, Selita 67

Chadian
Déby, Idriss 30
Habré, Hissène 6

Congolese
Kabila, Joseph 30
Kintaudi, Leon 62
Lumumba, Patrice 33
Mudimbe, V.Y. 61

Costa Rican
McDonald, Erroll 1

Cuban
Ferrer, Ibrahim 41
Güines, Tata 69
León, Tania 13
Portuondo, Omara 53
Quirot, Ana 13
Velez-Rodriguez, Argelia 56

Dominican (from Dominica)
Charles, Pierre 52

Dominican (from Dominican Republic)
Charles, Mary Eugenia 10, 55
Ortiz, David 52
Sosa, Sammy 21, 44
Virgil, Ozzie 48

Dutch
Liberia-Peters, Maria Philomena 12

Eritrean
Keflezighi, Meb 49

Ethiopian
Aberra, Amsale 67
Gabre-Medhin, Tsegaye 64
Gebrselassie, Haile 70
Gerima, Haile 38
Haile Selassie 7
Kebede, Liya 59
Meles Zenawi 3
Mengistu, Haile Mariam 65
Samuelsson, Marcus 53

French
Baker, Josephine 3
Baldwin, James 1
Bebey, Francis 45
Bonaly, Surya 7
Chase-Riboud, Barbara 20, 46

Dieudonné 67
Fanon, Frantz 44
Henry, Thierry 66
Kanouté, Fred 68
Noah, Yannick 4, 60
Tanner, Henry Ossawa 1

Gabonese
Bongo, Omar 1

Gambian
Jammeh, Yahya 23
Peters, Lenrie 43

German
Massaquoi, Hans J. 30
Watts, Andre 42

Ghanaian
Adu, Freddy 67
Aidoo, Ama Ata 38
Ali, Mohammed Naseehu 60
Annan, Kofi Atta 15, 48
Appiah, Kwame Anthony 67
Armah, Ayi Kwei 49
Awoonor, Kofi 37
DuBois, Shirley Graham 21
Jawara, Dawda Kairaba 11
Kufuor, John Agyekum 54
Mensah, Thomas 48
Nkrumah, Kwame 3
Rawlings, Jerry 9
Rawlings, Nana Konadu Agyeman 13
Yeboah, Emmanuel Ofosu 53

Grenadian
Bishop, Maurice 39
Isaac, Julius 34

Guinea-Bissauan
Vieira, Joao 14

Guinean
Conté, Lansana 7
Diallo, Amadou 27
Niane, Katoucha 70
Touré, Sekou 6

Guyanese
Amos, Valerie 41
Beaton, Norman 14
Burnham, Forbes 66
Carter, Martin 49
Dabydeen, David 48
D'Aguiar, Fred 50
Damas, Léon-Gontran 46
Dathorne, O. R. 52
Griffith, Patrick A. 64
Jagan, Cheddi 16
Lefel, Edith 41
van Sertima, Ivan 25

Haitian
Aristide, Jean-Bertrand 6, 45
Auguste, Rose-Anne 13
Beauvais, Garcelle 29
Charlemagne, Manno 11
Christophe, Henri 9
Danticat, Edwidge 15, 68
Delice, Ronald 48
Delice, Rony 48
Jean, Wyclef 20
Laferriere, Dany 33
Laraque, Paul 67
Magloire, Paul Eugène 68

Pascal-Trouillot, Ertha 3
Peck, Raoul 32
Pierre, Andre 17
Siméus, Dumas M. 25
Verna, Gelsy 70

Irish
Mumba, Samantha 29

Italian
Esposito, Giancarlo 9

Ivorian
Bedie, Henri Konan 21
Blondy, Alpha 30
Dadié, Bernard 34
Gbagbo, Laurent 43
Guéï, Robert 66
Houphouët-Boigny, Félix 4, 64
Ouattara 43

Jamaican
Ashley, Maurice 15, 47
Barnes, John 53
Barrett, Lindsay 43
Beenie Man 32
Belafonte, Harry 4
Bennett, Louise 69
Berry, James 41
Channer, Colin 36
Cliff, Jimmy 28
Cliff, Michelle 42
Cooper, Afua 53
Cox, Renée 67
Curling, Alvin 34
Dunbar, Sly 34
Ewing, Patrick A. 17
Fagan, Garth 18
50 Cent 46
Figueroa, John J. 40
Garvey, Marcus 1
Goodison, Lorna 71
Griffiths, Marcia 29
Hammond, Lenn 34
Hearne, John Edgar Caulwell 45
Heavy, D 58
Johnson, Ben 1
Johnson, Linton Kwesi 37
Joseph, Kathie-Ann 56
Kong, B. Waine 50
Manley, Edna 26
Manley, Ruth 34
Marley, Bob 5
Marley, Rita 32, 70
Marley, Ziggy 41
McKay, Claude 6
Moody, Ronald 30
Morrison, Keith 13
Mowatt, Judy 38
Palmer, Everard 37
Patterson, Orlando 4
Patterson, P. J. 6, 20
Perry, Ruth 19
Reece, E. Albert 63
Rhoden, Wayne 70
Rogers, Joel Augustus 30
Senior, Olive 37
Shaggy 31
Shakespeare, Robbie 34
Simpson-Miller, Portia 62
Taylor, Karin 34
Tosh, Peter 9

White, Willard 53

Kenyan
Cheruiyot, Robert 69
Juma, Calestous 57
Kariuki, J. M. 67
Kenyatta, Jomo 5
Kibaki, Mwai 60
Kobia, Samuel 43
Loroupe, Tegla 59
Maathai, Wangari 43
Mazrui, Ali A. 12
Moi, Daniel Arap 1, 35
Mutu, Wangechi 44
Mwangi, Meja 40
Ngilu, Charity 58
Ngugi wa Thiong'o 29, 61
Odinga, Raila 67
Otunga, Maurice Michael 55
Tergat, Paul 59
Wambugu, Florence 42

Lesothoian
Mofolo, Thomas 37

Liberian
Conneh, Sekou Damate, Jr. 51
Fuller, Solomon Carter, Jr. 15
Keith, Rachel Boone 63
Perry, Ruth 15
Sawyer, Amos 2
Sirleaf, Ellen Johnson 71
Taylor, Charles 20
Weah, George 58

Malawian
Banda, Hastings Kamuzu 6, 54
Kayira, Legson 40
Muluzi, Bakili 14

Malian
Touré, Amadou Toumani 18

Martinican
Césaire, Aimé 48, 69

Mozambican
Chissano, Joaquim 7, 55, 67
Couto, Mia 45
Diogo, Luisa Dias 63
Machel, Graca Simbine 16
Machel, Samora Moises 8
Mutola, Maria 12

Namibian
Mbuende, Kaire 12
Nujoma, Samuel 10

Nigerian
Abacha, Sani 11, 70
Abiola, Moshood 70
Abubakar, Abdulsalami 66
Achebe, Chinua 6
Adichie, Chimamanda Ngozi 64
Ade, King Sunny 41
Ake, Claude 30
Akinola, Peter Jasper 65
Akpan, Uwem 70
Akunyili, Dora Nkem 58
Amadi, Elechi 40
Arinze, Francis Cardinal 19
Azikiwe, Nnamdi 13
Babangida, Ibrahim 4
Bandele, Biyi 68
Clark-Bekedermo, J. P. 44

Darego, Agbani 52
Ekwensi, Cyprian 37
Emeagwali, Philip 30
Emecheta, Buchi 30
Fela 1, 42
Kuti, Femi 47
Lawal, Kase L. 45
Obasanjo, Olusegun 5, 22
Obasanjo, Stella 32, 56
Ogunlesi, Adebayo O. 37
Okara, Gabriel 37
Okosuns, Sonny 71
Olajuwon, Hakeem 2
Olatunji, Babatunde 36
Olojede, Dele 59
Olopade, Olufunmilayo Falusi 58
Onwueme, Tess Osonye 23
Onwurah, Ngozi 38
Rotimi, Ola 1
Sade 15
Saro-Wiwa, Kenule 39
Siji 56
Sowande, Fela 39
Soyinka, Wole 4
Tutuola, Amos 30
Wiwa, Ken 67
Yar'adua, Umaru 69

Nigerien
Mamadou, Tandja 33

Panamanian
Bailey, Preston 64
Williams, Juan 35

Puerto Rican
Schomburg, Arthur Alfonso 9

Rhodesian
Brutus, Dennis 38

Russian
Khanga, Yelena 6

Rwandan
Bizimungu, Pasteur 19
Habyarimana, Juvenal 8
Ilibagiza, Immaculée 66
Kagame, Paul 54
Rusesabagina, Paul 60

St. Kitts and Nevis
Douglas, Denzil Llewellyn 53

Saint Lucian
Compton, John 65

Senegalese
Acogny, Germaine 55
Akon 68
Ba, Mariama 30
Boye, Madior 30
Diop, Birago 53
Diop, Cheikh Anta 4
Diouf, Abdou 3
Maal, Baaba 66
Mbaye, Mariétou 31
Mboup, Souleymane 10
N'Dour, Youssou 1, 53
Sané, Pierre Gabriel 21
Sembène, Ousmane 13, 62
Senghor, Augustin Diamancoune 66
Senghor, Léopold Sédar 12, 66
Sy, Oumou 65
Wade, Abdoulaye 66

Sierra Leonean
Beah, Ishmael 69
Cheney-Coker, Syl 43
Jones, Monty 66
Kabbah, Ahmad Tejan 23

Somalian
Ali, Ayaan Hirsi 58
Ali Mahdi Mohamed 5
Dirie, Waris 56
Farah, Nuruddin 27
Iman 4, 33
Roble, Abdi 71

South African
Abrahams, Peter 39
Adams, Paul 50
Biko, Steven 4
Brutus, Dennis 38
Buthelezi, Mangosuthu Gatsha 9
Butler, Jonathan 28
Chweneyagae, Presley 63
Grae, Jean 51
Hani, Chris 6
Head, Bessie 28
Ka Dinizulu, Mcwayizeni 29
Kente, Gibson 52
Khumalo, Leleti 51
Kuzwayo, Ellen 68
LaGuma, Alex 30
Luthuli, Albert 13
Mabuza, Lindiwe 18
Mabuza-Suttle, Felicia 43
Mahlasela, Vusi 65
Makeba, Miriam 2, 50
Mandela, Nelson 1, 14
Mandela, Winnie 2, 35
Masekela, Barbara 18
Masekela, Hugh 1
Mathabane, Mark 5
Mbeki, Thabo Mvuyelwa 14
Mhlaba, Raymond 55
Mphalele, Es'kia (Ezekiel) 40
Naki, Hamilton 63
Ngubane, Ben 33
Nkoli, Simon 60
Nkosi, Lewis 46
Ntshona, Winston 52
Nyanda, Siphiwe 21
Nzo, Alfred 15
Ramaphosa, Cyril 3
Ramphele, Mamphela 29
Sisulu, Albertina 57
Sisulu, Sheila Violet Makate 24
Sisulu, Walter 47
Thugwane, Josia 21
Tutu, Desmond (Mpilo) 6, 44
Tutu, Nontombi Naomi 57
Zuma, Jacob 33
Zuma, Nkosazana Dlamini 34

Sudanese
Bol, Manute 1
Nour, Nawal M. 56
Salih, Al-Tayyib 37
Wek, Alek 18, 63

Swazi
Mswati III 56

Swedish
Hendricks, Barbara 3, 67

Tanzanian
Mkapa, Benjamin 16
Mongella, Gertrude 11
Mollel, Tololwa 38
Mwinyi, Ali Hassan 1
Nyerere, Julius 5
Rugambwa, Laurean 20

Togolese
Eyadéma, Gnassingbé 7, 52
Gnassingbé, Faure 67
Soglo, Nicéphore 15

Trinidadian
Anthony, Michael 29
Auguste, Arnold A. 47
Brand, Dionne 32
Carmichael, Stokely 5, 26
Cartey, Wilfred 1992 47
Dymally, Mervyn 42
Guy, Rosa 5
Harris, Claire 34
Hendy, Francis 47
Hercules, Frank 44
Hill, Errol 40
Lushington, Augustus Nathaniel 56
Nakhid, David 25
Nunez, Elizabeth 62
Primus, Pearl 6
Shorty I, Ras 47
Toussaint, Lorraine 32
Williams, Eric Eustace 65

Tunisian
Memmi, Albert 37

Ugandan
Amin, Idi 42
Arac de Nyeko, Monica 66
Atim, Julian 66
Atyam, Angelina 55
Museveni, Yoweri 4
Mutebi, Ronald 25
Obote, Milton 63
Okaalet, Peter 58
Sentamu, John 58

Upper Voltan
Sankara, Thomas 17

West Indian
Césaire, Aimé 48, 69
Coombs, Orde M. 44
Innis, Roy 5
Kincaid, Jamaica 4
Knight, Gwendolyn 63
Rojas, Don 33
Staupers, Mabel K. 7
Pitt, David Thomas 10
Taylor, Susan L. 10
Walcott, Derek 5

Zairean
Kabila, Laurent 20
Mobutu Sese Seko 1, 56
Mutombo, Dikembe 7
Ongala, Remmy 9

Zambian
Kaunda, Kenneth 2
Zulu, Princess Kasune 54

Zimbabwean
Chideya, Farai 14
Chiluba, Frederick Jacob Titus 56
Marechera, Dambudzo 39
Mugabe, Robert 10, 71
Nkomo, Joshua 4, 65
Tsvangirai, Morgan 26
Vera, Yvonne 32

Cumulative Occupation Index

Volume numbers appear in **bold**

Art and design
Abele, Julian **55**
Aberra, Amsale **67**
Adjaye, David **38**
Allen, Tina **22**
Alston, Charles **33**
Amos, Emma **63**
Anderson, Ho Che **54**
Andrews, Benny **22, 59**
Andrews, Bert **13**
Armstrong, Robb **15**
Bailey, Preston **64**
Bailey, Radcliffe **19**
Bailey, Xenobia **11**
Barboza, Anthony **10**
Barnes, Ernie **16**
Barthe, Richmond **15**
Basquiat, Jean-Michel **5**
Bearden, Romare **2, 50**
Beasley, Phoebe **34**
Benberry, Cuesta **65**
Benjamin, Tritobia Hayes **53**
Biggers, John **20, 33**
Biggers, Sanford **62**
Blackburn, Robert **28**
Brandon, Barbara **3**
Brown, Donald **19**
Brown, Robert **65**
Burke, Selma **16**
Burroughs, Margaret Taylor **9**
Camp, Kimberly **19**
Campbell, E. Simms **13**
Campbell, Mary Schmidt **43**
Catlett, Elizabeth **2**
Chase-Riboud, Barbara **20, 46**
Colescott, Robert **69**
Collins, Paul **61**
Cortor, Eldzier **42**
Cowans, Adger W. **20**
Cox, Renée **67**
Crite, Alan Rohan **29**
De Veaux, Alexis **44**
DeCarava, Roy **42**
Delaney, Beauford **19**
Delaney, Joseph **30**
Delsarte, Louis **34**
Donaldson, Jeff **46**
Douglas, Aaron **7**
Driskell, David C. **7**
Dwight, Edward **65**
Edwards, Melvin **22**
El Wilson, Barbara **35**
Ewing, Patrick A. **17**

Fax, Elton **48**
Feelings, Tom **11, 47**
Fine, Sam **60**
Freeman, Leonard **27**
Fuller, Meta Vaux Warrick **27**
Gantt, Harvey **1**
Gilles, Ralph **61**
Gilliam, Sam **16**
Golden, Thelma **10, 55**
Goodnight, Paul **32**
Green, Jonathan **54**
Guyton, Tyree **9**
Hammons, David **69**
Harkless, Necia Desiree **19**
Harrington, Oliver W. **9**
Hathaway, Isaac Scott **33**
Hayden, Palmer **13**
Hayes, Cecil N. **46**
Honeywood, Varnette P. **54**
Hope, John **8**
Hudson, Cheryl **15**
Hudson, Wade **15**
Hunt, Richard **6**
Hunter, Clementine **45**
Hutson, Jean Blackwell **16**
Jackson, Earl **31**
Jackson, Vera **40**
John, Daymond **23**
Johnson, Jeh Vincent **44**
Johnson, William Henry **3**
Jones, Lois Mailou **13**
King, Robert Arthur **58**
Kitt, Sandra **23**
Knight, Gwendolyn **63**
Knox, Simmie **49**
Lawrence, Jacob **4, 28**
Lee, Annie Francis **22**
Lee-Smith, Hughie **5, 22**
Lewis, Edmonia **10**
Lewis, Norman **39**
Lewis, Samella **25**
Loving, Alvin, Jr., **35, 53**
Manley, Edna **26**
Marshall, Kerry James **59**
Mayhew, Richard **39**
McCullough, Geraldine **58**
McDuffie, Dwayne **62**
McGee, Charles **10**
McGruder, Aaron **28, 56**
Mitchell, Corinne **8**
Moody, Ronald **30**
Morrison, Keith **13**
Motley, Archibald, Jr. **30**
Moutoussamy-Ashe, Jeanne **7**

Mutu, Wangechi **44**
Myles, Kim **69**
N'Namdi, George R. **17**
Nugent, Richard Bruce **39**
Olden, Georg(e) **44**
Ouattara **43**
Perkins, Marion **38**
Pierre, Andre **17**
Pindell, Howardena **55**
Pinderhughes, John **47**
Pinkney, Jerry **15**
Piper, Adrian **71**
Pippin, Horace **9**
Porter, James A. **11**
Prophet, Nancy Elizabeth **42**
Puryear, Martin **42**
Reid, Senghor **55**
Ringgold, Faith **4**
Roble, Abdi **71**
Ruley, Ellis **38**
Saar, Alison **16**
Saint James, Synthia **12**
Sallee, Charles **38**
Sanders, Joseph R., Jr. **11**
Savage, Augusta **12**
Scott, John T. **65**
Sebree, Charles **40**
Serrano, Andres **3**
Shabazz, Attallah **6**
Shonibare, Yinka **58**
Simmons, Gary **58**
Simpson, Lorna **4, 36**
Sims, Lowery Stokes **27**
Sklarek, Norma Merrick **25**
Sleet, Moneta, Jr. **5**
Smith, Bruce W. **53**
Smith, Marvin **46**
Smith, Morgan **46**
Smith, Vincent D. **48**
Steave-Dickerson, Kia **57**
Stout, Renee **63**
Sudduth, Jimmy Lee **65**
Tanksley, Ann **37**
Tanner, Henry Ossawa **1**
Thomas, Alma **14**
Thrash, Dox **35**
Tolliver, Mose **60**
Tolliver, William **9**
Tooks, Lance **62**
VanDerZee, James **6**
Verna, Gelsy **70**
Wainwright, Joscelyn **46**
Walker, A'lelia **14**
Walker, Kara **16**

Washington, Alonzo **29**
Washington, James, Jr. **38**
Weems, Carrie Mae **63**
Wells, James Lesesne **10**
White, Charles **39**
White, Dondi **34**
White, John H. **27**
Wiley, Kehinde **62**
Williams, Billy Dee **8**
Williams, Clarence **70**
Williams, O. S. **13**
Williams, Paul R. **9**
Williams, William T. **11**
Wilson, Ellis **39**
Withers, Ernest C. **68**
Woodruff, Hale **9**

Business
Abbot, Robert Sengstacke **27**
Abdul-Jabbar, Kareem **8**
Abiola, Moshood **70**
Adams, Eula L. **39**
Adams, Jenoyne **60**
Adkins, Rod **41**
Ailey, Alvin **8**
Akil, Mara Brock **60**
Al-Amin, Jamil Abdullah **6**
Alexander, Archie Alphonso **14**
Allen, Byron **24**
Allen-Buillard, Melba **55**
Ames, Wilmer **27**
Amos, Wally **9**
Auguste, Donna **29**
Austin, Jim **63**
Austin, Gloria **63**
Avant, Clarence **19**
Baker, Dusty **8, 43**
Baker, Ella **5**
Baker, Gwendolyn Calvert **9**
Baker, Maxine **28**
Banks, Jeffrey **17**
Banks, Paula A. **68**
Banks, William **11**
Barden, Don H. **9, 20**
Barrett, Andrew C. **12**
Beal, Bernard B. **46**
Beamon, Bob **30**
Beasley, Phoebe **34**
Bell, James A. **50**
Bennett, Lerone, Jr. **5**
Bing, Dave **3, 59**
Blackshear, Leonard **52**
Blackwell, Robert D., Sr. **52**
Blayton, Jesse B., Sr. **55**

Bolden, Frank E. **44**
Borders, James **9**
Boston, Kelvin E. **25**
Boston, Lloyd **24**
Boyd, Edward **70**
Boyd, Gwendolyn **49**
Boyd, John W., Jr. **20**
Boyd, T. B., III **6**
Bradley, Jennette B. **40**
Brae, C. Michael **61**
Bridges, Shelia **36**
Bridgforth, Glinda **36**
Brimmer, Andrew F. **2, 48**
Bronner, Nathaniel H., Sr. **32**
Brown, Eddie C. **35**
Brown, Les **5**
Brown, Marie Dutton **12**
Brunson, Dorothy **1**
Bryant, John **26**
Burgess, Marjorie L. **55**
Burns, Ursula **60**
Burrell, Tom **21, 51**
Burroughs, Margaret Taylor **9**
Burrus, William Henry "Bill" **45**
Burt-Murray, Angela **59**
Busby, Jheryl **3**
Butler, George, Jr. **70**
Cain, Herman **15**
Caldwell, Earl **60**
Carter, Pamela Lynn **67**
CasSelle, Malcolm **11**
Chamberlain, Wilt **18, 47**
Chapman, Nathan A., Jr. **21**
Chappell, Emma **18**
Chase, Debra Martin **49**
Chase, Leah **57**
Chenault, Kenneth I. **4, 36**
Cherry, Deron **40**
Chisholm, Samuel J. **32**
Clark, Celeste **15**
Clark, Patrick **14**
Clay, William Lacy **8**
Clayton, Xernona **3, 45**
Cobbs, Price M. **9**
Colbert, Virgis William **17**
Coleman, Donald **24, 62**
Coleman, Ken **57**
Combs, Sean "Puffy" **17, 43**
Connerly, Ward **14**
Conyers, Nathan G. **24**
Cooper, Barry **33**
Cooper, Evern **40**
Corbi, Lana **42**
Cornelius, Don **4**
Cosby, Bill **7, 26, 59**
Cottrell, Comer **11**
Cox, William E. **68**
Creagh, Milton **27**
Cullers, Vincent T. **49**
Daniels-Carter, Valerie **23**
Darden, Calvin **38**
Dash, Darien **29**
Davis, Belva **61**
Davis, Ed **24**
Davis, Erroll B., Jr. **57**
Dawson, Matel "Mat," Jr. **39**
de Passe, Suzanne **25**
Dean, Mark **35**
Dee, Merri **55**
Delany, Bessie **12**
Delany, Martin R. **27**
Delany, Sadie **12**
DeVard, Jerri **61**

Diallo, Amadou **27**
Divine, Father **7**
Doley, Harold, Jr. **26**
Donald, Arnold Wayne **36**
Dre, Dr. **10, 14, 30**
Driver, David E. **11**
Ducksworth, Marilyn **12**
Easley, Annie J. **61**
Ebanks, Michelle **60**
Edelin, Ramona Hoage **19**
Edmonds, Tracey **16, 64**
Edmunds, Gladys **48**
Edwards, Trevor **54**
El Wilson, Barbara **35**
Elder, Lee **6**
Ellington, E. David **11**
Evans, Darryl **22**
Evers, Myrlie **8**
Farmer, Forest J. **1**
Farr, Mel **24**
Farrakhan, Louis **15**
Fauntroy, Walter E. **11**
Fletcher, Alphonse, Jr. **16**
Flowers, Sylester **50**
Ford, Harold E(ugene), Jr. **16, 70**
Forte, Linda Diane **54**
Foster, Jylla Moore **45**
Fowler, Reggie **51**
Franklin, Hardy R. **9**
Friday, Jeff **24**
Fryer, Roland G. **56**
Fudge, Ann **11, 55**
Fuller, S. B. **13**
Funderburg, I. Owen **38**
Gaines, Brenda **41**
Gardner, Chris **65**
Gardner, Edward G. **45**
Gaston, Arthur George **3, 38, 59**
Gibson, Kenneth Allen **6**
Gibson, Ted **66**
Gidron, Richard D. **68**
Gilles, Ralph **61**
Goings, Russell **59**
Goldsberry, Ronald **18**
Golston, Allan C. **55**
Gordon, Bruce S. **41, 53**
Gordon, Pamela **17**
Gordy, Berry, Jr. **1**
Goss, Carol A. **55**
Goss, Tom **23**
Grace, George H. **48**
Graham, Stedman **13**
Graves, Earl G. **1, 35**
Gray, Farrah **59**
Greely, M. Gasby **27**
Greene, Richard Thaddeus, Sr. **67**
Greenwood, Monique **38**
Griffith, Mark Winston **8**
Grooms, Henry R(andall) **50**
Hale, Lorraine **8**
Ham, Cynthia Parker **58**
Hamer, Fannie Lou **6**
Hamilton, Samuel C. **47**
Hammer, M. C. **20**
Handy, W. C. **8**
Hannah, Marc **10**
Hardison, Bethann **12**
Harrell, Andre **9, 30**
Harris, Alice **7**
Harris, Carla A. **67**
Harris, E. Lynn **12, 33**
Harris, Monica **18**
Harris, Richard E. **61**

Harvey, Steve **18, 58**
Harvey, William R. **42**
Hawkins, La-Van **17, 54**
Hayden, Carla D. **47**
Hazel, Darryl B. **50**
Henderson, Gordon **5**
Henry, Lenny **9, 52**
Hightower, Dennis F. **13**
Hill, Bonnie Guiton **20**
Hill, Calvin **19**
Hill, Janet **19**
Hill, Jesse, Jr. **13**
Hobson, Mellody **40**
Holland, Kimberly N. **62**
Holland, Robert, Jr. **11**
Holmes, Larry **20, 68**
Houston, Whitney **7**
Howroyd, Janice Bryant **42**
Hudlin, Reginald **9**
Hudlin, Warrington **9**
Hudson, Cheryl **15**
Hudson, Wade **15**
Huggins, Larry **21**
Hughes, Cathy **27**
Ibrahim, Mo **67**
Ice Cube **8, 30, 60**
Irvin, Vernon **65**
Jackson, George **19**
Jackson, Mannie **14**
Jackson, Michael **19, 53**
Jakes, Thomas "T.D." **17, 43**
James, Charles H., III **62**
James, Donna A. **51**
James, Juanita **13**
John, Daymond **23**
Johnson, Earvin "Magic" **3, 39**
Johnson, Eddie Bernice **8**
Johnson, George E. **29**
Johnson, John H. **3, 54**
Johnson, Kevin **70**
Johnson, Robert L. **3, 39**
Johnson, Sheila Crump **48**
Jolley, Willie **28**
Jones, Bobby **20**
Jones, Carl **7**
Jones, Caroline **29**
Jones, Ingrid Saunders **18**
Jones, Quincy **8, 30**
Jones, Thomas W. **41**
Jones, Wayne **53**
Jordan, Michael **6, 21**
Jordan, Montell **23**
Joyner, Marjorie Stewart **26**
Julian, Percy Lavon **6**
Kaigler, Denise **63**
Keith, Floyd A. **61**
Kelly, Patrick **3**
Kendrick, Erika **57**
Kidd, Mae Street **39**
Killingsworth, Cleve, Jr. **54**
Kimbro, Dennis **10**
King, Dexter **10**
King, Don **14**
Knight, Suge **11, 30**
Knowles, Tina **61**
Knowling, Robert E., Jr. **38**
Lane, Vincent **5**
Langhart Cohen, Janet **19, 60**
Lanier, Willie **33**
Laryea, Thomas Davies, III **67**
Lawal, Kase L. **45**
Lawless, Theodore K. **8**
Lawson, Jennifer **1, 50**

Leary, Kathryn D. **10**
Leavell, Dorothy R. **17**
Lee, Annie Francis **22**
Lee, Bertram M., Sr. **46**
Lee, Debra L. **62**
Leonard, Sugar Ray **15**
Lewellyn, J. Bruce **13**
Lewis, Aylwin **51**
Lewis, Byron E. **13**
Lewis, Delano **7**
Lewis, Edward T. **21**
Lewis, Reginald F. **6**
Lewis, William M., Jr. **40**
Ligging, Alfred, III **43**
Long, Eddie L. **29**
Lott, Ronnie **9**
Louis, Errol T. **8**
Lucas, John **7**
Lucy, William **50**
Madhubuti, Haki R. **7**
Madison, Paula **37**
Malone, Annie **13**
March, William Carrington **56**
Marshall, Bella **22**
Massenburg, Kedar **23**
Master P **21**
Matthews Shatteen, Westina **51**
Maynard, Robert C. **7**
Mays, Leslie A. **41**
Mays, William G. **34**
McCabe, Jewell Jackson **10**
McCann, Renetta **44**
McCoy, Elijah **8**
McDonald, Erroll **1**
McGee, James Madison **46**
McGuire, Raymond J. **57**
McLeod, Gus **27**
McPherson, David **32**
Micheaux, Oscar **7**
Millines Dziko, Trish **28**
Mills, Steve **47**
Mingo, Frank **32**
Monk, Art **38**
Monroe, Bryan **71**
Morgan, Garrett **1**
Morgan, Joe Leonard **9**
Morgan, Rose **11**
Morris, William "Bill" **51**
Morrison, Sam **50**
Moyo, Karega Kofi **36**
Moyo, Yvette Jackson **36**
Nanula, Richard D. **20**
Nelson Meigs, Andrea **48**
Nichols, Nichelle **11**
Norman, Christina **47**
Ogunlesi, Adebayo O. **37**
Olojede, Dele **59**
O'Neal, Stanley **38, 67**
Otis, Clarence, Jr. **55**
Packer, Daniel **56**
Parham, Marjorie B. **71**
Parks, Gordon **1, 35, 58**
Parsons, Richard Dean **11, 33**
Payton, Walter **11, 25**
Peck, Carolyn **23**
Perez, Anna **1**
Perkins, James, Jr. **55**
Perry, Laval **64**
Perry, Lowell **30**
Phillips, Charles E., Jr. **57**
Pinckney, Bill **42**
Pinkett, Randal **61**
Pleasant, Mary Ellen **9**

Potter, Myrtle **40**
Powell, Maxine **8**
Price, Frederick K.C. **21**
Price, Hugh B. **9, 54**
Procope, Ernesta **23**
Procope, John Levy **56**
Queen Latifah **1, 16, 58**
Quivers, Robin **61**
Ralph, Sheryl Lee **18**
Rand, A. Barry **6**
Reeves, Rachel J. **23**
Reid, Antonio "L.A." **28**
Rhone, Sylvia **2**
Rice, Linda Johnson **9, 41**
Rice, Norm **8**
Richardson, Donna **39**
Richie, Leroy C. **18**
Rideau, Iris **46**
Roberts, Mike **57**
Roberts, Roy S. **14**
Robertson, Oscar **26**
Robeson, Eslanda Goode **13**
Robinson, Jackie **6**
Robinson, Rachel **16**
Robinson, Randall **7, 46**
Roche, Joyce M. **17**
Rodgers, Johnathan **6, 51**
Rodriguez, Jimmy **47**
Rogers, John W., Jr. **5, 52**
Rojas, Don **33**
Ross, Charles **27**
Ross, Diana **8, 27**
Russell, Bill **8**
Russell, Herman Jerome **17**
Russell-McCloud, Patricia **17**
Saint James, Synthia **12**
Samara, Noah **15**
Samuelsson, Marcus **53**
Sanders, Dori **8**
Scott, C. A. **29**
Scott, Milton **51**
Sengstacke, John **18**
Shakur, Afeni **67**
Shropshire, Thomas B. **49**
Siméus, Dumas M. **25**
Simmons, Kimora Lee **51**
Simmons, Russell **1, 30**
Sims, Naomi **29**
Sinbad **1, 16**
Smith, B(arbara) **11**
Smith, Clarence O. **21**
Smith, Jane E. **24**
Smith, Joshua **10**
Smith, Willi **8**
Sneed, Paula A. **18**
Spaulding, Charles Clinton **9**
Staley, Dawn **57**
Stanford, Olivia Lee Dilworth **49**
Steinberg, Martha Jean "The Queen" **28**
Steward, David L. **36**
Stewart, Ella **39**
Stewart, Paul Wilbur **12**
Stinson, Denise L. **59**
Stringer, Vickie **58**
Sullivan, Leon H. **3, 30**
Sutton, Percy E. **42**
Taylor, Ephren W., II **61**
Taylor, Karin **34**
Taylor, Kristin Clark **8**
Taylor, Natalie **47**
Taylor, Susan L. **10**
Terrell, Dorothy A. **24**
Thomas, Franklin A. **5, 49**
Thomas, Isiah **7, 26, 65**
Thomas-Graham, Pamela **29**
Thompson, Cynthia Bramlett **50**
Thompson, Don **56**
Thompson, John W. **26**
Tribble, Israel, Jr. **8**
Trotter, Lloyd G. **56**
Trotter, Monroe **9**
Tuckson, Reed V. **71**
Tyson, Asha **39**
Ussery, Terdema, II **29**
Utendahl, John **23**
Van Peebles, Melvin **7**
VanDerZee, James **6**
Vaughn, Gladys Gary **47**
Vaughns, Cleopatra **46**
Walker, A'lelia **14**
Walker, Cedric "Ricky" **19**
Walker, Madame C. J. **7**
Walker, Maggie Lena **17**
Walker, T. J. **7**
Ward, Lloyd **21, 46**
Ware, Carl H. **30**
Washington, Alonzo **29**
Washington, Mary T. **57**
Washington, Regynald G. **44**
Washington, Val **12**
Wasow, Omar **15**
Watkins, Donald **35**
Watkins, Walter C., Jr., **24**
Wattleton, Faye **9**
Wein, Joyce **62**
Wek, Alek **18, 63**
Welburn, Edward T. **50**
Wells-Barnett, Ida B. **8**
Westbrook, Kelvin **50**
Wharton, Clifton R., Jr. **7**
White, Linda M. **45**
White, Walter F. **4**
Wiley, Ralph **8**
Wilkins, Ray **47**
Williams, Armstrong **29**
Williams, O. S. **13**
Williams, Paul R. **9**
Williams, Ronald A. **57**
Williams, Terrie **35**
Williams, Walter E. **4**
Williams, Wendy **62**
Willie, Louis, Jr. **68**
Wilson, Phill **9**
Wilson, Sunnie **7, 55**
Winfrey, Oprah **2, 15, 61**
Woods, Jacqueline **52**
Woods, Sylvia **34**
Woodson, Robert L. **10**
Wright, Antoinette **60**
Wright, Charles H. **35**
Wright, Deborah C. **25**
Wright, Rayfield **70**
Yoba, Malik **11**
Zollar, Alfred **40**

Dance

Acogny, Germaine **55**
Adams, Jenoyne **60**
Ailey, Alvin **8**
Alexander, Khandi **43**
Allen, Debbie **13, 42**
Atkins, Cholly **40**
Babatunde, Obba **35**
Baker, Josephine **3**
Bates, Peg Leg **14**
Beals, Jennifer **12**
Beatty, Talley **35**
Byrd, Donald **10**
Clarke, Hope **14**
Collins, Janet **33, 64**
Davis, Chuck **33**
Davis, Sammy, Jr. **18**
Diggs, Taye **25, 63**
Dove, Ulysses **5**
Dunham, Katherine **4, 59**
Ellington, Mercedes **34**
Fagan, Garth **18**
Falana, Lola **42**
Glover, Savion **14**
Guy, Jasmine **2**
Hall, Arthur **39**
Hammer, M. C. **20**
Henson, Darrin **33**
Hines, Gregory **1, 42**
Horne, Lena **5**
Jackson, Michael **19, 53**
Jamison, Judith **7, 67**
Johnson, Virginia **9**
Jones, Bill T. **1, 46**
Jones, Doris W. **62**
King, Alonzo **38**
LeTang, Henry **66**
McQueen, Butterfly **6, 54**
Miller, Bebe **3**
Mills, Florence **22**
Mitchell, Arthur **2, 47**
Moten, Etta **18**
Muse, Clarence Edouard **21**
Nash, Joe **55**
Nicholas, Fayard **20, 57**
Nicholas, Harold **20**
Nichols, Nichelle **11**
Powell, Maxine **8**
Premice, Josephine **41**
Primus, Pearl **6**
Ray, Gene Anthony **47**
Rhoden, Dwight **40**
Ribeiro, Alfonso **17**
Richardson, Desmond **39**
Robinson, Bill "Bojangles" **11**
Robinson, Cleo Parker **38**
Robinson, Fatima **34**
Robinson, LaVaughn **69**
Rodgers, Rod **36**
Rolle, Esther **13, 21**
Sims, Howard "Sandman" **48**
Slyde, Jimmy **70**
Spears, Warren **52**
Tyson, Andre **40**
Vereen, Ben **4**
Walker, Cedric "Ricky" **19**
Walker, Dianne **57**
Washington, Fredi **10**
Williams, Dudley **60**
Williams, Vanessa L. **4, 17**
Zollar, Jawole Willa Jo **28**

Education

Achebe, Chinua **6**
Adams, Leslie **39**
Adams-Ender, Clara **40**
Adkins, Rutherford H. **21**
Aidoo, Ama Ata **38**
Ake, Claude **30**
Alexander, Margaret Walker **22**
Allen, Robert L. **38**
Allen, Samuel W. **38**
Allen-Buillard, Melba **55**
Alston, Charles **33**
Amadi, Elechi **40**
Anderson, Charles Edward **37**
Appiah, Kwame Anthony **67**
Archer, Dennis **7**
Archie-Hudson, Marguerite **44**
Aristide, Jean-Bertrand **6, 45**
Asante, Molefi Kete **3**
Aubert, Alvin **41**
Awoonor, Kofi **37**
Bacon-Bercey, June **38**
Bahati, Wambui **60**
Baiocchi, Regina Harris **41**
Baker, Augusta **38**
Baker, Gwendolyn Calvert **9**
Baker, Houston A., Jr. **6**
Ballard, Allen Butler, Jr. **40**
Bambara, Toni Cade **10**
Baraka, Amiri **1, 38**
Barbee, Lloyd Augustus **71**
Barboza, Anthony **10**
Barnett, Marguerite **46**
Bath, Patricia E. **37**
Batiste, Alvin **66**
Beckham, Barry **41**
Bell, Derrick **6**
Benberry, Cuesta **65**
Benjamin, Tritobia Hayes **53**
Berry, Bertice **8, 55**
Berry, Mary Frances **7**
Bethune, Mary McLeod **4**
Biggers, John **20, 33**
Black, Albert **51**
Black, Keith Lanier **18**
Blassingame, John Wesley **40**
Blockson, Charles L. **42**
Bluitt, Juliann S. **14**
Bobo, Lawrence **60**
Bogle, Donald **34**
Bolden, Tonya **32**
Bosley, Freeman, Jr. **7**
Boyd, T. B., III **6**
Bradley, David Henry, Jr. **39**
Branch, William Blackwell **39**
Brathwaite, Kamau **36**
Braun, Carol Moseley **4, 42**
Briscoe, Marlin **37**
Brooks, Avery **9**
Brown, Claude **38**
Brown, Joyce F. **25**
Brown, Sterling Allen **10, 64**
Brown, Uzee **42**
Brown, Wesley **23**
Brown, Willa **40**
Bruce, Blanche Kelso **33**
Brutus, Dennis **38**
Bryan, Ashley F. **41**
Burke, Selma **16**
Burke, Yvonne Braithwaite **42**
Burks, Mary Fair **40**
Burnim, Mickey L. **48**
Burroughs, Margaret Taylor **9**
Burton, LeVar **8**
Butler, Paul D. **17**
Callender, Clive O. **3**
Campbell, Bebe Moore **6, 24, 59**
Campbell, Mary Schmidt **43**
Cannon, Katie **10**
Carby, Hazel **27**
Cardozo, Francis L. **33**
Carnegie, Herbert **25**
Carruthers, George R. **40**
Carter, Joye Maureen **41**

Carter, Kenneth **53**
Carter, Warrick L. **27**
Cartey, Wilfred **47**
Carver, George Washington **4**
Cary, Lorene **3**
Cary, Mary Ann Shadd **30**
Catlett, Elizabeth **2**
Cayton, Horace **26**
Chaney, John **67**
Cheney-Coker, Syl **43**
Clark, Joe **1**
Clark, Kenneth B. **5, 52**
Clark, Septima **7**
Clarke, Cheryl **32**
Clarke, George **32**
Clarke, John Henrik **20**
Clayton, Constance **1**
Cleaver, Kathleen Neal **29**
Clements, George **2**
Clemmons, Reginal G. **41**
Clifton, Lucille **14, 64**
Cobb, Jewel Plummer **42**
Cobb, W. Montague **39**
Cobb, William Jelani **59**
Cobbs, Price M. **9**
Cohen, Anthony **15**
Cole, Johnnetta B. **5, 43**
Coleman, William F., III **61**
Colescott, Robert **69**
Collins, Janet **33, 64**
Collins, Marva **3, 71**
Collins, Patricia Hill **67**
Comer, James P. **6**
Cone, James H. **3**
Coney, PonJola **48**
Cook, Mercer **40**
Cook, Samuel DuBois **14**
Cook, Toni **23**
Cooper Cafritz, Peggy **43**
Cooper, Afua **53**
Cooper, Anna Julia **20**
Cooper, Edward S. **6**
Copeland, Michael **47**
Cortez, Jayne **43**
Cosby, Bill **7, 26, 59**
Cotter, Joseph Seamon, Sr. **40**
Cottrell, Comer **11**
Cox, Joseph Mason Andrew **51**
Cox, William E. **68**
Creagh, Milton **27**
Crew, Rudolph F. **16**
Crew, Spencer R. **55**
Cross, Dolores E. **23**
Crouch, Stanley **11**
Cruse, Harold **54**
Cullen, Countee **8**
Daly, Marie Maynard **37**
Dathorne, O.R. **52**
Davis, Allison **12**
Davis, Angela **5**
Davis, Arthur P. **41**
Davis, Charles T. **48**
Davis, Erroll B., Jr. **57**
Davis, George **36**
Dawson, William Levi **39**
Days, Drew S., III **10**
Deconge-Watson, Lovenia **55**
Delany, Sadie **12**
Delany, Samuel R., Jr. **9**
Delco, Wilhemina R. **33**
Delsarte, Louis **34**
Dennard, Brazeal **37**
DePriest, James **37**

Dickens, Helen Octavia **14, 64**
Diop, Cheikh Anta **4**
Dixon, Margaret **14**
Dodson, Howard, Jr. **7, 52**
Dodson, Owen Vincent **38**
Donaldson, Jeff **46**
Douglas, Aaron **7**
Dove, Rita **6**
Dove, Ulysses **5**
Draper, Sharon Mills **16, 43**
Driskell, David C. **7**
Drummond, William J. **40**
Du Bois, David Graham **45**
Dumas, Henry **41**
Dunbar-Nelson, Alice Ruth Moore **44**
Dunnigan, Alice Allison **41**
Dunston, Georgia Mae **48**
Dymally, Mervyn **42**
Dyson, Michael Eric **11, 40**
Early, Gerald **15**
Edelin, Ramona Hoage **19**
Edelman, Marian Wright **5, 42**
Edley, Christopher **2, 48**
Edley, Christopher F., Jr. **48**
Edwards, Harry **2**
Elders, Joycelyn **6**
Elliot, Lorris **37**
Ellis, Clarence A. **38**
Ellison, Ralph **7**
Epps, Archie C., III **45**
Evans, Mari **26**
Falconer, Etta Zuber **59**
Fauset, Jessie **7**
Favors, Steve **23**
Feelings, Muriel **44**
Figueroa, John J. **40**
Fleming, Raymond **48**
Fletcher, Bill, Jr. **41**
Floyd, Elson S. **41**
Ford, Jack **39**
Foster, Ezola **28**
Foster, Henry W., Jr. **26**
Francis, Norman (C.) **60**
Franklin, John Hope **5**
Franklin, Robert M. **13**
Frazier, E. Franklin **10**
Freeman, Al, Jr. **11**
Fryer, Roland G. **56**
Fuller, A. Oveta **43**
Fuller, Arthur **27**
Fuller, Howard L. **37**
Fuller, Solomon Carter, Jr. **15**
Futrell, Mary Hatwood **33**
Gaines, Ernest J. **7**
Gates, Henry Louis, Jr. **3, 38, 67**
Gates, Sylvester James, Jr. **15**
Gayle, Addison, Jr. **41**
George, Zelma Watson **42**
Gerima, Haile **38**
Gibson, Donald Bernard **40**
Giddings, Paula **11**
Gill, Gerald **69**
Giovanni, Nikki **9, 39**
Golden, Marita **19**
Gomes, Peter J. **15**
Gomez, Jewelle **30**
Goodison, Lorna **71**
Granville, Evelyn Boyd **36**
Greenfield, Eloise **9**
Guinier, Lani **7, 30**
Guy-Sheftall, Beverly **13**
Hageman, Hans and Ivan **36**

Hale, Lorraine **8**
Halliburton, Warren J. **49**
Hammonds, Evelynn **69**
Handy, W. C. **8**
Hansberry, William Leo **11**
Harding, Vincent **67**
Harkless, Necia Desiree **19**
Harper, Michael S. **34**
Harris, Alice **7**
Harris, Barry **68**
Harris, Jay T. **19**
Harris, Patricia Roberts **2**
Harsh, Vivian Gordon **14**
Harvey, William R. **42**
Haskins, James **36, 54**
Hathaway, Isaac Scott **33**
Hayden, Carla D. **47**
Hayden, Robert **12**
Haynes, George Edmund **8**
Henderson, Stephen E. **45**
Henries, A. Doris Banks **44**
Herenton, Willie W. **24**
Hill, Andrew **66**
Hill, Anita **5, 65**
Hill, Bonnie Guiton **20**
Hill, Errol **40**
Hill, Leslie Pinckney **44**
Hilliard, Asa Grant, III **66**
Hine, Darlene Clark **24**
Hinton, William Augustus **8**
Hoagland, Everett H. **45**
Hogan, Beverly Wade **50**
Holland, Endesha Ida Mae **3, 57**
Holt, Nora **38**
hooks, Bell **5**
Hope, John **8**
Horton, James Oliver **58**
Houston, Charles Hamilton **4**
Hoyte, Lenon **50**
Hrabowski, Freeman A., III **22**
Huggins, Nathan Irvin **52**
Hughes, Ebony **57**
Hull, Akasha Gloria **45**
Humphries, Frederick **20**
Hunt, Richard **6**
Hutcherson, Hilda Yvonne **54**
Hutson, Jean Blackwell **16**
Imes, Elmer Samuel **39**
Jackson, Edison O. **67**
Jackson, Fred James **25**
Jackson, Vera **40**
Jarret, Vernon D. **42**
Jarvis, Charlene Drew **21**
Jarvis, Erich **67**
Jeffries, Leonard **8**
Jenifer, Franklyn G. **2**
Jenkins, Ella **15**
Johns, Vernon **38**
Johnson, Hazel **22**
Johnson, James Weldon **5**
Johnson, Katherine (Coleman Goble) **61**
Jones, Bobby **20**
Jones, Clara Stanton **51**
Jones, Edward P. **43, 67**
Jones, Gayl **37**
Jones, Ingrid Saunders **18**
Jones, Lois Mailou **13**
Joplin, Scott **6**
Jordan, Barbara **4**
Jordan, June **7, 35**
Josey, E. J. **10**
Just, Ernest Everett **3**

Karenga, Maulana **10, 71**
Kay, Ulysses **37**
Keith, Damon J. **16**
Kennedy, Florynce **12, 33**
Kennedy, Randall **40**
Kilpatrick, Carolyn Cheeks **16**
Kimbro, Dennis **10**
King, Preston **28**
King, Reatha Clark **65**
Kittles, Rick **51**
Komunyakaa, Yusef **9**
Kunjufu, Jawanza **3, 50**
Ladner, Joyce A. **42**
Lawrence, Jacob **4, 28**
Lawrence-Lightfoot, Sara **10**
Lee, Annie Francis **22**
Lee, Joe A. **45**
Leevy, Carrol M. **42**
Leffall, Lasalle **3, 64**
Lester, Julius **9**
Lewis, David Levering **9**
Lewis, Norman **39**
Lewis, Samella **25**
Lewis, Shirley A. R. **14**
Lewis, Thomas **19**
Liberia-Peters, Maria Philomena **12**
Lincoln, C. Eric **38**
Lindsey, Tommie **51**
Locke, Alain **10**
Logan, Rayford W. **40**
Lomax, Michael L. **58**
Long, Loretta **58**
Long, Richard Alexander **65**
Lorde, Audre **6**
Loury, Glenn **36**
Loving, Alvin, Jr. **35, 53**
Lowry, A. Leon **60**
Lucy Foster, Autherine **35**
Lyttle, Hulda Margaret **14**
Madhubuti, Haki R. **7**
Major, Clarence **9**
Malveaux, Floyd **54**
Manley, Audrey Forbes **16**
Marable, Manning **10**
Markham, E. A. **37**
Marsalis, Wynton **16**
Marshall, Paule **7**
Masekela, Barbara **18**
Mason, Ronald **27**
Massey, Walter E. **5, 45**
Massie, Samuel P., Jr. **29**
Mayhew, Richard **39**
Maynard, Robert C. **7**
Maynor, Dorothy **19**
Mayo, Whitman **32**
Mays, Benjamin E. **7**
McCarty, Osceola **16**
McCullough, Geraldine **58**
McKay, Nellie Yvonne **17, 57**
McMillan, Terry **4, 17, 53**
McMurray, Georgia L. **36**
McPherson, James Alan **70**
McWhorter, John **35**
Meek, Carrie **6**
Mell, Patricia **49**
Memmi, Albert **37**
Meredith, James H. **11**
Millender-McDonald, Juanita **21, 61**
Mitchell, Corinne **8**
Mitchell, Nicole **66**
Mitchell, Sharon **99**
Mofolo, Thomas Mokopu **37**
Mollel, Tololwa **38**

Mongella, Gertrude 11
Mooney, Paul 37
Moore, Barbara C. 49
Moore, Harry T. 29
Moore, Melba 21
Morrison, Keith 13
Morrison, Toni 15
Moses, Robert Parris 11
Mphalele, Es'kia (Ezekiel) 40
Mudimbe, V.Y. 61
Mullen, Harryette 34
Murray, Pauli 38
Nabrit, Samuel Milton 47
Nance, Cynthia 71
Naylor, Gloria 10, 42
Neal, Larry 38
Newkirk, Pamela 69
Newman, Lester C. 51
N'Namdi, George R. 17
Norman, Maidie 20
Norton, Eleanor Holmes 7
Nour, Nawal M. 56
Ogletree, Charles, Jr. 12, 47
Ojikutu, Bisola 65
Oliver, Kimberly 60
Onwueme, Tess Osonye 23
Onwurah, Ngozi 38
Owens, Helen 48
Owens, Major 6
Page, Alan 7
Paige, Rod 29
Painter, Nell Irvin 24
Palmer, Everard 37
Parker, Kellis E. 30
Parks, Suzan-Lori 34
Patterson, Frederick Douglass 12
Patterson, Mary Jane 54
Patterson, Orlando 4
Payton, Benjamin F. 23
Perry, Warren 56
Peters, Margaret and Matilda 43
Pickett, Cecil 39
Pinckney, Bill 42
Pindell, Howardena 55
Piper, Adrian 71
Player, Willa B. 43
Porter, James A. 11
Poussaint, Alvin F. 5, 67
Price, Florence 37
Price, Glenda 22
Price, Richard 51
Primus, Pearl 6
Prophet, Nancy Elizabeth 42
Purnell, Silas 59
Puryear, Martin 42
Quarles, Benjamin Arthur 18
Quigless, Helen G. 49
Rahman, Aishah 37
Ramphele, Mamphela 29
Reagon, Bernice Johnson 7
Reddick, Lawrence Dunbar 20
Redding, J. Saunders 26
Redmond, Eugene 23
Reid, Irvin D. 20
Ribeau, Sidney 70
Rice, Louise Allen 54
Richards, Hilda 49
Ringgold, Faith 4
Robinson, Sharon 22
Robinson, Spottswood W., III 22
Rodriguez, Cheryl 64
Rogers, Joel Augustus 30
Rollins, Charlemae Hill 27
Ross-Lee, Barbara 67
Russell-McCloud, Patricia 17
Salih, Al-Tayyib 37
Sallee, Charles Louis, Jr. 38
Satcher, David 7, 57
Schomburg, Arthur Alfonso 9
Sears, Stephanie 53
Senior, Olive 37
Shabazz, Betty 7, 26
Shange, Ntozake 8
Shipp, E. R. 15
Shirley, George 33
Simmons, Ruth J. 13, 38
Sinkford, Jeanne C. 13
Sisulu, Sheila Violet Makate 24
Sizemore, Barbara A. 26
Smith, Anna Deavere 6
Smith, Barbara 28
Smith, Jessie Carney 35
Smith, John L. 22
Smith, Mary Carter 26
Smith, Tubby 18
Snowden, Frank M., Jr. 67
Southern, Eileen 56
Sowande, Fela 39
Soyinka, Wole 4
Spears, Warren 52
Spikes, Dolores 18
Spriggs, William 67
Stanford, John 20
Steele, Claude Mason 13
Steele, Shelby 13
Stephens, Charlotte Andrews 14
Stewart, Maria W. Miller 19
Stone, Chuck 9
Sudarkasa, Niara 4
Sullivan, Louis 8
Swygert, H. Patrick 22
Tancil, Gladys Quander 59
Tanksley, Ann 37
Tatum, Beverly Daniel 42
Taylor, Helen (Lavon Hollingshed) 30
Taylor, Susie King 13
Terrell, Mary Church 9
Thomas, Alma 14
Thomas, Michael 69
Thurman, Howard 3
Tillis, Frederick 40
Tolson, Melvin 37
Tribble, Israel, Jr. 8
Trueheart, William E. 49
Tucker, Rosina 14
Turnbull, Charles Wesley 62
Turnbull, Walter 13, 60
Tutu, Desmond 6
Tutu, Nontombi Naomi 57
Tutuola, Amos 30
Tyson, Andre 40
Tyson, Asha 39
Tyson, Neil deGrasse 15, 65
Usry, James L. 23
van Sertima, Ivan 25
Vaughn, Viola 70
Vega, Marta Moreno 61
Velez-Rodriguez, Argelia 56
Verna, Gelsy 70
Wade-Gayles, Gloria Jean 41
Walcott, Derek 5
Walker, George 37
Wallace, Michele Faith 13
Wallace, Perry E. 47
Wallace, Phyllis A. 9
Washington, Booker T. 4
Watkins, Shirley R. 17
Wattleton, Faye 9
Weaver, Afaa Michael 37
Wedgeworth, Robert W. 42
Wells, Henrietta Bell 69
Wells, James Lesesne 10
Wells-Barnett, Ida B. 8
Welsing, Frances Cress 5
Wesley, Dorothy Porter 19
West, Cornel 5, 33
Wharton, Clifton R., Jr. 7
White, Charles 39
White, Lois Jean 20
Wilkens, J. Ernest, Jr. 43
Wilkins, Roger 2
Williams, David Rudyard 50
Williams, Fannie Barrier 27
Williams, Gregory 11
Williams, Patricia 11, 54
Williams, Sherley Anne 25
Williams, Walter E. 4
Wilson, William Julius 22
Woodruff, Hale 9
Woodson, Carter G. 2
Worrill, Conrad 12
Wright, Antoinette 60
Xuma, Madie Hall 59
Yancy, Dorothy Cowser 42
Young, Jean Childs 14
Zook, Kristal Brent 62

Fashion

Aberra, Amsale 67
Bailey, Xenobia 11
Banks, Jeffrey 17
Banks, Tyra 11, 50
Barboza, Anthony 10
Beals, Jennifer 12
Beckford, Tyson 11, 68
Berry, Halle 4, 19, 57
Boateng, Ozwald 35
Bond, Beverly 53
Boyd, Suzanne 52
Bridges, Sheila 36
Brown, Joyce F. 25
Burrows, Stephen 31
Campbell, Naomi 1, 31
Common 31, 63
Darego, Agbani 52
Dash, Damon 31
Davidson, Jaye 5
De' Alexander, Quinton 57
Delice, Ronald 48
Delice, Rony 48
Dirie, Waris 56
Ebanks, Selita 67
Evans, Etu 55
Gaskins, Eric 64
Gibson, Ted 66
Hall, Kevan 61
Harold, Erika 54
Henderson, Gordon 5
Hendy, Francis 47
Iman 4, 33
Iman, Chanel 66
John, Daymond 23
Johnson, Beverly 2
Jones, Carl 7
Kodjoe, Boris 34
Kani, Karl 10
Kebede, Liya 59
Kelly, Patrick 3
Lars, Byron 32
Malone, Maurice 32
Michele, Michael 31
Niane, Katoucha 70
Onwurah, Ngozi 38
Powell, Maxine 8
Reese, Tracy 54
Rhymes, Busta 31
Robinson, Patrick 19, 71
Rochon, Lela 16
Rowell, Victoria 13, 68
Sims, Naomi 29
Smaltz, Audrey 12
Smith, B(arbara) 11
Smith, Willi 8
Smythe Haith, Mabel 61
Steele, Lawrence 28
Stoney, Michael 50
Sy, Oumou 65
Talley, André Leon 56
Taylor, Karin 34
Walker, T. J. 7
Webb, Veronica 10
Wek, Alek 18, 63

Film

Aaliyah 30
Akinnuoye-Agbaje, Adewale 56
Akomfrah, John 37
Alexander, Khandi 43
Allain, Stephanie 49
Allen, Debbie 13, 42
Amos, John 8, 62
Anderson, Anthony 51
Anderson, Eddie "Rochester" 30
Awoonor, Kofi 37
Babatunde, Obba 35
Baker, Josephine 3
Banks, Michelle 59
Banks, Tyra 11, 50
Barclay, Paris 37
Barnett, Etta Moten 56
Bassett, Angela 6, 23, 62
Beach, Michael 26
Beals, Jennifer 12
Beckford, Tyson 11, 68
Belafonte, Harry 4, 65
Bellamy, Bill 12
Bennett, Louise 69
Bentley, Lamont 53
Berry, Fred "Rerun" 48
Berry, Halle 4, 19, 57
Beyoncé 39, 70
Blackwood, Maureen 37
Blacque, Taurean 58
Bleu, Corbin 65
Bogle, Donald 34
Bonet, Lisa 58
Brady, Wayne 32, 71
Braugher, Andre 13, 58
Breeze, Jean "Binta" 37
Brooks, Golden 62
Brooks, Hadda 40
Brown, Jim 11
Brown, Tony 3
Browne, Roscoe Lee 66
Burnett, Charles 16, 68
Byrd, Michelle 19
Byrd, Robert 11
Calloway, Cab 14
Campbell, Naomi 1, 31
Campbell Martin, Tisha 8, 42
Cannon, Nick 47

Cannon, Reuben 50
Carroll, Diahann 9
Carson, Lisa Nicole 21
Cash, Rosalind 28
Cedric the Entertainer 29, 60
Chase, Debra Martin 49
Cheadle, Don 19, 52
Chestnut, Morris 31
Chong, Rae Dawn 62
Chweneyagae, Presley 63
Clash, Kevin 14
Cliff, Jimmy 28
Combs, Sean "Puffy" 17, 43
Cortez, Jayne 43
Cosby, Bill 7, 26, 59
Crothers, Scatman 19
Curry, Mark 17
Curtis-Hall, Vondie 17
Dandridge, Dorothy 3
Daniels, Lee Louis 36
Dash, Julie 4
David, Keith 27
Davidson, Jaye 5
Davidson, Tommy 21
Davis, Eisa 68
Davis, Guy 36
Davis, Ossie 5, 50
Davis, Sammy, Jr. 18
de Passe, Suzanne 25
Dee, Ruby 8, 50, 68
Devine, Loretta 24
Dickerson, Ernest 6, 17
Diesel, Vin 29
Dieudonné 67
Diggs, Taye 25, 63
Dixon, Ivan 69
DMX 28, 64
Dourdan, Gary 37
Driskell, David C. 7
Duke, Bill 3
Duncan, Michael Clarke 26
Dunham, Katherine 4, 59
Dutton, Charles S. 4, 22
Earthquake 55
Edmonds, Kenneth "Babyface" 10, 31
Ejiofor, Chiwetel 67
Elder, Lonne, III 38
Elise, Kimberly 32
Emmanuel, Alphonsia 38
Epps, Omar 23, 59
Esposito, Giancarlo 9
Evans, Darryl 22
Everett, Francine 23
Faison, Donald 50
Faison, Frankie 55
Fetchit, Stepin 32
Fishburne, Laurence 4, 22, 70
Fisher, Antwone 40
Fox, Rick 27
Fox, Vivica A. 15, 53
Foxx, Jamie 15, 48
Foxx, Redd 2
Franklin, Carl 11
Freeman, Al, Jr. 11
Freeman, Morgan 2, 20, 62
Freeman, Yvette 27
Friday, Jeff 24
Fuller, Charles 8
Fuqua, Antoine 35
Gaye, Nona 56
George, Nelson 12
Gerima, Haile 38

Gibson, Tyrese 27, 62
Givens, Adele 62
Givens, Robin 4, 25, 58
Glover, Danny 1, 24
Glover, Savion 14
Goldberg, Whoopi 4, 33, 69
Gooding, Cuba, Jr. 16, 62
Gordon, Dexter 25
Gordy, Berry, Jr. 1
Gossett, Louis, Jr. 7
Gray, F. Gary 14, 49
Greaves, William 38
Grier, David Alan 28
Grier, Pam 9, 31
Guillaume, Robert 3, 48
Gunn, Moses 10
Guy, Jasmine 2
Hall, Arsenio 58
Hall, Juanita 62
Hamilton, Lisa Gay 71
Hampton, Henry 6
Hardison, Kadeem 22
Harewood, David 52
Harper, Hill 32, 65
Harris, Leslie 6
Harris, Naomie 55
Harris, Robin 7
Hawkins, Screamin' Jay 30
Hayes, Isaac 20, 58
Hayes, Teddy 40
Haysbert, Dennis 42
Hemsley, Sherman 19
Henriques, Julian 37
Henry, Lenny 9, 52
Henson, Darrin 33
Henson, Taraji 58
Hill, Dulé 29
Hill, Lauryn 20, 53
Hines, Gregory 1, 42
Horne, Lena 5
Hounsou, Djimon 19, 45
Houston, Whitney 7, 28
Howard, Sherri 36
Howard, Terrence 59
Hudlin, Reginald 9
Hudlin, Warrington 9
Hudson, Jennifer 63
Hughes, Albert 7
Hughes, Allen 7
Hurt, Byron 61
Ice Cube 8, 30, 60
Ice-T 6, 31
Iman 4, 33
Ingram, Rex 5
Jackson, George 19
Jackson, Janet 6, 30, 68
Jackson, Samuel 8, 19, 63
Jean, Michaëlle; 70
Jean-Baptiste, Marianne 17, 46
Johnson, Beverly 2
Jones, James Earl 3, 49
Jones, Orlando 30
Jones, Quincy 8, 30
Julien, Isaac 3
Kelley, Elijah 65
Keys, Alicia 32, 68
Khumalo, Leleti 51
King, Regina 22, 45
King, Woodie, Jr. 27
Kirby, George 14
Kitt, Eartha 16
Kool Moe Dee 37
Kotto, Yaphet 7

Kunjufu, Jawanza 3, 50
La Salle, Eriq 12
LaBelle, Patti 13, 30
Lane, Charles 3
Lathan, Sanaa 27
Lawrence, Martin 6, 27, 60
Lee, Joie 1
Lee, Spike 5, 19
Lemmons, Kasi 20
LeNoire, Rosetta 37
Lester, Adrian 46
Lewis, Samella 25
Lil' Kim 28
Lincoln, Abbey 3
Lindo, Delroy 18, 45
LisaRaye 27
LL Cool J 16, 49
Long, Nia 17
Love, Darlene 23
Lover, Ed 10
Luke, Derek 61
Lynch, Shola 61
Mabley, Jackie "Moms" 15
Mac, Bernie 29, 61
Malco, Romany 71
Marsalis, Branford 34
Martin, Darnell 43
Martin, Helen 31
Master P 21
McDaniel, Hattie 5
McKee, Lonette 12
McKinney, Nina Mae 40
McQueen, Butterfly 6, 54
Meadows, Tim 30
Micheaux, Oscar 7
Michele, Michael 31
Mitchell, Elvis 67
Mitchell, Kel 66
Mo'Nique 35
Mooney, Paul 37
Moore, Chante 26
Moore, Melba 21
Moore, Shemar 21
Morris, Garrett 31
Morris, Greg 28
Morton, Joe 18
Mos Def 30
Moses, Gilbert 12
Moss, Carlton 17
Murphy, Eddie 4, 20, 61
Muse, Clarence Edouard 21
Nas 33
Nash, Johnny 40
Nash, Niecy 66
Neal, Elise 29
Newton, Thandie 26
Nicholas, Fayard 20, 57
Nicholas, Harold 20
Nichols, Nichelle 11
Norman, Maidie 20
Odetta 37
Okonedo, Sophie 67
O'Neal, Ron 46
Onwurah, Ngozi 38
Packer, Will 71
Palmer, Keke 68
Parks, Gordon 1, 35, 58
Parker, Nicole Ari 52
Patton, Paula 62
Payne, Allen 13
Peck, Raoul 32
Perrineau, Harold, Jr. 51
Perry, Tyler 54

Phifer, Mekhi 25
Pinkett Smith, Jada 10, 41
Poitier, Sidney 11, 36
Poitier, Sydney Tamiia 65
Pratt, Kyla 57
Prince 18, 65
Prince-Bythewood, Gina 31
Pryor, Richard 3, 24, 56
Queen Latifah 1, 16, 58
Ralph, Sheryl Lee 18
Randle, Theresa 16
Reddick, Lance 52
Reid, Tim 56
Reese, Della 6, 20
Reuben, Gloria 15
Rhames, Ving 14, 50
Rhimes, Shonda Lynn 67
Rhymes, Busta 31
Richards, Beah 30
Richardson, LaTanya 71
Richardson, Salli 68
Ridley, John 69
Riggs, Marlon 5, 44
Roberts, Darryl 70
Robinson, Matt 69
Robinson, Shaun 36
Rochon, Lela 16
Rock, Chris 3, 22, 66
Rock, The 29, 66
Rodrigues, Percy 68
Rolle, Esther 13, 21
Rollins, Howard E., Jr. 16
Rose, Anika Noni 70
Ross, Diana 8, 27
Roundtree, Richard 27
Rowell, Victoria 13, 68
Rupaul 17
Russell, Nipsey 66
St. Jacques, Raymond 8
St. John, Kristoff 25
Schultz, Michael A. 6
Scott, Hazel 66
Seal 14
Sembène, Ousmane 13, 62
Shakur, Tupac 14
Shepherd, Sherri 55
Simmons, Henry 55
Simpson, O. J. 15
Sinbad 1, 16
Singleton, John 2, 30
Sisqo 30
Smith, Anjela Lauren 44
Smith, Anna Deavere 6, 44
Smith, Roger Guenveur 12
Smith, Will 8, 18, 53
Snipes, Wesley 3, 24, 67
Sullivan, Maxine 37
Tate, Larenz 15
Taylor, Meshach 4
Taylor, Regina 9, 46
Thigpen, Lynne 17, 41
Thomas, Sean Patrick 35
Thompson, Kenan 52
Thurman, Wallace 16
Tillman, George, Jr. 20
Torres, Gina 52
Torry, Guy 31
Toussaint, Lorraine 32
Townsend, Robert 4, 23
Tucker, Chris 13, 23, 62
Tunie, Tamara 63
Turner, Tina 6, 27
Tyler, Aisha N. 36

Tyson, Cicely **7, 51**
Uggams, Leslie **23**
Underwood, Blair **7, 27**
Union, Gabrielle **31**
Usher **23, 56**
Van Lierop, Robert **53**
Van Peebles, Mario **2, 51**
Van Peebles, Melvin **7**
Vance, Courtney B. **15, 60**
Vanity **67**
Vereen, Ben **4**
Walker, Eamonn **37**
Ward, Douglas Turner **42**
Warfield, Marsha **2**
Warner, Malcolm-Jamal **22, 36**
Warren, Michael **27**
Warwick, Dionne **18**
Washington, Denzel **1, 16**
Washington, Fredi **10**
Washington, Kerry **46**
Waters, Ethel **7**
Wayans, Damon **8, 41**
Wayans, Keenen Ivory **18**
Wayans, Marlon **29**
Wayans, Shawn **29**
Weathers, Carl **10**
Webb, Veronica **10**
Whitaker, Forest **2, 49, 67**
White, Michael Jai **71**
Whitfield, Lynn **18**
Williams, Billy Dee **8**
Williams, Clarence, III **26**
Williams, Marco **53**
Williams, Russell, II **70**
Williams, Samm-Art **21**
Williams, Saul **31**
Williams, Vanessa A. **32, 66**
Williams, Vanessa L. **4, 17**
Williamson, Fred **67**
Williamson, Mykelti **22**
Wilson, Debra **38**
Wilson, Dorien **55**
Winfield, Paul **2, 45**
Winfrey, Oprah **2, 15, 61**
Witherspoon, John **38**
Woodard, Alfre **9**
Wright, Jeffrey **54**
Yarbrough, Cedric **51**
Yoba, Malik **11**

Government and politics--international
Abacha, Sani **11, 70**
Abbott, Diane **9**
Abiola, Moshood **70**
Abubakar, Abdulsalami **66**
Achebe, Chinua **6**
Akunyili, Dora Nkem **58**
Ali, Ayaan Hirsi **58**
Ali Mahdi Mohamed **5**
Amadi, Elechi **40**
Amin, Idi **42**
Amos, Valerie **41**
Annan, Kofi Atta **15, 48**
Aristide, Jean-Bertrand **6, 45**
Arthur, Owen **33**
Augustine, Jean **53**
Awoonor, Kofi **37**
Azikiwe, Nnamdi **13**
Babangida, Ibrahim **4**
Baker, Gwendolyn Calvert **9**
Banda, Hastings Kamuzu **6, 54**
Barrow, Dean **69**
Bedie, Henri Konan **21**
Berry, Mary Frances **7**
Biko, Steven **4**
Bishop, Maurice **39**
Biya, Paul **28**
Bizimungu, Pasteur **19**
Boateng, Paul Yaw **56**
Bongo, Omar **1**
Boye, Madior **30**
Brown, Rosemary **62**
Bunche, Ralph J. **5**
Burnham, Forbes **66**
Buthelezi, Mangosuthu Gatsha **9**
Césaire, Aimé **48, 69**
Charlemagne, Manno **11**
Charles, Mary Eugenia **10, 55**
Charles, Pierre **52**
Chiluba, Frederick Jacob Titus **56**
Chissano, Joaquim **7, 55, 67**
Christie, Perry Gladstone **53**
Christophe, Henri **9**
Compton, John **65**
Conneh, Sekou Damate, Jr. **51**
Conté, Lansana **7**
Cools, Anne **64**
Curling, Alvin **34**
da Silva, Benedita **5**
Dadié, Bernard **34**
Davis, Ruth **37**
Déby, Idriss **30**
Diogo, Luisa Dias **63**
Diop, Cheikh Anta **4**
Diouf, Abdou **3**
dos Santos, José Eduardo **43**
Douglas, Denzil Llewellyn **53**
Ekwensi, Cyprian **37**
Eyadéma, Gnassingbé **7, 52**
Fela **1, 42**
Frazer, Jendayi **68**
Gbagbo, Laurent **43**
Gnassingbé, Faure **67**
Gordon, Pamela **17**
Grant, Bernie **57**
Habré, Hissène **6**
Habyarimana, Juvenal **8**
Haile Selassie **7**
Haley, George Williford Boyce **21**
Hani, Chris **6**
Houphouët-Boigny, Félix **4, 64**
Ifill, Gwen **28**
Ingraham, Hubert A. **19**
Isaac, Julius **34**
Jagan, Cheddi **16**
Jammeh, Yahya **23**
Jawara, Dawda Kairaba **11**
Jean, Michaëlle; **70**
Ka Dinizulu, Mcwayizeni **29**
Kabbah, Ahmad Tejan **23**
Kabila, Joseph **30**
Kabila, Laurent **20**
Kabunda, Kenneth **2**
Kagame, Paul **54**
Kenyatta, Jomo **5**
Kerekou, Ahmed (Mathieu) **1**
Kibaki, Mwai **60**
King, Oona **27**
Kariuki, J. M. **67**
Kufuor, John Agyekum **54**
Laraque, Paul **67**
Liberia-Peters, Maria Philomena **12**
Lumumba, Patrice **33**
Luthuli, Albert **13**
Maathai, Wangari **43**
Mabuza, Lindiwe **18**
Machel, Samora Moises **8**
Magloire, Paul Eugène **68**
Mamadou, Tandja **33**
Mandela, Nelson **1, 14**
Mandela, Winnie **2, 35**
Masekela, Barbara **18**
Masire, Quett **5**
Mbeki, Thabo Mvuyelwa **14**
Mbuende, Kaire **12**
Meles Zenawi **3**
Mengistu, Haile Mariam **65**
Mhlaba, Raymond **55**
Mkapa, Benjamin **16**
Mobutu Sese Seko **1, 56**
Mogae, Festus Gontebanye **19**
Moi, Daniel Arap **1, 35**
Mongella, Gertrude **11**
Mswati III **56**
Mugabe, Robert **10, 71**
Muluzi, Bakili **14**
Museveni, Yoweri **4**
Mutebi, Ronald **25**
Mwinyi, Ali Hassan **1**
Ndadaye, Melchior **7**
Neto, António Agostinho **43**
Ngilu, Charity **58**
Ngubane, Ben **33**
Nkoli, Simon **60**
Nkomo, Joshua **4, 65**
Nkrumah, Kwame **3**
Ntaryamira, Cyprien **8**
Nujoma, Samuel **10**
Nyanda, Siphiwe **21**
Nyerere, Julius **5**
Nzo, Alfred **15**
Obasanjo, Olusegun **5, 22**
Obasanjo, Stella **32, 56**
Obote, Milton **63**
Odinga, Raila **67**
Okara, Gabriel **37**
Oyono, Ferdinand **38**
Pascal-Trouillot, Ertha **3**
Patterson, P. J. **6, 20**
Pereira, Aristides **30**
Perkins, Edward **5**
Perry, Ruth **15**
Pitt, David Thomas **10**
Pitta, Celso **17**
Poitier, Sidney **11, 36**
Ramaphosa, Cyril **3**
Rawlings, Jerry **9**
Rawlings, Nana Konadu Agyeman **13**
Rice, Condoleezza **3, 28**
Roberto, Holden **65**
Robinson, Randall **7, 46**
Sampson, Edith S. **4**
Sankara, Thomas **17**
Savimbi, Jonas **2, 34**
Sawyer, Amos **2**
Senghor, Augustin Diamacoune **66**
Senghor, Léopold Sédar **12, 66**
Simpson-Miller, Portia **62**
Sirleaf, Ellen Johnson **71**
Sisulu, Walter **47**
Skinner, Kiron K. **65**
Smith, Jennifer **21**
Soglo, Nicephore **15**
Soyinka, Wole **4**
Spencer, Winston Baldwin **68**
Taylor, Charles **20**
Taylor, John (David Beckett) **16**
Todman, Terence A. **55**
Touré, Amadou Toumani **18**
Touré, Sekou **6**
Tsvangirai, Morgan **26**
Tutu, Desmond (Mpilo) **6, 44**
Van Lierop, Robert **53**
Vieira, Joao **14**
Wade, Abdoulaye **66**
Weah, George **58**
Wharton, Clifton R., Jr. **7**
Wharton, Clifton Reginald, Sr. **36**
Williams, Eric Eustace **65**
Wiwa, Ken **67**
Yar'adua, Umaru **69**
Zuma, Jacob G. **33**
Zuma, Nkosazana Dlamini **34**

Government and politics--U.S.
Adams, Floyd, Jr. **12**
Alexander, Archie Alphonso **14**
Alexander, Clifford **26**
Ali, Muhammad **2, 16, 52**
Allen, Claude **68**
Allen, Ethel D. **13**
Archer, Dennis **7, 36**
Arrington, Richard **24**
Avant, Clarence **19**
Baker, Thurbert **22**
Ballance, Frank W. **41**
Baltimore, Richard Lewis, III **71**
Barbee, Lloyd Augustus **71**
Barden, Don H. **9, 20**
Barrett, Andrew C. **12**
Barrett, Jacqueline **28**
Barry, Marion S(hepilov, Jr.) **7, 44**
Bass, Karen **70**
Bell, Michael **40**
Bellamy, Terry **58**
Belton, Sharon Sayles **9, 16**
Berry, Mary Frances **7**
Berry, Theodore M. **31**
Bethune, Mary McLeod **4**
Blackwell, Kenneth, Sr. **61**
Blackwell, Unita **17**
Bond, Julian **2, 35**
Booker, Cory Anthony **68**
Bosley, Freeman, Jr. **7**
Bowman, Bertie **71**
Brooks, Tyrone **59**
Brown, Byrd **49**
Boykin, Keith **14**
Bradley, Jennette B. **40**
Bradley, Thomas **2**
Braun, Carol Moseley **4, 42**
Brazile, Donna **25, 70**
Brimmer, Andrew F. **2, 48**
Brooke, Edward **8**
Brown, Cora **33**
Brown, Corrine **24**
Brown, Elaine **8**
Brown, George Leslie **62**
Brown, Jesse **6, 41**
Brown, Lee Patrick **24**
Brown, Les **5**
Brown, Ron **5**
Brown, Willie L., Jr. **7**
Bruce, Blanche K. **33**
Bryant, Wayne R. **6**
Buckley, Victoria (Vicki) **24**
Bunche, Ralph J. **5**
Burke, Yvonne Braithwaite **42**
Burris, Chuck **21**
Burris, Roland W. **25**

Butler, Jerry **26**
Caesar, Shirley **19**
Campbell, Bill **9**
Cardozo, Francis L. **33**
Carson, André **69**
Carson, Julia **23, 69**
Carter, Pamela Lynn **67**
Carter, Robert L. **51**
Chavis, Benjamin **6**
Chisholm, Shirley **2, 50**
Christian-Green, Donna M. **17**
Clay, William Lacy **8**
Clayton, Eva M. **20**
Cleaver, Eldridge **5**
Cleaver, Emanuel **4, 45, 68**
Clyburn, James E. **21, 71**
Coleman, Mary **46**
Coleman, Michael B. **28**
Collins, Barbara-Rose **7**
Collins, Cardiss **10**
Colter, Cyrus J. **36**
Connerly, Ward **14**
Conyers, John, Jr. **4, 45**
Cook, Mercer **40**
Cose, Ellis **5, 50**
Craig-Jones, Ellen Walker **44**
Crockett, George W., Jr. **10, 64**
Cummings, Elijah E. **24**
Cunningham, Evelyn **23**
Currie, Betty **21**
Davis, Angela **5**
Davis, Artur **41**
Davis, Benjamin O., Jr. **2, 43**
Davis, Benjamin O., Sr. **4**
Davis, Danny K. **24**
Davis, James E. **50**
Days, Drew S., III **10**
Delany, Martin R. **27**
Delco, Wilhemina R. **33**
Dellums, Ronald **2**
Diggs, Charles R. **21**
Dinkins, David **4**
Dixon, Julian C. **24**
Dixon, Sharon Pratt **1**
Dixon, Sheila **68**
Dougherty, Mary Pearl **47**
Du Bois, W. E. B. **3**
Dudley, Edward R. **58**
Dukes, Hazel Nell **56**
Dunbar-Nelson, Alice Ruth Moore **44**
Dymally, Mervyn **42**
Easley, Annie J. **61**
Edmonds, Terry **17**
Elders, Joycelyn **6**
Ellison, Keith **59**
Espy, Mike **6**
Farmer, James **2, 64**
Farrakhan, Louis **2**
Fattah, Chaka **11, 70**
Fauntroy, Walter E. **11**
Felix, Larry R. **64**
Fenty, Adrian **60**
Ferguson, Roger W. **25**
Fields, C. Virginia **25**
Fields, Cleo **13**
Flake, Floyd H. **18**
Fletcher, Arthur A. **63**
Flipper, Henry O. **3**
Ford, Harold E(ugene) **42**
Ford, Harold E(ugene), Jr. **16, 70**
Ford, Jack **39**
Ford, Johnny **70**

Fortune, T. Thomas **6**
Foster, Ezola **28**
Franklin, Shirley **34**
Franks, Gary **2**
Frazer, Jendayi **68**
Fulani, Lenora **11**
Gantt, Harvey **1**
Garrett, Joyce Finley **59**
Garvey, Marcus **1**
Gibson, Johnnie Mae **23**
Gibson, Kenneth Allen **6**
Gibson, William F. **6**
Goode, W. Wilson **4**
Gravely, Samuel L., Jr. **5, 49**
Gray, William H., III **3**
Grimké, Archibald H. **9**
Guinier, Lani **7, 30**
Haley, George Williford Boyce **21**
Hamer, Fannie Lou **6**
Harmon, Clarence **26**
Harris, Alice **7**
Harris, Patricia Roberts **2**
Harvard, Beverly **11**
Hastie, William H. **8**
Hastings, Alcee L. **16**
Hatcher, Richard G. **55**
Hawkins, Augustus F. **68**
Hayes, James C. **10**
Henderson, Thelton E. **68**
Henry, Aaron **19**
Herenton, Willie W. **24**
Herman, Alexis M. **15**
Hernandez, Aileen Clarke **13**
Hill, Bonnie Guiton **20**
Hilliard, Earl F. **24**
Hobson, Julius W. **44**
Holder, Eric H., Jr. **9**
Holmes, Amy **69**
Ifill, Gwen **28**
Irving, Larry, Jr. **12**
Irvis, K. Leroy **67**
Jackson, Alphonso R. **48**
Jackson, George **14**
Jackson, Jesse **1**
Jackson, Jesse, Jr. **14, 27, 45**
Jackson Lee, Sheila **20**
Jackson, Mae **57**
Jackson, Maynard **2, 41**
Jackson, Shirley Ann **12**
Jacob, John E. **2**
James, Sharpe **23, 69**
Jarvis, Charlene Drew **21**
Jefferson, William J. **25**
Johnson, Eddie Bernice **8**
Johnson, Harvey, Jr. **24**
Johnson, James Weldon **5**
Johnson, Katherine (Coleman Goble) **61**
Johnson, Kevin **70**
Johnson, Norma L. Holloway **17**
Johnson, Robert T. **17**
Jones, Elaine R. **7, 45**
Jordan, Barbara **4**
Jordan, Vernon **3, 35**
Kennard, William Earl **18**
Keyes, Alan L. **11**
Kidd, Mae Street **39**
Kilpatrick, Carolyn Cheeks **16**
Kilpatrick, Kwame **34, 71**
Kincaid, Bernard **28**
King, Martin Luther, III **20**
Kirk, Ron **11**
Lafontant, Jewel Stradford **3, 51**

Lee, Barbara **25**
Leland, Mickey **2**
Lewis, Delano **7**
Lewis, John **2, 46**
Majette, Denise **41**
Mallett, Conrad, Jr. **16**
Mallory, Mark **62**
Marsh, Henry, III **32**
Marshall, Bella **22**
Marshall, Thurgood **1, 44**
Martin, Louis E. **16**
Martin, Ruby Grant **49**
McCall, H. Carl **27**
McGee, James Madison **46**
McKinney, Cynthia Ann **11, 52**
McKissick, Floyd B. **3**
Meek, Carrie **6, 36**
Meek, Kendrick **41**
Meeks, Gregory **25**
Meredith, James H. **11**
Metcalfe, Ralph **26**
Mfume, Kweisi **6, 41**
Millender-McDonald, Juanita **21, 61**
Mitchell, Parren J. **42, 66**
Moore, Gwendolynne S. **55**
Moore, Minyon **45**
Morial, Ernest "Dutch" **26**
Morial, Marc H. **20, 51**
Morton, Azie Taylor **48**
Moses, Robert Parris **11**
Murrell, Sylvia Marilyn **49**
Nagin, C. Ray **42, 57**
Nix, Robert N.C., Jr. **51**
Norton, Eleanor Holmes **7**
Nutter, Michael **69**
Obama, Barack **49**
O'Leary, Hazel **6**
Owens, Major **6**
Page, Alan **7**
Paige, Rod **29**
Paterson, Basil A. **69**
Paterson, David A. **59**
Patrick, Deval **12, 61**
Patterson, Louise **25**
Payne, Donald M. **2, 57**
Payne, William D. **60**
Perez, Anna **1**
Perkins, Edward **5**
Perkins, James, Jr. **55**
Perry, Lowell **30**
Pinchback, P. B. S. **9**
Powell, Adam Clayton, Jr. **3**
Powell, Colin **1, 28**
Powell, Debra A. **23**
Powell, Michael **32**
Raines, Franklin Delano **14**
Randolph, A. Philip **3**
Rangel, Charles **3, 52**
Raoul, Kwame **55**
Reeves, Gregory **49**
Reeves, Triette Lipsey **27**
Rice, Condoleezza **3, 28**
Rice, Norm **8**
Richardson, Rupert **67**
Robinson, Bishop L. **66**
Robinson, Randall **7, 46**
Rogers, Joe **27**
Ross, Don **27**
Rush, Bobby **26**
Rustin, Bayard **4**
Sampson, Edith S. **4**
Sanders, Malika **48**
Satcher, David **7, 57**

Sayles Belton, Sharon **9**
Schmoke, Kurt **1, 48**
Scott, David **41**
Scott, Robert C. **23**
Sears-Collins, Leah J. **5**
Shakur, Assata **6**
Shavers, Cheryl **31**
Sharpton, Al **21**
Simpson, Carole **6, 30**
Sisulu, Sheila Violet Makate **24**
Smith, Nate **49**
Smythe Haith, Mabel **61**
Slater, Rodney E. **15**
Stanton, Robert **20**
Staupers, Mabel K. **7**
Steele, Michael **38**
Stokes, Carl B. **10**
Stokes, Louis **3**
Stone, Chuck **9**
Street, John F. **24**
Sullivan, Louis **8**
Sutton, Percy E. **42**
Terry, Clark **39**
Thomas, Clarence **2, 39, 65**
Thompson, Bennie G. **26**
Thompson, Larry D. **39**
Thompson, William C. **35**
Todman, Terence A. **55**
Toote, Gloria E.A. **64**
Towns, Edolphus **19**
Tribble, Israel, Jr. **8**
Trotter, Donne E. **28**
Tubbs Jones, Stephanie **24**
Tucker, C. Delores **12, 56**
Turnbull, Charles Wesley **62**
Turner, Henry McNeal **5**
Usry, James L. **23**
Vaughn, Gladys Gary **47**
Von Lipsey, Roderick K. **11**
Wallace, Phyllis A. **9**
Washington, Harold **6**
Washington, Val **12**
Washington, Walter **45**
Waters, Maxine **3, 67**
Watkins, Shirley R. **17**
Watson, Diane **41**
Watt, Melvin **26**
Watts, J. C., Jr. **14, 38**
Weaver, Robert C. **8, 46**
Webb, Wellington **3**
Wharton, Clifton Reginald, Sr. **36**
Wharton, Clifton R., Jr. **7**
Wheat, Alan **14**
White, Jesse **22**
White, Michael R. **5**
Wilder, L. Douglas **3, 48**
Wilkins, Roger **2**
Williams, Anthony **21**
Williams, Eddie N. **44**
Williams, George Washington **18**
Williams, Hosea Lorenzo **15, 31**
Williams, Maggie **7, 71**
Wilson, Sunnie **7, 55**
Wynn, Albert **25**
Young, Andrew **3, 48**

Law

Alexander, Clifford **26**
Alexander, Joyce London **18**
Alexander, Sadie Tanner Mossell **22**
Allen, Samuel W. **38**
Amaker, Norman **63**

Archer, Dennis **7, 36**
Arnwine, Barbara **28**
Bailey, Clyde **45**
Banks, William **11**
Barbee, Lloyd Augustus **71**
Barrett, Andrew C. **12**
Barrett, Jacqueline **28**
Baugh, David **23**
Bell, Derrick **6**
Berry, Mary Frances **7**
Berry, Theodore M. **31**
Bishop, Sanford D., Jr. **24**
Bolin, Jane **22, 59**
Bolton, Terrell D. **25**
Booker, Cory Anthony **68**
Bosley, Freeman, Jr. **7**
Boykin, Keith **14**
Bradley, Thomas **2**
Braun, Carol Moseley **4, 42**
Brooke, Edward **8**
Brown, Byrd **49**
Brown, Cora **33**
Brown, Cupcake **63**
Brown, Homer S. **47**
Brown, Janice Rogers **43**
Brown, Joe **29**
Brown, Lee Patrick **1, 24**
Brown, Ron **5**
Brown, Willie L., Jr. **7**
Bryant, Wayne R. **6**
Bryant, William Benson **61**
Bully-Cummings, Ella **48**
Burke, Yvonne Braithwaite **42**
Burris, Roland W. **25**
Butler, Louis **70**
Butler, Paul D. **17**
Bynoe, Peter C.B. **40**
Campbell, Bill **9**
Carter, Pamela Lynn **67**
Carter, Robert L. **51**
Carter, Stephen L. **4**
Cashin, Sheryll **63**
Chambers, Julius **3**
Cleaver, Kathleen Neal **29**
Clendenon, Donn **26, 56**
Cochran, Johnnie **11, 39, 52**
Colter, Cyrus J. **36**
Conyers, John, Jr. **4, 45**
Crockett, George W., Jr. **10, 64**
Darden, Christopher **13**
Davis, Artur **41**
Days, Drew S., III **10**
DeFrantz, Anita **37**
Diggs-Taylor, Anna **20**
Dillard, Godfrey J. **45**
Dinkins, David **4**
Dixon, Sharon Pratt **1**
Edelman, Marian Wright **5, 42**
Edley, Christopher **2, 48**
Edley, Christopher F., Jr. **48**
Ellington, E. David **11**
Ephriam, Mablean **29**
Espy, Mike **6**
Farmer-Paellmann, Deadria **43**
Fields, Cleo **13**
Finner-Williams, Paris Michele **62**
Ford, Wallace **58**
Frazier-Lyde, Jacqui **31**
Freeman, Charles **19**
Gary, Willie E. **12**
Gibson, Johnnie Mae **23**
Glover, Nathaniel, Jr. **12**
Gomez-Preston, Cheryl **9**

Graham, Lawrence Otis **12**
Gray, Fred **37**
Gray, Willie **46**
Greenhouse, Bunnatine "Bunny" **57**
Grimké, Archibald H. **9**
Guinier, Lani **7, 30**
Haley, George Williford Boyce **21**
Hall, Elliott S. **24**
Harris, Kamala D. **64**
Harris, Patricia Roberts **2**
Harvard, Beverly **11**
Hassell, Leroy Rountree, Sr. **41**
Hastie, William H. **8**
Hastings, Alcee L. **16**
Hatcher, Richard G. **55**
Hatchett, Glenda **32**
Hawkins, Augustus F. **68**
Hawkins, Steven **14**
Hayes, Dennis **54**
Haywood, Margaret A. **24**
Henderson, Thelton E. **68**
Higginbotham, A. Leon, Jr. **13, 25**
Hill, Anita **5, 65**
Hillard, Terry **25**
Hills, Oliver W. **24**
Holder, Eric H., Jr. **9**
Hollowell, Donald L. **57**
Holton, Hugh, Jr. **39**
Hooks, Benjamin L. **2**
Houston, Charles Hamilton **4**
Hubbard, Arnette Rhinehart **38**
Hunter, Billy **22**
Hurtt, Harold **46**
Isaac, Julius **34**
Jackson Lee, Sheila **20**
Jackson, Maynard **2, 41**
Johnson, Harry E. **57**
Johnson, James Weldon **5**
Johnson, Norma L. Holloway **17**
Jones, Elaine R. **7, 45**
Jones, Van **70**
Jordan, Vernon E. **3, 35**
Kearse, Amalya Lyle **12**
Keith, Damon J. **16**
Kennard, William Earl **18**
Kennedy, Florynce **12, 33**
Kennedy, Randall **40**
Kibaki, Mwai **60**
King, Bernice **4**
Kirk, Ron **11**
Lafontant, Jewel Stradford **3, 51**
Lewis, Delano **7**
Lewis, Reginald F. **6**
Lloyd, Reginald **64**
Majette, Denise **41**
Mallett, Conrad, Jr. **16**
Mandela, Nelson **1, 14**
Marsh, Henry, III **32**
Marshall, Thurgood **1, 44**
Mathis, Greg **26**
McAnulty, William E., Jr. **66**
McCrary Anthony, Crystal **70**
McDonald, Gabrielle Kirk **20**
McDougall, Gay J. **11, 43**
McKinnon, Isaiah **9**
McKissick, Floyd B. **3**
McPhail, Sharon **2**
Meek, Kendrick **41**
Meeks, Gregory **25**
Moose, Charles **40**
Morial, Ernest "Dutch" **26**
Motley, Constance Baker **10, 55**
Muhammad, Ava **31**

Murray, Pauli **38**
Nance, Cynthia **71**
Napoleon, Benny N. **23**
Nix, Robert N.C., Jr. **51**
Noble, Ronald **46**
Norton, Eleanor Holmes **7**
Nunn, Annetta **43**
Obama, Barack **49**
Obama, Michelle **61**
Ogletree, Charles, Jr. **12, 47**
Ogunlesi, Adebayo O. **37**
O'Leary, Hazel **6**
Oliver, Jerry **37**
Page, Alan **7**
Paker, Kellis E. **30**
Parks, Bernard C. **17**
Parsons, James **14**
Parsons, Richard Dean **11, 33**
Pascal-Trouillot, Ertha **3**
Paterson, Basil A. **69**
Patrick, Deval **12**
Payne, Ulice **42**
Payton, John **48**
Perry, Lowell **30**
Philip, Marlene Nourbese **32**
Pincham, R. Eugene, Sr. **69**
Powell, Michael **32**
Quince, Peggy A. **69**
Ramsey, Charles H. **21, 69**
Raoul, Kwame **55**
Ray, Charlotte E. **60**
Redding, Louis L. **26**
Reynolds, Star Jones **10, 27, 61**
Rice, Constance LaMay **60**
Richie, Leroy C. **18**
Robinson, Bishop L. **66**
Robinson, Malcolm S. **44**
Robinson, Randall **7, 46**
Russell-McCloud, Patricia **17**
Sampson, Edith S. **4**
Schmoke, Kurt **1, 48**
Sears-Collins, Leah J. **5**
Solomon, Jimmie Lee **38**
Sparks, Corinne Etta **53**
Steele, Michael **38**
Stokes, Carl B. **10**
Stokes, Louis **3**
Stout, Juanita Kidd **24**
Sutton, Percy E. **42**
Taylor, John (David Beckett) **16**
Thomas, Arthur Ray **52**
Thomas, Clarence **2, 39, 65**
Thomas, Franklin A. **5, 49**
Thompson, Larry D. **39**
Touré, Faya Ora Rose **56**
Tubbs Jones, Stephanie **24**
Van Lierop, Robert **53**
Vanzant, Iyanla **17, 47**
Wagner, Annice **22**
Wainwright, Joscelyn **46**
Walker, Cora T. **68**
Wallace, Perry E. **47**
Ward, Benjamin **68**
Washington, Harold **6**
Watkins, Donald **35**
Watt, Melvin **26**
Wharton, Clifton Reginald, Sr. **36**
Wilder, L. Douglas **3, 48**
Wilkins, Roger **2**
Williams, Evelyn **10**
Williams, Gregory **11**
Williams, Patricia **11, 54**
Williams, Willie L. **4**

Wilson, Jimmy **45**
Wright, Bruce McMarion **3, 52**
Wynn, Albert **25**

Military
Abacha, Sani **11, 70**
Adams Early, Charity **13, 34**
Adams-Ender, Clara **40**
Alexander, Margaret Walker **22**
Amin, Idi **42**
Babangida, Ibrahim **4**
Baker, Vernon Joseph **65**
Black, Barry C. **47**
Bolden, Charles F., Jr. **7**
Brashear, Carl **29**
Brown, Erroll M. **23**
Brown, Jesse **6, 41**
Brown, Jesse Leroy **31**
Brown, Willa **40**
Bullard, Eugene **12**
Cadoria, Sherian Grace **14**
Chissano, Joaquim **7, 55, 67**
Christophe, Henri **9**
Clemmons, Reginal G. **41**
Conté, Lansana **7**
Cooke, Marcia **60**
Davis, Benjamin O., Jr. **2, 43**
Davis, Benjamin O., Sr. **4**
Drew, Alvin, Jr. **67**
Duggins, George **64**
Europe, James Reese **10**
Eyadéma, Gnassingbé **7, 52**
Fields, Evelyn J. **27**
Flipper, Henry O. **3**
Gravely, Samuel L., Jr. **5, 49**
Gregory, Frederick **8, 51**
Guéï, Robert **66**
Habré, Hissène **6**
Habyarimana, Juvenal **8**
Harris, Marcelite Jordan **16**
Honoré, Russel L. **64**
Howard, Michelle **28**
Jackson, Fred James **25**
James, Daniel, Jr. **16**
Johnson, Hazel **22**
Johnson, Shoshana **47**
Kagame, Paul **54**
Kerekou, Ahmed (Mathieu) **1**
Laraque, Paul **67**
Lawrence, Robert H., Jr. **16**
Lyles, Lester **31**
Magloire, Paul Eugène **68**
Matthews, Mark **59**
Miller, Dorie **29**
Nyanda, Siphiwe **21**
Obasanjo, Olusegun **5, 22**
Petersen, Frank E. **31**
Powell, Colin **1, 28**
Pratt, Geronimo **18**
Rawlings, Jerry **9**
Reason, J. Paul **19**
Scantlebury, Janna **47**
Snow, Samuel **71**
Stanford, John **20**
Staupers, Mabel K. **7**
Stokes, Louis **3**
Touré, Amadou Toumani **18**
Vieira, Joao **14**
Von Lipsey, Roderick K. **11**
Watkins, Perry **12**
West, Togo, D., Jr. **16**
Wilson, Jimmy **45**

Wright, Lewin 43

Music

Aaliyah 30
Ace, Johnny 36
Adams, Johnny 39
Adams, Leslie 39
Adams, Oleta 18
Adams, Yolanda 17, 67
Adderley, Julian "Cannonball" 30
Adderley, Nat 29
Ade, King Sunny 41
Akon 68
Albright, Gerald 23
Alert, Kool DJ 33
Amerie 52
Anderson, Carl 48
Anderson, Marian 2, 33
Ardoin, Alphonse 65
Armatrading, Joan 32
Armstrong, Louis 2
Armstrong, Vanessa Bell 24
Arroyo, Marina 30
Ashanti 37
Ashford, Nickolas 21
Atkins, Juan 50
Austin, Lovie 40
Austin, Patti 24
Avant, Clarence 19
Ayers, Roy 16
Badu, Erykah 22
Bailey, Buster 38
Bailey, DeFord 33
Bailey, Philip 63
Baiocchi, Regina Harris 41
Baker, Anita 21, 48
Baker, Josephine 3
Baker, LaVern 26
Ballard, Hank 41
Bambaataa, Afrika 34
Banner, David 55
Barker, Danny 32
Barnes, Roosevelt "Booba" 33
Barrino, Fantasia 53
Basie, Count 23
Bassey, Shirley 25
Batiste, Alvin 66
Battle, Kathleen 70
Baylor, Helen 36
Bebey, Francis 45
Bechet, Sidney 18
Beenie Man 32
Belafonte, Harry 4, 65
Belle, Regina 1, 51
Benét, Eric 28
Benjamin, Andre 45
Bentley, Lamont 53
Berry, Chuck 29
Beverly, Frankie 25
Beyoncé 39, 70
Bibb, Eric 49
Black Thought 63
Blake, Eubie 29
Blakey, Art 37
Blanchard, Terence 43
Bland, Bobby "Blue" 36
Bleu, Corbin 65
Blige, Mary J. 20, 34, 60
Blondy, Alpha 30
Blow, Kurtis 31
Bolden, Buddy 39
Bond, Beverly 53
Bonds, Margaret 39

Bonga, Kuenda 13
Bow Wow 35
Bradley, J. Robert 65
Brae, C. Michael 61
Brandy 14, 34
Braxton, Toni 15, 61
Bridgewater, Dee Dee 32
Brooks, Avery 9
Brooks, Hadda 40
Brown, Angela M. 54
Brown, Bobby 58
Brown, Charles 23
Brown, Clarence Gatemouth 59
Brown, Foxy 25
Brown, James 15, 60
Brown, Oscar, Jr. 53
Brown, Patrick "Sleepy" 50
Brown, Uzee 42
Bumbry, Grace 5
Burke, Solomon 31
Burleigh, Henry Thacker 56
Burns, Eddie 44
Burnside, R.L. 56
Busby, Jheryl 3
Butler, George, Jr. 70
Butler, Jerry 26
Butler, Jonathan 28
Caesar, Shirley 19
Cage, Byron 53
Calloway, Cab 1
Campbell Martin, Tisha 8, 42
Cannon, Nick 47
Carey, Mariah 32, 53, 69
Carr, Kurt 56
Carr, Leroy 49
Carroll, Diahann 9
Cartier, Xam Wilson 41
Carter, Benny 46
Carter, Betty 19
Carter, Nell 39
Carter, Regina 23
Carter, Warrick L. 27
Cee-Lo 70
Chanté, Keshia 50
Chapman, Tracy 26
Charlemagne, Manno 11
Charles, Ray 16, 48
Cheatham, Doc 17
Checker, Chubby 28
Chenault, John 40
Christie, Angella 36
Chuck D 9
Ciara 56
Clark, Mattie Moss 61
Clark-Cole, Dorinda 66
Clarke, Kenny 27
Clark-Sheard, Karen 22
Clemons, Clarence 41
Cleveland, James 19
Cliff, Jimmy 28
Clinton, George 9
Cole, Keyshia 63
Cole, Nat King 17
Cole, Natalie 17, 60
Coleman, Ornette 39, 69
Collins, Albert 12
Collins, Bootsy 31
Collins, Lyn 53
Coltrane, Alice 70
Coltrane, John 19
Coltrane, Ravi 71
Combs, Sean "Puffy" 17, 43
Common 31, 63

Cook, Charles "Doc" 44
Cook, Will Marion 40
Cooke, Sam 17
Cortez, Jayne 43
Count Basie 23
Cowboy Troy 54
Cox, Deborah 28
Cox, Ida 42
Craig, Carl 31, 71
Crawford, Randy 19
Cray, Robert 30
Creagh, Milton 27
Crocker, Frankie 29
Crothers, Scatman 19
Crouch, Andraé 27
Crouch, Stanley 11
Crowder, Henry 16
Daemyon, Jerald 64
D'Angelo 27
Dara, Olu 35
Dash, Damon 31
Dash, Darien 29
David, Craig 31, 53
Davis, Anthony 11
Davis, Gary 41
Davis, Guy 36
Davis, Miles 4
Davis, Sammy, Jr. 18
Davis, Tyrone 54
Dawson, William Levi 39
de Passe, Suzanne 25
Deezer D 53
Dennard, Brazeal 37
Dickenson, Vic 38
Diddley, Bo 39
Dixon, Dean 68
Dixon, Willie 4
DJ Jazzy Jeff 32
Dobbs, Mattiwilda 34
Domino, Fats 20
Donegan, Dorothy 19
Dorsey, Lee 65
Dorsey, Thomas 15
Downing, Will 19
Dre, Dr. 10, 14, 30
Duke, George 21
Dumas, Henry 41
Dunner, Leslie B. 45
Duplechan, Larry 55
Dupri, Jermaine 13, 46
Dupri, Jermaine 13
Dworkin, Aaron P. 52
Earthquake 55
Eckstine, Billy 28
Edmonds, Kenneth "Babyface" 10, 31
Edmonds, Tracey 16, 64
Edwards, Esther Gordy 43
Eldridge, Roy 37
Ellington, Duke 5
Elliott, Missy "Misdemeanor" 31
Escobar, Damien 56
Escobar, Tourie 56
Estes, Simon 28
Estes, Sleepy John 33
Eubanks, Kevin 15
Europe, James Reese 10
Evans, Faith 22
Eve 29
Evora, Cesaria 12
Falana, Lola 42
Farmer, Art 38

Fela 1, 42
Ferrell, Rachelle 29
Ferrer, Ibrahim 41
Fiasco, Lupe 64
50 Cent 46
Fitzgerald, Ella 8, 18
Flack, Roberta 19
Flanagan, Tommy 69
Flavor Flav 67
Foster, George "Pops" 40
Foxx, Jamie 15, 48
Franklin, Aretha 11, 44
Franklin, Kirk 15, 49
Freelon, Nnenna 32
Freeman, Paul 39
Freeman, Yvette 27
Fuqua, Antoine 35
Gaines, Grady 38
Garrett, Sean 57
Gaye, Marvin 2
Gaye, Nona 56
Gaynor, Gloria 36
George, Zelma Watson 42
Gibson, Althea 8, 43
Gibson, Tyrese 27, 62
Gil, Gilberto 53
Gill, Johnny 51
Gillespie, Dizzy 1
Ginuwine 35
Glover, Corey 34
Goapele 55
Golson, Benny 37
Gordon, Dexter 25
Gordy, Berry, Jr. 1
Gotti, Irv 39
Grae, Jean 51
Grandmaster Flash 33, 60
Graves, Denyce Antoinette 19, 57
Gray, F. Gary 14, 49
Gray, Macy 29
Greaves, William 38
Greely, M. Gasby 27
Green, Al 13, 47
Green, Grant 56
Griffin, Johnny 71
Griffin, LaShell 51
Griffiths, Marcia 29
Güines, Tata 69
Guy, Buddy 31
Haddon, Dietrick 55
Hailey, JoJo 22
Hailey, K-Ci 22
Hall, Aaron 57
Hall, Juanita 62
Hamilton, Anthony 61
Hammer, M. C. 20
Hammond, Fred 23
Hammond, Lenn 34
Hampton, Lionel 17, 41
Hancock, Herbie 20, 67
Handy, W. C. 8
Hardin Armstrong, Lil 39
Harper, Ben 34, 62
Harrell, Andre 9, 30
Harris, Barry 68
Harris, Corey 39
Hart, Alvin Youngblood 61
Hathaway, Donny 18
Hathaway, Lalah 57
Hawkins, Coleman 9
Hawkins, Erskine 14
Hawkins, Screamin' Jay 30
Hawkins, Tramaine 16

Hayes, Isaac 20, 58
Hayes, Roland 4
Hayes, Teddy 40
Heavy, D 58
Hemphill, Jessie Mae 33, 59
Henderson, Fletcher 32
Hendricks, Barbara 3, 67
Hendrix, Jimi 10
Hendryx, Nona 56
Henry, Clarence "Frogman" 46
Higginsen, Vy 65
Higginbotham, J. C. 37
Hill, Andrew 66
Hill, Lauryn 20, 53
Hinderas, Natalie 5
Hines, Earl "Fatha" 39
Hinton, Milt 30
Holiday, Billie 1
Holland-Dozier-Holland 36
Holloway, Brenda 65
Holmes, Clint 57
Holt, Nora 38
Hooker, John Lee 30
Horn, Shirley 32, 56
Horne, Lena 5
House, Son 8
Houston, Cissy 20
Houston, Whitney 7, 28
Howlin' Wolf 9
Hudson, Jennifer 63
Humphrey, Bobbi 20
Hunter, Alberta 42
Hutch, Willie 62
Hyman, Phyllis 19
Ice Cube 8, 30, 60
Ice-T 6, 31
India.Arie 34
Isley, Ronald 25, 56
Ja Rule 35
Jackson, Fred James 25
Jackson, George 19
Jackson, Hal 41
Jackson, Isaiah 3
Jackson, Janet 6, 30, 68
Jackson, John 36
Jackson, Mahalia 5
Jackson, Michael 19, 53
Jackson, Millie 25
Jackson, Milt 26
Jackson, Randy 40
Jacquet, Illinois 49
Jaheim 58
Jamal, Ahmad 69
Jamelia 51
Jamerson, James 59
James, Etta 13, 52
James, Rick 17
James, Skip 38
Jarreau, Al 21, 65
Jay-Z 27, 69
Jean, Wyclef 20
Jean-Baptiste, Marianne 17, 46
Jenkins, Ella 15
Jennings, Lyfe 56, 69
Jerkins, Rodney 31
Jimmy Jam 13
Johnson, Beverly 2
Johnson, Buddy 36
Johnson, J. J. 37
Johnson, James Weldon 5
Johnson, Johnnie 56
Johnson, Robert 2
Jones, Bobby 20
Jones, Donell 29
Jones, Elvin 14, 68
Jones, Etta 35
Jones, Hank 57
Jones, Jonah 39
Jones, Quincy 8, 30
Jones, Thad 68
Joplin, Scott 6
Jordan, Montell 23
Jordan, Ronny 26
Joyner, Matilda Sissieretta 15
Joyner, Tom 19
Kay, Ulysses 37
Kee, John P. 43
Kelley, Elijah 65
Kelly, R. 18, 44, 71
Kelis 58
Kem 47
Kendricks, Eddie 22
Kenoly, Ron 45
Kenyatta, Robin 54
Keys, Alicia 32, 68
Khan, Chaka 12, 50
Kidjo, Anjelique 50
Killings, Debra 57
King, B. B. 7
King, Coretta Scott 3, 57
Kitt, Eartha 16
Klugh, Earl 59
Knight, Gladys 16, 66
Knight, Suge 11, 30
Knowles, Tina 61
Knuckles, Frankie 42
Kool Moe Dee 37
Kravitz, Lenny 10, 34
KRS-One 34
Kuti, Femi 47
LaBelle, Patti 13, 30
Larrieux, Amel 63
Lattimore, Kenny 35
León, Tania 13
Lefel, Edith 41
Legend, John 67
Lester, Julius 9
Levert, Eddie 70
Levert, Gerald 22, 59
Lewis, Ananda 28
Lewis, Butch 71
Lewis, Henry 38
Lewis, Ramsey 35, 70
Lewis, Terry 13
Lil' Kim 28
Lil Wayne 66
Liles, Kevin 42
Lincoln, Abbey 3
Lipscomb, Mance 49
Lister, Marquita 65
Little Milton 36, 54
Little Richard 15
Little Walter 36
LL Cool J 16, 49
Locke, Eddie 44
Lopes, Lisa "Left Eye" 36
Love, Darlene 23
Love, Laura 50
Love, Ed 58
Lover, Ed 10
Lucien, Jon 66
Luckett, Letoya 61
Ludacris 37, 60
Lymon, Frankie 22
Maal, Baaba 66
Madhubuti, Haki R. 7
Mahal, Taj 39
Mahlasela, Vusi 65
Majors, Jeff 41
Makeba, Miriam 2, 50
Mario 71
Marley, Bob 5
Marley, Rita 32, 70
Marley, Ziggy 41
Marrow, Queen Esther 24
Marsalis, Branford 34
Marsalis, Delfeayo 41
Marsalis, Wynton 16
Martin, Roberta 58
Martin, Sara 38
Mary Mary 34
Mase 24
Masekela, Hugh 1
Massenburg, Kedar 23
Master P 21
Mathis, Johnny 20
Maxwell 20
May, Derrick 41
Mayfield, Curtis 2, 43
Maynor, Dorothy 19
MC Lyte 34
McBride, James 35
McClendon, Lisa 61
McClurkin, Donnie 25
McCoo, Marilyn 53
McDaniel, Hattie 5
McFerrin, Bobby 68
McKee, Lonette 12
McKinney, Nina Mae 40
McKnight, Brian 18, 34
McPherson, David 32
Memphis Minnie 33
Miles, Buddy 69
Mills, Stephanie 36
Mingus, Charles 15
Mitchell, Leona 42
Mitchell, Nicole 66
Mo', Keb' 36
Monica 21
Monk, Thelonious 1
Moore, Chante 26
Moore, Dorothy Rudd 46
Moore, Johnny B. 38
Moore, Melba 21
Moore, Undine Smith 28
Morton, Jelly Roll 29
Mos Def 30
Moses, Gilbert 12
Moss, J 64
Moten, Etta 18
Mowatt, Judy 38
Mullen, Nicole C. 45
Mumba, Samantha 29
Murphy, Eddie 4, 20, 61
Murray, Tai 47
Muse, Clarence Edouard 21
Musiq 37
Mya 35
Nas 33
Nascimento, Milton 2, 64
Nash, Johnny 40
Ndegéocello, Me'Shell 15
N'Dour, Youssou 1, 53
Neal, Raful 44
Neale, Haydain 52
Nelly 32
Neville, Aaron 21
Ne-Yo 65
Nicholas, Fayard 20, 57
Nicholas, Harold 20
Noah, Yannick 4, 60
Norman, Jessye 5
Notorious B.I.G. 20
Odetta 37
Okosuns, Sonny 71
Ol' Dirty Bastard 52
Olatunji, Babatunde 36
Oliver, Joe "King" 42
O'Neal, Shaquille 8, 30
Ongala, Remmy 9
Osborne, Jeffrey 26
Otis, Clyde 67
OutKast 35
Owens, Jack 38
P.M. Dawn 54
Palmer, Keke 68
Palmer, Rissi 65
Parker, Charlie 20
Parks, Gordon 1, 35, 58
Patton, Antwan 45
Payne, Freda 58
Pena, Paul 58
Pendergrass, Teddy 22
Peoples, Dottie 22
Perkins, Pinetop 70
Perren, Freddie 60
Perry, Ruth 19
Peterson, James 38
Peterson, Marvin "Hannibal" 27
Peterson, Oscar 52
Phillips, Helen L. 63
Phipps, Wintley 59
Portuondo, Omara 53
Powell, Maxine 8
Powell, Bud 24
Pratt, Awadagin 31
Premice, Josephine 41
Preston, Billy 39, 59
Price, Florence 37
Price, Kelly 23
Price, Leontyne 1
Pride, Charley 26
Prince 18, 65
Pritchard, Robert Starling 21
Pryor, Rain 65
Queen Latifah 1, 16, 58
Rainey, Ma 33
Ralph, Sheryl Lee 18
Randall, Alice 38
Rawls, Lou 17, 57
Razaf, Andy 19
Reagon, Bernice Johnson 7
Record, Eugene 60
Redman, Joshua 30
Reed, A. C. 36
Reed, Jimmy 38
Reese, Della 6, 20
Reeves, Dianne 32
Reid, Antonio "L.A." 28
Reid, Vernon 34
Rhoden, Wayne 70
Rhone, Sylvia 2
Rhymes, Busta 31
Richie, Lionel 27, 65
Rihanna 65
Riperton, Minnie 32
Roach, Max 21, 63
Roberts, Marcus 19
Robeson, Paul 2
Robinson, Fenton 38
Robinson, Reginald R. 53
Robinson, Smokey 3, 49

Rogers, Jimmy 38
Rollins, Sonny 37
Ross, Diana 8, 27
Ross, Isaiah "Doc" 40
Roxanne Shante 33
Rucker, Darius 34
Run-DMC 31
Rupaul 17
Rush, Otis 38
Rushen, Patrice 12
Rushing, Jimmy 37
Russell, Brenda 52
Sade 15
Sample, Joe 51
Sanders, Pharoah 64
Sangare, Oumou 18
Scarlett, Millicent 49
Schuyler, Philippa 50
Scott, George 55
Scott, Hazel 66
Scott, Jill 29
Scott, "Little" Jimmy 48
Seal 14
Seals, Son 56
Shaggy 31
Shakur, Afeni 67
Shakur, Tupac 14
Sheard, Kierra "Kiki" 61
Shirley, George 33
Short, Bobby 52
Shorty I, Ras 47
Siji 56
Silver, Horace 26
Simmons, Russell 1, 30
Simone, Nina 15, 41
Simpson, Valerie 21
Simpson-Hoffman, N'kenge 52
Sisqo 30
Sissle, Noble 29
Sister Souljah 11
Sledge, Percy 39
Sly & Robbie 34
Smith, Bessie 3
Smith, Cladys "Jabbo" 32
Smith, Dr. Lonnie 49
Smith, Lonnie Liston 49
Smith, Mamie 32
Smith, Stuff 37
Smith, Trixie 34
Smith, Will 8, 18, 53
Snoop Dogg 35
Southern, Eileen 56
Sowande, Fela 39
Sparks, Jordin 66
Spence, Joseph 49
Stampley, Micah 54
Stanford, Olivia Lee Dilworth 49
Staples, "Pops" 32
Staples, Mavis 50
Staton, Candi 27
Staton, Dakota 62
Steinberg, Martha Jean "The Queen" 28
Stew 69
Still, William Grant 37
Stone, Angie 31
Stoute, Steve 38
Strayhorn, Billy 31
Streeter, Sarah 45
Studdard, Ruben 46
Sullivan, Maxine 37
Summer, Donna 25
Sun Ra 60
Sundiata, Sekou 66
Sweat, Keith 19
Sykes, Roosevelt 20
Tait, Michael 57
Tamar-kali 63
Tamia 24, 55
Tampa Red 63
Tatum, Art 28
Taylor, Billy 23
Taylor, Cecil 70
Taylor, Koko 40
Terrell, Tammi 32
Terry, Clark 39
Tharpe, Rosetta 65
The Supremes 33
The Tempations 33
Thomas, Irma 29
Thomas, Rufus 20
Thornton, Big Mama 33
Three Mo' Tenors 35
Thurston, Stephen J. 49
Tillis, Frederick 40
Timbaland 32
Tinsley, Boyd 50
Tisdale, Wayman 50
TLC 34
Tonex 54
Tosh, Peter 9
Toussaint, Allen 60
Tresvant, Ralph 57
Turnbull, Walter 13, 60
Turner, Ike 68
Turner, Tina 6, 27
Uggams, Leslie 23
Usher 23, 56
Valentino, Bobby 62
Vandross, Luther 13, 48, 59
Vanity 67
Vaughan, Sarah 13
Vereen, Ben 4
Verrett, Shirley 66
Walker, Albertina 10, 58
Walker, Cedric "Ricky" 19
Walker, George 37
Walker, Hezekiah 34
Wallace, Sippie 1
Waller, Fats 29
Warwick, Dionne 18
Washington, Dinah 22
Washington, Grover, Jr. 17, 44
Waters, Benny 26
Waters, Ethel 7
Waters, Muddy 34
Watley, Jody 54
Watson, Johnny "Guitar" 18
Watts, Andre 42
Watts, Reggie 52
Webster, Katie 29
Wein, Joyce 62
Welch, Elisabeth 52
Wells, Mary 28
West, Kanye 52
Whalum, Kirk 37, 64
White, Barry 13, 41
White, Josh, Jr. 52
White, Maurice 29
White, Willard 53
Wilkins, Thomas Alphonso 71
will.i.am 64
Williams, Bert 18
Williams, Clarence 33
Williams, Deniece 36
Williams, Denise 40
Williams, Joe 5, 25
Williams, Mary Lou 15
Williams, Pharrell 47
Williams, Saul 31
Williams, Tony 67
Williams, Vanessa L. 4, 17
Wilson, Cassandra 16
Wilson, Charlie 31
Wilson, Gerald 49
Wilson, Jackie 60
Wilson, Mary 28
Wilson, Nancy 10
Wilson, Natalie 38
Wilson, Sunnie 7, 55
Winans, Angie 36
Winans, BeBe 14
Winans, CeCe 14, 43
Winans, Debbie 36
Winans, Marvin L. 17
Winans, Ronald 54
Winans, Vickie 24
Withers, Bill 61
Withers-Mendes, Elisabeth 64
Womack, Bobby 60
Wonder, Stevie 11, 53
Woods, Georgie 57
Woods, Scott 55
Yarbrough, Camille 40
Yoba, Malik 11
York, Vincent 40
Young Jeezy 63
Young, Lester 37

Religion

Abernathy, Ralph David 1
Adams, Yolanda 17, 67
Agyeman, Jaramogi Abebe 10, 63
Akinola, Peter Jasper 65
Akpan, Uwem 70
Al-Amin, Jamil Abdullah 6
Anthony, Wendell 25
Arinze, Francis Cardinal 19
Aristide, Jean-Bertrand 6, 45
Armstrong, Vanessa Bell 24
Austin, Junius C. 44
Banks, William 11
Baylor, Helen 36
Bell, Ralph S. 5
Ben-Israel, Ben Ami 11
Black, Barry C. 47
Blanks, Deborah K. 69
Boyd, T. B., III 6
Bryant, John R. 45
Burgess, John 46
Butts, Calvin O., III 9
Bynum, Juanita 31, 71
Cage, Byron 53
Caldwell, Kirbyjon 55
Cardozo, Francis L. 33
Carr, Kurt 56
Caesar, Shirley 19
Cannon, Katie 10
Chavis, Benjamin 6
Cleaver, Emanuel 4, 45, 68
Clements, George 2
Cleveland, James 19
Colemon, Johnnie 11
Collins, Janet 33, 64
Coltrane, Alice 70
Cone, James H. 3
Cook, Suzan D. Johnson 22
Crouch, Andraé 27
DeLille, Henriette 30
Divine, Father 7
Dyson, Michael Eric 11, 40
Elmore, Ronn 21
Fabre, Shelton 71
Farrakhan, Louis 2, 15
Fauntroy, Walter E. 11
Flake, Floyd H. 18
Forbes, James A., Jr. 71
Foreman, George 15
Franklin, C. L. 68
Franklin, Kirk 15, 49
Franklin, Robert M. 13
Gaither, Israel L. 65
Gantin, Bernardin 70
Gilmore, Marshall 46
Gomes, Peter J. 15
Gray, Darius 69
Gray, William H., III 3
Green, Al 13, 47
Gregory, Wilton 37
Grier, Roosevelt 13
Haddon, Dietrick 55
Haile Selassie 7
Harding, Vincent 67
Harris, Barbara 12
Hawkins, Tramaine 16
Hayes, James C. 10
Healy, James Augustine 30
Hooks, Benjamin L. 2
Howard, M. William, Jr. 26
Jackson, Jesse 1, 27
Jakes, Thomas "T. D." 17, 43
Jemison, Major L. 48
Johns, Vernon 38
Jones, Absalom 52
Jones, Alex 64
Jones, Bobby 20
Jones, E. Edward, Sr. 45
Jones, William A., Jr. 61
Karim, Benjamin 61
Kelly, Leontine 33
King, Barbara 22
King, Bernice 4
King, Martin Luther, Jr. 1
Kobia, Samuel 43
Lester, Julius 9
Lewis-Thornton, Rae 32
Lincoln, C. Eric 38
Little Richard 15
Long, Eddie L. 29
Lowery, Joseph 2
Lowry, A. Leon 60
Lyons, Henry 12
Majors, Jeff 41
Marino, Eugene Antonio 30
Maxis, Theresa 62
Mays, Benjamin E. 7
McClurkin, Donnie 25
McKenzie, Vashti M. 29
Morgan, Gertrude 63
Moss, J 64
Muhammad, Ava 31
Muhammad, Elijah 4
Muhammad, Khallid Abdul 10, 31
Muhammed, W. Deen 27
Murray, Cecil 12, 47
Okaalet, Peter 58
Otunga, Maurice Michael 55
Patterson, Gilbert Earl 41
Phipps, Wintley 59
Pierre, Andre 17
Powell, Adam Clayton, Jr. 3
Price, Frederick K. C. 21

Reems, Ernestine Cleveland 27
Reese, Della 6, 20
Riley, Helen Caldwell Day 13
Rugambwa, Laurean 20
Scott, George 55
Senghor, Augustin Diamancoune 66
Sentamu, John 58
Shabazz, Betty 7, 26
Sharpton, Al 21
Shaw, William J. 30
Shuttlesworth, Fred 47
Slocumb, Jonathan 52
Somé, Malidoma Patrice 10
Stallings, George A., Jr. 6
Stampley, Micah 54
Steinberg, Martha Jean "The Queen" 28
Sullivan, Leon H. 3, 30
Thurman, Howard 3
Tillard, Conrad 47
Tolton, Augustine 62
Tonex 54
Turner, Henry McNeal 5
Tutu, Desmond (Mpilo) 6, 44
Vanity 67
Vanzant, Iyanla 17, 47
Waddles, Charleszetta "Mother" 10, 49
Walker, Hezekiah 34
Walker, John T. 50
Washington, James Melvin 50
Waters, Ethel 7
Weeks, Thomas, III 70
Weems, Renita J. 44
West, Cornel 5, 33
White, Reggie 6, 50
White-Hammond, Gloria 61
Williams, Frederick (B.) 63
Williams, Hosea Lorenzo 15, 31
Williams, Preston Warren, II 64
Wilson, Natalie 38
Winans, BeBe 14
Winans, CeCe 14, 43
Winans, Marvin L. 17
Winans, Ronald 54
Wright, Jeremiah A., Jr. 45, 69
Wright, Nathan, Jr. 56
Wyatt, Addie L. 56
X, Malcolm 1
York, Dwight D. 71
Youngblood, Johnny Ray 8

Science and technology
Adams-Campbell, Lucille L. 60
Adkins, Rod 41
Adkins, Rutherford H. 21
Alcorn, George Edward, Jr. 59
Alexander, Archie Alphonso 14
Allen, Ethel D. 13
Anderson, Charles Edward 37
Anderson, Michael P. 40
Anderson, Norman B. 45
Anderson, William G(ilchrist) 57
Atim, Julian 66
Auguste, Donna 29
Auguste, Rose-Anne 13
Bacon-Bercey, June 38
Banda, Hastings Kamuzu 6, 54
Bath, Patricia E. 37
Benjamin, Regina 20
Benson, Angela 34
Black, Keith Lanier 18
Bluford, Guy 2, 35

Bluitt, Juliann S. 14
Bolden, Charles F., Jr. 7
Brown, Vivian 27
Brown, Willa 40
Bullard, Eugene 12
Callender, Clive O. 3
Campbell, Donald J. 66
Canady, Alexa 28
Cargill, Victoria A. 43
Carroll, L. Natalie 44
Carruthers, George R. 40
Carson, Benjamin 1, 35
Carter, Joye Maureen 41
Carver, George Washington 4
CasSelle, Malcolm 11
Chatard, Peter 44
Chinn, May Edward 26
Christian, Spencer 15
Cobb, W. Montague 39
Cobbs, Price M. 9
Cole, Rebecca 38
Coleman, Bessie 9
Coleman, Ken 57
Comer, James P. 6
Coney, PonJola 48
Cooper, Edward S. 6
Cornwell, Edward E., III 70
Daly, Marie Maynard 37
Davis, Allison 12
Dean, Mark 35
Deconge-Watson, Lovenia 55
Delany, Bessie 12
Delany, Martin R. 27
Dickens, Helen Octavia 14, 64
Diop, Cheikh Anta 4
Drew, Alvin, Jr. 67
Drew, Charles Richard 7
Dunham, Katherine 4, 59
Dunston, Georgia Mae 48
Edwards, Willarda V. 59
Elders, Joycelyn 6
Ellington, E. David 11
Ellis, Clarence A. 38
Emeagwali, Dale 31
Emeagwali, Philip 30
Ericsson-Jackson, Aprille 28
Fields, Evelyn J. 27
Fisher, Rudolph 17
Flipper, Henry O. 3
Flowers, Sylester 50
Foster, Henry W., Jr. 26
Freeman, Harold P. 23
Fulani, Lenora 11
Fuller, A. Oveta 43
Fuller, Arthur 27
Fuller, Solomon Carter, Jr. 15
Gaston, Marilyn Hughes 60
Gates, Sylvester James, Jr. 15
Gayle, Helene D. 3, 46
Gibson, Kenneth Allen 6
Gibson, William F. 6
Gilliard, Steve 69
Gourdine, Meredith 33
Grant, Augustus O. 71
Granville, Evelyn Boyd 36
Gray, Ida 41
Gregory, Frederick 8, 51
Griffin, Anthony 71
Griffin, Bessie Blout 43
Griffith, Patrick A. 64
Hall, Lloyd A. 8
Hammonds, Evelynn 69
Hannah, Marc 10

Harris, Mary Styles 31
Haywood, Jimmy 58
Henderson, Cornelius Langston 26
Henson, Matthew 2
Hillary, Barbara 65
Hinton, William Augustus 8
Howard, Ayanna 65
Hutcherson, Hilda Yvonne 54
Ibrahim, Mo 67
Imes, Elmer Samuel 39
Irving, Larry, Jr. 12
Jackson, Shirley Ann 12
Jarvis, Erich 67
Jawara, Dawda Kairaba 11
Jemison, Mae C. 1, 35
Jenifer, Franklyn G. 2
Johnson, Eddie Bernice 8
Johnson, Lonnie G. 32
Jones, Edith Mae Irby 65
Jones, Frederick McKinley 68
Jones, Monty 66
Jones, Randy 35
Jones, Wayne 53
Joseph, Kathie-Ann 56
Julian, Percy Lavon 6
Juma, Calestous 57
Just, Ernest Everett 3
Keith, Rachel Boone 63
Kenney, John A., Jr. 48
King, Reatha Clark 65
Kintaudi, Leon 62
Kittles, Rick 51
Knowling, Robert E., Jr. 38
Kong, B. Waine 50
Kountz, Samuel L. 10
Laryea, Thomas Davies, III 67
Latimer, Lewis H. 4
Lavizzo-Mourey, Risa 48
Lawless, Theodore K. 8
Lawrence, Robert H., Jr. 16
Leevy, Carrol M. 42
Leffall, Lasalle 3, 64
Lewis, Delano 7
Logan, Onnie Lee 14
Lushington, Augustus Nathaniel 56
Lyttle, Hulda Margaret 14
Madison, Romell 45
Malveaux, Floyd 54
Manley, Audrey Forbes 16
Massey, Walter E. 5, 45
Massie, Samuel P., Jr. 29
Maxey, Randall 46
Mays, William G. 34
Mboup, Souleymane 10
McCoy, Elijah 8
McNair, Ronald 3, 58
Mensah, Thomas 48
Miller, Warren F., Jr. 53
Millines Dziko, Trish 28
Mills, Joseph C. 51
Morgan, Garrett 1
Murray, Pauli 38
Nabrit, Samuel Milton 47
Naki, Hamilton 63
Neto, António Agostinho 43
Nour, Nawal M. 56
Ojikutu, Bisola 65
Olopade, Olufunmilayo Falusi 58
O'Leary, Hazel 6
Osborne, Na'taki 54
Pace, Betty 59
Perry, Warren 56
Person, Waverly 9, 51

Peters, Lenrie 43
Pickett, Cecil 39
Pierre, Percy Anthony 46
Pinn, Vivian Winona 49
Pitt, David Thomas 10
Poussaint, Alvin F. 5, 67
Price, Richard 51
Prothrow-Stith, Deborah 10
Quarterman, Lloyd Albert 4
Rabb, Maurice F., Jr. 58
Randolph, Linda A. 52
Reece, E. Albert 63
Reese, Milous J., Jr. 51
Riley, Helen Caldwell Day 13
Robeson, Eslanda Goode 13
Robinson, Rachel 16
Roker, Al 12, 49
Ross-Lee, Barbara 67
Samara, Noah 15
Satcher, David 7, 57
Seacole, Mary 54
Shabazz, Betty 7, 26
Shavers, Cheryl 31
Sigur, Wanda 44
Sinkford, Jeanne C. 13
Slaughter, John Brooks 53
Smith, Ian 62
Smith, Richard 51
Staples, Brent 8
Staupers, Mabel K. 7
Stewart, Ella 39
Sullivan, Louis 8
Sweet, Ossian 68
Taylor, Susan C. 62
Terrell, Dorothy A. 24
Thomas, Vivien 9
Thornton, Yvonne S. 69
Tuckson, Reed V. 71
Tyson, Neil deGrasse 15, 65
Wambugu, Florence 42
Washington, Patrice Clarke 12
Watkins, Levi, Jr. 9
Wein, Joyce 62
Welsing, Frances Cress 5
Westbrooks, Bobby 51
White-Hammond, Gloria 61
Wilkens, J. Ernest, Jr. 43
Williams, Daniel Hale 2
Williams, David Rudyard 50
Williams, O. S. 13
Wisdom, Kimberlydawn 57
Witt, Edwin T. 26
Woods, Granville T. 5
Wright, Louis Tompkins 4
Young, Roger Arliner 29

Social issues
Aaron, Hank 5
Abbot, Robert Sengstacke 27
Abbott, Diane 9
Abdul-Jabbar, Kareem 8
Abernathy, Ralph David 1
Abu-Jamal, Mumia 15
Achebe, Chinua 6
Adams, Sheila J. 25
Agyeman, Jaramogi Abebe 10, 63
Ake, Claude 30
Al-Amin, Jamil Abdullah 6
Alexander, Clifford 26
Alexander, Sadie Tanner Mossell 22
Ali, Muhammad 2, 16, 52
Allen, Ethel D. 13

Amaker, Norman **63**
Andrews, Benny **22, 59**
Angelou, Maya **1, 15**
Annan, Kofi Atta **15, 48**
Anthony, Wendell **25**
Appiah, Kwame Anthony **67**
Arac de Nyeko, Monica **66**
Archer, Dennis **7**
Aristide, Jean-Bertrand **6, 45**
Arnwine, Barbara **28**
Asante, Molefi Kete **3**
Ashe, Arthur **1, 18**
Atyam, Angelina **55**
Auguste, Rose-Anne **13**
Autrey, Wesley **68**
Azikiwe, Nnamdi **13**
Avery, Byllye Y. **66**
Ba, Mariama **30**
Baisden, Michael **25, 66**
Baker, Ella **5**
Baker, Gwendolyn Calvert **9**
Baker, Houston A., Jr. **6**
Baker, Josephine **3**
Baker, Thurbert **22**
Baldwin, James **1**
Banks, Paula A. **68**
Baraka, Amiri **1, 38**
Barbee, Lloyd Augustus **71**
Barlow, Roosevelt **49**
Barnett, Etta Moten **56**
Bass, Charlotta Spears **40**
Bates, Daisy **13**
Beals, Melba Patillo **15**
Belafonte, Harry **4, 65**
Bell, Derrick **6**
Bell, Ralph S. **5**
Bennett, Lerone, Jr. **5**
Berry, Bertice **8, 55**
Berry, Mary Frances **7**
Berrysmith, Don Reginald **49**
Bethune, Mary McLeod **4**
Betsch, MaVynee **28**
Bibb, Henry and Mary **54**
Biko, Steven **4**
Birch, Glynn R. **61**
Black, Albert **51**
Blackwell, Unita **17**
Bobo, Lawrence **60**
Bolin, Jane **22, 59**
Bond, Julian **2, 35**
Bonga, Kuenda **13**
Booker, Cory Anthony **68**
Bosley, Freeman, Jr. **7**
Boyd, Gwendolyn **49**
Boyd, John W., Jr. **20**
Boyd, T. B., III **6**
Boykin, Keith **14**
Bradley, David Henry, Jr. **39**
Braun, Carol Moseley **4, 42**
Broadbent, Hydeia **36**
Brooke, Edward **8**
Brown, Byrd **49**
Brown, Cora **33**
Brown, Eddie C. **35**
Brown, Elaine **8**
Brown, Homer S. **47**
Brown, Jesse **6, 41**
Brown, Jim **11**
Brown, Lee P. **1**
Brown, Les **5**
Brown, Lloyd Louis **10 42**
Brown, Oscar, Jr. **53**
Brown, Tony **3**

Brown, Willa **40**
Brown, Zora Kramer **12**
Brutus, Dennis **38**
Bryant, Wayne R. **6**
Bullock, Steve **22**
Bunche, Ralph J. **5**
Burks, Mary Fair **40**
Burroughs, Margaret Taylor **9**
Butler, Paul D. **17**
Butts, Calvin O., III **9**
Campbell, Bebe Moore **6, 24, 59**
Canada, Geoffrey **23**
Carby, Hazel **27**
Carmichael, Stokely **5, 26**
Carr, Johnnie **69**
Carter, Mandy **11**
Carter, Robert L. **51**
Carter, Rubin **26**
Carter, Stephen L. **4**
Cary, Lorene **3**
Cary, Mary Ann Shadd **30**
Cayton, Horace **26**
Chavis, Benjamin **6**
Chideya, Farai **14, 61**
Childress, Alice **15**
Chissano, Joaquim **7, 55, 67**
Christophe, Henri **9**
Chuck D **9**
Clark, Joe **1**
Clark, Kenneth B. **5, 52**
Clark, Septima **7**
Clay, William Lacy **8**
Clayton, Mayme Agnew **62**
Claytor, Helen **14, 52**
Cleaver, Eldridge **5**
Cleaver, Kathleen Neal **29**
Clements, George **2**
Cobbs, Price M. **9**
Cole, Johnnetta B. **5, 43**
Cole, Lorraine **48**
Collins, Barbara-Rose **7**
Collins, Patricia Hill **67**
Comer, James P. **6**
Cone, James H. **3**
Connerly, Ward **14**
Conté, Lansana **7**
Conyers, John, Jr. **4, 45**
Cook, Toni **23**
Cooke, Marvel **31**
Cooper, Anna Julia **20**
Cooper, Edward S. **6**
Cooper, Margaret J. **46**
Cosby, Bill **7, 26, 59**
Cosby, Camille **14**
Cose, Ellis **5, 50**
Creagh, Milton **27**
Crew, Spencer R. **55**
Crockett, George W., Jr. **10, 64**
Crouch, Stanley **11**
Cruse, Harold **54**
Cummings, Elijah E. **24**
Cunningham, Evelyn **23**
da Silva, Benedita **5**
Dash, Julie **4**
Davis, Angela **5**
Davis, Artur **41**
Davis, Danny K. **24**
Davis, Ossie **5, 50**
Dawson, Matel "Mat," Jr. **39**
Dawson, Michael C. **63**
DeBaptiste, George **32**
Dee, Ruby **8, 50, 68**
Delany, Martin R. **27**

Dellums, Ronald **2**
Dent, Thomas C. **50**
Diallo, Amadou **27**
Dickerson, Ernest **6**
Dieudonné **67**
Diop, Cheikh Anta **4**
Dirie, Waris **56**
Divine, Father **7**
Dixon, Margaret **14**
Dodson, Howard, Jr. **7, 52**
Dortch, Thomas W., Jr. **45**
Dove, Rita **6**
Drew, Charles Richard **7**
Du Bois, W. E. B. **3**
DuBois, Shirley Graham **21**
Duggins, George **64**
Dukes, Hazel Nell **56**
Dumas, Henry **41**
Dunham, Katherine **4, 59**
Early, Gerald **15**
Edelin, Ramona Hoage **19**
Edelman, Marian Wright **5, 42**
Edley, Christopher **2, 48**
Edwards, Harry **2**
Elder, Larry **25**
Elder, Lee **6**
Elders, Joycelyn **6**
Ellison, Ralph **7**
Esposito, Giancarlo **9**
Espy, Mike **6**
Eugene-Richard, Margie **63**
Europe, James Reese **10**
Evers, Medgar **3**
Evers, Myrlie **8**
Farmer, James **2, 64**
Farris, Isaac Newton, Jr. **63**
Farrakhan, Louis **15**
Fauntroy, Walter E. **11**
Fauset, Jessie **7**
Fela **1, 42**
Fields, C. Virginia **25**
Finner-Williams, Paris Michele **62**
Flavor Flav **67**
Fletcher, Bill, Jr. **41**
Forbes, James A., Jr. **71**
Foreman, George **15**
Forman, James **7, 51**
Fortune, T. Thomas **6**
Foster, Marie **48**
Franklin, C. L. **68**
Franklin, Hardy R. **9**
Franklin, John Hope **5**
Franklin, Robert M. **13**
Frazier, E. Franklin **10**
Fulani, Lenora **11**
Fuller, Arthur **27**
Fuller, Charles **8**
Gaines, Ernest J. **7**
Gardner, Chris **65**
Garvey, Marcus **1**
Gates, Henry Louis, Jr. **3, 38, 67**
Gayle, Helene D. **3**
George, Zelma Watson **42**
Gibson, Kenneth Allen **6**
Gibson, William F. **6**
Gilbert, Christopher **50**
Gist, Carole **1**
Goldberg, Whoopi **4, 33, 69**
Golden, Marita **19**
Golston, Allan C. **55**
Gomez, Jewelle **30**
Gomez-Preston, Cheryl **9**
Goss, Carol A. **55**

Gossett, Louis, Jr. **7**
Graham, Lawrence Otis **12**
Gray, Fred **37**
Greene, Petey **65**
Gregory, Dick **1, 54**
Gregory, Wilton **37**
Grier, Roosevelt **13**
Griffith, Mark Winston **8**
Grimké, Archibald H. **9**
Guinier, Lani **7, 30**
Guy, Rosa **5**
Guy-Sheftall, Beverly **13**
Hale, Lorraine **8**
Haley, Alex **4**
Hall, Elliott S. **24**
Hamblin, Ken **10**
Hamer, Fannie Lou **6**
Hampton, Fred **18**
Hampton, Henry **6**
Hani, Chris **6**
Hansberry, Lorraine **6**
Hansberry, William Leo **11**
Harding, Vincent **67**
Harper, Frances Ellen Watkins **11**
Harrington, Oliver W. **9**
Harris, Alice **7**
Harris, Leslie **6**
Harris, Marcelite Jordan **16**
Harris, Patricia Roberts **2**
Hastings, Alcee L. **16**
Hawkins, Augustus F. **68**
Hawkins, Steven **14**
Hayes, Dennis **54**
Haynes, George Edmund **8**
Hedgeman, Anna Arnold **22**
Height, Dorothy I. **2, 23**
Henderson, Thelton E. **68**
Henderson, Wade J. **14**
Henderson, Zelma **71**
Henry, Aaron **19**
Henry, Lenny **9, 52**
Hernandez, Aileen Clarke **13**
Hernton, Calvin C. **51**
Hill, Anita **5, 65**
Hill, Jesse, Jr. **13**
Hill, Lauryn **20, 53**
Hill, Oliver W. **24, 63**
Hilliard, Asa Grant, III **66**
Hilliard, David **7**
Holland, Endesha Ida Mae **3, 57**
hooks, bell **5**
Hooks, Benjamin L. **2**
Horne, Lena **5**
Houston, Charles Hamilton **4**
Howard, M. William, Jr. **26**
Hoyte, Lenon **50**
Hubbard, Arnette Rhinehart **38**
Huggins, Nathan Irvin **52**
Hughes, Albert **7**
Hughes, Allen **7**
Hughes, Langston **4**
Hunter-Gault, Charlayne **6, 31**
Hutchinson, Earl Ofari **24**
Hutson, Jean Blackwell **16**
Ibrahim, Mo **67**
Iceberg Slim **11**
Ice-T **6, 31**
Iman **4, 33**
Ingram, Rex **5**
Innis, Roy **5**
Irvis, K. Leroy **67**
Jackson, Edison O. **67**
Jackson, Fred James **25**

Jackson, George **14**
Jackson, Janet **6, 30, 68**
Jackson, Jesse **1, 27**
Jackson, Judith D. **57**
Jackson, Mahalia **5**
Jacob, John E. **2**
Jagan, Cheddi **16**
James, Daniel, Jr. **16**
Jealous, Benjamin **70**
Jean, Wyclef **20**
Jeffries, Leonard **8**
Johnson, Charles S. **12**
Johnson, Earvin "Magic" **3, 39**
Johnson, James Weldon **5**
Johnson, Kevin **70**
Jolley, Willie **28**
Jones, Elaine R. **7, 45**
Jones, Van **70**
Jones, William A., Jr. **61**
Jordan, Barbara **4**
Jordan, June **7, 35**
Jordan, Vernon E. **3, 35**
Joseph, Kathie-Ann **56**
Josey, E. J. **10**
Joyner, Marjorie Stewart **26**
Joyner, Tom **19**
Julian, Percy Lavon **6**
Karim, Benjamin **61**
Kaunda, Kenneth **2**
Keith, Damon J. **16**
Kennedy, Florynce **12, 33**
Khanga, Yelena **6**
Kidd, Mae Street **39**
King, B. B. **7**
King, Bernice **4**
King, Coretta Scott **3, 57**
King, Dexter **10**
King, Martin Luther, III **20**
King, Martin Luther, Jr. **1**
King, Preston **28**
King, Yolanda **6**
Kitt, Eartha **16**
Kuzwayo, Ellen **68**
Ladner, Joyce A. **42**
LaGuma, Alex **30**
Lampkin, Daisy **19**
Lane, Charles **3**
Lane, Vincent **5**
Laraque, Paul **67**
Lee, Canada **8**
Lee, Spike **5, 19**
Leland, Mickey **2**
Lester, Julius **9**
Lewis, Ananda **28**
Lewis, Delano **7**
Lewis, John **2, 46**
Lewis, Thomas **19**
Lewis-Thornton, Rae **32**
Little, Robert L. **2**
Logan, Rayford W. **40**
Long, Eddie L. **29**
Lorde, Audre **6**
Louis, Errol T. **8**
Loving, Mildred **69**
Lowery, Joseph **2**
Lowry, A. Leon **60**
Lucas, John **7**
Lucy Foster, Autherine **35**
Lucy, William **50**
Maathai, Wangari **43**
Mabuza-Suttle, Felicia **43**
Madhubuti, Haki R. **7**
Madison, Joseph E. **17**

Makeba, Miriam **2, 50**
Malone Jones, Vivian **59**
Malveaux, Julianne **32, 70**
Mandela, Nelson **1, 14**
Mandela, Winnie **2, 35**
Manley, Audrey Forbes **16**
Marable, Manning **10**
Marley, Bob **5**
Marshall, Paule **7**
Marshall, Thurgood **1, 44**
Martin, Louis E. **16**
Masekela, Barbara **18**
Masekela, Hugh **1**
Mason, Ronald **27**
Mathabane, Mark **5**
Maynard, Robert C. **7**
Mays, Benjamin E. **7**
McCabe, Jewell Jackson **10**
McCarty, Osceola **16**
McDaniel, Hattie **5**
McDougall, Gay J. **11, 43**
McKay, Claude **6**
McKenzie, Vashti M. **29**
McKinney Hammond, Michelle **51**
McKissick, Floyd B. **3**
McMurray, Georgia L. **36**
McQueen, Butterfly **6, 54**
McWhorter, John **35**
Meek, Carrie **6, 36**
Meredith, James H. **11**
Mfume, Kweisi **6, 41**
Mhlaba, Raymond **55**
Micheaux, Oscar **7**
Millender-McDonald, Juanita **21, 61**
Miller-Travis, Vernice **64**
Millines Dziko, Trish **28**
Mkapa, Benjamin **16**
Mongella, Gertrude **11**
Moore, Gwendolynne S. **55**
Moore, Harry T. **29**
Morgan, Irene **65**
Morial, Ernest "Dutch" **26**
Morrison, Toni **2**
Moses, Robert Parris **11**
Mosley, Walter **5, 25, 68**
Mossell, Gertrude Bustill **40**
Motley, Constance Baker **10, 55**
Moutoussamy-Ashe, Jeanne **7**
Mowry, Jess **7**
Muhammad, Elijah **4**
Muhammad, Khallid Abdul **10, 31**
Murphy, Laura M. **43**
Murray, Pauli **38**
Ndadaye, Melchior **7**
Nelson, Jill **6, 54**
Newton, Huey **2**
Niane, Katoucha **70**
Nkoli, Simon **60**
Nkrumah, Kwame **3**
Norman, Pat **10**
Norton, Eleanor Holmes **7**
Nour, Nawal M. **56**
Nzo, Alfred **15**
Obasanjo, Olusegun **5**
Oglesby, Zena **12**
Ojikutu, Bisola **65**
O'Leary, Hazel **6**
Osborne, Na'taki **54**
Owens, Major **6**
Page, Alan **7**
Page, Clarence **4**
Paige, Satchel **7**
Parker, Kellis E. **30**

Parker, Pat **19**
Parks, Rosa **1, 35, 56**
Parr, Russ **51**
Patterson, Frederick Douglass **12**
Patterson, Louise **25**
Patterson, Orlando **4**
Patterson, P. J. **6, 20**
Perkins, Edward **5**
Pitt, David Thomas **10**
Pleasant, Mary Ellen **9**
Plessy, Homer Adolph **31**
Pough, Terrell **58**
Poussaint, Alvin F. **5, 67**
Powell, Adam Clayton, Jr. **3**
Powell, Kevin **31**
Pratt, Geronimo **18**
Pressley, Condace L. **41**
Price, Hugh B. **9, 54**
Primus, Pearl **6**
Pritchard, Robert Starling **21**
Prothrow-Stith, Deborah **10**
Quarles, Benjamin Arthur **18**
Quigless, Helen G. **49**
Ramaphosa, Cyril **3**
Ramphele, Mamphela **29**
Ramsey, Charles H. **21, 69**
Rand, A. Barry **6**
Randolph, A. Philip **3**
Randolph, Linda A. **52**
Rangel, Charles **3, 52**
Rawlings, Nana Konadu Agyeman **13**
Reagon, Bernice Johnson **7**
Reed, Ishmael **8**
Rice, Louise Allen **54**
Rice, Norm **8**
Richards, Hilda **49**
Richardson, Rupert **67**
Riggs, Marlon **5**
Riley, Helen Caldwell Day **13**
Ringgold, Faith **4**
Robeson, Eslanda Goode **13**
Robeson, Paul **2**
Robinson, Jackie **6**
Robinson, Rachel **16**
Robinson, Randall **7, 46**
Robinson, Sharon **22**
Robinson, Spottswood W., III **22**
Roble, Abdi **71**
Rodriguez, Cheryl **64**
Rowan, Carl T. **1, 30**
Rowell, Victoria **13, 68**
Rusesabagina, Paul **60**
Rustin, Bayard **4**
Sampson, Edith S. **4**
Sané, Pierre Gabriel **21**
Sanders, Malika **48**
Sapphire **14**
Saro-Wiwa, Kenule **39**
Satcher, David **7, 57**
Savimbi, Jonas **2, 34**
Sawyer, Amos **2**
Sayles Belton, Sharon **9, 16**
Scantlebury-White, Velma **64**
Schomburg, Arthur Alfonso **9**
Seacole, Mary **54**
Seale, Bobby **3**
Sears, Stephanie **53**
Seele, Pernessa **46**
Senghor, Léopold Sédar **12**
Shabazz, Attallah **6**
Shabazz, Betty **7, 26**
Shakur, Afeni **67**

Shakur, Assata **6**
Shinhoster, Earl **32**
Shuttlesworth, Fred **47**
Sifford, Charlie **4, 49**
Simone, Nina **15, 41**
Simpson, Carole **6, 30**
Sister Souljah **11**
Sisulu, Albertina **57**
Sisulu, Sheila Violet Makate **24**
Sleet, Moneta, Jr. **5**
Smith, Anna Deavere **6**
Smith, Barbara **11**
Smith, Damu **54**
Smith, Greg **28**
Smith, Kemba **70**
Smith, Marie F. **70**
Smith, Nate **49**
Snowden, Frank M., Jr. **67**
Soyinka, Wole **4**
Spriggs, William **67**
Stallings, George A., Jr. **6**
Staupers, Mabel K. **7**
Steele, Claude Mason **13**
Steele, Shelby **13**
Stewart, Alison **13**
Stewart, Ella **39**
Stewart, Maria W. Miller **19**
Stone, Chuck **9**
Sullivan, Leon H. **3, 30**
Sutton, Percy E. **42**
Sweet, Ossian **68**
Tate, Eleanora E. **20, 55**
Taulbert, Clifton Lemoure **19**
Taylor, Mildred D. **26**
Taylor, Susan L. **10**
Terrell, Mary Church **9**
Thomas, Arthur Ray **52**
Thomas, Franklin A. **5, 49**
Thomas, Isiah **7, 26, 65**
Thompson, Bennie G. **26**
Thompson, Cynthia Bramlett **50**
Thurman, Howard **3**
Thurman, Wallace **16**
Till, Emmett **7**
Toomer, Jean **6**
Tosh, Peter **9**
Touré, Askia (Muhammad Abu Bakr el) **47**
Touré, Faya Ora Rose **56**
Tribble, Israel, Jr. **8**
Trotter, Donne E. **28**
Trotter, Monroe **9**
Tsvangirai, Morgan **26**
Tubman, Harriet **9**
Tucker, C. Delores **12, 56**
Tucker, Cynthia **15, 61**
Tucker, Rosina **14**
Tutu, Desmond **6**
Tyree, Omar Rashad **21**
Underwood, Blair **7, 27**
Van Peebles, Melvin **7**
Vanzant, Iyanla **17, 47**
Vaughn, Viola **70**
Vega, Marta Moreno **61**
Velez-Rodriguez, Argelia **56**
Vincent, Marjorie Judith **2**
Waddles, Charleszetta "Mother" **10, 49**
Walcott, Derek **5**
Walker, A'lelia **14**
Walker, Alice **1, 43**
Walker, Bernita Ruth **53**
Walker, Cedric "Ricky" **19**

Walker, Madame C. J. **7**
Wallace, Joaquin **49**
Wallace, Michele Faith **13**
Wallace, Phyllis A. **9**
Washington, Booker T. **4**
Washington, Fredi **10**
Washington, Harold **6**
Waters, Maxine **3, 67**
Wattleton, Faye **9**
Wells, Henrietta Bell **69**
Wells, James Lesesne **10**
Wells-Barnett, Ida B. **8**
Welsing, Frances Cress **5**
West, Cornel **5, 33**
White, Michael R. **5**
White, Reggie **6, 50**
White, Walter F. **4**
White, Willye **67**
White-Hammond, Gloria **61**
Wideman, John Edgar **5**
Wilkins, Roger **2**
Wilkins, Roy **4**
Williams, Armstrong **29**
Williams, Evelyn **10**
Williams, Fannie Barrier **27**
Williams, George Washington **18**
Williams, Hosea Lorenzo **15, 31**
Williams, Maggie **7, 71**
Williams, Montel **4, 57**
Williams, Patricia **11, 54**
Williams, Robert F. **11**
Williams, Stanley "Tookie" **29, 57**
Williams, Walter E. **4**
Williams, Willie L. **4**
Wilson, August **7, 33, 55**
Wilson, Phill **9**
Wilson, Sunnie **7, 55**
Wilson, William Julius **22**
Winfield, Paul **2, 45**
Winfrey, Oprah **2, 15, 61**
Withers, Ernest C. **68**
Wiwa, Ken **67**
Wolfe, George C. **6, 43**
Woodson, Robert L. **10**
Worrill, Conrad **12**
Wright, Charles H. **35**
Wright, Louis Tompkins **4**
Wright, Nathan, Jr. **56**
Wright, Richard **5**
Wyatt, Addie L. **56**
X, Malcolm **1**
Xuma, Madie Hall **59**
Yancy, Dorothy Cowser **42**
Yarbrough, Camille **40**
Yeboah, Emmanuel Ofosu **53**
Yoba, Malik **11**
Young, Andrew **3, 48**
Young, Jean Childs **14**
Young, Whitney M., Jr. **4**
Youngblood, Johnny Ray **8**
Zulu, Princess Kasune **54**

Sports

Aaron, Hank **5**
Abdul-Jabbar, Kareem **8**
Abdur-Rahim, Shareef **28**
Adams, Paul **50**
Adu, Freddy **67**
Alexander, Shaun **58**
Ali, Laila **27, 63**
Ali, Muhammad **2, 16, 52**
Allen, Marcus **20**
Amaker, Tommy **62**
Amos, John **8, 62**
Anderson, Elmer **25**
Anderson, Jamal **22**
Anderson, Mike **63**
Anderson, Viv **58**
Anthony, Carmelo **46**
Artest, Ron **52**
Ashe, Arthur **1, 18**
Ashford, Emmett **22**
Ashford, Evelyn **63**
Ashley, Maurice **15, 47**
Baines, Harold **32**
Baker, Dusty **8, 43**
Banks, Ernie **33**
Barber, Ronde **41**
Barber, Tiki **57**
Barkley, Charles **5, 66**
Barnes, Ernie **16**
Barnes, John **53**
Barnes, Steven **54**
Barney, Lem **26**
Barnhill, David **30**
Baylor, Don **6**
Beamon, Bob **30**
Beasley, Jamar **29**
Bell, James "Cool Papa" **36**
Belle, Albert **10**
Bettis, Jerome **64**
Bickerstaff, Bernie **21**
Bing, Dave **3, 59**
Blair, Paul **36**
Blake, James **43**
Blanks, Billy **22**
Blanton, Dain **29**
Bogues, Tyrone "Muggsy" **56**
Bol, Manute **1**
Bolton-Holifield, Ruthie **28**
Bonaly, Surya **7**
Bonds, Barry **6, 34, 63**
Bonds, Bobby **43**
Bowe, Riddick **6**
Brand, Elton **31**
Brandon, Terrell **16**
Branham, George, III **50**
Brashear, Donald **39**
Brathwaite, Fred **35**
Briscoe, Marlin **37**
Brock, Lou **18**
Brooks, Aaron **33**
Brooks, Derrick **43**
Brown, James **22**
Brown, Jim **11**
Brown, Sean **52**
Brown, Willard **36**
Bruce, Isaac **26**
Bryant, Kobe **15, 31, 71**
Buchanan, Ray **32**
Bush, Reggie **59**
Butler, Leroy, III **17**
Bynoe, Peter C.B. **40**
Campanella, Roy **25**
Carew, Rod **20**
Carnegie, Herbert **25**
Carter, Anson **24**
Carter, Butch **27**
Carter, Cris **21**
Carter, Joe **30**
Carter, Kenneth **53**
Carter, Rubin **26**
Carter, Vince **26**
Cash, Swin **59**
Catchings, Tamika **43**
Chamberlain, Wilt **18, 47**
Chaney, John **67**
Charleston, Oscar **39**
Cheeks, Maurice **47**
Cherry, Deron **40**
Cheruiyot, Robert **69**
Christie, Linford **8**
Claiborne, Loretta **34**
Clay, Bryan Ezra **57**
Clemons, Michael "Pinball" **64**
Clendenon, Donn **26, 56**
Clifton, Nathaniel "Sweetwater" **47**
Coachman, Alice **18**
Coleman, Leonard S., Jr. **12**
Cooper, Andy "Lefty" **63**
Cooper, Charles "Chuck" **47**
Cooper, Cynthia **17**
Cooper, Michael **31**
Copeland, Michael **47**
Corley, Tony **62**
Cottrell, Comer **11**
Crennel, Romeo **54**
Crooks, Garth **53**
Croom, Sylvester **50**
Culpepper, Daunte **32**
Cunningham, Randall **23**
Dandridge, Ray **36**
Davis, Ernie **48**
Davis, Mike **41**
Davis, Piper **19**
Davis, Shani **58**
Davis, Terrell **20**
Dawes, Dominique **11**
Day, Leon **39**
DeFrantz, Anita **37**
Devers, Gail **7**
Dickerson, Eric **27**
Dixon, George **52**
Doby, Lawrence Eugene, Sr. **16, 41**
Doig, Jason **45**
Dorrell, Karl **52**
dos Santos, Manuel Francisco **65**
Drew, Charles Richard **7**
Drexler, Clyde **4, 61**
Dumars, Joe **16, 65**
Duncan, Tim **20**
Dungy, Tony **17, 42, 59**
Dunn, Jerry **27**
Dye, Jermaine **58**
Edwards, Harry **2**
Edwards, Herman **51**
Edwards, Teresa **14**
Elder, Lee **6**
Ellerbe, Brian **22**
Elliott, Sean **26**
Ellis, Jimmy **44**
Ervin, Anthony **66**
Erving, Julius **18, 47**
Ewing, Patrick A. **17**
Farr, Mel **24**
Faulk, Marshall **35**
Felix, Allyson **48**
Fielder, Cecil **2**
Fielder, Prince Semien **68**
Flood, Curt **10**
Flowers, Vonetta **35**
Ford, Cheryl **45**
Foreman, George **1, 15**
Fowler, Reggie **51**
Fox, Rick **27**
Frazier, Joe **19**
Frazier-Lyde, Jacqui **31**
Freeman, Cathy **29**
Freeman, Marianna **23**
Fuhr, Grant **1, 49**
Fuller, Vivian **33**
Futch, Eddie **33**
Gaines, Clarence E., Sr. **55**
Gaither, Alonzo Smith (Jake) **14**
Garnett, Kevin **14, 70**
Garrison, Zina **2**
Gaston, Cito **71**
Gebrselassie, Haile **70**
Gentry, Alvin **23**
Gibson, Althea **8, 43**
Gibson, Bob **33**
Gibson, Josh **22**
Gibson, Truman K., Jr. **60**
Gilliam, Frank **23**
Gilliam, Joe **31**
Gooden, Dwight **20**
Gorden, W. C. **71**
Goss, Tom **23**
Gourdine, Meredith **33**
Gourdine, Simon **11**
Grand-Pierre, Jean-Luc **46**
Granderson, Curtis **66**
Gray, Yeshimbra "Shimmy" **55**
Green, A. C. **32**
Green, Darrell **39**
Green, Dennis **5, 45**
Greene, Joe **10**
Greene, Maurice **27**
Gregg, Eric **16**
Gregory, Ann **63**
Grier, Mike **43**
Grier, Roosevelt **1**
Griffey, Ken, Jr. **12**
Griffith, Yolanda **25**
Griffith-Joyner, Florence **28**
Gumbel, Bryant **14**
Gumbel, Greg **8**
Gwynn, Tony **18**
Hamilton, Lewis **66**
Hardaway, Anfernee (Penny) **13**
Hardaway, Tim **35**
Harris, Sylvia **70**
Harrison, Alvin **28**
Harrison, Calvin **28**
Haskins, Clem **23**
Heard, Gar **25**
Hearns, Thomas **29**
Henderson, Rickey **28**
Henry, Thierry **66**
Hickman, Fred **11**
Hill, Calvin **19**
Hill, Grant **13**
Hillary, Barbara **65**
Hilliard, Wendy **53**
Hines, Garrett **35**
Holdsclaw, Chamique **24**
Holland, Kimberly N. **62**
Holmes, Kelly **47**
Holmes, Larry **20, 68**
Holyfield, Evander **6**
Hopkins, Bernard **35, 69**
Horton, Andre **33**
Horton, Suki **33**
Howard, Desmond **16, 58**
Howard, Juwan **15**
Howard, Ryan **65**
Howard, Sherri **36**
Hunter, Billy **22**
Hunter, Torii **43**
Hyde, Cowan F. "Bubba" **47**
Iginla, Jarome **35**
Irvin, Michael **64**

Irvin, Monte **31**
Iverson, Allen **24, 46**
Jackson, Jamea **64**
Jackson, Mannie **14**
Jackson, Reggie **15**
Jackson, Tom **70**
Jacobs, Regina **38**
James, LeBron **46**
Jenkins, Fergie **46**
Jeter, Derek **27**
Johnson, Ben **1**
Johnson, Avery **62**
Johnson, Clifford "Connie" **52**
Johnson, Earvin "Magic" **3, 39**
Johnson, Jack **8**
Johnson, Kevin **70**
Johnson, Larry **28**
Johnson, Levi **48**
Johnson, Mamie "Peanut" **40**
Johnson, Michael **13**
Johnson, Rafer **33**
Johnson, Rodney Van **28**
Jones, Cobi N'Gai **18**
Jones, Ed "Too Tall" **46**
Jones, Lou **64**
Jones, Marion **21, 66**
Jones, Merlakia **34**
Jones, Randy **35**
Jones, Roy, Jr. **22**
Jordan, Michael **6, 21**
Joyner-Kersee, Jackie **5**
Justice, David **18**
Kaiser, Cecil **42**
Kanouté, Fred **68**
Keflezighi, Meb **49**
Keith, Floyd A. **61**
Kellogg, Clark **64**
Kennedy-Overton, Jayne Harris **46**
Kerry, Leon G. **46**
Kimbro, Henry A. **25**
King, Don **14**
Lacy, Sam **30, 46**
Ladd, Ernie **64**
Lanier, Bob **47**
Lanier, Willie **33**
Lankford, Ray **23**
Laraque, Georges **48**
Larkin, Barry **24**
Lashley, Bobby **63**
Lassiter, Roy **24**
Lee, Canada **8**
Lennox, Betty **31**
Leonard, Buck **67**
Leonard, Sugar Ray **15**
Leslie, Lisa **16**
Lester, Bill **42**
Lewis, Butch **71**
Lewis, Carl **4**
Lewis, Denise **33**
Lewis, Lennox **27**
Lewis, Marvin **51**
Lewis, Oliver **56**
Lewis, Ray **33**
Liston, Sonny **33**
Littlepage, Craig **35**
Lloyd, Earl **26**
Lloyd, John Henry "Pop" **30**
Lofton, James **42**
Lofton, Kenny **12**
Loroupe, Tegla **59**
Lott, Ronnie **9**
Louis, Joe **5**
Love, Nat **9**

Lowe, Sidney **64**
Lucas, John **7**
Mahorn, Rick **60**
Malone, Karl **18, 51**
Manigault, Earl "The Goat" **15**
Mariner, Jonathan **41**
Master P **21**
Mayers, Jamal **39**
Mays, Willie **3**
Mayweather, Floyd, Jr. **57**
McBride, Bryant **18**
McCarthy, Sandy **64**
McCray, Nikki **18**
McGriff, Fred **24**
McKegney, Tony **3**
McNabb, Donovan **29**
McNair, Steve **22, 47**
McNeil, Lori **1**
Metcalfe, Ralph **26**
Milla, Roger **2**
Miller, Cheryl **10**
Miller, Reggie **33**
Mills, Sam **33**
Milton, DeLisha **31**
Minor, DeWayne **32**
Mohammed, Nazr **64**
Monk, Art **38**
Montgomery, Tim **41**
Moon, Warren **8, 66**
Moorer, Michael **19**
Morgan, Joe Leonard **9**
Moses, Edwin **8**
Mosley, Shane **32**
Moss, Randy **23**
Motley, Marion **26**
Mourning, Alonzo **17, 44**
Mundine, Anthony **56**
Murray, Eddie **12**
Murray, Lenda **10**
Mutola, Maria **12**
Mutombo, Dikembe **7**
Nakhid, David **25**
Newcombe, Don **24**
Newsome, Ozzie **26**
Noah, Yannick **4, 60**
Olajuwon, Hakeem **2**
Oliver, Pam **54**
O'Neal, Shaquille **8, 30**
O'Neil, Buck **19, 59**
Onyewu, Oguchi **60**
O'Ree, Willie **5**
Ortiz, David **52**
Owens, Jesse **2**
Owens, Terrell **53**
Pace, Orlando **21**
Page, Alan **7**
Paige, Satchel **7**
Palmer, Violet **59**
Parish, Robert **43**
Parker, Jim **64**
Patterson, Floyd **19, 58**
Payne, Ulice **42**
Payton, Walter **11, 25**
Peck, Carolyn **23**
Peete, Calvin **11**
Peete, Rodney **60**
Pelé **7**
Perrot, Kim **23**
Perry, Lowell **30**
Peters, Margaret and Matilda **43**
Phillips, Teresa L. **42**
Pickett, Bill **11**
Pierce, Paul **71**

Pippen, Scottie **15**
Pollard, Fritz **53**
Powell, Mike **7**
Powell, Renee **34**
Pride, Charley **26**
Prince, Ron **64**
Prince, Tayshaun **68**
Puckett, Kirby **4, 58**
Quirot, Ana **13**
Randolph, Willie **53**
Rashad, Ahmad **18**
Ready, Stephanie **33**
Reese, Pokey **28**
Regis, Cyrille **51**
Rhoden, William C. **67**
Rhodes, Ray **14**
Ribbs, Willy T. **2**
Rice, Jerry **5, 55**
Richards, Sanya **66**
Richardson, Donna **39**
Richardson, Nolan **9**
Richmond, Mitch **19**
Rivers, Glenn "Doc" **25**
Robertson, Oscar **26**
Robinson, David **24**
Robinson, Eddie G. **10, 61**
Robinson, Frank **9**
Robinson, Jackie **6**
Robinson, Sugar Ray **18**
Robinson, Will **51, 69**
Rock, The **29, 66**
Rodman, Dennis **12, 44**
Rollins, Jimmy **70**
Ronaldinho **69**
Rose, Lionel **56**
Rubin, Chanda **37**
Rudolph, Wilma **4**
Russell, Bill **8**
St. Julien, Marlon **29**
Salvador, Bryce **51**
Sampson, Charles **13**
Sanders, Barry **1, 53**
Sanders, Deion **4, 31**
Sapp, Warren **38**
Sayers, Gale **28**
Scott, Stuart **34**
Scott, Wendell Oliver, Sr. **19**
Scurry, Briana **27**
Sharper, Darren **32**
Sheffield, Gary **16**
Shell, Art **1, 66**
Shippen, John **43**
Showers, Reggie **30**
Sifford, Charlie **4, 49**
Silas, Paul **24**
Simmons, Bob **29**
Simpson, O. J. **15**
Singletary, Mike **4**
Smith, Emmitt **7**
Smith, Hilton **29**
Smith, Lovie **66**
Smith, Stephen A. **69**
Smith, Tubby **18**
Solomon, Jimmie Lee **38**
Sosa, Sammy **21, 44**
Spiller, Bill **64**
Sprewell, Latrell **23**
Stackhouse, Jerry **30**
Staley, Dawn **57**
Stargell, Willie **29**
Stearns, Norman "Turkey" **31**
Steward, Emanuel **18**
Stewart, James "Bubba", Jr. **60**

Stewart, Kordell **21**
Stingley, Darryl **69**
Stone, Toni **15**
Stoudemire, Amaré **59**
Strahan, Michael **35**
Strawberry, Darryl **22**
Stringer, C. Vivian **13, 66**
Stringer, Korey **35**
Swann, Lynn **28**
Swoopes, Sheryl **12, 56**
Taylor, Jason **70**
Taylor, Jermain **60**
Taylor, Lawrence **25**
Taylor, Marshall Walter "Major" **62**
Tergat, Paul **59**
Thomas, Debi **26**
Thomas, Derrick **25**
Thomas, Emmitt **71**
Thomas, Frank **12, 51**
Thomas, Isiah **7, 26, 65**
Thompson, Tina **25**
Thrower, Willie **35**
Thugwane, Josia **21**
Tirico, Mike **68**
Tisdale, Wayman **50**
Tomlinson, LaDainian **65**
Tunnell, Emlen **54**
Tyson, Mike **28, 44**
Unseld, Wes **23**
Upshaw, Gene **18, 47**
Ussery, Terdema, II **29**
Vick, Michael **39**
Virgil, Ozzie **48**
Wade, Dwyane **61**
Walker, Herschel **1, 69**
Wallace, Ben **54**
Wallace, Perry E. **47**
Wallace, Rasheed **56**
Ward, Andre **62**
Ware, Andre **37**
Washington, Gene **63**
Washington, Kenny **50**
Washington, MaliVai **8**
Watson, Bob **25**
Watts, J. C., Jr. **14, 38**
Weah, George **58**
Weathers, Carl **10**
Webber, Chris **15, 30, 59**
Weekes, Kevin **67**
Westbrook, Peter **20**
Whitaker, Pernell **10**
White, Bill **1, 48**
White, Jesse **22**
White, Reggie **6, 50**
White, Willye **67**
Whitfield, Fred **23**
Williams, Lauryn **58**
Wilkens, Lenny **11**
Whitfield, Mal **60**
Wilbon, Michael **68**
Williams, Doug **22**
Williams, Ken **68**
Williams, Natalie **31**
Williams, Serena **20, 41**
Williams, Stevie **71**
Williams, Venus **17, 34, 62**
Williamson, Fred **67**
Willingham, Tyrone **43**
Willis, Bill **68**
Willis, Dontrelle **55**
Wilson, Sunnie **7, 55**
Winfield, Dave **5**
Winkfield, Jimmy **42**

Woodruff, John 68
Woods, Tiger 14, 31
Woodward, Lynette 67
Worthy, James 49
Wright, Rayfield 70
Yeboah, Emmanuel Ofosu 53
Young, Donald, Jr. 57
Young, Jimmy 54

Television
Akil, Mara Brock 60
Akinnuoye-Agbaje, Adewale 56
Alexander, Khandi 43
Allen, Byron 3
Allen, Debbie 13, 42
Allen, Marcus 20
Amos, John 8, 62
Anderson, Anthony 51
Anderson, Eddie "Rochester" 30
Arkadie, Kevin 17
Arnez J 53
Arnold, Tichina 63
Babatunde, Obba 35
Banks, Michelle 59
Banks, William 11
Barclay, Paris 37
Barden, Don H. 9
Bassett, Angela 6, 23, 62
Beach, Michael 26
Beaton, Norman 14
Beauvais, Garcelle 29
Belafonte, Harry 4, 65
Bellamy, Bill 12
Bennett, Louise 69
Bentley, Lamont 53
Berry, Bertice 8, 55
Berry, Fred "Rerun" 48
Berry, Halle 4, 19, 57
Blackmon, Brenda 58
Blackwood, Maureen 37
Blacque, Taurean 58
Blake, Asha 26
Bleu, Corbin 65
Bonet, Lisa 58
Boston, Kelvin E. 25
Bowser, Yvette Lee 17
Bradley, Ed 2, 59
Brady, Wayne 32, 71
Brandy 14, 34
Braugher, Andre 13, 58
Bridges, Todd 37
Brooks, Avery 9
Brooks, Golden 62
Brooks, Hadda 40
Brooks, Mehcad 62
Brown, James 22
Brown, Joe 29
Brown, Les 5
Brown, Tony 3
Brown, Vivian 27
Brown, Warren 61
Browne, Roscoe Lee 66
Bruce, Bruce 56
Burnett, Charles 16, 68
Burton, LeVar 8
Byrd, Eugene 64
Byrd, Robert 11
Caldwell, Benjamin 46
Cameron, Earl 44
Campbell, Naomi 1, 31
Campbell Martin, Tisha 8, 42
Cannon, Nick 47
Cannon, Reuben 50

Carroll, Diahann 9
Carson, Lisa Nicole 21
Carter, Nell 39
Cash, Rosalind 28
Cedric the Entertainer 29, 60
Chappelle, Dave 50
Cheadle, Don 19, 52
Chestnut, Morris 31
Chideya, Farai 14, 61
Christian, Spencer 15
Ciara, Barbara 69
Clash, Kevin 14
Clayton, Xernona 3, 45
Cole, Nat King 17
Cole, Natalie 17, 60
Coleman, Gary 35
Corbi, Lana 42
Cornelius, Don 4
Cosby, Bill 7, 26, 59
Crothers, Scatman 19
Curry, Mark 17
Curtis-Hall, Vondie 17
Davidson, Tommy 21
Davis, Eisa 68
Davis, Ossie 5, 50
Davis, Viola 34
de Passe, Suzanne 25
Dee, Ruby 8, 50, 68
Deezer D 53
Devine, Loretta 24
Dickerson, Eric 27
Dickerson, Ernest 6
Diggs, Taye 25, 63
Dixon, Ivan 69
Dourdan, Gary 37
Dre, Dr. 10
Duke, Bill 3
Dungey, Merrin 62
Dutton, Charles S. 4, 22
Earthquake 55
Ejiofor, Chiwetel 67
Elba, Idris 49
Elder, Larry 25
Elise, Kimberly 32
Emmanuel, Alphonsia 38
Ephriam, Mablean 29
Epperson, Sharon 54
Erving, Julius 18, 47
Esposito, Giancarlo 9
Eubanks, Kevin 15
Evans, Harry 25
Faison, Donald 50
Faison, Frankie 55
Falana, Lola 42
Fargas, Antonio 50
Fields, Kim 36
Fishburne, Laurence 4, 22, 70
Flavor Flav 67
Fox, Rick 27
Foxx, Jamie 15, 48
Foxx, Redd 2
Frazier, Kevin 58
Freeman, Aaron 52
Freeman, Al, Jr. 11
Freeman, Morgan 2, 20, 62
Freeman, Yvette 27
Gaines, Ernest J. 7
Gibson, Tyrese 27, 62
Givens, Adele 62
Givens, Robin 4, 25, 58
Glover, Danny 3, 24
Glover, Savion 14
Goldberg, Whoopi 4, 33, 69

Goode, Mal 13
Gooding, Cuba, Jr. 16, 62
Gordon, Ed 10, 53
Gossett, Louis, Jr. 7
Gray, Darius 69
Greely, M. Gasby 27
Greene, Petey 65
Grier, David Alan 28
Grier, Pam 9, 31
Guillaume, Robert 3, 48
Gumbel, Bryant 14
Gumbel, Greg 8
Gunn, Moses 10
Guy, Jasmine 2
Haley, Alex 4
Hall, Arsenio 58
Hamilton, Lisa Gay 71
Hampton, Henry 6
Harewood, David 52
Hardison, Kadeem 22
Harper, Hill 32, 65
Harrell, Andre 9, 30
Harris, Naomie 55
Harris, Robin 7
Harvey, Steve 18, 58
Hatchett, Glenda 32
Hayes, Isaac 20, 58
Haynes, Trudy 44
Haysbert, Dennis 42
Hemsley, Sherman 19
Henriques, Julian 37
Henry, Lenny 9, 52
Henson, Darrin 33
Hickman, Fred 11
Hill, Dulé 29
Hill, Lauryn 20, 53
Hinderas, Natalie 5
Hines, Gregory 1, 42
Holmes, Amy 69
Holt, Lester 66
Horne, Lena 5
Hounsou, Djimon 19, 45
Houston, Whitney 7, 28
Howard, Sherri 36
Howard, Terrence 59
Huggins, Edie 71
Hughley, D. L. 23
Hunter-Gault, Charlayne 6, 31
Hyman, Earle 25
Ice-T 6, 31
Ifill, Gwen 28
Iman 4, 33
Ingram, Rex 5
Jackson, George 19
Jackson, Janet 6, 30, 68
Jackson, Jesse 1
Jackson, Randy 40
Jackson, Tom 70
Jarret, Vernon D. 42
Joe, Yolanda 21
Johnson, Beverly 2
Johnson, Linton Kwesi 37
Johnson, Robert L. 3, 39
Johnson, Rodney Van 28
Jones, Bobby 20
Jones, James Earl 3, 49
Jones, Orlando 30
Jones, Quincy 8, 30
Kaufman, Monica 66
Kelley, Malcolm David 59
Kennedy-Overton, Jayne Harris 46
Keys, Alicia 32, 68
King, Gayle 19

King, Regina 22, 45
King, Woodie, Jr. 27
Kirby, George 14
Kitt, Eartha 16
Knight, Gladys 16, 66
Kodjoe, Boris 34
Kotto, Yaphet 7
La Salle, Eriq 12
LaBelle, Patti 13, 30
Langhart Cohen, Janet 19, 60
Lathan, Sanaa 27
Lawrence, Martin 6, 27, 60
Lawson, Jennifer 1, 50
Lemmons, Kasi 20
Lesure, James 64
Lewis, Ananda 28
Lewis, Byron E. 13
Lewis, Emmanuel 36
Lil' Kim 28
Lindo, Delroy 18, 45
LisaRaye 27
LL Cool J 16, 49
Lofton, James 42
Long, Loretta 58
Long, Nia 17
Lover, Ed 10
Luke, Derek 61
Lumbly, Carl 47
Mabrey, Vicki 26
Mabuza-Suttle, Felicia 43
Mac, Bernie 29, 61
Madison, Paula 37
Malco, Romany 71
Manigault-Stallworth, Omarosa 69
Martin, Helen 31
Martin, Jesse L. 31
Mathis, Greg 26
Mayo, Whitman 32
McCoo, Marilyn 53
McCrary Anthony, Crystal 70
McDaniel, Hattie 5
McEwen, Mark 5
McFarland, Roland 49
McGlowan, Angela 64
McKee, Lonette 12
McKenzie, Vashti M. 29
McKinney, Nina Mae 40
McQueen, Butterfly 6, 54
Meadows, Tim 30
Mercado-Valdes, Frank 43
Merkerson, S. Epatha 47
Michele, Michael 31
Mickelbury, Penny 28
Miller, Cheryl 10
Mitchell, Brian Stokes 21
Mitchell, Kel 66
Mitchell, Russ 21
Mo'Nique 35
Mooney, Paul 37
Moore, Chante 26
Moore, Melba 21
Moore, Shemar 21
Morgan, Joe Leonard 9
Morgan, Tracy 61
Morris, Garrett 31
Morris, Greg 28
Morton, Joe 18
Mos Def 30
Moses, Gilbert 12
Moss, Carlton 17
Murphy, Eddie 4, 20, 61
Muse, Clarence Edouard 21
Myles, Kim 69

Nash, Johnny 40
Nash, Niecy 66
Neal, Elise 29
Nichols, Nichelle 11
Nissel, Angela 42
Neville, Arthel 53
Norman, Christina 47
Norman, Maidie 20
Odetta 37
Okonedo, Sophie 67
Oliver, Pam 54
Onwurah, Ngozi 38
Orman, Roscoe 55
Palmer, Keke 68
Parker, Nicole Ari 52
Parr, Russ 51
Payne, Allen 13
Peete, Holly Robinson 20
Peete, Rodney 60
Perkins, Tony 24
Perrineau, Harold, Jr. 51
Perry, Lowell 30
Perry, Tyler 40
Phifer, Mekhi 25
Pickens, James, Jr. 59
Pinckney, Sandra 56
Pinkett Smith, Jada 10, 41
Pinkston, W. Randall 24
Pitts, Byron 71
Poitier, Sydney Tamiia 65
Price, Frederick K.C. 21
Price, Hugh B. 9, 54
Quarles, Norma 25
Queen Latifah 1, 16, 58
Quivers, Robin 61
Ralph, Sheryl Lee 18
Randle, Theresa 16
Rashad, Ahmad 18
Rashad, Phylicia 21
Raven 44
Ray, Gene Anthony 47
Reddick, Lance 52
Reese, Della 6, 20
Reid, Tim 56
Reuben, Gloria 15
Reynolds, Star Jones 10, 27, 61
Rhimes, Shonda Lynn 67
Ribeiro, Alfonso 17
Richards, Beah 30
Richardson, Donna 39
Richardson, LaTanya 71
Richardson, Salli 68
Ridley, John 69
Roberts, Deborah 35
Roberts, Robin 16, 54
Robinson, Matt 69
Robinson, Max 3
Robinson, Shaun 36
Rochon, Lela 16
Rock, Chris 3, 22, 66
Rock, The 29, 66
Rodgers, Johnathan 6, 51
Rodrigues, Percy 68
Roker, Al 12, 49
Roker, Roxie 68
Rolle, Esther 13, 21
Rollins, Howard E., Jr. 16
Ross, Diana 8, 27
Ross, Tracee Ellis 35
Roundtree, Richard 27
Rowan, Carl T. 1, 30
Rowell, Victoria 13, 68
Rudolph, Maya 46

Rupaul 17
Russell, Bill 8
Russell, Nipsey 66
St. Jacques, Raymond 8
St. John, Kristoff 25
St. Patrick, Mathew 48
Salters, Lisa 71
Sanford, Isabel 53
Schultz, Michael A. 6
Scott, Hazel 66
Scott, Stuart 34
Shaw, Bernard 2, 28
Shepherd, Sherri 55
Simmons, Henry 55
Simpson, Carole 6, 30
Simpson, O. J. 15
Sinbad 1, 16
Smiley, Tavis 20, 68
Smith, Anjela Lauren 44
Smith, B(arbara) 11
Smith, Ian 62
Smith, Roger Guenveur 12
Smith, Will 8, 18, 53
Stewart, Alison 13
Stokes, Carl B. 10
Stone, Chuck 9
Sykes, Wanda 48
Syler, Rene 53
Swann, Lynn 28
Tate, Larenz 15
Taylor, Jason 70
Taylor, Karin 34
Taylor, Meshach 4
Taylor, Regina 9, 46
Thigpen, Lynne 17, 41
Thomas-Graham, Pamela 29
Thomason, Marsha 47
Thompson, Kenan 52
Thoms, Tracie 61
Tirico, Mike 68
Torres, Gina 52
Torry, Guy 31
Toussaint, Lorraine 32
Townsend, Robert 4, 23
Tucker, Chris 13, 23, 62
Tunie, Tamara 63
Tyler, Aisha N. 36
Tyson, Cicely 7, 51
Uggams, Leslie 23
Underwood, Blair 7, 27
Union, Gabrielle 31
Usher 23, 56
Van Peebles, Mario 2, 51
Van Peebles, Melvin 7
Vaughn, Countess 53
Vereen, Ben 4
Walker, Eamonn 37
Ware, Andre 37
Warfield, Marsha 2
Warner, Malcolm-Jamal 22, 36
Warren, Michael 27
Warwick, Dionne 18
Washington, Denzel 1, 16
Washington, Isaiah 62
Watson, Carlos 50
Wattleton, Faye 9
Watts, Rolonda 9
Wayans, Damon 8, 41
Wayans, Keenen Ivory 18
Wayans, Marlon 29
Wayans, Shawn 29
Weathers, Carl 10
Whack, Rita Coburn 36

Whitfield, Lynn 1, 18
Wilbon, Michael 68
Wilkins, Roger 2
Williams, Armstrong 29
Williams, Billy Dee 8
Williams, Clarence, III 26
Williams, Juan 35
Williams, Malinda 57
Williams, Montel 4, 57
Williams, Russell, II 70
Williams, Samm-Art 21
Williams, Vanessa A. 32, 66
Williams, Vanessa L. 4, 17
Williams, Wendy 62
Williamson, Mykelti 22
Wilson, Chandra 57
Wilson, Debra 38
Wilson, Dorien 55
Wilson, Flip 21
Winfield, Paul 2, 45
Winfrey, Oprah 2, 15, 61
Witherspoon, John 38
Wright, Jeffrey 54
Yarbrough, Cedric 51
Yoba, Malik 11

Theater
Adams, Osceola Macarthy 31
Ailey, Alvin 8
Alexander, Khandi 43
Allen, Debbie 13, 42
Amos, John 8, 62
Anderson, Carl 48
Andrews, Bert 13
Angelou, Maya 1, 15
Anthony, Trey 63
Arkadie, Kevin 17
Armstrong, Vanessa Bell 24
Arnez J 53
Babatunde, Obba 35
Bandele, Biyi 68
Baraka, Amiri 1, 38
Barnett, Etta Moten 56
Barrett, Lindsay 43
Bassett, Angela 6, 23, 62
Beach, Michael 26
Beaton, Norman 14
Belafonte, Harry 4, 65
Bennett, Louise 69
Borders, James 9
Branch, William Blackwell 39
Brooks, Avery 9
Brown, Oscar, Jr. 53
Browne, Roscoe Lee 66
Bruce, Bruce 56
Caldwell, Benjamin 46
Calloway, Cab 14
Cameron, Earl 44
Campbell, Naomi 1
Campbell, Tisha 8
Carroll, Diahann 9
Carroll, Vinnette 29
Carter, Nell 39
Cash, Rosalind 28
Cheadle, Don 19, 52
Chenault, John 40
Childress, Alice 15
Clarke, Hope 14
Cleage, Pearl 17, 64
Cook, Will Marion 40
Corthron, Kia 43
Curtis-Hall, Vondie 17
Dadié, Bernard 34

David, Keith 27
Davis, Eisa 68
Davis, Ossie 5, 50
Davis, Sammy, Jr. 18
Davis, Viola 34
Dee, Ruby 8, 50, 68
Devine, Loretta 24
Dieudonné 67
Diggs, Taye 25, 63
Dixon, Ivan 69
Dodson, Owen Vincent 38
Dourdan, Gary 37
Duke, Bill 3
Dunham, Katherine 4, 59
Dutton, Charles S. 4, 22
Ejiofor, Chiwetel 67
Elba, Idris 49
Elder, Lonne, III 38
Emmanuel, Alphonsia 38
Epps, Mike 60
Esposito, Giancarlo 9
Europe, James Reese 10
Faison, Frankie 55
Falana, Lola 42
Fargas, Antonio 50
Fields, Felicia P. 60
Fishburne, Laurence 4, 22, 70
Franklin, J. E. 44
Freeman, Aaron 52
Freeman, Al, Jr. 11
Freeman, Morgan 2, 20, 62
Freeman, Yvette 27
Fuller, Charles 8
Givens, Adele 62
Glover, Danny 1, 24
Glover, Savion 14
Goldberg, Whoopi 4, 33, 69
Gordone, Charles 15
Gossett, Louis, Jr. 7
Graves, Denyce Antoinette 19, 57
Greaves, William 38
Grier, Pam 9, 31
Guillaume, Robert 3, 48
Gunn, Moses 10
Guy, Jasmine 2
Hall, Juanita 62
Hamilton, Lisa Gay 71
Hamlin, Larry Leon 49, 62
Hansberry, Lorraine 6
Harewood, David 52
Harris, Robin 7
Hayes, Teddy 40
Hemsley, Sherman 19
Higginsen, Vy 65
Hill, Dulé 29
Hill, Errol 40
Hines, Gregory 1, 42
Holder, Laurence 34
Holland, Endesha Ida Mae 3, 57
Horne, Lena 5
Hyman, Earle 25
Hyman, Phyllis 19
Ingram, Rex 5
Jackson, Millie 25
Jackson, Samuel 8, 19, 63
Jamison, Judith 7, 67
Jean-Baptiste, Marianne 17, 46
Johnson, Je'Caryous 63
Jones, James Earl 3, 49
Jones, Sarah 39
Joyner, Matilda Sissieretta 15
Kente, Gibson 52
Khumalo, Leleti 51

King, Woodie, Jr. 27
King, Yolanda 6
Kitt, Eartha 16
Kotto, Yaphet 7
La Salle, Eriq 12
Lampley, Oni Faida 43, 71
Lathan, Sanaa 27
Lee, Canada 8
Leggs, Kingsley 62
Lenox, Adriane 59
Lemmons, Kasi 20
LeNoire, Rosetta 37
Leon, Kenny 10
Lester, Adrian 46
Letson, Al 39
Lincoln, Abbey 3
Lindo, Delroy 18, 45
Lister, Marquita 65
Mabley, Jackie "Moms" 15
Marrow, Queen Esther 24
Martin, Helen 31
Martin, Jesse L. 31
McDaniel, Hattie 5
McDonald, Audra 20, 62
McFarlan, Tyron 60
McKee, Lonette 12
McQueen, Butterfly 6, 54
Mickelbury, Penny 28
Mills, Florence 22
Milner, Ron 39
Mitchell, Brian Stokes 21
Mollel, Tololwa 38
Moore, Melba 21
Morgan, Tracy 61
Moses, Gilbert 12
Moss, Carlton 17
Moss, Preacher 63
Moten, Etta 18
Muse, Clarence Edouard 21
Nicholas, Fayard 20, 57
Nicholas, Harold 20
Norman, Maidie 20
Nottage, Lynn 66
Ntshona, Winston 52
Okonedo, Sophie 67
Orlandersmith, Dael 42
Parks, Suzan-Lori 34
Payne, Allen 13
Perrineau, Harold, Jr. 51
Perry, Tyler 54
Powell, Maxine 8
Premice, Josephine 41
Primus, Pearl 6
Pryor, Rain 65
Ralph, Sheryl Lee 18
Randle, Theresa 16
Rashad, Phylicia 21
Raven 44
Reese, Della 6, 20
Reid, Tim 56
Rhames, Ving 14, 50
Richards, Beah 30
Richards, Lloyd 2
Richardson, Desmond 39
Richardson, LaTanya 71
Robeson, Paul 2
Rolle, Esther 13, 21
Rollins, Howard E., Jr. 16
Rose, Anika Noni 70
Rotimi, Ola 1
St. Jacques, Raymond 8
Schultz, Michael A. 6
Scott, Harold Russell, Jr. 61

Sanford, Isabel 53
Shabazz, Attallah 6
Shange, Ntozake 8
Slocumb, Jonathan 52
Smiley, Rickey 59
Smith, Anjela Lauren 44
Smith, Anna Deavere 6, 44
Smith, Roger Guenveur 12
Snipes, Wesley 3, 24, 67
Sommore 61
Soyinka, Wole 4
Stew 69
Sundiata, Sekou 66
Talbert, David 34
Taylor, Meshach 4
Taylor, Regina 9, 46
Taylor, Ron 35
Thigpen, Lynne 17, 41
Thompson, Tazewell 13
Thurman, Wallace 16
Torres, Gina 52
Toussaint, Lorraine 32
Townsend, Robert 4, 23
Tyson, Cicely 7, 51
Uggams, Leslie 23
Underwood, Blair 7, 27
Van Peebles, Melvin 7
Vance, Courtney B. 15, 60
Vereen, Ben 4
Verrett, Shirley 66
Walcott, Derek 5
Walker, Eamonn 37
Ward, Douglas Turner 42
Washington, Denzel 1, 16
Washington, Fredi 10
Waters, Ethel 7
Watts, Reggie 52
Whitaker, Forest 2, 49, 67
White, Willard 53
Whitfield, Lynn 18
Williams, Bert 18
Williams, Billy Dee 8
Williams, Clarence, III 26
Williams, Samm-Art 21
Williams, Vanessa L. 4, 17
Williamson, Mykelti 22
Wilson, August 7, 33, 55
Wilson, Dorien 55
Winfield, Paul 2, 45
Withers-Mendes, Elisabeth 64
Wolfe, George C. 6, 43
Woodard, Alfre 9
Wright, Jeffrey 54
Yarbrough, Cedric 51

Writing

Abrahams, Peter 39
Abu-Jamal, Mumia 15
Achebe, Chinua 6
Adams, Jenoyne 60
Adams-Ender, Clara 40
Adichie, Chimamanda Ngozi 64
Aidoo, Ama Ata 38
Ake, Claude 30
Akpan, Uwem 70
Al-Amin, Jamil Abdullah 6
Alexander, Margaret Walker 22
Ali, Hana Yasmeen 52
Ali, Mohammed Naseehu 60
Allen, Debbie 13, 42
Allen, Robert L. 38
Allen, Samuel W. 38
Amadi, Elechi 40

Ames, Wilmer 27
Anderson, Ho Che 54
Andrews, Raymond 4
Angelou, Maya 1, 15
Ansa, Tina McElroy 14
Anthony, Michael 29
Appiah, Kwame Anthony 67
Arac de Nyeko, Monica 66
Aristide, Jean-Bertrand 6, 45
Arkadie, Kevin 17
Armah, Ayi Kwei 49
Asante, Molefi Kete 3
Ashe, Arthur 1, 18
Ashley-Ward, Amelia 23
Asim, Jabari 71
Atkins, Cholly 40
Atkins, Russell 45
Aubert, Alvin 41
Auguste, Arnold A. 47
Awoonor, Kofi 37
Azikiwe, Nnamdi 13
Ba, Mariama 30
Bahati, Wambui 60
Bailey, Chauncey 68
Baiocchi, Regina Harris 41
Baisden, Michael 25, 66
Baker, Augusta 38
Baker, Houston A., Jr. 6
Baldwin, James 1
Ballard, Allen Butler, Jr. 40
Bambara, Toni Cade 10
Bandele, Asha 36
Bandele, Biyi 68
Baquet, Dean 63
Baraka, Amiri 1, 38
Barnes, Steven 54
Barnett, Amy Du Bois 46
Barrax, Gerald William 45
Barrett, Lindsay 43
Bass, Charlotta Spears 40
Bates, Karen Grigsby 40
Beah, Ishmael 69
Beals, Melba Patillo 15
Bebey, Francis 45
Beckham, Barry 41
Bell, Derrick 6
Bell, James Madison 40
Benberry, Cuesta 65
Bennett, George Harold "Hal" 45
Bennett, Gwendolyn B. 59
Bennett, Lerone, Jr. 5
Bennett, Louise 69
Benson, Angela 34
Berry, James 41
Berry, Mary Frances 7
Beti, Mongo 36
Bishop, Maurice 39
Blair, Jayson 50
Bland, Eleanor Taylor 39
Blassingame, John Wesley 40
Blockson, Charles L. 42
Bluitt, Juliann S. 14
Bolden, Tonya 32
Bontemps, Arna 8
Booker, Simeon 23
Borders, James 9
Boston, Lloyd 24
Boyd, Gerald M. 32, 59
Boyd, Suzanne 52
Bradley, David Henry, Jr. 39
Bradley, Ed 2, 59
Braithwaite, William Stanley 52
Branch, William Blackwell 39

Brand, Dionne 32
Brathwaite, Kamau 36
Brawley, Benjamin 44
Breeze, Jean "Binta" 37
Bridges, Sheila 36
Brimmer, Andrew F. 2, 48
Briscoe, Connie 15
Britt, Donna 28
Brooks, Gwendolyn 1, 28
Brower, William 49
Brown, Cecil M. 46
Brown, Claude 38
Brown, Elaine 8
Brown, Les 5
Brown, Lloyd Louis 10, 42
Brown, Marie Dutton 12
Brown, Sterling Allen 10, 64
Brown, Tony 3
Brown, Wesley 23
Browne, Roscoe Lee 66
Broyard, Anatole 68
Broyard, Bliss 68
Brutus, Dennis 38
Bryan, Ashley F. 41
Buckley, Gail Lumet 39
Bullins, Ed 25
Bunche, Ralph J. 5
Bunkley, Anita Richmond 39
Burgess, Marjorie L. 55
Burroughs, Margaret Taylor 9
Butler, Octavia 8, 43, 58
Bynum, Juanita 31, 71
Césaire, Aimé 48, 69
Caldwell, Earl 60
Campbell, Bebe Moore 6, 24, 59
Carby, Hazel 27
Carmichael, Stokely 5, 26
Carroll, Vinnette 29
Cartíer, Xam Wilson 41
Carter, Joye Maureen 41
Carter, Martin 49
Carter, Stephen L. 4
Cartey, Wilfred 47
Cary, Lorene 3
Cary, Mary Ann Shadd 30
Cayton, Horace 26
Chadiha, Jeffri 57
Chamberlain, Wilt 18, 47
Channer, Colin 36
Chase-Riboud, Barbara 20, 46
Chenault, John 40
Cheney-Coker, Syl 43
Chesnutt, Charles 29
Chideya, Farai 14, 61
Childress, Alice 15
Christian, Barbara T. 44
Clark, Kenneth B. 5, 52
Clark, Septima 7
Clark-Bekederemo, J. P. 44
Clarke, Austin C. 32
Clarke, Cheryl 32
Clarke, George 32
Cleage, Pearl 17, 64
Cleaver, Eldridge 5
Cliff, Michelle 42
Clifton, Lucille 14, 64
Cobb, William Jelani 59
Cobbs, Price M. 9
Cohen, Anthony 15
Cole, Johnnetta B. 5, 43
Coleman, Wanda 48
Collins, Patricia Hill 67
Colter, Cyrus J. 36

Comer, James P. 6
Common 31, 63
Cone, James H. 3
Cook, Suzan D. Johnson 22
Cooke, Marvel 31
Coombs, Orde M. 44
Cooper, Afua 53
Cooper, Andrew W. 36
Cooper, Anna Julia 20
Cooper, J. California 12
Cornish, Sam 50
Cortez, Jayne 43
Cosby, Bill 7, 26, 59
Cosby, Camille 14
Cose, Ellis 5, 50
Cotter, Joseph Seamon, Sr. 40
Couto, Mia 45
Cox, Joseph Mason Andrew 51
Creagh, Milton 27
Crouch, Stanley 11
Cruse, Harold 54
Crutchfield, James N. 55
Cullen, Countee 8
Cuney, William Waring 44
Cunningham, Evelyn 23
Curry, George E. 23
Curtis, Christopher Paul 26
Curtis-Hall, Vondie 17
Dabydeen, David 48
Dadié, Bernard 34
D'Aguiar, Fred 50
Damas, Léon-Gontran 46
Dandridge, Raymond Garfield 45
Danner, Margaret Esse 49
Danticat, Edwidge 15, 68
Dash, Leon 47
Datcher, Michael 60
Dathorne, O.R. 52
Davis, Allison 12
Davis, Angela 5
Davis, Charles T. 48
Davis, Eisa 68
Davis, Frank Marshall 47
Davis, George 36
Davis, Miles 4
Davis, Nolan 45
Davis, Ossie 5, 50
Davis, Thulani 61
Dawkins, Wayne 20
de Passe, Suzanne 25
De Veaux, Alexis 44
Deggans, Eric 71
Delany, Martin R. 27
Delany, Samuel R., Jr. 9
DeLoach, Nora 30
Demby, William 51
Dent, Thomas C. 50
Dickerson, Debra J. 60
Dickey, Eric Jerome 21, 56
Diesel, Vin 29
Diop, Birago 53
Diop, Cheikh Anta 4
Dodson, Howard, Jr. 7, 52
Dodson, Owen Vincent 38
Dove, Rita 6
Draper, Sharon Mills 16, 43
Driskell, David C. 7
Driver, David E. 11
Drummond, William J. 40
Du Bois, David Graham 45
Du Bois, W. E. B. 3
DuBois, Shirley Graham 21
Due, Tananarive 30

Dumas, Henry 41
Dunbar, Paul Laurence 8
Dunbar-Nelson, Alice Ruth Moore 44
Dunham, Katherine 4, 59
Dunnigan, Alice Allison 41
Duplechan, Larry 55
Dyson, Michael Eric 11, 40
Early, Gerald 15
Edmonds, Terry 17
Ekwensi, Cyprian 37
Elder, Lonne, III 38
Elliot, Lorris 37
Ellison, Ralph 7
Elmore, Ronn 21
Emanuel, James A. 46
Emecheta, Buchi 30
Estes, Rufus 29
Evans, Mari 26
Fabio, Sarah Webster 48
Fair, Ronald L. 47
Fanon, Frantz 44
Farah, Nuruddin 27
Farley, Christopher John 54
Farrakhan, Louis 15
Fauset, Jessie 7
Feelings, Muriel 44
Feelings, Tom 11, 47
Fields, Julia 45
Figueroa, John J. 40
Files, Lolita 35
Finner-Williams, Paris Michele 62
Fisher, Antwone 40
Fisher, Rudolph 17
Fleming, Raymond 48
Fletcher, Bill, Jr. 41
Forbes, Calvin 46
Ford, Clyde W. 40
Ford, Nick Aaron 44
Ford, Wallace 58
Forman, James 7, 51
Forrest, Leon 44
Fortune, T. Thomas 6
Foster, Cecil 32
Foster, Jylla Moore 45
Franklin, John Hope 5
Franklin, Robert M. 13
Frazier, E. Franklin 10
Frazier, Oscar 58
French, Albert 18
Fuller, Charles 8
Fuller, Hoyt 44
Gabre-Medhin, Tsegaye 64
Gaines, Ernest J. 7
Gardner, Chris 65
Gaston, Marilyn Hughes 60
Gates, Henry Louis, Jr. 3, 38, 67
Gayle, Addison, Jr. 41
Gaynor, Gloria 36
George, Nelson 12
Gibson, Althea 8, 43
Gibson, Donald Bernard 40
Giddings, Paula 11
Gilbert, Christopher 50
Gilliard, Steve 69
Giovanni, Nikki 9, 39
Gladwell, Malcolm 62
Goines, Donald 19
Golden, Marita 19
Gomez, Jewelle 30
Goodison, Lorna 71
Graham, Lawrence Otis 12
Graham, Lorenz 48

Grant, Gwendolyn Goldsby 28
Gray, Darius 69
Greaves, William 38
Greenfield, Eloise 9
Greenlee, Sam 48
Greenwood, Monique 38
Griffith, Mark Winston 8
Grimké, Archibald H. 9
Guinier, Lani 7, 30
Guy, Rosa 5
Guy-Sheftall, Beverly 13
Haley, Alex 4
Halliburton, Warren J. 49
Hamblin, Ken 10
Hamilton, Virginia 10
Hansberry, Lorraine 6
Harding, Vincent 67
Hare, Nathan 44
Harkless, Necia Desiree 19
Harper, Frances Ellen Watkins 11
Harper, Michael S. 34
Harrington, Oliver W. 9
Harris, Claire 34
Harris, Eddy L. 18
Harris, Jay 19
Harris, Leslie 6
Harris, Monica 18
Harrison, Alvin 28
Harrison, Calvin 28
Haskins, James 36, 54
Hayden, Robert 12
Hayes, Teddy 40
Haywood, Gar Anthony 43
Head, Bessie 28
Heard, Nathan C. 45
Hearne, John Edgar Caulwell 45
Hemphill, Essex 10
Henderson, David 53
Henderson, Stephen E. 45
Henries, A. Doris Banks 44
Henriques, Julian 37
Henry, Lenny 9, 52
Henson, Matthew 2
Herbert, Bob 63
Hercules, Frank 44
Hernton, Calvin C. 51
Hill, Donna 32
Hill, Errol 40
Hill, Leslie Pinckney 44
Hilliard, David 7
Hoagland, Everett H. 45
Hobson, Julius W. 44
Holland, Endesha Ida Mae 3, 57
Holmes, Shannon 70
Holt, Nora 38
Holton, Hugh, Jr. 39
hooks, bell 5
Horne, Frank 44
Hrabowski, Freeman A., III 22
Hudson, Cheryl 15
Hudson, Wade 15
Hughes, Langston 4
Hull, Akasha Gloria 45
Hunter-Gault, Charlayne 6, 31
Hurston, Zora Neale 3
Iceberg Slim 11
Ifill, Gwen 28
Ilibagiza, Immaculée 66
Jackson, Fred James 25
Jackson, George 14
Jackson, Sheneska 18
Jarret, Vernon D. 42
Jasper, Kenji 39

Jenkins, Beverly 14
Joachim, Paulin 34
Joe, Yolanda 21
Johnson, Angela 52
Johnson, Charles 1
Johnson, Charles S. 12
Johnson, Georgia Douglas 41
Johnson, James Weldon 5
Johnson, John H. 3, 54
Johnson, Linton Kwesi 37
Johnson, Mat 31
Johnson, R. M. 36
Jolley, Willie 28
Jones, Edward P. 43, 67
Jones, Gayl 37
Jones, Orlando 30
Jones, Sarah 39
Jordan, June 7, 35
Josey, E. J. 10
July, William 27
Just, Ernest Everett 3
Kamau, Kwadwo Agymah 28
Karenga, Maulana 10, 71
Kariuki, J. M. 67
Kay, Jackie 37
Kayira, Legson 40
Kearney, Janis 54
Kendrick, Erika 57
Kennedy, Adrienne 11
Kennedy, Florynce 12, 33
Kennedy, Randall 40
Khanga, Yelena 6
Killens, John O. 54
Kimbro, Dennis 10
Kincaid, Jamaica 4
King, Colbert I. 69
King, Coretta Scott 3, 57
King, Preston 28
King, Woodie, Jr. 27
King, Yolanda 6
Kitt, Sandra 23
Knight, Etheridge 37
Kobia, Samuel 43
Komunyakaa, Yusef 9
Kotto, Yaphet 7
Kunjufu, Jawanza 3, 50
Lacy, Sam 30, 46
Ladner, Joyce A. 42
Laferriere, Dany 33
LaGuma, Alex 30
Lamming, George 35
Lampley, Oni Faida 43, 71
Larsen, Nella 10
Lawrence, Martin 6, 27, 60
Lawrence-Lightfoot, Sara 10
Lemmons, Kasi 20
Lester, Julius 9
Letson, Al 39
Lewis, David Levering 9
Lewis, Samella 25
Lincoln, C. Eric 38
Little, Benilde 21
Locke, Alain 10
Lorde, Audre 6
Louis, Errol T. 8
Loury, Glenn 36
Lowe, Herbert 57
Mabry, Marcus 70
Mabuza-Suttle, Felicia 43
Madhubuti, Haki R. 7
Madison, Paula 37
Major, Clarence 9
Makeba, Miriam 2, 50

Malveaux, Julianne 32, 70
Manley, Ruth 34
Marechera, Dambudzo 39
Markham, E. A. 37
Marshall, Paule 7
Martin, Roland S. 49
Mason, Felicia 31
Massaquoi, Hans J. 30
Mathabane, Mark 5
Maynard, Robert C. 7
Mays, Benjamin E. 7
Mbaye, Mariétou 31
McBride, James 35
McCall, Nathan 8
McCrary Anthony, Crystal 70
McDuffie, Dwayne 62
McFadden, Bernice L. 39
McGruder, Robert 22, 35
McKay, Claude 6
McKinney Hammond, Michelle 51
McKinney-Whetstone, Diane 27
McMillan, Rosalynn A. 36
McMillan, Terry 4, 17, 53
McPherson, James Alan 70
Memmi, Albert 37
Mengestu, Dinaw 66
Meredith, James H. 11
Mfume, Kweisi 6, 41
Micheaux, Oscar 7
Mickelbury, Penny 28
Milner, Ron 39
Mitchell, Elvis 67
Mitchell, Loften 31
Mitchell, Russ 21
Mitchell, Sharon 36
Mofolo, Thomas Mokopu 37
Mollel, Tololwa 38
Monroe, Bryan 71
Monroe, Mary 35
Moore, Jessica Care 30
Morrison, Toni 2, 15
Mosley, Walter 5, 25, 68
Moss, Carlton 17
Mossell, Gertrude Bustill 40
Moutoussamy-Ashe, Jeanne 7
Mowry, Jess 7
Mphalele, Es'kia (Ezekiel) 40
Mudimbe, V.Y. 61
Mugo, Micere Githae 32
Mullen, Harryette 34
Murphy, John H. 42
Murray, Albert L. 33
Murray, Pauli 38
Mwangi, Meja 40
Myers, Walter Dean 8, 70
Naylor, Gloria 10, 42
Neal, Larry 38
Nelson, Jill 6, 54
Neto, António Agostinho 43
Newkirk, Pamela 69
Newton, Huey 2
Ngugi wa Thiong'o 29, 61
Nissel, Angela 42
Nkosi, Lewis 46
Nkrumah, Kwame 3
Nugent, Richard Bruce 39
Nunez, Elizabeth 62

Okara, Gabriel 37
Ojikutu, Bayo 66
Oliver, John J., Jr. 48
Onwueme, Tess Osonye 23
Orlandersmith, Dael 42
Owens, Major 6
Oyono, Ferdinand 38
Packer, Z.Z. 64
Page, Clarence 4
Painter, Nell Irvin 24
Palmer, Everard 37
Parker, Pat 19
Parker, Star 70
Parks, Suzan-Lori 34
Patterson, Orlando 4
Payne, Ethel L. 28
Peters, Lenrie 43
Petry, Ann 19
Philip, Marlene Nourbese 32
Piper, Adrian 71
Pitts, Leonard, Jr. 54
Poitier, Sidney 11, 36
Poussaint, Alvin F. 5, 67
Powell, Adam Clayton, Jr. 3
Powell, Kevin 31
Pressley, Condace L. 41
Prince, Richard E. 71
Prince-Bythewood, Gina 31
Pryor, Rain 65
Pryor, Richard 3, 24, 56
Quarles, Benjamin Arthur 18
Rahman, Aishah 37
Randall, Alice 38
Randall, Dudley 8, 55
Raspberry, William 2
Reagon, Bernice Johnson 7
Reddick, Lawrence Dunbar 20
Redding, J. Saunders 26
Redmond, Eugene 23
Reed, Ishmael 8
Rhimes, Shonda Lynn 67
Rhoden, William C. 67
Rice, Condoleezza 3, 28
Richards, Beah 30
Ridley, John 69
Riggs, Marlon 5
Riley, Rochelle 50
Ringgold, Faith 4
Robeson, Eslanda Goode 13
Robinson, Aminah 50
Robinson, Matt 69
Rock, The 29, 66
Rodman, Dennis 12
Rogers, Joel Augustus 30
Rotimi, Ola 1
Rowan, Carl T. 1, 30
Sadlier, Rosemary 62
Saint James, Synthia 12
St. John, Kristoff 25
Salih, Al-Tayyib 37
Sanchez, Sonia 17, 51
Sanders, Dori 8
Sapphire 14
Saro-Wiwa, Kenule 39
Schomburg, Arthur Alfonso 9
Schuyler, George Samuel 40
Seale, Bobby 3

Sembène, Ousmane 13, 62
Senghor, Léopold Sédar 12, 66
Sengstacke, John 18
Senior, Olive 37
Shabazz, Attallah 6
Shabazz, Ilyasah 36
Shakur, Assata 6
Shange, Ntozake 8
Shaw, Bernard 2, 28
Shipp, E. R. 15
Simone, Nina 15, 41
Simpson, Carole 6, 30
Singleton, John 2, 30
Sister Souljah 11
Skinner, Kiron K. 65
Smiley, Tavis 20, 68
Smith, Anna Deavere 6
Smith, B(arbara) 11
Smith, Barbara 28
Smith, Bruce W. 53
Smith, Danyel 61
Smith, Jessie Carney 35
Smith, Mary Carter 26
Smith, Stephen A. 69
Smith, Zadie 51
Snowden, Frank M., Jr. 67
Somé, Malidoma Patrice 10
Southgate, Martha 58
Sowell, Thomas 2
Soyinka, Wole 4
Spencer, Anne 27
Spriggs, William 67
Staples, Brent 8
Stewart, Alison 13
Stone, Chuck 9
Stringer, Vickie 58
Sundiata, Sekou 66
Tademy, Lalita 36
Talbert, David 34
Talley, André Leon 56
Tate, Eleanora E. 20, 55
Taulbert, Clifton Lemoure 19
Taylor, Kristin Clark 8
Taylor, Mildred D. 26
Taylor, Susan C. 62
Taylor, Susan L. 10
Thomas, Michael 69
Thomas, Trisha R. 65
Thomas-Graham, Pamela 29
Thornton, Yvonne S. 69
Thurman, Howard 3
Tillis, Frederick 40
Tolson, Melvin 37
Toomer, Jean 6
Touré, Askia (Muhammad Abu Bakr el) 47
Townsend, Robert 4
Trotter, Monroe 9
Tucker, Cynthia 15, 61
Turner, Henry McNeal 5
Turner, Tina 6, 27
Tutu, Desmond 6
Tutuola, Amos 30
Tyree, Omar Rashad 21
Tyson, Asha 39
Tyson, Neil deGrasse 15, 65
Van Peebles, Melvin 7

van Sertima, Ivan 25
Vega, Marta Moreno 61
Vera, Yvonne 32
Verdelle, A. J. 26
Wade-Gayles, Gloria Jean 41
Walcott, Derek 5
Walker, Alice 1, 43
Walker, Margaret 29
Walker, Rebecca 50
Wallace, Michele Faith 13
Wallace, Phyllis A. 9
Ward, Douglas Turner 42
Washington, Booker T. 4
Washington, Harriet A. 69
Washington, James, Jr. 38
Washington, Laura S. 18
Waters, Ethel 7
Wattleton, Faye 9
Wayans, Damon 8, 41
Weaver, Afaa Michael 37
Webb, Veronica 10
Weems, Renita J. 44
Wells-Barnett, Ida B. 8
Wesley, Dorothy Porter 19
Wesley, Valerie Wilson 18
West, Cornel 5, 33
West, Dorothy 12, 54
Whack, Rita Coburn 36
Wharton, Clifton R., Jr. 7
Whitaker, Mark 21, 47
White, Walter F. 4
Whitfield, Van 34
Wideman, John Edgar 5
Wilbekin, Emil 63
Wiley, Ralph 8
Wilkerson, Isabel 71
Wilkins, Roger 2
Wilkins, Roy 4
Williams, Armstrong 29
Williams, Fannie Barrier 27
Williams, George Washington 18
Williams, John A. 27
Williams, Juan 35
Williams, Patricia 11, 54
Williams, Robert F. 11
Williams, Samm-Art 21
Williams, Saul 31
Williams, Sherley Anne 25
Williams, Stanley "Tookie" 29, 57
Williams, Wendy 62
Wilson, August 7, 33, 55
Wilson, Mary 28
Wilson, William Julius 22
Winans, Marvin L. 17
Wiwa, Ken 67
Wolfe, George C. 6, 43
Woods, Mattiebelle 63
Woods, Scott 55
Woods, Teri 69
Woodson, Carter G. 2
Worrill, Conrad 12
Wright, Bruce McMarion 3, 52
Wright, Richard 5
X, Marvin 45
Yarbrough, Camille 40
Yette, Samuel F. 63
Young, Whitney M., Jr., 4
Youngblood, Shay 32
Zane 71
Zook, Kristal Brent 62

Cumulative Subject Index

Volume numbers appear in **bold**

A Better Chance
Lewis, William M., Jr. **40**

A Harvest Biotech Foundation International
Wambugu, Florence **42**

AA
See Alcoholics Anonymous

AAAS
See American Association for the Advancement of Science

Aaron Gunner series
Haywood, Gar Anthony **43**

AARP
Dixon, Margaret **14**
Smith, Marie F. **70**

ABC
See American Broadcasting Company

Abstract expressionism
Lewis, Norman **39**

A. C. Green Youth Foundation
Green, A. C. **32**

Academy awards
Austin, Patti **24**
Freeman, Morgan **2, 20, 62**
Goldberg, Whoopi **4, 33, 69**
Gooding, Cuba, Jr. **16, 62**
Gossett, Louis, Jr. **7**
Jean-Baptiste, Marianne **17, 46**
McDaniel, Hattie **5**
Poitier, Sidney **11, 36**
Prince **18, 65**
Richie, Lionel **27, 65**
Washington, Denzel **1, 16**
Whitaker, Forest **2, 49, 67**
Williams, Russell, II **70**
Wonder, Stevie **11, 53**

Academy of Praise
Kenoly, Ron **45**

A cappella
Cooke, Sam **17**
Reagon, Bernice Johnson **7**

Access Hollywood
Robinson, Shaun **36**

ACDL
See Association for Constitutional Democracy in Liberia

ACLU
See American Civil Liberties Union

Acquired immune deficiency syndrome (AIDS)
Ashe, Arthur **1, 18**
Atim, Julian **66**
Broadbent, Hydeia **36**
Cargill, Victoria A. **43**
Gayle, Helene D. **3, 46**
Hale, Lorraine **8**
Johnson, Earvin "Magic" **3, 39**
Lewis-Thornton, Rae **32**
Mboup, Souleymane **10**
Moutoussamy-Ashe, Jeanne **7**
Norman, Pat **10**
Ojikutu, Bisola **65**
Okaalet, Peter **58**
Pickett, Cecil **39**
Riggs, Marlon **5, 44**
Satcher, David **7, 57**
Seele, Pernessa **46**
Wilson, Phill **9**
Zulu, Princess Kasune **54**

Act*1 Personnel Services
Howroyd, Janice Bryant **42**

ACT-SO
See Afro-Academic Cultural, Technological, and Scientific Olympics

Acting
Aaliyah **30**
Adams, Osceola Macarthy **31**
Ailey, Alvin **8**
Akinnuoye-Agbaje, Adewale **56**
Alexander, Khandi **43**
Allen, Debbie **13, 42**
Amos, John **8, 62**
Anderson, Anthony **51**
Anderson, Carl **48**
Anderson, Eddie "Rochester" **30**
Angelou, Maya **1, 15**
Armstrong, Vanessa Bell **24**
Ashanti **37**
Babatunde, Obba **35**
Bahati, Wambui **60**
Baker, Josephine **3**
Banks, Michelle **59**
Banks, Tyra **11, 50**
Barnett, Etta Moten **56**
Bassett, Angela **6, 23, 62**
Beach, Michael **26**
Beals, Jennifer **12**
Beaton, Norman **14**
Beauvais, Garcelle **29**
Bennett, Louise **69**
Bentley, Lamont **53**
Berry, Fred "Rerun" **48**
Berry, Halle **4, 19, 57**
Beyoncé **39, 70**
Blacque, Taurean **58**
Blanks, Billy **22**
Blige, Mary J. **20, 34, 60**
Bonet, Lisa **58**
Borders, James **9**
Bow Wow **35**
Brady, Wayne **32, 71**
Branch, William Blackwell **39**
Braugher, Andre **13, 58**
Bridges, Todd **37**
Brooks, Avery **9**
Brooks, Golden **62**
Brooks, Mehcad **62**
Brown, Jim **11**
Browne, Roscoe Lee **66**
Byrd, Eugene **64**
Caesar, Shirley **19**
Calloway, Cab **14**
Cameron, Earl **44**
Campbell, Naomi **1, 31**
Campbell-Martin, Tisha **8, 42**
Cannon, Nick **47**
Carroll, Diahann **9**
Carson, Lisa Nicole **21**
Carey, Mariah **32, 53, 69**
Cash, Rosalind **28**
Cedric the Entertainer **29, 60**
Cheadle, Don **19, 52**
Chestnut, Morris **31**
Childress, Alice **15**
Chong, Rae Dawn **62**
Chweneyagae, Presley **63**
Clarke, Hope **14**
Cliff, Jimmy **28**
Cole, Nat King **17**
Cole, Natalie **17, 60**
Coleman, Gary **35**
Combs, Sean "Puffy" **17, 43**
Cosby, Bill **7, 26, 59**
Crothers, Scatman **19**
Curry, Mark **17**
Curtis-Hall, Vondie **17**
Dandridge, Dorothy **3**
David, Keith **27**
Davidson, Jaye **5**
Davis, Eisa **68**
Davis, Guy **36**
Davis, Ossie **5, 50**
Davis, Sammy, Jr. **18**
Davis, Viola **34**
Dee, Ruby **8, 50, 68**
Devine, Loretta **24**
Diesel, Vin **29**
Diggs, Taye **25, 63**
Dixon, Ivan **69**
DMX **28, 64**
Dourdan, Gary **37**
Duke, Bill **3**
Duncan, Michael Clarke **26**
Dungey, Merrin **62**
Dutton, Charles S. **4, 22**
Ejiofor, Chiwetel **67**
Elba, Idris **49**
Elise, Kimberly **32**
Emmanuel, Alphonsia **38**
Epps, Mike **60**
Epps, Omar **23, 59**
Esposito, Giancarlo **9**
Everett, Francine **23**
Faison, Donald **50**
Faison, Frankie **55**
Falana, Lola **42**
Fargas, Antonio **50**
Fields, Felicia P. **60**
Fields, Kim **36**
Fetchit, Stepin **32**
Fishburne, Laurence **4, 22, 70**
Fox, Rick **27**
Fox, Vivica A. **15, 53**
Foxx, Jamie **15, 48**
Foxx, Redd **2**
Freeman, Al, Jr. **11**
Freeman, Morgan **2, 20, 62**
Freeman, Yvette **27**
Gaye, Nona **56**
Gibson, Althea **8, 43**
Gibson, Tyrese **27, 62**
Ginuwine **35**
Givens, Adele **62**
Givens, Robin **4, 25, 58**
Glover, Danny **1, 24**
Goldberg, Whoopi **4, 33, 69**
Gooding, Cuba, Jr. **16, 62**
Gordon, Dexter **25**
Gossett, Louis, Jr. **7**
Greaves, William **38**
Grier, David Alan **28**

Grier, Pam **9, 31**
Guillaume, Robert **3, 48**
Gunn, Moses **10**
Guy, Jasmine **2**
Hall, Arsenio **58**
Hamilton, Lisa Gay **71**
Hamlin, Larry Leon **49, 62**
Hammer, M. C. **20**
Hammond, Fred **23**
Hardison, Kadeem **22**
Harewood, David **52**
Harper, Hill **32, 65**
Harris, Naomie **55**
Harris, Robin **7**
Harvey, Steve **18, 58**
Hawkins, Screamin' Jay **30**
Hayes, Isaac **20, 58**
Haysbert, Dennis **42**
Hemsley, Sherman **19**
Henry, Lenny **9, 52**
Henson, Taraji **58**
Hill, Dulé **29**
Hill, Lauryn **20, 53**
Hines, Gregory **1, 42**
Horne, Lena **5**
Hounsou, Djimon **19, 45**
Houston, Whitney **7, 28**
Howard, Sherri **36**
Howard, Terrence **59**
Hudson, Jennifer **63**
Hughley, D. L. **23**
Hyman, Earle **25**
Ice Cube **8, 30, 60**
Iman **4, 33**
Ingram, Rex **5**
Ja Rule **35**
Jackson, Janet **6, 30, 68**
Jackson, Michael **19, 53**
Jackson, Millie **25**
Jackson, Samuel **8, 19, 63**
Jean-Baptiste, Marianne **17, 46**
Johnson, Rafer **33**
Johnson, Rodney Van **28**
Jones, James Earl **3, 49**
Jones, Orlando **30**
Kelley, Elijah **65**
Kelley, Malcolm David **59**
Kennedy-Overton, Jayne Harris **46**
Khumalo, Leleti **51**
King, Regina **22, 45**
King, Woodie, Jr. **27**
Kirby, George **14**
Kitt, Eartha **16**
Knight, Gladys **16, 66**
Kodhoe, Boris **34**
Kotto, Yaphet **7**
La Salle, Eriq **12**
LaBelle, Patti **13, 30**
Lampley, Oni Faida **43, 71**
Lane, Charles **3**
Lassiter, Roy **24**
Lathan, Sanaa **27**
Lawrence, Martin **6, 27, 60**
Lee, Canada **8**
Lee, Joie **1**
Lee, Spike **5, 19**
Leggs, Kingsley **62**
Lemmons, Kasi **20**
LeNoire, Rosetta **37**
Lenox, Adriane **59**
Lester, Adrian **46**
Lesure, James **64**
Lewis, Emmanuel **36**

Lil' Kim **28**
Lincoln, Abbey **3**
Lindo, Delroy **18, 45**
LisaRaye **27**
LL Cool J **16, 49**
Love, Darlene **23**
Luke, Derek **61**
Lumbly, Carl **47**
Mabley, Jackie "Moms" **15**
Mac, Bernie **29, 61**
Malco, Romany **71**
Mario **71**
Marrow, Queen Esther **24**
Martin, Helen **31**
Martin, Jesse L. **31**
Master P **21**
Mayo, Whitman **32**
McDaniel, Hattie **5**
McDonald, Audra **20, 62**
McKee, Lonette **12**
McKinney, Nina Mae **40**
McQueen, Butterfly **6, 54**
Meadows, Tim **30**
Merkerson, S. Epatha **47**
Michele, Michael **31**
Mitchell, Brian Stokes **21**
Mitchell, Kel **66**
Mo'Nique **35**
Moore, Chante **26**
Moore, Melba **21**
Moore, Shemar **21**
Morris, Garrett **31**
Morris, Greg **28**
Morton, Joe **18**
Mos Def **30**
Moten, Etta **18**
Murphy, Eddie **4, 20, 61**
Muse, Clarence Edouard **21**
Nash, Johnny **40**
Nash, Niecy **66**
Neal, Elise **29**
Newton, Thandie **26**
Nicholas, Fayard **20, 57**
Nicholas, Harold **20**
Nichols, Nichelle **11**
Norman, Maidie **20**
Notorious B.I.G. **20**
Ntshona, Winston **52**
Okonedo, Sophie **67**
O'Neal, Ron **46**
Orlandersmith, Dael **42**
Orman, Roscoe **55**
Parker, Nicole Ari **52**
Patton, Paula **62**
Payne, Allen **13**
Payne, Freda **58**
Peete, Holly Robinson **20**
Perrineau, Harold, Jr. **51**
Perry, Tyler **40, 54**
Phifer, Mekhi **25**
Pickens, James, Jr. **59**
Pinkett Smith, Jada **10, 41**
Poitier, Sidney **11, 36**
Poitier, Sydney Tamiia **65**
Pratt, Kyla **57**
Premice, Josephine **41**
Prince **18, 65**
Pryor, Rain **65**
Pryor, Richard **3, 24, 56**
Queen Latifah **1, 16, 58**
Randle, Theresa **16**
Rashad, Phylicia **21**
Raven **44**

Ray, Gene Anthony **47**
Reddick, Lance **52**
Reese, Della **6, 20**
Reid, Tim **56**
Reuben, Gloria **15**
Rhames, Ving **14, 50**
Rhymes, Busta **31**
Ribeiro, Alfonso **17**
Richards, Beah **30**
Richards, Lloyd **2**
Richardson, LaTanya **71**
Richardson, Salli **68**
Robeson, Paul **2**
Robinson, Shaun **36**
Rock, Chris **3, 22, 66**
Rock, The **29 66**
Rodgers, Rod **36**
Rodrigues, Percy **68**
Roker, Roxie **68**
Rolle, Esther **13, 21**
Rose, Anika Noni **70**
Ross, Diana **8, 27**
Ross, Tracee Ellis **35**
Roundtree, Richard **27**
Rowell, Victoria **13, 68**
Rudolph, Maya **46**
Russell, Nipsey **66**
St. Jacques, Raymond **8**
St. John, Kristoff **25**
St. Patrick, Mathew **48**
Scott, Hazel **66**
Shakur, Tupac **14**
Simmons, Henry **55**
Sinbad **1, 16**
Sisqo **30**
Smith, Anjela Lauren **44**
Smith, Anna Deavere **6, 44**
Smith, Barbara **11**
Smith, Roger Guenveur **12**
Smith, Will **8, 18, 53**
Snipes, Wesley **3, 24, 67**
Snoop Dogg **35**
Sommore **61**
Tamia **24, 55**
Tate, Larenz **15**
Taylor, Meshach **4**
Taylor, Regina **9, 46**
Taylor, Ron **35**
Thomas, Sean Patrick **35**
Thomason, Marsha **47**
Thompson, Kenan **52**
Thompson, Tazewell **13**
Thoms, Tracie **61**
Torres, Gina **52**
Torry, Guy **31**
Toussaint, Lorraine **32**
Townsend, Robert **4, 23**
Tucker, Chris **13, 23, 62**
Tunie, Tamara **63**
Turner, Tina **6, 27**
Tyler, Aisha N. **36**
Tyson, Cicely **7, 51**
Uggams, Leslie **23**
Underwood, Blair **7, 27**
Union, Gabrielle **31**
Usher **23, 56**
Van Peebles, Mario **2, 51**
Van Peebles, Melvin **7**
Vance, Courtney B. **15, 60**
Vanity **67**
Vereen, Ben **4**
Walker, Eamonn **37**
Ward, Douglas Turner **42**

Warfield, Marsha **2**
Warner, Malcolm-Jamal **22, 36**
Warren, Michael **27**
Washington, Denzel **1, 16**
Washington, Fredi **10**
Washington, Isaiah **62**
Washington, Kerry **46**
Waters, Ethel **7**
Wayans, Damon **8, 41**
Wayans, Keenen Ivory **18**
Wayans, Marlon **29**
Wayans, Shawn **29**
Weathers, Carl **10**
Webb, Veronica **10**
Whitaker, Forest **2, 49, 67**
White, Michael Jai **71**
Whitfield, Lynn **18**
Williams, Bert **18**
Williams, Billy Dee **8**
Williams, Clarence, III **26**
Wilson, Chandra **57**
Wilson, Dorien **55**
Williams, Joe **5, 25**
Williams, Malinda **57**
Williams, Samm-Art **21**
Williams, Saul **31**
Williams, Vanessa A. **32, 66**
Williams, Vanessa L. **4, 17**
Williamson, Fred **67**
Williamson, Mykelti **22**
Wilson, Debra **38**
Wilson, Flip **21**
Winfield, Paul **2, 45**
Winfrey, Oprah **2, 15, 61**
Withers-Mendes, Elisabeth **64**
Witherspoon, John **38**
Woodard, Alfre **9**
Wright, Jeffrey **54**
Yarbrough, Cedric **51**
Yoba, Malik **11**

Active Ministers Engaged in Nurturance (AMEN)
King, Bernice **4**

Actors Equity Association
Lewis, Emmanuel **36**

Actuarial science
Hill, Jesse, Jr. **13**

ACT UP
See AIDS Coalition to Unleash Power

Acustar, Inc.
Farmer, Forest **1**

ADC
See Agricultural Development Council

Addiction Research and Treatment Corporation
Cooper, Andrew W. **36**

Adoption and foster care
Baker, Josephine **3**
Blacque, Taurean **58**
Clements, George **2**
Gossett, Louis, Jr. **7**
Hale, Clara **16**
Hale, Lorraine **8**
Oglesby, Zena **12**

Rowell, Victoria **13, 68**

Adventures in Movement (AIM)
Morgan, Joe Leonard **9**

Advertising
Barboza, Anthony **10**
Boyd, Edward **70**
Burrell, Tom **21, 51**
Campbell, E. Simms **13**
Chisholm, Samuel J. **32**
Coleman, Donald **24, 62**
Cullers, Vincent T. **49**
Johnson, Beverly **2**
Jones, Caroline R. **29**
Jordan, Montell **23**
Lewis, Byron E. **13**
McKinney Hammond, Michelle **51**
Mingo, Frank **32**
Olden, Georg(e) **44**
Pinderhughes, John **47**
Roche, Joyce M. **17**

Advocates Scene
Seale, Bobby **3**

Aetna
Williams, Ronald A. **57**

AFCEA
See Armed Forces Communications and Electronics Associations

Affirmative action
Arnwine, Barbara **28**
Berry, Mary Frances **7**
Carter, Stephen L. **4**
Edley, Christopher F., Jr. **48**
Higginbotham, A. Leon, Jr. **13, 25**
Maynard, Robert C. **7**
Norton, Eleanor Holmes **7**
Rand, A. Barry **6**
Thompson, Bennie G. **26**
Waters, Maxine **3, 67**

AFL-CIO
See American Federation of Labor and Congress of Industrial Organizations

African/African-American Summit
Sullivan, Leon H. **3, 30**

African American Catholic Congregation
Stallings, George A., Jr. **6**

African American Dance Ensemble
Davis, Chuck **33**

African American folklore
Bailey, Xenobia **11**
Brown, Sterling Allen **10, 64**
Driskell, David C. **7**
Ellison, Ralph **7**
Gaines, Ernest J. **7**
Hamilton, Virginia **10**
Hughes, Langston **4**
Hurston, Zora Neale **3**
Lester, Julius **9**
Morrison, Toni **2, 15**
Primus, Pearl **6**
Tillman, George, Jr. **20**

Williams, Bert **18**
Yarbrough, Camille **40**

African American folk music
Cuney, William Waring **44**
Handy, W. C. **8**
House, Son **8**
Johnson, James Weldon **5**
Lester, Julius **9**
Southern, Eileen **56**

African American history
Angelou, Maya **1, 15**
Appiah, Kwame Anthony **67**
Ashe, Arthur **1, 18**
Benberry, Cuesta **65**
Bennett, Lerone, Jr. **5**
Berry, Mary Frances **7**
Blackshear, Leonard **52**
Blockson, Charles L. **42**
Burroughs, Margaret Taylor **9**
Camp, Kimberly **19**
Chase-Riboud, Barbara **20, 46**
Cheadle, Don **19, 52**
Clarke, John Henrik **20**
Clayton, Mayme Agnew **62**
Cobb, William Jelani **59**
Coombs, Orde M. **44**
Cooper, Anna Julia **20**
Dodson, Howard, Jr. **7, 52**
Douglas, Aaron **7**
Du Bois, W. E. B. **3**
DuBois, Shirley Graham **21**
Dyson, Michael Eric **11, 40**
Feelings, Tom **11, 47**
Franklin, John Hope **5**
Gaines, Ernest J. **7**
Gates, Henry Louis, Jr. **3, 38, 67**
Gill, Gerald **69**
Haley, Alex **4**
Halliburton, Warren J. **49**
Harkless, Necia Desiree **19**
Harris, Richard E. **61**
Hine, Darlene Clark **24**
Hughes, Langston **4**
Johnson, James Weldon **5**
Jones, Edward P. **43, 67**
Lewis, David Levering **9**
Madhubuti, Haki R. **7**
Marable, Manning **10**
Morrison, Toni **2**
Painter, Nell Irvin **24**
Pritchard, Robert Starling **21**
Quarles, Benjamin Arthur **18**
Reagon, Bernice Johnson **7**
Ringgold, Faith **4**
Schomburg, Arthur Alfonso **9**
Southern, Eileen **56**
Tancil, Gladys Quander **59**
Wilson, August **7, 33, 55**
Woodson, Carter G. **2**
Yarbrough, Camille **40**

African American Images
Kunjufu, Jawanza **3, 50**

African American literature
Andrews, Raymond **4**
Angelou, Maya **1, 15**
Appiah, Kwame Anthony **67**
Baisden, Michael **25, 66**
Baker, Houston A., Jr. **6**
Baldwin, James **1**
Bambara, Toni Cade **1**

Baraka, Amiri **1, 38**
Bennett, George Harold "Hal" **45**
Bontemps, Arna **8**
Briscoe, Connie **15**
Brooks, Gwendolyn **1, 28**
Brown, Claude **38**
Brown, Wesley **23**
Burroughs, Margaret Taylor **9**
Campbell, Bebe Moore **6, 24, 59**
Cary, Lorene **3**
Childress, Alice **15**
Cleage, Pearl **17, 64**
Cullen, Countee **8**
Curtis, Christopher Paul **26**
Davis, Arthur P. **41**
Davis, Nolan **45**
Dickey, Eric Jerome **21, 56**
Dove, Rita **6**
Du Bois, W. E. B. **3**
Dunbar, Paul Laurence **8**
Ellison, Ralph **7**
Evans, Mari **26**
Fair, Ronald L. **47**
Fauset, Jessie **7**
Feelings, Tom **11, 47**
Fisher, Rudolph **17**
Ford, Nick Aaron **44**
Fuller, Charles **8**
Gaines, Ernest J. **7**
Gates, Henry Louis, Jr. **3, 38, 67**
Gayle, Addison, Jr. **41**
Gibson, Donald Bernard **40**
Giddings, Paula **11**
Giovanni, Nikki **9, 39**
Goines, Donald **19**
Golden, Marita **19**
Guy, Rosa **5**
Haley, Alex **4**
Hansberry, Lorraine **6**
Harper, Frances Ellen Watkins **11**
Heard, Nathan C. **45**
Himes, Chester **8**
Holland, Endesha Ida Mae **3, 57**
Holmes, Shannon **70**
Hughes, Langston **4**
Hull, Akasha Gloria **45**
Hurston, Zora Neale **3**
Iceberg Slim **11**
Joe, Yolanda **21**
Johnson, Charles **1**
Johnson, James Weldon **5**
Jones, Gayl **37**
Jordan, June **7, 35**
July, William **27**
Kitt, Sandra **23**
Larsen, Nella **10**
Lester, Julius **9**
Little, Benilde **21**
Lorde, Audre **6**
Madhubuti, Haki R. **7**
Major, Clarence **9**
Marshall, Paule **7**
McKay, Claude **6**
McKay, Nellie Yvonne **17, 57**
McKinney-Whetstone, Diane **27**
McMillan, Terry **4, 17, 53**
McPherson, James Alan **70**
Morrison, Toni **2, 15**
Mowry, Jess **7**
Myers, Walter Dean **8, 20**
Naylor, Gloria **10, 42**
Painter, Nell Irvin **24**
Petry, Ann **19**

Pinkney, Jerry **15**
Rahman, Aishah **37**
Randall, Dudley **8, 55**
Redding, J. Saunders **26**
Redmond, Eugene **23**
Reed, Ishmael **8**
Ringgold, Faith **4**
Sanchez, Sonia **17, 51**
Schomburg, Arthur Alfonso **9**
Schuyler, George Samuel **40**
Shange, Ntozake **8**
Smith, Mary Carter **26**
Taylor, Mildred D. **26**
Thomas, Trisha R. **65**
Thurman, Wallace **16**
Toomer, Jean **6**
Tyree, Omar Rashad **21**
Van Peebles, Melvin **7**
Verdelle, A. J. **26**
Walker, Alice **1, 43**
Wesley, Valerie Wilson **18**
Wideman, John Edgar **5**
Williams, John A. **27**
Williams, Sherley Anne **25**
Wilson, August **7, 33, 55**
Wolfe, George C. **6, 43**
Wright, Richard **5**
Yarbrough, Camille **40**

African American Research Library and Cultural Center
Morrison, Sam **50**

African American studies
Brawley, Benjamin **44**
Carby, Hazel **27**
Christian, Barbara T. **44**
De Veaux, Alexis **44**
Ford, Nick Aaron **44**
Hare, Nathan **44**
Henderson, Stephen E. **45**
Huggins, Nathan Irvin **52**
Long, Richard Alexander **65**

African Ancestry Inc.
Kittles, Rick **51**

African Burial Ground Project
Perry, Warren **56**

African Canadian literature
Elliott, Lorris **37**
Foster, Cecil **32**
Senior, Olive **37**

African Continental Telecommunications Ltd.
Sutton, Percy E. **42**

African dance
Acogny, Germaine **55**
Adams, Jenoyne **60**
Ailey, Alvin **8**
Davis, Chuck **33**
Fagan, Garth **18**
Primus, Pearl **6**

African Heritage Network
See The Heritage Network

African history
Appiah, Kwame Anthony **67**
Chase-Riboud, Barbara **20, 46**
Clarke, John Henrik **20**
Diop, Cheikh Anta **4**

Dodson, Howard, Jr. **7**, 52
DuBois, Shirley Graham **21**
Feelings, Muriel **44**
Halliburton, Warren J. **49**
Hansberry, William Leo **11**
Harkless, Necia Desiree **19**
Henries, A. Doris Banks **44**
Hilliard, Asa Grant, III **66**
Jawara, Dawda Kairaba **11**
Madhubuti, Haki R. **7**
Marshall, Paule **7**
van Sertima, Ivan **25**

African literature
Aidoo, Ama Ata **38**
Akpan, Uwem **70**
Appiah, Kwame Anthony **67**
Arac de Nyeko, Monica **66**
Armah, Ayi Kwei **49**
Awoonor, Kofi **37**
Bandele, Biyi **68**
Cartey, Wilfred **47**
Cheney-Coker, Syl **43**
Couto, Mia **45**
Dadié, Bernard **34**
Dathorne, O.R. **52**
Ekwensi, Cyprian **37**
Farah, Nuruddin **27**
Gabre-Medhin, Tsegaye **64**
Head, Bessie **28**
Kayira, Legson **40**
Memmi, Albert **37**
Mphalele, Es'kia **40**
Mwangi, Meja **40**
Oyono, Ferdinand **38**
Peters, Lenrie **43**
Salih, Al-Tayyib **37**

African Methodist Episcopal Church (AME)
Blanks, Deborah K. **69**
Bryant, John R. **45**
Flake, Floyd H. **18**
McKenzie, Vashti M. **29**
Mudimbe, V.Y. **61**
Murray, Cecil **12**, 47
Shuttlesworth, Fred **47**
Turner, Henry McNeal **5**
Youngblood, Johnny Ray **8**

African music
Ade, King Sunny **41**
Fela **1**, 42
Kidjo, Anjelique **50**
Kuti, Femi **47**
Maal, Baaba **66**
Makeba, Miriam **2**, 50
Mahlasela, Vusi **65**
Nascimento, Milton **2**, 64

African National Congress (ANC)
Baker, Ella **5**
Hani, Chris **6**
Ka Dinizulu, Mcwayizeni **29**
Kaunda, Kenneth **2**
Kuzwayo, Ellen **68**
Luthuli, Albert **13**
Mandela, Nelson **1**, 14
Mandela, Winnie **2**, 35
Masekela, Barbara **18**
Mbeki, Thabo Mvuyelwa **14**
Mhlaba, Raymond **55**
Nkomo, Joshua **4**, 65

Nyanda, Siphiwe **21**
Nzo, Alfred **15**
Ramaphosa, Cyril **3**
Sisulu, Albertina **57**
Sisulu, Walter **47**
Tutu, Desmond Mpilo **6**, 44
Weems, Renita J. **44**
Xuma, Madie Hall **59**
Zuma, Nkosazana Dlamini **34**

African Party for the Independence of Guinea and Cape Verde
Pereira, Aristides **30**

African Women's Health Center
Nour, Nawal M. **56**

Afro-Academic Cultural, Technological, and Scientific Olympics
Jarret, Vernon D. **42**

Afro-American Dance Ensemble
Hall, Arthur **39**

Afro-American League
Fortune, T. Thomas **6**

Afro-American Newspaper Company
Murphy, John H. **42**

Afro-Beat music
Fela **1**, 42

Afro-Brazilian music
Gil, Gilberto **53**

Afrocentricity
Asante, Molefi Kete **3**
Biggers, John **20**, 33
Diop, Cheikh Anta **4**
Hansberry, Lorraine **6**
Hansberry, William Leo **11**
Sanchez, Sonia **17**, 51
Turner, Henry McNeal **5**

Afro-Cuban music
Lefel, Edith **41**

Aftermath Entertainment
Dre, Dr. **10**, 14, 30

Agency for International Development (AID)
Gayle, Helene D. **3**, 46
Perkins, Edward **5**
Wilkins, Roger **2**

A. G. Gaston Boys and Girls Club
Gaston, Arthur George **3**, 38, 59

A. G. Gaston Motel
Gaston, Arthur George **3**, 38, 59

Agricultural Development Council (ADC)
Wharton, Clifton R., Jr. **7**

Agriculture
Boyd, John W., Jr. **20**
Carver, George Washington **4**
Espy, Mike **6**
Hall, Lloyd A. **8**

Jones, Monty **66**
Masire, Quett **5**
Obasanjo, Olusegun **5**
Sanders, Dori **8**
Wambugu, Florence **42**

AHA
See American Heart Association

AID
See Agency for International Development

AIDS
See Acquired Immune Deficiency Syndrome

AIDS Coalition to Unleash Power (ACT UP)
Norman, Pat **10**

AIDS Health Care Foundation
Wilson, Phill **9**

AIDS Prevention Team
Wilson, Phill **9**

AIDS research
Mboup, Souleymane **10**
Ojikutu, Bisola **65**

AIM
See Adventures in Movement

Akron Beacon Journal
Crutchfield, James N. **55**

Akwaaba Mansion Bed & Breakfast
Greenwood, Monique **38**

ALA
See American Library Association

Alabama state government
Davis, Artur **41**
Ford, Johnny **70**
Gray, Fred **37**

Alamerica Bank
Watkins, Donald **35**

Alcoholics Anonymous (AA)
Hilliard, David **7**
Lucas, John **7**

All Afrikan People's Revolutionary Party
Carmichael, Stokely **5**, 26
Moses, Robert Parris **11**

Alliance for Children
McMurray, Georgia L. **36**

Alliance Theatre
Leon, Kenny **10**

Allied Arts Academy
Bonds, Margaret **39**

Alligator Records
Harris, Corey **39**

Alpha & Omega Ministry
White, Reggie **6**, 50

Alpha Kappa Alpha Sorority
White, Linda M. **45**

Alvin Ailey American Dance Theater
Ailey, Alvin **8**
Clarke, Hope **14**

Dove, Ulysses **5**
Faison, George **16**
Jamison, Judith **7**, 67
Primus, Pearl **6**
Rhoden, Dwight **40**
Richardson, Desmond **39**
Spears, Warren **52**
Tyson, Andre **40**
Williams, Dudley **60**

Alvin Ailey Repertory Ensemble
Ailey, Alvin **8**
Miller, Bebe **3**

Amadou Diallo Foundation
Diallo, Amadou **27**

AMAS Repertory Theater
LeNoire, Rosetta **37**

Ambassadors
Braun, Carol Moseley **4**, 42
Cook, Mercer **40**
Dudley, Edward R. **58**
Dymally, Mervyn **42**
Frazer, Jendayi **68**
Todman, Terence A. **55**
Watson, Diane **41**
Whitfield, Mal **60**

AME
See African Methodist Episcopal Church

AMEN
See Active Ministers Engaged in Nurturance

American Academy of Arts and Sciences
Loury, Glenn **36**

American Art Award
Simpson, Lorna **4**, 36

American Association for the Advancement of Science (AAAS)
Cobb, W. Montague **39**
Massey, Walter E. **5**, 45
Pickett, Cecil **39**

American Association of University Women
Granville, Evelyn Boyd **36**

American Ballet Theatre
Dove, Ulysses **5**
Richardson, Desmond **39**

American Bar Association
Archer, Dennis **7**, 36
Pincham, R. Eugene, Sr. **69**
Thompson, Larry D. **39**
Walker, Cora T. **68**

American Basketball Association (ABA)
Chamberlain, Wilt **18**, 47
Erving, Julius **18**, 47

American Beach
Betsch, MaVynee **28**

American Book Award
Baraka, Amiri **1**, 38
Bates, Daisy **13**

Bradley, David Henry, Jr. **39**
Clark, Septima **7**
Gates, Henry Louis, Jr. **3, 38, 67**
Lorde, Audre **6**
Loury, Glenn **36**
Marshall, Paule **7**
Sanchez, Sonia **17, 51**
Walker, Alice **1, 43**

American Broadcasting Company (ABC)
Christian, Spencer **15**
Goode, Mal **13**
Jackson, Michael **19, 53**
Joyner, Tom **19**
Mickebury, Penny **28**
Reynolds, Star Jones **10, 27, 61**
Roberts, Robin **16, 54**
Robinson, Max **3**
Simpson, Carole **6, 30**
Winfrey, Oprah **2, 15, 61**

American Cancer Society
Ashe, Arthur **1, 18**
Leffall, Lasalle **3, 64**
Riperton, Minnie **32**
Thomas, Arthur Ray **52**

American Choral Directors Association
Adams, Leslie **39**

American Civil Liberties Union (ACLU)
Baugh, David **23**
Murphy, Laura M. **43**
Murray, Pauli **38**
Norton, Eleanor Holmes **7**
Pincham, R. Eugene, Sr. **69**

American Communist Party
Patterson, Louise **25**

American Community Housing Associates, Inc.
Lane, Vincent **5**

American Composers Alliance
Tillis, Frederick **40**

American Counseling Association
Mitchell, Sharon **36**

American Dance Guild
Hall, Arthur **39**

American Economic Association
Loury Glenn **36**

American Enterprise Institute
Woodson, Robert L. **10**

American Express Company
Adams, Eula L. **39**
Chenault, Kenneth I. **4, 36**

American Express Consumer Card Group, USA
Chenault, Kenneth I. **4, 36**

American Federation of Labor and Congress of Industrial Organizations (AFL-CIO)
Fletcher, Bill, Jr. **41**
Randolph, A. Philip **3**

American Federation of Television and Radio Artists
Falana, Lola **42**
Fields, Kim **36**
Lewis, Emmanuel **36**
Daniels, Lee Louis **36**

American Guild of Organists
Adams, Leslie **39**

American Heart Association (AHA)
Cooper, Edward S. **6**
Grant, Augustus O. **71**
Richardson, Donna **39**

American Idol
Hudson, Jennifer **63**
Jackson, Randy **40**

American Institute for the Prevention of Blindness
Bath, Patricia E. **37**

American Library Association (ALA)
Franklin, Hardy R. **9**
Hayden, Carla D. **47**
Jones, Clara Stanton **51**
Josey, E. J. **10**
McFadden, Bernice L. **39**
Rollins, Charlamae Hill **27**
Wedgeworth, Robert W. **42**

American Management Association
Cooper, Andrew W. **36**

American Negro Academy
Grimké, Archibald H. **9**
Schomburg, Arthur Alfonso **9**

American Negro Theater
Martin, Helen **31**

American Nuclear Society
Wilkens, J. Ernest, Jr. **43**

American Nurses' Association (ANA)
Kennedy, Adrienne **11**
Staupers, Mabel K. **7**

American Postal Worker's Union
Burrus, William Henry "Bill" **45**

American Psychological Association
Anderson, Norman B. **45**
Mitchell, Sharon **36**

American Red Cross
Bullock, Steve **22**
Drew, Charles Richard **7**

American Society of Magazine Editors
Curry, George E. **23**

American Tennis Association
Gibson, Althea **8, 43**
Peters, Margaret and Matilda **43**

American Writers Association
Schuyler, George Samuel **40**

America's Promise
Powell, Colin **1, 28**

Amistad Freedom Schooner
Pinckney, Bill **42**

Amos Fraser Bernard Consultants
Amos, Valerie **41**

Amsterdam News
Cooper, Andrew W. **36**
Holt, Nora **38**

ANA
See American Nurses' Association

ANC
See African National Congress

Angella Christie Sound Ministries
Christie, Angella **36**

Anglican church hierarchy
Akinola, Peter Jasper **65**
Tutu, Desmond Mpilo **6, 44**

Angolan government
dos Santos, José Eduardo **43**
Neto, António Agostinho **43**

Anheuser-Busch distribution
Cherry, Deron **40**

Anthropology
Asante, Molefi Kete **3**
Bunche, Ralph J. **5**
Cole, Johnnetta B. **5, 43**
Davis, Allison **12**
Diop, Cheikh Anta **4**
Dunham, Katherine **4, 59**
Hansberry, William Leo **11**
Morrison, Toni **2, 15**
Primus, Pearl **6**
Robeson, Eslanda Goode **13**
Rodriguez, Cheryl **64**

Antoinette Perry awards
See Tony awards

APA
See American Psychological Association

Apartheid
Abrahams, Peter **39**
Ashe, Arthur **18**
Berry, Mary Frances **7**
Biko, Steven **4**
Brutus, Dennis **38**
Butler, Jonathan **28**
Howard, M. William, Jr. **26**
Ka Dinizulu, Mcwayizeni **29**
Kuzwayo, Ellen **68**
LaGuma, Alex **30**
Luthuli, Albert **13**
Mahlasela, Vusi **65**
Makeba, Miriam **2, 50**
Mandela, Nelson **1, 14**
Mandela, Winnie **2, 35**
Masekela, Hugh **1**
Mathabane, Mark **5**
Mbeki, Thabo Mvuyelwa **14**
Mbuende, Kaire **12**
McDougall, Gay J. **11, 43**
Mhlaba, Raymond **55**
Mphalele, Es'kia **40**
Nkoli, Simon **60**
Ntshona, Winston **52**
Nyanda, Siphiwe **21**
Nzo, Alfred **15**
Ramaphosa, Cyril **3**
Ramphele, Mamphela **29**
Robinson, Randall **7, 46**
Sisulu, Albertina **57**
Sisulu, Walter **47**
Sullivan, Leon H. **13, 30**
Tutu, Desmond Mpilo **6, 44**

Apollo Theater
Sims, Howard "Sandman" **48**
Sutton, Percy E. **42**

Apollo
Williams, O. S. **13**

APWU
See American Postal Worker's Union

Arab-Israeli conflict
Bunche, Ralph J. **5**

Architecture
Abele, Julian **55**
Adjaye, David **38**
Gantt, Harvey **1**
Johnson, Jeh Vincent **44**
King, Robert Arthur **58**
Sklarek, Norma Merrick **25**
Williams, Paul R. **9**

Argonne National Laboratory
Massey, Walter E. **5, 45**
Quarterman, Lloyd Albert **4**
Massey, Walter E. **5, 45**

Ariel Capital Management
Rogers, John W., Jr. **5, 52**
Hobson, Mellody **40**

Arista Records
Lattimore, Kenny **35**
Reid, Antonio "L.A." **28**

Arkansas Department of Health
Elders, Joycelyn **6**

Armed Forces Communications and Electronics Associations (AFCEA)
Gravely, Samuel L., Jr. **5, 49**

Art history
Benjamin, Tritobia Hayes **53**
Campbell, Mary Schmidt **43**

Arthritis treatment
Julian, Percy Lavon **6**

Arthur Andersen
Scott, Milton **51**

Artists for a Free South Africa
Woodard, Alfre **9**

ASALH
See Association for the Study of Afro-American Life and History

ASH
See Association for the Sexually Harassed

Asheville, North Carolina, city government
Bellamy, Terry 58

Association for Constitutional Democracy in Liberia (ACDL)
Sawyer, Amos 2

Association for the Sexually Harassed (ASH)
Gomez-Preston, Cheryl 9

Assocation of Tennis Professionals (ATP)
Blake, James 43

Association of Volleyball Professionals (AVP)
Blanton, Dain 29

Astronauts
Anderson, Michael P. 40
Bluford, Guy 2, 35
Bolden, Charles F., Jr. 7
Gregory, Frederick 8, 51
Jemison, Mae C. 1, 35
Lawrence, Robert H., Jr. 16
McNair, Ronald 3, 58

Astrophysics
Alcorn, George Edward, Jr. 59
Carruthers, George R. 40

Atco-EastWest
Rhone, Sylvia 2

ATD Publishing
Tyson, Asha 39

Athletic administration
Goss, Tom 23
Littlepage, Craig 35

Atlanta Association of Black Journalists
Pressley, Condace L. 41

Atlanta Baptist College
See Morehouse College

Atlanta Beat
Scurry, Briana 27

Atlanta Board of Education
Mays, Benjamin E. 7

Atlanta Braves baseball team
Aaron, Hank 5
Baker, Dusty 8, 43
Justice, David 18
McGriff, Fred 24
Sanders, Deion 4, 31

Atlanta Chamber of Commerce
Hill, Jesse, Jr. 13

Atlanta city government
Campbell, Bill 9
Franklin, Shirley 34
Jackson, Maynard 2, 41
Williams, Hosea Lorenzo 15, 31
Young, Andrew 3, 48

Atlanta Falcons football team
Anderson, Jamal 22
Buchanan, Ray 32
Sanders, Deion 4, 31
Vick, Michael 39, 65

Atlanta Hawks basketball team
Silas, Paul 24
Wilkens, Lenny 11

Atlanta Life Insurance Company
Hill, Jesse, Jr. 13

Atlanta Negro Voters League
Hill, Jesse, Jr. 13

Atlanta Police Department
Brown, Lee Patrick 1, 24
Harvard, Beverly 11

Atlanta World
Scott, C. A. 29

Atlantic City city government
Usry, James L. 23

Atlantic Records
Franklin, Aretha 11, 44
Lil' Kim 28
Rhone, Sylvia 2

ATP
See Association of Tennis Professionals

Audelco awards
Holder, Laurence 34
Rodgers, Rod 36

Aurelian Honor Society Award
Lewis, William M., Jr. 40

Authors Guild
Davis, George 36
Gayle, Addison, Jr. 41
Schuyler, George Samuel 40

Authors League of America
Abrahams, Peter 39
Cotter, Joseph Seamon, Sr. 40
Davis, George 36
Gayle, Addison, Jr. 41

Automobile dealership
Farr, Mel 24
Gidron, Richard D. 68
Parker, Jim 64

Avery Institute for Social Change
Avery, Byllye Y. 66

Aviation
Brown, Jesse Leroy 31
Brown, Willa 40
Bullard, Eugene 12
Coleman, Bessie 9
McLeod, Gus 27
Petersen, Frank E. 31
Roy, Kenny 51

AVP
See Association of Volleyball Professionals

Baby Phat
Simmons, Kimora Lee 51

"Back to Africa" movement
Turner, Henry McNeal 5

Bad Boy Entertainment
Combs, Sean "Puffy" 17, 43
Harrell, Andre 9, 30
Notorious B.I.G. 20

Bahamian government
Christie, Perry Gladstone 53

Ballet
Ailey, Alvin 8
Allen, Debbie 13, 42
Collins, Janet 33, 64
Dove, Ulysses 5
Faison, George 16
Jamison, Judith 7, 67
Johnson, Virginia 9
Jones, Doris W. 62
Mitchell, Arthur 2, 47
Nichols, Nichelle 11
Parks, Gordon 1, 35, 58
Rhoden, Dwight 40
Richardson, Desmond 39
Rowell, Victoria 13, 68
Tyson, Andre 40

Balm in Gilead, The
Seele, Pernessa 46

Baltimore Black Sox baseball team
Day, Leon 39

Baltimore city government
Dixon, Sheila 68
Robinson, Bishop L. 66
Schmoke, Kurt 1, 48

Baltimore Colts football team
Barnes, Ernie 16
Parker, Jim 64

Baltimore Elite Giants baseball team
Campanella, Roy 25
Day, Leon 39
Kimbro, Henry A. 25

Baltimore Orioles baseball team
Baylor, Don 6
Blair, Paul 36
Carter, Joe 30
Jackson, Reggie 15
Robinson, Frank 9

Banking
Boyd, T. B., III 6
Bradley, Jennette B. 40
Bridgforth, Glinda 36
Brimmer, Andrew F. 2, 48
Bryant, John 26
Chapman, Nathan A., Jr. 21
Chappell, Emma 18
Ferguson, Roger W. 25
Forte, Linda Diane 54
Funderburg, I. Owen 38
Greene, Richard Thaddeus, Sr. 67
Griffith, Mark Winston 8
Harris, Carla A. 67
Lawless, Theodore K. 8
Louis, Errol T. 8
March, William Carrington 56
McGuire, Raymond J. 57
Morgan, Rose 11
Parsons, Richard Dean 11
Utendahl, John 23
Walker, Maggie Lena 17
Watkins, Walter C. 24
Willie, Louis, Jr. 68
Wright, Deborah C. 25

Baptist
Austin, Junius C. 44
Bradley, J. Robert 65
Davis, Gary 41
Forbes, James A., Jr. 71
Franklin, C. L. 68
Gomes, Peter J. 15
Jemison, Major L. 48
Jones, E. Edward, Sr. 45
Long, Eddie L. 29
Meek, Carrie 6
Meek, Kendrick 41
Thurston, Stephen J. 49

Baptist World Alliance Assembly
Mays, Benjamin E. 7

Barnett-Ader Gallery
Thomas, Alma 14

Barnum and Bailey Circus
McFarlan, Tyron 60

Baseball
Aaron, Hank 5
Anderson, Elmer 25
Ashford, Emmett 22
Baines, Harold 32
Baker, Dusty 8, 43
Banks, Ernie 33
Barnhill, David 30
Baylor, Don 6
Bell, James "Cool Papa" 36
Belle, Albert 10
Blair, Paul 36
Bonds, Barry 6, 34, 63
Bonds, Bobby 43
Brock, Lou 18
Brown, Willard 36
Campanella, Roy 25
Carew, Rod 20
Carter, Joe 30
Charleston, Oscar 39
Clendenon, Donn 26, 56
Coleman, Leonard S., Jr. 12
Cooper, Andy "Lefty" 63
Cottrell, Comer 11
Dandridge, Ray 36
Davis, Piper 19
Doby, Lawrence Eugene, Sr. 16
Day, Leon 39
Dye, Jermaine 58
Edwards, Harry 2
Fielder, Cecil 2
Fielder, Prince Semien 68
Flood, Curt 10
Gaston, Cito 71
Gibson, Bob 33
Gibson, Josh 22
Gooden, Dwight 20
Granderson, Curtis 66
Gregg, Eric 16
Griffey, Ken, Jr. 12
Hammer, M. C. 20
Henderson, Rickey 28
Howard, Ryan 65
Hunter, Torii 43
Hyde, Cowan F. "Bubba" 47
Irvin, Monte 31
Jackson, Reggie 15

Jenkins, Fergie **46**
Jeter, Derek **27**
Johnson, Clifford "Connie" **52**
Johnson, Mamie "Peanut" **40**
Justice, David **18**
Kaiser, Cecil **42**
Kimbro, Henry A. **25**
Lacy, Sam **30, 46**
Lankford, Ray **23**
Larkin, Barry **24**
Lloyd, John Henry "Pop" **30**
Lofton, Kenny **12**
Mariner, Jonathan **41**
Mays, Willie **3**
McGriff, Fred **24**
Morgan, Joe Leonard **9**
Murray, Eddie **12**
Newcombe, Don **24**
O'Neil, Buck **19, 59**
Ortiz, David **52**
Paige, Satchel **7**
Payne, Ulice **42**
Pride, Charley **26**
Puckett, Kirby **4, 58**
Randolph, Willie **53**
Reese, Pokey **28**
Robinson, Frank **9**
Robinson, Jackie **6**
Robinson, Sharon **22**
Rollins, Jimmy **70**
Sanders, Deion **4, 31**
Sheffield, Gary **16**
Smith, Hilton **29**
Sosa, Sammy **21, 44**
Stargell, Willie **29**
Stearnes, Norman "Turkey" **31**
Stone, Toni **15**
Strawberry, Darryl **22**
Thomas, Frank **12, 51**
Vaughn, Mo **16**
Virgil, Ozzie **48**
Watson, Bob **25**
White, Bill **1, 48**
Williams, Ken **68**
Willis, Dontrelle **55**
Winfield, Dave **5**

Baseball Hall of Fame
Bell, James "Cool Papa" **36**
Charleston, Oscar **39**
Day, Leon **39**
Doby, Lawrence Eugene, Sr. **16, 41**

Barbadian government
Arthur, Owen **33**

Basketball
Abdul-Jabbar, Kareem **8**
Abdur-Rahim, Shareef **28**
Amaker, Tommy **62**
Anderson, Mike **63**
Anthony, Carmelo **46**
Artest, Ron **52**
Barkley, Charles **5, 66**
Bing, Dave **3, 59**
Bogues, Tyrone "Muggsy" **56**
Bol, Manute **1**
Bolton-Holifield, Ruthie **28**
Brand, Elton **31**
Brandon, Terrell **16**
Bryant, Kobe **15, 31, 71**
Carter, Butch **27**
Carter, Kenneth **53**
Carter, Vince **26**
Catchings, Tamika **43**
Chamberlain, Wilt **18, 47**
Chaney, John **67**
Cheeks, Maurice **47**
Clifton, Nathaniel "Sweetwater" **47**
Cooper, Charles "Chuck" **47**
Cooper, Cynthia **17**
Cooper, Michael **31**
Davis, Mike **41**
Drexler, Clyde **4, 61**
Dumars, Joe **16, 65**
Duncan, Tim **20**
Dunn, Jerry **27**
Edwards, Harry **2**
Edwards, Teresa **14**
Ellerbe, Brian **22**
Elliott, Sean **26**
Ewing, Patrick A. **17**
Fox, Rick **27**
Freeman, Marianna **23**
Gaines, Clarence E., Sr. **55**
Garnett, Kevin **14, 70**
Gentry, Alvin **23**
Gossett, Louis, Jr. **7**
Gray, Yeshimbra "Shimmy" **55**
Green, A. C. **32**
Griffith, Yolanda **25**
Hardaway, Anfernee (Penny) **13**
Hardaway, Tim **35**
Haskins, Clem **23**
Haynes, Marques **22**
Heard, Gar **25**
Hill, Grant **13**
Holdsclaw, Chamique **24**
Howard, Juwan **15**
Hunter, Billy **22**
Iverson, Allen **24, 46**
James, LeBron **46**
Johnson, Avery **62**
Johnson, Earvin "Magic" **3, 39**
Johnson, Kevin **70**
Johnson, Larry **28**
Jones, Merlakia **34**
Jones, Roy, Jr. **22**
Jordan, Michael **6, 21**
Justice, David **18**
Kellogg, Clark **64**
Lanier, Bob **47**
Lennox, Betty **31**
Leslie, Lisa **16**
Lloyd, Earl **26**
Lofton, Kenny **12**
Lowe, Sidney **64**
Lucas, John **7**
Mahorn, Rick **60**
Malone, Karl **18, 51**
Manigault, Earl "The Goat" **15**
Master P **21**
Miller, Cheryl **10**
Miton, DeLisha **31**
Mohammed, Nazr **64**
Mourning, Alonzo **17, 44**
Mutombo, Dikembe **7**
Olajuwon, Hakeem **2**
O'Neal, Shaquille **8, 30**
Palmer, Violet **59**
Parish, Robert **43**
Peck, Carolyn **23**
Phillips, Teresa L. **42**
Pierce, Paul **71**
Pippen, Scottie **15**
Prince, Tayshaun **68**
Richardson, Nolan **9**
Richmond, Mitch **19**
Rivers, Glenn "Doc" **25**
Robertson, Oscar **26**
Robinson, David **24**
Robinson, Will **51, 69**
Russell, Bill **8**
Silas, Paul **24**
Smith, Stephen A. **69**
Smith, Tubby **18**
Sprewell, Latrell **23**
Stackhouse, Jerry **30**
Staley, Dawn **57**
Stoudemire, Amaré **59**
Stringer, C. Vivian **13, 66**
Swoopes, Sheryl **12, 56**
Thomas, Isiah **7, 26, 65**
Thompson, Tina **25**
Tisdale, Wayman **50**
Unseld, Wes **23**
Wallace, Ben **54**
Wallace, Perry E. **47**
Wallace, Rasheed **56**
Webber, Chris **15, 30, 59**
Wilkens, Lenny **11**
Williams, Natalie **31**
Woodward, Lynette **67**
Worthy, James **49**

Basketball Hall of Fame
Parish, Robert **43**

Bass
Foster, George "Pops" **40**
Jamerson, James **59**

BBC
See British Broadcasting Company

BCALA
See Black Caucus of the American Library Association

BDP
See Botswana Democratic Party

Beach Volleyball America (BVA)
Blanton, Dain **29**

Beale Streeters
Ace, Johnny **36**
Bland, Bobby "Blue" **36**
King, B.B. **7**

Bear, Stearns & Co.
Fletcher, Alphonso, Jr. **16**

Beatrice International
See TLC Beatrice International Holdings, Inc.

Beauty Salons and Products
Fine, Sam **60**
Gibson, Ted **66**
Stanford, Olivia Lee Dilworth **49**

Bebop
Carter, Betty **19**
Clarke, Kenny **27**
Coltrane, John **19**
Davis, Miles **4**
Eckstine, Billy **28**
Fitzgerald, Ella **8, 18**
Gillespie, Dizzy **1**
Gordon, Dexter **25**
Hancock, Herbie **20, 67**
Harris, Barry **68**
Hawkins, Coleman **9**
Jackson, Milt **26**
Parker, Charlie **20**
Powell, Bud **24**
Roach, Max **21, 63**
Vaughan, Sarah **13**

Bechuanaland Protectorate Legislative Council
Masire, Quett **5**

Beckham Publications Group Inc.
Beckham, Barry **41**

Bedford-Stuyvesant Restoration Corporation
Thomas, Franklin A. **5, 49**

Bell of Pennsylvania
Gordon, Bruce S. **41, 53**

Ben & Jerry's Homemade Ice Cream, Inc.
Holland, Robert, Jr. **11**

Bennett College
Cole, Johnnetta B. **5, 43**
Player, Willa B. **43**

Bessie award
Richardson, Desmond **39**

BET
See Black Entertainment Television

Bethann Management, Inc.
Hardison, Bethann **12**

Bethune-Cookman College
Bethune, Mary McLeod **4**
Joyner, Marjorie Stewart **26**

BFF
See Black Filmmaker Foundation

BGLLF
See Black Gay and Lesbian Leadership Forum

Big Easy Award
Adams, Johnny **39**

Bill and Melinda Gates Foundation
Golston, Allan C. **55**

Billy Graham Evangelistic Association
Bell, Ralph S. **5**
Waters, Ethel **7**

Bing Group, The
Bing, Dave **3, 59**
Lloyd, Earl **26**

Biology
Cobb, Jewel Plummer **42**
Pickett, Cecil **39**
Emeagwali, Dale **31**
Jarvis, Erich **67**
Just, Ernest Everett **3**
Malveaux, Floyd **54**

Biotechnology
Juma, Calestous **57**
Wambugu, Florence **42**

Birmingham city government
Kincaid, Bernard 28
Nunn, Annetta 43

Birmingham (AL) Police Department
Nunn, Annetta 43

Birth control
Elders, Joycelyn 6
Williams, Maggie 7, 71

Bishop College
Cottrell, Comer 11

Bismark Bisons baseball team
Dandridge, Ray 36

BLA
See Black Liberation Army

Black Aesthetic
Baker, Houston A., Jr. 6

Black Academy of Arts & Letters
White, Charles 39

Black Alliance for Educational Options
Fuller, Howard L. 37

Black American West Museum
Stewart, Paul Wilbur 12

Black Americans for Family Values
Foster, Ezola 28

Black and White Minstrel Show
Henry, Lenny 9, 52

Black arts movement
Barrett, Lindsay 43
Caldwell, Benjamin 46
Cornish, Sam 50
Cortez, Jayne 43
Cruse, Harold 54
Dent, Thomas C. 50
Donaldson, Jeff 46
Dumas, Henry 41
Gayle, Addison, Jr. 41
Giovanni, Nikki 9, 39
Henderson, David 53
Hoagland, Everett H. 45
Neal, Larry 38
Smith, Vincent D. 48
Touré, Askia (Muhammad Abu Bakr el) 47
X, Marvin 45

Black Cabinet
Hastie, William H. 8

Black Caucus of the American Library Association (BCALA)
Josey, E. J. 10

Black Christian Nationalist movement
Agyeman, Jaramogi Abebe 10, 63

Black Coaches Association (BCA)
Freeman, Marianna 23
Keith, Floyd A. 61

Black Consciousness movement
Biko, Steven 4
Fanon, Frantz 44
Fuller, Hoyt 44
Muhammad, Elijah 4
Ramaphosa, Cyril 3
Ramphele, Mamphela 29
Tutu, Desmond Mpilo 6, 44

Black Economic Union (BEU)
Brown, Jim 11

Black Enterprise magazine
Brimmer, Andrew F. 2, 48
Graves, Earl G. 1, 35
Wallace, Phyllis A. 9

Black Enterprise Corporate Executive of the Year
Chenault, Kenneth I. 5, 36
Steward, David L. 36

Black Entertainment Television (BET)
Ames, Wilmer 27
Gordon, Ed 10, 53
Greely, M. Gasby 27
Johnson, Robert L. 3, 39
Johnson, Sheila Crump 48
Jones, Bobby 20
Lee, Debra L. 62
McCrary Anthony, Crystal 70
Smiley, Tavis 20, 68

Black Filmmaker Foundation (BFF)
Hudlin, Reginald 9
Hudlin, Warrington 9
Jackson, George 19
Williams, Terrie 35

Black Filmmakers Hall of Fame
Browne, Roscoe Lee 66
Dee, Ruby 8, 50, 68
Dixon, Ivan 69
McKinney, Nina Mae 40

Black Gay and Lesbian Leadership Forum (BGLLF)
Wilson, Phill 9

Black Guerrilla Family (BGF)
Jackson, George 14

Black History Month
Woodson, Carter G. 2

Black Horizons on the Hill
Wilson, August 7, 33, 55

Black Liberation Army (BLA)
Shakur, Assata 6
Williams, Evelyn 10

Black literary theory
Gates, Henry Louis, Jr. 3, 38, 67

Black Manifesto
Forman, James 7, 51

Black Music Center
Moore, Undine Smith 28

Black Muslims
Abdul-Jabbar, Kareem 8
Ali, Muhammad 2, 16, 52
Farrakhan, Louis 2
Muhammad, Elijah 4
Muhammed, W. Deen 27
X, Malcolm 1

Black nationalism
Baker, Houston A., Jr. 6
Baraka, Amiri 1, 38
Caldwell, Benjamin 46
Carmichael, Stokely 5, 26
Donaldson, Jeff 46
Farrakhan, Louis 2
Forman, James 7, 51
Garvey, Marcus 1
Heard, Nathan C. 45
Innis, Roy 5
Muhammad, Elijah 4
Turner, Henry McNeal 5
X, Malcolm 1
York, Dwight D. 71

Black Oscar Awards
Daniels, Lee Louis 36

Black Panther Party (BPP)
Abu-Jamal, Mumia 15
Al-Amin, Jamil Abdullah 6
Brown, Elaine 8
Carmichael, Stokely 5
Cleaver, Eldridge 5
Cleaver, Kathleen Neal 29
Davis, Angela 5
Forman, James 7, 51
Hampton, Fred 18
Hilliard, David 7
Jackson, George 14
Neal, Larry 38
Newton, Huey 2
Pratt, Geronimo 18
Rush, Bobby 26
Shakur, Afeni 67
Seale, Bobby 3
Shakur, Assata 6

Black Power movement
Al-Amin, Jamil Abdullah 6
Baker, Houston A., Jr. 6
Brown, Elaine 8
Carmichael, Stokely 5, 26
Dodson, Howard, Jr. 7, 52
Donaldson, Jeff 46
Dumas, Henry 41
Giovanni, Nikki 9, 39
Hare, Nathan 44
McKissick, Floyd B. 3
Stone, Chuck 9

Blackside, Inc.
Hampton, Henry 6

Black theology
Cone, James H. 3

Black Think Tank
Hare, Nathan 44

Blackvoices.com
Cooper, Barry 33

Blackwell Consulting Services
Blackwell, Robert D., Sr. 52

Black World magazine
See *Negro Digest* magazine

Black Writers Conference
McMillan, Rosalynn A. 36

Blessed Martin House
Riley, Helen Caldwell Day 13

Blind Boys of Alabama
Scott, George 55

"Blood for Britain"
Drew, Charles Richard 7

Blood plasma research/preservation
Drew, Charles Richard 7

Blues
Ace, Johnny 36
Austin, Lovie 40
Barnes, Roosevelt "Booba" 33
Bibb, Eric 49
Bland, Bobby "Blue" 36
Brown, Charles 23
Burns, Eddie 44
Burnside, R. L. 56
Carr, Leroy 49
Clarke, Kenny 27
Collins, Albert 12
Cox, Ida 42
Cray, Robert 30
Davis, Gary 41
Davis, Guy 36
Davis, Tyrone 54
Dixon, Willie 4
Dorsey, Thomas 15
Estes, Sleepy John 33
Evora, Cesaria 12
Freeman, Yvette 27
Gaines, Grady 38
Guy, Buddy 31
Handy, W. C. 8
Harris, Corey 39
Hemphill, Jessie Mae 33, 59
Holiday, Billie 1
Hooker, John Lee 30
House, Son 8
Howlin' Wolf 9
Hunter, Alberta 42
Jean-Baptiste, Marianne 17, 46
Jackson, John 36
James, Skip 38
Johnson, Buddy 36
King, B. B. 7
Lipscomb, Mance 49
Little Milton 36
Little Walton 36
Mahal, Taj 39
Martin, Sara 38
Mo', Keb' 36
Moore, Johnny B. 38
Muse, Clarence Edouard 21
Neal, Raful 44
Odetta 37
Owens, Jack 38
Parker, Charlie 20
Pena, Paul 58
Perkins, Pinetop 70
Peterson, James 38
Rawls, Lou 17, 57
Reed, A. C. 36
Reed, Jimmy 38
Reese, Della 6, 20
Robinson, Fenton 38
Rogers, Jimmy 38

Ross, Isaiah "Doc" 40
Rush, Otis 38
Seals, Son 56
Smith, Bessie 3
Smith, Mamie 32
Smith, Trixie 34
Staples, Mavis 50
Staples, "Pops" 32
Streeter, Sarah 45
Sykes, Roosevelt 20
Tampa Red 63
Taylor, Koko 40
Turner, Ike 68
Wallace, Sippie 1
Washington, Dinah 22
Waters, Ethel 7
Waters, Muddy 34
Watson, Johnny "Guitar" 18
Webster, Katie 29
White, Josh, Jr. 52
Williams, Joe 5, 25
Wilson, August 7, 33, 55

Blues Hall of Fame
Little Milton 36

Blues Heaven Foundation
Dixon, Willie 4

Blues vernacular
Baker, Houston A., Jr. 6

Bobsledding
Flowers, Vonetta 35
Hines, Garrett 35
Jones, Randy 35
Moses, Edwin 8

Bodybuilding
Murray, Lenda 10

Boeing Company, The
Bell, James A. 50
Grooms, Henry R(andall) 50
Mills, Joseph C. 51

Bola Press
Cortez, Jayne 43

Bolero music
Ferrer, Ibrahim 41

Boogie music
Brooks, Hadda 40

Booker T. Washington Business College
Gaston, Arthur George 3, 38, 59

Booker T. Washington Insurance Company
Gaston, Arthur George 3, 38, 59
Willie, Louis, Jr. 68

The Boondocks
McGruder, Aaron 28, 56

Boston Bruins hockey team
O'Ree, Willie 5

Boston Celtics basketball team
Cooper, Charles "Chuck" 47
Fox, Rick 27
Garnett, Kevin 14, 70
Parish, Robert 43
Pierce, Paul 71

Russell, Bill 8
Silas, Paul 24

Boston Collective
Crite, Alan Rohan 29

Boston Red Sox baseball team
Baylor, Don 6
Ortiz, David 52
Vaughn, Mo 16

Boston University
Loury, Glenn 36
Mitchell, Sharon 36

Botany
Carver, George Washington 4

Botswana Democratic Party (BDP)
Masire, Quett 5
Mogae, Festus Gontebanye 19

Bountiful Blessings magazine
Patterson, Gilbert Earl 41

Bowling
Branham, George, III 50

Boxing
Ali, Laila 27, 63
Ali, Muhammad 2, 16, 52
Bowe, Riddick 6
Carter, Rubin 26
Dixon, George 52
Ellis, Jimmy 44
Foreman, George 1, 15
Frazier, Joe 19
Frazier-Lyde, Jacqui 31
Futch, Eddie 33
Gibson, Truman K., Jr. 60
Hearns, Thomas 29
Holmes, Larry 20, 68
Holyfield, Evander 6
Hopkins, Bernard 35, 69
Johnson, Jack 8
Jones, Roy, Jr. 22
King, Don 14
Lee, Canada 8
Leonard, Sugar Ray 15
Lewis, Butch 71
Lewis, Lennox 27
Louis, Joe 5
Mayweather, Floyd, Jr. 57
Moorer, Michael 19
Mosley, Shane 32
Mundine, Anthony 56
Patterson, Floyd 19, 58
Robinson, Sugar Ray 18
Rose, Lionel 56
Steward, Emanuel 18
Taylor, Jermain 60
Tyson, Mike 28, 44
Ward, Andre 62
Whitaker, Pernell 10
Young, Jimmy 54

Boys Choir of Harlem
Turnbull, Walter 13, 60

BPP
See Black Panther Party

Brazeal Dennard Chorale
Dennard, Brazeal 37

Brazilian Congress
da Silva, Benedita 5

Breast Cancer awareness
Riperton, Minnie 32

Breast Cancer Resource Committee
Brown, Zora Kramer 12

Bridgforth Financial Management Group
Bridgforth, Glinda 36

Bristol-Myers Squibb Inc.
Potter, Myrtle 40

British Broadcasting Company (BBC)
Figueroa, John J. 40

British Film Institute
Akomfrah, John 37

British government
Abbott, Diane 9
Amos, Valerie 41
Boateng, Paul Yaw 56
Grant, Bernie 57
King, Oona 27
Pitt, David Thomas 10

British Open golf tournament
Woods, Tiger 14, 31

British Parliament
See British government

Broadcasting
Allen, Byron 3, 24
Ashley, Maurice 15, 47
Banks, William 11
Barden, Don H. 9, 20
Bettis, Jerome 64
Blackmon, Brenda 58
Bradley, Ed 2, 59
Branch, William Blackwell 39
Brown, Les 5
Brown, Tony 3
Brown, Vivian 27
Brunson, Dorothy 1
Clayton, Xernona 3, 45
Cornelius, Don 4
Davis, Ossie 5, 50
Dee, Merri 55
Elder, Larry 25
Evans, Harry 25
Figueroa, John J. 40
Freeman, Aaron 52
Goode, Mal 13
Gumbel, Bryant 14
Gumbel, Greg 8
Hamblin, Ken 10
Hickman, Fred 11
Holt, Lester 66
Hunter-Gault, Charlayne 6, 31
Jackson, Hal 41
Johnson, Rafer 33
Johnson, Robert L. 3, 39
Jones, Bobby 20
Joyner, Tom 19
Kellogg, Clark 64
Kennedy-Overton, Jayne Harris 46
Langhart Cohen, Janet 19, 60
Lawson, Jennifer 1, 50
Lewis, Delano 7

Lofton, James 42
Long, Eddie L. 29
Mabrey, Vicki 26
Madison, Joseph E. 17
Madison, Paula 37
McEwen, Mark 5
McFarland, Roland 49
Mickelbury, Penny 28
Miller, Cheryl 10
Mitchell, Russ 21
Morgan, Joe Leonard 9
Neville, Arthel 53
Peete, Rodney 60
Pinckney, Sandra 56
Pinkston, W. Randall 24
Quarles, Norma 25
Reynolds, Star Jones 10, 27, 61
Roberts, Deborah 35
Roberts, Robin 16, 54
Robinson, Max 3
Rodgers, Johnathan 6, 51
Russell, Bill 8
Shaw, Bernard 2, 28
Simpson, Carole 6, 30
Simpson, O. J. 15
Smiley, Tavis 20, 68
Stewart, Alison 13
Stokes, Carl B. 10
Swann, Lynn 28
Syler, Rene 53
Tirico, Mike 68
Watts, Rolonda 9
White, Bill 1, 48
Williams, Armstrong 29
Williams, Juan 35
Williams, Montel 4, 57
Winfrey, Oprah 2, 15, 61

Broadside Press
Hoagland, Everett H. 45
Randall, Dudley 8, 55

Bronner Brothers
Bronner, Nathaniel H., Sr. 32

Brookings Institute
Ladner, Joyce A. 42

Brooklyn Academy of Music
Miller, Bebe 3

Brooklyn Dodgers baseball team
Campanella, Roy 25
Newcombe, Don 24
Robinson, Jackie 6

Brooklyn Eagles baseball team
Day, Leon 39

Brooks Bunch
Brooks, Derrick 43

Brotherhood of Sleeping Car Porters
Randolph, A. Philip 3
Tucker, Rosina 14

Brown Capital Management
Brown, Eddie C. 35

Brown University
Beckham, Barry 41
Gibson, Donald Bernard 40

Simmons, Ruth 13, 38

Brown v. Board of Education of Topeka
Bell, Derrick 6
Carter, Robert L. 51
Clark, Kenneth B. 5, 52
Franklin, John Hope 5
Henderson, Zelma 71
Hill, Oliver W. 24, 63
Houston, Charles Hamilton 4
Malone Jones, Vivian 59
Marshall, Thurgood 1, 44
Motley, Constance Baker 10, 55
Redding, Louis L. 26
Robinson, Spottswood W., III 22

Buena Vista Social Club
Ferrer, Ibrahim 41

Buffalo Bills football team
Lofton, James 42
Simpson, O. J. 15

Bull-riding
Sampson, Charles 13

Busing (anti-busing legislation)
Bosley, Freeman, Jr. 7

BVA
See Beach Volleyball America

Cabinet
See U.S. Cabinet

Cable News Network (CNN)
Chideya, Farai 14, 61
Hickman, Fred 11
Quarles, Norma 25
Shaw, Bernard 2, 28
Watson, Carlos 50

Calabash International Literary Festival
Channer, Colin 36

Calgary Flames hockey team
Iginla, Jarome 35

California Angels baseball team
See Los Angeles Angels baseball team

California Eagle newspaper
Bass, Charlotta Spears 40
Jackson, Vera 40

California State Assembly
Bass, Karen 70
Brown, Willie L., Jr. 7
Dixon, Julian C. 24
Dymally, Mervyn 42
Hawkins, Augustus F. 68
Lee, Barbara 25
Millender-McDonald, Juanita 21, 61
Waters, Maxine 3, 67

California state government
Bass, Karen 70
Brown, Janice Rogers 43
Dymally, Mervyn 42

Watson, Diane 41

California State University
Cobb, Jewel Plummer 42
Granville, Evelyn Boyd 36
Karenga, Maulana 10, 71

California Supreme Court
Brown, Janice Rogers 43

Calypso
Belafonte, Harry 4, 65
Jean, Wyclef 20
Premice, Josephine 41
Rhoden, Wayne 70

Camac Holdings, Inc.
Lawal, Kase L. 45

Cameroonian government
Biya, Paul 28
Oyono, Ferdinand 38

Canadian Agricultural Chemistry Association
Donald, Arnold Wayne 36

Canadian Football League (CFL)
Clemons, Michael "Pinball" 64
Gilliam, Frank 23
Moon, Warren 8, 66
Thrower, Willie 35
Weathers, Carl 10

Canadian government
Augustine, Jean 53
Brown, Rosemary 62
Cools, Anne 64
Jean, Michaëlle; 70
Sparks, Corinne Etta 53

Canadian Provincial baseball league
Kaiser, Cecil 42

Cancer research
Adams-Campbell, Lucille L. 60
Chinn, May Edward 26
Clark, Celeste 15
Daly, Marie Maynard 37
Dunston, Georgia Mae 48
Freeman, Harold P. 23
Leffall, Lasalle 3, 64
Olopade, Olufunmilayo Falusi 58

Capital punishment
Hawkins, Steven 14

Cardiac research
Watkins, Levi, Jr. 9

CARE
Gossett, Louis, Jr. 7
Stone, Chuck 9

Caribbean Artists' Movement
Brathwaite, Kamau 36

Caribbean dance
Ailey, Alvin 8
Dunham, Katherine 4, 59
Fagan, Garth 18
Nichols, Nichelle 11

Primus, Pearl 6

Caribbean literature
Breeze, Jean "Binta" 37
Carter, Martin 49
Cartey, Wilfred 47
Dabydeen, David 48
Hearne, John Edgar Caulwell 45

Caroline Jones Advertising, Inc
Jones, Caroline R. 29

Casamance, Senegal
Senghor, Augustin Dimacoune 66

Casting
Cannon, Reuben 50

Catalyst Award (American Express)
Chenault, Kenneth I. 5, 36

Cartoonists
Armstrong, Robb 15
Brandon, Barbara 3
Brown, Robert 65
Campbell, E. Simms 13
Fax, Elton 48
Harrington, Oliver W. 9
McDuffie, Dwayne 62
McGruder, Aaron 28, 56
Smith, Bruce W. 53

Catholicism
See Roman Catholic Church

CBC
See Congressional Black Caucus

CBEA
See Council for a Black Economic Agenda

CBS
See Columbia Broadcasting System

CBS Television Stations Division
Rodgers, Johnathan 6, 51

CDC
See Centers for Disease Control and Prevention

CDF
See Children's Defense Fund

CEDBA
See Council for the Economic Development of Black Americans

Celebrities for a Drug-Free America
Vereen, Ben 4

Censorship
Butts, Calvin O., III 9
Ice-T 6, 31

Center of Hope Church
Reems, Ernestine Cleveland 27

Centers for Disease Control and Prevention (CDC)
Gayle, Helene D. 3
Satcher, David 7, 57

Wisdom, Kimberlydawn 57

Central Intercollegiate Athletic Association (CIAA)
Kerry, Leon G. 46
Yancy, Dorothy Cowser 42

Certified Public Accountant
Jones, Thomas W. 41
Washington, Mary T. 57

CFL
See Canadian Football League

CHA
See Chicago Housing Authority

Chadian government
Habré, Hissène 6

Challenged Athletes Foundation
Yeboah, Emmanuel Ofosu 53

Challenger
McNair, Ronald 3, 58

Challenger Air Pilot's Association
Brown, Willa 40

Chama cha Mapinduzi (Tanzania; Revolutionary Party)
Mkapa, Benjamin 16
Mongella, Gertrude 11
Nyerere, Julius 5

Chamber of Deputies (Brazil)
da Silva, Benedita 5

Chanteuses
Baker, Josephine 3
Dandridge, Dorothy 3
Horne, Lena 5
Kitt, Eartha 16
Lefel, Edith 41
Moore, Melba 21
Moten, Etta 18
Reese, Della 6, 20

Charles H. Wright Museum of African American History (CWMAAH)
Wright, Charles H. 35

Charles R. Drew University
Bath, Patricia E. 37

Charlotte Hornets basketball team
Bryant, Kobe 15, 31, 71
Parish, Robert 43

Charter Schools USA
Mariner, Jonathan 41

Che-Lumumba Club
Davis, Angela 5

Chemistry
Daly, Marie Maynard 37
Hall, Lloyd A. 8
Humphries, Frederick 20
Julian, Percy Lavon 6
King, Reatha Clark 65
Massie, Samuel Proctor, Jr. 29
Mays, William G. 34

Mensah, Thomas 48

Chemurgy
Carver, George Washington 4

Chesapeake and Potomac Telephone Company
Lewis, Delano 7

Chess
Ashley, Maurice 15, 47

Chess Records
Taylor, Koko 40

Chicago American Giants baseball team
Bell, James "Cool Papa" 36
Charleston, Oscar 39

Chicago Art League
Wilson, Ellis 39

Chicago Bears football team
Page, Alan 7
Payton, Walter 11, 25
Sayers, Gale 28
Singletary, Mike 4
Thrower, Willie 35

Chicago Black Arts Movement
Cortor, Eldzier 42
Sebree, Charles 40

Chicago Blaze basketball team
Catchings, Tamika 43

Chicago Bulls basketball team
Brand, Elton 31
Jordan, Michael 6, 21
Parish, Robert 43
Pippen, Scottie 15
Rodman, Dennis 12, 44

Chicago city government
Metcalfe, Ralph 26
Washington, Harold 6

Chicago Cubs baseball team
Baker, Dusty 8, 43
Banks, Ernie 33
Bonds, Bobby 43
Carter, Joe 30
Sosa, Sammy 21, 44

Chicago Defender
Abbott, Robert Sengstacke 27
Holt, Nora 38
Martin, Roland S. 49
Payne, Ethel L. 28

Chicago Defender Charities
Joyner, Marjorie Stewart 26

Chicago Eight
Seale, Bobby 3

Chicago Housing Authority (CHA)
Lane, Vincent 5

Chicago Library Board
Williams, Fannie Barrier 27

Chicago Negro Chamber of Commerce
Fuller, S. B. 13

Chicago Police Department
Hillard, Terry 25
Holton, Hugh, Jr. 39

Chicago Reporter
Washington, Laura S. 18

Chicago Tribune
Page, Clarence 4

Chicago White Sox baseball team
Baines, Harold 32
Bonds, Bobby 43
Doby, Lawrence Eugene, Sr. 16, 41
Johnson, Clifford "Connie" 52
Thomas, Frank 12, 51
Williams, Ken 68

Chicago Women's Club
Williams, Fannie Barrier 27

Child Care Trust
Obasanjo, Stella 32, 56

Child psychiatry
Comer, James P. 6

Child psychology
Hale, Lorraine 8

Child Welfare Administration
Little, Robert L. 2

Children's Defense Fund (CDF)
Edelman, Marian Wright 5, 42
Williams, Maggie 7, 71

Children's literature
Asim, Jabari 71
Berry, James 41
Bryan, Ashley F. 41
Common 31, 63
De Veaux, Alexis 44
Feelings, Muriel 44
Graham, Lorenz 48
Johnson, Angela 52
Mollel, Tololwa 38
Myers, Walter Dean 8, 20
Okara, Gabriel 37
Palmer, Everard 37
Yarbrough, Camille 40

Chi-Lites
Record, Eugene 60

Chiropractics
Ford, Clyde W. 40
Reese, Milous J., Jr. 51
Westbrooks, Bobby 51

Chisholm-Mingo Group, Inc.
Chisholm, Samuel J. 32
Mingo, Frank 32

Choreography
Acogny, Germaine 55
Ailey, Alvin 8
Alexander, Khandi 43
Allen, Debbie 13, 42
Atkins, Cholly 40
Babatunde, Obba 35
Beatty, Talley 35
Brooks, Avery 9
Byrd, Donald 10
Campbell-Martin, Tisha 8, 42

Collins, Janet 33, 64
Davis, Chuck 33
de Passe, Suzanne 25
Dove, Ulysses 5
Dunham, Katherine 4, 59
Ellington, Mercedes 34
Fagan, Garth 18
Faison, George 16
Glover, Savion 14
Hall, Arthur 39
Henson, Darrin 33
Jamison, Judith 7, 67
Johnson, Virginia 9
Jones, Bill T. 1
King, Alonzo 38
LeTang, Henry 66
Miller, Bebe 3
Mitchell, Arthur 2, 47
Nicholas, Fayard 20, 57
Nicholas, Harold 20
Primus, Pearl 6
Rhoden, Dwight 40
Richardson, Desmond 39
Robinson, Cleo Parker 38
Robinson, Fatima 34
Rodgers, Rod 36
Spears, Warren 52
Tyson, Andre 40
Zollar, Jawole 28

Christian Financial Ministries, Inc.
Ross, Charles 27

Christian Science Monitor
Khanga, Yelena 6

Chrysler Corporation
Colbert, Virgis William 17
Farmer, Forest 1
Gilles, Ralph 61
Richie, Leroy C. 18

Church for the Fellowship of All Peoples
Thurman, Howard 3

Church of God in Christ
Franklin, Robert M. 13
Hayes, James C. 10
Patterson, Gilbert Earl 41

CIAA
See Central Intercollegiate Athletic Association

Cincinnati city government
Berry, Theodore M. 31
Mallory, Mark 62

Cincinnati Reds baseball team
Blair, Paul 36
Larkin, Barry 24
Morgan, Joe Leonard 9
Reese, Pokey 28
Robinson, Frank 9
Sanders, Deion 4, 31

Cinematography
Dickerson, Ernest 6, 17

Citadel Press
Achebe, Chinua 6

Citigroup
Gaines, Brenda 41
Jones, Thomas W. 41

McGuire, Raymond J. 57

Citizens Federal Savings and Loan Association
Gaston, Arthur George 3, 38, 59
Willie, Louis, Jr. 68

Citizens for Affirmative Action's Preservation
Dillard, Godfrey J. 45

City Capital Corporation
Taylor, Ephren W., II 61

City government--U.S.
Archer, Dennis 7, 36
Barden, Don H. 9, 20
Barry, Marion S. 7, 44
Berry, Theodore M. 31
Bosley, Freeman, Jr. 7
Bradley, Thomas 2, 20
Brown, Lee P. 1, 24
Burris, Chuck 21
Caesar, Shirley 19
Campbell, Bill 9
Clayton, Constance 1
Cleaver, Emanuel 4, 45, 68
Craig-Jones, Ellen Walker 44
Dinkins, David 4
Dixon, Sharon Pratt 1
Evers, Myrlie 8
Fauntroy, Walter E. 11
Fields, C. Virginia 25
Ford, Jack 39
Ford, Johnny 70
Gibson, Kenneth Allen 6
Goode, W. Wilson 4
Harmon, Clarence 26
Hayes, James C. 10
Jackson, Maynard 2, 41
James, Sharpe 23, 69
Jarvis, Charlene Drew 21
Johnson, Eddie Bernice 8
Johnson, Harvey, Jr. 24
Kirk, Ron 11
Mallett, Conrad, Jr. 16
McPhail, Sharon 2
Metcalfe, Ralph 26
Millender-McDonald, Juanita 21, 61
Morial, Ernest "Dutch" 26
Morial, Marc H. 20, 51
Murrell, Sylvia Marilyn 49
Powell, Adam Clayton, Jr. 3
Powell, Debra A. 23
Rice, Norm 8
Sayles Belton, Sharon 9, 16
Schmoke, Kurt 1, 48
Stokes, Carl B. 10
Street, John F. 24
Usry, James L. 23
Washington, Harold 6
Webb, Wellington 3
White, Michael R. 5
Williams, Anthony 21
Young, Andrew 3, 48
Young, Coleman 1, 20

City Sun newspaper
Cooper, Andrew W. 36

City University of New York
Ballard, Allen Butler, Jr. 40
Davis, George 36
Gayle, Addison, Jr. 41

Shabazz, Ilyasah 36

Civil rights

Abbott, Diane 9
Abernathy, Ralph 1
Agyeman, Jaramogi Abebe 10, 63
Al-Amin, Jamil Abdullah 6
Alexander, Clifford 26
Ali, Ayaan Hirsi 58
Ali, Muhammad 2, 16, 52
Amaker, Norman 63
Angelou, Maya 1, 15
Anthony, Wendell 25
Aristide, Jean-Bertrand 6, 45
Arnwine, Barbara 28
Baker, Ella 5
Baker, Houston A., Jr. 6
Baker, Josephine 3
Ballance, Frank W. 41
Barbee, Lloyd Augustus 71
Bass, Charlotta Spears 40
Bates, Daisy 13
Baugh, David 23
Beals, Melba Patillo 15
Belafonte, Harry 4, 65
Bell, Derrick 6
Bell, James Madison 40
Bennett, Lerone, Jr. 5
Berry, Mary Frances 7
Berry, Theodore M. 31
Biko, Steven 4
Bishop, Sanford D., Jr. 24
Bond, Julian 2, 35
Booker, Simeon 23
Boyd, John W., Jr. 20
Bradle, David Henry, Jr. 39
Brooks, Tyrone 59
Brown, Byrd 49
Brown, Elaine 8
Brown, Homer S. 47
Brown, Tony 3
Brown, Wesley 23
Brown, Willa 40
Burks, Mary Fair 40
Caldwell, Earl 60
Campbell, Bebe Moore 6, 24, 59
Carmichael, Stokely 5, 26
Carr, Johnnie 69
Carter, Mandy 11
Carter, Rubin 26
Carter, Stephen L. 4
Cary, Mary Ann Shadd 30
Cayton, Horace 26
Chambers, Julius 3
Chavis, Benjamin 6
Clark, Septima 7
Clay, William Lacy 8
Cleaver, Eldridge 5
Cleaver, Kathleen Neal 29
Clyburn, James E. 21, 71
Cobb, W. Montague 39
Cobbs, Price M. 9
Cooper, Anna Julia 20
Cosby, Bill 7, 26, 59
Crockett, George W., Jr. 10, 64
Cunningham, Evelyn 23
Davis, Angela 5
Davis, Artur 41
Davis, James E. 50
Days, Drew S., III 10
Dee, Ruby 8, 50, 68
Dent, Thomas C. 50
Diallo, Amadou 27
Diggs, Charles C. 21
Diggs-Taylor, Anna 20
Divine, Father 7
Dodson, Howard, Jr. 7, 52
Du Bois, W. E. B. 3
Dudley, Edward R. 58
Dukes, Hazel Nell 56
Dumas, Henry 41
Edelman, Marian Wright 5, 42
Ellison, Ralph 7
Evers, Medgar 3
Evers, Myrlie 8
Farmer, James 2, 64
Farmer-Paellmann, Deadria 43
Fauntroy, Walter E. 11
Fletcher, Bill, Jr. 41
Forman, James 7, 51
Fortune, T. Thomas 6
Foster, Marie 48
Franklin, C. L. 68
Franklin, John Hope 5
Gaines, Ernest J. 7
George, Zelma Watson 42
Gibson, William F. 6
Gray, Fred 37
Gregory, Dick 1, 54
Grimké, Archibald H. 9
Guinier, Lani 7, 30
Haley, Alex 4
Haley, George Williford Boyce 21
Hall, Elliott S. 24
Hamer, Fannie Lou 6
Hampton, Fred 18
Hampton, Henry 6
Hansberry, Lorraine 6
Harding, Vincent 67
Harper, Frances Ellen Watkins 11
Harris, Patricia Roberts 2
Hastie, William H. 8
Hatcher, Richard G. 55
Hawkins, Augustus F. 68
Hawkins, Steven 14
Hayes, Dennis 54
Hedgeman, Anna Arnold 22
Height, Dorothy I. 2, 23
Henderson, Thelton E. 68
Henderson, Wade J. 14
Henry, Aaron 19
Higginbotham, A. Leon, Jr. 13, 25
Hill, Jesse, Jr. 13
Hill, Oliver W. 24, 63
Hilliard, David 7
Hobson, Julius W. 44
Holland, Endesha Ida Mae 3, 57
Hollowell, Donald L. 57
hooks, bell 5
hooks, Benjamin L. 2
Horne, Lena 5
Houston, Charles Hamilton 4
Howard, M. William, Jr. 26
Hughes, Langston 4
Innis, Roy 5
Irvis, K. Leroy 67
Jackson, Alexine Clement 22
Jackson, Jesse 1, 27
James, Daniel, Jr. 16
Jarret, Vernon D. 42
Johns, Vernon 38
Johnson, Eddie Bernice 8
Johnson, Georgia Douglas 41
Johnson, James Weldon 5
Johnson, Norma L. Holloway 17
Jones, Elaine R. 7, 45
Jones, William A., Jr. 61
Jordan, Barbara 4
Jordan, June 7, 35
Jordan, Vernon E. 3, 35
Julian, Percy Lavon 6
Karim, Benjamin 61
Kennedy, Florynce 12, 33
Kenyatta, Jomo 5
Kidd, Mae Street 39
King, Bernice 4
King, Coretta Scott 3, 57
King, Martin Luther, Jr. 1
King, Martin Luther, III 20
King, Preston 28
King, Yolanda 6
Ladner, Joyce A. 42
Lampkin, Daisy 19
Lee, Spike 5, 19
Lester, Julius 9
Lewis, John 2, 46
Logan, Rayford W. 40
Lorde, Audre 6
Loving, Mildred 69
Lowery, Joseph 2
Lowry, A. Leon 60
Lucy Foster, Autherine 35
Makeba, Miriam 2, 50
Malone Jones, Vivian 59
Mandela, Nelson 1, 14
Mandela, Winnie 2, 35
Martin, Louis E. 16
Martin, Ruby Grant 49
Mayfield, Curtis 2, 43
Mays, Benjamin E. 7
Mbeki, Thabo Mvuyelwa 14
McDonald, Gabrielle Kirk 20
McDougall, Gay J. 11, 43
McKissick, Floyd B. 3
Meek, Carrie 6
Meredith, James H. 11
Metcalfe, Ralph 26
Morgan, Irene 65
Moore, Barbara C. 49
Moore, Harry T. 29
Morial, Ernest "Dutch" 26
Morrison, Toni 2, 15
Moses, Robert Parris 11
Motley, Constance Baker 10, 55
Mowry, Jess 7
Murphy, Laura M. 43
Murray, Pauli 38
Ndadaye, Melchior 7
Nelson, Jill 6, 54
Newton, Huey 2
Nkoli, Simon 60
Nkomo, Joshua 4, 65
Norman, Pat 10
Norton, Eleanor Holmes 7
Nunn, Annetta 43
Nzo, Alfred 15
Parker, Kellis E. 30
Parks, Rosa 1, 35, 56
Patrick, Deval 12, 61
Patterson, Louise 25
Patterson, Orlando 4
Perkins, Edward 5
Pincham, R. Eugene, Sr. 69
Pinchback, P. B. S. 9
Player, Willa B. 43
Pleasant, Mary Ellen 9
Plessy, Homer Adolph 31
Poitier, Sidney 11, 36
Powell, Adam Clayton, Jr. 3
Price, Hugh B. 9, 54
Ramaphosa, Cyril 3
Randolph, A. Philip 3
Reagon, Bernice Johnson 7
Redding, Louis L. 26
Riggs, Marlon 5, 44
Robeson, Paul 2
Robinson, Jackie 6
Robinson, Rachel 16
Robinson, Randall 7, 46
Robinson, Sharon 22
Robinson, Spottswood W., III 22
Rowan, Carl T. 1, 30
Rush, Bobby 26
Rustin, Bayard 4
Sadlier, Rosemary 62
Sané, Pierre Gabriel 21
Sanders, Malika 48
Saro-Wiwa, Kenule 39
Seale, Bobby 3
Shabazz, Attallah 6
Shabazz, Betty 7, 26
Shakur, Assata 6
Shinhoster, Earl 32
Shuttlesworth, Fred 47
Simone, Nina 15, 41
Sisulu, Albertina 57
Sisulu, Sheila Violet Makate 24
Sleet, Moneta, Jr. 5
Smith, Barbara 28
Staupers, Mabel K. 7
Sullivan, Leon H. 3, 30
Sutton, Percy E. 42
Sweet, Ossian 68
Thompson, Bennie G. 26
Thurman, Howard 3
Till, Emmett 7
Touré, Faya Ora Rose 56
Trotter, Monroe 9
Tsvangirai, Morgan 26
Turner, Henry McNeal 5
Tutu, Desmond Mpilo 6, 44
Underwood, Blair 7
Walker, Rebecca 50
Washington, Booker T. 4
Washington, Fredi 10
Watt, Melvin 26
Weaver, Robert C. 8, 46
Wells, James Lesesne 10
Wells-Barnett, Ida B. 8
West, Cornel 5
White, Walter F. 4
Wideman, John Edgar 5
Wilkins, Roy 4
Williams, Evelyn 10
Williams, Fannie Barrier 27
Williams, Hosea Lorenzo 15, 31
Williams, Robert F. 11
Williams, Walter E. 4
Wilson, August 7, 33, 55
Wilson, Sunnie 7, 55
Wilson, William Julius 22
Woodson, Robert L. 10
Wright, Nathan, Jr. 56
X, Malcolm 1
Yoba, Malik 11
Young, Andrew 3, 48
Young, Jean Childs 14
Young, Whitney M., Jr. 4

Civilian Pilots Training Program

Brown, Willa 40

Classical music
Adams, Leslie 39
Baiocchi, Regina Harris 41
Bonds, Margaret 39
Brown, Uzee 42
Burleigh, Henry Thacker 56
Cook, Will Marion 40
Dawson, William Levi 39
DePriest, James 37
Dixon, Dean 68
Dunner, Leslie B. 45
Freeman, Paul 39
Kay, Ulysses 37
Lewis, Henry 38
McFerrin, Bobby 68
Moore, Dorothy Rudd 46
Murray, Tai 47
Pratt, Awadagin 31
Price, Florence 37
Schuyler, Philippa 50
Sowande, Fela 39
Still, William Grant 37
Tillis, Frederick 40
Walker, George 37
Wilkins, Thomas Alphonso 71
Williams, Denise 40

Classical singers
Anderson, Marian 2, 33
Battle, Kathleen 70
Bumbry, Grace 5
Burleigh, Henry Thacker 56
Hayes, Roland 4
Hendricks, Barbara 3, 67
Lister, Marquita 65
Norman, Jessye 5
Price, Leontyne 1
Three Mo' Tenors 35
Williams, Denise 40

Clearview Golf Club
Powell, Renee 34

Cleo Parker Robinson Dance Ensemble
Robinson, Cleo Parker 38

Clergy
Anthony, Wendell 25
Austin, Junius C. 44
Black, Barry C. 47
Burgess, John 46
Caesar, Shirley 19
Caldwell, Kirbyjon 55
Cleveland, James 19
Cook, Suzan D. Johnson 22
Dyson, Michael Eric 11, 40
Gilmore, Marshall 46
Gomes, Peter J. 15
Gregory, Wilton 37
Howard, M. William, Jr. 26
Jakes, Thomas "T.D." 17, 43
James, Skip 38
Jemison, Major L. 48
Johns, Vernon 38
Jones, Absalom 52
Jones, Alex 64
Jones, William A., Jr. 61
Karim, Benjamin 61
Kelly, Leontine 33
King, Barbara 22
Kobia, Samuel 43
Lincoln, C. Eric 38
Long, Eddie L. 29
Maxis, Theresa 62
McClurkin, Donnie 25
McKenzie, Vashti M. 29
Morgan, Gertrude 63
Okaalet, Peter 58
Otunga, Maurice Michael 55
Phipps, Wintley 59
Reese, Della 6, 20
Sentamu, John 58
Shuttlesworth, Fred 47
Thurston, Stephen J. 49
Tillard, Conrad 47
Tolton, Augustine 62
Walker, John T. 50
Washington, James Melvin 50
Weems, Renita J. 44
White-Hammond, Gloria 61
Williams, David Rudyard 50
Williams, Frederick (B.) 63
Williams, Preston Warren, II 64
Winans, Marvin L. 17
Wright, Nathan, Jr. 56

Cleveland Browns football team
Brown, Jim 11
Crennel, Romeo 54
Hill, Calvin 19
Motley, Marion 26
Newsome, Ozzie 26
Willis, Bill 68

Cleveland Cavaliers basketball team
Brandon, Terrell 16
Wilkens, Lenny 11

Cleveland city government
Stokes, Carl B. 10
White, Michael R. 5

Cleveland Foundation
Adams, Leslie 39

Cleveland Indians baseball team
Belle, Albert 10
Bonds, Bobby 43
Carter, Joe 30
Doby, Lawrence Eugene, Sr. 16, 41
Justice, David 18
Lofton, Kenny 12
Murray, Eddie 12
Paige, Satchel 7
Robinson, Frank 9

Cleveland Rockers basketball team
Jones, Merlakia 34

CLIO Awards
Lewis, Emmanuel 36

Clothing design
Aberra, Amsale 67
Bailey, Xenobia 11
Burrows, Stephen 31
Gaskins, Eric 64
Henderson, Gordon 5
John, Daymond 23
Jones, Carl 7
Kani, Karl 10
Kelly, Patrick 3
Lars, Byron 32
Malone, Maurice 32
Pinkett Smith, Jada 10, 41
Robinson, Patrick 19, 71
Smith, Willi 8
Walker, T. J. 7

CNBC
Epperson, Sharon 54
Thomas-Graham, Pamela 29

CNN
See Cable News Network

CNU
See Cameroon National Union

Coaching
Amaker, Tommy 62
Anderson, Mike 63
Ashley, Maurice 15, 47
Baker, Dusty 8, 43
Baylor, Don 6
Bickerstaff, Bernie 21
Bonds, Bobby 43
Campanella, Roy 25
Carew, Rod 20
Carter, Butch 27
Carter, Kenneth 53
Chaney, John 67
Cheeks, Maurice 47
Cooper, Michael 31
Crennel, Romeo 54
Davis, Mike 41
Dorrell, Karl 52
Dungy, Tony 17, 42, 59
Dunn, Jerry 27
Edwards, Herman 51
Ellerbe, Brian 22
Freeman, Marianna 23
Gaines, Clarence E., Sr. 55
Gaither, Alonzo Smith (Jake) 14
Gaston, Cito 71
Gentry, Alvin 23
Gibson, Althea 8, 43
Gibson, Bob 33
Gorden, W. C. 71
Gray, Yeshimbra "Shimmy" 55
Green, Dennis 5, 45
Greene, Joe 10
Haskins, Clem 23
Heard, Gar 25
Johnson, Avery 62
Keith, Floyd A. 61
Lewis, Marvin 51
Lofton, James 42
Miller, Cheryl 10
O'Neil, Buck 19, 59
Parish, Robert 43
Phillips, Teresa L. 42
Rhodes, Ray 14
Richardson, Nolan 9
Rivers, Glenn "Doc" 25
Robinson, Eddie G. 10, 61
Robinson, Will 51, 69
Russell, Bill 8
Shell, Art 1, 66
Silas, Paul 24
Simmons, Bob 29
Smith, Lovie 66
Smith, Tubby 18
Stringer, C. Vivian 13, 66
Thomas, Emmitt 71
Tunnell, Emlen 54
White, Jesse 22
Williams, Doug 22
Willingham, Tyrone 43

Coalition of Black Trade Unionists
Lucy, William 50
Wyatt, Addie L. 56

Coca-Cola Company
Ware, Carl T. 30

Coca-Cola Foundation
Jones, Ingrid Saunders 18

COHAR
See Committee on Appeal for Human Rights

Collage
Andrews, Benny 22, 59
Bearden, Romare 2, 50
Driskell, David C. 7
Pindell, Howardena 55
Robinson, Aminah 50
Thomas, Mickalene 61
Verna, Gelsy 70

College and university administration
Archie-Hudson, Marguerite 44
Barnett, Marguerite 46
Burnim, Mickey L. 48
Christian, Barbara T. 44
Davis, Erroll B., Jr. 57
Ford, Nick Aaron 44
Hill, Leslie Pinckney 44
Hogan, Beverly Wade 50
Horne, Frank 44
Jackson, Edison O. 67
King, Reatha Clark 65
Lee, Joe A. 45
Massey, Walter E. 5, 45
Mell, Patricia 49
Nance, Cynthia 71
Newman, Lester C. 51
Ribeau, Sidney 70
Trueheart, William E. 49

Colorado Rockies baseball team
Baylor, Don 6

Colorado state government
Brown, George Leslie 62
Rogers, Joe 27

Columbia Broadcasting System (CBS)
Bradley, Ed 2, 59
Dourdan, Gary 37
Kellogg, Clark 64
Mabrey, Vicki 26
McEwen, Mark 5
Mitchell, Russ 21
Olden, Georg(e) 44
Pinkston, W. Randall 24
Pitts, Byron 71
Rashad, Phylicia 21
Rodgers, Johnathan 6, 51
Taylor, Meshach 4
Ware, Andre 37

Columbia Records
Jackson, Randy 40
Knowles, Tina 61
Olatunji, Babatunde 36

Williams, Deniece 36

Columbia space shuttle
Anderson, Michael P. 40

Columbus city government
Bradley, Jennette B. 40
Coleman, Michael 28

Comedy
Allen, Byron 3, 24
Amos, John 8, 62
Anderson, Anthony 51
Anderson, Eddie "Rochester" 30
Anthony, Trey 63
Arnez J 53
Beaton, Norman 14
Bellamy, Bill 12
Berry, Bertice 8, 55
Brady, Wayne 32, 71
Bruce, Bruce 56
Campbell-Martin, Tisha 8, 42
Cannon, Nick 47
Cedric the Entertainer 29, 60
Chappelle, Dave 50
Cosby, Bill 7, 26, 59
Curry, Mark 17
Davidson, Tommy 21
Davis, Sammy, Jr. 18
Dieudonné 67
Earthquake 55
Epps, Mike 60
Foxx, Jamie 15, 48
Foxx, Redd 2
Freeman, Aaron 52
Givens, Adele 62
Goldberg, Whoopi 4, 33, 69
Gregory, Dick 1, 54
Harris, Robin 7
Harvey, Steve 18, 58
Henry, Lenny 9, 52
Hughley, D. L. 23
Kirby, George 14
Lawrence, Martin 6, 27, 60
Mabley, Jackie "Moms" 15
Mac, Bernie 29, 61
Mayo, Whitman 32
McEwen, Mark 5
Meadows, Tim 30
Mo'Nique 35
Mooney, Paul 37
Moore, Melba 21
Morgan, Tracy 61
Morris, Garrett 31
Moss, Preacher 63
Murphy, Eddie 4, 20, 61
Nash, Niecy 66
Perry, Tyler 40, 54
Pryor, Rain 65
Pryor, Richard 3, 24, 56
Rashad, Phylicia 21
Reese, Della 6, 20
Rock, Chris 3, 22, 66
Russell, Nipsey 66
Schultz, Michael A. 6
Shepherd, Sherri 55
Sinbad 1, 16
Slocumb, Jonathan 52
Smiley, Rickey 59
Smith, Will 8, 18
Sommore 61
Sykes, Wanda 48
Taylor, Meshach 4
Thompson, Kenan 52
Torry, Guy 31
Townsend, Robert 4, 23
Tucker, Chris 13, 23, 62
Tyler, Aisha N. 36
Warfield, Marsha 2
Wayans, Damon 8, 41
Wayans, Keenen Ivory 18
Wayans, Marlon 29
Wayans, Shawn 29
Wilson, Debra 38
Wilson, Flip 21
Witherspoon, John 38
Yarbrough, Cedric 51

Comer Method
Comer, James P. 6

Comerica Bank
Forte, Linda Diane 54

Commercial art
Freeman, Leonard 27

Commission for Racial Justice
Chavis, Benjamin 6

Committee on Appeal for Human Rights (COHAR)
Bond, Julian 2, 35

Communist Party
Brown, Lloyd Louis 42
Davis, Angela 5
Du Bois, W. E. B. 3
Jagan, Cheddi 16
Wright, Richard 5

Complete Energy Partners
Scott, Milton 51

Complexions dance troupe
Rhoden, Dwight 40
Richardson, Desmond 39
Tyson, Andre 40

Computer graphics
Coleman, Ken 57
Hannah, Marc 10

Computer science
Adkins, Rod 41
Auguste, Donna 29
Dean, Mark 35
Easley, Annie J. 61
Ellis, Clarence 38
Emeagwali, Philip 30
Hannah, Marc 10
Irvin, Vernon 65
Laryea, Thomas Davies, III 67
Mensah, Thomas 48
Millines Dziko, Trish 28
Zollar, Alfred 40

Conceptual art
Allen, Tina 22
Bailey, Xenobia 11
Piper, Adrian 71
Robinson, Aminah 50
Simpson, Lorna 4, 36

Concerned Black Men
Holder, Eric H., Jr. 9

Concerned Parents Association (Uganda)
Atyam, Angelina 55

Conductors
Calloway, Cab 14
Cook, Will Marion 40
Dawson, William Levi 39
DePriest, James 37
Dixon, Dean 68
Dunner, Leslie B. 45
Freeman, Paul 39
Jackson, Isaiah 3
León, Tania 13
Lewis, Henry 38

Co-nect Schools
Fuller, Arthur 27

Congressional Black Caucus (CBC)
Christian-Green, Donna M. 17
Clay, William Lacy 8
Clyburn, James E. 21, 71
Collins, Cardiss 10
Conyers, John, Jr. 4, 45
Dellums, Ronald 2
Diggs, Charles C. 21
Fauntroy, Walter E. 11
Gray, William H., III 3
Hastings, Alcee L. 16
Hawkins, Augustus F. 68
Johnson, Eddie Bernice 8
Mfume, Kweisi 6, 41
Mitchell, Parren J. 42, 66
Owens, Major 6
Payton, John 48
Rangel, Charles 3, 52
Scott, Robert C. 23
Stokes, Louis 3
Thompson, Bennie G. 26
Towns, Edolphus 19

Congressional Black Caucus Higher Education Braintrust
Owens, Major 6

Congress of Racial Equality (CORE)
Dee, Ruby 8, 50, 68
Farmer, James 2, 64
Hobson, Julius W. 44
Innis, Roy 5
Jackson, Jesse 1, 27
McKissick, Floyd B. 3
Rustin, Bayard 4

Contemporary Christian music
Griffin, LaShell 51
Tait, Michael 57

Continental Basketball Association (CBA)
Davis, Mike 41
Thomas, Isiah 7, 26, 65
Ussery, Terdema, II 29

Convention People's Party (Ghana; CPP)
Nkrumah, Kwame 3

Cook County Circuit Court
Sampson, Edith S. 4

Cooking
Brown, Warren 61
Chase, Leah 57
Clark, Patrick 14
Estes, Rufus 29
Evans, Darryl 22
Roker, Al 12, 49
Samuelsson, Marcus 53

Coppin State College
Blair, Paul 36

CORE
See Congress of Racial Equality

Coretta Scott King Awards
Haskins, James 36, 54

Coronet
Oliver, Joe "King" 42

Corporation for Public Broadcasting (CPB)
Brown, Tony 3

Cosmetology
Cottrell, Comer 11
Fuller, S. B. 13
Morgan, Rose 11
Powell, Maxine 8
Roche, Joyce M. 17
Walker, A'lelia 14
Walker, Madame C. J. 7

Cotton Club Revue
Johnson, Buddy 36

Council for a Black Economic Agenda (CBEA)
Woodson, Robert L. 10

Council for Social Action of the Congregational Christian Churches
Julian, Percy Lavon 6

Council for the Economic Development of Black Americans (CEDBA)
Brown, Tony 3

Council on Legal Education Opportunities (CLEO)
Henderson, Wade J. 14
Henry, Aaron 19

Count Basie Orchestra
Eldridge, Roy 37
Johnson, J. J. 37
Rushing, Jimmy 37
Williams, Joe 5, 25
Young, Lester 37

Country music
Bailey, DeFord 33
Cowboy Troy 54
Palmer, Rissi 65
Pride, Charley 26
Randall, Alice 38

Covad Communications
Knowling, Robert 38

Cowboys
Love, Nat 9
Pickett, Bill 11

CPB
See Corporation for Public Broadcasting

CPDM
See Cameroon People's Democratic Movement

CPP
See Convention People's Party

Creative Artists Agency
Nelson Meigs, Andrea **48**

Credit Suisse First Boston, Inc.
Ogunlesi, Adebayo **37**

Creole music
Ardoin, Alphonse **65**

Cress Theory of Color-Confrontation and Racism
Welsing, Frances Cress **5**

Cricket
Adams, Paul **50**

Crisis
Du Bois, W. E. B. **3**
Fauset, Jessie **7**
Wilkins, Roy **4**

Critics' Choice Award
Channer, Colin **36**

Cross Colours
Jones, Carl **7**
Kani, Karl **10**
Walker, T. J. **7**

Crown Media
Corbi, Lana **42**

Crucial Films
Henry, Lenny **9, 52**

Crusader
Williams, Robert F. **11**

CTRN
See Transitional Committee for National Recovery (Guinea)

Cuban League
Charleston, Oscar **39**
Day, Leon **39**

Cuban music
Ferrer, Ibrahim **41**
Portuondo, Omara **53**

Cubism
Bearden, Romare **2, 50**
Green, Jonathan **54**

Culinary arts
Clark, Patrick **14**

Cultural Hangups
Ham, Cynthia Parker **58**

Cultural pluralism
Locke, Alain **10**

Cumulative voting
Guinier, Lani **7, 30**

Curator/exhibition designer
Camp, Kimberly **19**
Campbell, Mary Schmidt **43**
Golden, Thelma **10, 55**
Hoyte, Lenon **50**

Hutson, Jean Blackwell **16**
Pindell, Howardena **55**
Sanders, Joseph R., Jr. **11**
Sims, Lowery Stokes **27**
Stewart, Paul Wilbur **12**

Cycling
Taylor, Marshall Walter "Major" **62**
Yeboah, Emmanuel Ofosu **53**

Cytogenetics
Satcher, David **7, 57**

Dallas city government
Johnson, Eddie Bernice **8**
Kirk, Ron **11**

Dallas Cowboys football team
Hill, Calvin **19**
Irvin, Michael **64**
Jones, Ed "Too Tall" **46**
Sanders, Deion **4, 31**
Smith, Emmitt **7**
Wright, Rayfield **70**

Dallas Mavericks basketball team
Ussery, Terdema **29**

Dallas Police Department
Bolton, Terrell D. **25**

Dance
LeTang, Henry **66**

DanceAfrica
Davis, Chuck **33**

Dance Theatre of Harlem
Johnson, Virginia **9**
King, Alonzo **38**
Mitchell, Arthur **2, 47**
Nicholas, Fayard **20, 57**
Nicholas, Harold **20**
Tyson, Cicely **7, 51**

Darkchild Records
Jerkins, Rodney **31**

Darrell Green Youth Life Foundation
Green, Darrell **39**

DAV
See Disabled American Veterans

David M. Winfield Foundation
Winfield, Dave **5**

Daytona Institute
See Bethune-Cookman College

Dayton Philharmonic Orchestra
Jackson, Isaiah **3**

D.C. Black Repertory Theater
Reagon, Bernice Johnson **7**

D.C. sniper
Moose, Charles **40**

Death Row Records
Dre, Dr. **10, 14, 30**
Hammer, M. C. **20**
Knight, Suge **11, 30**

Shakur, Tupac **14**

De Beers Botswana
See Debswana
Allen, Debbie **13, 42**

Debswana
Masire, Quett **5**

Decca Records
Hardin Armstrong, Lil **39**

Def Jam Records
Brown, Foxy **25**
DMX **28, 64**
Gotti, Irv **39**
Jay-Z **27, 69**
Jordan, Montell **23**
Liles, Kevin **42**
LL Cool J **16, 49**
Simmons, Russell **1, 30**

Def Jam South Records
Ludacris **37, 60**

Def Poetry Jam
Letson, Al **39**

Defense Communications Agency
Gravely, Samuel L., Jr. **5, 49**

Delta Sigma Theta Sorority
Rice, Louise Allen **54**

Democratic National Committee (DNC)
Brown, Ron **5**
Brown, Willie L., Jr. **7**
Dixon, Sharon Pratt **1**
Fattah, Chaka **11, 70**
Hamer, Fannie Lou **6**
Jackson, Maynard **2, 41**
Jordan, Barbara **4**
Joyner, Marjorie Stewart **26**
Mallett, Conrad, Jr. **16**
Martin, Louis E. **16**
Moore, Minyon **45**
Waters, Maxine **3, 67**
Williams, Maggie **7, 71**

Democratic National Convention
Allen, Ethel D. **13**
Brown, Ron **5**
Brown, Willie L., Jr. **7**
Dixon, Sharon Pratt **1**
Hamer, Fannie Lou **6**
Herman, Alexis M. **15**
Jordan, Barbara **4**
Millender-McDonald, Juanita **21, 61**
Waters, Maxine **3, 67**
Williams, Maggie **7, 71**

Democratic Socialists of America (DSA)
Marable, Manning **10**
West, Cornel **5**

Dentistry
Bluitt, Juliann S. **14**
Delany, Bessie **12**
Gray, Ida **41**
Madison, Romell **45**

Sinkford, Jeanne C. **13**

Denver Broncos football team
Barnes, Ernie **16**
Briscoe, Marlin **37**
Davis, Terrell **20**
Jackson, Tom **70**

Denver city government
Webb, Wellington **3**

Denver Nuggets basketball team
Bickerstaff, Bernie **21**
Bynoe, Peter C. B. **40**
Hardaway, Tim **35**
Lee, Bertram M., Sr. **46**
Mutombo, Dikembe **7**

DePaul University
Braun, Carol Moseley **4, 42**
Sizemore, Barbara A. **26**

Depression/The Great Depression
Hampton, Henry **6**

Dermatology
Taylor, Susan C. **62**

Desert Shield
See Operation Desert Shield

Desert Storm
See Operation Desert Storm

Destiny's Child
Beyoncé **39, 70**
Knowles, Tina **61**
Luckett, Letoya **61**

Detective fiction
Bates, Karen Grigsby **40**
Bland, Eleanor Taylor **39**
DeLoach, Nora **30**
Hayes, Teddy **40**
Haywood, Gar Anthony **43**
Himes, Chester **8**
Holton, Hugh, Jr. **39**
Mosley, Walter **5, 25, 68**
Wesley, Valerie Wilson **18**

Detroit Bible Institute
Patterson, Gilbert Earl **41**

Detroit city government
Archer, Dennis **7, 36**
Collins, Barbara-Rose **7**
Crockett, George W., Jr. **10, 64**
Garrett, Joyce Finley **59**
Kilpatrick, Kwame **34, 71**
Marshall, Bella **22**
Young, Coleman **1, 20**

Detroit College of Law
Archer, Dennis **7, 36**

Detroit Golden Gloves
Wilson, Sunnie **7, 55**

Detroit Lions football team
Barney, Lem **26**
Farr, Mel **24**
Johnson, Levi **48**
Sanders, Barry **1, 53**

Ware, Andre 37

Detroit Pistons basketball team
Bing, Dave 3, 59
Dumars, Joe 16, 65
Gentry, Alvin 23
Hill, Grant 13
Lanier, Bob 47
Lloyd, Earl 26
Lowe, Sidney 64
Mahorn, Rick 60
Mohammed, Nazr 64
Prince, Tayshaun 68
Robinson, Will 51, 69
Stackhouse, Jerry 30
Thomas, Isiah 7, 26, 65
Wallace, Ben 54
Webber, Chris 15, 30, 59

Detroit Police Department
Bully-Cummings, Ella 48
Gomez-Preston, Cheryl 9
McKinnon, Isaiah 9
Napoleon, Benny N. 23

Detroit Public Schools
Coleman, William F., III 61

Detroit Stars baseball team
Kaiser, Cecil 42

Detroit Tigers baseball team
Fielder, Cecil 2
Granderson, Curtis 66
Sheffield, Gary 16
Virgil, Ozzie 48

Detroit Wolves baseball team
Dandridge, Ray 36

Diabetes
Wisdom, Kimberlydawn 57

Diamond mining
Masire, Quett 5

Dictators
Abacha, Sani 11, 70
Amin, Idi 42
Biya, Paul 28
Eyadéma, Gnassingbé 7, 52
Habré, Hissène 6
Kabila, Laurent 20
Meles Zenawi 3
Mengistu, Haile Mariam 65
Moi, Daniel Arap 1, 35
Mswati III 56
Mugabe, Robert 10, 71
Touré, Sekou 6

Digital divide
Adkins, Rod 41

Dillard University
Cook, Samuel DuBois 14
Lomax, Michael L. 58

Dime Savings Bank
Parsons, Richard Dean 11

Diner's Club
Gaines, Brenda 41

Diplomatic Corps
See U.S. Department of State

Directing
Akomfrah, John 37
Barclay, Paris 37

Branch, William Blackwell 39
Chong, Rae Dawn 62
Dixon, Ivan 69
Hines, Gregory 1, 42
Milner, Ron 39
Perry, Tyler 40, 54
Scott, Harold Russell, Jr. 61
Thompson, Tazewell 13
Ward, Douglas Turner 42
Warner, Malcolm-Jamal 22, 36
Whack, Rita Coburn 36
Wolfe, George C. 6, 43

Director's Guild of America
Barclay, Paris 37

Disabled American Veterans (DAV)
Brown, Jesse 6, 41

Disco
Gaynor, Gloria 36
Payne, Freda 58
Perren, Freddie 60
Staton, Candi 27
Summer, Donna 25

Distance running
Cheruiyot, Robert 69
Loroupe, Tegla 59
Tergat, Paul 59

Diving
Brashear, Carl 29

DJ
Alert, Kool DJ Red 32
Atkins, Juan 50
Bond, Beverly 53
DJ Jazzy Jeff 32
Grandmaster Flash 33, 60
Knuckles, Frankie 42
Love, Ed 58

DNC
See Democratic National Committee

Documentary film
Blackwood, Maureen 37
Branch, William Blackwell 39
Byrd, Robert 11
Dash, Julie 4
Davis, Ossie 5, 50
Gray, Darius 69
Greaves, William 38
Hampton, Henry 6
Henry, Lenny 9, 52
Hudlin, Reginald 9
Hudlin, Warrington 9
Hurt, Byron 61
Jean, Michaëlle; 70
Julien, Isaac 3
Lee, Spike 5, 19
Lynch, Shola 61
Peck, Raoul 32
Riggs, Marlon 5, 44
Whack, Rita Coburn 36
Williams, Marco 53

Dollmaking
El Wilson, Barbara 35

Dominica government
Charles, Pierre 52

Donald Byrd/The Group
Byrd, Donald 10

Donnaerobics
Richardson, Donna 39

Dove Award
Baylor, Helen 36
Winans, CeCe 14, 43

Down Beat Jazz Hall of Fame
Terry, Clark 39

Dr. Martin Luther King Boys and Girls Club
Gaines, Brenda 41

Drama Desk Awards
Carter, Nell 39
Taylor, Ron 35

Drawing
Simmons, Gary 58

Dreamland Orchestra
Cook, Charles "Doc" 44

Drug abuse prevention
Brown, Les 5
Clements, George 2
Creagh, Milton 27
Hale, Lorraine 8
Harris, Alice 7
Lucas, John 7
Rangel, Charles 3, 52

Drug synthesis
Julian, Percy Lavon 6
Pickett, Cecil 39

Drums
Blakey, Art 37
Güines, Tata 69
Jones, Elvin 14, 68
Locke, Eddie 44
Miles, Buddy 69
Williams, Tony 67

DSA
See Democratic Socialists of America

Dub poetry
Breeze, Jean "Binta" 37
Johnson, Linton Kwesi 37

Duke Ellington School of Arts
Cooper Cafritz, Peggy 43

Duke Records
Bland, Bobby "Blue" 36

Dunham Dance Company
Dunham, Katherine 4, 59

DuSable Museum of African American History
Burroughs, Margaret Taylor 9
Wright, Antoinette 60

Dynegy
Scott, Milton 51

E Street Band
Clemons, Clarence 41

Earthquake Early Alerting Service
Person, Waverly 9, 51

East Harlem School at Exodus House
Hageman, Hans 36
Hageman, Ivan 36

East St. Louis city government
Powell, Debra A. 23

Ebenezer Baptist Church
King, Bernice 4

Ebonics
Cook, Toni 23

Ebony magazine
Bennett, Lerone, Jr. 5
Branch, William Blackwell 39
Cullers, Vincent T. 49
Fuller, Hoyt 44
Johnson, John H. 3, 54
Massaquoi, Hans J. 30
Rice, Linda Johnson 9, 41
Sleet, Moneta, Jr. 5

Ebony Museum of African American History
See DuSable Museum of African American History

E.C. Reems Women's International Ministries
Reems, Ernestine Cleveland 27

Economic Community of West African States (ECOWAS)
Sawyer, Amos 2

Economic Regulatory Administration
O'Leary, Hazel 6

Economics
Ake, Claude 30
Arthur, Owen 33
Boyd, T. B., III 6
Brimmer, Andrew F. 2, 48
Brown, Tony 3
Divine, Father 7
Fryer, Roland G. 56
Gibson, William F. 6
Hamer, Fannie Lou 6
Hampton, Henry 6
Juma, Calestous 57
Machel, Graca Simbine 16
Malveaux, Julianne 32, 70
Masire, Quett 5
Pitta, Celso 17
Raines, Franklin Delano 14
Robinson, Randall 7, 46
Sowell, Thomas 2
Spriggs, William 67
Sullivan, Leon H. 3, 30
Van Peebles, Melvin 7
Wallace, Phyllis A. 9
Wharton, Clifton R., Jr. 7
White, Michael R. 5
Williams, Walter E. 4

ECOWAS
See Economic Community of West African States

Edelman Public Relations
Barrett, Andrew C. 12

Editing
Aubert, Alvin 41
Bass, Charlotta Spears 40
Brown, Lloyd Louis 42
Curry, George E. 23
Delany, Martin R. 27
Dumas, Henry 41
Murphy, John H. 42
Schuyler, George Samuel 40

Edmonds Entertainment
Edmonds, Kenneth "Babyface" 10, 31
Edmonds, Tracey 16, 64
Tillman, George, Jr. 20

Edmonton Oilers hockey team
Fuhr, Grant 1, 49
Grier, Mike 43
Laraque, Georges 48

Educational Testing Service
Stone, Chuck 9

EEC
See European Economic Community

EEOC
See Equal Employment Opportunity Commission

Egyptology
Diop, Cheikh Anta 4

Elder Foundation
Elder, Lee 6

Electronic music
Craig, Carl 31, 71

Elektra Records
McPherson, David 32

***Emerge (Savoy)* magazine**
Ames, Wilmer 27
Curry, George E. 23

Emmy awards
Allen, Debbie 13, 42
Amos, John 8, 62
Ashe, Arthur 1, 18
Barclay, Paris 37
Belafonte, Harry 4, 65
Bradley, Ed 2, 59
Branch, William Blackwell 39
Brown, James 22
Brown, Les 5
Browne, Roscoe Lee 66
Carter, Nell 39
Clayton, Xernona 3, 45
Cosby, Bill 7, 26, 59
Curtis-Hall, Vondie 17
Dee, Ruby 8, 50, 68
Foxx, Redd 2
Freeman, Al, Jr. 11
Goldberg, Whoopi 4, 33, 69
Gossett, Louis, Jr. 7
Guillaume, Robert 3, 48
Gumbel, Greg 8
Hunter-Gault, Charlayne 6, 31
Jones, James Earl 3, 49
La Salle, Eriq 12
Mabrey, Vicki 26
McQueen, Butterfly 6, 54
Moore, Shemar 21

Parks, Gordon 1, 35, 58
Pinkston, W. Randall 24
Quarles, Norma 25
Richards, Beah 30
Robinson, Max 3
Rock, Chris 3, 22, 66
Rolle, Esther 13, 21
St. John, Kristoff 25
Stokes, Carl B. 10
Taylor, Billy 23
Thigpen, Lynne 17, 41
Tyson, Cicely 7, 51
Uggams, Leslie 23
Wayans, Damon 8, 41
Whack, Rita Coburn 36
Whitfield, Lynn 18
Williams, Montel 4, 57
Williams, Russell, II 70
Williams, Sherley Anne 25
Winfrey, Oprah 2, 15, 61
Woodard, Alfre 9

Emory University
Cole, Johnnetta B. 5, 43

Endocrinology
Elders, Joycelyn 6

Energy studies
Cose, Ellis 5, 50
O'Leary, Hazel 6

Engineering
Alexander, Archie Alphonso 14
Anderson, Charles Edward 37
Auguste, Donna 29
Benson, Angela 34
Boyd, Gwendolyn 49
Burns, Ursula 60
Emeagwali, Philip 30
Ericsson-Jackson, Aprille 28
Gibson, Kenneth Allen 6
Gourdine, Meredith 33
Grooms, Henry R(andall) 50
Hannah, Marc 10
Henderson, Cornelius Langston 26
Howard, Ayanna 65
Jones, Wayne 53
Laryea, Thomas Davies, III 67
McCoy, Elijah 8
Miller, Warren F., Jr. 53
Mills, Joseph C. 51
Pierre, Percy Anthony 46
Price, Richard 51
Sigur, Wanda 44
Slaughter, John Brooks 53
Trotter, Lloyd G. 56
Wilkens, J. Ernest, Jr. 43
Williams, O. S. 13

Entertainment promotion
Lewis, Butch 71

Environmental issues
Chavis, Benjamin 6
Eugene-Richard, Margie 63
Hill, Bonnie Guiton 20
Jones, Van 70
Miller-Travis, Vernice 64
Osborne, Na'taki 54

Epic Records
McPherson, David 32
Mo', Keb' 36

Epidemiology
Gayle, Helene D. 3

Episcopal Diocese of Massachusetts
Harris, Barbara 12

Episcopalian
Burgess, John 46
Jones, Absalom 52
Walker, John T. 50
Williams, Frederick (B.) 63

EPRDF
See Ethiopian People's Revolutionary Democratic Front

Equal Employment Opportunity Commission (EEOC)
Alexander, Clifford 26
Hill, Anita 5, 65
Lewis, Delano 7
Norton, Eleanor Holmes 7
Thomas, Clarence 2, 39, 65
Wallace, Phyllis A. 9

Equality Now
Jones, Sarah 39

Esalen Institute
Olatunji, Babatunde 36

ESPN
Jackson, Tom 70
Roberts, Robin 16, 54
Salters, Lisa 71
Scott, Stuart 34
Smith, Stephen A. 69
Tirico, Mike 68
Wilbon, Michael 68

***Essence* magazine**
Bandele, Asha 36
Burt-Murray, Angela 59
Channer, Colin 36
De Veaux, Alexis 44
Ebanks, Michelle 60
Grant, Gwendolyn Goldsby 28
Greenwood, Monique 38
Lewis, Edward T. 21
Parks, Gordon 1, 35, 58
Smith, Clarence O. 21
Taylor, Susan L. 10
Wesley, Valerie Wilson 18

***Essence* Award**
Broadbent, Hydeia 36
McMurray, Georgia L. 36

Essence Communications
Lewis, Edward T. 21
Smith, Clarence O. 21
Taylor, Susan L. 10

Essence, the Television Program
Taylor, Susan L. 10

Ethiopian government
Haile Selassie 7
Meles Zenawi 3
Mengistu, Haile Mariam 65

Etiquette
Bates, Karen Grigsby 40

Eugene O'Neill Theater
Richards, Lloyd 2

European Economic Community (EEC)
Diouf, Abdou 3

Evangelical church
Weeks, Thomas, III 70

Event planning
Bailey, Preston 64

Executive Leadership Council
Jackson, Mannie 14

Exiled heads of state
Aristide, Jean-Bertrand 6, 45

Exploration
Henson, Matthew 2

***Eyes on the Prize* series**
Hampton, Henry 6

F & M Schaefer Brewing Co.
Cooper, Andrew W. 36

Fairbanks city government
Hayes, James C. 10

FAIRR
See Foundation for the Advancement of Inmate Rehabilitation and Recreation

Fair Share Agreements
Gibson, William F. 6

Famine relief
See World hunger

Famous Amos Cookie Corporation
Amos, Wally 9

FAN
See Forces Armées du Nord (Chad)

Fannie Mae
Jackson, Maynard 2, 41

FANT
See Forces Amrées Nationales Tchadiennes

Fashion
Aberra, Amsale 67
Boateng, Ozwald 35
Boyd, Suzanne 52
Darego, Agbani 52
Delice, Ronald 48
Delice, Rony 48
Evans, Etu 55
Fine, Sam 60
Gaskins, Eric 64
Hall, Kevan 61
Hendy, Francis 47
Knowles, Tina 61
Lars, Byron 32
Malone, Maurice 32
Reese, Tracy 54
Sade 15
Simmons, Kimora Lee 51
Smaltz, Audrey 12
Steele, Lawrence 28
Stoney, Michael 50

Sy, Oumou **65**
Talley, André Leon **56**

Fashion Institute of Technology (FIT)
Brown, Joyce F. **25**

Fast 50 Awards
Steward, David L. **36**

FCC
See Federal Communications Commission

Federal Bureau of Investigation (FBI)
Gibson, Johnnie Mae **23**
Harvard, Beverly **11**

Federal Communications Commission (FCC)
Barrett, Andrew C. **12**
Hooks, Benjamin L. **2**
Hughes, Cathy **27**
Kennard, William Earl **18**
Powell, Michael **32**
Russell-McCloud, Patricia A. **17**

Federal Court of Canada
Isaac, Julius **34**

Federal Energy Administration
O'Leary, Hazel **6**

Federal Reserve Bank
Brimmer, Andrew F. **2, 48**
Ferguson, Roger W. **25**

Federal Set-Aside Program
Mitchell, Parren J. **42, 66**

Federation of Nigeria
Sowande, Fela **39**

Feed the Hungry program
Williams, Hosea Lorenzo **15, 31**

Fellowship of Reconciliation (FOR)
Farmer, James **2, 64**
Rustin, Bayard **4**

Feminist studies
Carby, Hazel **27**
Christian, Barbara T. **44**
De Veaux, Alexis **44**
Hull, Akasha Gloria **45**
Smith, Barbara **28**
Walker, Rebecca **50**

Fencing
Westbrook, Peter **20**

Fiction
Adams, Jenoyne **60**
Adichie, Chimamanda Ngozi **64**
Alexander, Margaret Walker **22**
Ali, Mohammed Naseehu **60**
Amadi, Elechi **40**
Anthony, Michael **29**
Ansa, Tina McElroy **14**
Armah, Ayi Kwei **49**
Ba, Mariama **30**
Baiocchi, Regina Harris **41**
Baisden, Michael **25, 66**
Ballard, Allen Butler, Jr. **40**

Bandele, Biyi **68**
Barrett, Lindsay **43**
Bates, Karen Grigsby **40**
Beckham, Barry **41**
Benson, Angela **34**
Berry, James **41**
Bland, Eleanor Taylor **39**
Bolden, Tonya **32**
Bradley, David Henry, Jr. **39**
Brand, Dionne **32**
Briscoe, Connie **15**
Brown, Cecil M. **46**
Brown, Lloyd Louis **42**
Bunkley, Anita Richmond **39**
Butler, Octavia **8, 43, 58**
Campbell, Bebe Moore **6, 24, 59**
Cartiér, Xam Wilson **41**
Chase-Riboud, Barbara **20, 46**
Cheney-Coker, Syl **43**
Chesnutt, Charles **29**
Clarke, Austin **32**
Cleage, Pearl **17, 64**
Cliff, Michelle **42**
Creagh, Milton **27**
Curtis, Christopher Paul **26**
Danticat, Edwidge **15, 68**
Dathorne, O.R. **52**
Demby, William **51**
Diop, Birago **53**
Draper, Sharon Mills **16, 43**
Due, Tananarive **30**
Dumas, Henry **41**
Dunbar-Nelson, Alice Ruth Moore **44**
Duplechan, Larry **55**
Emecheta, Buchi **30**
Fair, Ronald L. **47**
Farah, Nuruddin **27**
Farley, Christopher John **54**
Files, Lolita **35**
Ford, Nick Aaron **44**
Ford, Wallace **58**
Forrest, Leon **44**
Gomez, Jewelle **30**
Gray, Darius **69**
Greenlee, Sam **48**
Harris, E. Lynn **12, 33**
Haywood, Gar Anthony **43**
Hercules, Frank **44**
Hill, Donna **32**
Holton, Hugh, Jr. **39**
Horne, Frank **44**
Jackson, Sheneska **18**
Jakes, Thomas "T.D." **17, 43**
Jasper, Kenji **39**
Jenkins, Beverly **14**
Johnson, Georgia Douglas **41**
Johnson, Mat **31**
Jones, Edward P. **43, 67**
Jones, Gayl **37**
Kamau, Kwadwo Agymah **28**
Kay, Jackie **37**
Kayira, Legson **40**
Kendrick, Erika **57**
Killens, John O. **54**
Laferriere, Dany **33**
LaGuma, Alex **30**
Lamming, George **35**
Marechera, Dambudzo **39**
Markham, E.A. **37**
Mason, Felicia **31**
Mbaye, Mariétou **31**
McCrary Anthony, Crystal **70**

McFadden, Bernice L. **39**
McKinney-Whetstone, Diane **27**
McMillan, Terry **4, 17, 53**
Memmi, Albert **37**
Mengestu, Dinaw **66**
Monroe, Mary **35**
Mosley, Walter **5, 25, 68**
Mossell, Gertrude Bustill **40**
Mphalele, Es'kia **40**
Mwangi, Meja **40**
Naylor, Gloria **10, 42**
Ngugi wa Thiong'o **29, 61**
Nkosi, Lewis **46**
Nugent, Richard Bruce **39**
Nunez, Elizabeth **62**
Okara, Gabriel **37**
Ojikutu, Bayo **66**
Packer, Z.Z. **64**
Peters, Lenrie **43**
Philip, Marlene Nourbese **32**
Randall, Alice **38**
Ridley, John **69**
Saro-Wiwa, Kenule **39**
Schuyler, George Samuel **40**
Senior, Olive **37**
Smith, Danyel **40**
Smith, Zadie **51**
Southgate, Martha **58**
Tate, Eleanora E. **20, 55**
Taylor, Mildred D. **26**
Thomas, Michael **69**
Thomas-Graham, Pamela **29**
Tutuola, Amos **30**
Vera, Yvonne **32**
Verdelle, A. J. **26**
Walker, Margaret **29**
Weaver, Afaa Michael **37**
Whitfield, Van **34**
Williams, Sherley Anne **25**
Williams, Stanley "Tookie" **29, 57**
Woods, Teri **69**
Yarbrough, Camille **40**
Youngblood, Shay **32**
Zane **71**

Figure skating
Bonaly, Surya **7**
Thomas, Debi **26**

Film criticism
Mitchell, Elvis **67**

Film direction
Akomfrah, John **37**
Allain, Stephanie **49**
Allen, Debbie **13, 42**
Blackwood, Maureen **37**
Burnett, Charles **16, 68**
Byrd, Robert **11**
Campbell-Martin, Tisha **8, 42**
Cortez, Jayne **43**
Curtis-Hall, Vondie **17**
Dash, Julie **4**
Davis, Ossie **5, 50**
Dickerson, Ernest **6, 17**
Diesel, Vin **29**
Duke, Bill **3**
Franklin, Carl **11**
Freeman, Al, Jr. **11**
Fuqua, Antoine **35**
Gerima, Haile **38**
Gray, Darius **69**
Gray, F. Gary **14, 49**
Greaves, William **38**

Harris, Leslie **6**
Hayes, Teddy **40**
Henriques, Julian **37**
Hines, Gregory **1, 42**
Hudlin, Reginald **9**
Hudlin, Warrington **9**
Hughes, Albert **7**
Hughes, Allen **7**
Hurt, Byron **61**
Jackson, George **19**
Julien, Isaac **3**
Lane, Charles **3**
Lee, Spike **5, 19**
Lemmons, Kasi **20**
Lewis, Samella **25**
Martin, Darnell **43**
Micheaux, Oscar **7**
Morton, Joe **18**
Moses, Gilbert **12**
Moss, Carlton **17**
Mwangi, Meja **40**
Onwurah, Ngozi **38**
Peck, Raoul **32**
Perry, Tyler **40, 54**
Poitier, Sidney **11, 36**
Prince-Bythewood, Gina **31**
Riggs, Marlon **5, 44**
Roberts, Darryl **70**
St. Jacques, Raymond **8**
Schultz, Michael A. **6**
Sembène, Ousmane **13, 62**
Singleton, John **2, 30**
Smith, Roger Guenveur **12**
Tillman, George, Jr. **20**
Townsend, Robert **4, 23**
Tyler, Aisha N. **36**
Underwood, Blair **7**
Van Peebles, Mario **2, 51**
Van Peebles, Melvin **7**
Ward, Douglas Turner **42**
Wayans, Damon **8, 41**
Wayans, Keenen Ivory **18**
Whitaker, Forest **2, 49, 67**

Film production
Allain, Stephanie **49**
Chase, Debra Martin **49**
Daniels, Lee Louis **36**
Gerima, Haile **38**
Greaves, William **38**
Hines, Gregory **1, 42**
Lewis, Emmanuel **36**
Martin, Darnell **43**
Onwurah, Ngozi **38**
Packer, Will **71**
Patton, Paula **62**
Poitier, Sidney **11, 36**
Randall, Alice **38**
Robinson, Matt **69**
Tyler, Aisha N. **36**
Van Lierop, Robert **53**
Ward, Douglas Turner **42**
Whitaker, Forest **2, 49, 67**
Williams, Marco **53**
Williams, Russell, II **70**
Williamson, Fred **67**

Film scores
Blanchard, Terence **43**
Crouch, Andraé **27**
Hancock, Herbie **20, 67**
Jean-Baptiste, Marianne **17, 46**
Jones, Quincy **8, 30**

Prince 18, 65

Finance
Adams, Eula L. 39
Banks, Jeffrey 17
Bell, James A. 50
Boston, Kelvin E. 25
Bryant, John 26
Chapman, Nathan A., Jr. 21
Doley, Harold, Jr. 26
Epperson, Sharon 54
Ferguson, Roger W. 25
Fletcher, Alphonse, Jr. 16
Funderburg, I. Owen 38
Gaines, Brenda 41
Griffith, Mark Winston 8
Harris, Carla A. 67
Hobson, Mellody 40
Jones, Thomas W. 41
Lawless, Theodore K. 8
Lewis, William M., Jr. 40
Louis, Errol T. 8
Marshall, Bella 22
O'Neal, Stanley 38, 67
Rogers, John W., Jr. 5, 52
Ross, Charles 27
Thompson, William C. 35

Firefighters
Barlow, Roosevelt 49
Bell, Michael 40

First Data Corporation
Adams, Eula L. 39

Fisk University
Harvey, William R. 42
Imes, Elmer Samuel 39
Johnson, Charles S. 12
Phillips, Teresa L. 42
Smith, John L. 22

Fitness
Richardson, Donna 39
Smith, Ian 62

Florida A & M University
Gaither, Alonzo Smith (Jake) 14
Humphries, Frederick 20
Meek, Kendrick 41

Florida International baseball league
Kaiser, Cecil 42

Florida Marlins baseball team
Mariner, Jonathan 41
Sheffield, Gary 16

Florida state government
Brown, Corrine 24
Meek, Carrie 6
Meek, Kendrick 41
Tribble, Israel, Jr. 8

Florida State Supreme Court
Quince, Peggy A. 69

Fluoride chemistry
Quarterman, Lloyd Albert 4

Focus Detroit Electronic Music Festival
May, Derrick 41

Folk music
Bailey, DeFord 33
Chapman, Tracy 26
Charlemagne, Manno 11
Cuney, William Waring 44
Davis, Gary 41
Dawson, William Levi 39
Harper, Ben 34, 62
Jenkins, Ella 15
Love, Laura 50
Odetta 37
Spence, Joseph 49
Williams, Denise 40
Wilson, Cassandra 16

Football
Alexander, Shaun 58
Allen, Marcus 20
Amos, John 8, 62
Anderson, Jamal 22
Barber, Ronde 41
Barber, Tiki 57
Barney, Lem 26
Bettis, Jerome 64
Briscoe, Marlin 37
Brooks, Aaron 33
Brooks, Derrick 43
Brown, James 22
Brown, Jim 11
Bruce, Isaac 26
Buchanan, Ray 32
Bush, Reggie 59
Butler, LeRoy, III 17
Carter, Cris 21
Cherry, Deron 40
Clemons, Michael "Pinball" 64
Crennel, Romeo 54
Croom, Sylvester 50
Culpepper, Daunte 32
Cunningham, Randall 23
Davis, Ernie 48
Davis, Terrell 20
Dickerson, Eric 27
Dorrell, Karl 52
Dungy, Tony 17, 42, 59
Edwards, Harry 2
Farr, Mel 24
Faulk, Marshall 35
Fowler, Reggie 51
Gaither, Alonzo Smith (Jake) 14
Gilliam, Frank 23
Gilliam, Joe 31
Gorden, W. C. 71
Green, Darrell 39
Green, Dennis 5, 45
Greene, Joe 10
Grier, Roosevelt 13
Hill, Calvin 19
Irvin, Michael 64
Johnson, Levi 48
Jones, Ed "Too Tall" 46
Keith, Floyd A. 61
Ladd, Ernie 64
Lanier, Willie 33
Lewis, Marvin 51
Lofton, James 42
Lott, Ronnie 9
McNair, Steve 22, 47
McNabb, Donovan 29
Monk, Art 38
Moon, Warren 8, 66
Moss, Randy 23
Motley, Marion 26
Newsome, Ozzie 26
Owens, Terrell 53
Pace, Orlando 21
Page, Alan 7
Parker, Jim 64
Payton, Walter 11, 25
Perry, Lowell 30
Pollard, Fritz 53
Prince, Ron 64
Rashad, Ahmad 18
Rice, Jerry 5, 55
Robinson, Eddie G. 10, 61
Sanders, Barry 1, 53
Sanders, Deion 4, 31
Sapp, Warren 38
Sayers, Gale 28
Sharper, Darren 32
Shell, Art 1, 66
Simmons, Bob 29
Simpson, O. J. 15
Singletary, Mike 4
Smith, Emmitt 7
Smith, Lovie 66
Stewart, Kordell 21
Stingley, Darryl 69
Strahan, Michael 35
Stringer, Korey 35
Swann, Lynn 28
Taylor, Lawrence 25
Thomas, Derrick 25
Thomas, Emmitt 71
Thrower, Willie 35
Tomlinson, LaDainian 65
Upshaw, Gene 18, 47
Vick, Michael 39, 65
Walker, Herschel 1, 69
Ware, Andre 37
Watts, J. C., Jr. 14, 38
Weathers, Carl 10
White, Reggie 6, 50
Williams, Doug 22
Willingham, Tyrone 43
Willis, Bill 68
Wright, Rayfield 70

Football Hall of Fame, professional
Lofton, James 42
Sayers, Gale 28
Swann, Lynn 28
Willis, Bill 68
Wright, Rayfield 70

FOR
See Fellowship of Reconciliation

Forces Armées du Nord (Chad; FAN)
Déby, Idriss 30
Habré, Hissène 6

Ford Foundation
Thomas, Franklin A. 5, 49
Franklin, Robert M. 13

Ford Motor Company
Cherry, Deron 40
Dawson, Matel "Mat," Jr. 39
Goldsberry, Ronald 18
Hazel, Darryl B. 50
McMillan, Rosalynn A. 36

Fordham University
Blair, Paul 36
McMurray, Georgia L. 36

Foreign policy
Bunche, Ralph J. 5
Frazer, Jendayi 68
Rice, Condoleezza 3, 28
Robinson, Randall 7, 46

Forensic science
Griffin, Bessie Blout 43

Forest Club
Wilson, Sunnie 7, 55

40 Acres and a Mule Filmworks
Dickerson, Ernest 6, 17
Lee, Spike 5, 19

Foster care
Hale, Clara 16
Hale, Lorraine 8

Foundation for the Advancement of Inmate Rehabilitation and Recreation (FAIRR)
King, B. B. 7

Fox Broadcasting Company
Corbi, Lana 42
McFarland, Roland 49
Oliver, Pam 54

FPI
See Ivorian Popular Front

Frank H. Williams Caribbean Cultural Center African Diaspora Institute
Vega, Marta Moreno 61

Freddie Mac Corporation
Baker, Maxine 28

Freddie Mac Foundation
Baker, Maxine 28

Frederick Douglass Caring Award
Broadbent, Hydeia 36

Frederick Douglass Memorial Hospital
Mossell, Gertrude Bustill 40

Freedom Farm Cooperative
Hamer, Fannie Lou 6

Free Southern Theater (FST)
Borders, James 9

FRELIMO
See Front for the Liberation of Mozambique

French West Africa
Diouf, Abdou 3

FRODEBU
See Front for Democracy in Burundi

FRONASA
See Front for National Salvation (Uganda)

Front for Democracy in Burundi (FRODEBU)
Ndadaye, Melchior 7
Ntaryamira, Cyprien 8

Front for National Salvation (Uganda; FRONASA)
Museveni, Yoweri 4

Front for the Liberation of Mozambique (FRELIMO)
Chissano, Joaquim 7, 55, 67
Machel, Graca Simbine 16
Machel, Samora Moises 8

FST
See Free Southern Theater

Full Gospel Baptist
Long, Eddie L. 29

FullerMusic
Fuller, Arthur 27

Fulton County Juvenile Court
Hatchett, Glenda 32

Funeral homes
March, William Carrington 56

Funk Brothers
Jamerson, James 59

Funk music
Ayers, Roy 16
Brown, James 15, 60
Clinton, George 9
Collins, Bootsy 31
Collins, Lyn 53
Love, Laura 50
Richie, Lionel 27, 65
Watson, Johnny "Guitar" 18

Fusion
Davis, Miles 4
Jones, Quincy 8, 30
Williams, Tony 67

FWP Union
Nugent, Richard Bruce 39

Gangs
Williams, Stanley "Tookie" 29, 57

Gary, Indiana, city government
Hatcher, Richard G. 55

Gary, Williams, Parenti, Finney, Lewis & McManus
Gary, Willie E. 12

Gary Enterprises
Gary, Willie E. 12

Gary Post-Tribune
Ross, Don 27

Gassaway, Crosson, Turner & Parsons
Parsons, James 14

Gay and Lesbian Activism
De Veaux, Alexis 44

Gay Men of Color Consortium
Wilson, Phill 9

Genealogy
Blockson, Charles L. 42
Dash, Julie 4
Haley, Alex 4

General Hospital **TV series**
Cash, Rosalind 28

General Motors Corporation
O'Neal, Stanley 38, 67
Roberts, Roy S. 14

Welburn, Edward T. 50

Genetech
Potter, Myrtle 40

Genetics
Dunston, Georgia Mae 48
Harris, Mary Styles 31
Kittles, Rick 51
Olopade, Olufunmilayo Falusi 58

Geometric symbolism
Douglas, Aaron 7

Geophysics
Person, Waverly 9, 51

George Foster Peabody Broadcasting Award
Bradley, Ed 2, 59
Hunter-Gault, Charlayne 6, 31
Shaw, Bernard 2

George Mason University
Dunn, Jerry 27

George Washington University
Carter, Joye Maureen 41

Georgia state government
Baker, Thurbert 22
Bishop, Sanford D., Jr. 24
Bond, Julian 2, 35
Brooks, Tyrone 59
Majette, Denise 41
McKinney, Cynthia Ann 11, 52
Scott, David 41
Williams, Hosea Lorenzo 15, 31

Georgia State Supreme Court
Sears-Collins, Leah J. 5

Ghanaian government
Awoonor, Kofi 37
Kufuor, John Agyekum 54

Girl Scouts of the USA
Thompson, Cynthia Bramlett 50

Glaucoma treatment
Julian, Percy Lavon 6

Glidden Company
Julian, Percy Lavon 6

GLM Group
McMurray, Georgia L. 36

Goddard Space Flight Center
Ericsson-Jackson, Aprille 28

Gold Mind, Inc.
Elliott, Missy 31

Golden Globe awards
Allen, Debbie 13, 42
Bassett, Angela 6, 23, 62
Carroll, Diahann 9
Freeman, Morgan 2, 20, 62
Ross, Diana 8, 27
Taylor, Regina 9, 46

Golden Pen award
McFadden, Bernice L. 39

Golden State Warriors basketball team
Edwards, Harry 2
Lucas, John 7

Parish, Robert 43
Sprewell, Latrell 23

Golf
Elder, Lee 6
Gibson, Althea 8, 43
Gregory, Ann 63
Jackson, Fred James 25
Peete, Calvin 11
Richmond, Mitch 19
Shippen, John 43
Sifford, Charlie 4, 49
Spiller, Bill 64
Webber, Chris 15, 30, 59
Woods, Tiger 14, 31

Goodwill ambassador
Terry, Clark 39

Goodwill Games
Swoopes, Sheryl 12, 56

Gospel music
Adams, Oleta 18
Adams, Yolanda 17, 67
Armstrong, Vanessa Bell 24
Baylor Helen 36
Bonds, Margaret 39
Bradley, J. Robert 65
Caesar, Shirley 19
Cage, Byron 53
Clark, Mattie Moss 61
Clark-Cole, Dorinda 66
Clark-Sheard, Karen 22
Cleveland, James 19
Christie, Angella 36
Cooke, Sam 17
Crouch, Andraé 27
Davis, Gary 41
Dorsey, Thomas 15
Franklin, Aretha 11, 44
Franklin, Kirk 15, 49
Gaynor, Gloria 36
Green, Al 13, 47
Haddon, Dietrick 55
Hammond, Fred 23
Hawkins, Tramaine 16
Higginsen, Vy 65
Houston, Cissy 20
Jackson, Mahalia 5
Jakes, Thomas "T.D." 17, 43
Jones, Bobby 20
Kee, John P. 43
Kenoly, Ron 45
Killings, Debra 57
Knight, Gladys 16, 66
Lassiter, Roy 24
Little Richard 15
Majors, Jeff 41
Marrow, Queen Esther 24
Martin, Roberta 58
Mary Mary 34
Mayfield, Curtis 2, 43
McClendon, Lisa 61
McClurkin, Donnie 25
Mills, Stephanie 36
Monica 21
Moss, J 64
Mullen, Nicole C. 45
Peoples, Dottie 22
Phipps, Wintley 59
Preston, Billy 39, 59
Reagon, Bernice Johnson 7
Reese, Della 6, 20

Scott, George 55
Sheard, Kierra "Kiki" 61
Stampley, Micah 54
Staples, Mavis 50
Staples, "Pops" 32
Staton, Candi 27
Steinberg, Martha Jean "The Queen" 28
Tharpe, Rosetta 65
Tonex 54
Walker, Albertina 10, 58
Walker, Hezekiah 34
Washington, Dinah 22
West, Kanye 52
Whalum, Kirk 37, 64
Williams, Deniece 36
Wilson, Natalie 38
Winans, Angie 36
Winans, BeBe 14
Winans, CeCe 14, 43
Winans, Debbie 36
Winans, Marvin L. 17
Winans, Ronald 54
Winans, Vickie 24

Gospel theater
Perry, Tyler 40, 54

Graffiti art
White, Dondi 34

Grambling State University
Favors, Steve 23

Grammy awards
Adams, Oleta 18
Adderley, Nat 29
Badu, Erykah 22
Battle, Kathleen 70
Belafonte, Harry 4, 65
Beyoncé 39, 70
Blige, Mary J. 20, 34, 60
Brandy 14, 34
Caesar, Shirley 19
Chapman, Tracy 26
Cleveland, James 19
Cole, Natalie 17, 60
Combs, Sean "Puffy" 17, 43
Cosby, Bill 7, 26, 59
Cray, Robert 30
Crouch, Andraé 27
Davis, Miles 4
Dee, Ruby 8, 50, 68
Edmonds, Kenneth "Babyface" 10, 31
Ellington, Duke 5
Ferrer, Ibrahim 41
Fitzgerald, Ella 8
Franklin, Aretha 11, 44
Gaye, Marvin 2
Gaynor, Gloria 36
Gibson, Tyrese 27, 62
Glover, Corey 34
Goldberg, Whoopi 4, 33, 69
Gray, Macy 29
Guy, Buddy 31
Hammer, M. C. 20
Hathaway, Donny 18
Hawkins, Tramaine 16
Hill, Lauryn 20, 53
Holland-Dozier-Holland 36
Hooker, John Lee 30
Houston, Cissy 20
Houston, Whitney 7, 28

Isley, Ronald 25, 56
Jackson, Janet 6, 30, 68
Jackson, Michael 19, 53
James, Etta 13, 52
Jay-Z 27, 69
Jean, Wyclef 20
Jimmy Jam 13
Jones, Bobby 20
Jones, Quincy 8, 30
Kee, John P. 43
Kelly, R. 18, 44, 71
Keys, Alicia 32, 68
Knight, Gladys 16, 66
Knuckles, Frankie 42
LaBelle, Patti 13, 30
Legend, John 67
Lewis, Terry 13
Lopes, Lisa "Left Eye" 36
Mahal, Taj 39
Makeba, Miriam 2, 50
Marley, Ziggy 41
Marsalis, Branford 34
Mills, Stephanie 36
Mo', Keb' 36
Murphy, Eddie 4, 20, 61
Norman, Jessye 5
Olatunji, Babatunde 36
Perkins, Pinetop 70
Poitier, Sidney 11, 36
Price, Leontyne 1
Pride, Charley 26
Prince 18, 65
Queen Latifah 1, 16, 58
Reagon, Bernice Johnson 7
Redding, Otis 16
Reid, Vernon 34
Richie, Lionel 27, 65
Robinson, Smokey 3, 49
Ross, Isaiah "Doc" 40
Rucker, Darius 34
Sade 15
Shaggy 31
Smith, Will 8, 18
Summer, Donna 25
Turner, Tina 6, 27
Walker, Hezekiah 34
Warwick, Dionne 18
White, Barry 13, 41
White, Maurice 29
Williams, Deniece 36
Williams, Joe 5, 25
Wilson, Nancy 10
Winans, CeCe 14, 43
Winans, Marvin L. 17
Wonder, Stevie 11, 53

Grand Ole Opry
Bailey, DeFord 33

Graphic novels
Anderson, Ho Che 54
McDuffie, Dwayne 62
Tooks, Lance 62

Greater Emmanuel Temple of Faith
Jakes, Thomas "T.D." 17, 43

Green Bay Packers football team
Brooks, Aaron 33
Butler, Leroy, III 17
Howard, Desmond 16, 58
Lofton, James 42

Sharper, Darren 32
White, Reggie 6, 50

Green Belt Movement
Maathai, Wangari 43

Grenadian government
Bishop, Maurice 39

Groupe de Recherche Chorégraphique de
Dove, Ulysses 5

Guardian
Trotter, Monroe 9

Guggenheim fellowship
Rollins, Sonny 37
Taylor, Cecil 70
Wilson, Ellis 39

Guitar
Ade, King Sunny 41
Barker, Danny 32
Barnes, Roosevelt "Booba" 33
Bibb, Eric 49
Brown, Clarence Gatemouth 59
Butler, Jonathan 28
Burns, Eddie 44
Burnside, R. L. 56
Collins, Bootsy 31
Cray, Robert 30
Davis, Gary 41
Diddley, Bo 39
Estes, Sleepy John 33
Green, Grant 56
Guy, Buddy 31
Harris, Corey 39
Hemphill, Jessie Mae 33, 59
Hendrix, Jimi 10
House, Son 8
Hooker, John Lee 30
Howlin' Wolf 9
Jean, Wyclef 20
Johnson, Robert 2
Jordan, Ronny 26
Killings, Debra 57
King, B. B. 7
Klugh, Earl 59
Kravitz, Lenny 10, 34
Lipscomb, Mance 49
Marley, Bob 5
Mayfield, Curtis 2, 43
Ndegéocello, Me'Shell 15
Ongala, Remmy 9
Pena, Paul 58
Seals, Son 56
Spence, Joseph 49
Staples, Mavis 50
Staples, "Pops" 32
Watson, Johnny "Guitar" 18
Wilson, Cassandra 16

Gulf War
Powell, Colin 1, 28
Shaw, Bernard 2
Von Lipsey, Roderick K. 11

Gurdjieff Institute
Toomer, Jean 6

Guyanese government
Burnham, Forbes 66

Gymnastics
Dawes, Dominique 11
Hilliard, Wendy 53

White, Jesse 22

Hair care
Cottrell, Comer 11
Fuller, S. B. 13
Gibson, Ted 66
Johnson, George E. 29
Joyner, Marjorie Stewart 26
Malone, Annie 13
Roche, Joyce M. 17
Walker, Madame C. J. 7

Haitian refugees
Ashe, Arthur 1, 18
Dunham, Katherine 4, 59
Jean, Wyclef 20
Robinson, Randall 7, 46

Hal Jackson's Talented Teens International
Jackson, Hal 41

Hale House
Hale, Clara 16
Hale, Lorraine 8

Hallmark Channel
Corbi, Lana 42

Hampton University
Harvey, William R. 42

Handy Award
Hunter, Alberta 42

Harlem Artist Guild
Nugent, Richard Bruce 39
Wilson, Ellis 39

Harlem Cultural Council
Nugent, Richard Bruce 39

Harlem Globetrotters
Chamberlain, Wilt 18, 47
Haynes, Marques 22
Jackson, Mannie 14
Woodward, Lynette 67

Harlem Junior Tennis League
Blake, James 43

Harlem Renaissance
Alexander, Margaret Walker 22
Bennett, Gwendolyn B. 59
Christian, Barbara T. 44
Cullen, Countee 8
Cuney, William Waring 44
Dandridge, Raymond Garfield 45
Davis, Arthur P. 41
Delaney, Beauford 19
Ellington, Duke 5
Fauset, Jessie 7
Fisher, Rudolph 17
Frazier, E. Franklin 10
Horne, Frank 44
Hughes, Langston 4
Hurston, Zora Neale 3
Imes, Elmer Samuel 39
Johnson, Georgia Douglas 41
Johnson, James Weldon 5
Johnson, William Henry 3
Larsen, Nella 10
Locke, Alain 10
McKay, Claude 6
Mills, Florence 22
Nugent, Richard Bruce 39

Petry, Ann 19
Thurman, Wallace 16
Toomer, Jean 6
VanDerZee, James 6
West, Dorothy 12, 54
Wilson, Ellis 39

Harlem Writers Guild
Guy, Rosa 5
Killens, John O. 54
Wesley, Valerie Wilson 18

Harlem Youth Opportunities Unlimited (HARYOU)
Clark, Kenneth B. 5, 52

Harmonica
Bailey, DeFord 33
Barnes, Roosevelt "Booba" 33
Burns, Eddie 44
Howlin' Wolf 9
Neal, Raful 44
Ross, Isaiah "Doc" 40

Harness racing
Minor, DeWayne 32

Harp
Coltrane, Alice 70
Majors, Jeff 41

Harriet Tubman Home for Aged and Indigent Colored People
Tubman, Harriet 9

Harrisburg Giants baseball team
Charleston, Oscar 39

Harvard Law School
Bell, Derrick 6
Dickerson, Debra J. 60
Ogletree, Charles, Jr. 12, 47

Harvard University
Amaker, Tommy 62
Epps, Archie C., III 45
Hammonds, Evelynn 69
Huggins, Nathan Irvin 52
Loury, Glenn 36

HARYOU
See Harlem Youth Opportunities Unlimited

Hazelitt Award for Excellence in Arts
Bradley, David Henry, Jr. 39

Head Start
Edelman, Marian Wright 5, 42
Taylor, Helen (Lavon Hollingshed) 30

Health care reform
Adams-Campbell, Lucille L. 60
Berrysmith, Don Reginald 49
Brown, Jesse 6, 41
Carroll, L. Natalie 44
Cole, Lorraine 48
Cooper, Edward S. 6
Davis, Angela 5
Dirie, Waris 56
Gibson, Kenneth A. 6
Hughes, Ebony 57
Kintaudi, Leon 62

Lavizzo-Mourey, Risa **48**
Norman, Pat **10**
Potter, Myrtle **40**
Richardson, Rupert **67**
Satcher, David **7, 57**
Tuckson, Reed V. **71**
Vaughn, Viola **70**
Williams, Daniel Hale **2**
Williams, David Rudyard **50**

Heart disease
Cooper, Edward S. **6**
Grant, Augustus O. **71**

Heidelberg Project
Guyton, Tyree **9**

Heisman Trophy
Bush, Reggie **59**
Ware, Andre **37**

The Heritage Network
Mercado-Valdes, Frank **43**

HEW
See U.S. Department of Health, Education, and Welfare

HHS
See U.S. Department of Health and Human Services

Hip-hop music
Akon **68**
Ashanti **37**
Benjamin, Andre **45**
Fiasco, Lupe **64**
Garrett, Sean **57**
Jennings, Lyfe **56, 69**
Lil Wayne **66**
Patton, Antwan **45**
Smith, Danyel **40**
will.i.am **64**
Williams, Pharrell **47**

Historians
Ballard, Allen Butler, Jr. **40**
Benberry, Cuesta **65**
Berry, Mary Frances **7**
Blassingame, John Wesley **40**
Blockson, Charles L. **42**
Bogle, Donald **34**
Chase-Riboud, Barbara **20, 46**
Cooper, Afua **53**
Cooper, Anna Julia **20**
Cruse, Harold **54**
Diop, Cheikh Anta **4**
Dodson, Howard, Jr. **7, 52**
Du Bois, W. E. B. **3**
Franklin, John Hope **5**
Gates, Henry Louis, Jr. **3, 38, 67**
Giddings, Paula **11**
Gill, Gerald **69**
Hammonds, Evelynn **69**
Logan, Rayford W. **40**
Nash, Joe **55**
Hansberry, William Leo **11**
Harkless, Necia Desiree **19**
Hine, Darlene Clark **24**
Horton, James Oliver **58**
Huggins, Nathan Irvin **52**
Marable, Manning **10**
Painter, Nell Irvin **24**
Patterson, Orlando **4**
Quarles, Benjamin Arthur **18**
Reagon, Bernice Johnson **7**
Reddick, Lawrence Dunbar **20**
Rogers, Joel Augustus **30**
Sadlier, Rosemary **62**
Schomburg, Arthur Alfonso **9**
Skinner, Kiron K. **65**
Snowden, Frank M., Jr. **67**
van Sertima, Ivan **25**
Washington, James Melvin **50**
Williams, George Washington **18**
Woodson, Carter G. **2**

Hitman Records
Brae, C. Michael **61**

Hockey
Brashear, Donald **39**
Brathwaite, Fred **35**
Brown, James **22**
Brown, Sean **52**
Carnegie, Herbert **25**
Doig, Jason **45**
Fuhr, Grant **1, 49**
Grand-Pierre, Jean-Luc **46**
Grier, Mike **43**
Iginla, Jarome **35**
Mayers, Jamal **39**
McBride, Bryant **18**
McCarthy, Sandy **64**
McKegney, Tony **3**
O'Ree, Willie **5**
Salvador, Bryce **51**
Weekes, Kevin **67**

Homestead Grays baseball team
Charleston, Oscar **39**
Day, Leon **39**

Homosexuality
Carter, Mandy **11**
Clarke, Cheryl **32**
Delany, Samuel R., Jr. **9**
Gomes, Peter J. **15**
Harris, E. Lynn **12, 33**
Hemphill, Essex **10**
Julien, Isaac **3**
Lorde, Audre **6**
Norman, Pat **10**
Nugent, Richard Bruce **39**
Parker, Pat **19**
Riggs, Marlon **5, 44**
Rupaul **17**
Wilson, Phill **9**

Honeywell Corporation
Jackson, Mannie **14**

Horse racing
Harris, Sylvia **70**
St. Julien, Marlon **29**
Winkfield, Jimmy **42**

House music
Knuckles, Frankie **42**

House of Representatives
See U.S. House of Representatives

Housing Authority of New Orleans
Mason, Ronald **27**

Houston Astros baseball team
Morgan, Joe Leonard **9**
Watson, Bob **25**

Houston Comets basketball team
Perrot, Kim **23**
Thompson, Tina **25**

Houston Oilers football team
McNair, Steve **22, 47**
Moon, Warren **8, 66**

Houston Rockets basketball team
Lucas, John **7**
Olajuwon, Hakeem **2**

Howard University
Adams-Campbell, Lucille L. **60**
Benjamin, Tritobia Hayes **53**
Cardozo, Francis L. **33**
Carter, Joye Maureen **41**
Cobb, W. Montague **39**
Davis, Arthur P. **41**
Dodson, Owen **38**
Gerima, Haile **38**
Jenifer, Franklyn G. **2**
Ladner, Joyce A. **42**
Locke, Alain **10**
Logan, Rayford W. **40**
Malveaux, Floyd **54**
Mays, Benjamin E. **7**
Neal, Larry **38**
Payton, Benjamin F. **23**
Porter, James A. **11**
Reid, Irvin D. **20**
Ribeau, Sidney **70**
Robinson, Spottswood W., III **22**
Snowden, Frank M., Jr. **67**
Sowande, Fela **39**
Spriggs, William **67**
Swygert, H. Patrick **22**
Wells, James Lesesne **10**
Wesley, Dorothy Porter **19**
White, Charles **39**
Young, Roger Arliner **29**

HRCF
See Human Rights Campaign Fund

Hubbard Hospital
Lyttle, Hulda Margaret **14**

HUD
See U.S. Department of Housing and Urban Development

Hugo awards
Butler, Octavia **8, 43, 58**
Delany, Samuel R., Jr. **9**

Hull-Ottawa Canadiens hockey team
O'Ree, Willie **5**

Human resources
Howroyd, Janice Bryant **42**

Human Rights Campaign Fund (HRCF)
Carter, Mandy **11**

Hunter College
DeCarava, Roy **42**
Mayhew, Richard **39**
Thomas, Michael **69**

Hurdle
Devers, Gail **7**

IBF
See International Boxing Federation

IBM
Adkins, Rod **41**
Blackwell, Robert D., Sr. **52**
Chenault, Kenneth I. **5, 36**
Dean, Mark **35**
Foster, Jylla Moore **45**
Thompson, John W. **26**
Zollar, Alfred **40**

IBM's National Black Family Technology Awareness
Adkins, Rod **41**

Ice Hockey in Harlem
Mayers, Jamal **39**

Ice skating
See Figure skating

Igbo people/traditions
Achebe, Chinua **6**

IHRLG
See International Human Rights Law Group

I-Iman Cosmetics
Iman **4, 33**

Ile Ife Films
Hall, Arthur **39**

Illinois state government
Braun, Carol Moseley **4, 42**
Burris, Roland W. **25**
Colter, Cyrus J. **36**
Obama, Barack **49**
Raoul, Kwame **55**
Trotter, Donne E. **28**
Washington, Harold **6**
White, Jesse **22**

Illustrations
Anderson, Ho Che **54**
Biggers, John **20, 33**
Bryan, Ashley F. **41**
Campbell, E. Simms **13**
Fax, Elton **48**
Honeywood, Varnette P. **54**
Hudson, Cheryl **15**
Kitt, Sandra **23**
Pinkney, Jerry **15**
Saint James, Synthia **12**

Imani Temple
Stallings, George A., Jr. **6**

IMF
See International Monetary Fund

Imhotep National Conference on Hospital Integration
Cobb, W. Montague **39**

Indecorp, Inc.
Johnson, George E. **29**

Indiana Fever basketball team
Catchings, Tamika **43**

Indiana state government
Carson, Julia **23, 69**
Carter, Pamela Lynn **67**

Indianapolis ABCs baseball team
Charleston, Oscar 39

Indianapolis Clowns baseball team
Charleston, Oscar 39
Johnson, Mamie "Peanut" 40

Indianapolis Colts football team
Dickerson, Eric 27
Dungy, Tony 17, 42, 59

Indianapolis Crawfords baseball team
Charleston, Oscar 39
Kaiser, Cecil 42

Indianapolis 500
Ribbs, Willy T. 2

Information technology
Blackwell, Robert D., Sr. 52
Coleman, Ken 57
Pinkett, Randal 61
Smith, Joshua 10
Woods, Jacqueline 52
Zollar, Alfred 40

In Friendship
Baker, Ella 5

Inkatha
Buthelezi, Mangosuthu Gatsha 9

Inner City Broadcasting Corporation
Jackson, Hal 41
Sutton, Percy E. 42

Institute for Black Parenting
Oglesby, Zena 12

Institute for Journalism Education
Harris, Jay T. 19
Maynard, Robert C. 7

Institute for Research in African American Studies
Marable, Manning 10

Institute of Positive Education
Madhubuti, Haki R. 7

Institute of Social and Religious Research
Mays, Benjamin E. 7

Insurance
Hill, Jesse, Jr. 13
James, Donna A. 51
Kidd, Mae Street 39
Killingsworth, Cleve, Jr. 54
Procope, Ernesta 23
Procope, John Levy 56
Spaulding, Charles Clinton 9
Vaughns, Cleopatra 46
Williams, Ronald A. 57
Willie, Louis, Jr. 68

Interior design
Bridges, Sheila 36
De' Alexander, Quinton 57
Ham, Cynthia Parker 58
Hayes, Cecil N. 46

King, Robert Arthur 58
Myles, Kim 69
Steave-Dickerson, Kia 57
Taylor, Karin 34

Internal Revenue Service
Colter, Cyrus J. 36

International ambassadors
Davis, Ruth 37
Poitier, Sidney 11, 36
Smythe Haith, Mabel 61
Todman, Terence A. 55
Wharton, Clifton Reginald, Sr. 36

International Association of Fire Chiefs
Bell, Michael 40
Day, Leon 39

International Boxing Federation (IBF)
Ali, Muhammad 2, 16, 52
Hearns, Thomas 29
Hopkins, Bernard 35, 69
Lewis, Lennox 27
Moorer, Michael 19
Mosley, Shane 32
Tyson, Mike 28, 44
Whitaker, Pernell 10

International Federation of Library Associations and Institutions
Wedgeworth, Robert W. 42

International Free and Accepted Masons and Eastern Star
Banks, William 11

International Human Rights Law Group (IHRLG)
McDougall, Gay J. 11, 43

International Ladies' Auxiliary
Tucker, Rosina 14

International law
Payne, Ulice 42

International Monetary Fund (IMF)
Babangida, Ibrahim 4
Chissano, Joaquim 7, 55, 67
Conté, Lansana 7
Diouf, Abdou 3
Patterson, P. J. 6, 20

International Olympic Committee (IOC)
DeFrantz, Anita 37

International Workers Organization (IWO)
Patterson, Louise 25

Internet
Cooper, Barry 33
Gilliard, Steve 69
Knowling, Robert 38
Thomas-Graham, Pamela 29

Internet security
Thompson, John W. 26

Interpol
Noble, Ronald 46

Interscope Geffen A & M Records
Stoute, Steve 38

***In the Black* television show**
Jones, Caroline R. 29

Inventions
Johnson, Lonnie 32
Jones, Frederick McKinley 68
Julian, Percy Lavon 6
Latimer, Lewis H. 4
McCoy, Elijah 8
Morgan, Garrett 1
Woods, Granville T. 5

Investment management
Beal, Bernard B. 46
Bryant, John 26
Ford, Wallace 58
Gardner, Chris 65
Goings, Russell 59
Harris, Carla A. 67
Procope, Ernesta 23
Rogers, John W., Jr. 5, 52
Utendahl, John 23

Island Def Jam Music Group
Liles, Kevin 42

Island Records
Ade, King Sunny 41

Ivorian Popular Front (FPI)
Gbagbo, Laurent 43

Ivory Coast government
Gbagbo, Laurent 43
Guéï, Robert 66

Jackie Robinson Foundation
Robinson, Rachel 16

Jackson Securities, Inc.
Jackson, Maynard 2, 41

Jackson University
Mason, Ronald 27

Jacksonville Jaguars football team
Cherry, Deron 40

jacksoul
Neale, Haydain 52

Jamaican government
Simpson-Miller, Portia 62

Janet-Bi Company
Acogny, Germaine 55

Jazz
Adderley, Julian "Cannonball" 30
Adderley, Nat 29
Albright, Gerald 23
Anderson, Carl 48
Armstrong, Louis 2
Austin, Lovie 40
Austin, Patti 24
Ayers, Roy 16
Barker, Danny 32
Bailey, Buster 38
Bailey, Philip 63
Basie, Count 23

Batiste, Alvin 66
Bechet, Sidney 18
Belle, Regina 1, 51
Blakey, Art 37
Blanchard, Terence 43
Bolden, Buddy 39
Bridgewater, Dee Dee 32
Brooks, Avery 9
Butler, Jonathan 28
Calloway, Cab 14
Carter, Benny 46
Carter, Betty 19
Carter, Regina 23
Carter, Warrick L. 27
Cartiér, Xam Wilson 41
Charles, Ray 16, 48
Cheatham, Doc 17
Clarke, Kenny 27
Cole, Nat King 17
Coleman, Ornette 39, 69
Coltrane, Alice 70
Coltrane, John 19
Coltrane, Ravi 71
Cook, Charles "Doc" 44
Count Basie 23
Crawford, Randy 19
Crothers, Scatman 19
Crouch, Stanley 11
Crowder, Henry 16
Daemyon, Jerald 64
Dara, Olu 35
Davis, Anthony 11
Davis, Frank Marshall 47
Davis, Miles 4
Dickenson, Vic 38
Donegan, Dorothy 19
Downing, Will 19
Duke, George 21
Dumas, Henry 41
Eckstine, Billy 28
Eldridge, Roy 37
Ellington, Duke 5
Ellison, Ralph 7
Eubanks, Kevin 15
Farmer, Art 38
Ferrell, Rachelle 29
Fitzgerald, Ella 8, 18
Flanagan, Tommy 69
Foster, George "Pops" 40
Freelon, Nnenna 32
Freeman, Yvette 27
Fuller, Arthur 27
Gillespie, Dizzy 1
Golson, Benny 37
Gordon, Dexter 25
Green, Grant 56
Griffin, Johnny 71
Güines, Tata 69
Hampton, Lionel 17, 41
Hancock, Herbie 20, 67
Hardin Armstrong, Lil 39
Harris, Barry 68
Hathaway, Lalah 57
Hawkins, Coleman 9
Henderson, Fletcher 32
Higginbotham, J. C. 37
Hill, Andrew 66
Hines, Earl "Fatha" 39
Hinton, Milt 30
Holiday, Billie 1
Horn, Shirley 32, 56
Hyman, Phyllis 19
Jackson, Milt 26

Jacquet, Illinois 49
Jamal, Ahmad 69
James, Etta 13, 52
Jarreau, Al 21, 65
Johnson, Buddy 36
Johnson, J. J. 37
Jones, Elvin 14, 68
Jones, Etta 35
Jones, Hank 57
Jones, Jonah 39
Jones, Quincy 8, 30
Jones, Thad 68
Jordan, Ronny 26
Kenyatta, Robin 54
Klugh, Earl 59
Lewis, Ramsey 35, 70
Lincoln, Abbey 3
Locke, Eddie 44
Lucien, Jon 66
Madhubuti, Haki R. 7
Marsalis, Branford 34
Marsalis, Delfeayo 41
Marsalis, Wynton 16
McBride, James 35
Mills, Florence 22
Mingus, Charles 15
Mitchell, Nicole 66
Monk, Thelonious 1
Moore, Melba 21
Morton, Jelly Roll 29
Muse, Clarence Edouard 21
Nascimento, Milton 2, 64
Oliver, Joe "King" 42
Parker, Charlie 20
Payne, Freda 58
Peterson, Marvin "Hannibal" 27
Peterson, Oscar 52
Powell, Bud 24
Redman, Joshua 30
Reese, Della 6, 20
Reeves, Dianne 32
Roach, Max 21, 63
Roberts, Marcus 19
Rollins, Sonny 37
Ross, Diana 8, 27
Rushing, Jimmy 37
Sample, Joe 51
Scarlett, Millicent 49
Scott, Hazel 66
Scott, "Little" Jimmy 48
Silver, Horace 26
Simpson-Hoffman, N'kenge 52
Sissle, Noble 29
Smith, Bessie 3
Smith, Cladys "Jabbo" 32
Smith, Dr. Lonnie 49
Smith, Lonnie Liston 49
Smith, Stuff 37
Staton, Dakota 62
Strayhorn, Billy 31
Sullivan, Maxine 37
Sun Ra 60
Swann, Lynn 28
Tampa Red 63
Taylor, Billy 23
Taylor, Cecil 70
Terry, Clark 39
Tisdale, Wayman 50
Vaughan, Sarah 13
Waller, Fats 29
Washington, Dinah 22
Washington, Grover, Jr. 17, 44
Waters, Benny 26

Watson, Johnny "Guitar" 18
Watts, Reggie 52
Webster, Katie 29
Wein, Joyce 62
Whalum, Kirk 37, 64
White, Maurice 29
Williams, Joe 5, 25
Williams, Mary Lou 15
Williams, Tony 67
Wilson, Cassandra 16
Wilson, Gerald 49
Wilson, Nancy 10
York, Vincent 40
Young, Lester 37

Jazzistry
York, Vincent 40

Jet magazine
Bennett, Lerone, Jr. 5
Johnson, John H. 3, 54
Massaquoi, Hans J. 30
Sleet, Moneta, Jr. 5

Jive Records
McPherson, David 32

Jockeys
Harris, Sylvia 70
Lewis, Oliver 56
Winkfield, Jimmy 42

John Lucas Enterprises
Lucas, John 7

Johnny Ace with the New Blues Sound
Ace, Johnny 36

Johnson C. Smith University
Yancy, Dorothy Cowser 42

Johnson Products
Johnson, George E. 29

Johnson Publishing Company, Inc.
Bennett, Lerone, Jr. 5
Booker, Simeon 23
Johnson, John H. 3, 54
Monroe, Bryan 71
Rice, Linda Johnson 9, 41
Sleet, Moneta, Jr. 5

Joint Center for Political Studies
Williams, Eddie N. 44

Joint Chiefs of Staff
See U.S. Joint Chiefs of Staff

Joint Regional Terrorism Task Force
Bell, Michael 40

Jones Haywood School of Ballet
Jones, Doris W. 62

Journalism
Abbott, Robert Sengstacke 27
Abrahams, Peter 39
Abu-Jamal, Mumia 15
Ansa, Tina McElroy 14
Ashley-Ward, Amelia 23
Asim, Jabari 71
Auguste, Arnold A. 47

Azikiwe, Nnamdi 13
Bailey, Chauncey 68
Baquet, Dean 63
Barden, Don H. 9, 20
Barnett, Amy Du Bois 46
Barrett, Lindsay 43
Bass, Charlotta Spears 40
Bates, Karen Grigsby 40
Bennett, Gwendolyn B. 59
Bennett, Lerone, Jr. 5
Blair, Jayson 50
Blake, Asha 26
Bolden, Frank E. 44
Booker, Simeon 23
Borders, James 9
Boyd, Gerald M. 32, 59
Boyd, Suzanne 52
Bradley, Ed 2, 59
Britt, Donna 28
Brower, William 49
Brown, George Leslie 62
Brown, Lloyd Louis 42
Brown, Tony 3
Buckley, Gail Lumet 39
Burt-Murray, Angela 59
Caldwell, Earl 60
Campbell, Bebe Moore 6, 24, 59
Cary, Mary Ann Shadd 30
Cayton, Horace 26
Chadiha, Jeffri 57
Chideya, Farai 14, 61
Ciara, Barbara 69
Cooke, Marvel 31
Cooper, Barry 33
Cose, Ellis 5, 50
Crouch, Stanley 11
Crutchfield, James N. 55
Cullen, Countee 8
Cunningham, Evelyn 23
Dash, Leon 47
Datcher, Michael 60
Davis, Belva 61
Davis, Frank Marshall 47
Davis, Thulani 61
Dawkins, Wayne 20
Deggans, Eric 71
Drummond, William J. 40
Due, Tananarive 30
Dunbar, Paul Laurence 8
Dunnigan, Alice Allison 41
Edmonds, Terry 17
Epperson, Sharon 54
Farley, Christopher John 54
Forman, James 7, 51
Fortune, T. Thomas 6
Fuller, Hoyt 44
Giddings, Paula 11
Gilliard, Steve 69
Goode, Mal 13
Gordon, Ed 10, 53
Grimké, Archibald H. 9
Gumbel, Bryant 14
Gumbel, Greg 8
Hansberry, Lorraine 6
Hare, Nathan 44
Harrington, Oliver W. 9
Harris, Claire 34
Harris, Jay 19
Harris, Richard E. 61
Haynes, Trudy 44
Henriques, Julian 37
Herbert, Bob 63
Hickman, Fred 11

Holt, Lester 66
Huggins, Edie 71
Hunter-Gault, Charlayne 6, 31
Ifill, Gwen 28
Jarret, Vernon D. 42
Jasper, Kenji 39
Jealous, Benjamin 70
Joachim, Paulin 34
Johnson, Georgia Douglas 41
Johnson, James Weldon 5
Kaufman, Monica 66
Kearney, Janis 54
Khanga, Yelena 6
Killens, John O. 54
King, Colbert I. 69
Knight, Etheridge 37
LaGuma, Alex 30
Lacy, Sam 30, 46
Lampkin, Daisy 19
Leavell, Dorothy R. 17
Lewis, Edward T. 21
Lowe, Herbert 57
Mabrey, Vicki 26
Mabry, Marcus 70
Mabuza-Suttle, Felicia 43
Madison, Paula 37
Martin, Louis E. 16
Martin, Roland S. 49
Mason, Felicia 31
Maynard, Robert C. 7
McBride, James 35
McCall, Nathan 8
McGruder, Robert 22, 35
McKay, Claude 6
Mickelbury, Penny 28
Mitchell, Elvis 67
Mitchell, Russ 21
Mkapa, Benjamin 16
Monroe, Bryan 71
Mossell, Gertrude Bustill 40
Murphy, John H. 42
Murray, Pauli 38
Nelson, Jill 6, 54
Neville, Arthel 53
Newkirk, Pamela 69
Nkosi, Lewis 46
Oliver, Pam 54
Olojede, Dele 59
Page, Clarence 4
Palmer, Everard 37
Parham, Marjorie B. 71
Parker, Star 70
Parks, Gordon 1, 35, 58
Payne, Ethel L. 28
Perez, Anna 1
Perkins, Tony 24
Pinkston, W. Randall 24
Pitts, Byron 71
Pitts, Leonard, Jr. 54
Pressley, Condace L. 41
Price, Hugh B. 9, 54
Prince, Richard E. 71
Quarles, Norma 25
Raspberry, William 2
Reed, Ishmael 8
Reeves, Rachel J. 23
Rhoden, William C. 67
Riley, Rochelle 50
Roberts, Robin 16, 54
Robinson, Max 3
Rodgers, Johnathan 6, 51
Rowan, Carl T. 1, 30
Salih, Al-Tayyib 37

Salters, Lisa **71**
Sanders, Pharoah **64**
Schuyler, George Samuel **40**
Schuyler, Philippa **50**
Senior, Olive **37**
Shaw, Bernard **2, 28**
Shipp, E. R. **15**
Simpson, Carole **6, 30**
Smith, Clarence O. **21**
Smith, Danyel **40**
Smith, Stephen A. **69**
Sowell, Thomas **2**
Staples, Brent **8**
Stewart, Alison **13**
Stokes, Carl B. **10**
Stone, Chuck **9**
Syler, Rene **53**
Tate, Eleanora E. **20, 55**
Taylor, Kristin Clark **8**
Taylor, Susan L. **10**
Thurman, Wallace **16**
Tolson, Melvin B. **37**
Trotter, Monroe **9**
Tucker, Cynthia **15, 61**
Wallace, Michele Faith **13**
Washington, Harriet A. **69**
Watson, Carlos **50**
Watts, Rolonda **9**
Webb, Veronica **10**
Wells-Barnett, Ida B. **8**
Wesley, Valerie Wilson **18**
Whitaker, Mark **21, 47**
Wilbekin, Emil **63**
Wilbon, Michael **68**
Wiley, Ralph **8**
Wilkerson, Isabel **71**
Wilkins, Roger **2**
Williams, Armstrong **29**
Williams, Clarence **70**
Williams, Juan **35**
Williams, Patricia **11, 54**
Wiwa, Ken **67**
Woods, Mattiebelle **63**
Yette, Samuel F. **63**
Zook, Kristal Brent **62**

Journal of Negro History
Woodson, Carter G. **2**

Juanita Bynum Ministries
Bynum, Juanita **31, 71**

Juju music
Ade, King Sunny **41**

Just Us Books
Hudson, Cheryl **15**
Hudson, Wade **15**

Kansas City Athletics baseball team
Paige, Satchel **7**

Kansas City Chiefs football team
Allen, Marcus **20**
Cherry, Deron **40**
Dungy, Tony **17, 42, 59**
Thomas, Derrick **25**
Thomas, Emmitt **71**

Kansas City government
Cleaver, Emanuel **4, 45, 68**

Kansas City Monarchs baseball team
Bell, James "Cool Papa" **36**
Brown, Willard **36**

Kansas State University
Prince, Ron **64**

KANU
See Kenya African National Union

Kappa Alpha Psi
Hamilton, Samuel C. **47**

Karl Kani Infinity
Kani, Karl **10**

KAU
See Kenya African Union

KCA
See Kikuyu Central Association

Kentucky Derby
Winkfield, Jimmy **42**

Kentucky Negro Educational Association
Cotter, Joseph Seamon, Sr. **40**

Kentucky state government
Kidd, Mae Street **39**

Kenya African National Union (KANU)
Kariuki, J. M. **67**
Kenyatta, Jomo **5**
Kibaki, Mwai **60**
Moi, Daniel Arap **1, 35**
Ngilu, Charity **58**
Odinga, Raila **67**

Kenya African Union (KAU)
Kenyatta, Jomo **5**

Kenya National Council of Churchs (NCCK)
Kobia, Samuel **43**

Kenyan government
Kariuki, J. M. **67**
Kibaki, Mwai **60**
Maathai, Wangari **43**
Moi, Daniel Arap **1, 35**
Ngilu, Charity **58**
Odinga, Raila **67**

Kikuyu Central Association (KCA)
Kenyatta, Jomo **5**

King Center
See Martin Luther King Jr. Center for Nonviolent Social Change

King Oliver's Creole Band
Armstrong, (Daniel) Louis **2**
Hardin Armstrong, Lil **39**
Oliver, Joe "King" **42**

King Sunny Ade Foundation
Ade, King Sunny **41**

King's Troop of the Royal Horse Artillery
Scantlebury, Janna **47**

Kitchen Table: Women of Color Press
Smith, Barbara **28**

Kmart Holding Corporation
Lewis, Aylwin **51**

Koko Taylor's Celebrity
Taylor, Koko **40**

Kraft General Foods
Fudge, Ann (Marie) **11, 55**
Sneed, Paula A. **18**

Kunta Kinte–Alex Haley Foundation
Blackshear, Leonard **52**

Kwanzaa
Karenga, Maulana **10, 71**

Kwazulu Territorial Authority
Buthelezi, Mangosuthu Gatsha **9**

Labour Party
Amos, Valerie **41**

Ladies Professional Golfers' Association (LPGA)
Gibson, Althea **8, 43**
Powell, Renee **34**

LaFace Records
Benjamin, Andre **45**
Edmonds, Kenneth "Babyface" **10, 31**
OutKast **35**
Patton, Antwan **45**
Reid, Antonio "L.A." **28**

Lamb of God Ministry
Falana, Lola **42**

Langston (OK) city government
Tolson, Melvin B. **37**

LAPD
See Los Angeles Police Department

Latin American folk music
Nascimento, Milton **2, 64**

Latin baseball leagues
Kaiser, Cecil **42**

Law enforcement
Alexander, Joyce London **18**
Barrett, Jacquelyn **28**
Bolton, Terrell D. **25**
Bradley, Thomas **2, 20**
Brown, Lee P. **1, 24**
Freeman, Charles **19**
Gibson, Johnnie Mae **23**
Glover, Nathaniel, Jr. **12**
Gomez-Preston, Cheryl **9**
Harvard, Beverly **11**
Hillard, Terry **25**
Holton, Hugh, Jr. **39**
Hurtt, Harold **46**
Johnson, Norma L. Holloway **17**
Johnson, Robert T. **17**
Keith, Damon J. **16**
McKinnon, Isaiah **9**
Moose, Charles **40**
Napoleon, Benny N. **23**
Noble, Ronald **46**
Oliver, Jerry **37**
Parks, Bernard C. **17**
Ramsey, Charles H. **21, 69**
Robinson, Bishop L. **66**
Schmoke, Kurt **1, 48**
Smith, Richard **51**
Thomas, Franklin A. **5, 49**
Wainwright, Joscelyn **46**
Ward, Benjamin **68**
Williams, Willie L. **4**
Wilson, Jimmy **45**

Lawrence Steele Design
Steele, Lawrence **28**

Lawyers' Committee for Civil Rights Under Law
Arnwine, Barbara **28**
Hubbard, Arnette **38**
McDougall, Gay J. **11, 43**

LDF
See NAACP Legal Defense and Educational Fund

Leadership Conference on Civil Rights (LCCR)
Henderson, Wade J. **14**

League of Nations
Haile Selassie **7**

League of Women Voters
Meek, Carrie **36**

Leary Group Inc.
Leary, Kathryn D. **10**

"Leave No Child Behind"
Edelman, Marian Wright **5, 42**

Lee Elder Scholarship Fund
Elder, Lee **6**

Legal Defense Fund
See NAACP Legal Defense and Educational Fund

Les Brown Unlimited, Inc.
Brown, Les **5**

Lexicography
Major, Clarence **9**

Liberation theology
West, Cornel **5**

Liberian government
Henries, A. Doris Banks **44**
Sirleaf, Ellen Johnson **71**
Weah, George **58**

Liberians United for Reconciliation and Democracy (LURD)
Conneh, Sekou Damate, Jr. **51**

Library science
Bontemps, Arna **8**
Franklin, Hardy R. **9**
Harsh, Vivian Gordon **14**
Hutson, Jean Blackwell **16**
Jones, Clara Stanton **51**
Josey, E. J. **10**
Kitt, Sandra **23**
Larsen, Nella **10**
Morrison, Sam **50**

Owens, Major **6**
Rollins, Charlemae Hill **27**
Schomburg, Arthur Alfonso **9**
Smith, Jessie Carney **35**
Spencer, Anne **27**
Wedgeworth, Robert W. **42**
Wesley, Dorothy Porter **19**

Librettos
Chenault, John **40**

Lincoln University
Cuney, William Waring **44**
Randall, Dudley **8, 55**
Sudarkasa, Niara **4**

LISC
See Local Initiative Support Corporation

Listen Up Foundation
Jones, Quincy **8, 30**

Literacy Volunteers of America
Amos, Wally **9**

Literary criticism
Baker, Houston A., Jr. **6**
Braithwaite, William Stanley **52**
Brown, Sterling Allen **10, 64**
Broyard, Anatole **68**
Cartey, Wilfred **47**
Christian, Barbara T. **44**
Cook, Mercer **40**
De Veaux, Alexis **44**
Emanuel, James A. **46**
Fleming, Raymond **48**
Ford, Nick Aaron **44**
Fuller, Hoyt **44**
Joachim, Paulin **34**
Mugo, Micere Githae **32**
Ngugi wa Thiong'o **29, 61**
Redding, J. Saunders **26**
Reed, Ishmael **8**
Smith, Barbara **28**
Wesley, Valerie Wilson **18**
West, Cornel **5**

Literary Hall of Fame for Writers of African Descent
Colter, Cyrus J. **36**

Lithography
White, Charles **39**

Little Junior Project
Fuller, Arthur **27**

"Little Paris" group
Thomas, Alma **14**

"Little Rock Nine"
Bates, Daisy **13**

Liver research
Leevy, Carrol M. **42**

Lobbying
Brooke, Edward **8**
Brown, Elaine **8**
Brown, Jesse **6, 41**
Brown, Ron **5**
Edelman, Marian Wright **5, 42**
Lee, Canada **8**
Mallett, Conrad, Jr. **16**
Reeves, Gregory **49**

Robinson, Randall **7, 46**

Local Initiative Support Corporation (LISC)
Thomas, Franklin A. **5, 49**

Long jump
Lewis, Carl **4**
Powell, Mike **7**

Los Angeles Angels baseball team
Baylor, Don **6**
Bonds, Bobby **43**
Carew, Rod **20**
Robinson, Frank **9**
Winfield, Dave **5**

Los Angeles city government
Bradley, Thomas **2, 20**
Evers, Myrlie **8**

Los Angeles Clippers basketball team
Brand, Elton **31**

Los Angeles Dodgers baseball team
Baker, Dusty **8, 43**
Newcombe, Don **24**
Robinson, Frank **9**
Strawberry, Darryl **22**

Los Angeles Lakers basketball team
Abdul-Jabbar, Kareem **8**
Bryant, Kobe **15, 31, 71**
Chamberlain, Wilt **18, 47**
Fox, Rick **27**
Green, A. C. **32**
Johnson, Earvin "Magic" **3, 39**
O'Neal, Shaquille **8, 30**
Worthy, James **49**

Los Angeles Philharmonic
Lewis, Henry **38**

Los Angeles Police Department (LAPD)
Parks, Bernard C. **17**
Smith, Richard **51**
Williams, Willie L. **4**

Los Angeles Raiders football team
Allen, Marcus **20**
Lofton, James **42**
Lott, Ronnie **9**
Shell, Art **1, 66**

Los Angeles Rams football team
Dickerson, Eric **27**
Washington, Kenny **50**

Los Angeles Sparks basketball team
Leslie, Lisa **16**

Los Angeles Times newspaper
Baquet, Dean **63**
Drummond, William J. **40**

Lost-Found Nation of Islam
Ali, Muhammad **2, 16, 52**
Ellison, Keith **59**
Farrakhan, Louis **2, 15**

Heard, Nathan C. **45**
Karim, Benjamin **61**
Muhammad, Ava **31**
Muhammad, Elijah **4**
Muhammad, Khallid Abdul **10, 31**
Muhammed, W. Deen **27**
Sutton, Percy E. **42**
Tillard, Conrad **47**
X, Malcolm **1**
X, Marvin **45**

Louisiana Disaster Recovery Authority
Francis, Norman (C.) **60**

Louisiana state government
Fields, Cleo **13**
Jefferson, William J. **25**
Morial, Ernest "Dutch" **26**
Pinchback, P. B. S. **9**
Richardson, Rupert **67**

LPGA
See Ladies Professional Golfers' Association

Lunar surface ultraviolet camera
See Ultraviolet camera/spectrograph (UVC)

Lynching (anti-lynching legislation)
Johnson, James Weldon **5**
Moore, Harry T. **29**
Till, Emmett **7**

Lyrics
Crouch, Andraé **27**
D'Angelo **27**
Dunbar, Paul Laurence **8**
Fitzgerald, Ella **8**
Jean, Wyclef **20**
Johnson, James Weldon **5**
KRS-One **34**
Lil' Kim **28**
MC Lyte **34**
Randall, Alice **38**
Run-DMC **31**

MacArthur Foundation Fellowship
Butler, Octavia **8, 43, 58**
Hammons, David **69**
Olopade, Olufunmilayo Falusi **58**
Parks, Suzan-Lori **34**
Taylor, Cecil **70**

MacNeil/Lehrer NewsHour
Hunter-Gault, Charlayne **6, 31**

Mad TV
Jones, Orlando **30**
Wilson, Debra **38**

Madame C. J. Walker Manufacturing Company
Joyner, Marjorie Stewart **26**
Walker, A'lelia **14**
Walker, Madame C. J. **7**

Major League Baseball
Howard, Ryan **65**
Mariner, Jonathan **41**

Solomon, Jimmie Lee **38**

Major League Baseball Players Association
Blair, Paul **36**
Howard, Ryan **65**

Major League Baseball Properties
Doby, Lawrence Eugene, Sr. **16, 41**

Maktub
Watts, Reggie **52**

Malaco Records
Bland, Bobby "Blue" **36**

Malawi Congress Party (MCP)
Banda, Hastings Kamuzu **6, 54**

Manhattan Project
Quarterman, Lloyd Albert **4**
Wilkens, J. Ernest, Jr. **43**

MARC Corp.
See Metropolitan Applied Research Center

March on Washington/Freedom March
Baker, Josephine **3**
Belafonte, Harry **4, 65**
Bunche, Ralph J. **5**
Davis, Ossie **5, 50**
Fauntroy, Walter E. **11**
Forman, James **7, 51**
Franklin, John Hope **5**
Hedgeman, Anna Arnold **22**
Horne, Lena **5**
Jackson, Mahalia **5**
King, Coretta Scott **3, 57**
King, Martin Luther, Jr. **1**
Lewis, John **2, 46**
Meredith, James H. **11**
Randolph, A. Philip **3**
Rustin, Bayard **4**
Sleet, Moneta, Jr. **5**
Wilkins, Roy **4**
Young, Whitney M., Jr. **4**

Marketing
DeVard, Jerri **61**
Edwards, Trevor **54**
Kaigler, Denise **63**
Kendrick, Erika **57**

Martial arts
Barnes, Steven **54**
Copeland, Michael **47**

Martin Luther King Jr. Center for Nonviolent Social Change
Dodson, Howard, Jr. **7, 52**
Farris, Isaac Newton, Jr. **63**
King, Bernice **4**
King, Coretta Scott **3, 57**
King, Dexter **10**
King, Martin Luther, Jr. **1**
King, Yolanda **6**

Martin Luther King Jr. Drum Major Award
Broadbent, Hydeia **36**
Mfume, Kweisi **6, 41**

Martin Luther King Jr. National Memorial Project
Johnson, Harry E. 57

Marxism
Baraka, Amiri 1, 38
Bishop, Maurice 39
Jagan, Cheddi 16
Machel, Samora Moises 8
Nkrumah, Kwame 3
Sankara, Thomas 17

Maryland Mustangs basketball team
Parish, Robert 43

Maryland state government
Steele, Michael 38

Massachusetts state government
Brooke, Edward 8

Masters Golf Tournament
Elder, Lee 6
Woods, Tiger 14, 31

Mathematics
Alcorn, George Edward, Jr. 59
Deconge-Watson, Lovenia 55
Emeagwali, Philip 30
Falconer, Etta Zuber 59
Gates, Sylvester James, Jr. 15
Johnson, Katherine (Coleman Goble) 61
Price, Richard 51
Wilkens, J. Ernest, Jr. 43

MAXIMA Corporation
Smith, Joshua 10

Maxwell House Coffee Company
Fudge, Ann (Marie) 11, 55

McCall Pattern Company
Lewis, Reginald F. 6

McDonald's Corporation
Thompson, Don 56

McGill University (Canada)
Elliott, Lorris 37

MCP
See Malawi Congress Party

Medical examiners
Carter, Joye Maureen 41

Medicine
Adams-Campbell, Lucille L. 60
Anderson, William G(ilchrist), D.O. 57
Atim, Julian 66
Banda, Hastings Kamuzu 6, 54
Benjamin, Regina 20
Black, Keith Lanier 18
Callender, Clive O. 3
Canady, Alexa 28
Carroll, L. Natalie 44
Carson, Benjamin 1, 35
Carter, Joye Maureen 41
Chatard, Peter 44
Chinn, May Edward 26
Christian-Green, Donna M. 17
Cobb, W. Montague 39
Cole, Rebecca 38
Comer, James P. 6
Coney, PonJola 48
Cooper, Edward S. 6
Cornwell, Edward E., III 70
Dickens, Helen Octavia 14, 64
Drew, Charles Richard 7
Edwards, Willarda V. 59
Elders, Joycelyn 6
Fisher, Rudolph 17
Flowers, Sylester 50
Foster, Henry W., Jr. 26
Freeman, Harold P. 23
Fuller, Solomon Carter, Jr. 15
Gayle, Helene D. 3
Gibson, William F. 6
Grant, Augustus O. 71
Griffin, Anthony 71
Griffith, Patrick A. 64
Hinton, William Augustus 8
Hutcherson, Hilda Yvonne 54
Jemison, Mae C. 1, 35
Johnson, R. M. 36
Jones, Edith Mae Irby 65
Joseph, Kathie-Ann 56
Keith, Rachel Boone 63
Kenney, John A., Jr. 48
Kintaudi, Leon 62
Kong, B. Waine 50
Kountz, Samuel L. 10
Lavizzo-Mourey, Risa 48
Lawless, Theodore K. 8
Leffall, Lasalle 3, 64
Logan, Onnie Lee 14
Malveaux, Floyd 54
Maxey, Randall 46
Naki, Hamilton 63
Nour, Nawal M. 56
Okaalet, Peter 58
Olopade, Olufunmilayo Falusi 58
Pace, Betty 59
Pinn, Vivian Winona 49
Pitt, David Thomas 10
Poussaint, Alvin F. 5, 67
Rabb, Maurice F., Jr. 58
Randolph, Linda A. 52
Reece, E. Albert 63
Ross-Lee, Barbara 67
Satcher, David 7, 57
Scantlebury-White, Velma 64
Smith, Ian 62
Stewart, Ella 39
Sullivan, Louis 8
Sweet, Ossian 68
Taylor, Susan C. 62
Thomas, Claudia Lynn 64
Thomas, Vivien 9
Thornton, Yvonne S. 69
Tuckson, Reed V. 71
Washington, Harriet A. 69
Watkins, Levi, Jr. 9
Welsing, Frances Cress 5
White-Hammond, Gloria 61
Williams, Daniel Hale 2
Witt, Edwin T. 26
Wright, Charles H. 35
Wright, Louis Tompkins 4

Meharry Medical College
Coney, PonJola 48
Foster, Henry W., Jr. 26
Griffith, Patrick A. 64
Lyttle, Hulda Margaret 14

Melanin theory of racism
See Cress Theory of Color Confrontation and Racism

Melody Makers
Marley, Ziggy 41

Men's movement
Somé, Malidoma Patrice 10

Merce Cunningham Dance Company
Dove, Ulysses 5

Merrill Lynch & Co., Inc.
Ford, Harold E(ugene), Jr. 16, 70
Matthews Shatteen, Westina 51
O'Neal, Stanley 38, 67

MESBICs
See Minority Enterprise Small Business Investment Corporations

Meteorology
Anderson, Charles Edward 37
Bacon-Bercey, June 38

Metropolitan Applied Research Center (MARC Corp.)
Clark, Kenneth B. 5, 52

Metropolitan Opera
Anderson, Marian 2, 33
Battle, Kathleen 70
Brown, Angela M. 54
Collins, Janet 33, 64
Dobbs, Mattiwilda 34
Phillips, Helen L. 63

Mexican baseball league
Bell, James "Cool Papa" 36
Dandridge, Ray 36

MFDP
See Mississippi Freedom Democratic Party

Miami Dolphins football team
Greene, Joe 10

Michigan House of Representatives
Collins, Barbara-Rose 7
Kilpatrick, Carolyn Cheeks 16
Kilpatrick, Kwame 34, 71
Reeves, Triette Lipsey 27

Michigan state government
Brown, Cora 33

Michigan State Supreme Court
Archer, Dennis 7, 36
Mallett, Conrad, Jr. 16

Michigan State University
Wharton, Clifton R., Jr. 7
Willingham, Tyrone 43

Microsoft Corporation
Millines Dziko, Trish 28

Midwest Stamping
Thompson, Cynthia Bramlett 50

Midwifery
Logan, Onnie Lee 14
Robinson, Sharon 22

Military police
Cadoria, Sherian Grace 14

Millennium Digital Media
Westbrook, Kelvin 50

Miller Brewing Company
Colbert, Virgis William 17
Shropshire, Thomas B. 49

Millinery
Bailey, Xenobia 11

Million Man March
Farrakhan, Louis 2, 15
Hawkins, La-Van 17, 54
Worrill, Conrad 12

Milwaukee Braves baseball team
Aaron, Hank 5

Milwaukee Brewers baseball team
Aaron, Hank 5
Baylor, Don 6
Fielder, Prince Semien 68
Payne, Ulice 42
Sheffield, Gary 16

Milwaukee Bucks basketball team
Abdul-Jabbar, Kareem 8
Lucas, John 7
Robertson, Oscar 26

Mingo-Jones Advertising
Chisholm, Samuel J. 32
Jones, Caroline R. 29
Mingo, Frank 32

Minneapolis city government
Sayles Belton, Sharon 9, 16

Minneapolis Millers baseball team
Dandridge, Ray 36

Minnesota State Supreme Court
Page, Alan 7

Minnesota Timberwolves basketball team
Garnett, Kevin 14, 70

Minnesota Twins baseball team
Baylor, Don 6
Carew, Rod 20
Hunter, Torii 43
Puckett, Kirby 4, 58
Winfield, Dave 5

Minnesota Vikings football team
Carter, Cris 21
Culpepper, Daunte 32
Cunningham, Randall 23
Dungy, Tony 17, 42, 59
Fowler, Reggie 51
Gilliam, Frank 23
Green, Dennis 5, 45

Moon, Warren **8, 66**
Moss, Randy **23**
Page, Alan **7**
Rashad, Ahmad **18**
Stringer, Korey **35**

Minority Business Enterprise Legal Defense and Education Fund
Mitchell, Parren J. **42, 66**

Minority Business Resource Center
Hill, Jesse, Jr. **13**

Minority Enterprise Small Business Investment Corporations (MESBICs)
Lewis, Reginald F. **6**

Minstrel shows
McDaniel, Hattie **5**

Miracle Network Telethon
Warner, Malcolm-Jamal **22, 36**

Miss America
Dunlap, Ericka **55**
Harold, Erika **54**
Vincent, Marjorie Judith **2**
Williams, Vanessa L. **4, 17**

Miss Collegiate African-American Pageant
Mercado-Valdes, Frank **43**

Miss USA
Gist, Carole **1**

Miss World
Darego, Agbani **52**

Mississippi Freedom Democratic Party (MFDP)
Baker, Ella **5**
Blackwell, Unita **17**
Hamer, Fannie Lou **6**
Henry, Aaron **19**
Norton, Eleanor Holmes **7**

Mississippi state government
Hamer, Fannie Lou **6**

MLA
See Modern Language Association of America

Model Inner City Community Organization (MICCO)
Fauntroy, Walter E. **11**

Modeling
Allen-Buillard, Melba **55**
Banks, Tyra **11, 50**
Beckford, Tyson **11, 68**
Berry, Halle **4, 19, 57**
Campbell, Naomi **1, 31**
Darego, Agbani **52**
Dirie, Waris **56**
Ebanks, Selita **67**
Gibson, Tyrese **27, 62**
Hardison, Bethann **12**
Hounsou, Djimon **19, 45**
Houston, Whitney **7, 28**
Iman **4, 33**
Iman, Chanel **66**
Johnson, Beverly **2**

Kebede, Liya **59**
Kodjoe, Boris **34**
Langhart Cohen, Janet **19, 60**
Leslie, Lisa **16**
LisaRaye **27**
Michele, Michael **31**
Niane, Katoucha **70**
Onwurah, Ngozi **38**
Powell, Maxine **8**
Rochon, Lela **16**
Simmons, Kimora Lee **51**
Sims, Naomi **29**
Smith, Barbara **11**
Tamia **24, 55**
Taylor, Karin **34**
Tyson, Cicely **7, 51**
Watley, Jody **54**
Webb, Veronica **10**
Wek, Alek **18, 63**

Modern dance
Ailey, Alvin **8**
Allen, Debbie **13, 42**
Byrd, Donald **10**
Collins, Janet **33, 64**
Davis, Chuck **33**
Diggs, Taye **25, 63**
Dove, Ulysses **5**
Fagan, Garth **18**
Faison, George **16**
Henson, Darrin **33**
Jamison, Judith **7, 67**
Jones, Bill T. **1, 46**
King, Alonzo **38**
Kitt, Eartha **16**
Miller, Bebe **3**
Primus, Pearl **6**
Spears, Warren **52**
Vereen, Ben **4**
Williams, Dudley **60**

Modern Language Association of America (MLA)
Baker, Houston A., Jr. **6**

Modern Records
Brooks, Hadda **40**

Monoprinting
Honeywood, Varnette P. **54**

Montgomery bus boycott
Abernathy, Ralph David **1**
Baker, Ella **5**
Burks, Mary Fair **40**
Carr, Johnnie **69**
Jackson, Mahalia **5**
Killens, John O. **54**
King, Martin Luther, Jr. **1**
Parks, Rosa **1, 35, 56**
Rustin, Bayard **4**

Montgomery County (MD) Police Department
Moose, Charles **40**

Montreal Canadiens hockey team
Brashear, Donald **39**

Montreal Expos baseball team
Doby, Lawrence Eugene, Sr. **16, 41**

Morehouse College
Brown, Uzee **42**
Hope, John **8**
Mays, Benjamin E. **7**

Morgan Stanley
Lewis, William M., Jr. **40**

Morna
Evora, Cesaria **12**

Morris Brown College
Cross, Dolores E. **23**

Moscow World News
Khanga, Yelena **6**
Sullivan, Louis **8**

Motivational speaking
Bahati, Wambui **60**
Baisden, Michael **66**
Brown, Les **5**
Bunkley, Anita Richmond **39**
Creagh, Milton **27**
Gardner, Chris **65**
Grant, Gwendolyn Goldsby **28**
Gray, Farrah **59**
Jolley, Willie **28**
July, William **27**
Kimbro, Dennis **10**
Russell-McCloud, Patricia **17**
Tyson, Asha **39**

Motor City Giants baseball team
Kaiser, Cecil **42**

Motorcycle racing
Showers, Reggie **30**
Stewart, James "Bubba," Jr. **60**

Motown Records
Atkins, Cholly **40**
Bizimungu, Pasteur **19**
Busby, Jheryl **3**
de Passe, Suzanne **25**
Edwards, Esther Gordy **43**
Gaye, Marvin **2**
Gordy, Berry, Jr. **1**
Harrell, Andre **9, 30**
Holland-Dozier-Holland **36**
Holloway, Brenda **65**
Hutch, Willie **62**
Jackson, George **19**
Jackson, Michael **19, 53**
Jamerson, James **59**
Kendricks, Eddie **22**
Knight, Gladys **16, 66**
Massenburg, Kedar **23**
Powell, Maxine **8**
Richie, Lionel **27, 65**
Robinson, Smokey **3, 49**
Ross, Diana **8, 27**
Terrell, Tammi **32**
Wells, Mary **28**
Wilson, Mary **28**
Wonder, Stevie **11, 53**

Mt. Holyoke College
Tatum, Beverly Daniel **42**

Mouvement Revolutionnaire National pour la Developpement (Rwanda; MRND)
Habyarimana, Juvenal **8**

MOVE
Goode, W. Wilson **4**
Wideman, John Edgar **5**

Movement for Assemblies of the People
Bishop, Maurice **39**

Movement for Democratic Change (MDC)
Tsvangirai, Morgan **26**

Movement for the Survival of the Ogoni People
Saro-Wiwa, Kenule **39**
Wiwa, Ken **67**

Movimento Popular de Libertação de Angola (MPLA)
dos Santos, José Eduardo **43**
Neto, António Agostinho **43**

Mozambican government
Diogo, Luisa Dias **63**

MPLA
See Movimento Popular de Libertação de Angola

MPS
See Patriotic Movement of Salvation

MRND
See Mouvement Revolutionnaire National pour la Developpement

MTV Jams
Bellamy, Bill **12**

Muddy Waters
Little Walter **36**

Multimedia art
Bailey, Xenobia **11**
Robinson, Aminah **50**
Simpson, Lorna **4, 36**

Multiple sclerosis
Falana, Lola **42**

Muppets, The
Clash, Kevin **14**

Murals
Alston, Charles **33**
Biggers, John **20, 33**
Douglas, Aaron **7**
Lee-Smith, Hughie **5**
Walker, Kara **16**

Murder Inc.
Ashanti **37**
Gotti, Irv **39**
Ja Rule **35**

Museum of Modern Art
Pindell, Howardena **55**

Music Critics Circle
Holt, Nora **38**

Music One, Inc.
Majors, Jeff **41**

Music publishing
Combs, Sean "Puffy" **17, 43**
Cooke, Sam **17**
Edmonds, Tracey **16, 64**
Gordy, Berry, Jr. **1**
Handy, W. C. **8**
Holland-Dozier-Holland **36**
Humphrey, Bobbi **20**

Ice Cube 8, 30, 60
Jackson, George 19
Jackson, Michael 19, 53
James, Rick 17
Knight, Suge 11, 30
Lewis, Emmanuel 36
Master P 21
Mayfield, Curtis 2, 43
Otis, Clyde 67
Prince 18, 65
Redding, Otis 16
Ross, Diana 8, 27
Shakur, Afeni 67
Shorty, Ras I 47

Music Television (MTV)
Bellamy, Bill 12
Chideya, Farai 14, 61
Norman, Christina 47
Powell, Kevin 31

Musical composition
Armatrading, Joan 32
Ashford, Nickolas 21
Baiocchi, Regina Harris 41
Ballard, Hank 41
Bebey, Francis 45
Blanchard, Terence 43
Blige, Mary J. 20, 34, 60
Bonds, Margaret 39
Bonga, Kuenda 13
Braxton, Toni 15, 61
Brown, Patrick "Sleepy" 50
Brown, Uzee 42
Burke, Solomon 31
Burleigh, Henry Thacker 56
Caesar, Shirley 19
Carter, Warrick L. 27
Chapman, Tracy 26
Charlemagne, Manno 11
Charles, Ray 16, 48
Cleveland, James 19
Cole, Natalie 17, 60
Coleman, Ornette 39, 69
Collins, Bootsy 31
Combs, Sean "Puffy" 17, 43
Cook, Will Marion 40
Davis, Anthony 11
Davis, Miles 4
Davis, Sammy, Jr. 18
Dawson, William Levi 39
Diddley, Bo 39
Domino, Fats 20
Ellington, Duke 5
Elliott, Missy 31
Europe, James Reese 10
Evans, Faith 22
Freeman, Paul 39
Fuller, Arthur 27
Garrett, Sean 57
Gaynor, Gloria 36
George, Nelson 12
Gillespie, Dizzy 1
Golson, Benny 37
Gordy, Berry, Jr. 1
Green, Al 13, 47
Hailey, JoJo 22
Hailey, K-Ci 22
Hammer, M. C. 20
Handy, W. C. 8
Harris, Corey 39
Hathaway, Donny 18
Hayes, Isaac 20, 58

Hayes, Teddy 40
Hill, Lauryn 20, 53
Holland-Dozier-Holland 36
Holmes, Clint 57
Holt, Nora 38
Humphrey, Bobbi 20
Hutch, Willie 62
Isley, Ronald 25, 56
Jackson, Fred James 25
Jackson, Michael 19, 53
Jackson, Randy 40
James, Rick 17
Jean, Wyclef 20
Jean-Baptiste, Marianne 17, 46
Jerkins, Rodney 31
Johnson, Buddy 36
Johnson, Georgia Douglas 41
Jones, Jonah 39
Jones, Quincy 8, 30
Jones, Thad 68
Joplin, Scott 6
Jordan, Montell 23
Jordan, Ronny 26
Kay, Ulysses 37
Kee, John P. 43
Kelly, R. 18, 44, 71
Keys, Alicia 32, 68
Kidjo, Anjelique 50
Killings, Debra 57
King, B. B. 7
León, Tania 13
Lincoln, Abbey 3
Little Milton 36, 54
Little Walter 36
Lopes, Lisa "Left Eye" 36
Mahlasela, Vusi 65
Majors, Jeff 41
Marsalis, Delfeayo 41
Marsalis, Wynton 16
Martin, Roberta 58
Master P 21
Maxwell 20
Mayfield, Curtis 2, 43
McClurkin, Donnie 25
McFerrin, Bobby 68
Mills, Stephanie 36
Mitchell, Brian Stokes 21
Mo', Keb' 36
Monica 21
Moore, Chante 26
Moore, Dorothy Rudd 46
Moore, Undine Smith 28
Muse, Clarence Edouard 21
Nash, Johnny 40
Ndegéocello, Me'Shell 15
Osborne, Jeffrey 26
Otis, Clyde 67
Pratt, Awadagin 31
Price, Florence 37
Prince 18, 65
Pritchard, Robert Starling 21
Reagon, Bernice Johnson 7
Redding, Otis 16
Reed, A. C. 36
Reid, Antonio "L.A." 28
Roach, Max 21, 63
Robinson, Reginald R. 53
Run-DMC 31
Rushen, Patrice 12
Russell, Brenda 52
Sangare, Oumou 18
Shorty, Ras I 47
Silver, Horace 26

Simone, Nina 15, 41
Simpson, Valerie 21
Sowande, Fela 39
Still, William Grant 37
Strayhorn, Billy 31
Sundiata, Sekou 66
Sweat, Keith 19
Tillis, Frederick 40
Usher 23, 56
Van Peebles, Melvin 7
Walker, George 37
Warwick, Dionne 18
Washington, Grover, Jr. 17, 44
Williams, Deniece 36
Williams, Tony 67
Winans, Angie 36
Winans, Debbie 36
Withers, Bill 61

Musicology
George, Zelma Watson 42

Muslim Mosque, Inc.
X, Malcolm 1

Mysteries
Bland, Eleanor Taylor 39
Creagh, Milton 27
DeLoach, Nora 30
Himes, Chester 8
Holton, Hugh, Jr. 39
Mickelbury, Penny 28
Mosley, Walter 5, 25, 68
Thomas-Graham 29
Wesley, Valerie Wilson 18

The Mystery
Delany, Martin R. 27

Mystic Seaport Museum
Pinckney, Bill 42

NAACP
See National Association for the Advancement of Colored People

NAACP Image Awards
Fields, Kim 36
Lawrence, Martin 6, 27, 60
Okonedo, Sophie 67
Rhimes, Shonda Lynn 67
Warner, Malcolm-Jamal 22, 36

NAACP Legal Defense and Educational Fund (LDF)
Bell, Derrick 6
Carter, Robert L. 51
Chambers, Julius 3
Edelman, Marian Wright 5, 42
Guinier, Lani 7, 30
Jones, Elaine R. 7, 45
Julian, Percy Lavon 6
Marshall, Thurgood 1, 44
Motley, Constance Baker 10, 55
Rice, Constance LaMay 60
Smith, Kemba 70
Smythe Haith, Mabel 61

NABJ
See National Association of Black Journalists

NAC
See Nyasaland African Congress

NACGN
See National Association of Colored Graduate Nurses

NACW
See National Association of Colored Women

NAG
See Nonviolent Action Group

NASA
See National Aeronautics and Space Administration

NASCAR
See National Association of Stock Car Auto Racing

NASCAR Craftsman Truck series
Lester, Bill 42

NASCAR Diversity Council
Lester, Bill 42

Nation
Wilkins, Roger 2

Nation of Islam
See Lost-Found Nation of Islam

National Academy of Design
White, Charles 39

National Action Council for Minorities in Engineering
Pierre, Percy Anthony 46
Slaughter, John Brooks 53

National Action Network
Sharpton, Al 21

National Aeronautics and Space Administration (NASA)
Anderson, Michael P. 40
Bluford, Guy 2, 35
Bolden, Charles F., Jr. 7
Campbell, Donald J. 66
Carruthers, George R. 40
Drew, Alvin, Jr. 67
Easley, Annie J. 61
Gregory, Frederick 8, 51
Jemison, Mae C. 1, 35
Johnson, Katherine (Coleman Goble) 61
McNair, Ronald 3, 58
Mills, Joseph C. 51
Nichols, Nichelle 11
Sigur, Wanda 44

National Afro-American Council
Fortune, T. Thomas 6
Mossell, Gertrude Bustill 40

National Airmen's Association of America
Brown, Willa 40

National Alliance of Postal and Federal Employees
McGee, James Madison 46

National Alliance Party (NAP)
Fulani, Lenora 11

National Association for the Advancement of Colored People (NAACP)
Anderson, William G(ilchrist), D.O. 57
Anthony, Wendell 25
Austin, Junius C. 44
Baker, Ella 5
Ballance, Frank W. 41
Bates, Daisy 13
Bell, Derrick 6
Bond, Julian 2, 35
Bontemps, Arna 8
Brooks, Gwendolyn 1
Brown, Homer S. 47
Bunche, Ralph J. 5
Chambers, Julius 3
Chavis, Benjamin 6
Clark, Kenneth B. 5, 52
Clark, Septima 7
Cobb, W. Montague 39
Colter, Cyrus, J. 36
Cotter, Joseph Seamon, Sr. 40
Creagh, Milton 27
Days, Drew S., III 10
Dee, Ruby 8, 50, 68
DuBois, Shirley Graham 21
Du Bois, W. E. B. 3
Dukes, Hazel Nell 56
Edelman, Marian Wright 5, 42
Evers, Medgar 3
Evers, Myrlie 8
Farmer, James 2, 64
Ford, Clyde W. 40
Fuller, S. B. 13
Gibson, William F. 6
Grimké, Archibald H. 9
Hampton, Fred 18
Harrington, Oliver W. 9
Hayes, Dennis 54
Henderson, Wade 14
Hobson, Julius W. 44
Hollowell, Donald L. 57
Hooks, Benjamin L. 2
Horne, Lena 5
Houston, Charles Hamilton 4
Jackson, Vera 40
Jealous, Benjamin 70
Johnson, James Weldon 5
Jordan, Vernon E. 3, 35
Kidd, Mae Street 39
Lampkin, Daisy 19
Madison, Joseph E. 17
Marshall, Thurgood 1, 44
McKissick, Floyd B. 3
McPhail, Sharon 2
Meek, Carrie 36
Meredith, James H. 11
Mfume, Kweisi 6, 41
Mitchell, Sharon 36
Moore, Harry T. 29
Morgan, Irene 65
Moses, Robert Parris 11
Motley, Constance Baker 10, 55
Moyo, Yvette Jackson 36
Owens, Major 6
Payton, John 48
Richardson, Rupert 67
Rustin, Bayard 4
Sutton, Percy E. 42
Terrell, Mary Church 9
Tucker, C. Delores 12, 56
Van Lierop, Robert 53

White, Walter F. 4
Wilkins, Roger 2
Wilkins, Roy 4
Williams, Hosea Lorenzo 15, 31
Williams, Robert F. 11
Wright, Louis Tompkins 4

National Association of Black Journalists (NABJ)
Curry, George E. 23
Dawkins, Wayne 20
Harris, Jay T. 19
Jarret, Vernon D. 42
Lowe, Herbert 57
Madison, Paula 37
Pressley, Condace L. 41
Rice, Linda Johnson 9, 41
Shipp, E. R. 15
Stone, Chuck 9
Washington, Laura S. 18

National Association of Colored Graduate Nurses (NACGN)
Staupers, Mabel K. 7

National Association of Colored Women (NACW)
Bethune, Mary McLeod 4
Cooper, Margaret J. 46
Harper, Frances Ellen Watkins 11
Lampkin, Daisy 19
Stewart, Ella 39
Terrell, Mary Church 9

National Association of Negro Business and Professional Women's Clubs
Vaughns, Cleopatra 46

National Association of Negro Musicians
Bonds, Margaret 39
Brown, Uzee 42

National Association of Regulatory Utility Commissioners
Colter, Cyrus, J. 36

National Association of Social Workers
Jackson, Judith D. 57
McMurray, Georgia L. 36

National Association of Stock Car Auto Racing
Lester, Bill 42

National Baptist Convention USA
Bradley, J. Robert 65
Jones, E. Edward, Sr. 45
Lyons, Henry 12
Shaw, William J. 30
Thurston, Stephen J. 49

National Baptist Publishing Board
Boyd, T. B., III 6

National Baptist Sunday Church School and Baptist Training Union Congress
Boyd, T. B., III 6

National Bar Association
Alexander, Joyce London 18

Alexander, Sadie Tanner Mossell 22
Archer, Dennis 7, 36
Bailey, Clyde 45
Hubbard, Arnette 38
McPhail, Sharon 2
Pincham, R. Eugene, Sr. 69
Quince, Peggy A. 69
Ray, Charlotte E. 60
Robinson, Malcolm S. 44
Thompson, Larry D. 39
Walker, Cora T. 68

National Basketball Association (NBA)
Abdul-Jabbar, Kareem 8
Abdur-Rahim, Shareef 28
Anthony, Carmelo 46
Barkley, Charles 5, 66
Bing, Dave 3, 59
Bol, Manute 1
Brandon, Terrell 16
Bryant, Kobe 15, 31, 71
Bynoe, Peter C. B. 40
Carter, Vince 26
Chamberlain, Wilt 18, 47
Cheeks, Maurice 47
Clifton, Nathaniel "Sweetwater" 47
Cooper, Charles "Chuck" 47
Drexler, Clyde 4, 61
Duncan, Tim 20
Elliott, Sean 26
Erving, Julius 18, 47
Ewing, Patrick A. 17
Garnett, Kevin 14, 70
Gourdine, Simon 11
Green, A. C. 32
Hardaway, Anfernee (Penny) 13
Hardaway, Tim 35
Heard, Gar 25
Hill, Grant 13
Howard, Juwan 15
Hunter, Billy 22
Johnson, Avery 62
Johnson, Earvin "Magic" 3, 39
Johnson, Larry 28
Jordan, Michael 6, 21
Lanier, Bob 47
Lowe, Sidney 64
Lucas, John 7
Mahorn, Rick 60
Mohammed, Nazr 64
Mourning, Alonzo 17, 44
Mutombo, Dikembe 7
Olajuwon, Hakeem 2
O'Neal, Shaquille 8, 30
Palmer, Violet 59
Parish, Robert 43
Pierce, Paul 71
Pippen, Scottie 15
Prince, Tayshaun 68
Rivers, Glenn "Doc" 25
Robertson, Oscar 26
Robinson, David 24
Rodman, Dennis 12, 44
Russell, Bill 8
Silas, Paul 24
Sprewell, Latrell 23
Stoudemire, Amaré 59
Thomas, Isiah 7, 26, 65
Tisdale, Wayman 50
Wade, Dwyane 61
Wallace, Ben 54

Wallace, Rasheed 56
Webber, Chris 15, 30, 59
Wilkens, Lenny 11
Worthy, James 49

National Basketball Players Association
Erving, Julius 18, 47
Ewing, Patrick A. 17
Gourdine, Simon 11
Hunter, Billy 22

National Black Arts Festival (NBAF)
Borders, James 9
Brooks, Avery 9

National Black College Hall of Fame
Dortch, Thomas W., Jr. 45

National Black Farmers Association (NBFA)
Boyd, John W., Jr. 20

National Black Fine Art Show
Wainwright, Joscelyn 46

National Black Gay and Lesbian Conference
Wilson, Phill 9

National Black Gay and Lesbian Leadership Forum (NBGLLF)
Boykin, Keith 14
Carter, Mandy 11

National Black Theatre Festival
Hamlin, Larry Leon 49, 62

National Black Women's Health Project
Avery, Byllye Y. 66

National Book Award
Ellison, Ralph 7
Haley, Alex 4
Johnson, Charles 1
Patterson, Orlando 4

National Broadcasting Company (NBC)
Allen, Byron 3, 24
Cosby, Bill 7, 26, 59
Grier, David Alan 28
Gumbel, Bryant 14
Hinderas, Natalie 5
Holt, Lester 66
Ifill, Gwen 28
Johnson, Rodney Van 28
Madison, Paula 37
Rashad, Phylicia 21
Reuben, Gloria 15
Reynolds, Star Jones 10, 27, 61
Roker, Al 12, 49
Simpson, Carole 6, 30
Stokes, Carl B. 10
Thomas-Graham, Pamela 29
Williams, Montel 4, 57
Wilson, Flip 21

National Brotherhood of Skiers (NBS)
Horton, Andre 33
Horton, Suki 33

National Center for Neighborhood Enterprise (NCNE)
Woodson, Robert L. 10

National Coalition of 100 Black Women (NCBW)
Mays, Leslie A. 41
McCabe, Jewell Jackson 10

National Coalition to Abolish the Death Penalty (NCADP)
Hawkins, Steven 14

National Commission for Democracy (Ghana; NCD)
Rawlings, Jerry 9

National Conference on Black Lawyers (NCBL)
McDougall, Gay J. 11, 43

National Council of Churches
Howard, M. William, Jr. 26

National Council of Negro Women (NCNW)
Bethune, Mary McLeod 4
Blackwell, Unita 17
Cole, Johnnetta B. 5, 43
Hamer, Fannie Lou 6
Height, Dorothy I. 2, 23
Horne, Lena 5
Lampkin, Daisy 19
Sampson, Edith S. 4
Smith, Jane E. 24
Staupers, Mabel K. 7

National Council of Nigeria and the Cameroons (NCNC)
Azikiwe, Nnamdi 13

National Council of Teachers of Mathematics
Granville, Evelyn Boyd 36

National Council on the Arts
Robinson, Cleo Parker 38

National Cowboys of Color Museum and Hall of Fame
Austin, Gloria 63
Austin, Jim 63

National Defence Council (Ghana; NDC)
Rawlings, Jerry 9

National Dental Association
Madison, Romell 45

National Earthquake Information Center (NEIC)
Person, Waverly 9, 51

National Education Association (NEA)
Futrell, Mary Hatwood 33

National Endowment for the Arts (NEA)
Bradley, David Henry, Jr. 39
Hall, Arthur 39
Hemphill, Essex 10
Serrano, Andres 3
Williams, John A. 27
Williams, William T. 11

National Endowment for the Arts Jazz Hall of Fame
Terry, Clark 39

National Endowment for the Humanities
Gibson, Donald Bernard 40

National Equal Rights League (NERL)
Trotter, Monroe 9

National Football League (NFL)
Allen, Marcus 20
Barber, Tiki 57
Barney, Lem 26
Bettis, Jerome 64
Briscoe, Marlin 37
Brooks, Aaron 33
Brooks, Derrick 43
Brown, Jim 11
Bruce, Isaac 26
Butler, Leroy, III 17
Cherry, Deron 40
Crennel, Romeo 54
Croom, Sylvester 50
Culpepper, Daunte 32
Cunningham, Randall 23
Davis, Terrell 20
Dickerson, Eric 27
Edwards, Herman 51
Farr, Mel 24
Faulk, Marshall 35
Fowler, Reggie 51
Gilliam, Frank 23
Gilliam, Joe 31
Green, Darrell 39
Green, Dennis 5, 45
Greene, Joe 10
Hill, Calvin 19
Howard, Desmond 16, 58
Irvin, Michael 64
Jackson, Tom 70
Johnson, Levi 48
Ladd, Ernie 64
Lofton, James 42
Lott, Ronnie 9
Monk, Art 38
Moon, Warren 8, 66
Moss, Randy 23
Motley, Marion 26
Newsome, Ozzie 26
Oliver, Pam 54
Owens, Terrell 53
Pace, Orlando 21
Page, Alan 7
Payton, Walter 11, 25
Peete, Rodney 60
Rhodes, Ray 14
Rice, Jerry 5, 55
Sanders, Barry 1, 53
Sanders, Deion 4, 31
Sapp, Warren 38
Sayers, Gale 28
Sharper, Darren 32
Shell, Art 1, 66
Simpson, O.J. 15
Singletary, Mike 4
Smith, Emmitt 7
Stewart, Kordell 21
Stingley, Darryl 69
Strahan, Michael 35
Stringer, Korey 35
Swann, Lynn 28
Taylor, Jason 70
Taylor, Lawrence 25
Thomas, Derrick 25
Thomas, Emmitt 71
Thrower, Willie 35
Tomlinson, LaDainian 65
Tunnell, Emlen 54
Upshaw, Gene 18, 47
Vick, Michael 39, 65
Walker, Herschel 1, 69
Ware, Andre 37
Washington, Kenny 50
White, Reggie 6, 50
Williams, Doug 22
Williamson, Fred 67
Wright, Rayfield 70

National Heritage "Living Treasure" Fellowship
Jackson, John 36

National Hockey League (NHL)
Brashear, Donald 39
Brathwaite, Fred 35
Brown, Sean 52
Fuhr, Grant 1, 49
Grier, Mike 43
Iginla, Jarome 35
Laraque, Georges 48
Mayers, Jamal 39
McBride, Bryant 18
McCarthy, Sandy 64
McKegney, Tony 3
O'Ree, Willie 5
Salvador, Bryce 51
Weekes, Kevin 67

National Immigration Forum
Jones, Sarah 39

National Information Infrastructure (NII)
Lewis, Delano 7

National Institute of Arts & Letters
Lewis, Norman 39
White, Charles 39

National Institute of Education
Baker, Gwendolyn Calvert 9

National Institutes of Health (NIH)
Cargill, Victoria A. 43
Dunston, Georgia Mae 48
Pinn, Vivian Winona 49

National Inventors Hall of Fame
Carruthers, George R. 40

National Lawn & Garden Distributor Association
Donald, Arnold Wayne 36

National Medical Association
Cole, Lorraine 48
Maxey, Randall 46
Ojikutu, Bisola 65

National Minority Business Council
Leary, Kathryn D. 10

National Museum of American History
Crew, Spencer R. 55
Reagon, Bernice Johnson 7

National Negro Congress
Bunche, Ralph J. 5

National Negro Suffrage League
Trotter, Monroe 9

National Network for African American Women and the Law
Arnwine, Barbara 28

National Newspaper Publishers Association
Cooper, Andrew W. 36
Jealous, Benjamin 70
Oliver, John J., Jr. 48

National Oceanic and Atmospheric Administration
Bacon-Bercey, June 38
Fields, Evelyn J. 27

National Organization for Women (NOW)
Hernandez, Aileen Clarke 13
Kennedy, Florynce 12, 33
Meek, Carrie 6, 36
Murray, Pauli 38

National Poetry Slam
Letson, Al 39

National Political Congress of Black Women
Chisholm, Shirley 2, 50
Tucker, C. Delores 12, 56
Waters, Maxine 3, 67

National Public Radio (NPR)
Abu-Jamal, Mumia 15
Bates, Karen Grigsby 40
Drummond, William J. 40
Early, Gerald 15
Lewis, Delano 7
Mitchell, Elvis 67
Smiley, Tavis 20, 68
Zook, Kristal Brent 62

National Resistance Army (Uganda; NRA)
Museveni, Yoweri 4

National Resistance Movement
Museveni, Yoweri 4

National Revolutionary Movement for Development
See Mouvement Revolutionnaire National pour la Developpment

National Rifle Association (NRA)
Williams, Robert F. 11

National Science Foundation (NSF)
Massey, Walter E. **5, 45**

National security adviser
Rice, Condoleezza **3, 28**

National Security Council
Frazer, Jendayi **68**
Powell, Colin **1, 28**
Rice, Condoleezza **3, 28**

National Society of Black Engineers
Donald, Arnold Wayne **36**
Price, Richard **51**

National Underground Railroad Freedom Center
Crew, Spencer R. **55**

National Union for the Total Independence of Angola (UNITA)
Roberto, Holden **65**
Savimbi, Jonas **2, 34**

National Union of Mineworkers (South Africa; NUM)
Ramaphosa, Cyril **3**

National Urban Affairs Council
Cooper, Andrew W. **36**

National Urban Coalition (NUC)
Edelin, Ramona Hoage **19**

National Urban League
Brown, Ron **5**
Gordon, Bruce S. **41, 53**
Greely, M. Gasby **27**
Haynes, George Edmund **8**
Jacob, John E. **2**
Jordan, Vernon E. **3, 35**
Price, Hugh B. **9, 54**
Spriggs, William **67**
Young, Whitney M., Jr. **4**

National War College
Clemmons, Reginal G. **41**

National Wildlife Federation
Osborne, Na'taki **54**

National Women's Basketball League (NWBL)
Catchings, Tamika **43**

National Women's Hall of Fame
Kelly, Leontine **33**

National Women's Political Caucus
Hamer, Fannie Lou **6**

National Youth Administration (NYA)
Bethune, Mary McLeod **4**
Primus, Pearl **6**

Nationwide
James, Donna A. **51**

Nature Boy Enterprises
Yoba, Malik **11**

Naval Research Laboratory (NRL)
Carruthers, George R. **40**

NBA
See National Basketball Association

NBAF
See National Black Arts Festival

NBC
See National Broadcasting Company

NBGLLF
See National Black Gay and Lesbian Leadership Forum

NCBL
See National Conference on Black Lawyers

NCBW
See National Coalition of 100 Black Women

NCCK
See Kenya National Council of Churches

NCD
See National Commission for Democracy

NCNE
See National Center for Neighborhood Enterprise

NCNW
See National Council of Negro Women

NDC
See National Defence Council

NEA
See National Education Association; National Endowment for the Arts

Nebula awards
Butler, Octavia **8, 43, 58**
Delany, Samuel R., Jr. **9**

Négritude
Césaire, Aimé **48, 69**
Damas, Léon-Gontran **46**

Negro American Labor Council
Randolph, A. Philip **3**

Negro American Political League
Trotter, Monroe **9**

Negro Digest **magazine**
Fuller, Hoyt **44**
Johnson, John H. **3, 54**

Negro Ensemble Company
Cash, Rosalind **28**
Rolle, Esther **13, 21**
Schultz, Michael A. **6**
Taylor, Susan L. **10**
Ward, Douglas Turner **42**

Negro History Bulletin
Woodson, Carter G. **2**

Negro Leagues
Banks, Ernie **33**
Barnhill, David **30**
Bell, James "Cool Papa" **36**
Brown, Willard **36**
Campanella, Roy **25**
Charleston, Oscar **39**
Dandridge, Ray **36**
Davis, Piper **19**
Day, Leon **39**
Gibson, Josh **22**
Howard, Ryan **65**
Hyde, Cowan F. "Bubba" **47**
Irvin, Monte **31**
Johnson, Clifford "Connie" **52**
Johnson, Mamie "Peanut" **40**
Kaiser, Cecil **42**
Kimbro, Henry A. **25**
Leonard, Buck **67**
Lloyd, John Henry "Pop" **30**
O'Neil, Buck **19, 59**
Paige, Satchel **7**
Pride, Charley **26**
Smith, Hilton **29**
Stearnes, Norman "Turkey" **31**
Stone, Toni **15**

Negro World
Fortune, T. Thomas **6**

NEIC
See National Earthquake Information Center

Neo-hoodoo
Reed, Ishmael **8**

Nequai Cosmetics
Taylor, Susan L. **10**

NERL
See National Equal Rights League

Netherlands Antilles
Liberia-Peters, Maria Philomena **12**

Netherlands government
Ali, Ayaan Hirsi **58**

NetNoir Inc.
CasSelle, Malcolm **11**
Ellington, E. David **11**

Neurosurgery
Black, Keith Lanier **18**
Canady, Alexa **28**
Carson, Benjamin **1, 35**

Neustadt International Prize for Literature
Brathwaite, Kamau **36**

New Birth Missionary Baptist Church
Long, Eddie L. **29**

New Black Muslims
Muhammad, Khallid Abdul **10, 31**

New Black Panther Party
Muhammad, Khallid, Abdul **10, 31**

New Concept Development Center
Madhubuti, Haki R. **7**

New Dance Group
Primus, Pearl **6**

New Danish Dance Theatre
Spears, Warren **52**

New Edition
Gill, Johnny **51**

New Jack Swing music
Brown, Bobby **58**
Hall, Aaron **57**

New Jersey Family Development Act
Bryant, Wayne R. **6**

New Jersey General Assembly
Bryant, Wayne R. **6**
Payne, William D. **60**

New Jersey Nets
Doby, Lawrence Eugene, Sr. **16, 41**

New Jewel Movement
Bishop, Maurice **39**

New Life Community Choir
Kee, John P. **43**

New Life Fellowship Church
Kee, John P. **43**

New Negro movement
See Harlem Renaissance

New Orleans city government
Nagin, C. Ray **42, 57**

New Orleans Saints football team
Brooks, Aaron **33**
Mills, Sam **33**

New Patriotic Party (Ghana)
Kufuor, John Agyekum **54**

New York Age
Fortune, T. Thomas **6**

New York City government
Campbell, Mary Schmidt **43**
Crew, Rudolph F. **16**
Dinkins, David **4**
Fields, C. Virginia **25**
Ford, Wallace **58**
Hageman, Hans **36**
Paterson, Basil A. **69**
Sutton, Percy E. **42**
Thompson, William **35**

New York Coalition of 100 Black Woman
Wein, Joyce **62**

New York Daily News
Cose, Ellis **5, 50**

New York Drama Critics Circle Award
Hansberry, Lorraine **6**

New York Freeman
Fortune, T. Thomas **6**

New York Giants baseball team
Dandridge, Ray **36**
Mays, Willie **3**
Tunnell, Emlen **54**

New York Giants football team
Barber, Tiki **57**
Strahan, Michael **35**

Taylor, Lawrence 25

New York Globe
Fortune, T. Thomas 6

New York Hip Hop Theater Festival
Jones, Sarah 39

New York Institute for Social Therapy and Research
Fulani, Lenora 11

New York Jets football team
Lott, Ronnie 9

New York Knicks basketball team
Ewing, Patrick A. 17
Johnson, Larry 28
Sprewell, Latrell 23

New York Mets baseball team
Clendenon, Donn 26, 56

New York Philharmonic
DePriest, James 37

New York Public Library
Baker, Augusta 38
Dodson, Howard, Jr. 7, 52
Schomburg, Arthur Alfonso 9

New York Shakespeare Festival
Browne, Roscoe Lee 66
Gunn, Moses 10
Wolfe, George C. 6, 43

New York state government
McCall, H. Carl 27
Paterson, Basil A. 69
Paterson, David A. 59

New York State Senate
McCall, H. Carl 27
Motley, Constance Baker 10, 55
Owens, Major 6
Paterson, Basil A. 69

New York State Supreme Court
Dudley, Edward R. 58
Wright, Bruce McMarion 3, 52

New York Stock Exchange
Doley, Harold, Jr. 26

New York Sun
Fortune, T. Thomas 6

New York Times
Blair, Jayson 50
Boyd, Gerald M. 32, 59
Broyard, Anatole 68
Caldwell, Earl 60
Davis, George 36
Hunter-Gault, Charlayne 6, 31
Ifill, Gwen 28
Mabry, Marcus 70
Price, Hugh B. 9, 54
Rhoden, William C. 67
Wilkins, Roger 2

New York University
Brathwaite, Kamau 36
Campbell, Mary Schmidt 43

Newkirk, Pamela 69

New York Yankees baseball team
Baylor, Don 6
Bonds, Bobby 43
Jackson, Reggie 15
Jeter, Derek 27
Strawberry, Darryl 22
Watson, Bob 25
Winfield, Dave 5

Newark city government
Booker, Cory Anthony 68
Gibson, Kenneth Allen 6
James, Sharpe 23, 69

Newark Dodgers baseball team
Dandridge, Ray 36

Newark Eagles baseball team
Dandridge, Ray, Sr. 16, 41

Newark Housing Authority
Gibson, Kenneth Allen 6

The News Hour with Jim Lehrer TV series
Ifill, Gwen 28

Newsday
Olojede, Dele 59

Newsweek
Mabry, Marcus 70

NFL
See National Football League

NHL
See National Hockey League

Niagara movement
Du Bois, W. E. B. 3
Hope, John 8
Trotter, Monroe 9

Nickelodeon
Thompson, Kenan 52

Nigerian Armed Forces
Abacha, Sani 11, 70
Abiola, Moshood 70
Babangida, Ibrahim 4
Obasanjo, Olusegun 5, 22

Nigerian Association of Patriotic Writers and Artists
Barrett, Lindsay 43

Nigerian government
Abiola, Moshood 70
Abubakar, Abdulsalami 66
Akunyili, Dora Nkem 58
Yar'adua, Umaru 69

Nigerian literature
Achebe, Chinua 6
Akpan, Uwem 70
Amadi, Elechi 40
Bandele, Biyi 68
Barrett, Lindsay 43
Ekwensi, Cyprian 37
Onwueme, Tess Osonye 23
Rotimi, Ola 1
Saro-Wiwa, Kenule 39

Soyinka, Wole 4

NIH
See National Institutes of Health

NII
See National Information Infrastructure

Nike
Edwards, Trevor 54

1960 Masks
Soyinka, Wole 4

Nobel Peace Prize
Annan, Kofi Atta 15, 48
Bunche, Ralph J. 5
King, Martin Luther, Jr. 1
Luthuli, Albert 13
Tutu, Desmond Mpilo 6, 44

Nobel Prize for Literature
Morrison, Toni 2, 15
Soyinka, Wole 4
Walcott, Derek 5

Noma Award for Publishing in African
Ba, Mariama 30

Nonfiction
Abrahams, Peter 39
Adams-Ender, Clara 40
Ali, Hana Yasmeen 52
Allen, Debbie 13, 42
Allen, Robert L. 38
Atkins, Cholly 40
Baisden, Michael 66
Ballard, Allen Butler, Jr. 40
Beah, Ishmael 69
Blassingame, John Wesley 40
Blockson, Charles L. 42
Bogle, Donald 34
Brown, Cecil M. 46
Brown, Lloyd Louis 42
Broyard, Bliss 68
Buckley, Gail Lumet 39
Carby, Hazel 27
Carter, Joye Maureen 41
Cashin, Sheryll 63
Cobb, William Jelani 59
Cole, Johnnetta B. 5, 43
Cook, Mercer 40
Cox, Joseph Mason Andrew 51
Crew, Spencer R. 55
Cruse, Harold 54
Datcher, Michael 60
Davis, Arthur P. 41
Davis, Thulani 61
Dickerson, Debra J. 60
Dunnigan, Alice Allison 41
Edelman, Marian Wright 5, 42
Elliott, Lorris 37
Fax, Elton 48
Fine, Sam 60
Finner-Williams, Paris Michele 62
Fisher, Antwone 40
Fletcher, Bill, Jr. 41
Ford, Clyde W. 40
Foster, Cecil 32
Gayle, Addison, Jr. 41
Gibson, Donald Bernard 40
Gladwell, Malcolm 62
Greenwood, Monique 38

Harrison, Alvin 28
Harrison, Calvin 28
Henderson, David 53
Henries, A. Doris Banks 44
Henriques, Julian 37
Hercules, Frank 44
Hernton, Calvin C. 51
Hill, Errol 40
Hobson, Julius W. 44
Horne, Frank 44
Ilibagiza, Immaculée 66
Jakes, Thomas "T.D." 17, 43
Jolley, Willie 28
Jordan, Vernon E. 7, 35
Kayira, Legson 40
Kearney, Janis 54
Kennedy, Randall 40
Knight, Etheridge 37
Kobia, Samuel 43
Ladner, Joyce A. 42
Lampley, Oni Faida 43, 71
Lincoln, C. Eric 38
Long, Eddie L. 29
Mabuza-Suttle, Felicia 43
Malveaux, Julianne 32, 70
Manley, Ruth 34
Matthews Shatteen, Westina 51
McBride, James 35
McKenzie, Vashti M. 29
McKinney Hammond, Michelle 51
McWhorter, John 35
Mossell, Gertrude Bustill 40
Murray, Pauli 38
Myers, Walter Dean 8, 20
Naylor, Gloria 10, 42
Newkirk, Pamela 69
Nissel, Angela 42
Parks, Rosa 1, 35, 56
Pitts, Leonard, Jr. 54
Rusesabagina, Paul 60
Sadlier, Rosemary 62
Smith, Jessie Carney 35
Thornton, Yvonne S. 69
Tillis, Frederick 40
Wade-Gayles, Gloria Jean 41
Walker, Rebecca 50
Wambugu, Florence 42
Wilkens, J. Ernest, Jr. 43
Williams, Terrie 35
Williams, Wendy 62
Wiwa, Ken 67
Wright, Nathan, Jr. 56
Zook, Kristal Brent 62

Nonviolent Action Group (NAG)
Al-Amin, Jamil Abdullah 6

North Carolina Mutual Life Insurance
Spaulding, Charles Clinton 9

North Carolina state government
Ballance, Frank W. 41

North Carolina State University
Lowe, Sidney 64

North Pole
Delany, Martin R. 27
Henson, Matthew 2
Hillary, Barbara 65

McLeod, Gus 27

Notre Dame Univeristy
Willingham, Tyrone 43

NOW
See National Organization for Women

NPR
See National Public Radio

NRA
See National Resistance Army (Uganda); National Rifle Association

NRL
See Naval Research Laboratory

NSF
See National Science Foundation

Nuclear energy
O'Leary, Hazel 6
Packer, Daniel 56
Quarterman, Lloyd Albert 4

Nuclear Regulatory Commission
Jackson, Shirley Ann 12

Nucleus
King, Yolanda 6
Shabazz, Attallah 6

NUM
See National Union of Mineworkers (South Africa)

Nursing
Adams-Ender, Clara 40
Auguste, Rose-Anne 13
Hillary, Barbara 65
Hughes, Ebony 57
Hunter, Alberta 42
Johnson, Eddie Bernice 8
Johnson, Hazel 22
Johnson, Mamie "Peanut" 40
Larsen, Nella 10
Lyttle, Hulda Margaret 14
Richards, Hilda 49
Riley, Helen Caldwell Day 13
Robinson, Rachel 16
Robinson, Sharon 22
Seacole, Mary 54
Shabazz, Betty 7, 26
Staupers, Mabel K. 7
Taylor, Susie King 13

Nursing agency
Daniels, Lee Louis 36

Nutrition
Clark, Celeste 15
Gregory, Dick 1, 54
Smith, Ian 62
Watkins, Shirley R. 17

Nuwaubianism
York, Dwight D. 71

NWBL
See National Women's Basketball League

NYA
See National Youth Administration

Nyasaland African Congress (NAC)
Banda, Hastings Kamuzu 6, 54

Oakland Athletics baseball team
Baker, Dusty 8, 43
Baylor, Don 6
Henderson, Rickey 28
Jackson, Reggie 15
Morgan, Joe Leonard 9

Oakland Oaks baseball team
Dandridge, Ray 36

Oakland Raiders football team
Howard, Desmond 16, 58
Upshaw, Gene 18, 47

Oakland Tribune
Bailey, Chauncey 68
Maynard, Robert C. 7

OAR
See Office of AIDS Research

OAU
See Organization of African Unity

Obie awards
Browne, Roscoe Lee 66
Carter, Nell 39
Freeman, Yvette 27
Orlandersmith, Dael 42
Thigpen, Lynne 17, 41

OBSSR
See Office of Behavioral and Social Sciences Research

OECS
See Organization of Eastern Caribbean States

Office of AIDS Research (OAR)
Cargill, Victoria A. 43

Office of Behavioral and Social Science Research
Anderson, Norman B. 45

Office of Civil Rights
See U.S. Department of Education

Office of Management and Budget
Raines, Franklin Delano 14

Office of Public Liaison
Herman, Alexis M. 15

Ohio House of Representatives
Stokes, Carl B. 10

Ohio state government
Brown, Les 5
Ford, Jack 39
Stokes, Carl B. 10
Williams, George Washington 18

Ohio State Senate
White, Michael R. 5

Ohio Women's Hall of Fame
Craig-Jones, Ellen Walker 44
Stewart, Ella 39

OIC
See Opportunities Industrialization Centers of America, Inc.

OKeh record label
Brooks, Hadda 40
Mo', Keb' 36

Oklahoma Eagle
Ross, Don 27

Oklahoma Hall of Fame
Mitchell, Leona 42

Oklahoma House of Representatives
Ross, Don 27

Olatunji Center for African Culture
Olatunji, Babatunde 36

Olympics
Abdur-Rahim, Shareef 28
Ali, Muhammad 2, 16, 52
Beamon, Bob 30
Bonaly, Surya 7
Bowe, Riddick 6
Carter, Vince 26
Cash, Swin 59
Christie, Linford 8
Clay, Bryan Ezra 57
Coachman, Alice 18
Davis, Shani 58
Dawes, Dominique 11
DeFrantz, Anita 37
Devers, Gail 7
Edwards, Harry 2
Edwards, Teresa 14
Ervin, Anthony 66
Ewing, Patrick A. 17
Felix, Allyson 48
Flowers, Vonetta 35
Ford, Cheryl 45
Freeman, Cathy 29
Garrison, Zina 2
Gebrselassie, Haile 70
Gourdine, Meredith 33
Greene, Maurice 27
Griffith, Yolanda 25
Griffith-Joyner, Florence 28
Hardaway, Anfernee (Penny) 13
Hardaway, Tim 35
Harrison, Alvin 28
Harrison, Calvin 28
Hill, Grant 13
Hines, Garrett 35
Holmes, Kelly 47
Holyfield, Evander 6
Howard, Sherri 36
Iginla, Jarome 35
Johnson, Ben 1
Johnson, Michael 13
Johnson, Rafer 33
Jones, Lou 64
Jones, Randy 35
Joyner-Kersee, Jackie 5
Keflezighi, Meb 49
Leslie, Lisa 16
Lewis, Carl 4
Malone, Karl 18, 51
Metcalfe, Ralph 26
Miller, Cheryl 10
Montgomery, Tim 41
Moses, Edwin 8

Mutola, Maria 12
Owens, Jesse 2
Pippen, Scottie 15
Powell, Mike 7
Quirot, Ana 13
Richards, Sanya 66
Robertson, Oscar 26
Rudolph, Wilma 4
Russell, Bill 8
Scurry, Briana 27
Swoopes, Sheryl 12, 56
Thomas, Debi 26
Thugwane, Josia 21
Ward, Andre 62
Ward, Lloyd 21, 46
Westbrook, Peter 20
Whitaker, Pernell 10
White, Willye 67
Whitfield, Mal 60
Wilkens, Lenny 11
Williams, Lauryn 58
Woodruff, John 68
Woodward, Lynette 67

On a Roll Radio
Smith, Greg 28

Oncology
Leffall, Lasalle 3, 64

One Church, One Child
Clements, George 2

100 Black Men of America
Dortch, Thomas W., Jr. 45

One Way-Productions
Naylor, Gloria 10, 42

Ontario Legislature
Curling, Alvin 34

Onyx Opera
Brown, Uzee 42

Onyx Theater Company
Banks, Michelle 59

OPC
See Ovambo People's Congress

Opera
Adams, Leslie 39
Anderson, Marian 2, 33
Arroyo, Martina 30
Battle, Kathleen 70
Brooks, Avery 9
Brown, Angela M. 54
Brown, Uzee 42
Bumbry, Grace 5
Davis, Anthony 11
Dobbs, Mattiwilda 34
Estes, Simon 28
Freeman, Paul 39
Graves, Denyce Antoinette 19, 57
Greely, M. Gasby 27
Hendricks, Barbara 3, 67
Joplin, Scott 6
Joyner, Matilda Sissieretta 15
Lister, Marquita 65
Maynor, Dorothy 19
McDonald, Audra 20, 62
Mitchell, Leona 42
Norman, Jessye 5
Phillips, Helen L. 63
Price, Leontyne 1

Simpson-Hoffman, N'kenge 52
Still, William Grant 37
Three Mo' Tenors 35
Verrett, Shirley 66
White, Willard 53

Operation Desert Shield
Powell, Colin 1, 28

Operation Desert Storm
Powell, Colin 1, 28

Operation HOPE
Bryant, John 26

Ophthalmology
Bath, Patricia E. 37

OPO
See Ovamboland People's Organization

Opportunities Industrialization Centers of America, Inc. (OIC)
Sullivan, Leon H. 3, 30

Ora Nelle Records
Little Walter 36

Oracle Corporation
Phillips, Charles E., Jr. 57
Woods, Jacqueline 52

Organization of African States
Museveni, Yoweri 4

Organization of African Unity (OAU)
Diouf, Abdou 3
Haile Selassie 7
Kaunda, Kenneth 2
Kenyatta, Jomo 5
Nkrumah, Kwame 3
Nujoma, Samuel 10
Nyerere, Julius 5
Touré, Sekou 6

Organization of Afro-American Unity
Feelings, Muriel 44
X, Malcolm 1

Organization of Eastern Caribbean States (OECS)
Charles, Mary Eugenia 10, 55

Organization of Women Writers of African Descent
Cortez, Jayne 43

Organization Us
Karenga, Maulana 10, 71

Orisun Repertory
Soyinka, Wole 4

Orlando Magic basketball team
Erving, Julius 18, 47
O'Neal, Shaquille 8, 30
Rivers, Glenn "Doc" 25

Orlando Miracle basketball team
Peck, Carolyn 23

Osteopathy
Allen, Ethel D. 13

Anderson, William G(ilchrist), D.O. 57
Ross-Lee, Barbara 67

Ovambo People's Congress (South Africa; OPC)
Nujoma, Samuel 10

Ovamboland People's Organization (South Africa; OPO)
Nujoma, Samuel 10

Overbrook Entertainment
Pinkett Smith, Jada 10, 41

Page Education Foundation
Page, Alan 7

PAIGC
See African Party for the Independence of Guinea and Cape Verde

Paine College
Lewis, Shirley A. R. 14

Painting
Alston, Charles 33
Amos, Emma 63
Andrews, Benny 22, 59
Bailey, Radcliffe 19
Barthe, Richmond 15
Basquiat, Jean-Michel 5
Bearden, Romare 2, 50
Beasley, Phoebe 34
Biggers, John 20, 33
Campbell, E. Simms 13
Colescott, Robert 69
Collins, Paul 61
Cortor, Eldzier 42
Cowans, Adger W. 20
Crite, Alan Rohan 29
Delaney, Beauford 19
Delaney, Joseph 30
Delsarte, Louis 34
Douglas, Aaron 7
Driskell, David C. 7
Ewing, Patrick A. 17
Flood, Curt 10
Freeman, Leonard 27
Gilliam, Sam 16
Goodnight, Paul 32
Green, Jonathan 54
Guyton, Tyree 9
Harkless, Necia Desiree 19
Hayden, Palmer 13
Honeywood, Varnette P. 54
Hunter, Clementine 45
Jackson, Earl 31
Johnson, William Henry 3
Jones, Lois Mailou 13
Knight, Gwendolyn 63
Knox, Simmie 49
Lawrence, Jacob 4, 28
Lee, Annie Francis 22
Lee-Smith, Hughie 5, 22
Lewis, Norman 39
Lewis, Samella 25
Loving, Alvin, Jr. 35, 53
Marshall, Kerry James 59
Mayhew, Richard 39
Major, Clarence 9
McGee, Charles 10
Mitchell, Corinne 8
Motley, Archibald, Jr. 30
Mutu, Wangechi 44

Nugent, Richard Bruce 39
Ouattara 43
Pierre, Andre 17
Pindell, Howardena 55
Pippin, Horace 9
Porter, James A. 11
Reid, Senghor 55
Ringgold, Faith 4
Ruley, Ellis 38
Sallee, Charles 38
Sebree, Charles 40
Smith, Vincent D. 48
Sudduth, Jimmy Lee 65
Tanksley, Ann 37
Tanner, Henry Ossawa 1
Thomas, Alma 14
Thomas, Mickalene 61
Tolliver, Mose 60
Tolliver, William 9
Verna, Gelsy 70
Washington, James, Jr. 38
Wells, James Lesesne 10
White, Charles 39
Wiley, Kehinde 62
Williams, Billy Dee 8
Williams, William T. 11
Wilson, Ellis 39
Woodruff, Hale 9

Pan African Congress
Logan, Rayford W. 40

Pan African Orthodox Christian Church
Agyeman, Jaramogi Abebe 10, 63

Pan-Africanism
Carmichael, Stokely 5, 26
Clarke, John Henrik 20
Du Bois, David Graham 45
Du Bois, W. E. B. 3
Garvey, Marcus 1
Haile Selassie 7
Kenyatta, Jomo 5
Madhubuti, Haki R. 7
Marshall, Paule 7
Nkrumah, Kwame 3
Nyerere, Julius 5
Touré, Sekou 6
Turner, Henry McNeal 5

Papal Medal
Hampton, Lionel 17, 41

Parents of Watts (POW)
Harris, Alice 7

Parti Démocratique de la Côte d'Ivoire (Democratic Party of the Ivory Coast; PDCI)
Bedie, Henri Konan 21
Houphouët-Boigny, Félix 4, 64

Partido Africano da Independencia da Guine e Cabo Verde (PAIGC)
Vieira, Joao 14

Party for Unity and Progress (Guinea; PUP)
Conté, Lansana 7

PATC
See Performing Arts Training Center

Pathology
Fuller, Solomon Carter, Jr. 15

Patriot Party
Fulani, Lenora 11

Patriotic Alliance for Reconstruction and Construction (PARC)
Jammeh, Yahya 23

Patriotic Movement of Salvation (MPS)
Déby, Idriss 30

PBS
See Public Broadcasting Service

PDCI
See Parti Démocratique de la Côte d'Ivoire (Democratic Party of the Ivory Coast)

PDP
See People's Democratic Party

Peace and Freedom Party
Cleaver, Eldridge 5

Peace Corps
See U.S. Peace Corps

Peck School of the Fine Arts
Tyson, Andre 40

Pediatrics
Carson, Benjamin 1, 35
Elders, Joycelyn 6
Witt, Edwin T. 26
Zuma, Nkosazana Dlamini 34

Peg Leg Bates Country Club
Bates, Peg Leg 14

PEN/Faulkner award
Bradley, David Henry, Jr. 39
Mayhew, Richard 39

Pennsylvania state government
Allen, Ethel D. 13
Brown, Homer S. 47
Fattah, Chaka 11, 70
Irvis, K. Leroy 67
Nix, Robert N. C., Jr. 51

Pennsylvania State University
Dunn, Jerry 27

People United to Serve Humanity (PUSH)
Jackson, Jesse 1, 27
Jackson, Jesse, Jr. 14, 45

People's Association for Human Rights
Williams, Robert F. 11

People's Choice Awards
Lewis, Emmanuel 36

People's Democratic Party (Nigeria; PDP)
Obasanjo, Stella 32
Yar'adua, Umaru 69

People's Liberation Army of Namibia (PLAN)
Nujoma, Samuel 10

People's National Party (Jamaica; PNP)
Patterson, P. J. **6, 20**

People's Progressive Party (PPP)
Jagan, Cheddi **16**
Jawara, Dawda Kairaba **11**

People's Revolutionary government
Bishop, Maurice **39**

PepsiCo Inc.
Banks, Paula A. **68**
Boyd, Edward **70**
Harvey, William R. **42**

Performing Arts Training Center (PATC)
Dunham, Katherine **4, 59**

Perkins Prize
Jones, Thomas W. **41**

PGA
See Professional Golfers' Association

Pharmaceutical research
Pickett, Cecil **39**

Pharmaceuticals
Flowers, Sylester **50**
Potter, Myrtle **40**

Pharmacist
Akunyili, Dora Nkem **58**
Flowers, Sylester **50**
Pickett, Cecil **39**
Stewart, Ella **39**

Phelps Stokes Fund
Patterson, Frederick Douglass **12**

Phi Beta Sigma Fraternity
Thomas, Arthur Ray **52**

Philadelphia city government
Allen, Ethel D. **13**
Goode, W. Wilson **4**
Nutter, Michael **69**
Street, John F. **24**

Philadelphia Eagles football team
Cunningham, Randall **23**
McNabb, Donovan **29**
Rhodes, Ray **14**
White, Reggie **6, 50**

Philadelphia Flyers hockey team
Brashear, Donald **39**
Charleston, Oscar **39**

Philadelphia Phillies baseball team
Howard, Ryan **65**
Morgan, Joe Leonard **9**
Rollins, Jimmy **70**

Philadelphia public schools
Clayton, Constance **1**

Philadelphia 76ers basketball team
Barkley, Charles **5, 66**
Bol, Manute **1**
Chamberlain, Wilt **18, 47**
Erving, Julius **18, 47**
Iverson, Allen **24, 46**
Lucas, John **7**
Stackhouse, Jerry **30**

Philadelphia Stars baseball team
Charleston, Oscar **39**

Philadelphia Warriors
Chamberlain, Wilt **18, 47**

Philanthropy
Banks, Paula A. **68**
Brown, Eddie C. **35**
Cooper, Evern **40**
Cosby, Bill **7, 26, 59**
Cosby, Camille **14**
Dawson, Matel "Mat," Jr. **39**
Edley, Christopher **2, 48**
Gardner, Chris **65**
Golden, Marita **19**
Gray, Willie **46**
Johnson, Kevin **70**
Johnson, Sheila Crump **48**
Lavizzo-Mourey, Risa **48**
Malone, Annie **13**
McCarty, Osceola **16**
Millines Dziko, Trish **28**
Pleasant, Mary Ellen **9**
Reeves, Rachel J. **23**
Thomas, Franklin A. **5, 49**
Waddles, Charleszetta "Mother" **10, 49**
Walker, Madame C. J. **7**
Wein, Joyce **62**
White, Reggie **6, 50**
Williams, Fannie Barrier **27**
Wonder, Stevie **11, 53**

Philosophy
Appiah, Kwame Anthony **67**
Baker, Houston A., Jr. **6**
Davis, Angela **5**
Piper, Adrian **71**
Toomer, Jean **6**
West, Cornel **5**

Phoenix Suns basketball team
Barkley, Charles **5, 66**
Heard, Gar **25**
Johnson, Kevin **70**

Photography
Andrews, Bert **13**
Barboza, Anthony **10**
Cowans, Adger W. **20**
Cox, Renée **67**
DeCarava, Roy **42**
Hinton, Milt **30**
Jackson, Vera **40**
Lester, Julius **9**
Moutoussamy-Ashe, Jeanne **7**
Parks, Gordon **1, 35, 58**
Pinderhughes, John **47**
Robeson, Eslanda Goode **13**
Roble, Abdi **71**
Serrano, Andres **3**
Simpson, Lorna **4, 36**
Sleet, Moneta, Jr. **5**
Smith, Marvin **46**
Smith, Morgan **46**
Tanner, Henry Ossawa **1**
Thomas, Mickalene **61**
VanDerZee, James **6**
Weems, Carrie Mae **63**
White, John H. **27**
Williams, Clarence **70**
Withers, Ernest C. **68**

Photojournalism
Ashley-Ward, Amelia **23**
DeCarava, Roy **42**
Jackson, Vera **40**
Moutoussamy-Ashe, Jeanne **7**
Parks, Gordon **1, 35, 58**
Sleet, Moneta, Jr. **5**
Van Lierop, Robert **53**
White, John H. **27**
Williams, Clarence **70**
Withers, Ernest C. **68**
Yette, Samuel F. **63**

Physical therapy
Elders, Joycelyn **6**
Griffin, Bessie Blout **43**

Physics
Adkins, Rutherford H. **21**
Carruthers, George R. **40**
Gates, Sylvester James, Jr. **15**
Gourdine, Meredith **33**
Imes, Elmer Samuel **39**
Jackson, Shirley Ann **12**
Massey, Walter E. **5, 45**
Tyson, Neil deGrasse **15, 65**

Piano
Adams, Leslie **39**
Austin, Lovie **40**
Basie, Count **23**
Bonds, Margaret **39**
Brooks, Hadda **40**
Cartiér, Xam Wilson **41**
Cole, Nat King **17**
Coltrane, Alice **70**
Cook, Charles "Doc" **44**
Domino, Fats **20**
Donegan, Dorothy **19**
Duke, George **21**
Ellington, Duke **5**
Flanagan, Tommy **69**
Hancock, Herbie **20, 67**
Hardin Armstrong, Lil **39**
Harris, Barry **68**
Hayes, Isaac **20, 58**
Hinderas, Natalie **5**
Hines, Earl "Fatha" **39**
Horn, Shirley **32, 56**
Jamal, Ahmad **69**
Johnson, Johnnie **56**
Jones, Hank **57**
Joplin, Scott **6**
Keys, Alicia **32, 68**
Monk, Thelonious **1**
Perkins, Pinetop **70**
Peterson, Oscar **52**
Powell, Bud **24**
Pratt, Awadagin **31**
Preston, Billy **39, 59**
Price, Florence **37**
Pritchard, Robert Starling **21**
Roberts, Marcus **19**
Robinson, Reginald R. **53**
Sample, Joe **51**
Schuyler, Philippa **50**
Scott, Hazel **66**
Silver, Horace **26**
Simone, Nina **15, 41**
Sun Ra **60**
Swann, Lynn **28**
Southern, Eileen **56**
Sykes, Roosevelt **20**
Taylor, Billy **23**
Taylor, Cecil **70**
Turner, Ike **68**
Vaughan, Sarah **13**
Walker, George **37**
Waller, Fats **29**
Watts, Andre **42**
Webster, Katie **29**
Williams, Mary Lou **15**

Pittsburgh Crawfords
See Indianapolis Crawfords

Pittsburgh Homestead Grays baseball team
Charleston, Oscar **39**
Kaiser, Cecil **42**
Leonard, Buck **67**

Pittsburgh Pirates baseball team
Bonds, Barry **6, 34, 63**
Clendenon, Donn **26, 56**
Stargell, Willie **29**

Pittsburgh Steelers football team
Dungy, Tony **17, 42, 59**
Gilliam, Joe **31**
Greene, Joe **10**
Perry, Lowell **30**
Stargell, Willie **29**
Stewart, Kordell **21**
Swann, Lynn **28**

PLAN
See People's Liberation Army of Namibia

Planned Parenthood Federation of America Inc.
Wattleton, Faye **9**

Playboy
Brown, Robert **65**
Taylor, Karin **34**

Playwright
Allen, Debbie **13, 42**
Anthony, Trey **63**
Arkadie, Kevin **17**
Baldwin, James **1**
Bandele, Biyi **68**
Barrett, Lindsay **43**
Beckham, Barry **41**
Branch, William Blackwell **39**
Brown, Cecil M. **46**
Brown, Oscar, Jr. **53**
Bullins, Ed **25**
Caldwell, Benjamin **46**
Carroll, Vinnette **29**
Césaire, Aimé **48, 69**
Cheadle, Don **19, 52**
Chenault, John **40**
Childress, Alice **15**
Clark-Bekederno, J. P. **44**
Clarke, George **32**
Cleage, Pearl **17, 64**
Corthron, Kia **43**
Cotter, Joseph Seamon, Sr. **40**

Cox, Joseph Mason Andrew **51**
Dadié, Bernard **34**
Davis, Eisa **68**
De Veaux, Alexis **44**
Dent, Thomas C. **50**
Dodson, Owen **38**
Elder, Larry, III **38**
Evans, Mari **26**
Farah, Nuruddin **27**
Franklin, J. E. **44**
Gordone, Charles **15**
Hansberry, Lorraine **6**
Hayes, Teddy **40**
Hill, Errol **40**
Hill, Leslie Pinckney **44**
Holder, Laurence **34**
Hughes, Langston **4**
Jean-Baptiste, Marianne **17, 46**
Johnson, Georgia Douglas **41**
Johnson, Je'Caryous **63**
Jones, Sarah **39**
Kennedy, Adrienne **11**
Kente, Gibson **52**
King, Woodie, Jr. **27**
Lampley, Oni Faida **43, 71**
Long, Richard Alexander **65**
Marechera, Dambudzo **39**
Milner, Ron **39**
Mitchell, Loften **31**
Moss, Carlton **17**
Mugo, Micere Githae **32**
Nottage, Lynn **66**
Onwueme, Tess Osonye **23**
Orlandersmith, Dael **42**
Parks, Suzan-Lori **34**
Perry, Tyler **40, 54**
Rahman, Aishah **37**
Richards, Beah **30**
Sanchez, Sonia **17, 51**
Schuyler, George Samuel **40**
Sebree, Charles **40**
Smith, Anna Deavere **6, 44**
Talbert, David **34**
Taylor, Regina **9, 46**
Thurman, Wallace **17**
Tolson, Melvin B. **37**
Walcott, Derek **5**
Ward, Douglas Turner **42**
Williams, Samm-Art **21**
Wilson, August **7, 33, 55**
Wolfe, George C. **6, 43**
Youngblood, Shay **32**

PNP
See People's National Party (Jamaica)

Podium Records
Patterson, Gilbert Earl **41**

Poet laureate (U.S.)
Dove, Rita **6**

Poetry
Adams, Jenoyne **60**
Alexander, Margaret Walker **22**
Allen, Samuel L. **38**
Angelou, Maya **1, 15**
Atkins, Russell **45**
Aubert, Alvin **41**
Baiocchi, Regina Harris **41**
Bandele, Asha **36**
Barrax, Gerald William **45**
Barrett, Lindsay **43**

Bell, James Madison **40**
Bennett, Gwendolyn B. **59**
Bennett, Louise **69**
Berry, James **41**
Bontemps, Arna **8**
Braithwaite, William Stanley **52**
Brand, Dionne **32**
Breeze, Jean "Binta" **37**
Brooks, Gwendolyn **1, 28**
Brown, Cecil M. **46**
Brutus, Dennis **38**
Burgess, Marjorie L. **55**
Carter, Martin **49**
Cartey, Wilfred **47**
Césaire, Aimé **48, 69**
Chenault, John **40**
Cheney-Coker, Syl **43**
Clark-Bekedermo, J. P. **44**
Clarke, Cheryl **32**
Clarke, George **32**
Cleage, Pearl **17, 64**
Cliff, Michelle **42**
Clifton, Lucille **14, 64**
Coleman, Wanda **48**
Cooper, Afua **53**
Cornish, Sam **50**
Cortez, Jayne **43**
Cotter, Joseph Seamon, Sr. **40**
Cox, Joseph Mason Andrew **51**
Cuney, William Waring **44**
Dabydeen, David **48**
Dadié, Bernard **34**
D'Aguiar, Fred **50**
Damas, Léon-Gontran **46**
Dandridge, Raymond Garfield **45**
Danner, Margaret Esse **49**
Datcher, Michael **60**
Davis, Charles T. **48**
Davis, Frank Marshall **47**
De Veaux, Alexis **44**
Dent, Thomas C. **50**
Dodson, Owen **38**
Dove, Rita **6**
Draper, Sharon Mills **16, 43**
Dumas, Henry **41**
Dunbar-Nelson, Alice Ruth Moore **44**
Emanuel, James A. **46**
Evans, Mari **26**
Fabio, Sarah Webster **48**
Fair, Ronald L. **47**
Figueroa, John J. **40**
Fisher, Antwone **40**
Fleming, Raymond **48**
Frazier, Oscar **58**
Forbes, Calvin **46**
Ford, Nick Aaron **44**
Gabre-Medhin, Tsegaye **64**
Gilbert, Christopher **50**
Goings, Russell **59**
Goodison, Lorna **71**
Harkless, Necia Desiree **19**
Harper, Frances Ellen Watkins **11**
Harper, Michael S. **34**
Harris, Claire **34**
Hayden, Robert **12**
Henderson, David **53**
Hernton, Calvin C. **51**
Hill, Leslie Pinckney **44**
Hoagland, Everett H. **45**
Horne, Frank **44**
Hughes, Langston **7**
Jackson, Fred James **25**

Joachim, Paulin **34**
Johnson, Georgia Douglas **41**
Johnson, Linton Kwesi **37**
Jones, Sarah **39**
Kay, Jackie **37**
Knight, Etheridge **37**
Laraque, Paul **67**
Letson, Al **39**
Lorde, Audre **6**
Manley, Ruth **34**
Marechera, Dambudzo **39**
Moore, Jessica Care **30**
Mugo, Micere Githae **32**
Mullen, Harryette **34**
Naylor, Gloria **10, 42**
Neto, António Agostinho **43**
Nugent, Richard Bruce **39**
Okara, Gabriel **37**
Parker, Pat **19**
Peters, Lenrie **43**
Philip, Marlene Nourbese **32**
Powell, Kevin **31**
Quigless, Helen G. **49**
Randall, Dudley **8, 55**
Redmond, Eugene **23**
Richards, Beah **30**
Sanchez, Sonia **17, 51**
Sapphire **14**
Senghor, Léopold Sédar **12**
Senior, Olive **37**
Smith, Mary Carter **26**
Spencer, Anne **27**
Sundiata, Sekou **66**
Tillis, Frederick **40**
Tolson, Melvin B. **37**
Touré, Askia (Muhammad Abu Bakr el) **47**
van Sertima, Ivan **25**
Walker, Margaret **29**
Washington, James, Jr. **38**
Weaver, Afaa Michael **37**
Williams, Saul **31**
Williams, Sherley Anne **25**
Woods, Scott **55**

Poetry Slam, Inc.
Woods, Scott **55**

Political science
Ake, Claude **30**
Dawson, Michael C. **63**
Skinner, Kiron K. **65**
Watson, Carlos **50**

Politics
Alexander, Archie Alphonso **14**
Allen, Claude **68**
Arthur, Owen **33**
Austin, Junius C. **44**
Baker, Thurbert **22**
Ballance, Frank W. **41**
Barrow, Dean **69**
Bass, Charlotta Spears **40**
Belton, Sharon Sayles **9, 16**
Bishop, Sanford D., Jr. **24**
Blackwell, Unita **17**
Boateng, Paul Yaw **56**
Booker, Cory Anthony **68**
Boye, Madior **30**
Brazile, Donna **25, 70**
Brown, Corrine **24**
Brown, Oscar, Jr. **53**
Buckley, Victoria (Vikki) **24**
Burris, Chuck **21**

Burris, Roland W. **25**
Butler, Jerry **26**
Césaire, Aimé **48, 69**
Chideya, Farai **14, 61**
Christian-Green, Donna M. **17**
Clayton, Eva M. **20**
Coleman, Mary **46**
Compton, John **65**
Connerly, Ward **14**
Cummings, Elijah E. **24**
Curling, Alvin **34**
Currie, Betty **21**
Davis, Artur **41**
Davis, James E. **50**
Dixon, Julian C. **24**
Dixon, Sheila **68**
dos Santos, José Eduardo **43**
Dymally, Mervyn **42**
Edmonds, Terry **17**
Ellison, Keith **59**
Fields, C. Virginia **25**
Fields, Julia **45**
Ford, Jack **39**
Gbagbo, Laurent **43**
Gordon, Pamela **17**
Greenlee, Sam **48**
Hatcher, Richard G. **55**
Henry, Aaron **19**
Herenton, Willie W. **24**
Hilliard, Earl F. **24**
Hobson, Julius W. **44**
Holmes, Amy **69**
Ingraham, Hubert A. **19**
Isaac, Julius **34**
Jackson Lee, Sheila **20**
Jackson, Mae **57**
James, Sharpe **23, 69**
Jammeh, Yahya **23**
Jarvis, Charlene Drew **21**
Jefferson, William J. **25**
Johnson, Harvey, Jr. **24**
Kabbah, Ahmad Tejan **23**
Kabila, Joseph **30**
Kariuki, J. M. **67**
Kidd, Mae Street **39**
Lee, Barbara **25**
Maathai, Wangari **43**
Magloire, Paul Eugène **68**
Majette, Denise **41**
Mamadou, Tandja **33**
McGlowan, Angela **64**
Meek, Carrie **6, 36**
Meek, Kendrick **41**
Meeks, Gregory **25**
Metcalfe, Ralph **26**
Millender-McDonald, Juanita **21, 61**
Moore, Gwendolynne S. **55**
Moore, Harry T. **29**
Morial, Ernest "Dutch" **26**
Morial, Marc H. **20, 51**
Nagin, C. Ray **42, 57**
Obasanjo, Olusegun **22**
Pereira, Aristides **30**
Perry, Ruth **15**
Pitta, Celso **17**
Powell, Debra A. **23**
Rush, Bobby **26**
Saro-Wiwa, Kenule **39**
Scott, David **41**
Scott, Robert C. **23**
Sisulu, Sheila Violet Makate **24**
Smith, Jennifer **21**
Spencer, Winston Baldwin **68**

Thompson, Bennie G. **26**
Touré, Amadou Toumani **18**
Tsvangirai, Morgan **26**
Watson, Diane **41**
Watt, Melvin **26**
Watts, J. C., Jr. **14, 38**
Wheat, Alan **14**
White, Jesse **22**
Williams, Anthony **21**
Williams, Eddie N. **44**
Williams, Eric Eustace **65**
Williams, George Washington **18**
Wiwa, Ken **67**
Wynn, Albert R. **25**
Yar'adua, Umaru **69**

Pop music
Ashanti **37**
Ashford, Nickolas **21**
Barrino, Fantasia **53**
Bassey, Shirley **25**
Bleu, Corbin **65**
Blige, Mary J. **20, 34, 60**
Brown, Bobby **58**
Butler, Jonathan **28**
Carey, Mariah **32, 53, 69**
Cee-Lo **70**
Chanté, Keshia **50**
Checker, Chubby **28**
Cole, Nat King **17**
Combs, Sean "Puffy" **17, 43**
Cox, Deborah **28**
David, Craig **31, 53**
Duke, George **21**
Edmonds, Kenneth "Babyface" **10, 31**
Ferrell, Rachelle **29**
Franklin, Aretha **11, 44**
Franklin, Kirk **15, 49**
Gray, Macy **29**
Hailey, JoJo **22**
Hailey, K-Ci **22**
Hammer, M. C. **20**
Hathaway, Lalah **57**
Hawkins, Screamin' Jay **30**
Hayes, Isaac **20, 58**
Hill, Lauryn **20, 53**
Holmes, Clint **57**
Houston, Cissy **20**
Houston, Whitney **7, 28**
Hudson, Jennifer **63**
Humphrey, Bobbi **20**
Isley, Ronald **25, 56**
Ja Rule **35**
Jackson, Janet **6, 30, 68**
Jackson, Michael **19, 53**
James, Rick **17**
Jarreau, Al **21, 65**
Jean, Wyclef **20**
Jones, Quincy **8, 30**
Jordan, Montell **23**
Kelis **58**
Kendricks, Eddie **22**
Keys, Alicia **32, 68**
Khan, Chaka **12, 50**
LaBelle, Patti **13, 30**
Love, Darlene **23**
Luckett, Letoya **61**
Massenburg, Kedar **23**
Mathis, Johnny **20**
McFerrin, Bobby **68**
Monica **21**
Moore, Chante **26**
Mumba, Samantha **29**
Mya **35**
Ne-Yo **65**
Neville, Aaron **21**
Noah, Yannick **4, 60**
Osborne, Jeffrey **26**
Otis, Clyde **67**
P.M. Dawn **54**
Palmer, Keke **68**
Preston, Billy **39, 59**
Prince **18, 65**
Reid, Antonio "L.A." **28**
Reid, Vernon **34**
Richie, Lionel **27, 65**
Rihanna **65**
Robinson, Smokey **3, 49**
Rucker, Darius **34**
Rupaul **17**
Sade **15**
Seal **14**
Senghor, Léopold Sédar **12**
Short, Bobby **52**
Simpson, Valerie **21**
Sisqo **30**
Staton, Candi **27**
Summer, Donna **25**
The Supremes **33**
Sweat, Keith **19**
The Temptations **33**
Thomas, Irma **29**
TLC **34**
Turner, Tina **6, 27**
Usher **23, 56**
Vanity **67**
Washington, Dinah **22**
Washington, Grover, Jr. **17, 44**
Washington, Val **12**
Welch, Elisabeth **52**
White, Barry **13, 41**
White, Josh, Jr. **52**
White, Maurice **29**
will.i.am **64**
Williams, Vanessa L. **4, 17**
Wilson, Jackie **60**
Wilson, Mary **28**
Wilson, Nancy **10**
Withers-Mendes, Elisabeth **64**
Wonder, Stevie **11, 53**

Portland (OR) Police Department
Moose, Charles **40**

Portland Trail Blazers basketball team
Drexler, Clyde **4, 61**
Wilkens, Lenny **11**

Potters' House
Jakes, Thomas "T. D." **17, 43**

POW
See Parents of Watts

PPP
See People's Progressive Party (Gambia)

Pratt Institute
Mayhew, Richard **39**

Presbyterianism
Cannon, Katie **10**

Pride Economic Enterprises
Barry, Marion S. **7, 44**

Princeton University
Blanks, Deborah K. **69**
Simmons, Ruth **13, 38**

Printmaking
Blackburn, Robert **28**
Tanksley, Ann **37**
Thrash, Dox **35**
Wells, James Lesesne **10**

Printmaking Workshop
Blackburn, Robert **28**
Tanksley, Ann **37**

Prison ministry
Bell, Ralph S. **5**

Professional Golfers' Association (PGA)
Elder, Lee **6**
Powell, Renee **34**
Sifford, Charlie **4, 49**
Woods, Tiger **14, 31**

Professional Women's Club of Chicago
Gray, Ida **41**

Progressive Labour Party
Smith, Jennifer **21**

Progressive Party
Bass, Charlotta Spears **40**

Project Teen Aid
McMurray, Georgia L. **36**

Pro-Line Corp.
Cottrell, Comer **11**

Proposition 209
Connerly, Ward **14**

Provincial Freeman
Cary, Mary Ann Shadd **30**

Psychiatry
Cobbs, Price M. **9**
Comer, James P. **6**
Fanon, Frantz **44**
Fuller, Solomon Carter, Jr. **15**
Poussaint, Alvin F. **5, 67**
Welsing, Frances Cress **5**

Psychic health
Ford, Clyde W. **40**

Psychology
Anderson, Norman B. **45**
Archie-Hudson, Marguerite **44**
Brown, Joyce F. **25**
Finner-Williams, Paris Michele **62**
Fulani, Lenora **11**
Gilbert, Christopher **50**
Hare, Nathan **44**
Hilliard, Asa Grant, III **66**
Staples, Brent **8**
Steele, Claude Mason **13**
Tatum, Beverly Daniel **42**

Psychotheraphy
Berrysmith, Don Reginald **49**
Ford, Clyde W. **40**

Public Broadcasting Service (PBS)
Brown, Les **5**
Davis, Ossie **5, 50**
Duke, Bill **3**
Hampton, Henry **6**
Hunter-Gault, Charlayne **6, 31**
Lawson, Jennifer **1, 50**
Lynch, Shola **61**
Riggs, Marlon **5, 44**
Roker, Al **12, 49**
Wilkins, Roger **2**

Public housing
Hamer, Fannie Lou **6**
Lane, Vincent **5**
Reems, Ernestine Cleveland **27**

Public relations
Barden, Don H. **9, 20**
Edmonds, Terry **17**
Graham, Stedman **13**
Hedgeman, Anna Arnold **22**
McCabe, Jewell Jackson **10**
Perez, Anna **1**
Pritchard, Robert Starling **21**
Rowan, Carl T. **1, 30**
Taylor, Kristin Clark **8**
Williams, Maggie **7, 71**

Public speaking
Bell, James Madison **40**
Kennedy, Randall **40**

Public television
Brown, Tony **3**
Creagh, Milton **27**
Ifill, Gwen **28**
Long, Loretta **58**

Publishing
Abbott, Robert Sengstacke **27**
Achebe, Chinua **6**
Ames, Wilmer **27**
Ashley-Ward, Amelia **23**
Aubert, Alvin **41**
Auguste, Arnold A. **47**
Baisden, Michael **25, 66**
Barden, Don H. **9, 20**
Bass, Charlotta Spears **40**
Bates, Daisy **13**
Boston, Lloyd **24**
Boyd, T. B., III **6**
Brown, Marie Dutton **12**
Cary, Mary Ann Shadd **30**
Coombs, Orde M. **44**
Cox, William E. **68**
Dawkins, Wayne **20**
Driver, David E. **11**
Ducksworth, Marilyn **12**
Dumas, Henry **41**
Fuller, Hoyt **44**
Giddings, Paula **11**
Graves, Earl G. **1, 35**
Harris, Jay **19**
Harris, Monica **18**
Hill, Bonnie Guiton **20**
Hudson, Cheryl **15**
Hudson, Wade **15**
James, Juanita **13**
Johnson, John H. **3, 54**
Jones, Quincy **8, 30**
Kunjufu, Jawanza **3, 50**
Lawson, Jennifer **1, 50**

Leavell, Dorothy R. **17**
Lewis, Edward T. **21**
Lorde, Audre **6**
Madhubuti, Haki R. **7**
Maynard, Robert C. **7**
McDonald, Erroll **1**
Moore, Jessica Care **30**
Morgan, Garrett **1**
Murphy, John H. **42**
Myers, Walter Dean **8, 20**
Parks, Gordon **1, 35, 58**
Perez, Anna **1**
Randall, Dudley **8, 55**
Scott, C. A. **29**
Sengstacke, John **18**
Smith, Clarence O. **21**
Stinson, Denise L. **59**
Stringer, Vickie **58**
Tyree, Omar Rashad **21**
Vanzant, Iyanla **17, 47**
Walker, Alice **1, 43**
Washington, Alonzo **29**
Washington, Laura S. **18**
Wells-Barnett, Ida B. **8**
Williams, Armstrong **29**
Williams, Patricia **11, 54**
Woods, Teri **69**

Pulitzer prize
Brooks, Gwendolyn **1, 28**
Dove, Rita **6**
Fuller, Charles **8**
Gordone, Charles **15**
Haley, Alex **4**
Komunyakaa, Yusef **9**
Lewis, David Levering **9**
McPherson, James Alan **70**
Morrison, Toni **2, 15**
Newkirk, Pamela **69**
Page, Clarence **4**
Parks, Suzan-Lori **34**
Shipp, E. R. **15**
Sleet, Moneta, Jr. **5**
Walker, Alice **1, 43**
Walker, George **37**
White, John H. **27**
Wilkins, Roger **2**
Wilson, August **7, 33, 55**

PUP
See Party for Unity and Progress (Guinea)

Puppeteer
Clash, Kevin **14**

PUSH
See People United to Serve Humanity

Quiltmaking
Benberry, Cuesta **65**
Ringgold, Faith **4**

Quincy Jones Media Group
Jones, Quincy **8, 30**

Qwest Records
Jones, Quincy **8, 30**

Race car driving
Hamilton, Lewis **66**
Lester, Bill **42**
Ribbs, Willy T. **2**

Scott, Wendell Oliver, Sr. **19**

Race relations
Abbott, Diane **9**
Achebe, Chinua **6**
Alexander, Clifford **26**
Anthony, Wendell **25**
Asante, Molefi Kete **3**
Baker, Ella **5**
Baker, Houston A., Jr. **6**
Baldwin, James **1**
Beals, Melba Patillo **15**
Bell, Derrick **6**
Bennett, Lerone, Jr. **5**
Bethune, Mary McLeod **4**
Bobo, Lawrence **60**
Booker, Simeon **23**
Bosley, Freeman, Jr. **7**
Boyd, T. B., III **6**
Bradley, David Henry, Jr. **39**
Branch, William Blackwell **39**
Brown, Elaine **8**
Bunche, Ralph J. **5**
Butler, Paul D. **17**
Butts, Calvin O., III **9**
Carter, Stephen L. **4**
Cary, Lorene **3**
Cashin, Sheryll **63**
Cayton, Horace **26**
Chavis, Benjamin **6**
Clark, Kenneth B. **5, 52**
Clark, Septima **7**
Cobbs, Price M. **9**
Cochran, Johnnie **11, 39, 52**
Cole, Johnnetta B. **5, 43**
Comer, James P. **6**
Cone, James H. **3**
Conyers, John, Jr. **4, 45**
Cook, Suzan D. Johnson **22**
Cook, Toni **23**
Cosby, Bill **7, 26, 59**
Cunningham, Evelyn **23**
Darden, Christopher **13**
Davis, Angela **5**
Davis, Benjamin O., Jr. **2, 43**
Davis, Benjamin O., Sr. **4**
Dee, Ruby **8, 50, 68**
Delany, Martin R. **27**
Dellums, Ronald **2**
Diallo, Amadou **27**
Dickerson, Debra J. **60**
Divine, Father **7**
DuBois, Shirley Graham **21**
Dunbar, Paul Laurence **8**
Dunbar-Nelson, Alice Ruth Moore **44**
Dyson, Michael Eric **11, 40**
Edelman, Marian Wright **5, 42**
Elder, Lee **6**
Ellison, Ralph **7**
Esposito, Giancarlo **9**
Farmer, James **2, 64**
Farmer-Paellmann, Deadria **43**
Farrakhan, Louis **2**
Fauset, Jessie **7**
Franklin, John Hope **5**
Fuller, Charles **8**
Gaines, Ernest J. **7**
Gibson, William F. **6**
Goode, W. Wilson **4**
Graham, Lawrence Otis **12**
Gregory, Dick **1, 54**
Grimké, Archibald H. **9**

Guinier, Lani **7, 30**
Guy, Rosa **5**
Haley, Alex **4**
Hall, Elliott S. **24**
Hampton, Henry **6**
Hansberry, Lorraine **6**
Harris, Alice **7**
Hastie, William H. **8**
Haynes, George Edmund **8**
Hedgeman, Anna Arnold **22**
Henry, Aaron **19**
Henry, Lenny **9, 52**
Hill, Oliver W. **24, 63**
hooks, bell **5**
Hooks, Benjamin L. **2**
Hope, John **8**
Howard, M. William, Jr. **26**
Ingram, Rex **5**
Innis, Roy **5**
Jeffries, Leonard **8**
Johnson, James Weldon **5**
Jones, Elaine R. **7, 45**
Jordan, Vernon E. **3, 35**
Khanga, Yelena **6**
King, Bernice **4**
King, Coretta Scott **3, 57**
King, Martin Luther, Jr. **1**
King, Yolanda **6**
Lane, Charles **3**
Lee, Spike **5, 19**
Lee-Smith, Hughie **5, 22**
Lorde, Audre **6**
Mabuza-Suttle, Felicia **43**
Mandela, Nelson **1, 14**
Martin, Louis E. **16**
Mathabane, Mark **5**
Maynard, Robert C. **7**
Mays, Benjamin E. **7**
McDougall, Gay J. **11, 43**
McKay, Claude **6**
Meredith, James H. **11**
Micheaux, Oscar **7**
Moore, Harry T. **29**
Mosley, Walter **5, 25, 68**
Muhammad, Khallid Abdul **10, 31**
Norton, Eleanor Holmes **7**
Page, Clarence **4**
Perkins, Edward **5**
Pitt, David Thomas **10**
Poussaint, Alvin F. **5, 67**
Price, Frederick K.C. **21**
Price, Hugh B. **9, 54**
Robeson, Paul **2**
Robinson, Spottswood W., III **22**
Sampson, Edith S. **4**
Shabazz, Attallah **6**
Sifford, Charlie **4, 49**
Simpson, Carole **6, 30**
Sister Souljah **11**
Sisulu, Sheila Violet Makate **24**
Smith, Anna Deavere **6, 44**
Sowell, Thomas **2**
Spaulding, Charles Clinton **9**
Staples, Brent **8**
Steele, Claude Mason **13**
Taulbert, Clifton Lemoure **19**
Till, Emmett **7**
Tutu, Desmond Mpilo **6, 44**
Tutu, Nontombi Naomi **57**
Tyree, Omar Rashad **21**
Walcott, Derek **5**
Walker, Maggie **17**
Washington, Booker T. **4**

Washington, Harold **6**
Wells-Barnett, Ida B. **8**
Welsing, Frances Cress **5**
West, Cornel **5**
Wideman, John Edgar **5**
Wiley, Ralph **8**
Wilkins, Roger **2**
Wilkins, Roy **4**
Williams, Fannie Barrier **27**
Williams, Gregory **11**
Williams, Hosea Lorenzo **15, 31**
Williams, Patricia **11, 54**
Williams, Walter E. **4**
Wilson, Sunnie **7, 55**
Wright, Richard **5**
Young, Whitney M., Jr. **4**

Radio
Abrahams, Peter **39**
Abu-Jamal, Mumia **15**
Alert, Kool DJ Red **33**
Anderson, Eddie "Rochester" **30**
Banks, William **11**
Bates, Karen Grigsby **40**
Beasley, Phoebe **34**
Blayton, Jesse B., Sr. **55**
Booker, Simeon **23**
Branch, William Blackwell **39**
Crocker, Frankie **29**
Dee, Ruby **8, 50, 68**
Dre, Dr. **10, 14, 30**
Elder, Larry **25**
Fuller, Charles **8**
Gibson, Truman K., Jr. **60**
Goode, Mal **13**
Greene, Petey **65**
Gumbel, Greg **8**
Hamblin, Ken **10**
Haynes, Trudy **44**
Holt, Nora **38**
Hughes, Cathy **27**
Jackson, Hal **41**
Jarret, Vernon D. **42**
Joe, Yolanda **21**
Joyner, Tom **19**
Keyes, Alan L. **11**
Lewis, Delano **7**
Lewis, Ramsey **35, 70**
Ligging, Alfred, III **43**
Love, Ed **58**
Lover, Ed **10**
Ludacris **37, 60**
Madison, Joseph E. **17**
Majors, Jeff **41**
Mickelbury, Penny **28**
Moss, Carlton **17**
Parr, Russ **51**
Pressley, Condace L. **41**
Quivers, Robin **61**
Samara, Noah **15**
Smiley, Rickey **59**
Smiley, Tavis **20, 68**
Smith, Greg **28**
Steinberg, Martha Jean "The Queen" **28**
Taylor, Billy **23**
Tirico, Mike **68**
Whack, Rita Coburn **36**
Williams, Armstrong **29**
Williams, Juan **35**
Williams, Wendy **62**
Woods, Georgie **57**

Yarbrough, Camille **40**

Radio Jamaica
Abrahams, Peter **39**

Radio One Inc.
Hughes, Cathy **27**
Ligging, Alfred, III **43**
Majors, Jeff **41**

Radio-Television News Directors Association
Pressley, Condace L. **41**

Ragtime
Blake, Eubie **29**
Europe, James Reese **10**
Joplin, Scott **6**
Robinson, Reginald R. **53**
Sissle, Noble **29**

Rainbow Coalition
Chappell, Emma **18**
Jackson, Jesse **1, 27**
Jackson, Jesse, Jr. **14, 45**
Moore, Minyon **45**

Rap music
Alert, Kool DJ Red **33**
Baker, Houston A., Jr. **6**
Bambaataa, Afrika **34**
Banner, David **55**
Benjamin, Andre **45**
Black Thought **63**
Blow, Kurtis **31**
Bow Wow **35**
Brown, Foxy **25**
Butts, Calvin O., III **9**
Cee-Lo **70**
Chuck D. **9**
Combs, Sean "Puffy" **17, 43**
Common **31, 63**
Deezer D **53**
DJ Jazzy Jeff **32**
DMX **28, 64**
Dre, Dr. **10, 14, 30**
Dupri, Jermaine **13, 46**
Dyson, Michael Eric **11, 40**
Elliott, Missy **31**
Eve **29**
50 Cent **46**
Flavor Flav **67**
Gotti, Irv **39**
Grae, Jean **51**
Grandmaster Flash **33, 60**
Gray, F. Gary **14, 49**
Hammer, M. C. **20**
Harrell, Andre **9, 30**
Heavy, D **58**
Hill, Lauryn **20, 53**
Ice Cube **8, 30, 60**
Ice-T **6, 31**
Ja Rule **35**
Jay-Z **27, 69**
Jean, Wyclef **20**
Jones, Quincy **8, 30**
Knight, Suge **11, 30**
KRS-One **34**
Lil' Kim **28**
Lil Wayne **66**
Liles, Kevin **42**
Lopes, Lisa "Left Eye" **36**
Lover, Ed **10**
Ludacris **37, 60**
Mase **24**

Master P **21**
MC Lyte **34**
Mos Def **30**
Nelly **32**
Notorious B.I.G. **20**
Ol' Dirty Bastard **52**
O'Neal, Shaquille **8, 30**
OutKast **35**
Queen Latifah **1, 16, 58**
Rhymes, Busta **31**
Run-DMC **31**
Shakur, Afeni **67**
Shakur, Tupac **14**
Simmons, Russell **1, 30**
Sister Souljah **11**
Smith, Will **8, 18, 53**
Snoop Dogg **35**
Timbaland **32**
Tucker, C. Delores **12, 56**
West, Kanye **52**
Yarbrough, Camille **40**
Young Jeezy **63**

Rassemblement Démocratique Africain (African Democratic Rally; RDA)
Houphouët-Boigny, Félix **4, 64**
Touré, Sekou **6**

Rastafarianism
Haile Selassie **7**
Marley, Bob **5**
Marley, Rita **32, 70**
Tosh, Peter **9**

RDA
See Rassemblement Démocratique Africain (African Democratic Rally)

Reader's Choice Award
Holton, Hugh, Jr. **39**

Reading Is Fundamental
Trueheart, William E. **49**

Real estate development
Barden, Don H. **9, 20**
Brooke, Edward **8**
Holmes, Larry **20, 68**
Lane, Vincent **5**
Marshall, Bella **22**
Russell, Herman Jerome **17**
Toote, Gloria E.A. **64**

"Real Men Cook"
Moyo, Karega Kofi **36**

Record producer
Albright, Gerald **23**
Ayers, Roy **16**
Bambaataa, Afrika **34**
Blige, Mary J. **20, 34, 60**
Butler, George, Jr. **70**
Coleman, Ornette **39, 69**
Combs, Sean "Puffy" **17, 43**
de Passe, Suzanne **25**
DJ Jazzy Jeff **32**
Dre, Dr. **10, 14, 30**
Duke, George **21**
Dupri, Jermaine **13, 46**
Edmonds, Kenneth "Babyface" **10, 31**
Elliott, Missy **31**
Gotti, Irv **39**

Hailey, JoJo **22**
Hailey, K-Ci **22**
Hammond, Fred **23**
Hill, Lauryn **20, 53**
Ice Cube **8, 30, 60**
Ja Rule **35**
Jackson, George **19**
Jackson, Michael **19, 53**
Jackson, Randy **40**
Jean, Wyclef **20**
Jerkins, Rodney **31**
Jimmy Jam **13**
Jones, Quincy **8, 30**
Kelly, R. **18, 44, 71**
Lewis, Terry **13**
Liles, Kevin **42**
Marley, Rita **32, 70**
Master P **21**
Mayfield, Curtis **2, 43**
Osborne, Jeffrey **26**
Prince **18, 65**
Queen Latifah **1, 16, 58**
Reid, Antonio "L.A." **28**
Sweat, Keith **19**
Timbaland **32**
Turner, Ike **68**
Vandross, Luther **13, 48, 59**
White, Barry **13, 41**
Williams, Pharrell **47**

Recording executives
Avant, Clarence **19**
Busby, Jheryl **3**
Butler, George, Jr. **70**
Combs, Sean "Puffy" **17, 43**
de Passe, Suzanne **25**
Dupri, Jermaine **13, 46**
Gordy, Berry, Jr. **1**
Harrell, Andre **9, 30**
Jackson, George **19**
Jackson, Randy **40**
Jimmy Jam **13**
Jones, Quincy **8, 30**
Knight, Suge **11, 30**
Lewis, Terry **13**
Liles, Kevin **42**
Massenburg, Kedar **23**
Master P **21**
Mayfield, Curtis **2, 43**
Queen Latifah **1, 16, 58**
Reid, Antonio "L.A." **28**
Rhone, Sylvia **2**
Robinson, Smokey **3, 49**
Simmons, Russell **1, 30**

Reform Party
Foster, Ezola **28**

Reggae
Beenie Man **32**
Blondy, Alpha **30**
Cliff, Jimmy **28**
Griffiths, Marcia **29**
Hammond, Lenn **34**
Johnson, Linton Kwesi **37**
Marley, Bob **5**
Marley, Rita **32, 70**
Marley, Ziggy **41**
Mowatt, Judy **38**
Perry, Ruth **19**
Rhoden, Wayne **70**
Shaggy **31**
Sly & Robbie **34**

Tosh, Peter **9**

Republican National Convention
Allen, Ethel D. **13**
Toote, Gloria E.A. **64**

Republic of New Africa (RNA)
Williams, Robert F. **11**

Resource Associates International
Moyo, Karega Kofi **36**
Moyo, Yvette Jackson **36**

Restaurants
Cain, Herman **15**
Daniels-Carter, Valerie **23**
Hawkins, La-Van **17, 54**
James, Charles H., III **62**
Otis, Clarence, Jr. **55**
Rodriguez, Jimmy **47**
Samuelsson, Marcus **53**
Smith, Barbara **11**
Thompson, Don **56**
Washington, Regynald G. **44**

Restitution Study Group, Inc.
Farmer-Paellmann, Deadria **43**

Revolutionary Party of Tanzania
See Chama cha Mapinduzi

Revolutionary People's Communication Network
Cleaver, Kathleen Neal **29**

Rheedlen Centers for Children and Families
Canada, Geoffrey **23**

Rhode Island School of Design
Prophet, Nancy Elizabeth **42**

Rhodes scholar
Kennedy, Randall **40**

Rhythm and blues/soul music
Ace, Johnny **36**
Aaliyah **30**
Adams, Johnny **39**
Adams, Oleta **18**
Akon **68**
Amerie **52**
Ashanti **37**
Ashford, Nickolas **21**
Austin, Patti **24**
Ayers, Roy **16**
Badu, Erykah **22**
Bailey, Philip **63**
Baker, Anita **21, 48**
Baker, LaVern **26**
Ballard, Hank **41**
Baylor, Helen **36**
Belle, Regina **1, 51**
Bénét, Eric **28**
Berry, Chuck **29**
Beverly, Frankie **25**
Beyoncé **39, 70**
Blige, Mary J. **20, 34, 60**
Brandy **14, 34**
Braxton, Toni **15, 61**
Brooks, Hadda **40**
Brown, Bobby **58**

Brown, Charles **23**
Brown, Clarence Gatemouth **59**
Brown, James **15, 60**
Brown, Oscar, Jr. **53**
Burke, Solomon **31**
Busby, Jheryl **3**
Butler, Jerry **26**
Campbell-Martin, Tisha **8, 42**
Carey, Mariah **32, 53, 69**
Charles, Ray **16, 48**
Ciara **56**
Clinton, George **9**
Cole, Keyshia **63**
Combs, Sean "Puffy" **17, 43**
Cooke, Sam **17**
Cox, Deborah **28**
D'Angelo **27**
David, Craig **31, 53**
Davis, Tyrone **54**
Diddley, Bo **39**
Domino, Fats **20**
Dorsey, Lee **65**
Downing, Will **19**
Dre, Dr. **14, 30**
Dupri, Jermaine **13, 46**
Edmonds, Kenneth "Babyface" **10, 31**
Elliott, Missy **31**
Escobar, Damien **56**
Escobar, Tourie **56**
Evans, Faith **22**
Foxx, Jamie **15, 48**
Franklin, Aretha **11, 44**
Garrett, Sean **57**
Gaye, Marvin **2**
Gaynor, Gloria **36**
Gibson, Tyrese **27, 62**
Gill, Johnny **51**
Ginuwine **35**
Goapele **55**
Gotti, Irv **39**
Gray, Macy **29**
Green, Al **13, 47**
Hailey, JoJo **22**
Hailey, K-Ci **22**
Hamilton, Anthony **61**
Hammer, M. C. **20**
Harris, Corey **39**
Hart, Alvin Youngblood **61**
Hathaway, Donny **18**
Hathaway, Lalah **57**
Hayes, Isaac **20, 58**
Hendryx, Nona **56**
Henry, Clarence "Frogman" **46**
Hall, Aaron **57**
Hill, Lauryn **20, 53**
Holloway, Brenda **65**
Houston, Cissy **20**
Houston, Whitney **7**
Hyman, Phyllis **19**
India.Arie **34**
Isley, Ronald **25, 56**
Ja Rule **35**
Jackson, Janet **6, 30, 68**
Jackson, Michael **19, 53**
Jackson, Millie **25**
Jaheim **58**
Jamelia **51**
James, Etta **13, 52**
James, Rick **17**
Jarreau, Al **21, 65**
Jean, Wyclef **20**
Jennings, Lyfe **56, 69**

Johnson, Robert **2**
Jones, Donell **29**
Jones, Quincy **8, 30**
Jordan, Montell **23**
Kelly, R. **18, 44, 71**
Kem **47**
Kendricks, Eddie **22**
Keys, Alicia **32, 68**
Knight, Gladys **16, 66**
LaBelle, Patti **13, 30**
Larrieux, Amel **63**
Lattimore, Kenny **35**
Legend, John **67**
Levert, Eddie **70**
Levert, Gerald **22, 59**
Little Richard **15**
Lopes, Lisa "Left Eye" **36**
Luckett, Letoya **61**
Mario **71**
Massenburg, Kedar **23**
Master P **21**
Maxwell **20**
Mayfield, Curtis **2, 43**
McCoo, Marilyn **53**
McKnight, Brian **18, 34**
Miles, Buddy **69**
Monica **21**
Moore, Chante **26**
Moore, Melba **21**
Musiq **37**
Mya **35**
Nash, Johnny **40**
Ndegéocello, Me'Shell **15**
Ne-Yo **65**
Neale, Haydain **52**
Neville, Aaron **21**
Notorious B.I.G. **20**
Otis, Clyde **67**
Pendergrass, Teddy **22**
Preston, Billy **39, 59**
Price, Kelly **23**
Prince **18, 65**
Record, Eugene **60**
Redding, Otis **16**
Reed, A. C. **36**
Richie, Lionel **27, 65**
Rihanna **65**
Riperton, Minnie **32**
Robinson, Smokey **3, 49**
Ross, Diana **8, 27**
Russell, Brenda **52**
Sade **15**
Sample, Joe **51**
Scott, Jill **29**
Scott, "Little" Jimmy **48**
Siji **56**
Simpson, Valerie **21**
Sisqo **30**
Sledge, Percy **39**
Sparks, Jordin **66**
Staples, Mavis **50**
Staples, "Pops" **32**
Staton, Candi **27**
Steinberg, Martha Jean "The Queen" **28**
Stone, Angie **31**
Studdard, Ruben **46**
The Supremes **33**
Sweat, Keith **19**
Tamia **24, 55**
The Temptations **33**
Terrell, Tammi **32**
Thomas, Irma **29**

Thomas, Rufus **20**
TLC **34**
Tresvant, Ralph **57**
Turner, Ike **68**
Turner, Tina **6, 27**
Usher **23, 56**
Valentino, Bobby **62**
Vandross, Luther **13, 48, 59**
West, Kanye **52**
Watley, Jody **54**
Watts, Reggie **52**
Wells, Mary **28**
White, Barry **13, 41**
Williams, Vanessa L. **4, 17**
Wilson, Cassandra **16**
Wilson, Mary **28**
Wilson, Charlie **31**
Wilson, Nancy **10**
Withers, Bill **61**
Wonder, Stevie **11, 53**
Womack, Bobby **60**

Richmond city government
Marsh, Henry **32**

RNA
See Republic of New Africa

Roberts Companies, The
Roberts, Mike **57**

Roc-A-Fella Films
Dash, Damon **31**

Roc-A-Fella Records
Dash, Damon **31**
Jay-Z **27, 69**

Roc-A-Wear
Dash, Damon **31**

Rock and Roll Hall of Fame
Ballard, Hank **41**
Bland, Bobby "Blue" **36**
Brown, Charles **23**
Diddley, Bo **39**
Franklin, Aretha **11, 44**
Holland-Dozier-Holland **36**
Hooker, John Lee **30**
Isley, Ronald **25, 56**
Jamerson, James **59**
James, Etta **13, 52**
Johnson, Johnnie **56**
Knight, Gladys **16, 66**
Mayfield, Curtis **2, 43**
Steinberg, Martha Jean "The Queen" **28**
Toussaint, Allen **60**
Turner, Ike **68**
Turner, Tina **6, 27**
Wilson, Jackie **60**
Wilson, Mary **28**
Wonder, Stevie **11, 53**

Rock music
Ballard, Hank **41**
Berry, Chuck **29**
Clemons, Clarence **41**
Clinton, George **9**
Diddley, Bo **39**
Domino, Fats **20**
Edwards, Esther Gordy **43**
Glover, Corey **34**
Hendrix, Jimi **10**
Ice-T **6, 31**

Johnson, Johnnie **56**
Kravitz, Lenny **10, 34**
Little Richard **15**
Lymon, Frankie **22**
Mayfield, Curtis **2, 43**
Miles, Buddy **69**
Preston, Billy **39, 59**
Prince **18, 65**
Reid, Vernon **34**
Run-DMC **31**
Stew **69**
Tait, Michael **57**
Tamar-kali **63**
Tinsley, Boyd **50**
Toussaint, Allen **60**
Turner, Ike **68**
Turner, Tina **6, 27**
will.i.am **64**
Wilson, Jackie **60**

Rockefeller Foundation
Price, Hugh B. **9, 54**

Rockets
Williams, O. S. **13**

Rodeo
Nash, Johnny **40**
Pickett, Bill **11**
Sampson, Charles **13**
Whitfield, Fred **23**

Roman Catholic Church
Akpan, Uwem **70**
Arinze, Francis Cardinal **19**
Aristide, Jean-Bertrand **6, 45**
Clements, George **2**
DeLille, Henriette **30**
Fabre, Shelton **71**
Gantin, Bernardin **70**
Gregory, Wilton D. **37**
Guy, Rosa **5**
Healy, James Augustine **30**
Jones, Alex **64**
Marino, Eugene Antonio **30**
Otunga, Maurice Michael **55**
Rugambwa, Laurean **20**
Senghor, Augustin Diamacoune **66**
Stallings, George A., Jr. **6**

Romance fiction
Bunkley, Anita Richmond **39**
Hill, Donna **32**

Rounder Records
Harris, Corey **39**

Royal Ballet
Jackson, Isaiah **3**

Royalty
Christophe, Henri **9**
Ka Dinizulu, Mcwayizeni **29**
Mswati III **56**
Mutebi, Ronald **25**

RPT
See Togolese People's Rally

Ruff Ryders Records
Eve **29**

Rugby
Mundine, Anthony **56**

Rush Artists Management Co.
Simmons, Russell **1, 30**

Russell-McCloud and Associates
Russell-McCloud, Patricia A. **17**

Rutgers University
Davis, George **36**
Gibson, Donald Bernard **40**

Rwandan government
Kagame, Paul **54**

Rwandese Patriotic Front
Kagame, Paul **54**

SAA
See Syndicat Agricole Africain

SACC
See South African Council of Churches

Sacramento Kings basketball team
Russell, Bill **8**
Webber, Chris **15, 30, 59**

Sacramento Monarchs basketball team
Griffith, Yolanda **25**

SADCC
See Southern African Development Coordination Conference

Sailing
Pinckney, Bill **42**

St. Kitts and Nevis government
Douglas, Denzil Llewellyn **53**

St. Louis Blues hockey team
Brathwaite, Fred **35**
Mayers, Jamal **39**

St. Louis Browns baseball team
Brown, Willard **36**
Paige, Satchel **7**

St. Louis Cardinals baseball team
Baylor, Don **6**
Bonds, Bobby **43**
Brock, Lou **18**
Flood, Curt **10**
Gibson, Bob **33**
Lankford, Ray **23**

St. Louis city government
Bosley, Freeman, Jr. **7**
Harmon, Clarence **26**

St. Louis Giants baseball team
Charleston, Oscar **39**

St. Louis Hawks basketball team
See Atlanta Hawks basketball team

St. Louis Rams football team
Bruce, Isaac **26**
Faulk, Marshall **35**

Pace, Orlando **21**

St. Louis Stars baseball team
Bell, James "Cool Papa" **36**

St. Louis' Twenty-Third Street Theater
Leggs, Kingsley **62**

Sainte Beuve Prize
Beti, Mongo **36**

Salvation Army
Gaither, Israel L. **65**

SAMM
See Stopping AIDS Is My Mission

Sammy Davis Jr. National Liver Institute University Hospital
Leevy, Carrol M. **42**

San Antonio Spurs basketball team
Duncan, Tim **20**
Elliott, Sean **26**
Lucas, John **7**
Mohammed, Nazr **64**
Robinson, David **24**

San Diego Chargers football team
Barnes, Ernie **16**
Lofton, James **42**
Tomlinson, LaDainian **65**

San Diego Conquistadors
Chamberlain, Wilt **18, 47**

San Diego Gulls hockey team
O'Ree, Willie **5**

San Diego Hawks hockey team
O'Ree, Willie **5**

San Diego Padres baseball team
Carter, Joe **30**
Gwynn, Tony **18**
McGriff, Fred **24**
Sheffield, Gary **16**
Winfield, Dave **5**

San Francisco 49ers football team
Edwards, Harry **2**
Green, Dennis **5, 45**
Lott, Ronnie **9**
Rice, Jerry **5, 55**
Simpson, O. J. **15**
Washington, Gene **63**

San Francisco Giants baseball team
Baker, Dusty **8**
Bonds, Barry **6, 34, 63**
Bonds, Bobby **43**
Carter, Joe **30**
Mays, Willie **3**
Morgan, Joe Leonard **9**
Robinson, Frank **9**
Strawberry, Darryl **22**

San Francisco Opera
Mitchell, Leona **42**

San Francisco public schools
Coleman, William F., III **61**

Sankofa Film and Video
Blackwood, Maureen **37**
Julien, Isaac **3**

Sankofa Video and Bookstore
Gerima, Haile **38**

Saturday Night Live
Meadows, Tim **30**
Morgan, Tracy **61**
Morris, Garrett **31**
Murphy, Eddie **4, 20, 61**
Rock, Chris **3, 22, 66**
Rudolph, Maya **46**
Thompson, Kenan **52**

Savoy Ballroom
Johnson, Buddy **36**

Saxophone
Adderley, Julian "Cannonball" **30**
Albright, Gerald **23**
Bechet, Sidney **18**
Clemons, Clarence **41**
Coltrane, John **19**
Coltrane, Ravi **71**
Golson, Benny **37**
Gordon, Dexter **25**
Griffin, Johnny **71**
Hawkins, Coleman **9**
Jacquet, Illinois **49**
Kay, Ulyssess **37**
Kenyatta, Robin **54**
Parker, Charlie **20**
Redman, Joshua **30**
Rollins, Sonny **37**
Sanders, Pharoah **64**
Washington, Grover, Jr. **17, 44**
Waters, Benny **26**
Whalum, Kirk **37, 64**
York, Vincent **40**
Young, Lester **37**

Schomburg Center for Research in Black Culture
Andrews, Bert **13**
Dodson, Howard, Jr. **7, 52**
Hutson, Jean Blackwell **16**
Morrison, Sam **50**
Reddick, Lawrence Dunbar **20**
Schomburg, Arthur Alfonso **9**

School desegregation
Fortune, T. Thomas **6**
Hamer, Fannie Lou **6**
Hobson, Julius W. **44**

Science fiction
Barnes, Steven **54**
Bell, Derrick **6**
Butler, Octavia **8, 43, 58**
Delany, Samuel R., Jr. **9**

SCLC
See Southern Christian Leadership Conference

Score One for Kids
Cherry, Deron **40**

Scotland Yard
Griffin, Bessie Blout **43**

Screen Actors Guild
Dixon, Ivan **69**
Fields, Kim **36**

Howard, Sherri **36**
Lewis, Emmanuel **36**
Poitier, Sidney **11, 36**

Screenplay writing
Akil, Mara Brock **60**
Brown, Cecil M. **46**
Campbell-Martin, Tisha **8, 42**
Chong, Rae Dawn **62**
Davis, Thulani **61**
Elder, Lonne, III **38**
Fisher, Antwone **40**
Greaves, William **38**
Ice Cube **8, 30, 60**
Jones, Orlando **30**
Martin, Darnell **43**
Nissel, Angela **42**
Prince-Bythewood, Gina **31**
Rhimes, Shonda Lynn **67**
Ridley, John **69**
Robinson, Matt **69**
Singleton, John **2, 30**

Sculpture
Allen, Tina **22**
Amos, Emma **63**
Bailey, Radcliffe **19**
Barthe, Richmond **15**
Biggers, John **20, 33**
Biggers, Sanford **62**
Brown, Donald **19**
Burke, Selma **16**
Catlett, Elizabeth **2**
Chase-Riboud, Barbara **20, 46**
Cortor, Eldzier **42**
Dwight, Edward **65**
Edwards, Melvin **22**
Fuller, Meta Vaux Warrick **27**
Guyton, Tyree **9**
Hammons, David **69**
Hathaway, Isaac Scott **33**
Hunt, Richard **6**
Lewis, Edmonia **10**
Lewis, Samella **25**
Manley, Edna **26**
Marshall, Kerry James **59**
McCullough, Geraldine **58**
McGee, Charles **10**
Moody, Ronald **30**
Perkins, Marion **38**
Prophet, Nancy Elizabeth **42**
Puryear, Martin **42**
Ringgold, Faith **4**
Saar, Alison **16**
Savage, Augusta **12**
Scott, John T. **65**
Shabazz, Attallah **6**
Simmons, Gary **58**
Stout, Renee **63**
Washington, James, Jr. **38**

Sean John clothing line
Combs, Sean "Puffy" **17, 43**

Seattle city government
Rice, Norm **8**

Seattle Mariners baseball team
Griffey, Ken, Jr. **12**

Seattle Supersonics basketball team
Bickerstaff, Bernie **21**
Lucas, John **7**

Russell, Bill **8**
Silas, Paul **24**
Wilkens, Lenny **11**

Second District Education and Policy Foundation
Burke, Yvonne Braithwaite **42**

Second Republic (Nigeria)
Obasanjo, Olusegun **5**

Seismology
Person, Waverly **9, 51**

Selma, Alabama, city government
Perkins, James, Jr. **55**

Senate Confirmation Hearings
Ogletree, Charles, Jr. **12, 47**

Senate Judiciary Subcommittee on the Consitution
Hageman, Hans **36**

Senegalese government
Senghor, Léopold Sédar **66**
Wade, Abdoulaye **66**

Sesame Street
Byrd, Eugene **64**
Clash, Kevin **14**
Glover, Savion **14**
Long, Loretta **58**
Orman, Roscoe **55**
Robinson, Matt **69**

Sexual harassment
Gomez-Preston, Cheryl **9**
Hill, Anita **5, 65**
Thomas, Clarence **2, 39, 65**

Share
Auguste, Arnold A. **47**

Sheila Bridges Design Inc.
Bridges, Sheila **36**

Shell Oil Company
Mays, Leslie A. **41**

Shrine of the Black Madonna
Agyeman, Jaramogi Abebe **10, 63**

Sickle cell anemia
Edwards, Willarda V. **59**
Pace, Betty **59**
Satcher, David **7, 57**

Sierra Leone People's Party (SLPP)
Kabbah, Ahmad Tejan **23**

Silicon Graphics Incorporated
Coleman, Ken **57**
Hannah, Marc **10**

Siméus Foods International
Siméus, Dumas M. **25**

Sisters of the Holy Family
DeLille, Henriette **30**

Skateboarding
Williams, Stevie **71**

Sketches
Crite, Alan Rohan **29**
Sallee, Charles **38**

Skiing
Horton, Andre **33**
Horton, Suki **33**

Skillman Foundation
Goss, Carol A. **55**

Slavery
Asante, Molefi Kete **3**
Bennett, Lerone, Jr. **5**
Bibb, Henry and Mary **54**
Blackshear, Leonard **52**
Blassingame, John Wesley **40**
Chase-Riboud, Barbara **20, 46**
Cooper, Anna Julia **20**
Douglas, Aaron **7**
Du Bois, W. E. B. **3**
Dunbar, Paul Laurence **8**
Farmer-Paellmann, Deadria **43**
Gaines, Ernest J. **7**
Haley, Alex **4**
Harper, Frances Ellen Watkins **11**
Huggins, Nathan Irvin **52**
Johnson, Charles **1**
Jones, Edward P. **43, 67**
Morrison, Toni **2, 15**
Muhammad, Elijah **4**
Patterson, Orlando **4**
Pleasant, Mary Ellen **9**
Stephens, Charlotte Andrews **14**
Stewart, Maria W. Miller **19**
Tancil, Gladys Quander **59**
Taylor, Susie King **13**
Tubman, Harriet **9**
X, Malcolm **1**

Small Business Association Hall of Fame
Steward, David L. **36**

Smart Books
Pinkett Smith, Jada **10, 41**

Smith College
Mayhew, Richard **39**
Simmons, Ruth **13, 38**

SNCC
See Student Nonviolent Coordinating Committee

Soccer
Adu, Freddy **67**
Anderson, Viv **58**
Barnes, John **53**
Beasley, Jamar **29**
Crooks, Garth **53**
dos Santos, Manuel Francisco **65**
Henry, Thierry **66**
Jones, Cobi N'Gai **18**
Kanouté, Fred **68**
Milla, Roger **2**
Nakhid, David **25**
Onyewu, Oguchi **60**
Pelé **7**
Regis, Cyrille **51**
Ronaldinho **69**
Scurry, Briana **27**
Weah, George **58**

Social disorganization theory
Frazier, E. Franklin **10**

Social science
Berry, Mary Frances **7**
Black, Albert **51**
Bobo, Lawrence **60**
Bunche, Ralph J. **5**
Cayton, Horace **26**
Clark, Kenneth B. **5, 52**
Cobbs, Price M. **9**
Collins, Patricia Hill **67**
Frazier, E. Franklin **10**
George, Zelma Watson **42**
Hare, Nathan **44**
Harris, Eddy L. **18**
Haynes, George Edmund **8**
Ladner, Joyce A. **42**
Lawrence-Lightfoot, Sara **10**
Marable, Manning **10**
Steele, Claude Mason **13**
Williams, David Rudyard **50**
Woodson, Robert L. **10**

Social Service Auxiliary
Mossell, Gertrude Bustill **40**

Social work
Auguste, Rose-Anne **13**
Berry, Bertice **8, 55**
Berrysmith, Don Reginald **49**
Brown, Cora **33**
Canada, Geoffrey **23**
Dunham, Katherine **4, 59**
Fields, C. Virginia **25**
Finner-Williams, Paris Michele **62**
Hale, Clara **16**
Hale, Lorraine **8**
Harris, Alice **7**
Haynes, George Edmund **8**
Jackson, Judith D. **57**
Jackson, Mae **57**
King, Barbara **22**
Lewis, Thomas **19**
Little, Robert L. **2**
Robinson, Rachel **16**
Sears, Stephanie **53**
Smith, Damu **54**
Vaughn, Viola **70**
Waddles, Charleszetta "Mother" **10, 49**
Walker, Bernita Ruth **53**
Wallace, Joaquin **49**
Wells, Henrietta Bell **69**
White-Hammond, Gloria **61**
Williams, Fannie Barrier **27**
Thrower, Willie **35**
Young, Whitney M., Jr. **4**

Socialist Party of Senegal
Diouf, Abdou **3**

Soft Sheen Products
Gardner, Edward G. **45**

Soledad Brothers
Jackson, George **14**

Soul City, NC
McKissick, Floyd B. **3**

Soul Train
Baylor, Helen **36**
Cornelius, Don **4**
D'Angelo **27**
Lil' Kim **28**
Winans, CeCe **14, 43**

Source music awards
Nelly **32**

South African Communist Party
Hani, Chris **6**
Mhlaba, Raymond **55**

South African Council of Churches (SACC)
Tutu, Desmond Mpilo **6, 44**

South African Defence Force (SADF)
Nujoma, Samuel **10**

South African government
Mhlaba, Raymond **55**
Sisulu, Walter **47**
Zuma, Nkosazana Dlamini **34**

South African literature
Abrahams, Peter **39**
Brutus, Dennis **38**
Head, Bessie **28**
Mathabane, Mark **5**
Mofolo, Thomas **37**
Mphalele, Es'kia **40**

South African Students' Organization
Biko, Steven **4**

South Carolina state government
Cardozo, Francis L. **33**

South West African People's Organization (SWAPO)
Nujoma, Samuel **10**

Southeastern University
Jarvis, Charlene Drew **21**

Southern African Development Community (SADC)
Mbuende, Kaire **12**

Southern African Development Coordination Conference (SADCC)
Masire, Quett **5**
Numjoma, Samuel **10**

Southern African Project
McDougall, Gay J. **11, 43**

Southern Christian Leadership Conference (SCLC)
Abernathy, Ralph **1**
Angelou, Maya **1, 15**
Baker, Ella **5**
Brooks, Tyrone **59**
Chavis, Benjamin **6**
Dee, Ruby **8, 50, 68**
Fauntroy, Walter E. **11**
Hooks, Benjamin L. **2**
Jackson, Jesse **1, 27**
Jones, William A., Jr. **61**
King, Martin Luther, Jr. **1**
King, Martin Luther, III **20**
Lowery, Joseph **2**
Moses, Robert Parris **11**
Rustin, Bayard **4**
Shuttlesworth, Fred **47**
Williams, Hosea Lorenzo **15, 31**

Young, Andrew **3, 48**

Southern Syncopated Orchestra
Cook, Will Marion **40**

Space shuttle
Anderson, Michael **40**
Bluford, Guy **2, 35**
Bolden, Charles F., Jr. **7**
Gregory, Frederick **8, 51**
Jemison, Mae C. **1, 35**
McNair, Ronald **3, 58**

Special Olympics
Clairborne, Loretta **34**

Spectroscopy
Quarterman, Lloyd Albert **4**

Speedskating
Davis, Shani **58**

Spelman College
Cobb, William Jelani **59**
Cole, Johnnetta B. **5, 43**
Falconer, Etta Zuber **59**
Price, Glenda **22**
Simmons, Ruth **13, 38**
Tatum, Beverly Daniel **42**
Wade-Gayles, Gloria Jean **41**

Sphinx Organization
Dworkin, Aaron P. **52**

Spingarn medal
Aaron, Hank **5**
Ailey, Alvin **8**
Anderson, Marian **2, 33**
Angelou, Maya **1, 15**
Bates, Daisy **13**
Bethune, Mary McLeod **4**
Bradley, Thomas **2, 20**
Brooke, Edward **8**
Bunche, Ralph J. **5**
Carver, George Washington **4**
Chesnutt, Charles **29**
Clark, Kenneth B. **5, 52**
Cosby, Bill **7, 26, 59**
Davis, Sammy, Jr. **18**
Drew, Charles Richard **7**
Du Bois, W. E. B. **3**
Ellington, Duke **5**
Evers, Medgar **3**
Franklin, John Hope **5**
Grimké, Archibald H. **9**
Haley, Alex **4**
Hastie, William H. **8**
Hayes, Roland **4**
Height, Dorothy I. **2, 23**
Higginbotham, A. Leon, Jr. **13, 25**
Hinton, William Augustus **8**
Hooks, Benjamin L. **2**
Horne, Lena **5**
Houston, Charles Hamilton **4**
Hughes, Langston **4**
Jackson, Jesse **1, 27**
Johnson, James Weldon **5**
Johnson, John H. **3, 54**
Jordan, Barbara **4**
Julian, Percy Lavon **6**
Just, Ernest Everett **3**
Keith, Damon **16**
King, Martin Luther, Jr. **1**
Lawless, Theodore K. **8**

Lawrence, Jacob **4**
Logan, Rayford **40**
Marshall, Thurgood **1, 44**
Mays, Benjamin E. **7**
Moore, Harry T. **29**
Parks, Gordon **1, 35, 58**
Parks, Rosa **1, 35, 56**
Powell, Colin **1, 28**
Price, Leontyne **1**
Randolph, A. Philip **3**
Robeson, Paul **2**
Robinson, Jackie **6**
Staupers, Mabel K. **7**
Sullivan, Leon H. **3, 30**
Weaver, Robert C. **8, 46**
White, Walter F. **4**
Wilder, L. Douglas **3, 48**
Wilkins, Roy **4**
Williams, Paul R. **9**
Woodson, Carter G. **2**
Wright, Louis Tompkins **4**
Wright, Richard **5**
Young, Andrew **3, 48**
Young, Coleman **1, 20**

Spiral Group
Mayhew, Richard **39**

Spirituals
Anderson, Marian **2, 33**
Carr, Kurt **56**
Hayes, Roland **4**
Jackson, Mahalia **5**
Joyner, Matilda Sissieretta **15**
Norman, Jessye **5**
Reese, Della **6, 20**
Robeson, Paul **2**
Williams, Denise **40**

Sports administration
Fuller, Vivian **33**
Kerry, Leon G. **46**
Lee, Bertram M., Sr. **46**
Mills, Steve **47**
Phillips, Teresa L. **42**
Randolph, Willie **53**

Sports agent
Holland, Kimberly N. **62**

Sports psychology
Edwards, Harry **2**

Stanford University
Bobo, Lawrence **60**
Rice, Condoleezza **3, 28**
Washington, Gene **63**
Willingham, Tyrone **43**

Starcom
McCann, Renetta **44**

State University of New York System
Ballard, Allen Butler, Jr. **40**
Baraka, Amiri **1, 38**
Wharton, Clifton R., Jr. **7**

Stay Fit Plus
Richardson, Donna **39**

Stellar Awards
Baylor, Helen **36**

Stonewall 25
Norman, Pat **10**

Stop the Violence Movement
KRS-One **34**
MC Lyte **34**

Stopping AIDS Is My Mission (SAMM)
Cargill, Victoria A. **43**

Storytelling
Baker, Augusta **38**
Bennett, Louise **69**

Structural Readjustment Program
Babangida, Ibrahim **4**

Student Nonviolent Coordinating Committee (SNCC)
Al-Amin, Jamil Abdullah **6**
Anderson, William G(ilchrist), D.O. **57**
Baker, Ella **5**
Barry, Marion S. **7, 44**
Blackwell, Unita **17**
Bond, Julian **2, 35**
Carmichael, Stokely **5, 26**
Clark, Septima **7**
Crouch, Stanley **11**
Davis, Angela **5**
Forman, James **7, 51**
Hamer, Fannie Lou **6**
Holland, Endesha Ida Mae **3, 57**
Lester, Julius **9**
Lewis, John **2, 46**
Moses, Robert Parris **11**
Norton, Eleanor Holmes **7**
Poussaint, Alvin F. **5, 67**
Reagon, Bernice Johnson **7**
Touré, Askia (Muhammad Abu Bakr el) **47**

Subway rescue
Autrey, Wesley **68**

Sugarfoots
El Wilson, Barbara **35**

Sun Microsystems
Tademy, Lalita **36**

Sundance Film Festival
Harris, Leslie **6**

Sunni Muslim
Muhammed, W. Deen **27**

Sunny Alade Records
Ade, King Sunny **41**

Supreme Court
See U.S. Supreme Court

Supreme Court of Haiti
Pascal-Trouillot, Ertha **3**

Surfing
Corley, Tony **62**

Surgeon General of the State of Michigan
Wisdom, Kimberlydawn **57**

Surrealism
Ellison, Ralph **7**
Lee-Smith, Hughie **5, 22**

SWAPO
See South West African People's Organization

Swaziland government
Mswati III **56**

Sweet Honey in the Rock
Reagon, Bernice Johnson **7**

Sylvia's Restaurant
Washington, Regynald G. **44**
Woods, Sylvia **34**

Syndicat Agricole Africain (SAA)
Houphouët-Boigny, Félix **4, 64**

Synthetic chemistry
Julian, Percy Lavon **6**

T. D. Jakes Ministry
Jakes, Thomas "T.D." **17, 43**

Talk Soup
Tyler, Aisha N. **36**

Talladega College
Archie-Hudson, Marguerite **44**

Tampa Bay Buccaneers football team
Barber, Ronde **41**
Brooks, Derrick **43**
Dungy, Tony **17, 42, 59**
Sapp, Warren **38**
Williams, Doug **22**

Tanga Consultative Congress (Tanzania)
Nujoma, Samuel **10**

Tanganyikan African National Union (TANU)
Nyerere, Julius **5**

TANU
See Tanganyikan African National Union

Tanzanian African National Union (TANU)
See Tanganyikan African National Union

Tap dancing
Atkins, Cholly **40**
Bates, Peg Leg **14**
Glover, Savion **14**
Hines, Gregory **1, 42**
Robinson, LaVaughn **69**
Sims, Howard "Sandman" **48**
Slyde, Jimmy **70**
Walker, Dianne **57**

TBS
See Turner Broadcasting System

Teacher of the Year Award
Draper, Sharon Mills **16, 43**
Oliver, Kimberly **60**

Teachers Insurance and Annuity Association and the College Retirement Equities Fund (TIAA-CREF)
Wharton, Clifton R., Jr. **7**

Teaching
Adams-Ender, Clara **40**
Alexander, Margaret Walker **22**

Amadi, Elechi **40**
Archie-Hudson, Marguerite **44**
Aubert, Alvin **41**
Baiocchi, Regina Harris **41**
Ballard, Allen Butler, Jr. **40**
Bibb, Henry and Mary **54**
Blassingame, John Wesley **40**
Branch, William Blackwell **39**
Brawley, Benjamin **44**
Brown, Uzee **42**
Brown, Willa **40**
Bryan, Ashley F. **41**
Campbell, Mary Schmidt **43**
Cardozo, Francis L. **33**
Carruthers, George R. **40**
Carter, Joye Maureen **41**
Chenault, John **40**
Cheney-Coker, Syl **43**
Clarke, John Henrik **20**
Clemmons, Reginal G. **41**
Cobb, Jewel Plummer **42**
Cobb, W. Montague **39**
Cole, Johnnetta B. **5, 43**
Colescott, Robert **69**
Collins, Patricia Hill **67**
Cook, Mercer **40**
Cooper Cafritz, Peggy **43**
Cortez, Jayne **43**
Cortor, Eldzier **42**
Cotter, Joseph Seamon, Sr. **40**
Davis, Arthur P. **41**
Davis, Gary **41**
De Veaux, Alexis **44**
Dennard, Brazeal **37**
Draper, Sharon Mills **16, 43**
Drummond, William J. **40**
Dumas, Henry **41**
Dunnigan, Alice Allison **41**
Dymally, Mervyn **42**
Early, Gerald **15**
Falconer, Etta Zuber **59**
Feelings, Muriel **44**
Figueroa, John J. **40**
Fletcher, Bill, Jr. **41**
Ford, Nick Aaron **44**
Forrest, Leon **44**
Fuller, A. Oveta **43**
Fuller, Arthur **27**
Fuller, Howard L. **37**
Gates, Sylvester James, Jr. **15**
Gayle, Addison, Jr. **41**
George, Zelma Watson **42**
Gibson, Donald Bernard **40**
Gill, Gerald **69**
Hall, Arthur **39**
Hammonds, Evelynn **69**
Harding, Vincent **67**
Hare, Nathan **44**
Harris, Barry **68**
Harvey, William R. **42**
Henries, A. Doris Banks **44**
Hill, Errol **40**
Hill, Leslie Pinckney **44**
Horne, Frank **44**
Humphries, Frederick **20**
Imes, Elmer Samuel **39**
Jackson, Fred James **25**
Jarret, Vernon D. **42**
Jarvis, Erich **67**
Kennedy, Randall **40**
Ladner, Joyce A. **42**
Leevy, Carrol M. **42**
Lewis, Norman **39**
Lindsey, Tommie **51**
Logan, Rayford W. **40**
Maathai, Wangari **43**
McCullough, Geraldine **58**
Mitchell, Parren J. **42, 66**
Moore, Harry T. **29**
Mphalele, Es'kia **40**
Naylor, Gloria **10, 42**
Norman, Maidie **20**
Oliver, Kimberly **60**
Owens, Helen **48**
Palmer, Everard **37**
Patterson, Mary Jane **54**
Peters, Margaret and Matilda **43**
Player, Willa B. **43**
Prophet, Nancy Elizabeth **42**
Puryear, Martin **42**
Ray, Charlotte E. **60**
Redmond, Eugene **23**
Reid, Senghor **55**
Ross-Lee, Barbara **67**
Simpson-Hoffman, N'kenge **52**
Smith, Anna Deavere **6, 44**
Smith, John L. **22**
Tatum, Beverly Daniel **42**
Tillis, Frederick **40**
Tutu, Nontombi Naomi **57**
Tyson, Andre **40**
Wambugu, Florence **42**
Watson, Diane **41**
Wells, Henrietta Bell **69**
Wilkens, J. Ernest, Jr. **43**
Yancy, Dorothy Cowser **42**
Yarbrough, Camille **40**
York, Vincent **40**

Techno music
Atkins, Juan **50**
Craig, Carl **31, 71**
May, Derrick **41**

Technology Access Foundation
Millines Dziko, Trish **28**

TEF
See Theological Education Fund

Telecommunications
Gordon, Bruce S. **41, 53**
Ibrahim, Mo **67**
Irvin, Vernon **65**
Wilkins, Ray **47**

Telemat Incorporated
Bynoe, Peter C. B. **40**

Television
Akil, Mara Brock **60**
Alexander, Khandi **43**
Anderson, Eddie "Rochester" **30**
Arkadie, Kevin **17**
Arnold, Tichina **63**
Banks, Tyra **11, 50**
Barclay, Paris **37**
Barrino, Fantasia **53**
Beach, Michael **26**
Bentley, Lamont **53**
Blacque, Taurean **58**
Blake, Asha **26**
Bonet, Lisa **58**
Bowser, Yvette Lee **17**
Brady, Wayne **32, 71**
Branch, William Blackwell **39**
Bridges, Todd **37**
Brooks, Golden **62**
Brooks, Hadda **40**
Brooks, Mehcad **62**
Brown, Bobby **58**
Brown, Joe **29**
Brown, Vivian **27**
Burnett, Charles **16, 68**
Carson, Lisa Nicole **21**
Carter, Nell **39**
Cash, Rosalind **28**
Cedric the Entertainer **29, 60**
Cheadle, Don **19, 52**
Coleman, Gary **35**
Corbi, Lana **42**
Cosby, Bill **7, 26, 59**
Creagh, Milton **27**
Curtis-Hall, Vondie **17**
Davis, Viola **34**
de Passe, Suzanne **25**
Deezer D **53**
Diggs, Taye **25, 63**
Dourdan, Gary **37**
Dungey, Merrin **62**
Earthquake **55**
Elba, Idris **49**
Elder, Larry **25**
Ephriam, Mablean **29**
Eubanks, Kevin **15**
Evans, Harry **25**
Faison, Donald **50**
Falana, Lola **42**
Fields, Kim **36**
Flavor Flav **67**
Fox, Rick **27**
Frazier, Kevin **58**
Freeman, Yvette **27**
Givens, Robin **4, 25, 58**
Gray, Willie **46**
Greely, M. Gasby **27**
Greene, Petey **65**
Grier, David Alan **28**
Hall, Arsenio **58**
Hardison, Kadeem **22**
Harewood, David **52**
Hatchett, Glenda **32**
Haynes, Trudy **44**
Haysbert, Dennis **42**
Hemsley, Sherman **19**
Henriques, Julian **37**
Hill, Lauryn **20, 53**
Houston, Whitney **7, 28**
Hughley, D. L. **23**
Hyman, Earle **25**
Jackson, George **19**
Jackson, Randy **40**
Jackson, Tom **70**
Jarret, Vernon D. **42**
Joe, Yolanda **21**
Johnson, Rodney Van **28**
Jones, Bobby **20**
Kodjoe, Boris **34**
Lathan, Sanaa **27**
Lesure, James **64**
Lewis, Emmanuel **36**
Long, Loretta **58**
Lumbly, Carl **47**
Mabuza-Suttle, Felicia **43**
Mac, Bernie **29, 61**
Mahorn, Rick **60**
Manigault-Stallworth, Omarosa **69**
Marsalis, Branford **34**
Martin, Helen **31**
Martin, Jesse L. **31**
Mathis, Greg **26**
McCrary Anthony, Crystal **70**
McFarland, Roland **49**
McGlowan, Angela **64**
McKenzie, Vashti M. **29**
McKinney, Nina Mae **40**
Meadows, Tim **30**
Mercado-Valdes, Frank **43**
Merkerson, S. Epatha **47**
Michele, Michael **31**
Mitchell, Brian Stokes **21**
Mitchell, Russ **21**
Moss, Carlton **16**
Nash, Johnny **40**
Nash, Niecy **66**
Neal, Elise **29**
Neville, Arthel **53**
Nissel, Angela **42**
Norman, Christina **47**
Orman, Roscoe **55**
Palmer, Keke **68**
Parker, Nicole Ari **52**
Perry, Tyler **40, 54**
Phifer, Mekhi **25**
Pickens, James, Jr. **59**
Pitts, Byron **71**
Pratt, Kyla **57**
Premice, Josephine **41**
Price, Frederick K. C. **21**
Quarles, Norma **25**
Ray, Gene Anthony **47**
Reddick, Lance **52**
Reynolds, Star Jones **10, 27, 61**
Rhimes, Shonda Lynn **67**
Richards, Beah **30**
Richardson, Salli **68**
Ridley, John **69**
Roberts, Deborah **35**
Robinson, Shaun **36**
Rock, Chris **3, 22, 66**
Rodrigues, Percy **68**
Roker, Al **12, 49**
Roker, Roxie **68**
Rollins, Howard E., Jr. **17**
Russell, Nipsey **66**
St. Patrick, Mathew **48**
Salters, Lisa **71**
Sanford, Isabel **53**
Shepherd, Sherri **55**
Simmons, Henry **55**
Smiley, Tavis **20, 68**
Snipes, Wesley **3, 24, 67**
Sykes, Wanda **48**
Taylor, Jason **70**
Taylor, Karin **34**
Taylor, Regina **9, 46**
Thigpen, Lynne **17, 41**
Thompson, Kenan **52**
Torres, Gina **52**
Tyler, Aisha N. **36**
Union, Gabrielle **31**
Usher **23, 56**
Vaughn, Countess **53**
Wainwright, Joscelyn **46**
Warner, Malcolm-Jamal **22, 36**
Warren, Michael **27**
Watson, Carlos **50**
Wayans, Damon **8, 41**
Wayans, Marlon **29**
Wayans, Shawn **29**
Whitaker, Forest **2, 49, 67**
Williams, Armstrong **29**
Williams, Clarence, III **26**

Williams, Serena 20
Williams, Vanessa A. 32, 66
Williams, Wendy 62
Williamson, Mykelti 22
Wilson, Chandra 57
Wilson, Dorien 55

Temple of Hip-Hop
KRS-One 34

Tennessee state government
Ford, Harold E(ugene) 42

Tennessee State University
Phillips, Teresa L. 42

Tennessee Titans football team
McNair, Steve 22, 47

Tennis
Ashe, Arthur 1, 18
Blake, James 43
Garrison, Zina 2
Gibson, Althea 8, 43
Jackson, Jamea 64
Lucas, John 7
McNeil, Lori 1
Noah, Yannick 4, 60
Peters, Margaret and Matilda 43
Rubin, Chanda 37
Washington, MaliVai 8
Williams, Samm-Art 21
Williams, Serena 20, 41
Williams, Venus 17, 34, 62
Young, Donald, Jr. 57

Terrie Williams Agency
Williams, Terrie 35

Texas House of Representatives
Delco, Wilhemina 33
Johnson, Eddie Bernice 8

Texas Rangers baseball team
Bonds, Bobby 43
Cottrell, Comer 11

Texas State Senate
Johnson, Eddie Bernice 8
Jordan, Barbara 4

Theatre Owner's Booking Association (TOBA)
Austin, Lovie 40
Cox, Ida 42

Theatrical direction
Hall, Juanita 62
Hayes, Teddy 40

Theatrical production
Hayes, Teddy 40
Perry, Tyler 40, 54

Thelonius Monk Institute of Jazz Performance
Blanchard, Terence 43

Theological Education Fund (TEF)
Gordon, Pamela 17
Tutu, Desmond Mpilo 6, 44

Theology
Franklin, Robert M. 13
Harding, Vincent 67

Wright, Jeremiah A., Jr. 45, 69

They All Played Baseball Foundation
Johnson, Mamie "Peanut" 40

Third World Press
Madhubuti, Haki R. 7
Moyo, Karega Kofi 36

Threads 4 Life
Jones, Carl 7
Kani, Karl 10
Walker, T. J. 7

Three Fifths Productions
Marsalis, Delfeayo 41

TIAA-CREF
See Teachers Insurance and Annuity Association and the College Retirement Equities Fund

Tiger Woods Foundation
Woods, Tiger 14, 31

Time-Warner Inc.
Ames, Wilmer 27
Parsons, Richard Dean 11, 33

TLC Beatrice International Holdings, Inc.
Lewis, Reginald F. 6

TLC Group L.P.
Lewis, Reginald F. 6

TOBA
See Theatre Owner's Booking Association

***Today* show**
Gumbel, Bryant 14

Togolese Army
Eyadéma, Gnassingbé 7, 52

Togolese People's Rally (RPT)
Eyadéma, Gnassingbé 7, 52
Gnassingbé, Faure 67

Toledo city government
Bell, Michael 40

Toledo Civic Hall of Fame
Stewart, Ella 39

The Tonight Show
Eubanks, Kevin 15

Tony awards
Allen, Debbie 13, 42
Belafonte, Harry 4, 65
Carroll, Diahann 9
Carter, Nell 39
Clarke, Hope 14
Davis, Viola 34
Faison, George 16
Falana, Lola 42
Fishburne, Laurence 4, 22, 70
Hall, Juanita 62
Horne, Lena 5
Hyman, Phyllis 19
Jones, James Earl 3, 49
McDonald, Audra 20, 62
Moore, Melba 21
Premice, Josephine 41
Richards, Lloyd 2

Rose, Anika Noni 70
Thigpen, Lynne 17, 41
Uggams, Leslie 23
Vereen, Ben 4
Wilson, August 7, 33, 55
Wolfe, George C. 6, 43

Top Dawg Productions
Gotti, Irv 39

Toronto Blue Jays baseball team
Carter, Joe 30
Gaston, Cito 71
McGriff, Fred 24
Winfield, Dave 5

Toronto Raptors basketball team
Carter, Butch 27
Carter, Vince 26
Thomas, Isiah 7, 26, 65

Tourism
Edmunds, Gladys 48
Roker, Al 12, 49

Track and field
Ashford, Evelyn 63
Beamon, Bob 30
Christie, Linford 8
Clay, Bryan Ezra 57
Devers, Gail 7
Felix, Allyson 48
Freeman, Cathy 29
Gebrselassie, Haile 70
Greene, Maurice 27
Griffith-Joyner, Florence 28
Harrison, Alvin 28
Harrison, Calvin 28
Holmes, Kelly 47
Jacobs, Regina 38
Johnson, Michael 13
Johnson, Rodney Van 28
Jones, Lou 64
Jones, Marion 21, 66
Joyner-Kersee, Jackie 5
Keflezighi, Meb 49
Lewis, Carl 4
Metcalfe, Ralph 26
Montgomery, Tim 41
Moses, Edwin 8
Mutola, Maria 12
Owens, Jesse 2
Pollard, Fritz 53
Powell, Mike 7
Quirot, Ana 13
Richards, Sanya 66
Rudolph, Wilma 4
Thugwane, Josia 21
White, Willye 67
Whitfield, Mal 60
Williams, Lauryn 58
Woodruff, John 68

TransAfrica Forum, Inc.
Fletcher, Bill, Jr. 41
Robinson, Randall 7, 46

Transition
Soyinka, Wole 4

Transitional Committee for National Recovery (Guinea;

CTRN)
Conté, Lansana 7

Transplant surgery
Callender, Clive O. 3
Kountz, Samuel L. 10

Transport and General Workers' Union
Morris, William "Bill" 51

Trans-Urban News Service
Cooper, Andrew W. 36

Treasurer of the United States
Morton, Azie Taylor 48

"Trial of the Century"
Cochran, Johnnie 11, 39, 52
Darden, Christopher 13
Simpson, O. J. 15

Trinidad Theatre Workshop
Walcott, Derek 5

Trombone
Marsalis, Delfeayo 41

Trumpet
Adderley, Nat 29
Armstrong, Louis 2
Blanchard, Terence 43
Dara, Olu 35
Davis, Miles 4
Eldridge, Roy 37
Ellison, Ralph 7
Farmer, Art 38
Gillespie, Dizzy 1
Jones, Jonah 39
Jones, Thad 68
Smith, Cladys "Jabbo" 32
Terry, Clark 39
Wilson, Gerald 49

Tulane University
Mason, Ronald 27

Turner Broadcasting System (TBS)
Clayton, Xernona 3, 45

Tuskegee Airmen
Brown, Willa 40
Davis, Benjamin O., Jr. 2, 43
James, Daniel, Jr. 16
Patterson, Frederick Douglass 12

Tuskegee Experiment Station
Carver, George Washington 4

Tuskegee Institute School of Music
Dawson, William Levi 39

Tuskegee University
Harvey, William R. 42
Payton, Benjamin F. 23

TV One
Ligging, Alfred, III 43

UAW
See United Auto Workers

UCC
See United Church of Christ

UFBL
See Universal Foundation for Better Living

UGA
See United Golf Association

Ugandan government
Amin, Idi 42
Obote, Milton 63

Ultraviolet camera/spectrograph (UVC)
Carruthers, George R. 40

Umkhonto we Sizwe
Hani, Chris 6
Mandela, Nelson 1, 14
Zuma, Jacob 33

UN
See United Nations

UNCF
See United Negro College Fund

Uncle Nonamé Cookie Company
Amos, Wally 9

Underground Railroad
Blockson, Charles L. 42
Cohen, Anthony 15
DeBaptiste, George 32

Unemployment and Poverty Action Committee
Forman, James 7, 51

UNESCO
See United Nations Educational, Scientific, and Cultural Organization

UNESCO Medals
Dadié, Bernard 34

UNIA
See Universal Negro Improvement Association

UNICEF
See United Nations Children's Fund

Unions
Brown, Lloyd Louis 42
Clay, William Lacy 8
Crockett, George W., Jr. 10, 64
Europe, James Reese 10
Farmer, James 2, 64
Fletcher, Bill, Jr. 41
Hilliard, David 7
Lucy, William 50
Morris, William "Bill" 51
Ramaphosa, Cyril 3
Randolph, A. Philip 3
Smith, Nate 49
Touré, Sekou 6
Wyatt, Addie L. 56

UNIP
See United National Independence Party

UNITA
See National Union for the Total Independence of Angola

United Auto Workers (UAW)
Dawson, Matel "Mat," Jr. 39
Fletcher, Bill, Jr. 41

United Bermuda Party
Gordon, Pamela 17

United Church of Christ (UCC)
Chavis, Benjamin 6
Forbes, James A., Jr. 71

United Democratic Front (UDF)
Muluzi, Bakili 14

United Golf Association (UGA)
Elder, Lee 6
Sifford, Charlie 4, 49

United Methodist Church
Caldwell, Kirbyjon 55
Lewis, Shirley A. R. 14

United National Independence Party (UNIP)
Kaunda, Kenneth 2

United Nations (UN)
Annan, Kofi Atta 15, 48
Bunche, Ralph J. 5
Cleaver, Emanuel 4, 45, 68
Diouf, Abdou 3
Juma, Calestous 57
Lafontant, Jewel Stradford 3, 51
McDonald, Gabrielle Kirk 20
Mongella, Gertrude 11
Perkins, Edward 5
Sampson, Edith S. 4
Young, Andrew 3, 48

United Nations Children's Fund (UNICEF)
Baker, Gwendolyn Calvert 9
Belafonte, Harry 4, 65
Machel, Graca Simbine 16
Weah, George 58

United Nations Educational, Scientific, and Cultural Organization (UNESCO)
Diop, Cheikh Anta 4
Frazier, E. Franklin 10
Machel, Graca Simbine 16
Smythe Haith, Mabel 61

United Negro College Fund (UNCF)
Boyd, T. B., III 6
Bunkley, Anita Richmond 39
Creagh, Milton 27
Dawson, Matel "Mat," Jr. 39
Edley, Christopher 2, 48
Gray, William H., III 3
Jordan, Vernon E. 3, 35
Lomax, Michael L. 58
Mays, Benjamin E. 7
Patterson, Frederick Douglass 12
Tillis, Frederick 40

United Parcel Service
Cooper, Evern 40
Darden, Calvin 38
Washington, Patrice Clarke 12

United Parcel Service Foundation
Cooper, Evern 40

United Somali Congress (USC)
Ali Mahdi Mohamed 5

United States Delegations
Shabazz, Ilyasah 36

United States Football League (USFL)
White, Reggie 6, 50
Williams, Doug 22

United Way
Donald, Arnold Wayne 36
Steward, David L. 36

United Workers Union of South Africa (UWUSA)
Buthelezi, Mangosuthu Gatsha 9

Universal Foundation for Better Living (UFBL)
Colemon, Johnnie 11
Reese, Della 6, 20

Universal Negro Improvement Association (UNIA)
Austin, Junius C. 44
Garvey, Marcus 1

University of Alabama
Davis, Mike 41
Lucy Foster, Autherine 35

University of California–Berkeley
Drummond, William J. 40
Edley, Christopher F., Jr. 48

University of Cape Town
Ramphele, Mamphela 29

University of Chicago Hospitals
Obama, Michelle 61

University of Colorado administration
Berry, Mary Frances 7

University of Delaware's Center for Counseling and Student Development
Mitchell, Sharon 36

University of Florida
Haskins, James 36, 54

University of Michigan
Amaker, Tommy 62
Dillard, Godfrey J. 45
Fuller, A. Oveta 43
Goss, Tom 23
Gray, Ida 41
Imes, Elmer Samuel 39

University of Missouri
Anderson, Mike 63
Floyd, Elson S. 41

University of North Carolina
Floyd, Elson S. 41

University of Texas
Granville, Evelyn Boyd 36

University of the West Indies
Brathwaite, Kamau 36
Hill, Errol 40

University of Virginia
Littlepage, Craig 35

UniverSoul Circus
Walker, Cedric "Ricky" 19

Upscale magazine
Bronner, Nathaniel H., Sr. 32

Uptown Music Theater
Marsalis, Delfeayo 41

Urban Bush Women
Zollar, Jawole 28

Urban League (regional)
Adams, Sheila J. 25
Clayton, Xernona 3, 45
Jacob, John E. 2
Mays, Benjamin E. 7
Young, Whitney M., Jr. 4

Urban renewal
Archer, Dennis 7, 36
Barry, Marion S. 7, 44
Bosley, Freeman, Jr. 7
Collins, Barbara-Rose 7
Harris, Alice 7
Lane, Vincent 5
Waters, Maxine 3, 67

Urban theater
Perry, Tyler 40, 54

Urbancrest, Ohio, government
Craig-Jones, Ellen Walker 44

U.S. Air Force
Anderson, Michael P. 40
Carter, Joye Maureen 41
Davis, Benjamin O., Jr. 2, 43
Drew, Alvin, Jr. 67
Dwight, Edward 65
Gregory, Frederick 8, 51
Harris, Marcelite Jordan 16
James, Daniel, Jr. 16
Johnson, Lonnie 32
Jones, Wayne 53
Lyles, Lester 31

U.S. Armed Forces Nurse Corps
Staupers, Mabel K. 7

U.S. Army
Adams-Ender, Clara 40
Baker, Vernon Joseph 65
Cadoria, Sherian Grace 14
Clemmons, Reginal G. 41
Davis, Benjamin O., Sr. 4
Delany, Martin R. 27
Flipper, Henry O. 3
Greenhouse, Bunnatine "Bunny" 57
Honoré, Russel L. 64
Jackson, Fred James 25
Johnson, Hazel 22
Johnson, Shoshana 47
Matthews, Mark 59
Powell, Colin 1, 28
Snow, Samuel 71

Stanford, John 20
Watkins, Perry 12
West, Togo D., Jr. 16

U.S. Army Air Corps
Anderson, Charles Edward 37

U.S. Atomic Energy Commission
Nabrit, Samuel Milton 47

U.S. Attorney's Office
Lafontant, Jewel Stradford 3, 51

U.S. Basketball League (USBL)
Lucas, John 7

USBL
See U.S. Basketball League

U.S. Bureau of Engraving and Printing
Felix, Larry R. 64

USC
See United Somali Congress

U.S. Cabinet
Brown, Ron 5
Elders, Joycelyn 6
Espy, Mike 6
Harris, Patricia Roberts 2
Herman, Alexis M. 15
O'Leary, Hazel 6
Powell, Colin 1, 28
Rice, Condoleezza 3, 28
Slater, Rodney E. 15
Sullivan, Louis 8
Weaver, Robert C. 8, 46

U.S. Circuit Court of Appeals
Hastie, William H. 8
Keith, Damon J. 16

U.S. Coast Guard
Brown, Erroll M. 23

U.S. Commission on Civil Rights
Berry, Mary Frances 7
Edley, Christopher 2, 48
Fletcher, Arthur A. 63

U.S. Conference of Catholic Bishops
Gregory, Wilton D. 37

U.S. Court of Appeals
Higginbotham, A. Leon, Jr. 13, 25
Kearse, Amalya Lyle 12
Ogunlesi, Adebayo 37

U.S. Department of Agriculture (USDA)
Espy, Mike 6
Vaughn, Gladys Gary 47
Watkins, Shirley R. 17
Williams, Hosea Lorenzo 15, 31

U.S. Department of Commerce
Brown, Ron 5
Irving, Larry, Jr. 12
Person, Waverly 9, 51
Shavers, Cheryl 31

Wilkins, Roger 2

U.S. Department of Defense
Greenhouse, Bunnatine "Bunny" 57
Tribble, Israel, Jr. 8

U.S. Department of Education
Hill, Anita 5, 65
Hill, Bonnie Guiton 20
Paige, Rod 29
Purnell, Silas 59
Thomas, Clarence 2, 39, 65
Tribble, Israel, Jr. 8
Velez-Rodriguez, Argelia 56

U.S. Department of Energy
O'Leary, Hazel 6

U.S. Department of Health and Human Services (HHS)
See also U.S. Department of Health, Education, and Welfare
Gaston, Marilyn Hughes 60

U.S. Department of Health, Education, and Welfare (HEW)
Bell, Derrick 6
Berry, Mary Frances 7
Harris, Patricia Roberts 2
Johnson, Eddie Bernice 8
Randolph, Linda A. 52
Sullivan, Louis 8

U.S. Department of Housing and Urban Development (HUD)
Blackwell, J. Kenneth, Sr. 61
Gaines, Brenda 41
Harris, Patricia Roberts 2
Jackson, Alphonso R. 48
Weaver, Robert C. 8, 46

U.S. Department of Justice
Bell, Derrick 6
Campbell, Bill 9
Days, Drew S., III 10
Guinier, Lani 7, 30
Holder, Eric H., Jr. 9
Lafontant, Jewel Stradford 3, 51
Lewis, Delano 7
Patrick, Deval 12, 61
Payton, John 48
Thompson, Larry D. 39
Wilkins, Roger 2

U.S. Department of Labor
Crockett, George W., Jr. 10, 64
Fletcher, Arthur A. 63
Herman, Alexis M. 15

U.S. Department of Social Services
Little, Robert L. 2

U.S. Department of State
Baltimore, Richard Lewis, III 71
Bethune, Mary McLeod 4
Bunche, Ralph J. 5
Davis, Ruth 37
Dougherty, Mary Pearl 47
Frazer, Jendayi 68
Garrett, Joyce Finley 59
Grimké, Archibald H. 9
Haley, George Williford Boyce 21
Harris, Patricia Roberts 2
Keyes, Alan L. 11

Lafontant, Jewel Stradford 3, 51
Perkins, Edward 5
Powell, Colin 1, 28
Rice, Condoleezza 3, 28
Stokes, Carl B. 10
Van Lierop, Robert 53
Wharton, Clifton R., Jr. 7
Wharton, Clifton Reginald, Sr. 36

U.S. Department of the Interior
Person, Waverly 9, 51

U.S. Department of Transportation
Davis, Benjamin O., Jr. 2, 43

U.S. Department of Veterans Affairs
Brown, Jesse 6, 41

U.S. Diplomatic Corps
See U.S. Department of State

U.S. District Attorney
Harris, Kamala D. 64
Lloyd, Reginald 64

U.S. District Court judge
Bryant, William Benson 61
Carter, Robert L. 51
Cooke, Marcia 60
Diggs-Taylor, Anna 20
Henderson, Thelton E. 68
Keith, Damon J. 16
Parsons, James 14

U.S. Dream Academy
Phipps, Wintley 59

U.S. Foreign Service
See U.S. Department of State

U.S. Geological Survey
Person, Waverly 9, 51

U.S. House of Representatives
Archie-Hudson, Marguerite 44
Ballance, Frank W. 41
Bishop, Sanford D., Jr. 24
Brown, Corrine 24
Burke, Yvonne Braithwaite 42
Carson, André 69
Carson, Julia 23, 69
Chisholm, Shirley 2, 50
Clay, William Lacy 8
Clayton, Eva M. 20
Cleaver, Emanuel 4, 45, 68
Clyburn, James E. 21, 71
Collins, Barbara-Rose 7
Collins, Cardiss 10
Conyers, John, Jr. 4, 45
Crockett, George W., Jr. 10, 64
Cummings, Elijah E. 24
Davis, Artur 41
Dellums, Ronald 2
Diggs, Charles C. 21
Dixon, Julian C. 24
Dymally, Mervyn 42
Ellison, Keith 59
Espy, Mike 6
Fattah, Chaka 11, 70
Fauntroy, Walter E. 11
Fields, Cleo 13
Flake, Floyd H. 18

Ford, Harold E(ugene) 42
Ford, Harold E(ugene), Jr. 16, 70
Franks, Gary 2
Gray, William H., III 3
Hastings, Alcee L. 16
Hawkins, Augustus F. 68
Hilliard, Earl F. 24
Jackson, Jesse, Jr. 14, 45
Jackson Lee, Sheila 20
Jefferson, William J. 25
Johnson, Eddie Bernice 8
Jordan, Barbara 4
Kilpatrick, Carolyn Cheeks 16
Lee, Barbara 25
Leland, Mickey 2
Lewis, John 2, 46
Majette, Denise 41
McKinney, Cynthia Ann 11, 52
Meek, Carrie 6
Meek, Kendrick 41
Meeks, Gregory 25
Metcalfe, Ralph 26
Mfume, Kweisi 6, 41
Millender-McDonald, Juanita 21, 61
Mitchell, Parren J. 42, 66
Moore, Gwendolynne S. 55
Norton, Eleanor Holmes 7
Owens, Major 6
Payne, Donald M. 2, 57
Pinchback, P. B. S. 9
Powell, Adam Clayton, Jr. 3
Rangel, Charles 3, 52
Rush, Bobby 26
Scott, David 41
Scott, Robert C. 23
Stokes, Louis 3
Towns, Edolphus 19
Tubbs Jones, Stephanie 24
Washington, Harold 6
Waters, Maxine 3, 67
Watson, Diane 41
Watt, Melvin 26
Watts, J.C. 14, 38
Wheat, Alan 14
Wynn, Albert R. 25
Young, Andrew 3, 48

U.S. Information Agency
Allen, Samuel 38

U.S. Joint Chiefs of Staff
Howard, Michelle 28
Powell, Colin 1, 28
Rice, Condoleezza 3, 28

U.S. Marines
Bolden, Charles F., Jr. 7
Brown, Jesse 6, 41
Petersen, Franke E. 31
Von Lipsey, Roderick K. 11

U.S. Navy
Black, Barry C. 47
Brashear, Carl 29
Brown, Jesse Leroy 31
Doby, Lawrence Eugene, Sr. 16, 41
Fields, Evelyn J. 27
Gravely, Samuel L., Jr. 5, 49
Howard, Michelle 28
Miller, Dorie 29
Pinckney, Bill 42
Reason, J. Paul 19

Wright, Lewin 43

U.S. Olympic Committee (USOC)
DeFrantz, Anita 37

U.S. Open golf tournament
Shippen, John 43
Woods, Tiger 14, 31

U.S. Open tennis tournament
Williams, Venus 17, 34, 62

U.S. Peace Corps
Days, Drew S., III 10
Johnson, Rafer 33
Lewis, Delano 7

U.S. Register of the Treasury
Bruce, Blanche Kelso 33

U.S. Senate
Black, Barry C. 47
Bowman, Bertie 71
Braun, Carol Moseley 4, 42
Brooke, Edward 8
Bruce, Blanche Kelso 33
Obama, Barack 49
Pinchback, P. B. S. 9

U.S. State Department
See U.S. Department of State

U.S. Supreme Court
Marshall, Thurgood 1, 44
Thomas, Clarence 2, 39, 65

U.S. Surgeon General
Elders, Joycelyn 6
Satcher, David 7, 57

U.S. Virgin Islands government
Hastie, William H. 8
Turnbull, Charles Wesley 62

USDA
See U.S. Department of Agriculture

USFL
See United States Football League

U.S.S. *Constitution*
Wright, Lewin 43

UVC
See Ultraviolet camera/spectrograph

UWUSA
See United Workers Union of South Africa

Vancouver Canucks hockey team
Brashear, Donald 39

Vancouver Grizzlies basketball team
Abdur-Rahim, Shareef 28

Vaudeville
Anderson, Eddie "Rochester" 30
Austin, Lovie 40
Bates, Peg Leg 14
Cox, Ida 42
Davis, Sammy, Jr. 18
Johnson, Jack 8
Martin, Sara 38

McDaniel, Hattie 5
Mills, Florence 22
Robinson, Bill "Bojangles" 11
Waters, Ethel 7

Verizon Communication
DeVard, Jerri 61
Gordon, Bruce S. 41, 53

Veterinary science
Jawara, Dawda Kairaba 11
Lushington, Augustus Nathaniel 56
Maathai, Wangari 43
Patterson, Frederick Douglass 12
Thomas, Vivien 9

Vibe
Jones, Quincy 8, 30
Smith, Danyel 40
Wilbekin, Emil 63

Vibraphone
Hampton, Lionel 17, 41

Victim's Bill of Rights
Dee, Merri 55

Video direction
Barclay, Paris 37
Fuqua, Antoine 35
Pinkett Smith, Jada 10, 41

Vietnam Veterans of America
Duggins, George 64

Village Voice
Cooper, Andrew W. 36
Crouch, Stanley 11

Violin
Daemyon, Jerald 64
Dworkin, Aaron P. 52
Escobar, Damien 56
Escobar, Tourie 56
Murray, Tai 47
Smith, Stuff 37
Tinsley, Boyd 50

VIP Memphis magazine
McMillan, Rosalynn A. 36

Virgin Records
Brooks, Hadda 40
Sledge, Percy 39

Virginia state government
Marsh, Henry 32
Martin, Ruby Grant 49
Wilder, L. Douglas 3, 48

Virginia State Supreme Court
Hassell, Leroy Rountree, Sr. 41

Virginia Tech University
Vick, Michael 39, 65

Virology
Fuller, A. Oveta 43

Vogue magazine
Talley, André Leon 56

Volleyball
Blanton, Dain 29

Voodoo
Dunham, Katherine 4, 59
Guy, Rosa 5

Hurston, Zora Neale 3
Pierre, Andre 17

Voting rights
Cary, Mary Ann Shadd 30
Clark, Septima 7
Forman, James 7, 51
Guinier, Lani 7, 30
Hamer, Fannie Lou 6
Harper, Frances Ellen Watkins 11
Hill, Jesse, Jr. 13
Johnson, Eddie Bernice 8
Lampkin, Daisy 19
Mandela, Nelson 1, 14
Moore, Harry T. 29
Moses, Robert Parris 11
Terrell, Mary Church 9
Touré, Faya Ora Rose 56
Trotter, Monroe 9
Tubman, Harriet 9
Wells-Barnett, Ida B. 8
Williams, Fannie Barrier 27
Williams, Hosea Lorenzo 15, 31
Woodard, Alfre 9

Vulcan Realty and Investment Company
Gaston, Arthur George 3, 38, 59

WAAC (Women's Auxiliary Army Corps)
See Women's Army Corps (WAC)

WAC
See Women's Army Corp

Wall Street
Lewis, William M., Jr. 40
McGuire, Raymond J. 57
Phillips, Charles E., Jr. 57

Wall Street Project
Jackson, Jesse 1, 27

Walter Payton Inc.
Payton, Walter 11, 25

War Resister's League (WRL)
Carter, Mandy 11

Washington Capitols basketball team
Lloyd, Earl 26

Washington Capitols hockey team
Grier, Mike 43

Washington Color Field group
Thomas, Alma 14

Washington, D.C., city government
Barry, Marion S. 7, 44
Cooper Cafritz, Peggy 43
Dixon, Sharon Pratt 1
Fauntroy, Walter E. 11
Fenty, Adrian 60
Hobson, Julius W. 44
Jarvis, Charlene Drew 21
Norton, Eleanor Holmes 7
Washington, Walter 45
Williams, Anthony 21

Washington, D.C., Commission on the Arts and Humani-

ties
Neal, Larry 38

Washington Mystics basketball team
McCray, Nikki 18

Washington Post
Britt, Donna 28
Davis, George 36
Ifill, Gwen 28
King, Colbert I. 69
Maynard, Robert C. 7
McCall, Nathan 8
Nelson, Jill 6, 54
Raspberry, William 2
Wilkins, Roger 2

Washington Redskins football team
Green, Darrell 39
Monk, Art 38
Sanders, Deion 4, 31

Washington State Higher Education Coordinating Board
Floyd, Elson S. 41

Washington Week in Review
TV Series
Ifill, Gwen 28

Washington Wizards basketball team
Bickerstaff, Bernie 21
Heard, Gar 25
Howard, Juwan 15
Lucas, John 7
Unseld, Wes 23
Webber, Chris 15, 30, 59

Watts Repetory Theater Company
Cortez, Jayne 43

WBA
See World Boxing Association

WBC
See World Boxing Council

WCC
See World Council of Churches

Weather
Brown, Vivian 27
Christian, Spencer 15
McEwen, Mark 5

Welfare reform
Bryant, Wayne R. 6
Carson, Julia 23, 69
Parker, Star 70
Wallace, Joaquin 49
Williams, Walter E. 4

Wellspring Gospel
Winans, CeCe 14, 43

WERD (radio station)
Blayton, Jesse B., Sr. 55

West Indian folk songs
Belafonte, Harry 4, 65
Rhoden, Wayne 70

West Indian folklore
Walcott, Derek 5

West Indian literature
Coombs, Orde M. 44
Guy, Rosa 5
Kincaid, Jamaica 4
Markham, E.A. 37
Marshall, Paule 7
McKay, Claude 6
Walcott, Derek 5

West Point
Davis, Benjamin O., Jr. 2, 43
Flipper, Henry O. 3

West Side Preparatory School
Collins, Marva 3, 71

Western Michigan University
Floyd, Elson S. 41

White House Conference on Civil Rights
Randolph, A. Philip 3

Whitney Museum of American Art
Golden, Thelma 10, 55
Simpson, Lorna 4, 36

WHO
See Women Helping Offenders

"Why Are You on This Planet?"
Yoba, Malik 11

William Morris Talent Agency
Amos, Wally 9

WillieWear Ltd.
Smith, Willi 8

Wilmington 10
Chavis, Benjamin 6

Wimbledon
Williams, Venus 17, 34, 62

Wine and Winemaking
Allen-Buillard, Melba 55
Rideau, Iris 46

Wisconsin State Supreme Court
Butler, Louis 70

WOMAD
See World of Music, Arts, and Dance

Women Helping Offenders (WHO)
Holland, Endesha Ida Mae 3, 57

Women's Army Corps (WAC)
Adams Earley, Charity 13, 34
Cadoria, Sherian Grace 14

Women's Auxiliary Army Corps
See Women's Army Corps

Women's issues
Allen, Ethel D. 13
Angelou, Maya 1, 15
Avery, Byllye Y. 66
Ba, Mariama 30
Baker, Ella 5
Berry, Mary Frances 7
Brown, Elaine 8
Campbell, Bebe Moore 6, 24, 59
Cannon, Katie 10
Cary, Mary Ann Shadd 30
Charles, Mary Eugenia 10, 55
Chinn, May Edward 26
Christian, Barbara T. 44
Christian-Green, Donna M. 17
Clark, Septima 7
Cole, Johnnetta B. 5, 43
Cooper, Anna Julia 20
Cunningham, Evelyn 23
Dash, Julie 4
Davis, Angela 5
Edelman, Marian Wright 5, 42
Elders, Joycelyn 6
Fauset, Jessie 7
Giddings, Paula 11
Goldberg, Whoopi 4, 33, 69
Gomez, Jewelle 30
Grimké, Archibald H. 9
Guy-Sheftall, Beverly 13
Hale, Clara 16
Hale, Lorraine 8
Hamer, Fannie Lou 6
Harper, Frances Ellen Watkins 11
Harris, Alice 7
Harris, Leslie 6
Harris, Patricia Roberts 2
Height, Dorothy I. 2, 23
Hernandez, Aileen Clarke 13
Hill, Anita 5, 65
Hine, Darlene Clark 24
Holland, Endesha Ida Mae 3, 57
hooks, bell 5
Hughes, Ebony 57
Jackson, Alexine Clement 22
Joe, Yolanda 21
Jordan, Barbara 4
Jordan, June 7, 35
Lampkin, Daisy 19
Larsen, Nella 10
Lorde, Audre 6
Maathai, Wangari 43
Marshall, Paule 7
Mbaye, Mariétou 31
McCabe, Jewell Jackson 10
McKenzie, Vashti M. 29
McMillan, Terry 4, 17, 53
Meek, Carrie 6
Millender-McDonald, Juanita 21, 61
Mongella, Gertrude 11
Morrison, Toni 2, 15
Mossell, Gertrude Bustill 40
Naylor, Gloria 10, 42
Nelson, Jill 6, 54
Niane, Katoucha 70
Nichols, Nichelle 11
Norman, Pat 10
Norton, Eleanor Holmes 7
Painter, Nell Irvin 24
Parker, Pat 19
Rawlings, Nana Konadu Agyeman 13
Ringgold, Faith 4
Shange, Ntozake 8
Simpson, Carole 6, 30
Smith, Jane E. 24
Terrell, Mary Church 9
Tubman, Harriet 9
Vanzant, Iyanla 17, 47
Walker, Alice 1, 43
Walker, Maggie Lena 17
Wallace, Michele Faith 13
Waters, Maxine 3, 67
Wattleton, Faye 9
Williams, Fannie Barrier 27
Winfrey, Oprah 2, 15, 61
Xuma, Madie Hall 59

Women's Leadership Forum
Shabazz, Ilyasah 36

Women's National Basketball Association (WNBA)
Burks, Mary Fair 40
Bolton-Holifield, Ruthie 28
Cash, Swin 59
Catchings, Tamika 43
Cooper, Cynthia 17
Edwards, Teresa 14
Ford, Cheryl 45
Griffith, Yolanda 25
Holdsclaw, Chamique 24
Jones, Merlakia 34
Lennox, Betty 31
Leslie, Lisa 16
McCray, Nikki 18
Milton, DeLisha 31
Peck, Carolyn 23
Perrot, Kim 23
Swoopes, Sheryl 12, 56
Thompson, Tina 25
Williams, Natalie 31
Woodward, Lynette 67

Women's Political Council
Burks, Mary Fair 40

Women's Strike for Peace
King, Coretta Scott 3, 57

Women's United Soccer Association (WUSA)
Scurry, Briana 27

Worker's Party (Brazil)
da Silva, Benedita 5

Workplace equity
Clark, Septima 7
Hill, Anita 5, 65
Nelson, Jill 6, 54
Simpson, Carole 6, 30

Works Progress (Projects) Administration (WPA)
Alexander, Margaret Walker 22
Baker, Ella 5
Blackburn, Robert 28
DeCarava, Roy 42
Douglas, Aaron 7
Dunham, Katherine 4, 59
Hall, Juanita 62
Lawrence, Jacob 4, 28
Lee-Smith, Hughie 5, 22
Murray, Pauli 38
Sallee, Charles 38
Sebree, Charles 40
Winkfield, Jimmy 42
Wright, Richard 5

World African Hebrew Israelite Community
Ben-Israel, Ben Ami 11

World Bank
Soglo, Nicéphore 15

World beat
Belafonte, Harry 4, 65
Fela 1, 42
Maal, Baaba 66
N'Dour, Youssou 1, 53
Okosuns, Sonny 71
Ongala, Remmy 9

World Boxing Association (WBA)
Ellis, Jimmy 44
Hearns, Thomas 29
Hopkins, Bernard 35, 69
Lewis, Lennox 27
Tyson, Mike 28, 44
Whitaker, Pernell 10

World Boxing Council (WBC)
Mosley, Shane 32
Tyson, Mike 28, 44
Whitaker, Pernell 10

World Council of Churches (WCC)
Kobia, Samuel 43
Mays, Benjamin E. 7
Tutu, Desmond Mpilo 6, 44

World Cup
dos Santos, Manuel Francisco 65
Milla, Roger 2
Pelé 7
Scurry, Briana 27

World hunger
Belafonte, Harry 4, 65
Iman 4, 33
Jones, Quincy 8, 30
Leland, Mickey 2
Masire, Quett 5
Obasanjo, Olusegun 5

World of Music, Arts, and Dance (WOMAD)
Ongala, Remmy 9

World Wide Technology
Steward, David L. 36

World Wrestling Entertainment (WWE) Hall of Fame
Ladd, Ernie 64

World Wrestling Federation (WWF)
Ladd, Ernie 64
Lashley, Bobby 63
Rock, The 29, 66

WPA
See Works Progress Administration

Wrestling
Ladd, Ernie 64
Lashley, Bobby 63
Rock, The 29, 66

WRL
See War Resister's League

WSB Radio
Pressley, Condace L. 41

WWF
See World Wrestling Federation

Xavier University of Louisiana
Francis, Norman (C.) **60**

Xerox Corp.
Burns, Ursula **60**
Rand, A. Barry **6**

Yab Yum Entertainment
Edmonds, Tracey **16, 64**

Yale Child Study Center
Comer, James P. **6**

Yale Repertory Theater
Dutton, Charles S. **4, 22**
Richards, Lloyd **2**
Wilson, August **7, 33, 55**

Yale School of Drama
Dutton, Charles S. **4, 22**
Richards, Lloyd **2**

Yale University
Blassingame, John Wesley **40**
Carby, Hazel **27**
Davis, Charles T. **48**
Hill, Errol **40**
Neal, Larry **38**

Ybor City Boys and Girls Club
Brooks, Derrick **43**

YMCA
See Young Men's Christian Associations

Yoruban folklore
Soyinka, Wole **4**
Vanzant, Iyanla **17, 47**

Young adult literature
Anderson, Ho Che **54**
Bolden, Tonya **32**
Ekwensi, Cyprian **37**
Johnson, Angela **52**

Young and Rubicam Brands
Fudge, Ann (Marie) **11, 55**

Young British Artists
Shonibare, Yinka **58**

Young Men's Christian Association (YMCA)
Butts, Calvin O., III **9**
Goode, Mal **13**
Hope, John **8**
Mays, Benjamin E. **7**

Young Negroes' Cooperative League
Baker, Ella **5**

Young Women's Christian Association (YWCA)
Baker, Ella **5**
Baker, Gwendolyn Calvert **9**
Clark, Septima **7**
Claytor, Helen **14, 52**
Hedgeman, Anna Arnold **22**
Height, Dorothy I. **2, 23**
Jackson, Alexine Clement **22**
Jenkins, Ella **15**
Sampson, Edith S. **4**
Stewart, Ella **39**
Xuma, Madie Hall **59**

Youth Pride Inc.
Barry, Marion S. **7, 44**

Youth Services Administration
Little, Robert L. **2**

YWCA
See Young Women's Christian Association

Zairian government
Mobutu Sese Seko **1, 56**

Zambian government
Chiluba, Frederick Jacob Titus **56**

ZCTU
See Zimbabwe Congress of Trade Unions

Zimbabwe Congress of Trade Unions (ZCTU)
Tsvangirai, Morgan **26**
Young, Roger Arliner **29**

Zimbabwean government
Mugabe, Robert **10, 71**
Nkomo, Joshua **4, 65**

Zouk music
Lefel, Edith **41**

ZTA
See Zululand Territorial Authority

Zululand Territorial Authority (ZTA)
Buthelezi, Mangosuthu Gatsha **9**

Cumulative Name Index

Volume numbers appear in **bold**

Aaliyah 1979-2001 **30**
Aaron, Hank 1934— **5**
Aaron, Henry Louis *See Aaron, Hank*
Abacha, Sani 1943—1998 **11, 70**
Abbott, Diane (Julie) 1953— **9**
Abbott, Robert Sengstacke 1868-1940 **27**
Abdul-Jabbar, Kareem 1947— **8**
Abdullah, Imaam Isa *See York, Dwight D.*
Abdulmajid, Iman Mohamed *See Iman*
Abdur-Rahim, Shareef 1976— **28**
Abele, Julian 1881-1950 **55**
Abernathy, Ralph David 1926-1990 **1**
Aberra, Amsale 1954— **67**
Abiola, Moshood 1937–1998 **70**
Abrahams, Peter 1919— **39**
Abu-Jamal, Mumia 1954— **15**
Abubakar, Abdulsalami 1942— **66**
Ace, Johnny 1929-1954 **36**
Achebe, (Albert) Chinua(lumogu) 1930— **6**
Acogny, Germaine 1944— **55**
Adams Earley, Charity (Edna) 1918— **13, 34**
Adams, Eula L. 1950— **39**
Adams, Floyd, Jr. 1945— **12**
Adams, H. Leslie *See Adams, Leslie*
Adams, Jenoyne (?)— **60**
Adams, Johnny 1932-1998 **39**
Adams, Leslie 1932— **39**
Adams, Oleta 19(?)(?)— **18**
Adams, Osceola Macarthy 1890-1983 **31**
Adams, Paul 1977— **50**
Adams, Sheila J. 1943— **25**
Adams, Yolanda 1961— **17, 67**
Adams-Campbell, Lucille L. 1953— **60**
Adams-Ender, Clara 1939— **40**
Adderley, Julian "Cannonball" 1928-1975 **30**
Adderley, Nat 1931-2000 **29**
Adderley, Nathaniel *See Adderley, Nat*
Ade, Sunny King 1946— **41**
Adeniyi, Sunday *See Ade, Sunny King*
Adichie, Chimamanda Ngozi 1977— **64**
Adjaye, David 1966— **38**

Adkins, Rod 1958— **41**
Adkins, Rutherford H. 1924-1998 **21**
Adu, Freddy 1989— **67**
Adu, Fredua Koranteng *See Adu, Freddy*
Adu, Helen Folasade *See Sade*
Agyeman Rawlings, Nana Konadu 1948— **13**
Agyeman, Jaramogi Abebe 1911-2000 **10, 63**
Aidoo, Ama Ata 1942— **38**
Aiken, Loretta Mary *See Mabley, Jackie "Moms"*
Ailey, Alvin 1931-1989 **8**
Ake, Claude 1939-1996 **30**
Akil, Mara Brock 1970— **60**
Akinnuoye-Agbaje, Adewale 1967— **56**
Akinola, Peter Jasper 1944— **65**
Akomfrah, John 1957— **37**
Akon 1973(?)— **68**
Akpan, Uwem 1971— **70**
Akunyili, Dora Nkem 1954— **58**
Al-Amin, Jamil Abdullah 1943— **6**
Albright, Gerald 1947— **23**
Alcindor, Ferdinand Lewis *See Abdul-Jabbar, Kareem*
Alcorn, George Edward, Jr. 1940— **59**
Alert, Kool DJ Red 19(?)(?)— **33**
Alexander, Archie Alphonso 1888-1958 **14**
Alexander, Clifford 1933— **26**
Alexander, John Marshall *See Ace, Johnny*
Alexander, Joyce London 1949— **18**
Alexander, Khandi 1957— **43**
Alexander, Margaret Walker 1915-1998 **22**
Alexander, Sadie Tanner Mossell 1898-1989 **22**
Alexander, Shaun 1977— **58**
Ali Mahdi Mohamed 1940— **5**
Ali, Ayaan Hirsi 1969— **58**
Ali, Hana Yasmeen 1976— **52**
Ali, Laila 1977— **27, 63**
Ali, Mohammed Naseehu 1971— **60**
Ali, Muhammad 1942— **2, 16, 52**
Allain, Stephanie 1959— **49**
Allen, Byron 1961— **3, 24**
Allen, Claude 1960— **68**
Allen, Debbie 1950— **13, 42**

Allen, Ethel D. 1929-1981 **13**
Allen, Marcus 1960— **20**
Allen, Richard 1760-1831 **14**
Allen, Robert L. 1942— **38**
Allen, Samuel W. 1917— **38**
Allen, Tina 1955— **22**
Allen-Buillard, Melba 1960— **55**
Alston, Charles Henry 1907-1997 **33**
Amadi, Elechi 1934— **40**
Amaker, Harold Tommy, Jr. *See Amaker, Tommy*
Amaker, Norman 1935-2000 **63**
Amaker, Tommy 1965— **62**
Amerie 1980— **52**
Ames, Wilmer 1950-1993 **27**
Amin, Idi 1925-2003 **42**
Amos, Emma 1938— **63**
Amos, John 1941— **8, 62**
Amos, Valerie 1954— **41**
Amos, Wally 1937— **9**
Anderson, Anthony 1970— **51**
Anderson, Carl 1945-2004 **48**
Anderson, Charles Edward 1919-1994 **37**
Anderson, Eddie "Rochester" 1905-1977 **30**
Anderson, Elmer 1941— **25**
Anderson, Ho Che 1969— **54**
Anderson, Jamal 1972— **22**
Anderson, Marian 1902— **2, 33**
Anderson, Michael P. 1959-2003 **40**
Anderson, Mike 1959— **63**
Anderson, Norman B. 1955— **45**
Anderson, Viv 1956— **58**
Anderson, William G(ilchrist), D.O. 1927— **57**
Andre 3000 *See Benjamin, Andre*
Andrews, Benny 1930-2006 **22, 59**
Andrews, Bert 1929-1993 **13**
Andrews, Mark *See Sisqo*
Andrews, Raymond 1934-1991 **4**
Angelou, Maya 1928— **1, 15**
Anna Marie *See Lincoln, Abbey*
Annan, Kofi Atta 1938— **15, 48**
Ansa, Tina McElroy 1949— **14**
Anthony, Carmelo 1984— **46**
Anthony, Crystal *See McCrary Anthony, Crystal*
Anthony, Michael 1930(?)— **29**
Anthony, Trey 1974— **63**
Anthony, Wendell 1950— **25**
Appiah, Kwame Anthony 1954— **67**
Arac de Nyeko, Monica 1979— **66**

Arach, Monica *See Arac de Nyeko, Monica*
Archer, Dennis (Wayne) 1942— **7, 36**
Archer, Michael D'Angelo *See D'Angelo*
Archer, Osceola *See Adams, Osceola Macarthy*
Archie-Hudson, Marguerite 1937— **44**
Ardoin, Alphonse 1915-2007 **65**
Arinze, Francis Cardinal 1932— **19**
Aristide, Jean-Bertrand 1953— **6, 45**
Arkadie, Kevin 1957— **17**
Armah, Ayi Kwei 1939— **49**
Armatrading, Joan 1950— **32**
Armstrong, (Daniel) Louis 1900-1971 **2**
Armstrong, Robb 1962— **15**
Armstrong, Vanessa Bell 1953— **24**
Arnez J, 1966(?)— **53**
Arnold, Monica *See Monica*
Arnold, Tichina 1971— **63**
Arnwine, Barbara 1951(?)— **28**
Arrington, Richard 1934— **24**
Arroyo, Martina 1936— **30**
Artest, Ron 1979— **52**
Arthur, Owen 1949— **33**
Asante, Molefi Kete 1942— **3**
Ashanti 1980— **37**
Ashe, Arthur Robert, Jr. 1943-1993 **1, 18**
Ashford, Emmett 1914-1980 **22**
Ashford, Evelyn 1957— **63**
Ashford, Nickolas 1942— **21**
Ashley, Maurice 1966— **15, 47**
Ashley-Ward, Amelia 1957— **23**
Asim, Jabari 1962— **71**
Atim, Julian 1980(?)— **66**
Atkins, Cholly 1930-2003 **40**
Atkins, David *See Sinbad*
Atkins, Erica 1972(?)— *See Mary Mary*
Atkins, Jeffrey *See Ja Rule*
Atkins, Juan 1962— **50**
Atkins, Russell 1926— **45**
Atkins, Tina 1975(?)— *See Mary Mary*
Atyam, Angelina 1946— **55**
Aubert, Alvin 1930— **41**
Auguste, Arnold A. 1946— **47**
Auguste, Donna 1958— **29**

261

Auguste, (Marie Carmele) Rose-Anne 1963— 13
Augustine, Jean 1937— 53
Austin, Gloria 1956— 63
Austin, Jim 1951— 63
Austin, Junius C. 1887-1968 44
Austin, Lovie 1887-1972 40
Austin, Patti 1948— 24
Autrey, Wesley 1956— 68
Avant, Clarence 19(?)(?)— 19
Avery, Byllye Y. 1937— 66
Awoonor, Kofi 1935— 37
Awoonor-Williams, George *See* Awoonor, Kofi
Awoyinka, Adesiji *See* Siji
Ayers, Roy 1940— 16
Azikiwe, Nnamdi 1904-1996 13
Ba, Mariama 1929-1981 30
Babangida, Ibrahim (Badamasi) 1941— 4
Babatunde, Obba 19(?)(?)— 35
Babyface *See* Edmonds, Kenneth "Babyface"
Bacon-Bercey, June 1942— 38
Badu, Erykah 1971(?)— 22
Bahati, Wambui 1950(?)— 60
Bailey, Buster 1902-1967 38
Bailey, Chauncey 1949–2007 68
Bailey, Clyde 1946— 45
Bailey, DeFord 1899-1982 33
Bailey, Pearl Mae 1918-1990 14
Bailey, Philip 1951— 63
Bailey, Preston 1948(?)— 64
Bailey, Radcliffe 1968— 19
Bailey, William C. *See* Bailey, Buster
Bailey, Xenobia 1955(?)— 11
Baines, Harold 1959— 32
Baiocchi, Regina Harris 1956— 41
Baisden, Michael 1963— 25, 66
Baker, Anita 1957— 21, 48
Baker, Augusta 1911-1998 38
Baker, Constance *See* Motley, Constance Baker
Baker, Dusty 1949— 8, 43
Baker, Ella 1903-1986 5
Baker, George *See* Divine, Father
Baker, Gwendolyn Calvert 1931— 9
Baker, Houston A(lfred), Jr. 1943— 6
Baker, Johnnie B., Jr. *See* Baker, Dusty
Baker, Josephine 1906-1975 3
Baker, LaVern 1929-1997 26
Baker, Maxine 1952— 28
Baker, Thurbert 1952— 22
Baker, Vernon Joseph 1919— 65
Balance, Frank W. 1942— 41
Baldwin, James 1924-1987 1
Ballard, Allen B(utler), Jr. 1930— 40
Ballard, Hank 1927-2003 41
Baltimore, Richard Lewis, III 1946— 71
Bambaataa, Afrika 1958— 34
Bambara, Toni Cade 1939— 10
Banda, Hastings Kamuzu 1898(?)-1997 6, 54
Bandele, Asha 1970(?)— 36
Bandele, Biyi 1967— 68
Bandele-Thomas, Biyi *See* Bandele, Biyi
Banks, A. Doris *See* Henries, A. Doris Banks

Banks, Ernie 1931— 33
Banks, Jeffrey 1953— 17
Banks, Michelle 1968(?)— 59
Banks, Paula A. 1950— 68
Banks, Tyra 1973— 11, 50
Banks, William (Venoid) 1903-1985 11
Banner, David 1975(?)— 55
Baquet, Dean 1956— 63
Baraka, Amiri 1934— 1, 38
Barbee, Lloyd Augustus 1925–2002 71
Barber, Atiim Kiambu *See* Barber, Tiki
Barber, Ronde 1975— 41
Barber, Tiki 1975— 57
Barboza, Anthony 1944— 10
Barclay, Paris 1957— 37
Barden, Don H. 1943— 9, 20
Barker, Danny 1909-1994 32
Barkley, Charles 1963— 5, 66
Barlow, Roosevelt 1917-2003 49
Barnes, Ernie 1938— 16
Barnes, John 1963— 53
Barnes, Roosevelt "Booba" 1936-1996 33
Barnes, Steven 1952— 54
Barnett, Amy Du Bois 1969— 46
Barnett, Etta Moten 1901-2004 18, 56
Barnett, Marguerite 1942-1992 46
Barney, Lem 1945— 26
Barnhill, David 1914-1983 30
Barrax, Gerald William 1933— 45
Barrett, Andrew C. 1942(?)— 12
Barrett, Jacqueline 1950— 28
Barrett, Lindsay 1941— 43
Barrett, Mario Dewar *See* Mario
Barrino, Fantasia 1984— 53
Barrow, Dean 1951— 69
Barrow, Joseph Louis *See* Louis, Joe
Barry, Marion S(hepilov, Jr.) 1936— 7, 44
Barthe, Richmond 1901-1989 15
Basie, William James *See* Count Basie
Basquiat, Jean-Michel 1960-1988 5
Bass, Charlotta Amanda Spears 1874-1969 40
Bass, Karen 1953— 70
Bassett, Angela 1958— 6, 23, 62
Bassey, Shirley 1937— 25
Bates, Clayton *See* Bates, Peg Leg
Bates, Daisy (Lee Gatson) 1914(?)— 13
Bates, Karen Grigsby 19(?)(?)— 40
Bates, Peg Leg 1907— 14
Bath, Patricia E. 1942— 37
Batiste, Alvin 1932-2007 66
Battle, Kathleen 1948— 70
Baugh, David 1947— 23
Baylor, Don(ald Edward) 1949— 6
Baylor, Helen 1953— 36
Beach, Michael 1963— 26
Beah, Ishmael 1980— 69
Beal, Bernard B. 1954(?)— 46
Beals, Jennifer 1963— 12
Beals, Melba Patillo 1941— 15
Beamon, Bob 1946— 30
Bearden, Romare 1912–1988 2, 50
Beasley, Jamar 1979— 29
Beasley, Myrlie *See* Evers, Myrlie

Beasley, Phoebe 1943— 34
Beaton, Norman Lugard 1934-1994 14
Beatty, Talley 1923(?)-1995 35
Beauvais, Garcelle 1966— 29
Bebey, Francis 1929-2001 45
Bechet, Sidney 1897-1959 18
Beck, Robert *See* Iceberg Slim
Beckford, Tyson 1970— 11, 68
Beckham, Barry 1944— 41
Bedie, Henri Konan 1934— 21
Beenie Man 1973— 32
Belafonte, Harold George, Jr. *See* Belafonte, Harry
Belafonte, Harry 1927— 4, 65
Bell, Derrick (Albert, Jr.) 1930— 6
Bell, James "Cool Papa" 1901-1991 36
Bell, James A. 1948— 50
Bell, James Madison 1826-1902 40
Bell, Michael 1955— 40
Bell, Ralph S. 1934— 5
Bell, Robert Mack 1943— 22
Bellamy, Bill 1967— 12
Bellamy, Terry 1972— 58
Belle, Albert (Jojuan) 1966— 10
Belle, Regina 1963— 1, 51
Belton, Sharon Sayles 1951— 9, 16
Benberry, Cuesta 1923-2007 65
Benét, Eric 1970— 28
Ben-Israel, Ben Ami 1940(?)— 11
Benjamin, Andre 1975— 45
Benjamin, Andre (3000) 1975(?)— *See* OutKast
Benjamin, Regina 1956— 20
Benjamin, Tritobia Hayes 1944— 53
Bennett, George Harold "Hal" 1930— 45
Bennett, Gwendolyn B. 1902-1981 59
Bennett, Lerone, Jr. 1928— 5
Bennett, Louise 1919–2006 69
Benson, Angela 19(?)(?)— 34
Bentley, Lamont 1973-2005 53
Berry, Bertice 1960— 8, 55
Berry, Charles Edward Anderson *See* Berry, Chuck
Berry, Chuck 1926— 29
Berry, Fred "Rerun" 1951-2003 48
Berry, Halle 1966— 4, 19, 57
Berry, James 1925— 41
Berry, Mary Frances 1938— 7
Berry, Theodore M. 1905-2000 31
Berrysmith, Don Reginald 1936— 49
Betha, Mason Durrell 1977(?)— 24
Bethune, Mary (Jane) McLeod 1875-1955 4
Beti, Mongo 1932-2001 36
Betsch, MaVynee 1935— 28
Bettis, Jerome 1972— 64
Beverly, Frankie 1946— 25
Beyoncé 1981— 39, 70
Beze, Dante Terrell *See* Mos Def
Bibb, Eric 1951— 49
Bibb, Henry 1815-1854 54
Bibb, Mary 1820-1877 54
Bickerstaff, Bernard Tyrone 1944— 21
Big Boi *See* Patton, Antwan
Biggers, John 1924-2001 20, 33

Biggers, Sanford 1970— 62
Biko, Stephen *See* Biko, Steven (Bantu)
Biko, Steven (Bantu) 1946-1977 4
Bing, Dave 1943— 3, 59
Birch, Glynn R. 195(?)— 61
Bishop, Eric *See* Foxx, Jamie
Bishop, Maurice 1944-1983 39
Bishop, Sanford D. Jr. 1947— 24
Biya, Paul 1933— 28
Biyidi-Awala, Alexandre *See* Beti, Mongo
Bizimungu, Pasteur 1951— 19
Black Thought 1972— 63
Black, Albert 1940— 51
Black, Barry C. 1948— 47
Black, Keith Lanier 1955— 18
Blackburn, Robert 1920— 28
Blackmon, Brenda 1952— 58
Blackshear, Leonard 1943— 52
Blackwell, Kenneth, Sr. 1948— 61
Blackwell, Robert D., Sr. 1937— 52
Blackwell, Unita 1933— 17
Blackwood, Maureen 1960— 37
Blacque, Taurean 1941— 58
Blair, Jayson 1976— 50
Blair, Maxine *See* Powell, Maxine
Blair, Paul 1944— 36
Blake, Asha 1961(?)— 26
Blake, Eubie 1883-1983 29
Blake, James 1979— 43
Blake, James Hubert *See* Blake, Eubie
Blakey, Art(hur) 1919-1990 37
Blanchard, Terence 1962— 43
Bland, Bobby "Blue" 1930— 36
Bland, Eleanor Taylor 1944— 39
Bland, Robert Calvin *See* Bland, Bobby "Blue"
Blanks, Billy 1955(?)— 22
Blanks, Deborah K. 1958— 69
Blanton, Dain 1971— 29
Blassingame, John Wesley 1940-2000 40
Blayton, Jesse B., Sr. 1897-1977 55
Bleu, Corbin 1989— 65
Blige, Mary J. 1971— 20, 34, 60
Blockson, Charles L. 1933— 42
Blondy, Alpha 1953— 30
Blow, Kurtis 1959— 31
Bluford, Guion Stewart, Jr. *See* Bluford, Guy
Bluford, Guy 1942— 2, 35
Bluitt, Juliann Stephanie 1938— 14
Boateng, Ozwald 1968— 35
Boateng, Paul Yaw 1951— 56
Bobo, Lawrence 1958— 60
Bogle, Donald 19(?)(?)— 34
Bogues, Tyrone "Muggsy" 1965— 56
Bol, Manute 1963— 1
Bolden, Buddy 1877-1931 39
Bolden, Charles F(rank), Jr. 1946— 7
Bolden, Charles Joseph *See* Bolden, Buddy
Bolden, Frank E. 1913-2003 44
Bolden, Tonya 1959— 32
Bolin, Jane 1908-2007 22, 59
Bolton, Terrell D. 1959(?)— 25
Bolton-Holifield, Ruthie 1967— 28
Bonaly, Surya 1973— 7

Bond, Beverly 1970— **53**
Bond, (Horace) Julian 1940— **2, 35**
Bonds, Barry 1964— **6, 34, 63**
Bonds, Bobby 1946— **43**
Bonds, Margaret 1913-1972 **39**
Bonet, Lisa 1967— **58**
Boney, Lisa Michelle *See Bonet, Lisa*
Bonga, Kuenda 1942— **13**
Bongo, Albert-Bernard *See Bongo, (El Hadj) Omar*
Bongo, (El Hadj) Omar 1935— **1**
Bontemps, Arna(ud Wendell) 1902-1973 **8**
Booker, Cory Anthony 1969— **68**
Booker, Simeon 1918— **23**
Borders, James (Buchanan, IV) 1949— **9**
Bosley, Freeman (Robertson), Jr. 1954— **7**
Boston, Kelvin E. 1955(?)— **25**
Boston, Lloyd 1970(?)— **24**
Bow Wow 1987— **35**
Bowe, Riddick (Lamont) 1967— **6**
Bowman, Bertie 1931— **71**
Bowman, Herbert *See Bowman, Bertie*
Bowser, Yvette Lee 1965(?)— **17**
Boyd, Edward 1914–2007 **70**
Boyd, Gerald M. 1950-2006 **32, 59**
Boyd, Gwendolyn 1955— **49**
Boyd, John W., Jr. 1965— **20**
Boyd, Suzanne 1963— **52**
Boyd, T(heophilus) B(artholomew), III 1947— **6**
Boye, Madior 1940— **30**
Boykin, Keith 1965— **14**
Bradley, David Henry, Jr. 1950— **39**
Bradley, Ed 1941-2006 **2, 59**
Bradley, J. Robert 1919-2007 **65**
Bradley, Jennette B. 1952— **40**
Bradley, Thomas 1917— **2, 20**
Brady, Wayne 1972— **32, 71**
Brae, C. Michael 1963(?)— **61**
Braithwaite, William Stanley 1878-1962 **52**
Branch, William Blackwell 1927— **39**
Brand, Dionne 1953— **32**
Brand, Elton 1979— **31**
Brandon, Barbara 1960(?)— **3**
Brandon, Thomas Terrell 1970— **16**
Brandy 1979— **14, 34**
Branham, George, III 1962— **50**
Brashear, Carl Maxie 1931— **29**
Brashear, Donald 1972— **39**
Brathwaite, Fred 1972— **35**
Brathwaite, Kamau 1930— **36**
Brathwaite, Lawson Edward *See Kamau Brathwaite*
Braugher, Andre 1962— **13, 58**
Braun, Carol (Elizabeth) Moseley 1947— **4, 42**
Brawley, Benjamin 1882-1939 **44**
Braxton, Toni 1968(?)— **15, 61**
Brazile, Donna 1959— **25, 70**
Breedlove, Sarah *See Walker, Madame C. J.*
Breeze, Jean "Binta" 1956— **37**
Bridges, Christopher *See Ludacris*
Bridges, Sheila 1964— **36**
Bridges, Todd 1965— **37**
Bridgewater, Dee Dee 1950— **32**
Bridgforth, Glinda 1952— **36**

Brimmer, Andrew F. 1926— **2, 48**
Briscoe, Connie 1952— **15**
Briscoe, Marlin 1946(?)— **37**
Britt, Donna 1954(?)— **28**
Broadbent, Hydeia 1984— **36**
Brock, Louis Clark 1939— **18**
Bronner, Nathaniel H., Sr. 1914-1993 **32**
Brooke, Edward (William, III) 1919— **8**
Brooks, Aaron 1976— **33**
Brooks, Avery 1949— **9**
Brooks, Derrick 1973— **43**
Brooks, Golden 1970— **62**
Brooks, Gwendolyn 1917-2000 **1, 28**
Brooks, Hadda 1916-2002 **40**
Brooks, Mehcad 1980— **62**
Brooks, Tyrone 1945— **59**
Brower, William 1916-2004 **49**
Brown Bomber, The *See Louis, Joe*
Brown, Buck *See Brown, Robert*
Brown, Andre *See Dre, Dr.*
Brown, Angela M. 1964(?)— **54**
Brown, Bobby 1969— **58**
Brown, Byrd 1930-2001 **49**
Brown, Cecil M. 1943— **46**
Brown, Charles 1922-1999 **23**
Brown, Clarence Gatemouth 1924-2005 **59**
Brown, Claude 1937-2002 **38**
Brown, Cora 1914-1972 **33**
Brown, Corrine 1946— **24**
Brown, Cupcake 1964— **63**
Brown, Donald 1963— **19**
Brown, Eddie C. 1940— **35**
Brown, Elaine 1943— **8**
Brown, Erroll M. 1950(?)— **23**
Brown, Foxy 1979— **25**
Brown, George Leslie 1926-2006 **62**
Brown, H. Rap *See Al-Amin, Jamil Abdullah*
Brown, Homer S. 1896-1977 **47**
Brown, Hubert Gerold *See Al-Amin, Jamil Abdullah*
Brown, James 1933-2006 **15, 60**
Brown, James 1951— **22**
Brown, James Nathaniel *See Brown, Jim*
Brown, James Willie, Jr. *See Komunyakaa, Yusef*
Brown, Janice Rogers 1949— **43**
Brown, Jesse 1944-2003 **6, 41**
Brown, Jesse Leroy 1926-1950 **31**
Brown, Jim 1936— **11**
Brown, Joe 19(?)(?)— **29**
Brown, Joyce F. 1946— **25**
Brown, Lee P(atrick) 1937— **1, 24**
Brown, Les(lie Calvin) 1945— **5**
Brown, Lloyd Louis 1913-2003 **42**
Brown, Oscar, Jr. 1926-2005 **53**
Brown, Patrick "Sleepy" 1970— **50**
Brown, Robert 1936-2007 **65**
Brown, Ron(ald Harmon) 1941— **5**
Brown, Rosemary 1930-2003 **62**
Brown, Sean 1976— **52**
Brown, Sterling Allen 1901-1989 **10, 64**
Brown, Tony 1933— **3**
Brown, Uzee 1950— **42**
Brown, Vivian 1964— **27**
Brown, Warren 1971(?)— **61**

Brown, Wesley 1945— **23**
Brown, Willa Beatrice 1906-1992 **40**
Brown, Willard 1911(?)-1996 **36**
Brown, William Anthony *See Brown, Tony*
Brown, Willie L., Jr. 1934— **7**
Brown, Zora Kramer 1949— **12**
Browne, Roscoe Lee 1925-2007 **66**
Broyard, Anatole 1920–1990 **68**
Broyard, Bliss 1966— **68**
Bruce, Blanche Kelso 1849-1898 **33**
Bruce, Bruce 19(?)(?)— **56**
Bruce, Isaac 1972— **26**
Brunson, Dorothy 1938— **1**
Brutus, Dennis 1924— **38**
Bryan, Ashley F. 1923— **41**
Bryant, John 1966— **26**
Bryant, John R. 1943— **45**
Bryant, Kobe 1978— **15, 31, 71**
Bryant, Wayne R(ichard) 1947— **6**
Bryant, William Benson 1911-2005 **61**
Buchanan, Ray 1971— **32**
Buckley, Gail Lumet 1937— **39**
Buckley, Victoria (Vikki) 1947-1999 **24**
Bullard, Eugene Jacques 1894-1961 **12**
Bullins, Ed 1935— **25**
Bullock, Anna Mae *See Turner, Tina*
Bullock, Steve 1936— **22**
Bully-Cummings, Ella 1957(?)— **48**
Bumbry, Grace (Ann) 1937— **5**
Bunche, Ralph J(ohnson) 1904-1971 **5**
Bunkley, Anita Richmond 19(?)(?)— **39**
Burgess, John 1909-2003 **46**
Burgess, Marjorie L. 1929— **55**
Burke, Selma Hortense 1900-1995 **16**
Burke, Solomon 1936— **31**
Burke, Yvonne Braithwaite 1932— **42**
Burks, Mary Fair 1920-1991 **40**
Burleigh, Henry Thacker 1866-1949 **56**
Burley, Mary Lou *See Williams, Mary Lou*
Burnett, Charles 1944— **16, 68**
Burnett, Chester Arthur *See Howlin' Wolf*
Burnett, Dorothy 1905-1995 **19**
Burnham, Forbes 1923-1985 **66**
Burnim, Mickey L. 1949— **48**
Burns, Eddie 1928— **44**
Burns, Ursula 1958— **60**
Burnside, R. L. 1926-2005 **56**
Burrell, Orville Richard *See Shaggy*
Burrell, Stanley Kirk *See Hammer, M. C.*
Burrell, Tom 1939— **21, 51**
Burris, Chuck 1951— **21**
Burris, Roland W. 1937— **25**
Burroughs, Margaret Taylor 1917— **9**
Burrows, Stephen 1943— **31**
Burrus, William Henry "Bill" 1936— **45**
Burt-Murray, Angela 1970— **59**

Burton, LeVar(dis Robert Martyn) 1957— **8**
Busby, Jheryl 1949(?)— **3**
Bush, Reggie 1985— **59**
Buthelezi, Mangosuthu Gatsha 1928— **9**
Butler, George, Jr. 1931–2008 **70**
Butler, Jerry 1939— **26**
Butler, Jonathan 1961— **28**
Butler, Leroy, III 1968— **17**
Butler, Louis 1952— **70**
Butler, Octavia 1947-2006 **8, 43, 58**
Butler, Paul D. 1961— **17**
Butts, Calvin O(tis), III 1950— **9**
Bynoe, Peter C. B. 1951— **40**
Bynum, Juanita 1959— **31, 71**
Byrd, Donald 1949— **10**
Byrd, Eugene 1975— **64**
Byrd, Michelle 1965— **19**
Byrd, Robert (Oliver Daniel, III) 1952— **11**
Byron, JoAnne Deborah *See Shakur, Assata*
Césaire, Aimé 1913–2008 **48, 69**
Cade, Toni *See Bambara, Toni Cade*
Cadoria, Sherian Grace 1940— **14**
Caesar, Shirley 1938— **19**
Cage, Byron 1965(?)— **53**
Cain, Herman 1945— **15**
Caldwell, Benjamin 1937— **46**
Caldwell, Earl 1941(?)— **60**
Caldwell, Kirbyjon 1953(?)— **55**
Calhoun, Cora *See Austin, Lovie*
Callaway, Thomas DeCarlo *See Cee-Lo*
Callender, Clive O(rville) 1936— **3**
Calloway, Cabell, III 1907-1994 **14**
Cameron, Earl 1917— **44**
Camp, Georgia Blanche Douglas *See Johnson, Georgia Douglas*
Camp, Kimberly 1956— **19**
Campanella, Roy 1921-1993 **25**
Campbell, Bebe Moore 1950-2006 **6, 24, 59**
Campbell, Bill 1954— **9**
Campbell, Charleszetta Lena *See Waddles, Charleszetta (Mother)*
Campbell, Donald J. 1935— **66**
Campbell, E(lmer) Simms 1906-1971 **13**
Campbell, Mary Schmidt 1947— **43**
Campbell, Milton *See Little Milton*
Campbell, Naomi 1970— **1, 31**
Campbell, Tisha *See Campbell-Martin, Tisha*
Campbell-Martin, Tisha 1969— **8, 42**
Canada, Geoffrey 1954— **23**
Canady, Alexa 1950— **28**
Canegata, Leonard Lionel Cornelius *See Lee, Canada*
Cannon, Katie 1950— **10**
Cannon, Nick 1980— **47**
Cannon, Reuben 1946— **50**
Carby, Hazel 1948— **27**
Cardozo, Francis L. 1837-1903 **33**
Carew, Rod 1945— **20**
Carey, Mariah 1970— **32, 53, 69**
Cargill, Victoria A. 19(?)(?)— **43**
Carmichael, Stokely 1941-1998 **5, 26**
Carnegie, Herbert 1919— **25**

Carr, Johnnie 1911–2008 **69**
Carr, Kurt 196(?)— **56**
Carr, Leroy 1905-1935 **49**
Carroll, Diahann 1935— **9**
Carroll, L. Natalie 1950— **44**
Carroll, Vinnette 1922— **29**
Carruthers, George R. 1939— **40**
Carson, André 1974— **69**
Carson, Benjamin 1951— **1, 35**
Carson, Josephine *See* Baker, Josephine
Carson, Julia 1938–2007 **23, 69**
Carson, Lisa Nicole 1969— **21**
Carter, Anson 1974— **24**
Carter, Ben *See* Ben-Israel, Ben Ami
Carter, Benny 1907-2003 **46**
Carter, Betty 1930— **19**
Carter, Butch 1958— **27**
Carter, Cris 1965— **21**
Carter, Dwayne Michael, Jr. *See* Lil Wayne
Carter, Joe 1960— **30**
Carter, Joye Maureen 1957— **41**
Carter, Kenneth 1959(?)— **53**
Carter, Mandy 1946— **11**
Carter, Martin 1927-1997 **49**
Carter, Nell 1948-2003 **39**
Carter, Pamela Lynn 1949— **67**
Carter, Regina 1966(?)— **23**
Carter, Robert L. 1917— **51**
Carter, Rubin 1937— **26**
Carter, Shawn *See* Jay-Z
Carter, Stephen L(isle) 1954— **4**
Carter, Vince 1977— **26**
Carter, Warrick L. 1942— **27**
Cartey, Wilfred 1931-1992 **47**
Cartiér, Xam Wilson 1949— **41**
Carver, George Washington 1861(?)-1943 **4**
Cary, Lorene 1956— **3**
Cary, Mary Ann Shadd 1823-1893 **30**
Cash, Rosalind 1938-1995 **28**
Cash, Swin 1979— **59**
Cashin, Sheryll 1962— **63**
CasSelle, Malcolm 1970— **11**
Catchings, Tamika 1979— **43**
Catlett, Elizabeth 1919— **2**
Cayton, Horace 1903-1970 **26**
Cedric the Entertainer 1964— **29, 60**
Cee-Lo 1974— **70**
Chadiha, Jeffri 1970— **57**
Chamberlain, Wilt 1936-1999 **18, 47**
Chambers, James *See* Cliff, Jimmy
Chambers, Julius (LeVonne) 1936— **3**
Chaney, John 1932— **67**
Channer, Colin 1963— **36**
Chanté, Keshia 1988— **50**
Chapman, Nathan A., Jr. 1957— **21**
Chapman, Tracy 1964— **26**
Chappell, Emma C. 1941— **18**
Chappelle, Dave 1973— **50**
Charlemagne, Emmanuel *See* Charlemagne, Manno
Charlemagne, Manno 1948— **11**
Charles, Mary Eugenia 1919-2005 **10, 55**
Charles, Pierre 1954-2004 **52**
Charles, Ray 1930-2004 **16, 48**

Charleston, Oscar 1896-1954 **39**
Chase, Debra Martin 1956(?)— **49**
Chase, Leah 1923— **57**
Chase-Riboud, Barbara 1939— **20, 46**
Chatard, Peter 1936— **44**
Chavis, Benjamin (Franklin, Jr.) 1948— **6**
Cheadle, Don 1964— **19, 52**
Cheatham, Doc 1905-1997 **17**
Checker, Chubby 1941— **28**
Cheeks, Maurice 1956— **47**
Chenault, John 1952— **40**
Chenault, Kenneth I. 1952— **4, 36**
Cheney-Coker, Syl 1945— **43**
Cheruiyot, Robert 1978— **69**
Cherry, Deron 1959— **40**
Chesimard, JoAnne (Deborah) *See* Shakur, Assata
Chesnutt, Charles 1858-1932 **29**
Chestnut, Morris 1969— **31**
Chideya, Farai 1969— **14, 61**
Chief Black Thunderbird Eagle *See* York, Dwight D.
Childress, Alice 1920-1994 **15**
Chiluba, Frederick Jacob Titus 1943— **56**
Chinn, May Edward 1896-1980 **26**
Chisholm, Samuel J. 1942— **32**
Chisholm, Shirley 1924-2005 **2, 50**
Chissano, Joaquim 1939— **7, 55, 67**
Chong, Rae Dawn 1961— **62**
Christian, Barbara T. 1946-2000 **44**
Christian, Spencer 1947— **15**
Christian-Green, Donna M. 1945— **17**
Christie, Angella **36**
Christie, Linford 1960— **8**
Christie, Perry Gladstone 1944— **53**
Christophe, Henri 1767-1820 **9**
Chuck D 1960— **9**
Church, Bruce *See* Bruce, Bruce
Chweneyagae, Presley 1984— **63**
Ciara 1985— **56**
Ciara, Barbara 195(?)— **69**
Claiborne, Loretta 1953— **34**
Clark, Celeste (Clesteen) Abraham 1953— **15**
Clark, Joe 1939— **1**
Clark, John Pepper *See* Clark-Bekedermo, J. P.
Clark, Kenneth B. 1914-2005 **5, 52**
Clark, Kristin *See* Taylor, Kristin Clark
Clark, Mattie Moss 1925-1994 **61**
Clark, Patrick 1955— **14**
Clark, Septima (Poinsette) 1898-1987 **7**
Clark-Bekedermo, J. P. 1935— **44**
Clark-Cole, Dorinda 1957— **66**
Clarke, Austin C. 1934— **32**
Clarke, Cheryl 1947— **32**
Clarke, George Elliott 1960— **32**
Clarke, Hope 1943(?)— **14**
Clarke, John Henrik 1915-1998 **20**
Clarke, Kenny 1914-1985 **27**
Clarke, Patrice Francise *See* Washington, Patrice Clarke
Clark-Sheard, Karen 19(?)(?)— **22**
Clash, Kevin 1961(?)— **14**
Clay, Bryan Ezra 1980— **57**

Clay, Cassius Marcellus, Jr. *See* Ali, Muhammad
Clay, William Lacy 1931— **8**
Clayton, Constance 1937— **1**
Clayton, Eva M. 1934— **20**
Clayton, Mayme Agnew 1923-2006 **62**
Clayton, Xernona 1930— **3, 45**
Claytor, Helen 1907-2005 **14, 52**
Cleage, Albert B., Jr. *See* Agyeman, Jaramogi Abebe
Cleage, Pearl 1948— **17, 64**
Cleaver, (Leroy) Eldridge 1935— **5, 45**
Cleaver, Emanuel (II) 1944— **4, 68**
Cleaver, Kathleen Neal 1945— **29**
Clements, George (Harold) 1932— **2**
Clemmons, Reginal G. 19(?)(?)— **41**
Clemons, Clarence 1942— **41**
Clemons, Michael "Pinball" 1965— **64**
Clendenon, Donn 1935-2005 **26, 56**
Cleveland, James 1932(?)-1991 **19**
Cliff, Jimmy 1948— **28**
Cliff, Michelle 1946— **42**
Clifton, Lucille 1936— **14, 64**
Clifton, Nathaniel "Sweetwater" 1922(?)-1990 **47**
Clinton, George (Edward) 1941— **9**
Clyburn, James E. 1940— **21, 71**
Coachman, Alice 1923— **18**
Cobb, Jewel Plummer 1924— **42**
Cobb, Monty *See* Cobb, W. Montague
Cobb, W. Montague 1904-1990 **39**
Cobb, William Jelani 1969— **59**
Cobbs, Price M(ashaw) 1928— **9**
Cochran, Johnnie 1937-2005 **11, 39, 52**
Cohen, Anthony 1963— **15**
Colbert, Virgis William 1939— **17**
Cole, Johnnetta B(etsch) 1936— **5, 43**
Cole, Keyshia 1983— **63**
Cole, Lorraine 195(?)— **48**
Cole, Nat King 1919-1965 **17**
Cole, Natalie 1950— **17, 60**
Cole, Rebecca 1846-1922 **38**
Coleman, Bessie 1892-1926 **9**
Coleman, Donald 1952— **24, 62**
Coleman, Gary 1968— **35**
Coleman, Ken 1942— **57**
Coleman, Leonard S., Jr. 1949— **12**
Coleman, Mary 1946— **46**
Coleman, Michael B. 1955(?)— **28**
Coleman, Ornette 1930— **39, 69**
Coleman, Troy *See* Cowboy Troy
Coleman, Wanda 1946— **48**
Coleman, William F., III 1955(?)— **61**
Colemon, Johnnie 1921(?)— **11**
Colescott, Robert 1925— **69**
Collins, Albert 1932-1993 **12**
Collins, Barbara-Rose 1939— **7**
Collins, Bootsy 1951— **31**
Collins, Cardiss 1931— **10**
Collins, Janet 1917-2003 **33, 64**
Collins, Lyn 1948-2005 **53**
Collins, Marva 1936— **3, 71**
Collins, Patricia Hill 1948— **67**
Collins, Paul 1936— **61**

Collins, William *See* Collins, Bootsy
Colter, Cyrus J. 1910-2002 **36**
Coltrane, Alice 1937–2007 **70**
Coltrane, John William 1926-1967 **19**
Coltrane, Ravi 1965— **71**
Combs, Sean "Puffy" 1969— **17, 43**
Comer, James P(ierpont) 1934— **6**
Common 1972— **31, 63**
Compton, John 1925-2007 **65**
Cone, James H. 1938— **3**
Coney, PonJola 1951— **48**
Conneh, Sekou Damate, Jr. 1960— **51**
Connerly, Ward 1939— **14**
Conté, Lansana 1944(?)— **7**
Conyers, John, Jr. 1929— **4, 45**
Conyers, Nathan G. 1932— **24**
Cook, Charles "Doc" 1891-1958 **44**
Cook, (Will) Mercer 1903-1987 **40**
Cook, Sam 1931-1964 **17**
Cook, Samuel DuBois 1928— **14**
Cook, Suzan D. Johnson 1957— **22**
Cook, Toni 1944— **23**
Cook, Victor Trent 19(?)(?)— *See* Three Mo' Tenors
Cook, Wesley *See* Abu-Jamal, Mumia
Cook, Will Marion 1869-1944 **40**
Cooke, Charles L. *See* Cook, Charles "Doc"
Cooke, Marcia 1954— **60**
Cooke, Marvel 1901(?)-2000 **31**
Cooks, Patricia 1944-1989 **19**
Cool Papa Bell *See* Bell, James "Cool Papa"
Cools, Anne 1943— **64**
Coombs, Orde M. 1939-1984 **44**
Cooper Cafritz, Peggy 1947— **43**
Cooper, Afua 1957— **53**
Cooper, Andrew Lewis *See* Cooper, Andy "Lefty"
Cooper, Andrew W. 1928-2002 **36**
Cooper, Andy "Lefty" 1898-1941 **63**
Cooper, Anna Julia 1858-1964 **20**
Cooper, Barry 1956— **33**
Cooper, Charles "Chuck" 1926-1984 **47**
Cooper, Cynthia 1963— **17**
Cooper, Edward S(awyer) 1926— **6**
Cooper, Evern 19(?)(?)— **40**
Cooper, J. California 19(?)(?)— **12**
Cooper, Margaret J. 194(?)— **46**
Cooper, Michael 1956— **31**
Copeland, Michael 1954— **47**
Corbi, Lana 1955— **42**
Corley, Tony 1949— **62**
Cornelius, Don 1936— **4**
Cornish, Sam 1935— **50**
Cornwell, Edward E., III 1956— **70**
Cortez, Jayne 1936— **43**
Corthron, Kia 1961— **43**
Cortor, Eldzier 1916— **42**
Cosby, Bill 1937— **7, 26, 59**
Cosby, Camille Olivia Hanks 1944— **14**
Cosby, William Henry, Jr. *See* Cosby, Bill
Cose, Ellis 1951— **5, 50**
Cotter, Joseph Seamon, Sr. 1861-1949 **40**
Cottrell, Comer 1931— **11**
Count Basie 1904-1984 **23**

Couto, Mia 1955— **45**
Coverley, Louise Bennett *See Bennett, Louise*
Cowans, Adger W. 1936— **20**
Cowboy Troy, 1970— **54**
Cox, Deborah 1974(?)— **28**
Cox, Ida 1896-1967 **42**
Cox, Joseph Mason Andrew 1930— **51**
Cox, Renée 1960— **67**
Cox, William E. 1942— **68**
Craig, Carl 1969— **31, 71**
Craig-Jones, Ellen Walker 1906-2000 **44**
Crawford, Randy 1952— **19**
Crawford, Veronica *See Crawford, Randy*
Cray, Robert 1953— **30**
Creagh, Milton 1957— **27**
Crennel, Romeo 1947— **54**
Crew, Rudolph F. 1950(?)— **16**
Crew, Spencer R. 1949— **55**
Crite, Alan Rohan 1910— **29**
Crocker, Frankie 1937-2000 **29**
Crockett, George W., Jr. 1909-1997 **10, 64**
Crooks, Garth 1958— **53**
Croom, Sylvester 1954— **50**
Cross, Dolores E. 1938— **23**
Crothers, Benjamin Sherman *See Crothers, Scatman*
Crothers, Scatman 1910-1986 **19**
Crouch, Andraé 1942— **27**
Crouch, Stanley 1945— **11**
Crowder, Henry 1895-1954(?) **16**
Crump, Lavell *See Banner, David*
Cruse, Harold 1916-2005 **54**
Crutchfield, James N. 1947— **55**
Cullen, Countee 1903-1946 **8**
Cullers, Vincent T. 1924(?)-2003 **49**
Culpepper, Daunte 1977— **32**
Cummings, Elijah E. 1951— **24**
Cuney, William Waring 1906-1976 **44**
Cunningham, Evelyn 1916— **23**
Cunningham, Randall 1963— **23**
Curling, Alvin 1939— **34**
Currie, Betty 1939(?)— **21**
Curry, George E. 1947— **23**
Curry, Mark 1964— **17**
Curtis, Christopher Paul 1954(?)— **26**
Curtis-Hall, Vondie 1956— **17**
da Silva, Benedita 1942— **5**
Dabydeen, David 1956— **48**
Dadié, Bernard 1916— **34**
Daemyon, Jerald 1970(?)— **64**
D'Aguiar, Fred 1960— **50**
Daly, Marie Maynard 1921— **37**
Damas, Léon-Gontran 1912-1978 **46**
Dandridge, Dorothy 1922-1965 **3**
Dandridge, Ray 1913-1994 **36**
Dandridge, Raymond Garfield 1882-1930 **45**
D'Angelo 1974— **27**
Daniels, Gertrude *See Haynes, Trudy*
Daniels, Lee Louis 1959— **36**
Daniels-Carter, Valerie 19(?)(?)— **23**
Danner, Margaret Esse 1915-1986 **49**
Danticat, Edwidge 1969— **15, 68**

Dara, Olu 1941— **335**
Darden, Calvin 1950— **38**
Darden, Christopher 1957— **13**
Darego, Agbani 1982— **52**
Dash, Damon 19(?)(?)— **31**
Dash, Darien 1972(?)— **29**
Dash, Julie 1952— **4**
Dash, Leon 1944— **47**
Datcher, Michael 1967— **60**
Dathorne, O. R. 1934— **52**
Davenport, Arthur *See Fattah, Chaka*
David, Craig 1981— **31, 53**
David, Keith 1954— **27**
Davidson, Jaye 1967(?)— **5**
Davidson, Tommy 1963(?)— **21**
Davis, Allison 1902-1983 **12**
Davis, Angela (Yvonne) 1944— **5**
Davis, Anthony 1951— **11**
Davis, Anthony Moses *See Beenie Man*
Davis, Arthur P. 1904-1996 **41**
Davis, Artur 1967— **41**
Davis, Belva 1932— **61**
Davis, Benjamin O(liver), Jr. 1912-2002 **2, 43**
Davis, Benjamin O(liver), Sr. 1877-1970 **4**
Davis, Charles T. 1918-1981 **48**
Davis, Chuck 1937— **33**
Davis, Danny K. 1941— **24**
Davis, Ed 1911-1999 **24**
Davis, Eisa 1971— **68**
Davis, Ernie 1939-1963 **48**
Davis, Erroll B., Jr. 1944— **57**
Davis, Frank Marshall 1905-1987 **47**
Davis, Gary 1896-1972 **41**
Davis, George 1939— **36**
Davis, Guy 1952— **36**
Davis, Jamelia Niela *See Jamelia*
Davis, James E. 1962-2003 **50**
Davis, Lorenzo "Piper" 1917-1997 **19**
Davis, Mike 1960— **41**
Davis, Miles (Dewey, III) 1926-1991 **4**
Davis, Nolan 1942— **45**
Davis, Ossie 1917-2005 **5, 50**
Davis, Ruth 1943— **37**
Davis, Sammy, Jr. 1925-1990 **18**
Davis, Shani 1982— **58**
Davis, Terrell 1972— **20**
Davis, Thulani 1948— **61**
Davis, Tyrone 1938-2005 **54**
Davis, Viola 1965— **34**
Dawes, Dominique (Margaux) 1976— **11**
Dawkins, Wayne 1955— **20**
Dawson, Matel "Mat," Jr. 1921-2002 **39**
Dawson, Michael C. 1951— **63**
Dawson, William Levi 1899-1900 **39**
Day, Leon 1916-1995 **39**
Days, Drew S(aunders, III) 1941— **10**
De' Alexander, Quinton 19??— **57**
de Assís Moreira, Ronaldo *See Ronaldinho*
de Carvalho, Barcelo *See Bonga, Kuenda*
de Passe, Suzanne 1948(?)— **25**
De Veaux, Alexis 1948— **44**

"Deadwood Dick" *See Love, Nat*
Dean, Mark E. 1957— **35**
DeBaptiste, George 1814(?)-1875 **32**
Déby, Idriss 1952— **30**
DeCarava, Roy 1919— **42**
Deconge-Watson, Lovenia 1933— **55**
Dee, Merri 1936— **55**
Dee, Ruby 1924— **8, 50, 68**
Deezer D 1965— **53**
DeFrantz, Anita 1952— **37**
Deggans, Eric 1965— **71**
Delaney, Beauford 1901-1979 **19**
Delaney, Joseph 1904-1991 **30**
Delany, Annie Elizabeth 1891-1995 **12**
Delany, Martin R. 1812-1885 **27**
Delany, Samuel R(ay), Jr. 1942— **9**
Delany, Sarah (Sadie) 1889— **12**
Delco, Wilhemina R. 1929— **33**
Delice, Ronald 1966— **48**
Delice, Rony 1966— **48**
DeLille, Henriette 1813-1862 **30**
Dellums, Ronald (Vernie) 1935— **2**
DeLoach, Nora 1940-2001 **30**
Delsarte, Louis 1944— **34**
Demby, William 1922— **51**
Dennard, Brazeal 1929— **37**
Dent, Thomas C. 1932-1998 **50**
Dent, Tom *See Dent, Thomas C.*
DePriest, James 1936— **37**
DeVard, Jerri 1957(?)— **61**
Devers, (Yolanda) Gail 1966— **7**
Devine, Loretta 1953— **24**
Devine, Major J. *See Divine, Father*
DeWese, Mohandas *See Kool Moe Dee*
Diallo, Amadou 1976-1999 **27**
Dickens, Helen Octavia 1909-2001 **14, 64**
Dickenson, Vic 1906-1984 **38**
Dickerson, Debra J. 1959— **60**
Dickerson, Eric 1960— **27**
Dickerson, Ernest 1952(?)— **6, 17**
Dickey, Eric Jerome 1961— **21, 56**
Diddley, Bo 1928— **39**
Diesel, Vin 1967(?)— **29**
Dieudonné 1966— **67**
Diggs, Charles C. 1922-1998 **21**
Diggs, Scott *See Diggs, Taye*
Diggs, Taye 1972— **25, 63**
Diggs-Taylor, Anna 1932— **20**
Dillard, Godfrey J. 1948— **45**
Dinkins, David (Norman) 1927— **4**
Diogo, Luisa Dias 1958— **63**
Diop, Birago 1906-1989 **53**
Diop, Cheikh Anta 1923-1986 **4**
Diouf, Abdou 1935— **3**
Dirie, Waris 1965(?)— **56**
Divine, Father 1877(?)-1965 **7**
Dixon, Dean 1915–1976 **68**
Dixon, George 1870-1909 **52**
Dixon, Ivan 1931–2008 **69**
Dixon, Julian C. 1934— **24**
Dixon, Margaret 192(?)— **14**
Dixon, Rodrick 19(?)(?)— *See Three Mo' Tenors*
Dixon, Sharon Pratt 1944— **1**
Dixon, Sheila 1953— **68**
Dixon, Willie (James) 1915-1992 **4**
DJ Jazzy Jeff 1965— **32**

"Deadwood Dick" *See Love, Nat*
DJ Red Alert *See Alert, Kool DJ Red*
DMC 1964— **31**
DMX 1970— **28, 64**
do Nascimento, Edson Arantes *See Pelé*
Dobbs, Mattiwilda 1925— **34**
Doby, Larry *See Doby, Lawrence Eugene, Sr.*
Doby, Lawrence Eugene, Sr. 1924-2003 **16, 41**
Dodson, Howard, Jr. 1939— **7, 52**
Dodson, Owen 1914-1983 **38**
Doig, Jason 1977— **45**
Doley, Harold, Jr. 1947— **26**
Domini, Rey *See Lorde, Audre (Geraldine)*
Domino, Fats 1928— **20**
Donald, Arnold Wayne 1954— **36**
Donaldson, Jeff 1932-2004 **46**
Donegan, Dorothy 1922-1998 **19**
Donovan, Kevin *See Bambaataa, Afrika*
Dorrell, Karl 1963— **52**
Dorsey, Lee 1926-1986 **65**
Dorsey, Thomas Andrew 1899-1993 **15**
Dortch, Thomas W., Jr. 1950— **45**
dos Santos, José Eduardo 1942— **43**
dos Santos, Manuel Francisco 1933 **65**
Dougherty, Mary Pearl 1915-2003 **47**
Douglas, Aaron 1899-1979 **7**
Douglas, Ashanti *See Ashanti*
Douglas, Denzil Llewellyn 1953— **53**
Douglas, Lizzie *See Memphis Minnie*
Dourdan, Gary 1966— **37**
Dove, Rita (Frances) 1952— **6**
Dove, Ulysses 1947— **5**
Downing, Will 19(?)(?)— **19**
Dozier, Lamont *See Holland-Dozier-Holland*
Dr. J *See Erving, Julius*
Draper, Sharon Mills 1952— **16, 43**
Drayton, William Jonathan, Jr. *See Flavor Flav*
Dre, Dr. 1965(?)— **10, 14, 30**
Drew, Alvin, Jr. 1962— **67**
Drew, Charles Richard 1904-1950 **7**
Drexler, Clyde 1962— **4, 61**
Driskell, David C(lyde) 1931— **7**
Driver, David E. 1955— **11**
Drummond, William J. 1944— **40**
Du Bois, David Graham 1925— **45**
Du Bois, W(illiam) E(dward) B(urghardt) 1868-1963 **3**
DuBois, Shirley Graham 1907-1977 **21**
Duchemin, Alamaine *See Maxis, Theresa*
Duchemin, Marie Almaide Maxis *See Maxis, Theresa*
Duchemin, Marie Teresa Maxis *See Maxis, Theresa*
Duchemin, Theresa Maxis *See Maxis, Theresa*
Ducksworth, Marilyn 1957— **12**
Dudley, Edward R. 1911-2005 **58**
Due, Tananarive 1966— **30**
Duggins, George 1943-2005 **64**

Duke, Bill 1943— **3**
Duke, George 1946— **21**
Dukes, Hazel Nell 1932— **56**
Dumars, Joe 1963— **16, 65**
Dumas, Henry 1934-1968 **41**
Dunbar, Alice *See Dunbar-Nelson, Alice Ruth Moore*
Dunbar, Paul Laurence 1872-1906 **8**
Dunbar, Sly 1952— *See Sly & Robbie*
Dunbar-Nelson, Alice Ruth Moore 1875-1935 **44**
Duncan, Michael Clarke 1957— **26**
Duncan, Tim 1976— **20**
Dungey, Merrin 1971— **62**
Dungy, Tony 1955— **17, 42, 59**
Dunham, Katherine 1910-2006 **4, 59**
Dunlap, Ericka 1982(?)— **55**
Dunn, Jerry 1953— **27**
Dunner, Leslie B. 1956— **45**
Dunnigan, Alice Allison 1906-1983 **41**
Dunston, Georgia Mae 1944— **48**
Duplechan, Larry 1956— **55**
Dupri, Jermaine 1972— **13, 46**
Dutton, Charles S. 1951— **4, 22**
Dutton, Marie Elizabeth 1940— **12**
Dwight, Edward 1933— **65**
Dworkin, Aaron P. 1970— **52**
Dye, Jermaine 1974— **58**
Dymally, Mervyn 1926— **42**
Dyson, Michael Eric 1958— **11, 40**
Early, Deloreese Patricia *See Reese, Della*
Early, Gerald (Lyn) 1952— **15**
Earthquake, 1963— **55**
Easley, Annie J. 1933— **61**
Ebanks, Michelle 1962— **60**
Ebanks, Selita 1983— **67**
Eckstein, William Clarence *See Eckstine, Billy*
Eckstine, Billy 1914-1993 **28**
Edelin, Ramona Hoage 1945— **19**
Edelman, Marian Wright 1939— **5, 42**
Edley, Christopher 1928-2003 **2, 48**
Edley, Christopher F., Jr. 1953— **48**
Edmonds, Kenneth "Babyface" 1958(?)— **10, 31**
Edmonds, Terry 1950(?)— **17**
Edmonds, Tracey 1967— **16, 64**
Edmunds, Gladys 1951(?)— **48**
Edwards, Eli *See McKay, Claude*
Edwards, Esther Gordy 1920(?)— **43**
Edwards, Harry 1942— **2**
Edwards, Herman 1954— **51**
Edwards, Melvin 1937— **22**
Edwards, Teresa 1964— **14**
Edwards, Trevor 1962— **54**
Edwards, Willarda V. 1951— **59**
Ejiofor, Chiwetal 1977(?)— **67**
Ekwensi, Cyprian 1921— **37**
El Wilson, Barbara 1959— **35**
Elba, Idris 1972— **49**
Elder, Larry 1952— **25**
Elder, (Robert) Lee 1934— **6**
Elder, Lonne, III 1931-1996 **38**
Elders, Joycelyn (Minnie) 1933— **6**
Eldridge, Roy 1911-1989 **37**
El-Hajj Malik El-Shabazz *See X, Malcolm*

Elise, Kimberly 1967— **32**
Ellerbe, Brian 1963— **22**
Ellington, Duke 1899-1974 **5**
Ellington, E. David 1960— **11**
Ellington, Edward Kennedy *See Ellington, Duke*
Ellington, Mercedes 1939— **34**
Elliott, Lorris 1931-1999 **37**
Elliott, Missy "Misdemeanor" 1971— **31**
Elliott, Sean 1968— **26**
Ellis, Clarence A. 1943— **38**
Ellis, Jimmy 1940— **44**
Ellison, Keith 1963— **59**
Ellison, Ralph (Waldo) 1914-1994 **7**
Elmore, Ronn 1957— **21**
El-Shabazz, El-Hajj Malik *See X, Malcolm*
Emanuel, James A. 1921— **46**
Emeagwali, Dale 1954— **31**
Emeagwali, Philip 1954— **30**
Emecheta, Buchi 1944— **30**
Emmanuel, Alphonsia 1956— **38**
Ensley, Carol Denis *See Nash, Niecy*
Ephriam, Mablean 1949(?)— **29**
Epperson, Sharon 1969(?)— **54**
Epps, Archie C., III 1937-2003 **45**
Epps, Mike 1970— **60**
Epps, Omar 1973— **23, 59**
Ericsson-Jackson, Aprille 19(?)(?)— **28**
Ervin, Anthony 1981— **66**
Erving, Julius 1950— **18, 47**
Escobar, Damien 1987— **56**
Escobar, Tourie 1985— **56**
Esposito, Giancarlo (Giusseppi Alessandro) 1958— **9**
Espy, Alphonso Michael *See Espy, Mike*
Espy, Mike 1953— **6**
Estes, Rufus 1857-19(?)(?) **29**
Estes, Simon 1938— **28**
Estes, Sleepy John 1899-1977 **33**
Eubanks, Kevin 1957— **15**
Eugene-Richard, Margie 1941— **63**
Europe, (William) James Reese 1880-1919 **10**
Evans, Darryl 1961— **22**
Evans, Ernest *See Checker, Chubby*
Evans, Etu 1969— **55**
Evans, Faith 1973(?)— **22**
Evans, Harry 1956(?)— **25**
Evans, Mari 1923— **26**
Eve 1979— **29**
Everett, Francine 1917-1999 **23**
Everett, Ronald McKinley *See Karenga, Maulana*
Evers, Medgar (Riley) 1925-1963 **3**
Evers, Myrlie 1933— **8**
Evora, Cesaria 1941— **12**
Ewing, Patrick Aloysius 1962— **17**
Eyadéma, Gnassingbé 1937-2005 **7, 52**
Fabio, Sarah Webster 1928-1979 **48**
Fabre, Shelton 1963— **71**
Fagan, Garth 1940— **18**
Fair, Ronald L. 1932— **47**
Faison, Donald 1974— **50**
Faison, Frankie 1949— **55**
Faison, George William 1946— **16**
Falana, Lola 1942— **42**

Falconer, Etta Zuber 1933-2002 **59**
Fanon, Frantz 1925-1961 **44**
Farah, Nuruddin 1945— **27**
Fargas, Antonio 1946(?)— **50**
Farley, Christopher John 1966— **54**
Farmer, Art(hur Stewart) 1928-1999 **38**
Farmer, Forest J(ackson) 1941— **1**
Farmer, James 1920-1999 **2, 64**
Farmer-Paellmann, Deadria 1966— **43**
Farr, Mel 1944— **24**
Farrakhan, Louis 1933— **2, 15**
Farris, Isaac Newton, Jr. 1962— **63**
Father Goose *See Rhoden, Wayne*
Fattah, Chaka 1956— **11, 70**
Faulk, Marshall 1973— **35**
Fauntroy, Walter E(dward) 1933— **11**
Fauset, Jessie (Redmon) 1882-1961 **7**
Favors, Steve 1948— **23**
Fax, Elton 1909-1993 **48**
Feaster, Robert Franklin *See Sundiata, Sekou*
Feelings, Muriel 1938— **44**
Feelings, Tom 1933-2003 **11, 47**
Fela 1938-1997 **1, 42**
Felix, Allyson 1985— **48**
Felix, Larry R. (?)— **64**
Fenty, Adrian 1970— **60**
Fentry, Robyn *See Rihanna*
Ferguson, Roger W. 1951— **25**
Ferrell, Rachelle 1961— **29**
Ferrer, Ibrahim 1927— **41**
Fetchit, Stepin 1892-1985 **32**
Fiasco, Lupe 1982— **64**
Fielder, Cecil (Grant) 1963— **2**
Fielder, Prince Semien 1984— **68**
Fields, C. Virginia 1946— **25**
Fields, Cleo 1962— **13**
Fields, Evelyn J. 1949— **27**
Fields, Felicia P. (?)— **60**
Fields, Julia 1938— **45**
Fields, Kim 1969— **36**
50 Cent 1976— **46**
Figueroa, John J. 1920-1999 **40**
Files, Lolita 1964(?)— **35**
Fine, Sam 1969— **60**
Finner-Williams, Paris Michele 1951— **62**
Fishburne, Larry *See Fishburne, Laurence*
Fishburne, Laurence 1961— **4, 22, 70**
Fisher, Antwone Quenton 1959— **40**
Fisher, Rudolph John Chauncey 1897-1934 **17**
Fitzgerald, Ella 1918-1996 **8, 18**
Flack, Roberta 1940— **19**
Flake, Floyd H. 1945— **18**
Flanagan, Tommy 1930-2001 **69**
Flash, Grandmaster *See Grandmaster Flash*
Flavor Flav 1959— **67**
Fleming, Raymond 1945— **48**
Fletcher, Alphonse, Jr. 1965— **16**
Fletcher, Arthur A. 1924-2005 **63**
Fletcher, Bill, Jr. 1954— **41**
Flipper, Henry O(ssian) 1856-1940 **3**
Flood, Curt(is) 1963— **10**
Flowers, Sylester 1935— **50**

Flowers, Vonetta 1973— **35**
Floyd, Elson S. 1956— **41**
Folks, Byron *See Allen, Byron*
Forbes, Audrey Manley 1934— **16**
Forbes, Calvin 1945— **46**
Forbes, James A., Jr. 1935— **71**
Ford, Cheryl 1981— **45**
Ford, Clyde W. 1951— **40**
Ford, Harold E(ugene) 1945— **42**
Ford, Harold E(ugene), Jr. 1970— **16, 70**
Ford, Jack 1947— **39**
Ford, Johnny 1942— **70**
Ford, Nick Aaron 1904–1982 **44**
Ford, Wallace 1950— **58**
Foreman, George 1948— **1, 15**
Forman, James 1928-2005 **7, 51**
Forrest, Leon 1937–1997 **44**
Forrest, Vernon 1971— **40**
Forte, Linda Diane 1952— **54**
Fortune, T(imothy) Thomas 1856-1928 **6**
Foster, Cecil (A.) 1954— **32**
Foster, Ezola 1938— **28**
Foster, George "Pops" 1892-1969 **40**
Foster, Henry W., Jr. 1933— **26**
Foster, Jylla Moore 1954— **45**
Foster, Marie 1917-2003 **48**
Fowler, Reggie 1959— **51**
Fowles, Gloria *See Gaynor, Gloria*
Fox, Rick 1969— **27**
Fox, Ulrich Alexander *See Fox, Rick*
Fox, Vivica A. **15, 53**
Foxx, Jamie 1967— **15, 48**
Foxx, Redd 1922-1991 **2**
Francis, Norman (C.) 1931— **60**
Franklin, Aretha 1942— **11, 44**
Franklin, C. L. 1915–1984 **68**
Franklin, Carl 1949— **11**
Franklin, Hardy R. 1929— **9**
Franklin, J.E. 1937— **44**
Franklin, John Hope 1915— **5**
Franklin, Kirk 1970(?)— **15, 49**
Franklin, Robert M(ichael) 1954— **13**
Franklin, Shirley 1945— **34**
Franks, Gary 1954(?)— **2**
Frazer, Jendayi 196(?)— **68**
Frazier, Edward Franklin 1894-1962 **10**
Frazier, Joe 1944— **19**
Frazier, Kevin 1964— **58**
Frazier, Oscar 1956-2005 **58**
Frazier-Lyde, Jacqui 1961— **31**
Fredericks, Henry Saint Claire *See Mahal, Taj*
Freelon, Nnenna 1954— **32**
Freeman, Aaron 1956— **52**
Freeman, Al(bert Cornelius), Jr. 1934— **11**
Freeman, Cathy 1973— **29**
Freeman, Charles Eldridge 1933— **19**
Freeman, Harold P. 1933— **23**
Freeman, Leonard 1950— **27**
Freeman, Marianna 1957— **23**
Freeman, Morgan 1937— **2, 20, 62**
Freeman, Paul 1936— **39**
Freeman, Yvette **27**
French, Albert 1943— **18**
Fresh Prince, The *See Smith, Will*

Friday, Jeff 1964(?)— **24**
Fryer, Roland G. 1977— **56**
Fudge, Ann (Marie) 1951— **11, 55**
Fuhr, Grant 1962— **1, 49**
Fulani, Lenora (Branch) 1950— **11**
Fuller, A. Oveta 1955— **43**
Fuller, Arthur 1972— **27**
Fuller, Charles (Henry) 1939— **8**
Fuller, Howard L. 1941— **37**
Fuller, Hoyt 1923-1981 **44**
Fuller, Meta Vaux Warrick 1877-1968 **27**
Fuller, S. B. 1895-1988 **13**
Fuller, Solomon Carter, Jr. 1872-1953 **15**
Fuller, Vivian 1954— **33**
Funderburg, I. Owen 1924-2002 **38**
Fuqua, Antoine 1966— **35**
Futch, Eddie 1911-2001 **33**
Gabre-Medhin, Tsegaye 1936-2006 **64**
Gaines, Brenda 19(?)(?)— **41**
Gaines, Clarence E., Sr. 1923-2005 **55**
Gaines, Ernest J(ames) 1933— **7**
Gaines, Grady 1934— **38**
Gaither, Israel L. 1944— **65**
Gaither, Jake 1903-1994 **14**
Gantin, Bernardin 1922–2008 **70**
Gantt, Harvey (Bernard) 1943— **1**
Gardner, Chris 1954— **65**
Gardner, Edward G. 1925— **45**
Garnett, Kevin (Maurice) 1976— **14, 70**
Garrett, Joyce Finley 1931-1997 **59**
Garrett, Sean 1979— **57**
Garrincha *See dos Santos, Manuel Francisco*
Garrison, Zina 1963— **2**
Garvey, Marcus 1887-1940 **1**
Gary, Willie Edward 1947— **12**
Gaskins, Eric 1958— **64**
Gaston, Arthur George 1892-1996 **3, 38, 59**
Gaston, Cito 1944— **71**
Gaston, Clarence Edwin *See Gaston, Cito*
Gaston, Marilyn Hughes 1939— **60**
Gates, Henry Louis, Jr. 1950— **3, 38, 67**
Gates, Sylvester James, Jr. 1950— **15**
Gay, Marvin Pentz, Jr. *See Gaye, Marvin*
Gaye, Marvin 1939-1984 **2**
Gaye, Nona 1974— **56**
Gayle, Addison, Jr. 1932-1991 **41**
Gayle, Helene D. 1955— **3, 46**
Gaynor, Gloria 1947— **36**
Gbagbo, Laurent 1945— **43**
Gebrselassie, Haile 1973— **70**
Gentry, Alvin 1954— **23**
George, Nelson 1957— **12**
George, Zelma Watson 1903-1994 **42**
Gerima, Haile 1946— **38**
Gibson, Althea 1927-2003 **8, 43**
Gibson, Bob 1935— **33**
Gibson, Donald Bernard 1933— **40**
Gibson, Johnnie Mae 1949— **23**
Gibson, Josh 1911-1947 **22**
Gibson, Kenneth Allen 1932— **6**
Gibson, Ted 1965— **66**

Gibson, Truman K., Jr. 1912-2005 **60**
Gibson, Tyrese 1978— **27, 62**
Gibson, William F(rank) 1933— **6**
Giddings, Paula (Jane) 1947— **11**
Gidron, Richard D. 1939–2007 **68**
Gil, Gilberto 1942— **53**
Gilbert, Christopher 1949— **50**
Gill, Gerald 1948–2007 **69**
Gill, Johnny 1966— **51**
Gilles, Ralph 1970— **61**
Gillespie, Dizzy 1917-1993 **1**
Gillespie, John Birks *See Gillespie, Dizzy*
Gilliam, Frank 1934(?)— **23**
Gilliam, Joe, Jr. 1950-2000 **31**
Gilliam, Sam 1933— **16**
Gilliard, Steve 1964–2007 **69**
Gilmore, Marshall 1931— **46**
Ginuwine 1975(?)— **35**
Giovanni, Nikki 1943— **9, 39**
Giovanni, Yolande Cornelia, Jr. *See Giovanni, Nikki*
Gist, Carole 1970(?)— **1**
Givens, Adele 19(?)(?)— **62**
Givens, Robin 1964— **4, 25, 58**
Gladwell, Malcolm 1963— **62**
Glover, Corey 1964— **34**
Glover, Danny 1948— **1, 24**
Glover, Nathaniel, Jr. 1943— **12**
Glover, Savion 1974— **14**
Gnassingbé, Faure 1966— **67**
Goapele 1977— **55**
"The Goat" *See Manigault, Earl "The Goat"*
Godbolt, James Titus *See Slyde, Jimmy*
Goines, Donald 1937(?)-1974 **19**
Goings, Russell 1932(?)— **59**
Goldberg, Whoopi 1955— **4, 33, 69**
Golden, Marita 1950— **19**
Golden, Thelma 1965— **10, 55**
Goldsberry, Ronald 1942— **18**
Golson, Benny 1929— **37**
Golston, Allan C. 1967(?)— **55**
Gomes, Peter J(ohn) 1942— **15**
Gomez, Jewelle 1948— **30**
Gomez-Preston, Cheryl 1954— **9**
Goode, Mal(vin Russell) 1908-1995 **13**
Goode, W(oodrow) Wilson 1938— **4**
Gooden, Dwight 1964— **20**
Gooden, Lolita *See Roxanne Shante*
Gooding, Cuba, Jr. 1968— **16, 62**
Goodison, Lorna 1947— **71**
Goodnight, Paul 1946— **32**
Gorden, W. C. 1930— **71**
Gorden, William C. *See Gorden, W. C.*
Gordon, Bruce S. 1946— **41, 53**
Gordon, Dexter 1923-1990 **25**
Gordon, Ed 1960— **10, 53**
Gordon, Pamela 1955— **17**
Gordone, Charles 1925-1995 **15**
Gordy, Berry, Jr. 1929— **1**
Goreed, Joseph *See Williams, Joe*
Goss, Carol A. 1947— **55**
Goss, Tom 1946— **23**
Gossett, Louis, Jr. 1936— **7**
Gotti, Irv 1971— **39**
Gourdine, Meredith 1929-1998 **33**

Gourdine, Simon (Peter) 1940— **11**
Grace, George H. 1948— **48**
Grae, Jean 1976— **51**
Graham, Lawrence Otis 1962— **12**
Graham, Lorenz 1902-1989 **48**
Graham, Stedman 1951(?)— **13**
Grandmaster Flash 1958— **33, 60**
Grand-Pierre, Jean-Luc 1977— **46**
Granderson, Curtis 1981— **66**
Grant, Augustus O. 1946(?)— **71**
Grant, Bernie 1944-2000 **57**
Grant, Gwendolyn Goldsby 19(?)(?)— **28**
Granville, Evelyn Boyd 1924— **36**
Gravely, Samuel L., Jr. 1922-2004 **5, 49**
Graves, Denyce Antoinette 1964— **19, 57**
Graves, Earl G(ilbert) 1935— **1, 35**
Gray, Darius 1945— **69**
Gray, F. Gary 1969— **14, 49**
Gray, Farrah 1984— **59**
Gray, Fred Sr. 1930— **37**
Gray, Frizzell *See Mfume, Kweisi*
Gray (Nelson Rollins), Ida 1867-1953 **41**
Gray, Macy 1970— **29**
Gray, William H., III 1941— **3**
Gray, Willie 1947— **46**
Gray, Yeshimbra "Shimmy" 1972— **55**
Greaves, William 1926— **38**
Greely, M. Gasby 1946— **27**
Greely, Margaret Gasby *See Greely, M. Gasby*
Green, A. C. 1963— **32**
Green, Al 1946— **13, 47**
Green, Cee-Lo *See Cee-Lo*
Green, Darrell 1960— **39**
Green, Dennis 1949— **5, 45**
Green, Grant 1935-1979 **56**
Green, Jonathan 1955— **54**
Greene, Joe 1946— **10**
Greene, Maurice 1974— **27**
Greene, Petey 1931-1984 **65**
Greene, Ralph Waldo *See Greene, Petey*
Greene, Richard Thaddeus, Sr. 1913-2006 **67**
Greenfield, Eloise 1929— **9**
Greenhouse, Bunnatine "Bunny" 1944— **57**
Greenlee, Sam 1930— **48**
Greenwood, Monique 1959— **38**
Gregg, Eric 1951— **16**
Gregory, Ann 1912-1990 **63**
Gregory, Dick 1932— **1, 54**
Gregory, Frederick 1941— **8, 51**
Gregory, Wilton 1947— **37**
Grier, David Alan 1955— **28**
Grier, Mike 1975— **43**
Grier, Pam(ala Suzette) 1949— **9, 31**
Grier, Roosevelt (Rosey) 1932— **13**
Griffey, George Kenneth, Jr. 1969— **12**
Griffin, Anthony 1960— **71**
Griffin, Bessie Blout 1914— **43**
Griffin, Johnny 1928–2008 **71**
Griffin, John Arnold, III *See Griffin, Johnny*
Griffin, LaShell 1967— **51**
Griffith, Mark Winston 1963— **8**
Griffith, Patrick A. 1944— **64**

Griffith, Yolanda 1970— **25**
Griffith-Joyner, Florence 1959-1998 **28**
Griffiths, Marcia 1948(?)— **29**
Grimké, Archibald H(enry) 1849-1930 **9**
Grooms, Henry R(andall) 1944— **50**
Guarionex *See Schomburg, Arthur Alfonso*
Guéï, Robert 1941-2002 **66**
Guillaume, Robert 1927— **3, 48**
Güines, Tata 1930–2008 **69**
Guinier, (Carol) Lani 1950— **7, 30**
Gumbel, Bryant Charles 1948— **14**
Gumbel, Greg 1946— **8**
Gunn, Moses 1929-1993 **10**
Guy, (George) Buddy 1936— **31**
Guy, Jasmine 1964(?)— **2**
Guy, Rosa 1925(?)— **5**
Guy-Sheftall, Beverly 1946— **13**
Guyton, Tyree 1955— **9**
Gwynn, Anthony Keith 1960— **18**
Habré, Hissène 1942— **6**
Habyarimana, Juvenal 1937-1994 **8**
Haddon, Dietrick 1973(?)— **55**
Hageman, Hans 19(?)(?)— **36**
Hageman, Ivan 19(?)(?)— **36**
Haile Selassie 1892-1975 **7**
Hailey, JoJo 1971— **22**
Hailey, K-Ci 1969— **22**
Hale, Clara 1902-1992 **16**
Hale, Lorraine 1926(?)— **8**
Haley, Alex (Palmer) 1921-1992 **4**
Haley, George Williford Boyce 1925— **21**
Hall, Aaron 1963— **57**
Hall, Arsenio 1955— **58**
Hall, Arthur 1943-2000 **39**
Hall, Elliott S. 1938(?)— **24**
Hall, Juanita 1901-1968 **62**
Hall, Kevan 19(?)(?)— **61**
Hall, Lloyd A(ugustus) 1894-1971 **8**
Halliburton, Warren J. 1924— **49**
Ham, Cynthia Parker 1970(?)— **58**
Hamblin, Ken 1940— **10**
Hamer, Fannie Lou (Townsend) 1917-1977 **6**
Hamilton, Anthony 1971— **61**
Hamilton, Lewis 1985— **66**
Hamilton, Lisa Gay 1964— **71**
Hamilton, Samuel C. 19(?)(?)— **47**
Hamilton, Virginia 1936— **10**
Hamlin, Larry Leon 1948-2007 **49, 62**
Hammer *See Hammer, M. C.*
Hammer, M. C. 1963— **20**
Hammond, Fred 1960— **23**
Hammond, Lenn 1970(?)— **34**
Hammonds, Evelynn 1953— **69**
Hammons, David 1943— **69**
Hampton, Fred 1948-1969 **18**
Hampton, Henry (Eugene, Jr.) 1940— **6**
Hampton, Lionel 1908(?)-2002 **17, 41**
Hancock, Herbie 1940— **20, 67**
Handy, W(illiam) C(hristopher) 1873-1937 **8**
Hani, Chris 1942-1993 **6**
Hani, Martin Thembisile *See Hani, Chris*
Hannah, Marc (Regis) 1956— **10**

Hansberry, Lorraine (Vivian) 1930-1965 **6**
Hansberry, William Leo 1894-1965 **11**
Hardaway, Anfernee (Deon) *See* Hardaway, Anfernee (Penny)
Hardaway, Anfernee (Penny) 1971— **13**
Hardaway, Penny *See* Hardaway, Anfernee (Penny)
Hardaway, Tim 1966— **35**
Hardin Armstrong, Lil 1898-1971 **39**
Hardin, Lillian Beatrice *See* Hardin Armstrong, Lil
Harding, Vincent 1931— **67**
Hardison, Bethann 19(?)(?)— **12**
Hardison, Kadeem 1966— **22**
Hardy, Nell *See* Carter, Nell
Hare, Nathan 1934— **44**
Harewood, David 1965— **52**
Harkless, Necia Desiree 1920— **19**
Harmon, Clarence 1940(?)— **26**
Harold, Erika 1980(?)— **54**
Harper, Ben 1969— **34, 62**
Harper, Frances E(llen) W(atkins) 1825-1911 **11**
Harper, Frank *See* Harper, Hill
Harper, Hill 1966— **32, 65**
Harper, Michael S. 1938— **34**
Harrell, Andre (O'Neal) 1962(?)— **9, 30**
Harrington, Oliver W(endell) 1912— **9**
Harris, "Sweet" Alice *See* Harris, Alice
Harris, Alice 1934— **7**
Harris, Barbara 1930— **12**
Harris, Barry 1929— **68**
Harris, Carla A. 1962— **67**
Harris, Ciara Princess *See* Ciara
Harris, Claire 1937— **34**
Harris, Corey 1969— **39**
Harris, E. Lynn 1957— **12, 33**
Harris, Eddy L. 1956— **18**
Harris, James, III *See* Jimmy Jam
Harris, Jay **19**
Harris, Kamala D. 1964— **64**
Harris, Leslie 1961— **6**
Harris, Marcelite Jordon 1943— **16**
Harris, Mary Styles 1949— **31**
Harris, Monica 1968— **18**
Harris, Naomie 1976— **55**
Harris, Patricia Roberts 1924-1985 **2**
Harris, Richard E. 1912(?)— **61**
Harris, Robin 1953-1990 **7**
Harris, Sylvia 1967(?)— **70**
Harrison, Alvin 1974— **28**
Harrison, Calvin 1974— **28**
Harrison, Mya *See* Mya
Harsh, Vivian Gordon 1890-1960 **14**
Hart, Alvin Youngblood 1963— **61**
Hart, Gregory Edward *See* Hart, Alvin Youngblood
Harvard, Beverly (Joyce Bailey) 1950— **11**
Harvey, Steve 1956— **18, 58**
Harvey, William R. 1941— **42**
Haskins, Clem 1943— **23**
Haskins, James 1941-2005 **36, 54**
Hassell, Leroy Rountree, Sr. 1955— **41**

Hastie, William H(enry) 1904-1976 **8**
Hastings, Alcee Lamar 1936— **16**
Hatcher, Richard G. 1933— **55**
Hatchett, Glenda 1951(?)— **32**
Hathaway, Donny 1945-1979 **18**
Hathaway, Isaac Scott 1874-1967 **33**
Hathaway, Lalah 1969— **57**
Haughton, Aaliyah *See* Aaliyah
Hawkins, "Screamin'" Jay 1929-2000 **30**
Hawkins, Adrienne Lita *See* Kennedy, Adrienne
Hawkins, Augustus F. 1907–2007 **68**
Hawkins, Coleman 1904-1969 **9**
Hawkins, Erskine Ramsey 1914-1993 **14**
Hawkins, Jamesetta *See* James, Etta
Hawkins, La-Van 1960— **17, 54**
Hawkins, Steven Wayne 1962— **14**
Hawkins, Tramaine Aunzola 1951— **16**
Hayden, Carla D. 1952— **47**
Hayden, Palmer 1890-1973 **13**
Hayden, Robert Earl 1913-1980 **12**
Hayes, Cecil N. 1945— **46**
Hayes, Dennis 1951— **54**
Hayes, Isaac 1942— **20, 58**
Hayes, James C. 1946— **10**
Hayes, Roland 1887-1977 **4**
Hayes, Teddy 1951— **40**
Haynes, Cornell, Jr. *See* Nelly
Haynes, George Edmund 1880-1960 **8**
Haynes, Marques 1926— **22**
Haynes, Trudy 1926— **44**
Haysbert, Dennis 1955— **42**
Haywood, Gar Anthony 1954— **43**
Haywood, Jimmy 1993(?)— **58**
Haywood, Margaret A. 1912— **24**
Hazel, Darryl B. 1949— **50**
Head, Bessie 1937-1986 **28**
Healy, James Augustine 1830-1900 **30**
Heard, Gar 1948— **25**
Heard, Nathan C. 1936-2004 **45**
Hearne, John Edgar Caulwell 1926-1994 **45**
Hearns, Thomas 1958— **29**
Heavy, D 1967— **58**
Hedgeman, Anna Arnold 1899-1990 **22**
Hedgeman, Peyton Cole *See* Hayden, Palmer
Height, Dorothy I(rene) 1912— **2, 23**
Hemphill, Essex 1957— **10**
Hemphill, Jessie Mae 1923-2006 **33, 59**
Hemsley, Sherman 1938— **19**
Henderson, Cornelius Langston 1888(?)-1976 **26**
Henderson, David 1942— **53**
Henderson, Fletcher 1897-1952 **32**
Henderson, Gordon 1957— **5**
Henderson, Natalie Leota *See* Hinderas, Natalie
Henderson, Rickey 1958— **28**
Henderson, Stephen E. 1925-1997 **45**
Henderson, Thelton E. 1933— **68**

Henderson, Wade 1944(?)— **14**
Henderson, Zelma 1920–2008 **71**
Hendricks, Barbara 1948— **3, 67**
Hendrix, James Marshall *See* Hendrix, Jimi
Hendrix, Jimi 1942-1970 **10**
Hendrix, Johnny Allen *See* Hendrix, Jimi
Hendryx, Nona 1944— **56**
Hendy, Francis 195(?)— **47**
Henries, A. Doris Banks 1913-1981 **44**
Henriques, Julian 1955(?)— **37**
Henry, Aaron Edd 1922-1997 **19**
Henry, Clarence "Frogman" 1937— **46**
Henry, Lenny 1958— **9, 52**
Henson, Darrin 1970(?)— **33**
Henson, Matthew (Alexander) 1866-1955 **2**
Henson, Taraji 1971— **58**
Henry, Thierry 1977— **66**
Herbert, Bob 1945— **63**
Hercules, Frank 1911-1996 **44**
Herenton, Willie W. 1940— **24**
Herman, Alexis Margaret 1947— **15**
Hernandez, Aileen Clarke 1926— **13**
Herton, Calvin C. 1932-2001 **51**
Hickman, Fred(erick Douglass) 1951— **11**
Higginbotham, A(loyisus) Leon, Jr. 1928-1998 **13, 25**
Higginbotham, Jack *See* Higginbotham, Jay C.
Higginbotham, Jay C. 1906-1973 **37**
Higginsen, Vy 1945(?)— **65**
Hightower, Dennis F(owler) 1941— **13**
Hill, Andrew 1931-2007 **66**
Hill, Anita 1956— **5, 65**
Hill, Beatrice *See* Moore, Melba
Hill, Bonnie Guiton 1941— **20**
Hill, Calvin 1947— **19**
Hill, Donna 1955— **32**
Hill, Dulé 1975(?)— **29**
Hill, Errol 1921— **40**
Hill, Grant (Henry) 1972— **13**
Hill, Janet 1947— **19**
Hill, Jesse, Jr. 1927— **13**
Hill, Lauryn 1975— **20, 53**
Hill, Leslie Pinckney 1880-1960 **44**
Hill, Oliver W. 1907-2007 **24, 63**
Hill, Tamia *See* Tamia
Hillard, Terry 1954— **25**
Hillary, Barbara 1923(?)— **65**
Hilliard, Asa Grant, III 1933-2007 **66**
Hilliard, David 1942— **7**
Hilliard, Earl F. 1942— **24**
Hilliard, Wendy 196(?)— **53**
Himes, Chester 1909-1984 **8**
Hinderas, Natalie 1927-1987 **5**
Hine, Darlene Clark 1947— **24**
Hines, Earl "Fatha" 1905-1983 **39**
Hines, Garrett 1969— **35**
Hines, Gregory (Oliver) 1946-2003 **1, 42**
Hinton, Milt 1910-2000 **30**
Hinton, William Augustus 1883-1959 **8**
Hoagland, Everett H. 1942— **45**
Hoagland, Jaheim *See* Jaheim

Hobson, Julius W. 1919-1977 **44**
Hobson, Mellody 1969— **40**
Hogan, Beverly Wade 1951— **50**
Holder, Eric H., Jr. 1951(?)— **9**
Holder, Laurence 1939— **34**
Holdsclaw, Chamique 1977— **24**
Holiday, Billie 1915-1959 **1**
Holland, Brian *See* Holland-Dozier-Holland
Holland, Eddie *See* Holland-Dozier-Holland
Holland, Endesha Ida Mae 1944-2006 **3, 57**
Holland, Kimberly N. 19(?)(?)— **62**
Holland, Robert, Jr. 1940— **11**
Holland-Dozier-Holland **36**
Holloway, Brenda 1946— **65**
Hollowell, Donald L. 1917-2004 **57**
Holmes, Amy 1973— **69**
Holmes, Clint 1946— **57**
Holmes, Kelly 1970— **47**
Holmes, Larry 1949— **20, 68**
Holmes, Shannon 1973(?)— **70**
Holt, Lester 1959— **66**
Holt, Nora 1885(?)-1974 **38**
Holte, Patricia Louise *See* LaBelle, Patti
Holton, Hugh, Jr. 1947-2001 **39**
Holyfield, Evander 1962— **6**
Honeywood, Varnette P. 1950— **54**
Honoré, Russel L. 1947— **64**
Hooker, John Lee 1917-2000 **30**
hooks, bell 1952— **5**
Hooks, Benjamin L(awson) 1925— **2**
Hope, John 1868-1936 **8**
Hopgood, Hadda *See* Brooks, Hadda
Hopkins, Bernard 1965— **35, 69**
Horn, Shirley 1934-2005 **32, 56**
Horne, Frank 1899-1974 **44**
Horne, Lena (Mary Calhoun) 1917— **5**
Horton, Andre 1979— **33**
Horton, James Oliver 1943— **58**
Horton, (Andreana) "Suki" 1982— **33**
Hounsou, Djimon 1964— **19, 45**
Houphouët, Dia *See* Houphouët-Boigny, Félix
Houphouët-Boigny, Félix 1905-1993 **4, 64**
House, Eddie James, Jr. *See* House, Son
House, Eugene *See* House, Son
House, Son 1902-1988 **8**
Houston, Charles Hamilton 1895-1950 **4**
Houston, Cissy 19(?)(?)— **20**
Houston, Whitney 1963— **7, 28**
Howard, Ayanna 1972— **65**
Howard, Corinne *See* Mitchell, Corinne
Howard, Desmond 1970— **16, 58**
Howard, Juwan Antonio 1973— **15**
Howard, M. William, Jr. 1946— **26**
Howard, Michelle 1960— **28**
Howard, Ryan 1979— **65**
Howard, Sherri 1962— **36**
Howard, Terrence Dashon 1969— **59**
Howlin' Wolf 1910-1976 **9**
Howroyd, Janice Bryant 1953— **42**
Hoyte, Lenon 1905-1999 **50**

Hrabowski, Freeman A., III 1950— **22**
Hubbard, Arnette 19(?)(?)— **38**
Hudlin, Reginald 1962(?)— **9**
Hudlin, Warrington, Jr. 1953(?)— **9**
Hudson, Cheryl 19(?)(?)— **15**
Hudson, Jennifer 1981— **63**
Hudson, Wade 1946— **15**
Huggins, Edie 1935–2008 **71**
Huggins, Larry 1950— **21**
Huggins, Nathan Irvin 1927-1989 **52**
Hughes, Albert 1972— **7**
Hughes, Allen 1972— **7**
Hughes, Cathy 1947(?)— **27**
Hughes, Ebony 1948— **57**
Hughes, (James Mercer) Langston 1902-1967 **4**
Hughley, Darryl Lynn 1964— **23**
Hull, Akasha Gloria 1944— **45**
Humphrey, Bobbi 1950— **20**
Humphries, Frederick 1935— **20**
Hunt, Richard (Howard) 1935— **6**
Hunter, Alberta 1895-1984 **42**
Hunter, Billy 1943— **22**
Hunter, Charlayne *See Hunter-Gault, Charlayne*
Hunter, Clementine 1887-1988 **45**
Hunter, George William *See Hunter, Billy*
Hunter, Torii 1975— **43**
Hunter-Gault, Charlayne 1942— **6, 31**
Hurston, Zora Neale 1891-1960 **3**
Hurt, Byron 1970— **61**
Hurtt, Harold 1947(?)— **46**
Hutch, Willie 1944-2005 **62**
Hutcherson, Hilda Yvonne 1955— **54**
Hutchinson, Earl Ofari 1945— **24**
Hutson, Jean Blackwell 1914— **16**
Hyde, Cowan F. "Bubba" 1908-2003 **47**
Hyman, Earle 1926— **25**
Hyman, Phyllis 1949(?)-1995 **19**
Ibrahim, Mo 1946— **67**
Ice Cube 1969— **8, 30, 60**
Iceberg Slim 1918-1992 **11**
Ice-T 1958(?)— **6, 31**
Ifill, Gwen 1955— **28**
Iginla, Jarome 1977— **35**
Ilibagiza, Immaculée 1972(?)— **66**
Iman 1955— **4, 33**
Iman, Chanel 1989— **66**
Imes, Elmer Samuel 1883-1941 **39**
India.Arie 1975— **34**
Ingraham, Hubert A. 1947— **19**
Ingram, Rex 1895-1969 **5**
Innis, Roy (Emile Alfredo) 1934— **5**
Irvin, Michael 1966— **64**
Irvin, (Monford Merrill) Monte 1919— **31**
Irvin, Vernon 1961— **65**
Irving, Clarence (Larry) 1955— **12**
Irvis, K. Leroy 1917(?)–2006 **67**
Isaac, Julius 1928— **34**
Isley, Ronald 1941— **25, 56**
Iverson, Allen 1975— **24, 46**
Ja Rule 1976— **35**
Jackson Lee, Sheila 1950— **20**
Jackson, Alexine Clement 1936— **22**
Jackson, Alphonso R. 1946— **48**
Jackson, Earl 1948— **31**

Jackson, Edison O. 1943(?)— **67**
Jackson, Fred James 1950— **25**
Jackson, George 1960(?)— **19**
Jackson, George Lester 1941-1971 **14**
Jackson, Hal 1915— **41**
Jackson, Isaiah (Allen) 1945— **3**
Jackson, Jamea 1986— **64**
Jackson, Janet 1966— **6, 30, 68**
Jackson, Jesse 1941— **1, 27**
Jackson, Jesse Louis, Jr. 1965— **14, 45**
Jackson, John 1924-2002 **36**
Jackson, Judith D. 1950— **57**
Jackson, Mae 1941-2005 **57**
Jackson, Mahalia 1911-1972 **5**
Jackson, Mannie 1939— **14**
Jackson, Maynard (Holbrook, Jr.) 1938-2003 **2, 41**
Jackson, Michael 1958— **19, 53**
Jackson, Millie 1944— **25**
Jackson, Milt 1923-1999 **26**
Jackson, O'Shea *See Ice Cube*
Jackson, Randy 1956— **40**
Jackson, Reginald Martinez 1946— **15**
Jackson, Samuel 1948— **8, 19, 63**
Jackson, Sheneska 1970(?)— **18**
Jackson, Shirley Ann 1946— **12**
Jackson, Tom 1951— **70**
Jackson, Vera 1912— **40**
Jaco, Wasalu Muhammad *See Fiasco, Lupe*
Jacob, John E(dward) 1934— **2**
Jacobs, Marion Walter *See Little Walter*
Jacobs, Regina 1963— **38**
Jacquet, Illinois 1922(?)-2004 **49**
Jagan, Cheddi 1918-1997 **16**
Jaheim 1978— **58**
Jakes, Thomas "T.D." 1957— **17, 43**
Jam, Jimmy *See Jimmy Jam*
Jamal, Ahmad 1930— **69**
Jamelia 1981— **51**
Jamerson, James 1936-1983 **59**
James, Charles H., III 1959(?)— **62**
James, Daniel "Chappie," Jr. 1920-1978 **16**
James, Donna A. 1957— **51**
James, Etta 1938— **13, 52**
James, Juanita (Therese) 1952— **13**
James, LeBron 1984— **46**
James, Sharpe 1936— **23, 69**
James, Skip 1902-1969 **38**
Jamison, Judith 1943— **7, 67**
Jammeh, Yahya 1965— **23**
Jarreau, Al 1940— **21, 65**
Jarret, Vernon D. 1921— **42**
Jarvis, Charlene Drew 1941— **21**
Jarvis, Erich 1965— **67**
Jasper, Kenji 1976(?)— **39**
Jawara, Dawda Kairaba 1924— **11**
Jay, Jam Master 1965— **31**
Jay-Z 1970— **27, 69**
Jealous, Benjamin 1973— **70**
Jean, Michaëlle 1957— **70**
Jean, Wyclef 1970— **20**
Jean-Baptiste, Marianne 1967— **17, 46**
Jeffers, Eve Jihan *See Eve*
Jefferson, William J. 1947— **25**

Jeffries, Leonard 1937— **8**
Jemison, Mae C. 1957— **1, 35**
Jemison, Major L. 1955(?)— **48**
Jenifer, Franklyn G(reen) 1939— **2**
Jenkins, Beverly 1951— **14**
Jenkins, Ella (Louise) 1924— **15**
Jenkins, Fergie 1943— **46**
Jenkins, Jay *See Young Jeezy*
Jennings, Chester *See Jennings, Lyfe*
Jennings, Lyfe 1973— **56, 69**
Jerkins, Rodney 1978(?)— **31**
Jeter, Derek 1974— **27**
Jimmy Jam 1959— **13**
Joachim, Paulin 1931— **34**
Joe, Yolanda 19(?)(?)— **21**
John, Daymond 1969(?)— **23**
Johns, Vernon 1892-1965 **38**
Johnson, Angela 1961— **52**
Johnson, Arnez *See Arnez J*
Johnson, Avery 1965— **62**
Johnson, Ben 1961— **1**
Johnson, Beverly 1952— **2**
Johnson, Buddy 1915-1977 **36**
Johnson, Carol Diann *See Carroll, Diahann*
Johnson, Caryn E. *See Goldberg, Whoopi*
Johnson, Charles 1948— **1**
Johnson, Charles Arthur *See St. Jacques, Raymond*
Johnson, Charles Spurgeon 1893-1956 **12**
Johnson, Clifford "Connie" 1922-2004 **52**
Johnson, Dwayne *See Rock, The*
Johnson, Earvin "Magic" 1959— **3, 39**
Johnson, Eddie Bernice 1935— **8**
Johnson, George E. 1927— **29**
Johnson, Georgia Douglas 1880-1966 **41**
Johnson, Harry E. 1954— **57**
Johnson, Harvey Jr. 1947(?)— **24**
Johnson, Hazel 1927— **22**
Johnson, J. J. 1924-2001 **37**
Johnson, Jack 1878-1946 **8**
Johnson, James Louis *See Johnson, J. J.*
Johnson, James Weldon 1871-1938 **5**
Johnson, James William *See Johnson, James Weldon*
Johnson, Je'Caryous 1977— **63**
Johnson, Jeh Vincent 1931— **44**
Johnson, John Arthur *See Johnson, Jack*
Johnson, John H. 1918-2005 **3, 54**
Johnson, Johnnie 1924-2005 **56**
Johnson, Katherine (Coleman Goble) 1918— **61**
Johnson, Kevin 1966— **70**
Johnson, Larry 1969— **28**
Johnson, Levi 1950— **48**
Johnson, Linton Kwesi 1952— **37**
Johnson, Lonnie G. 1949— **32**
Johnson, "Magic" *See Johnson, Earvin "Magic"*
Johnson, Mamie "Peanut" 1932— **40**
Johnson, Marguerite *See Angelou, Maya*
Johnson, Mat 1971(?)— **31**

Johnson, Michael (Duane) 1967— **13**
Johnson, Norma L. Holloway 1932— **17**
Johnson, R. M. 1968— **36**
Johnson, Rafer 1934— **33**
Johnson, Robert 1911-1938 **2**
Johnson, Robert L. 1946(?)— **3, 39**
Johnson, Robert T. 1948— **17**
Johnson, Rodney Van 19(?)(?)— **28**
Johnson, Sheila Crump 1949(?)— **48**
Johnson, Shoshana 1973— **47**
Johnson, Taalib *See Musiq*
Johnson, Virginia (Alma Fairfax) 1950— **9**
Johnson, William Henry 1901-1970 **3**
Johnson, Woodrow Wilson *See Johnson, Buddy*
Johnson-Brown, Hazel W. *See Johnson, Hazel*
Jolley, Willie 1956— **28**
Jones, Absalom 1746-1818 **52**
Jones, Alex 1941— **64**
Jones, Anthony *See Jones, Van*
Jones, Bill T. 1952— **1, 46**
Jones, Bobby 1939(?)— **20**
Jones, Carl 1955?— **7**
Jones, Caroline R. 1942— **29**
Jones, Clara Stanton 1913— **51**
Jones, Cobi N'Gai 1970— **18**
Jones, Donell 1973— **29**
Jones, Doris W. 1914(?)–2006 **62**
Jones, E. Edward, Sr. 1931— **45**
Jones, Ed "Too Tall" 1951— **46**
Jones, Edith Mae Irby 1927— **65**
Jones, Edward P. 1950— **43, 67**
Jones, Elaine R. 1944— **7, 45**
Jones, Elvin 1927–2004 **14, 68**
Jones, Etta 1928-2001 **35**
Jones, Frederick McKinley 1893–1961 **68**
Jones, Frederick Russell *See Jamal, Ahmad*
Jones, Gayl 1949— **37**
Jones, Hank 1918— **57**
Jones, Ingrid Saunders 1945— **18**
Jones, James Earl 1931— **3, 49**
Jones, Jonah 1909-2000 **39**
Jones, Kelis *See Kelis*
Jones, Kimberly Denise *See Lil' Kim*
Jones, Le Roi *See Baraka, Amiri*
Jones, Lillie Mae *See Carter, Betty*
Jones, Lois Mailou 1905— **13**
Jones, Lou 1932-2006 **64**
Jones, Marion 1975— **21, 66**
Jones, Merlakia 1973— **34**
Jones, Monty 1951(?)— **66**
Jones, Nasir *See Nas*
Jones, Orlando 1968— **30**
Jones, Quincy (Delight) 1933— **8, 30**
Jones, Randy 1969— **35**
Jones, Robert Elliott *See Jones, Jonah*
Jones, Roy Jr. 1969— **22**
Jones, Russell *See Ol' Dirty Bastard*
Jones, Ruth Lee *See Washington, Dinah*
Jones, Sarah 1974— **39**

Jones, Sissieretta *See* Joyner, Matilda Sissieretta
Jones, Star *See* Reynolds, Star Jones
Jones, Thad 1923–1986 **68**
Jones, Thomas W. 1949— **41**
Jones, Van 1968— **70**
Jones, Wayne 1952— **53**
Jones, William A., Jr. 1934-2006 **61**
Joplin, Scott 1868-1917 **6**
Jordan, Barbara (Charline) 1936— **4**
Jordan, Eric Benét *See* Benét, Eric
Jordan, June 1936— **7, 35**
Jordan, Michael (Jeffrey) 1963— **6, 21**
Jordan, Montell 1968(?)— **23**
Jordan, Ronny 1962— **26**
Jordan, Vernon E(ulion, Jr.) 1935— **3, 35**
Joseph, Kathie-Ann 1970(?)— **56**
Josey, E. J. 1924— **10**
Joyner, Jacqueline *See* Joyner-Kersee, Jackie
Joyner, Marjorie Stewart 1896-1994 **26**
Joyner, Matilda Sissieretta 1869(?)-1933 **15**
Joyner, Tom 1949(?)— **19**
Joyner-Kersee, Jackie 1962— **5**
Julian, Percy Lavon 1899–1975 **6**
Julien, Isaac 1960— **3**
July, William II 19(?)(?)— **27**
Juma, Calestous 1953— **57**
Just, Ernest Everett 1883-1941 **3**
Justice, David Christopher 1966— **18**
Ka Dinizulu, Israel *See* Ka Dinizulu, Mcwayizeni
Ka Dinizulu, Mcwayizeni 1932-1999 **29**
Kabbah, Ahmad Tejan 1932— **23**
Kabila, Joseph 1968(?)— **30**
Kabila, Laurent 1939— **20**
Kagame, Paul 1957— **54**
Kaigler, Denise 1962— **63**
Kaiser, Cecil 1916— **42**
Kamau, Johnstone *See* Kenyatta, Jomo
Kamau, Kwadwo Agymah 1960(?)— **28**
Kani, Karl 1968(?)— **10**
Kanouté, Fred 1977— **68**
Karenga, Maulana 1941— **10, 71**
Karim, Benjamin 1932-2005 **61**
Kariuki, J. M. 1929–1975 **67**
Katoucha *See* Niane, Katoucha
Kaufman, Monica 1948(?)— **66**
Kaunda, Kenneth (David) 1924— **2**
Kay, Jackie 1961— **37**
Kay, Ulysses 1917-1995 **37**
Kayira, Legson 1942— **40**
Kearney, Janis 1953— **54**
Kearse, Amalya Lyle 1937— **12**
Kebede, Liya 1978— **59**
Kee, John P. 1962— **43**
Keflezighi, Meb 1975— **49**
Keith, Damon Jerome 1922— **16**
Keith, Floyd A. 1948— **61**
Keith, Rachel Boone 1924-2007 **63**
Kelis 1979— **58**
Kelley, Elijah 1986— **65**
Kelley, Malcolm David 1992— **59**
Kellogg, Clark 1961— **64**

Kelly, Leontine 1920— **33**
Kelly, Patrick 1954(?)-1990 **3**
Kelly, R. 1967— **18, 44, 71**
Kelly, Robert Sylvester *See* Kelly, R.
Kelly, Sharon Pratt *See* Dixon, Sharon Pratt
Kem 196(?)— **47**
Kendrick, Erika 1975— **57**
Kendricks, Eddie 1939-1992 **22**
Kennard, William Earl 1957— **18**
Kennedy, Adrienne 1931— **11**
Kennedy, Florynce Rae 1916-2000 **12, 33**
Kennedy, Lelia McWilliams Robinson 1885-1931 **14**
Kennedy, Randall 1954— **40**
Kennedy-Overton, Jayne Harris 1951— **46**
Kenney, John A., Jr. 1914-2003 **48**
Kenoly, Ron 1944— **45**
Kente, Gibson 1932-2004 **52**
Kenyatta, Jomo 1891(?)-1978 **5**
Kenyatta, Robin 1942-2004 **54**
Kerekou, Ahmed (Mathieu) 1933— **1**
Kerry, Leon G. 1949(?)— **46**
Keyes, Alan L(ee) 1950— **11**
Keys, Alicia 1981— **32, 68**
Khan, Chaka 1953— **12, 50**
Khanga, Yelena 1962— **6**
Khumalo, Leleti 1970— **51**
Kibaki, Mwai 1931— **60**
Kidd, Mae Street 1904-1995 **39**
Kidjo, Anjelique 1960— **50**
Killens, John O. 1967-1987 **54**
Killings, Debra 196(?)— **57**
Killingsworth, Cleve, Jr. 1952— **54**
Kilpatrick, Carolyn Cheeks 1945— **16**
Kilpatrick, Kwame 1970— **34, 71**
Kimbro, Dennis (Paul) 1950— **10**
Kimbro, Henry A. 1912-1999 **25**
Kincaid, Bernard 1945— **28**
Kincaid, Jamaica 1949— **4**
King, Alonzo 19(?)(?)— **38**
King, B. B. 1925— **7**
King, Barbara 19(?)(?)— **22**
King, Bernice (Albertine) 1963— **4**
King, Colbert I. 1939— **69**
King, Coretta Scott 1927-2006 **3, 57**
King, Dexter (Scott) 1961— **10**
King, Don 1931— **14**
King, Gayle 1956— **19**
King, Martin Luther, III 1957— **20**
King, Martin Luther, Jr. 1929-1968 **1**
King, Oona 1967— **27**
King, Preston 1936— **28**
King, Reatha Clark 1938— **65**
King, Regina 1971— **22, 45**
King, Riley B. *See* King, B. B.
King, Robert Arthur 1945— **58**
King, Woodie Jr. 1937— **27**
King, Yolanda (Denise) 1955— **6**
KIntaudl, Leon 1949(?)— **62**
Kintaudi, Ngoma Miezi *See* Kintaudi, Leon
Kirby, George 1924-1995 **14**
Kirk, Ron 1954— **11**
Kitt, Eartha Mae 1928— **16**
Kitt, Sandra 1947— **23**

Kittles, Rick 1976(?)— **51**
Klugh, Earl 1953— **59**
Knight, Etheridge 1931-1991 **37**
Knight, Gladys 1944— **16, 66**
Knight, Gwendolyn 1913-2005 **63**
Knight, Marion, Jr. *See* Knight, Suge
Knight, Suge 1966— **11, 30**
Knowles, Beyoncé *See* Beyoncé
Knowles, Tina 1954(?)— **61**
Knowling, Robert Jr. 1955(?)— **38**
Knox, Simmie 1935— **49**
Knuckles, Frankie 1955— **42**
Kobia, Samuel 1947— **43**
Kodjoe, Boris 1973— **34**
Komunyakaa, Yusef 1941— **9**
Kone, Seydou *See* Blondy, Alpha
Kong, B. Waine 1943— **50**
Kool DJ Red Alert *See* Alert, Kool DJ Red
Kool Moe Dee 1963— **37**
Kotto, Yaphet (Fredrick) 1944— **7**
Kountz, Samuel L(ee) 1930-1981 **10**
Kravitz, Lenny 1964— **10, 34**
Kravitz, Leonard *See* Kravitz, Lenny
KRS-One 1965— **34**
Krute, Fred *See* Alert, Kool DJ Red
Kufuor, John Agyekum 1938— **54**
Kunjufu, Jawanza 1953— **3, 50**
Kuti, Fela Anikulapo *See* Fela
Kuti, Femi 1962— **47**
Kuzwayo, Ellen 1914–2006 **68**
Kyles, Cedric *See* Cedric the Entertainer
La Menthe, Ferdinand Joseph *See* Morton, Jelly Roll
La Salle, Eriq 1962— **12**
LaBelle, Patti 1944— **13, 30**
Lacy, Sam 1903-2003 **30, 46**
Ladd, Ernie 1938-2007 **64**
Ladner, Joyce A. 1943— **42**
Laferriere, Dany 1953— **33**
Lafontant, Jewel Stradford 1922-1997 **3, 51**
Lafontant-MANkarious, Jewel Stradford *See* Lafontant, Jewel Stradford
LaGuma, Alex 1925-1985 **30**
Lamming, George 1927— **35**
Lampkin, Daisy 1883(?)-1965 **19**
Lampley, Oni Faida 1959–2008 **43, 71**
Lampley, Vera *See* Lampley, Oni Faida
Lane, Charles 1953— **3**
Lane, Vincent 1942— **5**
Langhart Cohen, Janet 1941— **19, 60**
Lanier, Bob 1948— **47**
Lanier, Willie 1945— **33**
Lankford, Raymond Lewis 1967— **23**
Laraque, Georges 1976— **48**
Laraque, Paul 1920–2007 **67**
Larkin, Barry 1964— **24**
Larrieux, Amel 1973(?)— **63**
Lars, Byron 1965— **32**
Larsen, Nella 1891-1964 **10**
Laryea, Thomas Davies III 1979— **67**
Lashley, Bobby 1976— **63**

Lashley, Franklin Roberto *See* Lashley, Bobby
Lassiter, Roy 1969— **24**
Lathan, Sanaa 1971— **27**
Latimer, Lewis H(oward) 1848-1928 **4**
Lattimore, Kenny 1970(?)— **35**
Lavizzo-Mourey, Risa 1954— **48**
Lawal, Kase L. 19(?)(?)— **45**
Lawless, Theodore K(enneth) 1892-1971 **8**
Lawrence, Jacob (Armstead) 1917-2000 **4, 28**
Lawrence, Martin 1965— **6, 27, 60**
Lawrence, Robert Henry, Jr. 1935-1967 **16**
Lawrence-Lightfoot, Sara 1944— **10**
Lawson, Jennifer 1946— **1, 50**
Leary, Kathryn D. 1952— **10**
Leavell, Dorothy R. 1944— **17**
Lee, Annie Francis 1935— **22**
Lee, Barbara 1946— **25**
Lee, Bertram M., Sr. 1939-2003 **46**
Lee, Canada 1907-1952 **8**
Lee, Debra L. 1954— **62**
Lee, Don L(uther) *See* Madhubuti, Haki R.
Lee, Gabby *See* Lincoln, Abbey
Lee, Joe A. 1946(?)— **45**
Lee, Joie 1962(?)— **1**
Lee, Shelton Jackson *See* Lee, Spike
Lee, Spike 1957— **5, 19**
Lee-Smith, Hughie 1915— **5, 22**
Leevy, Carrol M. 1920— **42**
Lefel, Edith 1963-2003 **41**
Leffall, Lasalle, Jr. 1930— **3, 64**
Legend, John 1978— **67**
Leggs, Kingsley 196(?)— **62**
Leland, George Thomas *See* Leland, Mickey
Leland, Mickey 1944-1989 **2**
Lemmons, Kasi 1961— **20**
Lennox, Betty 1976— **31**
LeNoire, Rosetta 1911-2002 **37**
Lenox, Adriane 1956— **59**
Leon, Kenny 1957(?)— **10**
León, Tania 1943— **13**
Leonard, Buck 1907— **67**
Leonard, Sugar Ray 1956— **15**
Leonard, Walter Fenner *See* Leonard, Buck
Leslie, Lisa Deshaun 1972— **16**
Lester, Adrian 1968— **46**
Lester, Bill 1961— **42**
Lester, Julius 1939— **9**
Lesure, James 1975— **64**
LeTang, Henry 1915-2007 **66**
Letson, Al 1972— **39**
Levert, Eddie 1942— **70**
Levert, Gerald 1966-2006 **22, 59**
Lewellyn, J(ames) Bruce 1927— **13**
Lewis, Aylwin 1954(?)— **51**
Lewis, Butch 1946— **71**
Lewis, Byron E(ugene) 1931— **13**
Lewis, (Frederick) Carl(ton) 1961— **4**
Lewis, David Levering 1936— **9**
Lewis, Delano (Eugene) 1938— **7**
Lewis, Denise 1972— **33**
Lewis, (Mary) Edmonia 1845(?)-1911(?) **10**
Lewis, Edward T. 1940— **21**

Lewis, Emmanuel 1971— **36**
Lewis, Henry 1932-1996 **38**
Lewis, John 1940— **2, 46**
Lewis, Lennox 1965— **27**
Lewis, Marvin 1958— **51**
Lewis, Norman 1909-1979 **39**
Lewis, Oliver 1856-1924 **56**
Lewis, Ramsey 1935— **35, 70**
Lewis, Ray 1975— **33**
Lewis, Reginald F. 1942-1993 **6**
Lewis, Ronald *See* Lewis, *Butch*
Lewis, Samella 1924— **25**
Lewis, Shirley Ann Redd 1937— **14**
Lewis, Terry 1956— **13**
Lewis, Thomas 1939— **19**
Lewis, William M., Jr. 1956— **40**
Lewis-Thornton, Rae 1962— **32**
Ligging, Alfred III 1965— **43**
Lil' Bow Wow *See* Bow Wow
Lil' Kim 1975— **28**
Lil Wayne 1979— **66**
Lilakoi Moon *See* Bonet, Lisa
Liles, Kevin 1968— **42**
Lincoln, Abbey 1930— **3**
Lincoln, C(harles) Eric 1924-2000 **38**
Lindo, Delroy 1952— **18, 45**
Lindsey, Tommie 1951— **51**
Lipscomb, Mance 1895-1976 **49**
LisaRaye 1967— **27**
Lister, Marquita 1965(?) **65**
Liston, (Charles) Sonny 1928(?)-1970 **33**
Little Milton 1934-2005 **36, 54**
Little Richard 1932— **15**
Little Walter 1930-1968 **36**
Little, Benilde 1958— **21**
Little, Malcolm *See* X, Malcolm
Little, Robert L(angdon) 1938— **2**
Littlepage, Craig 1951— **35**
LL Cool J 1968— **16, 49**
Lloyd, Earl 1928(?)— **26**
Lloyd, John Henry "Pop" 1884-1965 **30**
Lloyd, Reginald 1967— **64**
Locke, Alain (LeRoy) 1886-1954 **10**
Locke, Eddie 1930— **44**
Lofton, James 1956— **42**
Lofton, Kenneth 1967— **12**
Lofton, Ramona 1950— **14**
Logan, Onnie Lee 1910(?)-1995 **14**
Logan, Rayford W. 1897-1982 **40**
Lomax, Michael L. 1947— **58**
Long, Eddie L. 19(?)(?)— **29**
Long, Loretta 1940— **58**
Long, Nia 1970— **17**
Long, Richard Alexander 1927— **65**
Lopes, Lisa " Left Eye" 1971-2002 **36**
Lord Pitt of Hampstead *See* Pitt, David Thomas
Lorde, Audre (Geraldine) 1934-1992 **6**
Lorenzo, Irving *See* Gotti, Irv
Loroupe, Tegla 1973— **59**
Lott, Ronnie 1959— **9**
Louis, Errol T. 1962— **8**
Louis, Joe 1914-1981 **5**
Loury, Glenn 1948— **36**
Love, Darlene 1941— **23**
Love, Ed 1932(?)— **58**
Love, Laura 1960— **50**
Love, Nat 1854-1921 **9**

Lover, Ed **10**
Loving, Alvin, Jr., 1935-2005 **35, 53**
Loving, Mildred 1939–2008 **69**
Lowe, Herbert 1962— **57**
Lowe, Sidney 1960— **64**
Lowery, Joseph E. 1924— **2**
Lowry, A. Leon 1913-2005 **60**
Lucas, John 1953— **7**
Lucien, Jon 1942-2007 **66**
Luckett, Letoya 1981— **61**
Lucy, William 1933— **50**
Lucy Foster, Autherine 1929— **35**
Ludacris, 1978— **37, 60**
Luke, Derek 1974— **61**
Lumbly, Carl 1952— **47**
Lumpkin, Elgin Baylor *See* Ginuwine
Lumumba, Patrice 1925-1961 **33**
Lushington, Augustus Nathaniel 1869-1939 **56**
Luthuli, Albert (John Mvumbi) 1898(?)-1967 **13**
Lyfe *See* Jennings, Lyfe
Lyle, Marcenia *See* Stone, Toni
Lyles, Lester Lawrence 1946— **31**
Lymon, Frankie 1942-1968 **22**
Lynch, Shola 1969— **61**
Lynn, Lonnie Rashid *See* Common
Lyons, Henry 1942(?)— **12**
Lyttle, Hulda Margaret 1889-1983 **14**
Maal, Baaba 1953— **66**
Maathai, Wangari 1940— **43**
Mabley, Jackie "Moms" 1897(?)-1975 **15**
Mabrey, Vicki 1957(?)— **26**
Mabry, Marcus 1967— **70**
Mabuza, Lindiwe 1938— **18**
Mabuza-Suttle, Felicia 1950— **43**
Mac, Bernie 1957— **29, 61**
Machel, Graca Simbine 1945— **16**
Machel, Samora Moises 1933-1986 **8**
Madhubuti, Haki R. 1942— **7**
Madikizela, Nkosikazi Nobandle Nomzamo Winifred *See* Mandela, Winnie
Madison, Joseph E. 1949— **17**
Madison, Paula 1952— **37**
Madison, Romell 1952— **45**
Magloire, Paul Eugène 1907–2001 **68**
Mahal, Taj 1942— **39**
Mahlasela, Vusi 1965— **65**
Mahorn, Rick 1958— **60**
Mainor, Dorothy Leigh 1910(?)-1996 **19**
Majette, Denise 1955— **41**
Major, Clarence 1936— **9**
Majors, Jeff 1960(?)— **41**
Makeba, Miriam 1932— **2, 50**
Malco, Romany 1968— **71**
Malcolm X *See* X, Malcolm
Mallett, Conrad, Jr. 1953— **16**
Mallory, Mark 1962— **62**
Malone Jones, Vivian 1942-2005 **59**
Malone, Annie (Minerva Turnbo Pope) 1869-1957 **13**
Malone, Karl 1963— **18, 51**
Malone, Maurice 1965— **32**
Malveaux, Floyd 1940— **54**
Malveaux, Julianne 1953— **32, 70**

Mamdou, Tandja 1938— **33**
Mandela, Nelson (Rolihlahla) 1918— **1, 14**
Mandela, Winnie 1934— **2, 35**
Manigault, Earl "The Goat" 1943— **15**
Manigault-Stallworth, Omarosa 1974— **69**
Manley, Audrey Forbes 1934— **16**
Manley, Edna 1900-1987 **26**
Manley, Ruth 1947— **34**
Marable, Manning 1950— **10**
March, William Carrington 1923-2002 **56**
Marchand, Inga *See* Foxy Brown
Marechera, Charles William *See* Marechera, Dambudzo
Marechera, Dambudzo 1952-1987 **39**
Marechera, Tambudzai *See* Marechera, Dambudzo
Mariner, Jonathan 1954(?)— **41**
Marino, Eugene Antonio 1934-2000 **30**
Mario 1986— **71**
Markham, E(dward) A(rchibald) 1939— **37**
Marley, Bob 1945-1981 **5**
Marley, David *See* Marley, Ziggy
Marley, Rita 1947— **32, 70**
Marley, Robert Nesta *See* Marley, Bob
Marley, Ziggy 1968— **41**
Marrow, Queen Esther 1943(?)— **24**
Marrow, Tracey *See* Ice-T
Marsalis, Branford 1960— **34**
Marsalis, Delfeayo 1965— **41**
Marsalis, Wynton 1961— **16**
Marsh, Henry L., III 1934(?)— **32**
Marshall, Bella 1950— **22**
Marshall, Gloria *See* Sudarkasa, Niara
Marshall, Kerry James 1955— **59**
Marshall, Paule 1929— **7**
Marshall, Thurgood 1908-1993 **1, 44**
Marshall, Valenza Pauline Burke *See* Marshall, Paule
Martha Jean "The Queen" *See* Steinberg, Martha Jean
Martin, Darnell 1964— **43**
Martin, Helen 1909-2000 **31**
Martin, Jesse L. 19(?)(?)— **31**
Martin, Louis Emanuel 1912-1997 **16**
Martin, Roberta 1907-1969 **58**
Martin, Roland S. 1969(?)— **49**
Martin, Ruby Grant 1933-2003 **49**
Martin, Sara 1884-1955 **38**
Marvin X *See* X, Marvin
Mary Mary **34**
Mase 1977(?)— **24**
Masekela, Barbara 1941— **18**
Masekela, Hugh (Ramopolo) 1939— **1**
Masire, Quett (Ketumile Joni) 1925— **5**
Mason, Felicia 1963(?)— **31**
Mason, Ronald 1949— **27**
Massaquoi, Hans J. 1926— **30**
Massenburg, Kedar 1964(?)— **23**
Massey, Brandon 1973— **40**

Massey, Walter E(ugene) 1938— **5, 45**
Massie, Samuel Proctor, Jr. 1919— **29**
Master P 1970— **21**
Mathabane, Johannes *See* Mathabane, Mark
Mathabane, Mark 1960— **5**
Mathis, Greg 1960— **26**
Mathis, Johnny 1935— **20**
Matthews, Denise *See* Vanity
Matthews, Mark 1894-2005 **59**
Matthews Shatteen, Westina 1948— **51**
Mauldin, Jermaine Dupri *See* Dupri, Jermaine
Maxey, Randall 1941— **46**
Maxis, Theresa 1810-1892 **62**
Maxwell 1973— **20**
May, Derrick 1963— **41**
Mayers, Jamal 1974— **39**
Mayfield, Curtis (Lee) 1942-1999 **2, 43**
Mayhew, Richard 1924— **39**
Maynard, Robert C(lyve) 1937-1993 **7**
Maynor, Dorothy 1910-1996 **19**
Mayo, Whitman 1930-2001 **32**
Mays, Benjamin E(lijah) 1894-1984 **7**
Mays, Leslie A. 19(?)(?)— **41**
Mays, William G. 1946— **34**
Mays, William Howard, Jr. *See* Mays, Willie
Mays, Willie 1931— **3**
Mayweather, Floyd, Jr. 1977— **57**
Mazrui, Ali Al'Amin 1933— **12**
M'bala M'bala, Dieudonné *See* Dieudonné
Mbaye, Mariétou 1948— **31**
Mbeki, Thabo Mvuyelwa 1942— **14**
Mboup, Souleymane 1951— **10**
Mbuende, Kaire Munionganda 1953— **12**
MC Lyte 1971— **34**
McAnulty, William E., Jr. 1947-2007 **66**
McBride, Bryant Scott 1965— **18**
McBride, James C. 1957— **35**
McCabe, Jewell Jackson 1945— **10**
McCall, H. Carl 1938(?)— **27**
McCall, Nathan 1955— **8**
McCann, Renetta 1957(?)— **44**
McCarthy, Sandy 1972— **64**
McCarty, Osceola 1908— **16**
McClendon, Lisa 1975(?)— **61**
McClurkin, Donnie 1961— **25**
McCoo, Marilyn 1943— **53**
McCoy, Elijah 1844-1929 **8**
McCrary, Crystal *See* McCrary Anthony, Crystal
McCrary Anthony, Crystal 1969— **70**
McCray, Nikki 1972— **18**
McCullough, Geraldine 1922— **58**
McDaniel, Hattie 1895-1952 **5**
McDaniels, Darryl *See* DMC
McDonald, Audra 1970— **20, 62**
McDonald, Erroll 1954(?)— **1**
McDonald, Gabrielle Kirk 1942— **20**
McDougall, Gay J. 1947— **11, 43**
McDuffie, Dwayne 1962— **62**
McEwen, Mark 1954— **5**

McFadden, Bernice L. 1966— **39**
McFarlan, Tyron 1971(?)— **60**
McFarland, Roland 1940— **49**
McFerrin, Bobby 1950— **68**
McFerrin, Robert, Jr. *See* McFerrin, Bobby
McGee, Charles 1924— **10**
McGee, James Madison 1940— **46**
McGlowan, Angela 1970(?)— **64**
McGriff, Fred 1963— **24**
McGruder, Aaron 1974— **28, 56**
McGruder, Robert 1942— **22, 35**
McGuire, Raymond J. 1957(?)(—) **57**
McIntosh, Winston Hubert *See* Tosh, Peter
McIntyre, Natalie *See* Gary, Macy
McKay, Claude 1889–1948 **6**
McKay, Festus Claudius *See* McKay, Claude
McKay, Nellie Yvonne 19(?)(?)–2006 **17, 57**
McKee, Lonette 1952— **12**
McKegney, Tony 1958— **3**
McKenzie, Vashti M. 1947— **29**
McKinney Hammond, Michelle 1957— **51**
McKinney, Cynthia Ann 1955— **11, 52**
McKinney, Nina Mae 1912-1967 **40**
McKinney-Whetstone, Diane 1954(?)— **27**
McKinnon, Ike *See* McKinnon, Isaiah
McKinnon, Isaiah 1943— **9**
McKissick, Floyd B(ixler) 1922-1981 **3**
McKnight, Brian 1969— **18, 34**
McLeod, Gus 1955(?)— **27**
McLeod, Gustavus *See* McLeod, Gus
McMillan, Rosalynn A. 1953— **36**
McMillan, Terry 1951— **4, 17, 53**
McMurray, Georgia L. 1934-1992 **36**
McNabb, Donovan 1976— **29**
McNair, Ronald 1950-1986 **3, 58**
McNair, Steve 1973— **22, 47**
McNeil, Lori 1964(?)— **1**
McPhail, Sharon 1948— **2**
McPherson, David 1968— **32**
McPherson, James Alan 1943— **70**
McQueen, Butterfly 1911-1995 **6, 54**
McQueen, Thelma *See* McQueen, Butterfly
McWhorter, John 1965— **35**
Meadows, Tim 1961— **30**
Meek, Carrie (Pittman) 1926— **6, 36**
Meek, Kendrick 1966— **41**
Meeks, Gregory 1953— **25**
Meles Zenawi 1955(?)— **3**
Mell, Patricia 1953— **49**
Memmi, Albert 1920— **37**
Memphis Minnie 1897-1973 **33**
Mengestu, Dinaw 1978— **66**
Mengistu, Haile Mariam 1937— **65**
Mensah, Thomas 1950— **48**
Mercado-Valdes, Frank 1962— **43**
Meredith, James H(oward) 1933— **11**
Merkerson, S. Epatha 1952— **47**
Messenger, The *See* Divine, Father

Metcalfe, Ralph 1910-1978 **26**
Meyer, June *See* Jordan, June
Mfume, Kweisi 1948— **6, 41**
Mhlaba, Raymond 1920-2005 **55**
Micheaux, Oscar (Devereaux) 1884-1951 **7**
Michele, Michael 1966— **31**
Mickelbury, Penny 1948— **28**
Milla, Roger 1952— **2**
Miles, Buddy 1947–2008 **69**
Miles, George Allen, Jr. *See* Miles, Buddy
Millender-McDonald, Juanita 1938-2007 **21, 61**
Miller, Bebe 1950— **3**
Miller, Cheryl 1964— **10**
Miller, Dorie 1919-1943 **29**
Miller, Doris *See* Miller, Dorie
Miller, Maria 1803-1879 **19**
Miller, Percy *See* Master P
Miller, Reggie 1965— **33**
Miller, Warren F., Jr. 1943— **53**
Miller-Travis, Vernice 1959— **64**
Millines Dziko, Trish 1957— **28**
Mills, Florence 1896-1927 **22**
Mills, Joseph C. 1946— **51**
Mills, Sam 1959— **33**
Mills, Stephanie 1957— **36**
Mills, Steve 1960(?)— **47**
Milner, Ron 1938— **39**
Milton, DeLisha 1974— **31**
Mingo, Frank L. 1939-1989 **32**
Mingus, Charles Jr. 1922-1979 **15**
Minor, DeWayne 1956— **32**
Mitchell, Arthur 1934— **2, 47**
Mitchell, Brian Stokes 1957— **21**
Mitchell, Corinne 1914-1993 **8**
Mitchell, Elvis 1958— **67**
Mitchell, Kel 1978— **66**
Mitchell, Leona 1949— **42**
Mitchell, Loften 1919-2001 **31**
Mitchell, Nicole 1967(?)— **66**
Mitchell, Parren J. 1922-2007 **42, 66**
Mitchell, Russ 1960— **21**
Mitchell, Sharon 1962— **36**
Mizell, Jason *See* Jay, Jam Master
Mkapa, Benjamin William 1938— **16**
Mo', Keb' 1952— **36**
Mobutu Sese Seko 1930-1997 **1, 56**
Mofolo, Thomas (Mokopu) 1876-1948 **37**
Mogae, Festus Gontebanye 1939— **19**
Mohamed, Ali Mahdi *See* Ali Mahdi Mohamed
Mohammed, Nazr 1977— **64**
Mohammed, W. Deen 1933— **27**
Mohammed, Warith Deen *See* Mohammed, W. Deen
Mohlabane, Goapele *See* Goapele
Moi, Daniel Arap 1924— **1, 35**
Mollel, Tololwa 1952— **38**
Mongella, Gertrude 1945— **11**
Monica 1980— **21**
Mo'Nique 1967— **35**
Monk, Art 1957— **38**
Monk, Thelonious (Sphere, Jr.) 1917-1982 **1**
Monroe, Bryan 1965— **71**
Monroe, Mary 19(?)(?)— **35**

Montgomery, Tim 1975— **41**
Moody, Ronald 1900-1984 **30**
Moon, Warren 1956— **8, 66**
Mooney, Paul 19(?)(?)— **37**
Moore, Alice Ruth *See* Dunbar-Nelson, Alice Ruth Moore
Moore, Barbara C. 1949— **49**
Moore, Bobby *See* Rashad, Ahmad
Moore, Chante 1970(?)— **26**
Moore, Dorothy Rudd 1940— **46**
Moore, Gwendolynne S. 1951— **55**
Moore, Harry T. 1905-1951 **29**
Moore, Jessica Care 1971— **30**
Moore, Johnny B. 1950— **38**
Moore, Kevin *See* Mo', Keb'
Moore, Melba 1945— **21**
Moore, Minyon 19(?)(?)— **45**
Moore, Shemar 1970— **21**
Moore, Undine Smith 1904-1989 **28**
Moorer, Lana *See* MC Lyte
Moorer, Michael 1967— **19**
Moose, Charles 1953— **40**
Morgan, Garrett (Augustus) 1877-1963 **1**
Morgan, Gertrude 1900-1986 **63**
Morgan, Irene 1917-2007 **65**
Morgan, Joe Leonard 1943— **9**
Morgan, Rose (Meta) 1912(?)— **11**
Morgan, Tracy 1968— **61**
Morganfield, McKinley *See* Muddy Waters
Morial, Ernest "Dutch" 1929-1989 **26**
Morial, Marc H. 1958— **20, 51**
Morris, Garrett 1937— **31**
Morris, Greg 1934-1996 **28**
Morris, William "Bill" 1938— **51**
Morris, Stevland Judkins *See* Wonder, Stevie
Morrison, Keith 1942— **13**
Morrison, Mary Thelma *See* Washington, Mary T.
Morrison, Sam 1936— **50**
Morrison, Toni 1931— **2, 15**
Morton, Azie Taylor 1936-2003 **48**
Morton, Jelly Roll 1885(?)-1941 **29**
Morton, Joe 1947— **18**
Mos Def 1973— **30**
Moseka, Aminata *See* Lincoln, Abbey
Moseley-Braun, Carol *See* Braun, Carol (Elizabeth) Moseley
Moses, Edwin 1955— **8**
Moses, Gilbert, III 1942-1995 **12**
Moses, Robert Parris 1935— **11**
Mosley, "Sugar" Shane 1971— **32**
Mosley, Tim *See* Timbaland
Mosley, Walter 1952— **5, 25, 68**
Moss, Bryant *See* Moss, Preacher
Moss, Carlton 1909-1997 **17**
Moss, J. (?)— **64**
Moss, Preacher 1967— **63**
Moss, Randy 1977— **23**
Moss, Shad Gregory *See* Lil' Bow Wow
Mossell, Gertrude Bustill 1855-1948 **40**
Moten, Etta *See* Barnett, Etta Moten
Motley, Archibald, Jr. 1891-1981 **30**
Motley, Constance Baker 1921-2005 **10, 55**
Motley, Marion 1920-1999 **26**

Mourning, Alonzo 1970— **17, 44**
Moutoussamy-Ashe, Jeanne 1951— **7**
Mowatt, Judy 1952(?)— **38**
Mowry, Jess 1960— **7**
Moyo, Karega Kofi 19(?)(?)— **36**
Moyo, Yvette Jackson 1953— **36**
Mphalele, Es'kia (Ezekiel) 1919— **40**
Mswati III 1968— **56**
Mudimbe, V. Y. 1941— **61**
Mugabe, Robert 1924— **10, 71**
Mugo, Madeleine *See* Mugo, Micere Githae
Mugo, Micere Githae 1942— **32**
Muhajir, El *See* X, Marvin
Muhammad, Ava 1951— **31**
Muhammad, Elijah 1897-1975 **4**
Muhammad, Khallid Abdul 1951(?)— **10, 31**
Mullen, Harryette 1953— **34**
Mullen, Nicole C. 1967— **45**
Muluzi, Elson Bakili 1943— **14**
Mumba, Samantha 1983— **29**
Mundine, Anthony 1975— **56**
Murphy, Eddie 1961— **4, 20, 61**
Murphy, Edward Regan *See* Murphy, Eddie
Murphy, John H. 1916— **42**
Murphy, Laura M. 1955— **43**
Murphy McKenzie, Vashti *See* McKenzie, Vashti M.
Murray, Albert L. 1916— **33**
Murray, Cecil 1929— **12, 47**
Murray, Eddie 1956— **12**
Murray, Lenda 1962— **10**
Murray, Pauli 1910-1985 **38**
Murray, Tai 1982— **47**
Murrell, Sylvia Marilyn 1947— **49**
Muse, Clarence Edouard 1889-1979 **21**
Museveni, Yoweri (Kaguta) 1944(?)— **4**
Musiq 1977— **37**
Mutebi, Ronald 1956— **25**
Mutola, Maria de Lurdes 1972— **12**
Mutombo, Dikembe 1966— **7**
Mutu, Wangechi 19(?)(?)— **44**
Mwangi, Meja 1948— **40**
Mwinyi, Ali Hassan 1925— **1**
Mya 1979— **35**
Myers, Dwight *See* Heavy D
Myers, Walter Dean 1937— **8, 70**
Myers, Walter Milton *See* Myers, Walter Dean
Myles, Kim 1974— **69**
Nabrit, Samuel Milton 1905-2003 **47**
Nagin, C. Ray 1956— **42, 57**
Nagin, Ray *See* Nagin, C. Ray
Nakhid, David 1964— **25**
Naki, Hamilton 1926-2005 **63**
Nance, Cynthia 1958— **71**
Nanula, Richard D. 1960— **20**
Napoleon, Benny N. 1956(?)— **23**
Nas 1973— **33**
Nascimento, Milton 1942— **2, 64**
Nash, Joe 1919-2005 **55**
Nash, Johnny 1940— **40**
Nash, Niecy 1970— **66**
Naylor, Gloria 1950— **10, 42**
Ndadaye, Melchior 1953-1993 **7**
Ndegeocello, Me'Shell 1968— **15**

N'Dour, Youssou 1959— **1, 53**
Ndungane, Winston Njongonkulu 1941— **16**
Ne-Yo 1982— **65**
Neal, Elise 1970— **29**
Neal, Larry 1937-1981 **38**
Neal, Raful 1936— **44**
Neale, Haydain 1970— **52**
Nelly 1978— **32**
Nelson Meigs, Andrea 1968— **48**
Nelson, Jill 1952— **6, 54**
Nelson, Prince Rogers *See Prince*
Neto, António Agostinho 1922— **43**
Nettles, Marva Deloise *See Collins, Marva*
Neville, Aaron 1941— **21**
Neville, Arthel 1962— **53**
Newcombe, Don 1926— **24**
Newkirk, Pamela 1957— **69**
Newman, Lester C. 1952— **51**
Newsome, Ozzie 1956— **26**
Newton, Huey (Percy) 1942-1989 **2**
Newton, Thandie 1972— **26**
Ngengi, Kamau wa *See Kenyatta, Jomo*
Ngilu, Charity 1952— **58**
Ngubane, (Baldwin Sipho) Ben 1941— **33**
Ngugi wa Thiong'o 1938— **29, 61**
Ngugi, James wa Thiong'o *See Ngugi wa Thiong'o*
Niane, Katoucha 1960-2008 **70**
Nicholas, Fayard 1914-2006 **20, 57, 61**
Nicholas, Harold 1921— **20**
Nichols, Grace *See Nichols, Nichelle*
Nichols, James Thomas *See Bell, James "Cool Papa"*
Nichols, Nichelle 1933(?)— **11**
Nissel, Angela 1974— **42**
Nix, Robert N.C., Jr. 1928-2003 **51**
Njongonkulu, Winston Ndungane 1941— **16**
Nkoli, Simon 1957-1998 **60**
Nkomo, Joshua 1917-1999 **4, 65**
Nkosi, Lewis 1936— **46**
Nkrumah, Kwame 1909-1972 **3**
N'Namdi, George R. 1946— **17**
Noah, Yannick 1960— **4, 60**
Noble, Ronald 1957— **46**
Norman, Christina 1960(?)— **47**
Norman, Jessye 1945— **5**
Norman, Maidie 1912-1998 **20**
Norman, Pat 1939— **10**
Norton, Eleanor Holmes 1937— **7**
Norwood, Brandy *See Brandy*
Notorious B.I.G. 1972-1997 **20**
Nottage, Cynthia DeLores *See Tucker, C. DeLores*
Nottage, Lynn 1964— **66**
Nour, Nawal M. 1965(?)— **56**
Ntaryamira, Cyprien 1955-1994 **8**
Ntshona, Winston 1941— **52**
Nugent, Richard Bruce 1906-1987 **39**
Nujoma, Samuel 1929— **10**
Nunez, Elizabeth 1944(?)— **62**
Nunn, Annetta 1959— **43**
Nutter, Michael 1958— **69**
Nuttin' but Stringz *See Escobar, Tourie, and Escobar, Damien*
Nyanda, Siphiwe 1950— **21**

Nyerere, Julius (Kambarage) 1922— **5**
Nzo, Alfred (Baphethuxolo) 1925— **15**
Obama, Barack 1961— **49**
Obama, Michelle 1964— **61**
Obasanjo, Olusegun 1937— **5, 22**
Obasanjo, Stella 1945-2005 **32, 56**
Obote, Milton 1925-2005 **63**
ODB *See Ol' Dirty Bastard*
Odetta 1939 **37**
Odinga, Raila 1945— **67**
Oglesby, Zena 1947— **12**
Ogletree, Charles, Jr. 1952— **12, 47**
Ogunlesi, Adebayo O. 19(?)(?)— **37**
Ojikutu, Bayo 1971— **66**
Ojikutu, Bisola 1974— **65**
Okaalet, Peter 1953— **58**
Okara, Gabriel 1921— **37**
Okonedo, Sophie 1969— **67**
Okosuns, Sonny 1947–2008 **71**
Ol' Dirty Bastard 1968-2004 **52**
Olajuwon, Akeem *See Olajuwon, Hakeem (Abdul Ajibola)*
Olajuwon, Hakeem (Abdul Ajibola) 1963— **2**
Olatunji, Babatunde 1927— **36**
Olden, Georg(e) 1920-1975 **44**
O'Leary, Hazel (Rollins) 1937— **6**
Oliver, Jerry 1947— **37**
Oliver, Joe "King" 1885-1938 **42**
Oliver, John J., Jr. 1945— **48**
Oliver, Kimberly 1976— **60**
Oliver, Pam 1961— **54**
Olojede, Dele 1961— **59**
Olopade, Olufunmilayo Falusi 1957(?)— **58**
O'Neal, Ron 1937-2004 **46**
O'Neal, Shaquille (Rashaun) 1972— **8, 30**
O'Neal, Stanley 1951— **38, 67**
O'Neil, Buck 1911-2006 **19, 59**
O'Neil, John Jordan *See O'Neil, Buck*
Ongala, Ramadhani Mtoro *See Ongala, Remmy*
Ongala, Remmy 1947— **9**
Onwueme, Tess Osonye 1955— **23**
Onwurah, Ngozi 1966(?)— **38**
Onyewu, Oguchi 1982— **60**
O'Ree, William Eldon *See O'Ree, Willie*
O'Ree, Willie 1935— **5**
Orlandersmith, Dael 1959— **42**
Orman, Roscoe 1944— **55**
Ortiz, David 1975— **52**
Osborne, Jeffrey 1948— **26**
Osborne, Na'taki 1974— **54**
Otis, Clarence, Jr. 1956— **55**
Otis, Clyde 1924— **67**
Otunga, Maurice Michael 1923-2003 **55**
Ouattara 1957— **43**
Ousmane, Sembène *See Sembène, Ousmane*
OutKast **35**
Owens, Dana *See Queen Latifah*
Owens, Helen 1937— **48**
Owens, J. C. *See Owens, Jesse*
Owens, Jack 1904-1997 **38**
Owens, James Cleveland *See Owens, Jesse*

Owens, Jesse 1913-1980 **2**
Owens, Major (Robert) 1936— **6**
Owens, Terrell 1973— **53**
Oyono, Ferdinand 1929— **38**
P. Diddy *See Combs, Sean "Puffy"*
P.M. Dawn, **54**
Pace, Betty 1954— **59**
Pace, Orlando 1975— **21**
Packer, Daniel 1947— **56**
Packer, Will 1974(?)— **71**
Packer, Z. Z. 1973— **64**
Page, Alan (Cedric) 1945— **7**
Page, Clarence 1947— **4**
Paige, Leroy Robert *See Paige, Satchel*
Paige, Rod 1933— **29**
Paige, Satchel 1906-1982 **7**
Painter, Nell Irvin 1942— **24**
Palmer, Everard 1930— **37**
Palmer, Keke 1993— **68**
Palmer, Rissi 1981— **65**
Palmer, Violet 1964— **59**
Parham, Marjorie B. 1918— **71**
Parish, Robert 1953— **43**
Parker, Charlie 1920-1955 **20**
Parker, Jim 1934-2005 **64**
Parker, Kellis E. 1942-2000 **30**
Parker, (Lawrence) Kris(hna) *See KRS-One*
Parker, LarStella Irby *See Parker, Star*
Parker, Nicole Ari 1970— **52**
Parker, Star 1956— **70**
Parks, Bernard C. 1943— **17**
Parks, Gordon 1912-2006 **1, 35, 58**
Parks, Rosa 1913-2005 **1, 35, 56**
Parks, Suzan-Lori 1964— **34**
Parr, Russ 196(?)— **51**
Parsons, James Benton 1911-1993 **14**
Parsons, Richard Dean 1948— **11, 33**
Pascal-Trouillot, Ertha 1943— **3**
Paterson, Basil A. 1926— **69**
Paterson, David A. 1954— **59**
Patillo, Melba Joy 1941— **15**
Patrick, Deval 1956— **12, 61**
Patterson, Floyd 1935-2006 **19, 58**
Patterson, Frederick Douglass 1901-1988 **12**
Patterson, Gilbert Earl 1939— **41**
Patterson, Louise 1901-1999 **25**
Patterson, Mary Jane 1840-1894 **54**
Patterson, Orlando 1940— **4**
Patterson, P(ercival) J(ames) 1936(?)— **6, 20**
Patton, Antwan 1975— **45**
Patton, Antwan "Big Boi" 1975(?)— *See OutKast*
Patton, Paula 1975— **62**
Payne, Allen 1962(?)— **13**
Payne, Donald M. 1934— **2, 57**
Payne, Ethel L. 1911-1991 **28**
Payne, Freda 1942— **58**
Payne, Ulice 1955— **42**
Payne, William D. 1932— **60**
Payton, Benjamin F. 1932— **23**
Payton, John 1946— **48**
Payton, Walter (Jerry) 1954–1999 **11, 25**
Pearman, Raven-Symone Christina *See Raven*

Peck, Carolyn 1966(?)— **23**
Peck, Raoul 1953— **32**
Peete, Calvin 1943— **11**
Peete, Holly Robinson 1965— **20**
Peete, Rodney 1966— **60**
Pelé 1940— **7**
Pena, Paul 1950-2005 **58**
Pendergrass, Teddy 1950— **22**
Penniman, Richard Wayne *See Little Richard*
Peoples, Dottie 19(?)(?)— **22**
Pereira, Aristides 1923— **30**
Perez, Anna 1951— **1**
Perkins, Anthony 1959(?)— **24**
Perkins, Edward (Joseph) 1928— **5**
Perkins, James, Jr. 1953(?)— **55**
Perkins, Joe Willie *See Perkins, Pinetop*
Perkins, Marion 1908-1961 **38**
Perkins, Pinetop 1913— **70**
Perren, Freddie 1943-2004 **60**
Perrineau, Harold, Jr. 1968— **51**
Perrot, Kim 1967-1999 **23**
Perry, Emmitt, Jr. *See Perry, Tyler*
Perry, Laval 195(?)— **64**
Perry, Lee "Scratch" 1936— **19**
Perry, Lincoln *See Fetchit, Stepin*
Perry, Lowell 1931-2001 **30**
Perry, Rainford Hugh *See Perry, Lee "Scratch"*
Perry, Ruth 1936— **19**
Perry, Ruth Sando 1939— **15**
Perry, Tyler 1969— **40, 54**
Perry, Warren 1942(?)— **56**
Person, Waverly 1927— **9, 51**
Peters, Lenrie 1932— **43**
Peters, Margaret and Matilda **43**
Peters, Maria Philomena 1941— **12**
Petersen, Frank E. 1932— **31**
Peterson, Hannibal *See Peterson, Marvin "Hannibal"*
Peterson, James 1937— **38**
Peterson, Marvin "Hannibal" 1948— **27**
Peterson, Oscar 1925— **52**
Petry, Ann 1909-1997 **19**
Phifer, Mekhi 1975— **25**
Philip, M. Nourbese *See Philip, Marlene Nourbese*
Philip, Marlene Nourbese 1947— **32**
Phillips, Charles E., Jr. 1959— **57**
Phillips, Helen L. 1919-2005 **63**
Phillips, Teresa L. 1958— **42**
Phipps, Wintley 1955— **59**
Pickens, James, Jr. 1954— **59**
Pickett, Bill 1870-1932 **11**
Pickett, Cecil 1945— **39**
Pierce, Paul 1977— **71**
Pierre, Andre 1915— **17**
Pierre, Percy Anthony 1939— **46**
Pincham, R. Eugene, Sr. 1925–2008 **69**
Pinchback, P(inckney) B(enton) S(tewart) 1837-1921 **9**
Pinckney, Bill 1935— **42**
Pinckney, Sandra 194(?)— **56**
Pindell, Howardena 1943— **55**
Pinderhughes, John 1946— **47**
Pinkett Smith, Jada 1971— **10, 41**
Pinkett, Jada *See Pinkett Smith, Jada*
Pinkett, Randal 1971— **61**

Pinkney, Jerry 1939— **15**
Pinkston, W. Randall 1950— **24**
Pinn, Vivian Winona 1941— **49**
Piper, Adrian 1948— **71**
Pippen, Scottie 1965— **15**
Pippin, Horace 1888-1946 **9**
Pitt, David Thomas 1913-1994 **10**
Pitta (do Nascimento), Celso (Roberto) 19(?)(?)— **17**
Pitts, Byron 1960— **71**
Pitts, Leonard, Jr. 1957— **54**
Player, Willa B. 1909-2003 **43**
Pleasant, Mary Ellen 1814-1904 **9**
Plessy, Homer Adolph 1862-1925 **31**
Poitier, Sidney 1927— **11, 36**
Poitier, Sydney Tamiia 1973— **65**
Pollard, Fritz 1894-1986 **53**
Poole, Elijah *See* Muhammad, Elijah
Porter, Countee Leroy *See* Cullin, Countee
Porter, Dorothy *See* Wesley, Dorothy Porter
Porter, James A(mos) 1905-1970 **11**
Portuondo, Omara 1930— **53**
Potter, Myrtle 1958— **40**
Pough, Terrell 1987(?)-2005 **58**
Poussaint, Alvin F. 1934— **5, 67**
Powell, Adam Clayton, Jr. 1908-1972 **3**
Powell, Bud 1924-1966 **24**
Powell, Colin (Luther) 1937— **1, 28**
Powell, Debra A. 1964— **23**
Powell, Kevin 1966— **31**
Powell, Maxine 1924— **8**
Powell, Michael Anthony *See* Powell, Mike
Powell, Michael K. 1963— **32**
Powell, Mike 1963— **7**
Powell, Renee 1946— **34**
Pratt Dixon, Sharon *See* Dixon, Sharon Pratt
Pratt, Awadagin 1966— **31**
Pratt, Geronimo 1947— **18**
Pratt, Kyla 1986— **57**
Premice, Josephine 1926-2001 **41**
Pressley, Condace L. 1964— **41**
Preston, Billy 1946-2006 **39, 59**
Preston, William Everett *See* Preston, Billy
Price, Florence 1887-1953 **37**
Price, Frederick K.C. 1932— **21**
Price, Glenda 1939— **22**
Price, Hugh B. 1941— **9, 54**
Price, Kelly 1973(?)— **23**
Price, Leontyne 1927— **1**
Price, Richard 1930(?)— **51**
Pride, Charley 1938(?)— **26**
Primus, Pearl 1919— **6**
Prince 1958— **18, 65**
Prince, Richard E. 1947— **71**
Prince, Ron 1969— **64**
Prince, Tayshaun 1980— **68**
Prince-Bythewood, Gina 1968— **31**
Pritchard, Robert Starling 1927— **21**
Procope, Ernesta 19(?)(?)— **23**
Procope, John Levy 1925-2005 **56**
Prophet, Nancy Elizabeth 1890-1960 **42**
Prothrow, Deborah Boutin *See* Prothrow-Stith, Deborah

Prothrow-Stith, Deborah 1954— **10**
Pryor, Rain 1969— **65**
Pryor, Richard 1940-2005 **3, 24, 56**
Puckett, Kirby 1960-2006 **4, 58**
Puff Daddy *See* Combs, Sean "Puffy"
Purnell, Silas 1923-2003 **59**
Puryear, Martin 1941— **42**
Quarles, Benjamin Arthur 1904-1996 **18**
Quarles, Norma 1936— **25**
Quarterman, Lloyd Albert 1918-1982 **4**
Queen Latifah 1970— **1, 16, 58**
Quigless, Helen G. 1944-2004 **49**
Quince, Peggy A. 1948— **69**
Quirot, Ana (Fidelia) 1963— **13**
Quivers, Robin 1952— **61**
Rabb, Maurice F., Jr. 1932-2005 **58**
Rabia, Aliyah *See* Staton, Dakota
Rahman, Aishah 1936— **37**
Raines, Franklin Delano 1949— **14**
Rainey, Ma 1886-1939 **33**
Ralph, Sheryl Lee 1956— **18**
Ramaphosa, (Matamela) Cyril 1952— **3**
Rambough, Lori Ann *See* Sommore
Ramphele, Mamphela 1947— **29**
Ramsey, Charles H. 1948— **21, 69**
Rand, A(ddison) Barry 1944— **6**
Randall, Alice 1959— **38**
Randall, Dudley 1914-2000 **8, 55**
Randle, Theresa 1967— **16**
Randolph, A(sa) Philip 1889-1979 **3**
Randolph, Linda A. 1941— **52**
Randolph, Willie 1954— **53**
Rangel, Charles 1930— **3, 52**
Rankin Don *See* Rhoden, Wayne
Raoul, Kwame 1964— **55**
Ras Tafari *See* Haile Selassie
Rashad, Ahmad 1949— **18**
Rashad, Phylicia 1948— **21**
Raspberry, William 1935— **2**
Raven, 1985— **44**
Raven-Symone *See* Raven
Rawlings, Jerry (John) 1947— **9**
Rawls, Lou 1936-2006 **17, 57**
Ray, Charlotte E. 1850-1911 **60**
Ray, Gene Anthony 1962-2003 **47**
Raymond, Usher, IV *See* Usher
Razaf, Andy 1895-1973 **19**
Razafkeriefo, Andreamentania Paul *See* Razaf, Andy
Ready, Stephanie 1975— **33**
Reagon, Bernice Johnson 1942— **7**
Reason, Joseph Paul 1943— **19**
Record, Eugene 1940-2005 **60**
Reddick, Lance 19(?)(?)— **52**
Reddick, Lawrence Dunbar 1910-1995 **20**
Redding, J. Saunders 1906-1988 **26**
Redding, Louis L. 1901-1998 **26**
Redding, Otis, Jr. 1941— **16**
Redman, Joshua 1969— **30**
Redmond, Eugene 1937— **23**
Reece, E. Albert 1950— **63**
Reed, A. C. 1926— **36**
Reed, Ishmael 1938— **8**
Reed, Jimmy 1925-1976 **38**
Reems, Ernestine Cleveland 1932— **27**
Reese, Calvin *See* Reese, Pokey

Reese, Della 1931— **6, 20**
Reese, Milous J., Jr. 1904— **51**
Reese, Pokey 1973— **28**
Reese, Tracy 1964— **54**
Reeves, Dianne 1956— **32**
Reeves, Gregory 1952— **49**
Reeves, Rachel J. 1950(?)— **23**
Reeves, Triette Lipsey 1963— **27**
Regis, Cyrille 1958— **51**
Reid, Antonio "L.A." 1958(?)— **28**
Reid, Irvin D. 1941— **20**
Reid, L.A. *See* Reid, Antonio "L.A."
Reid, Senghor 1976— **55**
Reid, Tim 1944— **56**
Reid, Vernon 1958— **34**
Reivers, Corbin Bleu *See* Corbin Bleu
Reuben, Gloria 19(?)(?)— **15**
Reynolds, Star Jones 1962(?)— **10, 27, 61**
Rhames, Ving 1959— **14, 50**
Rhimes, Shonda Lynn 1970— **67**
Rhoden, Dwight 1962— **40**
Rhoden, Wayne 1966— **70**
Rhoden, William C. 1950(?)— **67**
Rhodes, Ray 1950— **14**
Rhone, Sylvia 1952— **2**
Rhymes, Busta 1972— **31**
Ribbs, William Theodore, Jr. *See* Ribbs, Willy T.
Ribbs, Willy T. 1956— **2**
Ribeau, Sidney 1947(?)— **70**
Ribeiro, Alfonso 1971— **17**
Rice, Condoleezza 1954— **3, 28**
Rice, Constance LaMay 1956— **60**
Rice, Jerry 1962— **5, 55**
Rice, Linda Johnson 1958— **9, 41**
Rice, Louise Allen 1941— **54**
Rice, Norm(an Blann) 1943— **8**
Richards, Beah 1926-2000 **30**
Richards, Hilda 1936— **49**
Richards, Lloyd 1923(?)— **2**
Richards, Sanya 1985— **66**
Richardson, Desmond 1969— **39**
Richardson, Donna 1962— **39**
Richardson, Elaine Potter *See* Kincaid, Jamaica
Richardson, LaTanya 1949— **71**
Richardson, Nolan 1941— **9**
Richardson, Pat *See* Norman, Pat
Richardson, Rupert 1930–2008 **67**
Richardson, Salli 1967— **68**
Richie, Leroy C. 1941— **18**
Richie, Lionel 1949— **27, 65**
Richmond, Mitchell James 1965— **19**
Rideau, Iris 1940(?)— **46**
Ridenhour, Carlton *See* Chuck D.
Ridley, John 1965— **69**
Riggs, Marlon 1957–1994 **5, 44**
Rihanna 1988— **65**
Riley, Helen Caldwell Day 1926— **13**
Riley, Rochelle 1959(?)— **50**
Ringgold, Faith 1930— **4**
Riperton, Minnie 1947-1979 **32**
Rivers, Glenn "Doc" 1961— **25**
Roach, Max 1924-2007 **21, 63**
Roberto, Holden 1923-2007 **65**
Roberts, Darryl 1962(?)— **70**
Roberts, Deborah 1960— **35**
Roberts, James *See* Lover, Ed

Roberts, Kristina LaFerne *See* Zane
Roberts, Marcus 1963— **19**
Roberts, Marthaniel *See* Roberts, Marcus
Roberts, Mike 1948— **57**
Roberts, Robin 1960— **16, 54**
Roberts, Roy S. 1939(?)— **14**
Robertson, Oscar 1938— **26**
Robeson, Eslanda Goode 1896-1965 **13**
Robeson, Paul (Leroy Bustill) 1898-1976 **2**
Robinson, Aminah 1940— **50**
Robinson, Bill "Bojangles" 1878-1949 **11**
Robinson, Bishop L. 1927— **66**
Robinson, Cleo Parker 1948(?)— **38**
Robinson, David 1965— **24**
Robinson, Eddie G. 1919-2007 **10, 61**
Robinson, Fatima 19(?)(?)— **34**
Robinson, Fenton 1935-1997 **38**
Robinson, Frank 1935— **9**
Robinson, Jack Roosevelt *See* Robinson, Jackie
Robinson, Jackie 1919-1972 **6**
Robinson, LaVaughn 1927–2008 **69**
Robinson, Luther *See* Robinson, Bill "Bojangles"
Robinson, Malcolm S. 1948— **44**
Robinson, Matt 1937–2002 **69**
Robinson, Matthew, Jr. *See* Robinson, Matt
Robinson, Max 1939-1988 **3**
Robinson, Patrick 1966— **19, 71**
Robinson, Rachel 1922— **16**
Robinson, Randall 1941— **7, 46**
Robinson, Reginald R. 1972— **53**
Robinson, Sharon 1950— **22**
Robinson, Shaun 19(?)(?)— **36**
Robinson, Smokey 1940— **3, 49**
Robinson, Spottswood W., III 1916-1998 **22**
Robinson, Sugar Ray 1921— **18**
Robinson, Will 1911–2008 **51, 69**
Robinson, William, Jr. *See* Robinson, Smokey
Roble, Abdi 1964— **71**
Roche, Joyce M. 1947— **17**
Rochester *See* Anderson, Eddie "Rochester"
Rochon, Lela 1965(?)— **16**
Rock, Chris 1967(?)— **3, 22, 66**
Rock, The 1972— **29, 66**
Rodgers, Johnathan 1946— **6, 51**
Rodgers, Rod 1937-2002 **36**
Rodman, Dennis 1961— **12, 44**
Rodrigues, Percy 1918–2007 **68**
Rodriguez, Jimmy 1963(?)— **47**
Rodriguez, Cheryl 1952— **64**
Rogers, Jimmy 1924-1997 **38**
Rogers, Joe 1964— **27**
Rogers, Joel Augustus 1883(?)-1996 **30**
Rogers, John W., Jr. 1958— **5, 52**
Rogers, Kelis *See* Kelis
Rojas, Don 1949— **33**
Roker, Al 1954— **12, 49**
Roker, Roxie 1929–1995 **68**
Rolle, Esther 1920-1998 **13, 21**
Rollins, Charlemae Hill 1897-1979 **27**

Rollins, Howard E., Jr. 1950-1996 **16**
Rollins, Ida Gray Nelson *See Gray (Nelson Rollins), Ida*
Rollins, James Calvin, III *See Rollins, Jimmy*
Rollins, Jimmy 1978— **70**
Rollins, Sonny 1930— **37**
Ronaldinho 1980— **69**
Rooakhptah, Amunnubi *See York, Dwight D.*
Rose, Anika Noni 1972— **70**
Rose, Lionel 1948— **56**
Ross, Araminta *See Tubman, Harriet*
Ross, Charles 1957— **27**
Ross, Diana 1944— **8, 27**
Ross, Don 1941— **27**
Ross, Isaiah "Doc" 1925-1993 **40**
Ross, Tracee Ellis 1972— **35**
Ross-Lee, Barbara 1942— **67**
Rotimi, (Emmanuel Gladstone) Ola(wale) 1938— **1**
Roundtree, Richard 1942— **27**
Rowan, Carl T(homas) 1925— **1, 30**
Rowell, Victoria 1960— **13, 68**
Roxanne Shante 1969— **33**
Roy, Kenny 1990(?)— **51**
Rubin, Chanda 1976— **37**
Rucker, Darius 1966(?)— **34**
Rudolph, Maya 1972— **46**
Rudolph, Wilma (Glodean) 1940— **4**
Rugambwa, Laurean 1912-1997 **20**
Ruley, Ellis 1882-1959 **38**
Run 1964— **31**
Rupaul 1960— **17**
Rusesabagina, Paul 1954— **60**
Rush, Bobby 1946— **26**
Rush, Otis 1934— **38**
Rushen, Patrice 1954— **12**
Rushing, Jimmy 1903-1972 **37**
Russell, Bill 1934— **8**
Russell, Brenda 1944(?)— **52**
Russell, Herman Jerome 1931(?)— **17**
Russell, Nipsey 1924-2005 **66**
Russell, William Felton *See Russell, Bill*
Russell-McCloud, Patricia 1946— **17**
Rustin, Bayard 1910-1987 **4**
Saar, Alison 1956— **16**
Sade 1959— **15**
Sadler, Joseph *See Grandmaster Flash*
Sadlier, Rosemary 19(?)(?)— **62**
St. Jacques, Raymond 1930-1990 **8**
Saint James, Synthia 1949— **12**
St. John, Kristoff 1966— **25**
St. Julien, Marlon 1972— **29**
St. Patrick, Mathew 1969— **48**
Salih, Al-Tayyib 1929— **37**
Sallee, Charles 1911— **38**
Salters, Lisa 1966(?)— **71**
Salters, Alisia *See Salters, Lisa*
Salvador, Bryce 1976— **51**
Samara, Noah 1956— **15**
SAMO *See Basquiat, Jean-Michel*
Sample, Joe 1939— **51**
Sampson, Charles 1957— **13**

Sampson, Edith S(purlock) 1901-1979 **4**
Samuel, Sealhenry Olumide 1963— **14**
Samuelsson, Marcus 1970— **53**
Sané, Pierre Gabriel 1948-1998 **21**
Sanchez, Sonia 1934— **17, 51**
Sanders, Barry 1968— **1, 53**
Sanders, Deion (Luwynn) 1967— **4, 31**
Sanders, Dori(nda) 1935— **8**
Sanders, Joseph R(ichard, Jr.) 1954— **11**
Sanders, Malika 1973— **48**
Sanders, Pharoah 1940— **64**
Sanders, Rose M. *See Touré, Faya Ora Rose*
Sanford, Isabel 1917-2004 **53**
Sanford, John Elroy *See Foxx, Redd*
Sangare, Oumou 1968— **18**
Sankara, Thomas 1949-1987 **17**
Sapp, Warren 1972— **38**
Saro-Wiwa, Kenule 1941-1995 **39**
Satcher, David 1941— **7, 57**
Satchmo *See Armstrong, (Daniel) Louis*
Savage, Augusta Christine 1892(?)-1962 **12**
Savimbi, Jonas (Malheiro) 1934-2002 **2, 34**
Sawyer, Amos 1945— **2**
Sayers, Gale 1943— **28**
Sayles Belton, Sharon 1952(?)— **9, 16**
Scantlebury, Janna 1984(?)— **47**
Scantlebury-White, Velma 1955— **64**
Scarlett, Millicent 1971— **49**
Schmoke, Kurt 1949— **1, 48**
Schomburg, Arthur Alfonso 1874-1938 **9**
Schomburg, Arturo Alfonso *See Schomburg, Arthur Alfonso*
Schultz, Michael A. 1938— **6**
Schuyler, George Samuel 1895-1977 **40**
Schuyler, Philippa 1931-1967 **50**
Scott, C. A. 1908-2000 **29**
Scott, Coretta *See King, Coretta Scott*
Scott, Cornelius Adolphus *See Scott, C. A.*
Scott, David 1946— **41**
Scott, George 1929-2005 **55**
Scott, Harold Russell, Jr. 1935-2006 **61**
Scott, Hazel 1920-1981 **66**
Scott, Jill 1972— **29**
Scott, John T. 1940-2007 **65**
Scott, "Little" Jimmy 1925— **48**
Scott, Milton 1956— **51**
Scott, Robert C. 1947— **23**
Scott, Stuart 1965— **34**
Scott, Wendell Oliver, Sr. 1921-1990 **19**
Scruggs, Mary Elfrieda *See Williams, Mary Lou*
Scurry, Briana 1971— **27**
Seacole, Mary 1805-1881 **54**
Seal **14**
Seale, Bobby 1936— **3**
Seale, Robert George *See Seale, Bobby*

Seals, Frank *See Seals, Son*
Seals, Son 1942-2004 **56**
Sears, Stephanie 1964— **53**
Sears-Collins, Leah J(eanette) 1955— **5**
Sebree, Charles 1914-1985 **40**
Seele, Pernessa 1954— **46**
Selassie, Haile *See Haile Selassie*
Sembène, Ousmane 1923-2007 **13, 62**
Senghor, Augustin Diamacoune 1928-2007 **66**
Senghor, Léopold Sédar 1906-2001 **12, 66**
Sengstacke, John Herman Henry 1912-1997 **18**
Senior, Olive 1941— **37**
Sentamu, John 1949— **58**
Serrano, Andres 1951(?)— **3**
Shabazz, Attallah 1958— **6**
Shabazz, Betty 1936-1997 **7, 26**
Shabazz, Ilyasah 1962— **36**
Shaggy 1968— **31**
Shakespeare, Robbie 1953— *See Sly & Robbie*
Shakur, Afeni 1947— **67**
Shakur, Assata 1947— **6**
Shakur, Tupac Amaru 1971-1996 **14**
Shange, Ntozake 1948— **8**
Sharper, Darren 1975— **32**
Sharpton, Al 1954— **21**
Shavers, Cheryl 19(?)(?)— **31**
Shaw, Bernard 1940— **2, 28**
Shaw, William J. 1934— **30**
Sheard, Kierra "Kiki" 1987— **61**
Sheffey, Asa Bundy *See Hayden, Robert Earl*
Sheffield, Gary Antonian 1968— **16**
Shell, Art 1946— **1, 66**
Shepherd, Sherri 1970— **55**
Sherrod, Clayton 1944— **17**
Shinhoster, Earl 1950(?)-2000 **32**
Shipp, E. R. 1955— **15**
Shippen, John 1879-1968 **43**
Shirley, George I. 1934— **33**
Shonibare, Yinka 1962— **58**
Short, Bobby 1924-2005 **52**
Shorty I, Ras 1941-2000 **47**
Showers, Reggie 1964— **30**
Shropshire, Thomas B. 1925-2003 **49**
Shuttlesworth, Fred 1922— **47**
Sifford, Charlie 1922— **4, 49**
Sigur, Wanda 1958— **44**
Siji 1971(?)— **56**
Silas, Paul 1943— **24**
Silver, Horace 1928— **26**
Siméus, Dumas M. 1940— **25**
Simmons, Bob 1948— **29**
Simmons, Gary 1964— **58**
Simmons, Henry 1970— **55**
Simmons, Joseph *See Run*
Simmons, Kimora Lee 1975— **51**
Simmons, Russell 1957(?)— **1, 30**
Simmons, Ruth J. 1945— **13, 38**
Simone, Nina 1933-2003 **15, 41**
Simpson, Carole 1940— **6, 30**
Simpson, Lorna 1960— **4, 36**
Simpson, O. J. 1947— **15**
Simpson, Valerie 1946— **21**
Simpson-Hoffman, N'kenge 1975(?)— **52**

Simpson-Miller, Portia 1945— **62**
Sims, Howard "Sandman" 1917-2003 **48**
Sims, Lowery Stokes 1949— **27**
Sims, Naomi 1949— **29**
Sinbad 1957(?)— **1, 16**
Singletary, Michael *See Singletary, Mike*
Singletary, Mike 1958— **4**
Singleton, John 1968— **2, 30**
Sinkford, Jeanne C. 1933— **13**
Sirleaf, Ellen Johnson 1938— **71**
Sisqo 1976— **30**
Sissle, Noble 1889-1975 **29**
Sister Souljah 1964— **11**
Sisulu, Albertina 1918— **57**
Sisulu, Sheila Violet Makate 1948(?)— **24**
Sisulu, Walter 1912-2003 **47**
Sizemore, Barbara A. 1927— **26**
Skinner, Kiron K. 1962(?) **65**
Sklarek, Norma Merrick 1928— **25**
Slater, Rodney Earl 1955— **15**
Slaughter, John Brooks 1934— **53**
Sledge, Percy 1940— **39**
Sleet, Moneta (J.), Jr. 1926— **5**
Slocumb, Jonathan 19(?)(?)— **52**
Sly & Robbie **34**
Slyde, Jimmy 1927–2008 **70**
Smaltz, Audrey 1937(?)— **12**
Smiley, Rickey 1968— **59**
Smiley, Tavis 1964— **20, 68**
Smith, Anjela Lauren 1973— **44**
Smith, Anna Deavere 1950— **6, 44**
Smith, Arthur Lee, *See Asante, Molefi Kete*
Smith, B. *See Smith, B(arbara)*
Smith, B(arbara) 1949(?)— **11**
Smith, Barbara 1946— **28**
Smith, Bessie 1894-1937 **3**
Smith, Bruce W. 19(?)(?)— **53**
Smith, Cladys "Jabbo" 1908-1991 **32**
Smith, Clarence O. 1933— **21**
Smith, Damu 1951— **54**
Smith, Danyel 1966(?)— **40**
Smith, Dr. Lonnie 1942— **49**
Smith, Emmitt (III) 1969— **7**
Smith, Greg 1964— **28**
Smith, Hezekiah Leroy Gordon *See Smith, Stuff*
Smith, Hilton 1912-1983 **29**
Smith, Ian 1970(?)— **62**
Smith, Jabbo *See Smith, Cladys "Jabbo"*
Smith, Jane E. 1946— **24**
Smith, Jennifer 1947— **21**
Smith, Jessie Carney 1930— **35**
Smith, John L. 1938— **22**
Smith, Joshua (Isaac) 1941— **10**
Smith, Kemba 1971— **70**
Smith, Lonnie Liston 1940— **49**
Smith, Lovie 1958— **66**
Smith, Mamie 1883-1946 **32**
Smith, Marie F. 1939— **70**
Smith, Marvin 1910-2003 **46**
Smith, Mary Carter 1919— **26**
Smith, Morgan 1910-1993 **46**
Smith, Nate 1929— **49**
Smith, Orlando *See Smith, Tubby*
Smith, Richard 1957— **51**
Smith, Roger Guenveur 1960— **12**
Smith, Shaffer Chimere *See Ne-Yo*

Smith, Stephen A. 1967— **69**
Smith, Stuff 1909-1967 **37**
Smith, Trevor, Jr. *See Rhymes, Busta*
Smith, Trixie 1895-1943 **34**
Smith, Tubby 1951— **18**
Smith, Vincent D. 1929-2003 **48**
Smith, Walker, Jr. *See Robinson, Sugar Ray*
Smith, Will 1968— **8, 18, 53**
Smith, Willi (Donnell) 1948-1987 **8**
Smith, Zadie 1975— **51**
Smythe Haith, Mabel 1918-2006 **61**
Sneed, Paula A. 1947— **18**
Snipes, Wesley 1962— **3, 24, 67**
Snoop Dogg 1972— **35**
Snow, Samuel 1923–2008 **71**
Snowden, Frank M., Jr. 1911–2007 **67**
Soglo, Nicéphore 1935— **15**
Solomon, Jimmie Lee 1947(?)— **38**
Somé, Malidoma Patrice 1956— **10**
Sommore, 1966— **61**
Sosa, Sammy 1968— **21, 44**
Soto Alejo, Federico Arístides *See Güines, Tata*
Soulchild, Musiq *See Musiq*
Southern, Eileen 1920-2002 **56**
Southgate, Martha 1960(?)— **58**
Sowande, Fela 1905-1987 **39**
Sowande, Olufela Obafunmilayo *See Sowande, Fela*
Sowell, Thomas 1930— **2**
Soyinka, (Akinwande Olu) Wole 1934— **4**
Sparks, Corinne Etta 1953— **53**
Sparks, Jordin 1989— **66**
Spaulding, Charles Clinton 1874-1952 **9**
Spears, Warren 1954-2005 **52**
Spence, Joseph 1910-1984 **49**
Spencer, Anne 1882-1975 **27**
Spencer, Winston Baldwin 1948— **68**
Spikes, Dolores Margaret Richard 1936— **18**
Spiller, Bill 1913-1988 **64**
Sprewell, Latrell 1970— **23**
Spriggs, William 195(?)— **67**
Stackhouse, Jerry 1974— **30**
Staley, Dawn 1970— **57**
Stallings, George A(ugustus), Jr. 1948— **6**
Stampley, Micah 1971— **54**
Stanford, John 1938— **20**
Stanford, Olivia Lee Dilworth 1914-2004 **49**
Stanton, Robert 1940— **20**
Staples, "Pops" 1915-2000 **32**
Staples, Brent 1951— **8**
Staples, Mavis 1939(?)— **50**
Staples, Roebuck *See Staples, "Pops"*
Stargell, Willie "Pops" 1940(?)–2001 **29**
Staton, Candi 1940(?)— **27**
Staton, Dakota 1930(?)-2007 **62**
Staupers, Mabel K(eaton) 1890-1989 **7**
Stearnes, Norman "Turkey" 1901-1979 **31**
Steave-Dickerson, Kia 1970— **57**
Steele, Claude Mason 1946— **13**
Steele, Lawrence 1963— **28**

Steele, Michael 1958— **38**
Steele, Shelby 1946— **13**
Steinberg, Martha Jean 1930(?)-2000 **28**
Stephens, Charlotte Andrews 1854-1951 **14**
Stephens, John *See Legend, John*
Stephens, Myrtle *See Potter, Myrtle*
Stevens, Yvette *See Khan, Chaka*
Stew 1961— **69**
Steward, David L. 19(?)(?)— **36**
Steward, Emanuel 1944— **18**
Stewart, Alison 1966(?)— **13**
Stewart, Ella 1893-1987 **39**
Stewart, James "Bubba," Jr. 1985— **60**
Stewart, Kordell 1972— **21**
Stewart, Mark *See Stew*
Stewart, Paul Wilbur 1925— **12**
Still, William Grant 1895-1978 **37**
Stingley, Darryl 1951–2007 **69**
Stinson, Denise L. 1954— **59**
Stokes, Carl B(urton) 1927— **10**
Stokes, Louis 1925— **3**
Stone, Angie 1965(?)— **31**
Stone, Charles Sumner, Jr. *See Stone, Chuck*
Stone, Chuck 1924— **9**
Stone, Toni 1921-1996 **15**
Stoney, Michael 1969— **50**
Stott, Dorothy M. *See Stout, Renee*
Stott, Dot*See Stout, Renee*
Stoudemire, Amaré 1982— **59**
Stout, Juanita Kidd 1919-1998 **24**
Stout, Renee 1958— **63**
Stoute, Steve 1971(?)— **38**
Strahan, Michael 1971— **35**
Strawberry, Darryl 1962— **22**
Strayhorn, Billy 1915-1967 **31**
Street, John F. 1943(?)— **24**
Streeter, Sarah 1953— **45**
Stringer, C. Vivian 1948— **13**
Stringer, Korey 1974-2001 **35**
Stringer, C. Vivian 1948— **66**
Stringer, Vickie 196(?)— **58**
Stroman, Nathaniel *See Earthquake*
Studdard, Ruben 1978— **46**
Sudarkasa, Niara 1938— **4**
Sudduth, Jimmy Lee 1910-2007 **65**
Sullivan, Leon H(oward) 1922— **3, 30**
Sullivan, Louis (Wade) 1933— **8**
Sullivan, Maxine 1911-1987 **37**
Summer, Donna 1948— **25**
Sun Ra, 1914-1993 **60**
Sundiata, Sekou 1948-2007 **66**
Supremes, The **33**
Sutton, Percy E. 1920— **42**
Swann, Lynn 1952— **28**
Sweat, Keith 1961(?)— **19**
Sweet, Ossian 1895–1960 **68**
Swoopes, Sheryl 1971— **12, 56**
Swygert, H. Patrick 1943— **22**
Sy, Oumou 1952— **65**
Sykes, Roosevelt 1906-1984 **20**
Sykes, Wanda 1964— **48**
Syler, Rene 1963— **53**
Tademy, Lalita 1948— **36**
Tafari Makonnen *See Haile Selassie*
Tait, Michael 1966— **57**
Talbert, David 1966(?)— **34**

Talley, André Leon 1949(?)— **56**
Tamar-kali 1973(?)— **63**
Tamia 1975— **24, 55**
Tampa Red 1904(?)-1980 **63**
Tancil, Gladys Quander 1921-2002 **59**
Tanksley, Ann (Graves) 1934— **37**
Tanner, Henry Ossawa 1859-1937 **1**
Tate, Eleanora E. 1948— **20, 55**
Tate, Larenz 1975— **15**
Tatum, Art 1909-1956 **28**
Tatum, Beverly Daniel 1954— **42**
Taulbert, Clifton Lemoure 1945— **19**
Taylor, Billy 1921— **23**
Taylor, Cecil 1929— **70**
Taylor, Charles 1948— **20**
Taylor, Ephren W., II 1982— **61**
Taylor, Helen (Lavon Hollingshed) 1942-2000 **30**
Taylor, Jason 1974— **70**
Taylor, Jermain 1978— **60**
Taylor, John (David Beckett) 1952— **16**
Taylor, Karin 1971— **34**
Taylor, Koko 1935— **40**
Taylor, Kristin Clark 1959— **8**
Taylor, Lawrence 1959— **25**
Taylor, Marshall Walter "Major" 1878-1932 **62**
Taylor, Meshach 1947(?)— **4**
Taylor, Mildred D. 1943— **26**
Taylor, Natalie 1959— **47**
Taylor, Regina 1959(?)— **9, 46**
Taylor, Ron 1952-2002 **35**
Taylor, Susan C. 1957— **62**
Taylor, Susan L. 1946— **10**
Taylor, Susie King 1848-1912 **13**
Temptations, The **33**
Tergat, Paul 1969— **59**
Terrell, Dorothy A. 1945— **24**
Terrell, Mary (Elizabeth) Church 1863-1954 **9**
Terrell, Tammi 1945-1970 **32**
Terry, Clark 1920— **39**
Tharpe, Rosetta 1915-1973 **65**
The Artist *See Prince*
Thiam, Aliaune Akon *See Akon*
Thigpen, Lynne 1948-2003 **17, 41**
Thomas, Alma Woodsey 1891-1978 **14**
Thomas, Arthur Ray 1951— **52**
Thomas, Clarence 1948— **2, 39, 65**
Thomas, Claudia Lynn 1950— **64**
Thomas, Debi 1967— **26**
Thomas, Derrick 1967-2000 **25**
Thomas, Emmitt 1943— **71**
Thomas, Frank 1968— **12, 51**
Thomas, Franklin A. 1934— **5, 49**
Thomas, Irma 1941— **29**
Thomas, Isiah 1961— **7, 26, 65**
Thomas, Michael 1967— **69**
Thomas, Mickalene 1971— **61**
Thomas, Rozonda "Chilli" 1971— *See TLC*
Thomas, Rufus 1917— **20**
Thomas, Sean Patrick 1970— **35**
Thomas, Trisha R. 1964— **65**
Thomas, Vivien (T.) 1910-1985 **9**
Thomas-Graham, Pamela 1963(?)— **29**
Thomason, Marsha 1976— **47**

Thompson, Bennie G. 1948— **26**
Thompson, Cynthia Bramlett 1949— **50**
Thompson, Dearon *See Deezer D*
Thompson, Don 1963— **56**
Thompson, John W. 1949— **26**
Thompson, Kenan 1978— **52**
Thompson, Larry D. 1945— **39**
Thompson, Tazewell (Alfred, Jr.) 1954— **13**
Thompson, Tina 1975— **25**
Thompson, William C. 1953(?)— **35**
Thoms, Tracie 1975— **61**
Thornton, Big Mama 1926-1984 **33**
Thornton, Yvonne S. 1947— **69**
Thrash, Dox 1893-1965 **35**
Three Mo' Tenors **35**
Thrower, Willie 1930-2002 **35**
Thugwane, Josia 1971— **21**
Thurman, Howard 1900-1981 **3**
Thurman, Wallace Henry 1902-1934 **16**
Thurston, Stephen J. 1952— **49**
Till, Emmett (Louis) 1941-1955 **7**
Tillard, Conrad 1964— **47**
Tillis, Frederick 1930— **40**
Tillman, George, Jr. 1968— **20**
Timbaland 1971— **32**
Tinsley, Boyd 1964— **50**
Tirico, Michael *See Tirico, Mike*
Tirico, Mike 1966— **68**
Tisdale, Wayman 1964— **50**
TLC **34**
Todman, Terence A. 1926— **55**
Tolliver, Mose 1915(?)-2006 **60**
Tolliver, William (Mack) 1951— **9**
Tolson, Melvin B(eaunorus) 1898-1966 **37**
Tolton, Augustine 1854-1897 **62**
Tomlinson, LaDainian 1979— **65**
Tonex, 1978(?)— **54**
Tooks, Lance 1962— **62**
Toomer, Jean 1894-1967 **6**
Toomer, Nathan Pinchback *See Toomer, Jean*
Toote, Gloria E.A. 1931— **64**
Torres, Gina 1969— **52**
Torry, Guy 19(?)(?)— **31**
Tosh, Peter 1944-1987 **9**
Touré, Amadou Toumani 1948(?)— **18**
Touré, Askia (Muhammad Abu Bakr el) 1938— **47**
Touré, Faya Ora Rose 1945— **56**
Touré, Sekou 1922-1984 **6**
Toussaint, Allen 1938— **60**
Toussaint, Lorraine 1960— **32**
Townes, Jeffrey Allan *See DJ Jazzy Jeff*
Towns, Edolphus 1934— **19**
Townsend, Robert 1957— **4, 23**
Trammell, Kimberly N. *See Holland, Kimberly N.*
Tresvant, Ralph 1968— **57**
Tribble, Israel, Jr. 1940— **8**
Trotter, Donne E. 1950— **28**
Trotter, Lloyd G. 1945(?)— **56**
Trotter, (William) Monroe 1872-1934 **9**
Trotter, Tariq Luqmaan *See Black Thought*
Trouillot, Ertha Pascal *See Pascal-Trouillot, Ertha*
Trueheart, William E. 1942— **49**

Tsvangirai, Morgan 1952(?)— **26**
Tubbs Jones, Stephanie 1949— **24**
Tubman, Harriet 1820(?)-1913 **9**
Tucker, C. Delores 1927-2005 **12, 56**
Tucker, Chris 1972— **13, 23, 62**
Tucker, Cynthia 1955— **1561**
Tucker, Rosina Budd Harvey Corrothers 1881-1987 **14**
Tuckson, Reed V. 1951(?)— **71**
Tunie, Tamara 1959— **63**
Tunnell, Emlen 1925-1975 **54**
Ture, Kwame *See* Carmichael, Stokely
Turnbull, Charles Wesley 1935— **62**
Turnbull, Walter 1944— **13, 60**
Turner, Henry McNeal 1834-1915 **5**
Turner, Ike 1931–2007 **68**
Turner, Izear *See* Turner, Ike
Turner, Tina 1939— **6, 27**
Tutu, Desmond (Mpilo) 1931— **6, 44**
Tutu, Nontombi Naomi 1960— **57**
Tutuola, Amos 1920-1997 **30**
Tyler, Aisha N. 1970— **36**
Tyree, Omar Rashad 1969— **21**
Tyrese *See* Gibson, Tyrese
Tyson, Andre 1960— **40**
Tyson, Asha 1970— **39**
Tyson, Cicely 1933— **7, 51**
Tyson, Mike 1966— **28, 44**
Tyson, Neil deGrasse 1958— **15, 65**
Uggams, Leslie 1943— **23**
Underwood, Blair 1964— **7, 27**
Union, Gabrielle 1973— **31**
Unseld, Wes 1946— **23**
Upshaw, Gene 1945— **18, 47**
Usher 1978— **23, 56**
Usry, James L. 1922— **23**
Ussery, Terdema Lamar, II 1958— **29**
Utendahl, John 1956— **23**
Valentino, Bobby 1980— **62**
Van Lierop, Robert 1939— **53**
Van Peebles, Mario 1957— **2, 51**
Van Peebles, Melvin 1932— **7**
van Sertima, Ivan 1935— **25**
Vance, Courtney B. 1960— **15, 60**
VanDerZee, James (Augustus Joseph) 1886-1983 **6**
Vandross, Luther 1951-2005 **13, 48, 59**
Vanity 1959— **67**
Vann, Harold Moore *See* Muhammad, Khallid Abdul
Vanzant, Iyanla 1953— **17, 47**
Vaughan, Sarah (Lois) 1924-1990 **13**
Vaughn, Countess 1978— **53**
Vaughn, Gladys Gary 1942(?)— **47**
Vaughn, Mo 1967— **16**
Vaughn, Viola 1947— **70**
Vaughns, Cleopatra 1940— **46**
Vega, Marta Moreno 1942(?)— **61**
Velez-Rodriguez, Argelia 1936— **56**
Vera, Yvonne 1964— **32**
Verdelle, A. J. 1960— **26**
Vereen, Ben(jamin Augustus) 1946— **4**
Verna, Gelsy 1961–2008 **70**
Verrett, Shirley 1931— **66**
Vick, Michael 1980— **39, 65**
Vieira, Joao 1939— **14**
Vincent, Marjorie Judith 1965(?)— **2**
Vincent, Mark *See* Diesel, Vin
Virgil, Ozzie 1933— **48**
Von Lipsey, Roderick 1959— **11**
wa Ngengi, Kamau *See* Kenyatta, Jomo
Waddles, Charleszetta "Mother" 1912-2001 **10, 49**
Waddles, Mother *See* Waddles, Charleszetta "Mother"
Wade, Abdoulaye 1926— **66**
Wade, Dwyane 1982— **61**
Wade-Gayles, Gloria Jean 1937(?)— **41**
Wagner, Annice 1937— **22**
Wainwright, Joscelyn 1941— **46**
Walcott, Derek (Alton) 1930— **5**
Walcott, Louis Eugene 1933— **2, 15**
Walker, Albertina 1929— **10, 58**
Walker, Alice 1944— **1, 43**
Walker, Bernita Ruth 1946— **53**
Walker, Cedric "Ricky" 1953— **19**
Walker, Cora T. 1922–2006 **68**
Walker, Dianne 1951— **57**
Walker, Eamonn 1961(?)— **37**
Walker, George 1922— **37**
Walker, Herschel 1962— **1, 69**
Walker, Hezekiah 1962— **34**
Walker, John T. 1925–1989 **50**
Walker, Kara 1969— **16**
Walker, Kurt *See* Blow, Kurtis
Walker, Madame C. J. 1867-1919 **7**
Walker, Maggie Lena 1867(?)-1934 **17**
Walker, Margaret 1915-1998 **29**
Walker, Nellie Marian *See* Larsen, Nella
Walker, Rebecca 1969— **50**
Walker, T. J. 1961(?)— **7**
Walker, Thomas "T. J." *See* Walker, T. J.
Wallace, Ben 1974— **54**
Wallace, Joaquin 1965— **49**
Wallace, Michele Faith 1952— **13**
Wallace, Perry E. 1948— **47**
Wallace, Phyllis A(nn) 1920(?)-1993 **9**
Wallace, Rasheed 1974— **56**
Wallace, Ruby Ann *See* Dee, Ruby
Wallace, Sippie 1898-1986 **1**
Waller, Fats 1904-1943 **29**
Waller, Thomas Wright *See* Waller, Fats
Walton, Cora *See* Taylor, Koko
Wambugu, Florence 1953— **42**
Wamutombo, Dikembe Mutombo Mpolondo Mukamba Jean Jacque *See* Mutombo, Dikembe
Ward, Andre 1984— **62**
Ward, Benjamin 1926–2002 **68**
Ward, Douglas Turner 1930— **42**
Ward, Lloyd 1949— **21, 46**
Ware, Andre 1968— **37**
Ware, Carl H. 1943— **30**
Warfield, Marsha 1955— **2**
Warner, Malcolm Jamal 1970— **22, 36**
Warren, Michael 1946— **27**
Warren, Mike *See* Warren, Michael
Warwick, Dionne 1940— **18**
Washington, Alonzo 1967— **29**
Washington, Booker T(aliaferro) 1856-1915 **4**
Washington, Denzel 1954— **1, 16**
Washington, Dinah 1924-1963 **22**
Washington, Fred(er)i(cka Carolyn) 1903-1994 **10**
Washington, Gene 1947— **63**
Washington, Grover, Jr. 1943-1999 **17, 44**
Washington, Harold 1922–1987 **6**
Washington, Harriet A. 1951— **69**
Washington, Isaiah 1963— **62**
Washington, James, Jr. 1909(?)–2000 **38**
Washington, James Melvin 1948-1997 **50**
Washington, Kenny 1918-1971 **50**
Washington, Kerry 1977— **46**
Washington, Laura S. 1956(?)— **18**
Washington, MaliVai 1969— **8**
Washington, Mary T. 1906-2005 **57**
Washington, Patrice Clarke 1961— **12**
Washington, Regynald G. 1954(?)— **44**
Washington, Tamia Reneé *See* Tamia
Washington, Valores James 1903-1995 **12**
Washington, Walter 1915-2003 **45**
Washington Wylie, Mary T. *See* Washington, Mary T.
Wasow, Omar 1970— **15**
Waters, Benny 1902-1998 **26**
Waters, Ethel 1895-1977 **7**
Waters, Maxine 1938— **3, 67**
Waters, Muddy 1915-1983 **34**
Watkins, Donald 1948— **35**
Watkins, Frances Ellen *See* Harper, Frances Ellen Watkins
Watkins, Gloria Jean *See* hooks, bell
Watkins, Levi, Jr. 1945— **9**
Watkins, Perry James Henry 1948-1996 **12**
Watkins, Shirley R. 1938— **17**
Watkins, Tionne "T-Boz" 1970— *See* TLC
Watkins, Walter C. 1946— **24**
Watley, Jody 1959— **54**
Watson, Bob 1946— **25**
Watson, Carlos 1970— **50**
Watson, Diane 1933— **41**
Watson, Johnny "Guitar" 1935-1996 **18**
Watt, Melvin 1945— **26**
Wattleton, (Alyce) Faye 1943— **9**
Watts, Andre 1946— **42**
Watts, Julius Caesar, Jr. 1957— **14, 38**
Watts, Reggie 1972(?)— **52**
Watts, Rolonda 1959— **9**
Wayans, Damon 1961— **8, 41**
Wayans, Keenen Ivory 1958— **18**
Wayans, Marlon 1972— **29**
Wayans, Shawn 1971— **29**
Waymon, Eunice Kathleen *See* Simone, Nina
Weah, George 1966— **58**
Weathers, Carl 1948— **10**
Weaver, Afaa Michael 1951— **37**
Weaver, Michael S. *See* Weaver, Afaa Michael
Weaver, Robert C. 1907-1997 **8, 46**
Webb, Veronica 1965— **10**
Webb, Wellington, Jr. 1941— **3**
Webber, Chris 1973— **15, 30, 59**
Webster, Katie 1936-1999 **29**
Wedgeworth, Robert W. 1937— **42**
Weekes, Kevin 1975— **67**
Weeks, Thomas, III 1967— **70**
Weems, Carrie Mae 1953— **63**
Weems, Renita J. 1954— **44**
Wein, Joyce 1928-2005 **62**
Wek, Alek 1977— **18, 63**
Welburn, Edward T. 1950— **50**
Welch, Elisabeth 1908-2003 **52**
Wells, Henrietta Bell 1912–2008 **69**
Wells, James Lesesne 1902-1993 **10**
Wells, Mary 1943-1992 **28**
Wells-Barnett, Ida B(ell) 1862-1931 **8**
Welsing, Frances (Luella) Cress 1935— **5**
Wesley, Dorothy Porter 1905-1995 **19**
Wesley, Valerie Wilson 194(?)— **18**
West, Cornel (Ronald) 1953— **5, 33**
West, Dorothy 1907-1998 **12, 54**
West, Kanye 1977— **52**
West, Togo Dennis, Jr. 1942— **16**
Westbrook, Kelvin 1955— **50**
Westbrook, Peter 1952— **20**
Westbrooks, Bobby 1930(?)-1995 **51**
Whack, Rita Coburn 1958— **36**
Whalum, Kirk 1958— **37, 64**
Wharton, Clifton R(eginald), Jr. 1926— **7**
Wharton, Clifton Reginald, Sr. 1899-1990 **36**
Wheat, Alan Dupree 1951— **14**
Whitaker, "Sweet Pea" *See* Whitaker, Pernell
Whitaker, Forest 1961— **2, 49, 67**
Whitaker, Mark 1957— **21, 47**
Whitaker, Pernell 1964— **10**
White, Barry 1944-2003 **13, 41**
White, Bill 1933(?)— **1, 48**
White, Charles 1918-1979 **39**
White, (Donald) Dondi 1961-1998 **34**
White, Jesse 1934— **22**
White, John H. 1945— **27**
White, Josh, Jr. 1940— **52**
White, Linda M. 1942— **45**
White, Lois Jean 1938— **20**
White, Maurice 1941— **29**
White, Michael Jai 1967— **71**
White, Michael R(eed) 1951— **5**
White, Reggie 1961-2004 **6, 50**
White, Reginald Howard *See* White, Reggie
White, Walter F(rancis) 1893-1955 **4**
White, Willard 1946— **53**
White, William DeKova *See* White, Bill
White, Willye 1939— **67**
White-Hammond, Gloria 1951(?)— **61**
Whitfield, Fred 1967— **23**
Whitfield, Lynn 1954— **18**
Whitfield, Mal 1924— **60**
Whitfield, Van 1960(?)— **34**

Whittaker, Hudson *See Tampa Red*
Wideman, John Edgar 1941— **5**
Wilbekin, Emil 1968— **63**
Wilbon, Michael 1958— **68**
Wilder, L. Douglas 1931— **3, 48**
Wiley, Kehinde 1977— **62**
Wiley, Ralph 1952— **8**
Wilkens, J. Ernest, Jr. 1923— **43**
Wilkens, Lenny 1937— **11**
Wilkens, Leonard Randolph *See Wilkens, Lenny*
Wilkerson, Isabel 1961— **71**
Wilkins, Ray 1951— **47**
Wilkins, Roger (Wood) 1932— **2**
Wilkins, Roy 1901-1981 **4**
Wilkins, Thomas Alphonso 1956— **71**
will.i.am 1975— **64**
Williams, Alice Faye *See Shakur, Afeni*
Williams, Anthony 1951— **21**
Williams, Anthony Charles *See Tonex*
Williams, Armstrong 1959— **29**
Williams, Bert 1874-1922 **18**
Williams, Billy Dee 1937— **8**
Williams, Carl *See Kani, Karl*
Williams, Clarence 1893(?)-1965 **33**
Williams, Clarence 1967— **70**
Williams, Clarence, III 1939— **26**
Williams, Daniel Hale (III) 1856-1931 **2**
Williams, David Rudyard 1954— **50**
Williams, Deniece 1951— **36**
Williams, Denise 1958— **40**
Williams, Doug 1955— **22**
Williams, Dudley 1938— **60**
Williams, Eddie N. 1932— **44**
Williams, Eric Eustace 1911-1981 **65**
Williams, Evelyn 1922(?)— **10**
Williams, Fannie Barrier 1855-1944 **27**
Williams, Frederick (B.) 1939-2006 **63**
Williams, George Washington 1849-1891 **18**
Williams, Gertrude *See Morgan, Gertrude*
Williams, Gregory (Howard) 1943— **11**
Williams, Hosea Lorenzo 1926— **15, 31**
Williams, Joe 1918-1999 **5, 25**
Williams, John A. 1925— **27**
Williams, Juan 1954— **35**
Williams, Ken 1964— **68**
Williams, Lauryn 1983— **58**
Williams, Maggie 1954— **7, 71**

Williams, Malinda 1975— **57**
Williams, Marco 1956— **53**
Williams, Margaret Ann *See Williams, Maggie*
Williams, Mary Lou 1910-1981 **15**
Williams, Montel 1956— **4, 57**
Williams, Natalie 1970— **31**
Williams, O(swald) S. 1921— **13**
Williams, Patricia 1951— **11, 54**
Williams, Paul R(evere) 1894-1980 **9**
Williams, Paulette Linda *See Shange, Ntozake*
Williams, Pharrell 1973— **47**
Williams, Preston Warren, II 1939(?)— **64**
Williams, Robert F(ranklin) 1925— **11**
Williams, Robert Peter *See Guillaume, Robert*
Williams, Ronald A. 1949— **57**
Williams, Russell, II 1952— **70**
Williams, Samuel Arthur 1946— **21**
Williams, Saul 1972— **31**
Williams, Serena 1981— **20, 41**
Williams, Sherley Anne 1944-1999 **25**
Williams, Stanley "Tookie" 1953-2005 **29, 57**
Williams, Stevie 1979— **71**
Williams, Terrie M. 1954— **35**
Williams, Tony 1945–1997 **67**
Williams, Vanessa A. 1963— **32, 66**
Williams, Vanessa L. 1963— **4, 17**
Williams, Venus 1980— **17, 34, 62**
Williams, Walter E(dward) 1936— **4**
Williams, Wendy 1964— **62**
Williams, William December *See Williams, Billy Dee*
Williams, William T(homas) 1942— **11**
Williams, Willie L(awrence) 1943— **4**
Williamson, Fred 1938— **67**
Williamson, Lisa *See Sister Souljah*
Williamson, Mykelti 1957— **22**
Willie, Louis, Jr. 1923–2007 **68**
Willingham, Tyrone 1953— **43**
Willis, Bill 1921–2007 **68**
Willis, Cheryl *See Hudson, Cheryl*
Willis, Dontrelle 1982— **55**
Willis, William Karnet *See Willis, Bill*
Wilson, August 1945-2005 **7, 33, 55**
Wilson, Cassandra 1955— **16**
Wilson, Chandra 1969— **57**
Wilson, Charlie 1953— **31**
Wilson, Debra 1970(?)— **38**
Wilson, Dorien 1962(?)— **55**

Wilson, Ellis 1899-1977 **39**
Wilson, Flip 1933-1998 **21**
Wilson, Gerald 1918— **49**
Wilson, Jackie 1934-1984 **60**
Wilson, Jimmy 1946— **45**
Wilson, Mary 1944 **28**
Wilson, Nancy 1937— **10**
Wilson, Natalie 1972(?)— **38**
Wilson, Phill 1956— **9**
Wilson, Sunnie 1908-1999 **7, 55**
Wilson, William Julius 1935— **22**
Wilson, William Nathaniel *See Wilson, Sunnie*
Winans, Angie 1968— **36**
Winans, Benjamin 1962— **14**
Winans, CeCe 1964— **14, 43**
Winans, Debbie 1972— **36**
Winans, Marvin L. 1958— **17**
Winans, Ronald 1956-2005 **54**
Winans, Vickie 1953(?)— **24**
Winfield, Dave 1951— **5**
Winfield, David Mark *See Winfield, Dave*
Winfield, Paul (Edward) 1941-2004 **2, 45**
Winfrey, Oprah 1954— **2, 15, 61**
Winkfield, Jimmy 1882-1974 **42**
Wisdom, Kimberlydawn 1956— **57**
Withers, Bill 1938— **61**
Withers, Ernest C. 1922–2007 **68**
Withers-Mendes, Elisabeth 1973(?)— **64**
Witherspoon, John 1942— **38**
Witt, Edwin T. 1920— **26**
Wiwa, Ken 1968— **67**
Wofford, Chloe Anthony *See Morrison, Toni*
Wolfe, George C. 1954— **6, 43**
Womack, Bobby 1944— **60**
Wonder, Stevie 1950— **11, 53**
Woodard, Alfre 1953— **9**
Woodbridge, Hudson *See Tampa Red*
Woodruff, Hale (Aspacio) 1900-1980 **9**
Woodruff, John 1915–2007 **68**
Woods, Eldrick *See Woods, Tiger*
Woods, Georgie 1927-2005 **57**
Woods, Granville T. 1856-1910 **5**
Woods, Jacqueline 1962— **52**
Woods, Mattiebelle 1902-2005 **63**
Woods, Scott 1971— **55**
Woods, Sylvia 1926— **34**
Woods, Teri 1968— **69**
Woods, Tiger 1975— **14, 31**
Woodson, Carter G(odwin) 1875-1950 **2**
Woodson, Robert L. 1937— **10**
Woodward, Lynette 1959— **67**

Wooldridge, Anna Marie *See Lincoln, Abbey*
Worrill, Conrad 1941— **12**
Worthy, James 1961— **49**
Wright, Antoinette 195(?)— **60**
Wright, Bruce McMarion 1918-2005 **3, 52**
Wright, Charles H. 1918-2002 **35**
Wright, Deborah C. 1958— **25**
Wright, Jeffrey 1966— **54**
Wright, Jeremiah A., Jr. 1941— **45, 69**
Wright, Lewin 1962— **43**
Wright, Louis Tompkins 1891-1952 **4**
Wright, Nathan, Jr. 1923-2005 **56**
Wright, Rayfield 1945— **70**
Wright, Richard 1908-1960 **5**
Wyatt, Addie L. 1924— **56**
Wynn, Albert R. 1951— **25**
X, Malcolm 1925-1965 **1**
X, Marvin 1944— **45**
Xuma, Madie Hall 1894-1982 **59**
Yancy, Dorothy Cowser 1944— **42**
Yar'adua, Umaru 1951— **69**
Yarbrough, Camille 1938— **40**
Yarbrough, Cedric 1971— **51**
Yeboah, Emmanuel Ofosu 1977— **53**
Yette, Samuel F. 1929— **63**
Yoba, (Abdul-)Malik (Kashie) 1967— **11**
York, Dwight D. 1945— **71**
York, Malachi Z. *See York, Dwight D.*
York, Vincent 1952— **40**
Young Jeezy 1977— **63**
Young, Andre Ramelle *See Dre, Dr.*
Young, Andrew 1932— **3, 48**
Young, Coleman 1918-1997 **1, 20**
Young, Donald, Jr. 1989— **57**
Young, Jean Childs 1933-1994 **14**
Young, Jimmy 1948-2005 **54**
Young, Roger Arliner 1899-1964 **29**
Young, Thomas 194(?)— *See Three Mo' Tenors*
Young, Whitney M(oore), Jr. 1921-1971 **4**
Youngblood, Johnny Ray 1948— **8**
Youngblood, Shay 1959— **32**
Zane 1967(?)— **71**
Zollar, Alfred 1955(?)— **40**
Zollar, Jawole Willa Jo 1950— **28**
Zook, Kristal Brent 1966(?)— **62**
Zulu, Princess Kasune 1977— **54**
Zuma, Jacob G. 1942— **33**
Zuma, Nkosazana Dlamini 1949— **34**

Ref.
E
185.96
.C66

2009
v.71